THE LIFE OR LEGEND OF GAUDAMA

THE LIFE OR LEGEND OF GAUDAMA

THE BUDDHA OF THE BURMESE

WITH ANNOTATIONS

THE WAYS TO NEIBBAN, AND NOTICE ON THE PHONGYIES OR BURMESE MONKS.

BY THE

RIGHT REVEREND P. BIGANDET,

BISHOP OF RAMATHA,
VICAR APOSTOLIC OF AVA AND PEGU.

IN TWO VOLUMES

VOL. I

Third Edition.

GYAN

Published by

Gyan Publishing House
5, Ansari Road
Daryaganj, New Delhi-110002
Phone: 011-47034999, 9811692060
E-mail: books@gyanbooks.com

Distribution Network
gyanbooks.com
India, USA, Canada, UK, Australia, France

ISBN : 978-81-212-2810-7 (Set)
ISBN : 978-81-212-2811-4 (HB)
First Published, 1880

2nd Impression 2021

Printed at: Gyan Press, Delhi.

The
Life or Legend of Gaudama Vol. I
Author: P. Bigandet

THE LIFE OR LEGEND

OF

GAUDAMA

THE BUDDHA OF THE BURMESE.

With Annotations.

THE WAYS TO NEIBBAN, AND NOTICE ON THE PHONGYIES OR BURMESE MONKS.

BY THE

RIGHT REVEREND P. BIGANDET,

BISHOP OF RAMATHA,

VICAR APOSTOLIC OF AVA AND PEGU.

IN TWO VOLUMES.

VOL. I.

Third Edition.

LONDON:

TRÜBNER & CO., LUDGATE HILL.

1880.

ADVERTISEMENT TO THIRD EDITION.

THE origin of the present work dates back to the years 1852, 1853, 1854, and 1855, when portions of it appeared in the "Journal of the Indian Archipelago and Eastern Asia," edited by J. R. Logan of Penang (vols. vi., vii., viii., and ix.). The first complete edition was printed at Rangoon in Burmah in 1858, and a second, much enlarged, at the same place in 1866.

Very few copies of either of these editions reached Europe, and both are entirely out of print. The present third edition—a faithful reprint of the second—issued, with Bishop Bigandet's sanction, for the benefit of European and American scholars and readers, will, therefore, it is hoped, be gladly received.

Buddhism and Gautama, the faith and its founder, whose followers are between four and five hundred millions of the human race, were comparatively unknown in Europe but a generation ago, and yet this great faith had continued for four and twenty centuries to spread over the vast lands of the East, taking deep and enduring root in all, from Bhotan, Nepaul, and Ceylon, over Further

India to China Proper, Mongolia, Mantchooria, Tibet, and Japan.

Buddhism, as it is found in Burmah, has a particular claim to the attention of a diligent and attentive observer. We there have that religious creed or system as pure from adulteration as it can be after a lapse of so many centuries. Philosophy never flourished in Burmah, and, therefore, never modified the religious systems of the country. Hinduism never exercised any influence on the banks of the Irrawaddy. Chinese and Burmese have often met on battlefields, but the influence of the Middle Kingdom has never established itself in Burmah. In other words, Chinese Buddhism has never been able to penetrate into the customs and manners of the people, and has not attempted to communicate its own religion to its southern neighbours. It would seem that the true form of Buddhism is to be found in Burmah, and that a knowledge of that system can only be arrived at by the study of the religious books of Burmah, and by attentively observing the religious practices and ceremonies of the people. This is what Bishop Bigandet has endeavoured to do throughout his work.

Mr. Alabaster, the author of a very popular work on Siamese Buddhism, testifies to the great value of the Bishop's work, which, he remarks, is in one sense complete, for whereas the Siamese manuscript concludes with the attainment of omniscience, the Bishop had materials which enabled him to continue the story to the death of Nirwana (Neibban in the Burmese Pali form). He might have added that the work modestly entitled "Life of Gaudama" is a complete exposition of the great system of Eastern Asia. The metaphysical part, which is the very essence of the system, has received a due consideration, and the priesthood has been fully described. Moreover, the foot-notes help the ordinary reader in understanding clearly the text of the Legend.

Professor Albrecht Weber speaks also of the Bishop's work in terms of high commendation (see "Literarisches Centralblatt," 1870, No. 29, reprinted in "Indische Streifen," vol. iii.), whilst a still further testimony is accorded to its importance in the recent appearance of a French translation by Lieutenant Victor Gauvain.

LONDON, *December* 1879.

PREFACE TO THE FIRST EDITION.

WHETHER Buddhism be viewed in its extent and diffusion, or in the complex nature of its doctrines, it claims the serious attention of every inquiring mind.

In our own days it is, under different forms, the creed prevailing in Nepaul, Thibet, Mongolia, Corea, China, the Japanese Archipelago, Anam, Cambodia, Siam, the Shan States, Burmah, Arracan, and Ceylon. Its sway extends over nearly one-fourth of the human race.

Though based upon capital and revolting errors, Buddhism teaches a surprising number of the finest precepts and purest moral truths. From the abyss of its almost unfathomable darkness it sends forth rays of the brightest hue.

To the reflecting mind, the study of this religious system becomes the study of the history of one of the greatest religious enterprises that has ever been undertaken to elevate our nature above its low level, by uprooting the passions of the heart and dispelling the errors of the mind. A serious observer sees at a glance the dark and humiliating picture of the sad and barren results of the greatest and mightiest efforts of human wisdom, in its endeavours to find out the real cause of all human miseries, and to provide the remedies to cure the moral distempers to which our nature is subject. The fact of man's wretched and fallen condition was clearly perceived by the Buddhist philosopher, but he failed in his attempts to help man out of the difficulties which encompass him in all directions, and to bring him back to the path of truth and salvation. The efforts begun on the banks of the Ganges at an early period, and carried on with the greatest ardour and perseverance, have proved as abortive as those made at a later period throughout Greece and Italy by the greatest and brightest geniuses of antiquity. What a grand and irresistible demonstration both of the absolute inability of man to rescue from evil and attain good, and of the indispensable necessity of divine interference to help him in accomplishing that twofold achievement!

It may be said in favour of Buddhism, that no philosophico-religious system has ever upheld, to an equal degree, the notions of a saviour and deliverer, and of the necessity of his mission for procuring the salvation, in a Buddhist sense, of man. The *rôle* of Buddha, from beginning to end, is that of a deliverer, who preaches a law designed to secure to man deliverance from all the miseries under which he is labouring. But by an inexplicable and deplorable eccentricity, the pretended saviour, after having taught man the way to deliver himself from the tyranny of his passions, only leads him, after all, into the bottomless gulf of total annihilation.

Buddhism, such as we find it in Burmah, appears to have retained, to a great extent, its original character and primitive genuineness, exhibiting, as it does, the most correct forms and features of that Protean creed. At the epoch the Burmans left the northern valleys and settled in the country they now inhabit, they were a half-civilised Mongolian tribe, with no kind of worship, except a sort of geniolatry, much similar to what we see now existing among the various tribes bordering on Burmah. They were in the same condition when the first Buddhist missionaries arrived among them. Deposited in this almost virginal soil, the seed of Buddhism grew up freely without encountering any obstacle to check its growth.

Philosophy, which, in its too often erratic rambles in search of truth, changes, corrects, improves, destroys, and, in numberless ways, modifies all that it meets, never flourished in these parts; and, therefore, did not work on the religious institutions, which accordingly have remained up to this day nearly the same as they were when first imported into Burmah. The free discussion of religious and moral subjects, which constituted the very life of the Indian schools, and begat so many various, incoherent, and contradictory opinions on the most essential points of religion and philosophy, is the sign of an advanced state of civilisation, such as does not appear to have ever existed on the banks of the Irrawaddy.

Owing to its geographical position, and perhaps, also, to political causes, Burmah has ever remained out of the reach of Hindu influence, which in Nepaul has coloured Buddhism with Hindu myths, and habited it in gross forms of idolatry. In China, where there already subsisted at the time of the arrival of the preachers of the new doctrine the worship of heroes and ancestors, Buddhism, like an immense parasitic plant, extended itself all over the institutions which it covered rather than destroyed, allowing the ancient forms to subsist under the disguise it afforded them. But such was not the state of Burmah when visited by the first heralds of Buddhism.

The epoch of the introduction of Buddhism in Burmah has hitherto been a matter of conjecture. According to Burmese annals, Boudha-gautha, at the end of the fourth century of our era, brought from Ceylon a copy of the scriptures, and did for Burmah what Fa-Hian, the Chinese pilgrim, accomplished a few years afterwards in India and Ceylon for the benefit of his country. But Burmans maintain that they were followers of Buddha long before that epoch. If an inference may be drawn from analogy, it is probable that they are right in their assertion. China is fully as far from the ancient seat of Buddhism as Burmah. Yet it appears from the Chinese annals that the doctrines of the Indian philosopher were already propagated in some parts of that empire in the middle of the first century of our era, and probably at an earlier date. There is no improbability in concluding that, at least at the same time, Buddhist missionaries had penetrated into this country to propagate their tenets. According to Buddhistic annals, it was after the holding of the 3d Council, 236 after Gaudama's death, 207 B.C., that two missionaries carried religion to Thaton, the ruins of which are still to be seen between the mouths of the Tsitang and Salween rivers, and established Buddhism in Pegu. Be that as it may, we know, from the magnificent Buddhist monuments of Pagan, that that religion had reached, in the eleventh and twelfth centuries, a degree of splendour that has never since been equalled.

The Buddhist scriptures are divided into three great parts, the Thoots or instructions, the Wini or discipline, and the Abidama or metaphysics. Agreeably to this division, the matter of the following pages is arranged under three heads. The Life of Buddha, with some portions of his preaching, will convey notions of his principal teachings and doctrines. It is accompanied with copious annotations intended to explain the text, and to convey detailed notices of the system of Buddhism in general, and particularly as it is found existing in Burmah. We have added a few small dzats, or accounts of some of the former existences of Gaudama, and the summary of two large ones.

In the Notice on the Phongyies will be found the chief points of discipline fully explained and developed. We have endeavoured to render as complete as possible the account of the Buddhist Religious, or Phongyies. It is an exposition and practical illustration of the highest results that can be obtained under the influence of the doctrines of the Indian philosopher.

In the Ways to Neibban an attempt has been made to set forth and unfold the chief points of metaphysics upon which hinges the whole religious system. We confess that the summary of metaphysics is rather concise. We were reluctant to proceed too far in this subject, which, to the generality of readers, is an uninviting one.

A suggestion from Captain H. Hopkinson, Commissioner of the Martaban and Tenasserim Provinces, has induced us to add a few remarks on the names and situations of the principal towns and countries mentioned in the Legend, with the view of identifying them with modern sites and places.

It is hardly necessary to state here that the writer, when he undertook this work, had no other object in view than that of merely expounding the religious system of Buddhism as it is, explaining its doctrines and practices as correctly as it was in his power to do, regardless of their merits and demerits. His information has been derived from the perusal of the religious books of the Burmans, and from frequent conversations on religion, during several years, with the best informed among the laity and the religious whom he has had the chance of meeting.

The surest way perhaps of coming to at least an exact and accurate knowledge of the history and doctrines of Buddhism would be to give a translation of the Legends of Buddha, such as they are to be met with in all countries where Buddhism has established its sway, and to accompany these translations with an exposition of the various doctrinal points, such as they are held, understood, and believed by these various nations. This has already been done by eminent Orientalists, on Thibetan, Sanscrit, Cingalese, and Chinese originals. A similar work, executed by competent persons among the Shans, Siamese, Cambodians, and Cochin Chinese, would considerably help the savans in Europe, who have assumed the difficult task of expounding the Buddhist system in its complex and multifarious forms, to give a full, general, and comprehensive view of that great religious creed with all its variations.

The best way to undermine the foundations of a false creed and successfully attack it, is to lay it open to the eyes of all and exhibit it as it really is. Error never retains its hold over the mind except under the mask of truth which it contrives to assume. When deprived of the mask that has covered its emptiness and unreality, it vanishes away as a phantom and an illusion.

We are happy in having an opportunity of returning publicly our thanks to the worthy Commissioner of Pegu, Major A. P. Phayre, for his kind exertions in furthering the publication of this work. Not only is he an eminent Oriental scholar, and profoundly versed in all that has reference to Buddhism, but his great delight is to encourage every effort that tends to unfold and explain a creed which, despite all that has been written about it in the several countries where it flourishes, still contains many mysteries in the parts relating to its history and doctrines that require clearing up.

We have, with a deeply-felt distrust of our poor abilities, taken the best portion out of our limited stock of information concerning the Buddhist system as it exists in these parts, and, with a willing heart, presented it to the public. We hope that our example may induce others, whose stores of knowledge on this subject are fuller and richer than ours, to act in a similar spirit in aid of the prosecution of a great object, viz., the acquisition of a correct knowledge of the religion of nearly 300,000,000 of our fellow-men.

RANGOON, *October* 1858.

PREFACE TO THE SECOND EDITION.

THE First Edition of the Life of Gaudama being out of print for the last five or six years, we have, at the request of several highly esteemed persons, come to the determination of publishing a second and much-enlarged edition of the same Work. In carrying on the plan of improvement which we had in contemplation, we have been favoured by a happy circumstance. We have, after much labour, found and procured, in the Burmese capital, a very rare palm-leaf manuscript, the contents of which have supplied us with copious and interesting details respecting the sayings and doings of Gaudama.

The book is known under the Pali name of Tatha-gatha-oudana, the meaning of which is Joyful Utterance, or Praises, of the Tatha-gatha. The latter expression is one of the many titles given to Gaudama: it means, he who has come like all his predecessors. In the opinion of Buddhists, the Buddhas who appear throughout the duration of a world, or in the various series of succeeding worlds, have all the same mission to accomplish; they are gifted with the same perfect science, and are filled with similar feelings of compassion for and benevolence towards all beings. Hence the denomination which is fitly given to Gaudama, the last of them.

In the course of the Work will be found some particulars

concerning the author of the manuscript referred to, and the place where it was composed. We have only to state here that we have gathered therefrom much information on the condition of Gaudama, previous to his last existence, on the origin of the Kapilawot country, where he was born, and on the kings he has descended from. We have also met with many new details on the great intellectual working of Gaudama's mind, during the forty-nine days he spent in meditation around the Bodi-tree, particularly on the important theory of the twelve Nidanas, or causes and effects, which, with the four sublime truths, constitutes the very essence of the system. We have also found many important particulars concerning the whereabouts of Gaudama during the first twenty years of his public life, and the conversions he effected whilst engaged in the work of an itinerant preacher. Here, too, we have gleaned and selected a few of the instructions he delivered to the people that crowded about him. The story of Dewadat is narrated at great length. We have carefully written down what is said of the three Assemblies, or Councils, held at Radzagio, Wethalie, and Pataliputra, and what is mentioned of the kings who reigned in Magatha from Adzatathat to Dammathoka. We have mentioned the great fact of the spread of Buddhism beyond the boundaries of Magatha after the holding of the third Council, taking care to relate what we have found stated concerning its diffusion in Pegu and Burmah.

Numerous notes have been added to those of the First Edition, for the purpose of elucidating and explaining, as far as we are able, the principles of Buddhism and whatever is connected with that religious system.

RANGOON, *May* 1866.

CONTENTS.

LEGEND OR LIFE OF THE BURMESE BUDDHA, CALLED GAUDAMA.

CHAPTER IV

CHAPTER V.

CHAPTER VI.

CHAPTER VII.

PAGE

CHAPTER XI.

CHAPTER XII.

LEGEND OF THE BURMESE BUDDHA,

CALLED

GAUDAMA.

CHAPTER I.

Invocation of the Burmese translator—Slow but steady progress of Phralaong towards the Buddhaship—Promise made to him by the Buddha Deipinkara—Origin and beginning of the Kapilawot country and of its Rulers—Birth of Thoodaudana—His marriage with the Princess Maia—Rumour of the coming birth of a Buddha—Phralaong in the seat of Nats—Dream of Maia—Conception of Phralaong—Wonders attending that event.

I ADORE[1] Buddha who has gloriously emerged from the bottomless whirlpool of endless existences, who has extinguished the burning fire of anger and other passions, who

[1] All Buddhistic compositions are invariably prefaced with one of the following formulas of worship, always used by writers on religious subjects. The one relates to Buddha alone, and the other to the three most excellent things, ever deserving the highest veneration. The first, always written in Pali, beginning with the words *Namau tassa*, may be translated as follows: I adore thee, or rather adoration to, the blessed, perfect, and most intelligent. Here are proposed to the faith, admiration, and veneration of a true Buddhist, the three great characteristics of the founder of his religion, his goodness and benevolence, his supreme perfection, and his boundless knowledge. They form the essential qualifications of a being who has assumed to himself the task of bringing men out of the abyss of darkness and ignorance, and leading them to deliverance. Benevolence prompts him to undertake that great work, perfection fits him for such a high calling, and supreme science enables him to follow it up with a complete success. They are always held out to Buddhists as the three bright attributes and transcendent qualities inherent in that exalted personage, which are ever to attract and concentrate upon him the respect, love, and admiration of all his sincere followers.

The second formula may be considered as a short act of faith often repeated by Buddhists. It consists in saying—I take refuge in Buddha,

has opened and illuminated the fathomless abyss of dark ignorance, and who is the greatest and most excellent of all beings.

---

the Law, and the Assembly. This short profession of faith is often much enlarged by the religious zeal of writers and the fervent piety of devotees. From the instance of this legend we may remark how the compiler, with a soul warmed by fervour, is passing high encomiums upon each of the three sacred objects of veneration, or the sacred asylums wherein a Buddhist delights to dwell. There is no doubt that this formula is a very ancient one, probably coeval with the first age of Buddhism. The text of this legend bears out the correctness of this assertion. It appears that the repetition of this short sentence was the mark that distinguished converts. Ordinary hearers of the preachings of Buddha and his disciples evinced their adhesion to all that was delivered to them by repeating the sacred formula. It was then, and even now it is to Buddhists, what the celebrated Mahomedan declaration of faith—there is but one God, and Mahomed is his prophet—is to the followers of the Arabian Prophet. It is extremely important to have an accurate idea of the three sacred abodes in which the believer expects to find a sure shelter against all errors, doubts, and fears, and a resting-place where his soul may securely enjoy the undisturbed possession of truth. They constitute what is emphatically called the three precious things.

Phra and Buddha are two expressions which, though not having the same meaning, are used indiscriminately to designate the almost divine being, who after having gone, during myriads of successive existences, through the practice of all sorts of virtues, particularly self-denial and complete abnegation of all things, at last reaches to such a height of intellectual attainment that his mind becomes gifted with a perfect and universal intelligence or knowledge of all things. He is thus enabled to see and fathom the misery and wants of all mortal beings, and to devise means for relieving and filling them up. The law that he preaches is the wholesome balm designed to cure all moral distempers. He preaches it with unremitting zeal during a certain number of years, and commissions his chosen disciples to carry on the same benevolent and useful undertaking. Having laid on a firm basis his religious institution, he arrives at the state of Neibban. Buddha means wise, intelligent. Phra is an expression conveying the highest sense of respect, which was applied originally only to the author of Buddhism, but now, through a servile adulation, it is applied to the king, his ministers, all great personages, and often by inferiors to the lowest menials of Government. The word Phra, coupled with that of Thaking, which means Lord, is used by Christians in Burmah to express the idea of God, the supreme being.

From the foregoing lines the reader may easily infer that the author of Buddhism is a mere man, superior to all other beings, not in nature, but in science and perfection. He lays no claim whatever to any kind of superiority in nature; he exhibits himself to the eyes of his disciples as one of the children of men, who has been born and is doomed to die. He carries his pretensions no farther. The idea of a supreme being is nowhere mentioned by him. In the course of his religious disputations with the Brahmins, he combats the notion of a god, coolly establishing the most crude atheism. No one, it is true,

I adore the Law which the most excellent Buddha has published, which is infinitely high and incomparably profound, exceedingly acceptable, and most earnestly wished-

---

can deny that in certain Buddhistic countries the notion of an Adibudha, or supreme being, is to be found in writings as well as popular opinions, but we know that these writings are of a comparatively recent date, and contain many doctrines foreign to genuine Buddhism. This subject will, however, receive hereafter further developments.

The Law, the second object of veneration, is the body of doctrines delivered by Buddha to his disciples during the forty-five years of his public career. He came to the perfect knowledge of that law when he attained the Buddhaship under the shade of the Bodi tree. At that time his mind became indefinitely expanded; his science embraced all that exists; his penetrating and searching eye reached the farthest limits of the past, saw at a glance the present, and fathomed the secrets of the future. In that position, unclouded truth shone with radiant effulgence before him, and he knew the nature of all beings individually, their condition and situation, as well as all the relations subsisting between them. He understood at once the miseries and errors attending all rational beings, the hidden causes that generated them, and the springs they issued from. At the same time he perceived distinctly the means to be employed for putting an end to so many misfortunes, and the remedies to be used for the cure of those numberless and sad moral distempers. His omniscience pointed out to him the course those beings had to follow in order to retrace their steps back from the way of error, and enter the road that would lead to the coming out from the whirlpool of moral miseries in which they had hitherto wretchedly moved during countless existences. All that Gaudama said to the foregoing effect constitutes the law upon which so many high praises are lavished with such warm and fervent earnestness. A full and complete knowledge of that law, in the opinion of Buddhists, dispels at once the clouds of ignorance, which, like a thick mist, encompass all beings, and sheds bright rays of pure light which enlighten the understanding. Man is thus enabled to perceive distinctly the wretchedness of his position, and to discover the means wherewith he may extricate himself from the trammels of the passions and finally arrive at the state of Neibban, which is, as it shall be hereafter fully explained, exemption from all the miseries attending existence. The whole law is divided into three parts; the Abidama or metaphysics, Thouts or moral instructions, and the Wini or discipline. According to the opinion of the best informed among Buddhists, the law is eternal, without a beginning or an author that might have framed its precepts. No Buddha ever considered himself, or has ever been looked upon by others, as the inventor and originator of the law. He who becomes a Buddha is gifted with a boundless science that enables him to come to a perfect knowledge of all that constitutes the law: he is the fortunate discoverer of things already existing, but placed far beyond the reach of the human mind. In fact, the law is eternal, but has become, since the days of a former Buddha, obliterated from the minds of men, until a new one, by his omniscience, is enabled to win it back and preach it to all beings.

The third object of veneration is the Thanga, or Assembly. The meaning

for by Nats and men, capable to wipe off the stains of concupiscence, and is immutable.

I adore the Assembly of the Perfect, of the pure and illustrious Ariahs in their eight sublime states, who have overcome all the passions that torment other mortals, by eradicating the very root of concupiscence, and who are famous above all other beings.

I undertake to translate from the Pali[2] text the history

---

of the Pali word Thanga is nearly equivalent to that of church or congregation. In the time Gaudama lived the assembly was composed of all individuals who, becoming converts, embraced the mode of living of their preacher, and remained with him, or if they occasionally parted from him for a while, always kept a close intercourse with him, and spent a portion of their time in his company. Having left the world, they subjected themselves to certain disciplinary regulations, afterwards embodied in the great compilation called Wini. The members of the Assembly were divided into two classes; the Ariahs or venerables, who by their age, great proficiency in the knowledge of the law, and remarkable fervour in the assiduous practice of all its ordinances, occupied deservedly the first rank amongst the disciples of Buddha, and ranked foremost in the Assembly. The second class was composed of the Bickus, or simple mendicant Religious. It is difficult to assert with any degree of probability whether the Upasakas, or ordinary hearers, have ever been regarded as members of the Thanga, and forming a portion thereof. The Upasakas were believers, but continued to live in the world, and formed, as it were, the laity of the Buddhistic church. According to the opinion of Buddhists in these parts, the laity is not considered as forming or constituting a part of the Thanga; those only who abandon a secular life, put on the yellow canonical dress, and endeavour to tread in the footsteps of their great teacher, are entitled to the dignity of members of the Assembly, to which a veneration is paid similar to that offered to Buddha and the law. The Ariahs, or venerables, are divided into four classes, according to their greater or less proficiency in knowledge and moral worth. They are called Thotapan, Thakadagan, Anagam, and Arahat. In the class of Thotapan are included the individuals who have entered into the current, or stream, leading to deliverance, or, in other terms, who have stepped into the way of perfection. The Thotapan is as yet to be born four times ere he can obtain the deliverance. Those who belong to the second class glide rapidly down the stream, following steadily the way leading to perfection, and are to be born once more in the condition of Nat, and once in that of man. Those of the third class are to be born once in the condition of Nats. Finally, those of the fourth class have gone over the fourth and last way to perfection, reached the summit of science and spiritual attainments, and are ripe for the state of Neibban, which they infallibly obtain after their death. The Ariahs are again subdivided into eight classes, four of which include those who are following the four ways of perfection; the four others comprehend those who enjoy the reward of the duties practised in following the ways of perfection.

[2] The Burmese translator of the

of our most excellent Phra, from the period he left Toocita,[3] the fourth abode of Nats, to the time he entered into the state of Neibban.

Pali text gives us to understand that his intention is not to give the history of our Buddha during the countless existences that have preceded the last one, when he obtained the supreme intelligence. Buddhists keep five hundred and ten histories or legends of Buddha, purporting to give an account of as many of his former existences; and to enhance the value of such records, the contents are supposed to have been narrated by Buddha himself to his disciples and hearers. I have read most of them. Two hundred of these fabulous narrations are very short, and give few particulars regarding our Phra when he was as yet in the state of animal, man, and Nat. They are, except the heading and the conclusion, the very same fables and *contes* to be met with amongst all Asiatic nations, which have supplied with inexhaustible stores all ancient and modern fabulists. The last ten narratives are really very complete and interesting stories of ten existences of Buddha preceding the one we are about to describe, during which he is supposed to have practised the ten great virtues, the acquisition of which is an indispensable qualification for obtaining the exalted dignity of Phra. Some of these legends are really beautiful, interesting, and well-composed pieces of literature.

[3] Toocita, or the joyful abode, is one of the seats of the Nats. But in order to render more intelligible several passages of this work, it is almost indispensable to have an idea of the system adopted by Buddhists in assigning to rational beings their respective seats or abodes. There are thirty-one seats assigned to all beings, which we may suppose to be disposed on an immense scale, extending from the bottom of the earth to an incommensurable height above it. At the foot we find the four states of punishment, viz., hell, the states of Athourikes, Preithas, and animals. Next comes the abode of man. Above it are the six seats of Nats. These eleven seats are called the seats of passion, or concupiscence, because the beings residing therein are still subject to the influence of that passion, though not to an equal degree. Above the abodes of Nats we meet with the sixteen seats, called Rupa, disposed perpendicularly one above the other to an incalculable height. The inhabitants of those fanciful regions are called Brahmas, or perfect. They have freed themselves from concupiscence and almost all other passions, but still retain some affection for matter and material things. Hence the denomination of Rupa, or matter, given to the seats. The remaining portion of the scale is occupied by the four seats called Arupa or immaterials, for the beings inhabiting them are entirely delivered from all passions. They have, as it were, broken asunder even the smallest ties that would attach them to this material world. They have reached the summit of perfection; one step farther, and they enter into the state Neibban, the consummation, according to Buddhists, of all perfection. To sum up all the above in a few words: there are four states of punishment. The seat of man is a place of probation and trial. The six abodes of Nats are places of sensual pleasures and enjoyments. In the sixteen seats of Rupa are to be met those beings whose delights are of a more refined and almost purely spiritual nature, though retaining as yet some slight

Previous, however, to commencing the work, I will relate succinctly what is found in our books respecting the great Being who, by a slow but sure process, was qualifying himself for his great and high destiny. It is stated that all the following particulars were narrated by Gaudama himself to the great disciple Thariputra.

For seven thingies of worlds, he who was to become a Buddha felt, during that immense number of revolutions of nature, a thought for the Buddhaship awakening in his soul. This thought was succeeded by a wish, a desire, and a longing for that extraordinary calling. He began to understand that the practice of the virtues of the highest order was requisite to enable him to attain the glorious object of his ardent wishes, and no less than 125,000 Buddhas appeared during that space of time.

When the above period had at last come to an end, the inward workings of his soul prompted him to ask openly for the Buddhaship. The period of asking lasted nine thingies of worlds. It was brightened and illustrated by the successive manifestation of 987,000 Buddhas. In the beginning of this latter period, the future Gaudama was a prince of the name of Laukatara, ruler of the Nanda country. At that time there appeared in the country of Kapilawot a Buddha called Thakiamuni Paurana Gaudama. As he happened to travel through the Nanda country, with the twofold object of preaching the law and begging for his food, the ruler Laukatara made great offerings to him. Meanwhile, with a marked earnestness, he solicited at the feet of Thakiamuni the favour of becoming, at some future time, a Buddha like himself. He expressed the wish to be born in the same country, from the same father and mother, to have for his wife the very same queen, to ride the same horse, to be attended by the

affections for matter. In the four seats of Arupa are located those beings who are wholly disentangled from material affections, who delight only in the sublimest contemplation, soaring, as it were, in the boundless regions of pure spiritualism.

same companions and the same two great disciples on the right and on the left. To this request Thakiamuni replied in the affirmative, but he added that an immense length of time had still to elapse ere the objects of his petition could be fully granted. A similar application was repeatedly made to all the other succeeding Buddhas, and a like promise was held out to him.

The third period of four thingies of worlds was remarkable for the complete absence of all that could enlighten or illustrate the various states of existence. A complete moral and intellectual darkness was spread over all beings, and kept them wrapped up in utter darkness. No Buddhas, no Pitzekabuddhas appeared to illuminate by their doctrine and science the minds of men. No Tsekiawade, or king of the world, made his appearance to infuse life and energy in the midst of the universal slumbering.

But the hundred thousand revolutions of nature that followed were more fortunate. There flourished no less than twenty-seven Buddhas, from Tahingara, the first in the series, to Kathaba, the last one immediately preceding Gaudama.

During the period when the Buddha named Deipinkara was the teacher of all beings, our future Gaudama was born in the country of Amarawatti, from illustrious and rich parents belonging to the caste of Pounhas.

While still a youth, he lost both his parents and inherited their property.

In the midst of pleasure and plenty he one day made this reflection:—The riches that I now possess were my parents' property, but they have not been able to save them from the miseries attending death. They will not, alas! afford to me a better and more secure fate. When I go into the grave, they will not come along with me. This bodily frame I am clad in is not worthy to be pitied. Why should I bestow signs of compassion upon it? Filled with impurities, burdened by rottenness, it has all the elements of destruction in the compounded parts of its existence. Towards Neibban I will turn my regards; upon it my eyes shall be riveted. There is the tank in which all the impurities of passion may be washed away. Now I will forsake everything, and go forthwith in search of a teacher that will point out to me the way that leads to the state Neibban.

Full of these thoughts, the young man gave away to the needy all that he possessed, reserving nothing to himself. Freed from the trammels of riches, he withdrew into a lonely place, where the Nats had prepared beforehand all that was necessary to minister to his wants. He embraced the profession or mode of life of a Rahan, or perfect. Attired in the dress of his new profession, he lived for some time on this spot under the name of Thoomeda. Displeased, however, with the too easy mode of life he was leading, he left that spot, and contented himself with dwelling under the shade of trees. He, however, went forth from time to time in quest of his food.

A few years previous to the retirement of Thoomeda into solitude, he who was to be the Buddha Deipinkara migrated from one of the Nats' seats, and was incarnated in the womb of the Princess Thoomeda, wife of Thoodewa, king of the Ramawatti country. Subsequently he was married to the Princess Padouma, who bore unto him a son, named Oothabakanda. On the same year in which the child was born, the king left his palace on an elephant's back, withdrew into some lonely place, practised during ten months all sorts of self-inflicted penances, and, under the shade of the tree Gniaong Kiat, became a Buddha. On that occasion the earth quivered with great violence, but the hermit Thoomeda, being in ecstasy at that moment, knew nothing of the extraordinary occurrence.

On a certain day, Deipinkara was travelling through the country for the twofold purpose of preaching the law and collecting his food. Arrived near a place where the road was very bad, he stopped for a while until the road should be made passable. The people hastened from all parts to come and prepare the road for Deipinkara and his followers. Thoomeda, gifted with the privilege of travelling through the air, happened to pass over the spot where crowds of people were busily engaged in preparing and levelling a road. The hermit alighted on that spot, and inquired of the people what was the reason of their busy exertions. They told him that the most excellent Deipinkara was expected with a large retinue of disciples, and that they strained every nerve to have the road ready for them. Thoomeda begged to be permitted to bear a part in the good work, and asked that a certain extent of the road be assigned to him as his task. His request was granted, and he forthwith set to work with the greatest diligence. It was all but finished when Buddha Deipinkara, followed by forty thousand disciples, made his appearance. Thoomeda, actuated by an ardent desire of testifying his respect to the holy personage, without a moment's hesitation flung himself into the hollow that was as yet not filled, and lying on his belly, with his back upwards, bridged the place, and entreated the Buddha and his followers to cross the hollow by trampling over his body. Great and abundant shall be the merits that I, said he within himself, shall gain by this good work. No doubt I will receive from the mouth of Deipinkara the assurance that I shall, hereafter, obtain the Buddhaship. The Buddha, standing over him, admired the humble and fervent devotedness of Thoomeda. With one glance he perceived all that was going on in the hermit's mind, and with a loud voice, that could be heard by all his disciples, he assured him that four thingies and one hundred thousand worlds hence he would become a Buddha, the fourth that would appear during the world, called Badda. He went on to describe minutely the principal events that were to illustrate his future career. No sooner was this revelation made to him than Thoomeda hastened back to his forest. Sitting at the foot of a tree, he encouraged himself by fine comparisons to the practice of those virtues that were best suited to weaken in him the influence of the passions.

In the different existences that followed, Thoomeda, at all the periods of the appearance of some Buddhas, received a confirmation of the promise he had had from the lips of Deipinkara.

This present world we live in has been favoured above all others. Already three Buddhas have appeared, viz., Kaukkasan, Gaunagong, and Kathaba. These all belonged to the caste of Pounhas, and he who was to be hereafter our Gaudama, during the many existences he passed through, at the time of the manifestations of those three Buddhas, was always born of the same caste. Kathaba is said to have lived and preached during the ninth andrakap. It was he who, for the last time, assured the future Gaudama that he would obtain the Buddhaship during the tenth andrakap.

We will only mention his last existence in the seat of man, previous to the one in which he was to obtain the great prize he had laboured for with so much earnestness during innumerable existences. He became prince under the name of Wethandra, and practised to an eminent, nay heroic, degree the virtues of liberality and charity. To such an extent did he obey the dictates of his liberal heart, that, after having given away all the royal treasures, his white elephant, &c., he did not shrink from parting with his own wife, the Princess Madi, and his two children, Dzali and Gahna. He then died and migrated to the Toocita seat, and enjoyed the blissfulness and felicity of Nats, under the name of Saytakaytoo, during fifty-seven koudes of years.

The origin and beginning of the Kapilawot country, as well as of its rulers, are to be alluded to as briefly as possible. In the country of the middle, Mitzimadesa, the kings that ruled from the time of Mahathamadat to that of Ookakaritz, king of Benares, were 252,556 in number. The last-named monarch was married to five wives, and had children by them all. The first queen happening to die, the king became passionately enamoured of a young woman, whom he married. She soon presented him with a son, whom the king, pressed by his young wife's solicitations, declared heir-apparent, to the prejudice of his elder sons. As might have been expected, the four elder sons loudly complained of the preference given to their younger brother. To put an end to these domestic disputes, the king called his four sons and their five sisters, gave them a large retinue, and bade them go in a northerly direction, in search of a spot favourable for building a new city. They followed their father's advice. After long wandering through the forests, they came to a place where lived the Rathee Kapila, who, becoming acquainted with the object of their errand, desired them to stay with him and found a city. He also wished that on the very spot where his hut stood the king's palace should be erected. He predicted that this city would become great, powerful, and illustrious; that it would be a city of peace, since the animals in the forests lived peaceably, without ever attempting to inflict harm on each other. The proposal was cheerfully accepted. All the people set to work with great earnestness. When the work was completed, they offered the new city to Kapila, who was made their teacher. Hence the name of Kapilawottoo, or Kapilawot.

The four princes, finding that among their followers there were no daughters of the royal race whom they could marry, resolved, in order to keep pure the blood-royal, to marry their four younger sisters. The eldest one was raised to the dignity of queen-mother. Ookamukka, the eldest of the brothers, was the first king of Kapilawot. Whilst these things were taking place, the king of Benares, having been attacked with leprosy, had left his throne and retired to a forest north of his capital. There he found his cure under the shade of the kalau tree. At the same time the eldest sister, named Peya, who had become queen-mother, was seized with the same distemper, and went into the same forest. She met with the king, whom she knew not. By his advice she sat under the kalau tree, and the beneficent smell of the leaves soon worked a perfect cure. They were subsequently married, and had a numerous progeny. They settled on this spot, and built the city of Kaulya. The small river Rohani flowed between Kaulya and Kapilawot.*

From Ookamukka, the first king of Kapilawot, to Prince Wethandra, there are but seven successive kings. From Dzali, the son of Wethandra, to Dzeyathena, the great-grandfather of Gaudama, there were 82,002 kings. Let it be borne in mind, that, during that period of time, our Phralaong, or future of Gaudama, was in one of the Nats' seats. The princes of Kapilawot were wont to go and sport on the water of a lake somewhat distant from the

---

* When laying before the reader a short and concise account of the being who was to become the Buddha called Gaudama, the writer deems it necessary to make a general observation, which, he hopes, will greatly help the reader to understand correctly several passages of the following pages. Gaudama was a Hindu, brought up by Hindu masters, and initiated in all the knowledge possessed by the society he lived in. He accepted the fabulous genealogies of kings such as they were found in the writings of his days. The same may be said of the erroneous notions respecting our globe, the size and motions of the sun and the moon and other heavenly bodies, the explanations of many natural phenomena, the description of hell, of the seats of reward, &c. Teacher as he was of moral precepts, based upon metaphysical principles, Gaudama concerned himself very little about these things, which, in his eyes, were not worth the consideration of a sage. But he, or more probably his disciples, availed themselves of these notions for resting upon them some portions of their system, and giving them such developments as best suited their views. These notions, though wedded to the religious system originated by Gaudama, do not, strictly speaking, belong to it. They existed before his appearance in the schools of philosophy; they formed a part of the stock of knowledge possessed by the society in which he was reared. To account properly for these particulars and many others belonging to the disciplinary regulations, recourse must be had to the study of the ancient religion of the Hindus, Brahminism.

In the account of the foundation of the Kapilawot city, we find that the practice of leaving the eldest sister unmarried, and of the princes marrying their own sisters, is up to this day observed by the royal family of Burma. The eldest daughter of the reigning monarch is to remain unmarried during her parents' life, and the first queen is often, if not always, the sister or half-sister of the king. The same unnatural practice prevailed in the royal family of the ancient Persians.

city. They at first erected a temporary place of residence in the vicinity of that sheet of water, and finally built a city which received the name of Dewaha. It had likewise its kings of the same Thagiwi race. Dzeyathena, the king of Kapilawot, had a son named Thiahanoo, and a daughter named Yathaudara. Aukaka, king of Dewaha, his contemporary, had also a son and a daughter, Eetzana and Kitzana. Thiahanoo was married to Kitzana, who bore unto him five sons, Thoodaudana, Kanwaudana, Thoukkaudana, Thekkaudana, and Amittaudana; and two daughters, Amita and Pilita. Eetzana, the son of the king of Dewa, married Yathaudara, daughter of Dzeyathana, king of Kapilawot. From this marriage were born two sons, Thoopabuddha and Dantapani, and two daughters, Maia and Patzapati.

When Eetzana became king of Dewaha, a considerable error had crept into the calendar. A correction was deemed necessary. There lived a celebrated hermit, or Rathee, named Deweela, well versed in the science of calculation. After several consultations held on this important subject in the presence of the king, it was agreed that the Kaudza era of 8640 years should be done away with on a Saturday, the first of the moon of Tabaong, and that the new era should be made to begin on a Sunday, on the first day of the waxing moon of the month Tagoo. This was called the Eetzana era.

On the 10th of the new era, Thoodaudana was born in the city of Kapilawot; and on the twelfth year, Maia was born at Dewaha. In the days of the Buddha Wipathi, the future Maia was then the daughter of a Pounha. Her father, who tenderly loved her, gave her one day a fine nosegay with a great quantity of the choicest perfumes and essences. The young girl, delighted with these articles, hastened to the place where lived Wipathi, and with pious and fervent earnestness laid at his feet all that she had received from her father. Wipathi, admiring the fervent liberality of the damsel, assured her that she would hereafter become the mother of a Buddha, who was to be called Gaudama.

When Thoodaudana was eighteen years of age, his father, King Thiahanoo, called eight Pounhas skilled in the science of astrology, and directed them to go with a large retinue and splendid presents in search of a royal princess to be married to his son. The eight Pounhas departed. They visited several countries, but all in vain; they could not find one princess worthy of their master's son. At last they came to the city of Dewaha. They had no sooner arrived in sight of it than they saw many signs which prognosticated that in the city would be found an accomplished princess, in every respect qualified to become the wife of the heir to the throne of Kapilawot. At that time the young Maia had gone to enjoy herself in a garden outside the city. It was situated on a gently sloping ground, covered with all sorts of the finest and rarest trees. A small brook, winding its course in various directions, shed on every hand, from its gently murmuring waters, a delicious freshness. Thither the royal messengers resorted. They found the princess in the midst of her companions, outshining them all in beauty, like the moon among the stars. Admitted into her presence, the head of the deputation attempted to speak and explain the object of his visit; but he was so much overwhelmed by the beauty and the graceful and dignified appearance of the princess, that his voice failed him, and he fainted three times in succession. As each fit came on him several damsels ran to his assistance with pitchers of fresh water, and brought him back to his senses. Having recovered his spirits, the chief Pounha felt encouraged by some graceful and kind words from the lips of the princess. He explained to her, in the choicest expressions, the object of his mission; and with a faltering and timid tone of voice stated to her that he had come to entreat her to accept presents from, and the hand of, Prince Thoodaudana. Meanwhile he poured at her feet the brightest jewels and rarest articles. The princess, with a sweet voice, modestly replied that she was under the protection and care of her beloved parents, whose will she never resisted; that it was to them that this affair should be referred. For her own part, she had but one thing to do—to abide by her parents' wishes.

Satisfied with the answer, the Pounhas retired, and hastened to the palace of King Eetzana, to whom they related all that had just happened. The king graciously agreed to the proposal, and, in proof of his perfect satisfaction, sent in return a deputation with many presents to Prince Thoodaudana and his father. As might be expected, the royal messengers were well received at Kapilawot. Thiahanoo and his son set out with a countless retinue for the city of Dewaha. In a grove of mango-trees an immense building was erected, out of the city, for their reception and accommodation; and in the middle of that building a spacious hall was arranged with infinite art for the marriage ceremony. When all the preparations were completed, the bridegroom, attended by his father, King Thiahanoo and the chief of Brahmas, went out to meet the bride, who was coming from the garden, accompanied by her mother and the wife of the great Thagia. Both advanced towards the centre of the hall, near a stand raised for the occasion. Thoodaudana first stretched forth his hand and laid it over that place. Maia gracefully did the same. They then took each other's hands, in token of the mutual consent. At that auspicious moment all the musical instruments resounded, and proclaimed in gladdening airs the happy event. The Pounhas, holding the sacred shell in their hands, poured the blessed water over their heads, uttering all sorts of blessings. The parents and relatives joined in invoking upon the young couple the choicest benedictions. The king, princes, Pounhas, and nobles vied with each other in making presents, and wishing them all sorts of happiness.

When the festival was over, Thiahanoo desired to go back to his country with his son and daughter-in-law.

This was done with the utmost pomp and solemnity. On his return, he continued to govern his people with great prudence and wisdom, and at last died and migrated to one of the Nats' seats. He was succeeded by his son Thoodaudana, who, with his amiable wife, religiously observed the five precepts and the ten rules of kings. By his beneficence and liberality to all, he won the sincere affection of his people. It was on the twenty-eighth year of the new era that he was married. Soon after, he took for his second wife, Patzapati, the younger sister of Maia. Thoodaudana's sister, Amitau, was married to Thouppabuddha, the son of king Eetzana.

About four thingies,[4] an hundred thousand worlds ago,[5] the most excellent Buddha, who is infinitely wise

[4] Thingie is a number represented by a unit, followed by sixty-four ciphers; others say, one hundred and forty.

[5] Buddhists have different ways of classifying the series of worlds, which they suppose to succeed to each other, after the completion of a revolution of nature. As regards Buddhas, who appear at unequal intervals for illuminating and opening the way to deliverance to the then existing beings, worlds are divided into those which are favoured with the presence of one or several Buddhas, and those to which so eminent a benefit is denied. The present revolution of nature, which includes the period in which we live, has been privileged above all others. No less than five Buddhas, like five shining suns, are to shoot forth rays of incomparable brilliancy, and dispel the mist of thick darkness that encompasses all beings, according to their respective laws of demerits. Of these five, four, namely, Kaukassan, Gaunagong, Kathaba, Gaudama, have already performed their great task. The fifth, named Aremideia, is as yet to come. The religion of Gaudama is to last five thousand years, of which two thousand four hundred and eight are elapsed. The names of the twenty-eight last Buddhas are religiously preserved by Buddhists, together with their age, their stature, the names of the trees under which they have obtained the universal intelligence, their country, the names of their father and mother, and those of their two chief disciples. Deinpakara occupies the fourth place in the series. He is supposed to have been eighty cubits high, and to have lived one hundred thousand years.

It is not without interest to examine whether there have existed Buddhas previous to the time of Gaudama, and whether the twenty-eight Buddhas above alluded to are to be considered as mythological beings who have never existed. It cannot be denied that mention of former Buddhas is made in the earliest sacred records, but it seems difficult to infer therefrom that they are real beings. 1st. The circumstances respecting their extraordinary longevity, their immense stature, and the myriads of centuries that are supposed to have elapsed from the times of the first to those of Gaudama, are apparently conclusive proofs against

and far superior to the three orders of beings, the Brahmas, the Nats,[6] and men, received at the feet of the Phra Deipinkara the assurance that he would afterwards become

---

the reality of their existence. 2d. The names of those personages are found mentioned in the preachings of Gaudama, together with those individuals with whom he is supposed to have lived and conversed during former existences. Who has ever thought of giving any credence to those fables? They were used by Gaudama as so many means to give extension and solidity to the basis whereupon he intended to found his system. 3d. There are no historical records or monuments that can give countenance to the opposite opinion. The historical times begin with Gaudama, whilst there exist historical proofs of the existence of the rival creed of Brahminism anterior to the days of the acknowledged author of Buddhism.

It cannot be doubted that there existed in the days of Buddha, in the valley of the Ganges and in the Punjaub, a great number of philosophers, who led a retired life, devoting their time to study and the practice of virtue. Some of them occasionally sallied out of their retreats to go and deliver moral instructions to the people. The fame that attended those philosophers attracted round their lonely abodes crowds of hearers, eager to listen to their lectures and anxious to place themselves under their direction for learning the practice of virtue. In the pages of this legend will be found passages corroborating this assertion. Thence arose those multifarious schools, where were elaborated the many systems, opinions, &c., for which India has been celebrated from the remotest antiquity. The writer has had the patience to read two works full of disputations between Brahmins and Buddhists, as well as some books of the ethics of the latter. He has been astonished to find that in those days the art of arguing, disputing, defining, &c., had been carried to such a point of nicety as almost to leave the disciples of Aristotle far behind. It has been said that the gymnosophists whom Alexander the Great met in India, were Buddhist philosophers. But the particulars mentioned by Greek writers respecting their manners and doctrines contradict such a supposition. They are described as living in a state of complete nakedness, and as refusing to deliver instructions to the messenger of Alexander, unless he consented to strip himself of his clothes. On the other hand, we know that Buddha enjoined a strict modesty on his religious, and in the book of ordinations the candidate is first asked whether he comes provided with his canonical dress. The gymnosophists are represented as practising extraordinary austerities, and holding self-destruction in great esteem. These and other practices are quite at variance with all the prescriptions of the Wini, or book of discipline. It is further mentioned that the Macedonian hero met with other philosophers living in community; but whether these were Buddhists or not, it is impossible to decide. It can scarcely be believed that Buddhism in the days of Alexander could have already invaded the countries which the Grecian army conquered.

[6] Nat in Pali means Lord. Its signification is exactly equivalent to that of Dewa, Dewata. The Nats are an order of beings in the Buddhistic system, occupying six seats or abodes of happiness, placed in rising succession above the abode of man. They are spirits endowed with a body of so subtle and ethereal nature as

himself a Buddha. At this time he was a Rathee,[7] under the name of Thoomeda. During that immense space of time, he practised in the highest degree the ten great

to be able to move with the utmost rapidity from their seat to that of man, and *vice versa*. They play a conspicuous part in the affairs of this world, and are supposed to exercise a considerable degree of influence over man and other creatures. Fear, superstition, and ignorance have peopled all places with Nats. Every tree, forest, fountain, village, and town has its protecting Nat. Some among the Nats having lost their high station through misconduct, have been banished from their seats and doomed to drag a wretched existence in some gloomy recess. Their power for doing evil is supposed to be very great. Hence the excessive dread of those evil genii entertained by all Buddhists. Agood deal of their commonest superstitious rites have been devised for propitiating those enemies to all happiness, and averting the calamitous disasters which they seem to keep hanging over our heads.

Though the Nats' worship is universal among the Buddhists of all nations, it is but fair to state that it is contrary to the principles of genuine Buddhism and repugnant to its tenets. It is probable that it already existed among all the nations of Eastern Asia at the time they were converted to Buddhism.

The tribes that have not as yet been converted to Buddhism have no other worship but that of the Nats. To mention only the principal ones, such as the Karens, the Khyins, and the Singphos, they may differ in the mode of performing their religious rites and superstitious ceremonies, but the object is the same, honouring and propitiating the Nats. This worship is so deeply rooted in the minds of the wild and half-civilised tribes of Eastern Asia, that it has been, to a great extent, retained by the nations that have adopted Buddhism as their religious creed. The Burmans, for instance, from the king down to the lowest subject, privately and publicly indulge in the Nats' worship. As to the tribes that have remained outside the pale of Buddhism, they may be styled Nats' worshippers. Hence it may be inferred that previous to the introduction or the preaching of the tenets of the comparatively new religion in these parts, the worship of Nats was universal and predominating.

[7] Raci or Rathee means an hermit, a personage living by himself in some lonely and solitary recess, far from the contagious atmosphere of impure society, devoting his time to meditation and contemplation. His diet is of the coarsest kind, supplied to him by the forests he lives in; the skins of some wild animals afford him a sufficient dress. Most of those Rathees having reached an uncommon degree of extraordinary attainment, their bodies become spiritualised to a degree which enables them to travel from place to place by following an ærial course. In all Buddhistic legends, comedies, &c., they are often found interfering in the narrated stories and episodes.

There is no doubt but those devotees who, in the days of Buddha, spent their time in retreat, devoted to study and meditation, were Brahmins. In support of this assertion we have the highest possible native authority, the Institutes of Menoo, compiled probably during the eighth or ninth century before Christ. We find in that work, minutely described, the mode of life becoming a true Brahmin. During the third part of his life, a Brahmin must live as an anchorite in the woods. Clad in the bark of trees or the skins of animals,

virtues, the five renouncings, and the three mighty works of perfection.[8] Having become a great prince[9] under the name of Wethandra, he reached the acme of self-abnegation and renouncement to all the things of this world. After his death, he migrated to Toocita, the fourth abode of Nats. During his sojourn in that happy place, enjoying the fulness of pleasure allotted to the fortunate inhabitants of those blissful regions, a sudden and uncommon rumour, accompanied with an extraordinary commotion, proclaimed the gladdening tidings that a Phra was soon to make his appearance in this world.*

On hearing that a Phra was soon to make his appear-

---

with his hair and nails uncut, having no shelter whatever but that which is afforded him by the trees of the forest, keeping sometimes a strict silence, living on herbs and roots, he must train himself up to bearing with entire unconcern the cold of winter and the heat of summer. Such is the course of life, according to the Vedas, which the true Brahmin is bound to follow during the third portion of his existence. Some Buddhistic zealots have sometimes endeavoured to emulate the ancient Rathees in their singular mode of life. It is not quite unfrequent in our days to hear of some fervent Phongies who, during the three months of Lent, withdraw into solitude, to be more at liberty to devote their time to study and meditation. This observance, however, is practised by but very few individuals, and that, too, with a degree of laxity that indicates a marked decline of the pristine fervour that glowed in the soul of primitive Buddhists.

8 The three great works are; the assistance afforded to his parents and relatives, the great offerings he had made, coupled with a strict observance of the most difficult points of the law, and benevolent dispositions towards all beings indiscriminately.

9 This extraordinary monarch, called Tsekiawade, never makes his appearance during the period of time allotted to the publication and duration of the religious institutions of a Buddha.

---

* *Remark of the Burmese translator.*—There are three solemn occasions on which this great rumour is noised abroad. The first, when the Nats, guardians of this world, knowing that 100,000 years hence the end of this world is to come, show themselves amongst men with their heads hanging down, a sorrowful countenance, and tears streaming down their faces. They are clad in a red dress, and proclaim aloud to all mortals the destruction of this planet 100,000 years hence. They earnestly call upon men to devote themselves to the observance of the law, to the practice of virtue, the support of parents, and the respect due to virtuous personages. The second occasion is, when the same Nats proclaim to men that a thousand years hence a Buddha or Phra will appear amongst them; and the third is, when they come and announce to men that within a hundred years there will be in this world a mighty prince, whose unlimited sway shall extend over the four great islands.

ance amongst men, all the Nats, the peaceful inhabitants of the fortunate abode of Toocita, assembled in all haste and crowded around Phralaong,[10] eagerly inquiring of him, who was the fortunate Nat to whom was reserved the signal honour of attaining the incomparable dignity of Buddha. The reason which directed their steps towards Phralaong, and suggested their inquiry, was, that in him were already to be observed unmistakable signs, foreshadowing his future greatness.

No sooner did it become known that this incomparable destination was to be his happy lot, than Nats from all parts of the world resorted to the abode of Toocita, to meet Phralaong and to congratulate him upon this happy occasion. "Most glorious Nat," did they say to him, "you have practised most perfectly the ten great virtues;[11] the time is

---

[10] Here I make use of the expression Phralaong, or more correctly Phraalaong, to designate Buddha before he obtained the supreme knowledge, when he was, as it were, slowly and gradually gravitating towards the centre of matchless perfection. In that state it is said of him that he is not yet ripe.

This word involves a meaning which ought to be well understood. No single expression in our language can convey a correct idea of its import, and for this reason it has been retained through these pages. *Alaong* is a derivative from the verb *laong*, which means to be in an incipient way, in a way of progression towards something more perfect. A Buddha is at first a being in a very imperfect state; but passing through countless existences, he frees himself, by a slow process, from some of his imperfections; he acquires merits which enable him to rise in the scale of progress, science, and perfection. In perusing the narrative of the five hundred and ten former existences of Gaudama which have come down to us, we find that, when he was yet in the state of animal, he styled himself Phralaong. The Burmese have another expression of similar import to express the same meaning. They say of a being as yet in an imperfect condition that he is soft, tender as an unripe thing; and when he passes to the state of perfection, they say that he is ripe, that he has blossomed and expanded. They give to understand that he who is progressing towards the Buddhaship has in himself all the elements constitutive of a Buddha lying as yet concealed in himself; but when he reaches that state, then all that had hitherto remained in a state of unripeness bursts suddenly out of the bud and comes to full maturity. Similar expressions are often better calculated to give a clear insight into the true and real opinions of Buddhists than a lengthened and elaborate dissertation could do.

[11] The ten great virtues or duties are, liberality, observance of the precepts of the law, retreat into lonely places, wisdom, diligence, benevolence, patience, veracity, fortitude, and indifference. The five renounce-

now come for you to obtain the sublime nature of Buddha. During former existences, you most rigidly attended to the observance of the greatest precepts, and walked steadily in the path of the highest virtues; you then sighed after and longed for the happiness of Nats and Brahmas; but now you have most gloriously achieved the mightiest work, and reached the acme of perfection. It remains with you only to aspire at the full possession of the supreme intelligence, which will enable you to open to all Brahmas, Nats, and men the way to the deliverance from those endless series of countless existences [12] through which they are doomed

---

ments are, renouncing children, wife, goods, life, and one's self.

[12] Metempsychosis is one of the fundamental dogmas of Buddhism. That continual transition from one existence to another, from a state of happiness to one of unhappiness, and *vice versa*, forms a circle encompassing the Buddhist in every direction. He is doomed to fluctuate incessantly on the never-settled waters of existence. Hence his ardent wishes to be delivered from that most pitiable position, and his earnest longings for the ever-tranquil state of Neibban, the way to which Buddha alone can teach him by his precepts and his examples.

This dogma is common both to Brahmins and Buddhists. The originator and propagator of the creed of the latter found it already established; he had but to embody it among his own conceptions, and make it agree with his new ideas. His first teachers were Brahmins, and under their tuition he learned that dogma which may be considered as the basis on which hinge both systems. In fact, the two rival creeds have a common object in view, the elevating of the soul from those imperfections forced upon her by her connection with matter, and the setting of her free from the sway of passions, which keep her always linked to this world. According to the votaries of both creeds, transmigration has for its object the effecting of those several purposes. There is a curious opinion among Buddhists respecting the mode of transmigrations, and there is no doubt it is a very ancient one, belonging to the genuine productions of the earliest Buddhism. Transmigration, they say, is caused and entirely controlled by the influence of merits and demerits, but in such a way that a being who has come to his end transmits nothing of his entity to the being to be immediately reproduced. The latter is a being apart, independent of the former, created, it is true, by the influence of the late being's good or bad deeds, but having nothing in common with him. They explain this startling doctrine by the comparison of a tree successively producing and bearing fruits, of which some are good and some bad. The fruits, though coming from the same tree, have nothing in common, either with each other or with those that were previously grown, or may afterwards grow out of the same plant; they are distinct and separate. So they say, *kan*, or the influence of merits and demerits, produces successively beings totally distinct one from the other. This atheistic or materialistic doctrine is not generally known by the common people, who practically hold

to pass. Now the light of the law is extinguished, a universal darkness has overspread all minds. Men are more than ever slaves to their passions; there is a total lack of love among them; they hate each other, keep up quarrels, strifes and contentions, and mercilessly destroy each other. You alone can free them from the vicissitudes and miseries essentially connected with the present state of all beings. The time is at last come, when you are to become a Buddha."

Unwilling to return at once a positive answer, Phralaong modestly replied that he wanted some time to inquire particularly into the great circumstances always attending the coming of a Buddha in this world, viz., the epoch or time when a Buddha appears, the place which he chooses for his apparition or manifestation, the race or caste he is to be born from, and the age and quality of her who is to be his mother. As regards the first circumstance, Phralaong observed that the apparition of a Buddha could not have taken place during the previous period[13] of 100,000 years

---

that transmigration is effected in the manner professed and taught by Pythagoras and his school.

If between the adherents of the two creeds there is a perfect agreement respecting the means to be resorted to for reaching the point when man becomes free from miseries, ignorance, and imperfections, they are at variance as to the end to be arrived to. The Brahmin leads the perfected being to the supreme essence, in which he is merged as a drop of water in the ocean, losing his personality, to form a whole with the Divine substance. This is Pantheism. The Buddhist, ignoring a supreme being, conducts the individual that has become emancipated from the thraldom of passions to a state of complete isolation, called Neibban. This is, strictly speaking, Annihilation.

[13] The duration of a revolution of nature, or the time required for the formation of a world, its existence and destruction, is divided into four periods. The fourth period, or that which begins with the apparition of man on the earth until its destruction, is divided into sixty-four parts, called andrakaps. During one andrakap, the life of man increases gradually from ten years to an almost innumerable number of years; and having reached its maximum of duration, it decreases slowly to its former short duration of ten years. We live at present in that second part of an andrakap when the life of man is on the decline and decrease. If my memory serve me right, we have reached at present the ninth or tenth andrakap of the fourth period. Should the calculation of Buddhists ever prove correct, the deluded visionaries who look forward to an approaching Millennium, have still to wait long ere their darling wishes be realised.

Though it be somewhat tiresome and unpleasant to have to write down

and more that had just elapsed, because during that period the life of men was on the increase. The instructions on birth and death, as well as on the miseries of life, which

---

the absurd and ridiculous notions Burmans entertain respecting the organisation of matter, the origin, production, existence, duration, and end of the world, it appears quite necessary to give a brief account, and sketch an outline of their ideas on these subjects. The reader will then have the means of tracing up to their Hindu origin several of the many threads that link Buddhism to Brahminism, and better understand the various details hereafter to be given, and intended for establishing a great fact, viz., the Brahminical origin of the greater part of the Buddhistic institutions. He will, moreever, have the satisfaction of clearly discovering, buried in the rubbish of fabulous recitals, several important facts recorded in the Holy Scriptures.

Matter is eternal, but its organisation and all the changes attending it are caused and regulated by certain laws co-eternal with it. Both matter and the laws that act upon it are self-existing, independent of the action and control of any being, &c. As soon as a system of worlds is constituted, Buddhists boldly assert and perseveringly maintain that the law of merit and demerit is the sole principle that regulates and controls both the physical and moral world.

But how is a world brought into existence? Water, or rather rain, is the chief agent, operating in the reproduction of a system of nature. During an immense period of time rain pours down with an unabating violence in the space left by the last world that has been destroyed. Meanwhile strong winds, blowing from opposite directions, accumulate the water within definite and certain limits until it has filled the whole space. At last appears on the surface of water, floating like a greasy substance, the sediment deposited by water. In proportion as the water dries up under the unremitting action of the wind, that crust increases in size, until, by a slow, gradual, but sure process, it invariably assumes the shape and proportion of our planet, in the manner we are to describe. The centre of the earth, indeed of a world or system of nature, is occupied by a mountain of enormous size and elevation, called Mienmo. This is surrounded by seven ranges of mountains, separated from each other by streams, equalling, in breadth and depth, the height of the mountain forming its boundaries in the direction of the central elevation. The range nearest to the Mienmo rises to half its height. Each successive range is half the height of the range preceding it. Beyond the last stream are disposed four great islands, in the direction of the four points of the compass. Each of those four islands is surrounded by five hundred smaller ones. Beyond those there is water, reaching to the farthest limits of the world. The great island we inhabit is the southern one, called Dzampoudipa, from the Jambu, or Eugenia tree, growing upon it.

Our planet rests on a basis of water double the thickness of the earth; the water itself is lying on a mass of air that has a thickness double that of water. Below this aërial stratum is *laha*, or vacuum.

Let us see now in what manner our planet is peopled, and whence came its first inhabitants. From the seats of Brahmas which were beyond the range of destruction when the former world perished, three celestial beings, or, according to another version, six, came on the earth, remaining on it in a state of perfect happiness, occasion-

form the true characteristics of Buddha's law, would not then be received with sufficient interest and attention. Had any attempt been made at that time to preach on

ally revisiting, when it pleased them, their former seats of glory. This state of things lasts during a long period. At that time the two great luminaries of the day and the stars of night have not as yet made their appearance, but rays of incomparable brightness, emanating from the pure bodies of those new inhabitants, illuminate the globe. They feed at long intervals upon a certain gelatinous substance, of such a nutritious power that the smallest quantity is sufficient to support them for a long period. This delicious food is of the most perfect flavour. But it happens that at last it disappears, and is successively replaced by two other substances, one of which resembles the tender sprout of a tree. They are so nutritious and purified that in our present condition we can have no adequate idea of their properties. They too disappear, and are succeeded by a sort of rice called *Tha-le.* The inhabitants of the earth eat also of that rice. But alas! the consequences prove as fatal to them as the eating of the forbidden fruit proved to the happy denizens of Eden. The brightness that had hitherto encircled their bodies and illuminated the world vanishes away, and, to their utmost dismay, they find themselves, for the first time, sunk into an abyss of unknown darkness. The eating of that coarse food creates fæces and evacuations which, forcing their way out of the body, cause the appearance of what marks the distinction of the sexes. Passions, for the first time, burn and rage in the bosom of those hitherto passionless beings. They are deprived of the power to return to their celestial seats. Very soon jealousy, contentions, &c., follow in the train of the egotistical distinction of *mine* and *thine.* Finding themselves in the gloom of darkness, the unhappy beings sigh for and long after light, when, on a sudden, the sun, breaking down the barrier of darkness, bursts out, rolling, as it were, in a flood of light, which illuminates the whole world; but soon disappearing in the west below the horizon, darkness seems to resume its hold. New lamentations and bewailings arise on the part of men, when in a short time appears majestically the moon, spreading its silvery and trembling rays of light. At the same time the planets and stars take their respective stations in the sky, and begin their regular revolutions. The need of settling disputes that arise is soon felt by the new inhabitants; they agree to elect a chief, whom they invest with a sufficient authority for framing regulations which are to be obligatory on every member of society, and power for enforcing obedience to those regulations. Hence the origin of society.

Men, at first practising virtue, enjoyed a long life, the duration of which reached to the almost incredible length of a thingie. But they having much relaxed in the practice of virtue, it lessened proportionably to their want of fervour in the observance of the law, until, by their extreme wickedness, it dwindled to the short period of ten years. The same ascending and descending scale of human life, successively brought in by the law of merit and demerit, takes place sixty-four times, and constitutes an andrakap, or the duration of a world.

It remains only to mention rapidly some particulars regarding the end of a revolution of nature. The cause of such an event is the influence of the demerits, prevailing to such an extent as to be all-powerful in working out

these three great topics, the men of those days, to whom those great events would have appeared so distant, could not have been induced to look upon them with sufficient attention; the four great truths would have made no impression on their minds; vain and fruitless would have been the efforts to disentangle them from the ties of passions, then encompassing all beings, and to make them sigh after the deliverance from the miseries entailed upon mankind by birth, life, and death. The period when human life is under a hundred years' duration cannot at all be the proper period for such an important event, as the passions of men are then so many and so deeply rooted that Buddha would in vain attempt to preach his law. As the characters which a man traces over the smooth surface of unruffled water instantly disappear without leaving any mark behind, so the law and instructions that one should attempt to spread on the hardened hearts of men would make no lasting impression upon them. Hence he concluded that the present period, when the life of men was of about a hundred years' duration, was the proper one for the apparition of a Buddha. This first point having been disposed

---

destruction. Two solemn warnings of the approaching dissolution of our planet are given by Nats, one nearly 100,000 and the other 100 years before that event. The bearers of such sad news make their appearance on earth with marks of deep mourning, as best suited to afford additional weight to their exhortations. They earnestly call on men to repent of their sins and amend their lives. These last summonses are generally heeded by all mankind, so that men, when the world is destroyed, generally migrate, together with the victims of hell who have atoned for their past iniquities, to those seats of Brahmas that escape destruction. There are three great principles of demerit, concupiscence, anger, and ignorance. The world also is destroyed by the action of three different agents, fire, water, and wind. Concupiscence is the most common, though the less heinous of the three. Next comes anger, less prevailing, though it is more heinous; but ignorance is by far the most fatal of all moral distempers. The moral disorder then prevailing causes destruction by the agency that it sets in action. Concupiscence has for its agency fire; anger, water; ignorance, wind; but in the following proportion. Of sixty-four destructions of this world, fifty-six are caused by conflagration, seven by water, and one by wind. Their respective limits of duration stand as follows: conflagration reaches to the five lowest seats of Brahmas; water extends to the eighth seat, and the destructive violence of the wind is felt as far as the ninth seat.

of, Phralaong examined in what part of the globe a Buddha was to appear.

His regards glanced over the four great islands [14] and the 2000 small ones. He saw that the island of Dzapoudiba, the southern one, had always been the favourite place selected by all former Buddhas; he fixed upon it, too, for himself. That island, however, is a most extensive one, measuring in length 300 youdzanas, in breadth 252, and in circumference 900. He knew that on that island former Buddhas and semi-Buddhas, the two great Rahandas,[15] or disciples of the right and left, the prince whose sway is universal, &c., had all of them invariably fixed upon and selected that island, and, amidst the various countries on the island, that of Mitzima, the central one, where is to be found the district of Kapilawot. "Thither," said he, "shall I resort, and become a Buddha."

Having determined the place which he was to select for his terrestrial seat, Phralaong examined the race or caste from which he was to be born. The caste of the people

---

[14] Our planet or globe is composed, according to Buddhists, of the mountain Mienmo, being in height 82,000 youdzanas (1 youdzana is, according to some authorities, equal to little less than 12 English miles) above the surface of the earth, and in depth equal to its height. Around this huge and tall elevation are disposed the four great islands, according to the four points of the compass; and each of these again is surrounded by 500 small islands. The countries south of the great chain of the Himalaya are supposed to form the great island lying at the south.

It would be easy to give, at full length, the ridiculous notions entertained by Buddhists of these parts on geography and cosmography, &c., &c.; but the knowledge of such puerilities is scarcely worth the attention of a serious reader, who is anxious to acquire accurate information respecting a religious system, which was designed by its inventor to be the vehicle of moral doctrines, with but very few dogmas. Those speculations upon this material world have gradually found their place in the collection of sacred writings, but they are no part of the religious creed. They are of a Hindu origin, and convey Indian notions upon those various topics. These notions even do not belong to the system as expounded in the Vedas, but have been set forth at a comparatively modern epoch.

[15] A Rahanda is a being very far advanced in perfection, and gifted with high spiritual attainments, which impart to his mortal frame certain distinguished prerogatives, becoming almost spirits. Concupiscence is totally extinguished in a Rahanda; he may be said to be fit for the state Neibban. Several classes are assigned to Rahandas alone, according to their various degrees of advancement in the way of perfection.

and that of merchants appeared too low, and much wanting in respectability, and, moreover, no Buddha had ever come out therefrom. That of the Pounhas was in former times the most illustrious and respected, but that of princes, in those days, far surpassed it in power and consideration. He therefore fixed his choice upon the caste of princes, as most becoming his future high calling. "I choose," said he, "prince Thoodaudana for my father. As to the princess who is to become my mother, she must be distinguished by a modest deportment and chaste manners, and must never have tasted any intoxicating drink. During the duration of 100,000 worlds she must have lived in the practice of virtue, performing with a scrupulous exactitude all the rules and observances prescribed by the law. The great and glorious Princess Maia is the only person in whom all these conditions are to be found. Moreover, the period of her life shall be at an end ten months and seven days hence;[16] she shall be my mother."

Having thus maturely pondered over these four circumstances, Phralaong, turning to the Nats that surrounded him, anxiously expecting his answer, plainly and unreservedly told them that the time for his becoming Buddha had arrived, and bade them forthwith communicate this great news to all the Brahmas and Nats. He rose up, and, accompanied by all the Nats of Toocita, withdrew into the delightful garden of Nandawon. After a short sojourn in that place, he left the abode of Nats, descended into the seat of men, and incarnated in the womb of the glorious

[16] It is an immutable decree that she on whom has been conferred the singular honour of giving birth to a mortal who, during the course of his existence, is to become a Buddha, dies invariably seven days after her delivery, migrating to one of the delightful seats of Nats. The Burmese translator observes that a womb that has been, as it were, consecrated and sanctified by the presence of a child of so exalted a dignity, can never become afterwards the hidden abode of less dignified beings. It must be confessed that the conception of Phralaong in his mother's womb is wrapped up in a mysterious obscurity, appearing as it does to exclude the idea of conjugal intercourse. The Cochin-Chinese in their religious legends pretend that Buddha was conceived and born from Maia in a wonderful manner, not resembling at all what takes place according to the order of nature.

Maia, who at once understood that she was pregnant with a boy who would obtain the Buddhaship. At the same moment also the Princess Yathaudara, who was to be the wife of the son of Maia, descended from the seats of Nats, and was conceived in the womb of Amitau, the wife of Prince Thouppabuddha.

At that time the inhabitants of Kapilawot were busily engaged in celebrating, in the midst of extraordinary rejoicings, the festival of the constellation of Outarathan (July–August). But the virtuous Maia, without mixing amidst the crowds of those devoted to amusements, during the seven days that preceded the full moon of July, spent her time among her attendants, making offerings of flowers and perfumes. The day before the full moon she rose up at an early hour, bathed in perfumed water, and distributed to the needy four hundred thousand pieces of silver. Attired in her richest dress, she took her meal, and religiously performed all the pious observances usual on such occasions. This being done, she entered into her private apartment, and, lying on her couch, fell asleep and had the following dream:—

Four princes of Nats, of the abode of Tsadoomarit, took the princess with her couch, carried it to the Mount Himawonta,[17] and deposited it on an immense and magnificent rock, sixty youdzanas long, adorned with various colours, at the spot where a splendid tree, seven youdzanas high, extends its green and rich foliage. The four queens, wives of the four princes of Tsadoomarit, approaching the couch where Maia was reclining, took her to the banks of the lake Anawadat, washed her with the water of the lake, and spread over the couch flowers brought from the abode of Nats. Near the lake is a beautiful mountain of a silvery appearance, the summit whereof is crowned with a magni-

[17] The Mount Himawonta is famous in all Buddhistic compositions, as the scene where great and important events have happened. It is in all probability the Himalaya, as being the highest range of mountains ever known to Indian Buddhists.

ficent and lofty palace. On the east of the palace, in the side of the mount, is a splendid cave. Within the cave, a bed similar to that of the Nats was prepared. The princess was led to that place and sat on the bed, enjoying a delicious and refreshing rest. Opposite this mount, and facing the cave where Maia sat surrounded by her attendants, rose another mount, where Phralaong, under the shape of a young white elephant, was roaming over its sides in various directions. He was soon seen coming down that hill, and, ascending the one where the princess lay on her bed, directed his course towards the cave. On the extremity of his trunk, lifted up like a beautiful string of flowers, he carried a white lily. His voice, occasionally resounding through the air, could be heard distinctly by the inmates of the grotto, and indicated his approach. He soon entered the cave, turned three times round the couch whereupon sat the princess, then, standing for a while, he came nearer, opened her right side, and appeared to conceal himself in her womb.

In the morning, having awoke from her sleep, the queen related her dream to her husband. King Thoodaudana sent without delay for sixty-four Pounhas.[18] On a

[18] Pounhas are the Brahmins who, even in those days of remote antiquity, were considered as the wisest in their generation. They had already monopolised the lucrative trade of fortune-tellers, astrologers, &c., and it appears that they have contrived to retain it up to our own days. During my first stay in Burmah I became acquainted with a young Pounha, wearing the white dress, and getting his livelihood by telling the horoscopes of newly-born infants, and even grown-up people. I learned from him the mode of finding out by calculation the state of the heavens at any given hour whatever. This mode of calculation is entirely based on the Hindu system, and has evidently been borrowed from that people.

Though Brahmins in those days, as in our own, worked on popular ignorance and credulity in the manner abovementioned, we ought not to lose sight of the great fact, borne out by this legend in a most distinct and explicit way, that many among them devoted all their time, energies, and abilities to the acquirement of wisdom, and the observance of the most arduous practices. Their austere mode of life was to a great extent copied and imitated by the first religious of the Buddhist persuasion. Many ordinances and prescriptions of the Wini agree, in a remarkable degree, with those enforced by the Vedas. In the beginning, the resemblance must have been so great as to render the discrepancies scarcely perceptible, since

ground lined with cow-dung, where parched rice, flowers, and other offerings were carefully deposited and profusely spread, an appropriate place was reserved for the Pounhas. Butter, milk, and honey were served out to them in vases of gold and silver; moreover, several suits of apparel and five cows were offered to each of them as presents, as well as many other articles. These preliminaries being arranged, the prince narrated to them the dream, with a request for its explanation.

"Prince," answered the Pounhas, "banish from your mind all anxious thoughts, and be of a cheerful heart; the child whom the princess bears in her womb is not a girl but a boy. He will, after growing up, either live amongst men, and then become a mighty ruler, whose sway all the human race will acknowledge; or, withdrawing from the tumult of society, he will resort to some solitary place, and there embrace the profession of Rahan. In that condition he will disentangle himself from the miseries attending existence, and at last obtain the high dignity of Buddha." Such was the explanation of the dream. At the moment Phralaong entered into Maia's womb, a great commotion was felt throughout the four elements, and thirty-two wonders simultaneously appeared. A light of an incomparable brightness illuminated suddenly ten thousand worlds. The blind, desirous, as it were, to contemplate the glorious dignity of Phralaong, recovered their sight; the deaf heard distinctly every sound; the dumb spoke with fluency; those whose bodies were bent stood up in an erect position; the lame walked with ease and swiftness; prisoners saw their fetters unloosed, and found themselves restored to liberty; the fires of hell were extinguished; the ravenous cravings of the Preithas[19] were satiated; animals were

we read in this very work of an injunction made to the early converts, to bestow alms on the Pounhas as well as on the Bickus or mendicant religious, placing them both on a footing of perfect equality.

[19] Preitha is a being in a state of punishment and sufferings on account of sins committed in a former existence. He is doomed to live in the solitary recesses of uninhabited mountains, smarting under the pangs of never-

exempt from all infirmities; all rational beings uttered but words of peace and mutual benevolence; horses exhibited signs of an excessive joy; elephants, with a solemn and deep voice, expressed their contentment; musical instruments resounded of themselves with the most melodious harmony; gold and silver ornaments, worn at the arms and feet, without coming in contact, emitted pleasing sounds; all places became suddenly filled with a resplendent light; refreshing breezes blew gently all over the earth; abundant rain poured from the skies during the hot season, and springs of cool water burst out in every place, carrying through prepared beds their gently murmuring streams; birds of the air stood still, forgetting their usual flight; rivers suspended their course, seized with a mighty astonishment; sea water became fresh; the five sorts of lilies were to be seen in every direction; every description of flowers burst open, displaying the richness of their brilliant colours; from the branches of all trees and the bosom of the hardest rocks, flowers shot forth, exhibiting all around the most glowing, dazzling, and varied hues; lilies, seemingly rooted in the canopy of the skies, hung down, scattering their embalmed fragrance; showers of flowers poured from the firmament on the surface of the earth; the musical tunes of the Nats were heard by the rejoiced inhabitants of our globe; hundreds of thousands of worlds[20] suddenly approached each other, sometimes in the shape of an elegant nosegay, sometimes in that of a ball of flowers or of a spheroid; the choicest essences embalmed the whole atmosphere that encompasses this world. Such are the wonders that took place at the time Phralaong entered his mother's womb.

---

satiated hunger. His body, and particularly his stomach, are of gigantic dimensions, whilst his mouth is so small that a needle could scarcely be shoved into it.

[20] In the Buddhistic system of cosmogony, 100,000 worlds form one system, subject to the same immutable changes and revolutions as affect this one which we inhabit. They admit, indeed, that the number of worlds is unlimited, but they assert that those forming one system are simultaneously destroyed, reproduced and perfected, by virtue of certain eternal laws inherent in matter itself.

When this great event happened, four chiefs of Nats, from the seat of Tsadoomarit,[21] armed with swords, kept an uninterrupted watch round the palace, to avert any accident that might prove hurtful to the mother or her blessed fruit. From 10,000 worlds, four Nats from the same seat were actively engaged in driving away all Bilous[22] and other monsters, and forcing them to flee and hide themselves at the extremity of the earth. Maia, free from every disordered propensity, spent her time with her handmaids in the interior of her apartments. Her soul enjoyed, in a perfect calm, the sweetest happiness; fatigue and weariness never affected her unimpaired health. In his mother's womb, Phralaong appeared like the white thread passed through the purest and finest pearls; the womb itself resembled an elegant Dzedi.[23] *

[21] Tsadoomarit is the first of the six abodes of Nats. The description of the pleasures enjoyed by the inhabitants of that seat is replete with accounts of the grossest licentiousness.

[22] A Palou, or rather Bilou, is a monster with a human face, supposed to feed on human flesh. His eyes are of a deep red hue, and his body of so subtle a nature as never to project any shadow. Wonderful tales are told of this monster, which plays a considerable part in most of the Buddhistic writings.

[23] A Dzedi is a religious edifice of a conical form, supported on a square basis, and having its top covered with what the Burmese call an umbrella, resembling in its shape the musical instrument vulgarly called *chapeau chinois* by the French. On each side of the quadrangular basis are opened four niches, in the direction of the four cardinal points, destined to receive statues of Buddha. This monument is of every dimension in size, from the smallest, a few feet high, to the tallest, of one or two hundred feet high. It is to be seen in every direction, and in the neighbourhood of towns every elevation is crowned with one or several Dzedis.

The word Dzedi means a sacred depository, that is to say, a place where relics of Buddha were enshrined. The word has been extended since to places which have become

* *Remark of the Burmese Translator.*—It is to be borne in mind that mothers of Buddhas having had the singular privilege of giving birth to a child of so exalted a dignity, it would not be convenient or becoming that other mortals should receive life in the same womb; they therefore always die seven days after their delivery and migrate to the abode of Nats, called Toocita. It is usual with other mothers to be delivered, lying in an horizontal position, and sometimes before or after the tenth month. But with the mother of a Buddha the case is not the same; the time of her confinement invariably happens at the beginning of the tenth month, and she is always delivered in an erect and vertical position.

With the solicitous care and vigilant attention with which one carries about a thabeit[24] full of oil, the great Maia watched all her movements, and during ten months unremittingly laboured for the safe preservation of the precious fruit of her womb.

---

receptacles of the scriptures, or of the relics of distinguished religious, who had acquired eminence by their scientific and moral attainments. In the beginning, those Dzedis were a kind of *tumuli*, or mounds of earth or bricks, erected upon the shrine wherein relics were enclosed. In proportion as the followers of the Buddhistic faith increased in number, wealth, and influence, they erected Dzedis on a grander scale, bearing always a great resemblance in shape and form to the primitive ones. The stupas or topes discovered in the Punjaub, and in other parts of the Indian Peninsula, were real Buddhistic tumuli or Dzedis.

During succeeding ages, when relics could not be procured, the faithful continued to erect Dzedis, the sight of which was intended to remind them of the sacred relics, and they paid to those relics and monuments the same veneration as they would have offered to those enriched with those priceless objects. In Burmah, in particular, the zeal, or rather the rage, for building Dzedis has been carried to a degree scarcely to be credited by those who have not visited that country. In the following pages there will be found an attempt to describe the various forms given to those monuments.

[24] The thabeit is an open-mouthed pot, of a truncated spheroidical form, made of earth, iron, or brass, without ornaments, used by the Buddhist monks when going abroad, in their morning excursions, to receive the alms bestowed on them by the admirers of their holy mode of life.

CHAPTER II.

Birth of Buddha in a forest—Rejoicings on that occasion—Kaladewila—Prediction of the Pounhas—Vain efforts of Thoodaudana to thwart the effect of the Prediction.

THE time of her approaching confinement being close at hand, the princess solicited from her husband, King Thoodaudana, leave to go to the country of Dewah,[1] amongst her friends and relatives. As soon as her request was made known, the king ordered that the whole extent of the road between Kapilawot and Dewah should be per-

[1] This country of Dewah is one of the sixteen countries, so much celebrated in the Buddhistic annals, where the greatest religious events have taken place. They are placed in the centre, north, and north-west portions of Hindustan. In this place was born the celebrated Dewadat, who became brother-in-law to Buddha himself. But notwithstanding the close ties of relationship that united him to so saintly a personage, Dewadat is represented as the incarnation of evil, ever opposed to Buddha in his benevolent designs in favour of human kind. At last, in an attempt against his brother-in-law's life, he met with a condign punishment. The earth burst open under his feet, and, surrounded by devouring flames, he rolled down to the bottom of the lowest hell, acknowledging, however, in the accents of a true but tardy repentance, his errors and the unconquerable power of Buddha. Three red-hot iron bars transfix him perpendicularly, hanging him in an erect position, whilst three other bars pierce him through the shoulders and the side. For his repentance he is to be delivered hereafter from those torments, and restored to earth, in order to acquire merits that may entitle him to a better place in future existences. Some accounts mention that he is to become a Pietzega Buddha. This story respecting Dewadat has given rise in Burmah to a very strange misconception. The Burmese, with their usual thoughtlessness, on hearing of the particulars respecting the sufferings and mode of death of our Saviour, concluded that he must have been no other but Dewadat himself, and that, for holding opinions opposite to those of Buddha, he suffered such a punishment. The writer was not a little surprised to find in the writings of the old Barnabite missionaries a lengthened confutation of this erroneous supposition.

fectly levelled, and lined on both sides with plantain trees, and adorned with the finest ornaments. Jars, full of the purest water, were to be deposited all along the road at short intervals. A chair of gold was made ready for conveying the queen; and a thousand noblemen, attended by an innumerable retinue, were directed to accompany her during the journey. Between the two countries an immense forest of lofty Engyin trees extends to a great distance. As soon as the *cortège* reached it, five water-lilies shot forth spontaneously from the stem and the main branches of each tree, and innumerable birds of all kinds, by their melodious tunes, filled the air with the most ravishing music. Trees, similar in beauty to those growing in the seats of Nats, apparently sensible of the presence of the incarnated Buddha, seemed to share in the universal joy.

On beholding this wonderful appearance of all the lofty trees of the forest, the queen felt a desire to approach nearer and enjoy the marvellous sight offered to her astonished regards. Her noble attendants led her forthwith a short distance into the forest. Maia, seated on her couch, along with her sister Patzapati, desired her attendants to have it moved closer to an Engyin tree (*shorea robusta*), which she pointed out. Her wishes were immediately complied with. She then rose gently on her couch; her left hand, clasped round the neck of her sister, supported her in a standing position. With the right hand she tried to reach and break a small branch, which she wanted to carry away. On that very instant, as the slender rattan, heated by fire, bends down its tender head, all the branches lowered their extremities, offering themselves, as it were, to the hand of the queen, who unhesitatingly seized and broke the extremity of one of the young boughs. By virtue of a certain power inherent in her dignity, on a sudden all the winds blew gently throughout the forest. The attendants, having desired all the people to withdraw to a distance, disposed curtains all round the place the queen was standing on. Whilst she was in that position, admiring the slender bough she held in her hands, the moment of her confinement happened, and she was delivered of a son.*

Four chief Brahmas[2] received the new-born infant on a golden net-work, and placed him in the presence of the happy mother, saying, "Give yourself up, O Queen, to joy

* On the same day a son was born to Amitaudana, called Ananda. The wife of Thouppaboudha of Dewah was delivered of a daughter, called Yathaudara, who became afterwards the wife of Phralaong. Anouroudha, the son of Thookkaudana, was ushered into existence on the same solemn occasion. The above-named Ananda was first cousin to the Buddha, and subsequently became the amiable, faithful, and devoted disciple who, during twenty-five years, attended on the person of Buddha, and affectionately ministered to all his wants. After the death of his mother Maia, Phralaong was nursed and brought up with the greatest care by his aunt Patzapati, sometimes called Gautamee.

[2] According to Buddhistic notions, Buddha labours during his mortal career for the benefit of all living beings. His benevolent and compassionate heart, free from all partiality, feels an ardent desire of opening before them the way that leads to deliverance from the miseries of every succeeding existence, and of bringing them finally to the never troubled state of Neibban. Such a generous and benevolent disposition constitutes the genuine characteristic of Buddha. The Brahmas, inhabiting the sixteen seats of Rupa, are all but ripe for obtaining the crowning point of Buddhistic perfection. They only wait for the presence of a Buddha to unloose, by his preachings, the slender ties that keep them still connected with this material world. The Nats, though far less advanced in merits and perfection, eagerly look forward for the apparition of that great personage, who is to point out to them the means of freeing themselves from the influence of passions, and thereby destroying in them the principle of demerits. Men, also, in their state of probation and trial, want the mighty aid of a Buddha, who will enable them by his transcendent doctrine to advance in merits, so as either to arrive at once at the ever-quiescent state of Neibban, or progress gradually on the way. Hence, on his birth, Buddha is ministered to by those three sorts of intelligent beings, who are particularly destined to share in the blessings his coming is designed to shower on them.

The mission of a Buddha is that of a saviour. His great object, to make use of a Buddhistic expression, is, during his existence, to procure the deliverance of all the beings that will listen to his instructions and observe the precepts of the law. He is distinguished by feelings of compassion and an ardent love for all beings, as well as by an earnest desire of labouring for their welfare. These are the true characteristics of his heart. In this religious system mention is often made of Pitzegabuddhas, who have all the science and merits of a Buddha, but they are deficient in the above-mentioned qualities, which form, as it were, the essence of a true and genuine Buddha. They are never therefore honoured with the noble appellation of Buddha.

and rejoicing; here is the precious and wonderful fruit of your womb." *

From the hands of the four chiefs of Brahmas, four chiefs of Nats received the blessed child, whom they handed over to men, who placed him on a beautiful white cloth. But to the astonishment of all, he freed himself from the hands of those attending upon him, and stood in a firm and erect position on the ground, when casting a glance towards the east, more than one thousand worlds appeared like a perfectly levelled plain. All the Nats inhabiting those worlds made offerings of flowers and perfumes, exclaiming with exultation, "An exalted personage has made his appearance;—who can ever be compared to him? who has ever equalled him? He is indeed the most excellent of all beings." Phralaong looked again towards the three other directions. Raising his eyes upwards, and then lowering them down, he saw that there was no being equal to him. Conscious of his superiority, he jumped over a distance of seven lengths of a foot, in a northern direction, exclaiming,—"This is my last birth; there shall be to me no other state of existence; I am the greatest of all beings."[3] He then began to walk steadily in the same

* *Remarks of the Burmese Translator.*—When children are born they appear in this world covered all over their bodies with impure and disgusting substances. But an exception was made in favour of our infant Phralaong. He was born without the least stain of offending impurity; he was ushered into this world, pure and resplendent, like a fine ruby placed on a piece of the richest cloth of Kathika. He left his mother's womb with his feet and hands stretched out, exhibiting the dignified countenance of a Pundit descending from the place where he has expounded the law. Though both mother and child were exempt from the humiliating miseries common to all other human beings, there came down from the skies upon both, by way of a respectful offering, gentle showers of cold and warm water, succeeding each other alternately in a regular order.

[3] The Chinese, Cochin-Chinese, Cingalese, and Nepaulese Legends all agree in attributing to Phralaong the use of reason from the moment he was born, as well as the power of uttering with a proud accent the following words: "I am the greatest of all beings; this is my last existence." To his own eyes he must have appeared in this world without any competitor, since he knew already that he was destined to release countless beings from the trammels of existence, and lead them to a state of

direction. A chief of Brahmas held over his head the white umbrella.[4] A Nat carried the golden fan. Other Nats held in their hands the golden sword, the golden slippers, the cope set with the rarest precious stones, and other royal insignia.*

perfect rest, screened for ever from the incessant action of merits and demerits. He alone whose mind is deeply imbued with Buddhistic notions can boast exultingly that he has at length arrived at his last existence, and that, within a few years, he will escape out of the whirlpool of endless existences, wherein he has been turning and fluctuating from a state of happiness to one of wretchedness. This perpetual vicissitude is to him the greatest evil, the opposite of which is, therefore, the greatest good. No wonder, then, to hear our Phralaong, who was better acquainted with the miseries attending existence than any one else, exclaiming with the accents of a complete joy—"This is my last existence."

The Burmese translator seems delighted to remark that on two former occasions Phralaong, then an infant, had spoken distinct words, which he addressed to his mother. This happened in the beginning of the two existences during which he practised two of the ten great virtues. It took place first on the day he was born to that existence, when, under the name of Mahauthata, he displayed consummate skill and wisdom. The legend of Mahauthata is a very amusing performance, written in a very pure language, and relating stories about as credible as those we read in the Arabian Tales of a Thousand and One Nights. What surprised the writer not a little, was to find, in perusing that composition, a decision given by our Mahauthata, in a case perfectly similar to that which showed forth, in the presence of all Israel, the incomparable wisdom of Solomon. When Phralaong practised the last and most perfect of virtues, liberality, carried to its farthest limits, ending in perfect abnegation of self, and renouncing all that he possessed, he entered, too, into this world with the faculty of speech, and became a prince under the name of Wethandra. The legend of Wethandra is by far the best of all. Taking it as a mere romance, it is replete with circumstantial details well calculated to excite the finest emotions of the heart. The latter part, in particular, can scarcely be read without heart-moving feelings of pity and commiseration, on beholding our Phralaong parting willingly with all his property, with his wife and his lovely children, and finally offering his own person, to satisfy the ever-renewed calls on his unbounded generosity.

[4] In Burmah the use of the white umbrella is limited to the king and idols. The former can never move without having some one to hold over his head this distinguishing mark of royalty. Any one who has been introduced into the palace of Amerapoora will not have forgotten how great was his satisfaction on beholding the white umbrella towering above the sides of passages, and moving in the direction he was sitting in. He knew that the time of his expectation was at an end, and that in a moment he would behold the golden face.

* *Remarks of the Burmese Translator.*—In former existences, our Phralaong is said to have spoken a few words immediately after his birth, viz., when he was Mahauthata and Wethandra. In the first, he came into this world holding in his hands a small plant, which a Nat had brought

Thirty-two mighty wonders had proclaimed the incarnation of Phralaong in his mother's womb, and the same number of wonders announced his birth to the earth. Moreover, in that same moment were born the beautiful Yathaudara, Ananda, the son of Amitaudana, the noblemen Tsanda and Kaludari, and the horse Kantika. The great tree Bodi also sprung from the ground, in the forest of Oorouwela, about two youdzanas distant from the city of Radzagio, and in a north-easterly direction from that place, and the four golden vases suddenly reappeared.

The inhabitants of Dewah, joining those of Kapilawot, set out for the latter country with the newly-born infant, to whom they rendered the greatest honours. The Nats of the seat of Tawadeintha, on hearing that a son was born to King Thoodaudana, and that under the shade of the tree Bodi[5] he would become a true Buddha with a per-

and placed in his tender hands at that very moment. He showed it to his mother, who asked him what it was. "This is a medicinal plant," replied he, to his astonished mother. The plant was cast into a large jar full of water, and the virtualised liquid ever retained the power of curing every kind of bodily distemper. When he was born, or rather began the existence in which he was called Wethandra, he stretched out his hands asking something from his mother which he might bestow on the needy. The mother put at his disposal one thousand pieces of silver.

[5] In glancing over the genealogy of the twenty-eight last Buddhas, the writer has observed that every Buddha has always obtained the supreme intelligence under the shadow of some trees. Our Phralaong, as will be seen hereafter, attained to the exalted dignity of Buddha under the tree Baudhi (*ficus religiosa*), which grew up spontaneously at the very moment he was born. The writer has never been able to discover any well-grounded reason to account for this remarkable circumstance, so carefully noted down, relating the particulars attending the elevation of a being to this high station. For want of a better one, he will be permitted to hazard the following conjecture. Our Phralaong, previous to his becoming a Buddha, withdrew into solitude for the purpose of fitting himself for his future calling, in imitation of all his predecessors, leading an ascetic life, and devoting all his undivided attention and mental energies to meditation and contemplation, coupled with works of the most rigorous mortification. The senses, he knew well, were to be submitted to the uncontrolled sway of reason, by allowing to himself only what was barely requisite for supporting nature. Regardless of every comfort, his mind was bent upon acquiring the sublime knowledge of the principle and origin of all things, on fathoming the miseries of all beings, and on endeavouring to discover the most efficacious means of

fect knowledge of the four great truths, gave full vent to their boundless joy, hoisting unfurled flags and banners in every direction, in token of their indescribable rejoicings.

There was a celebrated Rathee, named Kaladewila, who had passed through the eight degrees of contemplation, and who was in the habit of resorting daily to the prince's palace for his food. On that very day, having taken his meal as usual, he ascended to the seat of Tawadeintha,[6] and found the fortunate inhabitants of that seat giving themselves up to uncommon rejoicings. He asked them the reason of such an unusual display of enrapturing transports of exultation. "It is," replied they to the inquiring Rathee, "because a son is born to King Thoodaudana, who will soon become a true Buddha. Like all former Buddhas, he will preach the law and exhibit in his person and throughout his life the greatest wonders and a most accomplished pattern of the highest virtues. We will hear the law from his very mouth."

On hearing the answer of the Nats, Kaladewila immediately left the seat of Tawadeintha, and directed his

---

affording them a thorough relief, by pointing out to them the road they had to follow in order to disentangle themselves from the trammels of existence, and arrive at a state of perfect rest. In common with all other ascetics, our Phralaong had no other shelter against the inclemency of the seasons but the protecting shadow of trees. It was under the cooling and refreshing foliage of the trees of the forests, that he spent his time in the placid and undisturbed work of meditation, acquiring gradually that matchless knowledge and consummate wisdom which he needed for carrying on to perfection the benevolent undertaking he had in contemplation.

[6] It is a maxim generally received amongst Buddhists, that he who has far advanced in the way of perfection acquires extraordinary privileges both in his soul and his body. The latter obtains a sort of spiritualised nature, or rather matter becomes so refined and purified that he is enabled to travel over distances with almost the rapidity of the thought of the mind. The former, by the help of continual meditation on the causes and nature of all things, enlarges incessantly its sphere of knowledge. The remembrance of the past revives in the mind. From the lofty position such a being is placed in, he calmly considers and watches the movement of events that will take place in future times. The more his mind expands, and the sphere of his knowledge extends, the greater are the perfections and refinements attending the coarser part of his being.

aërial course towards the palace of Thoodaudana. Having entered into the palace and occupied the place prepared for him, he conveyed to the king the good tidings of a son having been born unto him.

A few days after this message, the royal child was brought into the presence of his rejoicing father. Kaladewila was present on the occasion. Thoodaudana ordered that the child should be attired with the finest dress, and placed in the presence of the Rathee, in order to pay him his respects. But the child rose up and set his two feet on the curled hair of the venerable personage. The persons present on the occasion, not knowing that a Buddha in his last existence never bows down to any being, thought that the head of the imprudent child would be split into seven parts as a punishment for his unbecoming behaviour. But Kaladewila, rising up from his seat, and lifting up his hands to his forehead, bowed respectfully to the infant Phralaong. The king, astonished at such an unusual condescension from so eminent a personage, followed his example, and out of respect prostrated himself before his son.

By virtue of his great spiritual attainments, Kaladewila could recollect at once all that had taken place during the forty preceding worlds, and foresee all that would happen during the same number of future revolutions of nature. On seeing the high perfections shining forth in our Phralaong, he considered attentively whether he would become a Buddha or not. Having ascertained that such a dignity was reserved for him, he wished to know if the remaining period of his own existence would permit him to witness the happy moment when he would be a Buddha. To his deep regret, he foresaw that the end of his life would come before the occurrence of that great event, and that he would have then migrated to one of the seats of Arupa, and be, therefore, deprived of the favour of hearing the law from his mouth. This foresight caused a profound sadness in his heart, and abundant tears flowed from his eyes. But when he reflected on the future destiny of the blessed child, he could not contain within himself the pure joy that overflowed his soul. The people present on the occasion soon observed the opposite emotions which alternately affected the soul of Kaladewila. They asked him the reason of such an unusual occurrence. "I rejoice," said he, "at the glorious destiny of that child; but I feel sad and disconsolate when I think that it will not be given to me to see and contemplate him clothed with the dignity of Buddha. I bewail with tears my great misfortune."

With a view of assuaging his sorrow, Kaladewila, casting another glance towards future events, eagerly sought to discover if, among his relatives, there would not be at least one who would be so fortunate as to see Phralaong in the nature of Buddha. He saw with inexpressible delight that his nephew Nalaka would enjoy the blessing denied to himself. Thereupon he went in all haste to his sister's house, inquiring about her son. At his request the lad was brought into his presence. "Beloved nephew," said the venerable Rathee, "thirty-five years hence,[7] the son

---

[7] According to the prophecy of Kaladewila, Phralaong is to become Buddha when thirty-five years old. The total duration of his life being eighty years, it follows that he has lived as Buddha forty-five years. The advice of the old Rathee to his nephew Nalaka, to become a Rahan in order to better dispose himself to welcome the coming of Buddha, and listen with greater benefit to his preachings, leads me to make a remark and write down an observation that has been already alluded to. From this passage and many others which the reader will easily notice hereafter, as well as from the example of Buddha himself, one must suppose that at the time Phralaong was born, some institutions, the most important one at least, viz., that of the Rahans, recluses, or monks, already existed in a more or less perfect state. Relying solely on the authority of this Legend, no attempt at denying this supposition can ever be made. Kaladewila speaks of the order of Rahans as of a thing well known. Nalaka sends to the bazaar for the purchase of the dress and other articles he wanted for his new mode of life. Phralaong, on his way to his garden, sees a Rahan, whose habits and manners are described to him by his coachman. Having become Buddha, he meets with ascetics and recluses living in community, leading a life much resembling that which he is supposed to have hereafter instituted, holding but few opinions, which, according to his own standard, were heretical. From these facts flows the natural conclusion that Gandama is not the inventor or originator of all the Buddhistic disciplinary institutions. He found

of King Thoodaudana will become a Buddha; you will contemplate him in that sublime and exalted nature. From this day, therefore, you shall embrace the profession of Rahan." The young man, who descended from a long succession of wealthy noblemen, said within himself, "My uncle, indeed, never says anything but under the impulse of irresistible and cogent motives. I will follow his advice and will become a recluse." He immediately ordered the purchase of the insignia of his new profession, a patta, a thingan,[8] and other articles. His head was shaved, and he put on the yellow garb. Attired in his new dress, he looked all round, and saw that, amongst

---

among the multifarious sects of Brahminism many practices and ordinances which he approved of and incorporated or embodied in his new system. This is another proof, amounting to a demonstration, that Buddhism is an offshoot of the great Hindu system. In this respect, Gaudama borrowed largely from what he found existing in his own days, in the schools he resorted to, and re-echoed many tenets upheld by the masters under whom he studied the sciences and the training to morals and virtue. He enlarged and developed certain favourite theories and principles which had found favour with him; at the same time, for the purpose of leading his disciples to perfection, he enforced many disciplinary regulations, almost similar to those he had been subjected to during the years of his probation. He was certainly an ardent promoter of the perfected and improved system he endeavoured to introduce.

[8] The Thingan or Tsiwaran is composed of three parts—the thinbaing, resembling an ample petticoat, bound up to the waist, with a leathern girdle, and falling down to the heels; the kowot, which consists of a sort of cloak of a rectangular shape, covering the shoulders and breast, and reaching somewhat below the knee; and the dougout, which is a piece of cloth of the same shape, folded many times, thrown over the left shoulder when going abroad, and used to sit on when no proper seat has been prepared. The colour of these three pieces, constituting the dress of a recluse, is invariably yellow. The jack-tree supplies the material for dyeing the cloth yellow. In order to maintain a spirit of perfect poverty among the members of the order of the recluse, the Wini prescribes that the tsiwaran ought to be made up with rags picked up here and there, and sewed together. The rule, in this respect, at least as far as its spirit goes, is thoroughly disregarded, and has become almost a dead letter.

The hairs of the head and the beard, being too often objects which vanity turns to its own purposes, are, to say the least, mere superfluities. A stern contemner of worldly things must, of course, do away with things which may prove temptations to him, or at least afford him unnecessary trouble. Hence no layman can ever aspire to become a Rahan unless he has previously submitted to the operation of a complete shaving of the head, including even the eye-brows.

all beings, the Rahans are by far the most excellent. Then turning towards the place which Phralaong occupied, he prostrated himself five successive times in that direction, rose up, placed the patta in its bag, threw it over his shoulder, and directed his steps towards the solitude of Himawonta, where he devoted himself to all the exercises of his profession. At the time Phralaong became a Buddha, our hermit went to that great master, learnt from him the works that lead to the state of perfect stability of mind, returned back to his solitude, and attained to the perfection of Rahanda by the practice of the eminent works. Seven months after his return, the end of his existence arrived, when, disentangled from all the ties that had hitherto kept him in the world of passions, he reached the happy state of Neibban.

CHAPTER III.

A Name is given to the child—Prediction of the Pounhas respecting the child—Death of Maia—Miraculous occurrence at the child's cradle—Adolescence of the Phralaong—He sees the four signs—Return from the garden to the royal city.

FIVE days after the birth of Phralaong took place the ceremony of washing the head and giving him a name. In the apartment of the palace several kinds of perfumed wood and essences, such as sandal-wood, lignum, aloes, camphor, &c., were strewed profusely, as well as the most exquisitely scented flowers and parched rice. The nogana (a sort of beverage made of milk, sugar, and honey) was prepared in great abundance. One hundred and eighty Pounhas,[1] the most versed in the science of astrology, were

[1] Which of the two systems, Buddhism or Brahminism, is the most ancient? This is a question which learned Orientalists have in former days variously answered. If, however, some credit is to be given to this Legend, and the hero thereof is to be regarded as the author of Buddhism, the solution of that much-controverted question is comparatively easy, and seems to admit of no doubt. Priority of antiquity is decidedly in favour of Brahminism. At the time Buddha was born, and in his own country, we find already subsisting the great politico-religious fabric of Hinduism. The distinction of caste is already mentioned in several passages. We find the Pounhas or Brahmins already monopolising the lucrative trade of soothsaying, and regarded as the best informed among their countrymen. They are treated with great respect and consideration even by proud monarchs, who testify their regard for them by costly presents and every possible mark of distinction. It is true that their caste is not always spoken of with great regard by Buddhist authors; but this is to be attributed to the deadly enmity that prevailed at a later period between those two great rival sects, which have so long struggled for supremacy over the Indian Peninsula. The Brahminical creed is spoken of in very disparaging terms by Buddhists; and, as a matter of course, they have been reciprocally handled severely by their opponents. To

invited to partake of a splendid entertainment in the palace. The king made to every one of them costly presents, and desired them to examine carefully all the signs, prognosticating the future destiny of his son. Amidst that crowd of soothsayers, eight Pounhas were present, who explained the dream that Maia had in the beginning of her pregnancy. Seven of them, lifting up the index [2] of each hand of the child, were amazed at the wonderful signs their eyes met. "If this child," said they, "remain in the society of men, he will become a mighty ruler that will bring all nations under his sway; but if he embrace the profession of recluse, he will certainly become a Buddha." They began to foretell the incomparable glory and high honours that would attend his universal reign. The eighth Pounha, named Kauntagnia, the descendant of the celebrated son of Thoodata, and the youngest of all, raised up the index of one hand of the child. Struck with

---

those who feel inclined to regard Buddha as but a great reformer of a religious system already existing, the question will not appear cleared of all difficulty. But upon them rests the task of establishing on uncontrovertible grounds their hypothesis, ere any serious attention can be paid to the conclusion they would fain infer in favour of the superior antiquity of Buddhism. As for us, we believe Buddha to be the real author of the great religious system under examination. But, at the same time, we readily concede that many elements found existing in those days were seized upon by Buddha, and skilfully arranged so as to harmonise well with his plans.

[2] Superstition and ignorance seem to have been in all ages and under every climate the prolific source of human follies and mental delusions. Man has always been and will ever be the same ridiculously superstitious being, as long as his mind is left to itself, unenlightened by revelation. With few exceptions, the greatest men of Italy and Greece were as superstitious as the *vulgus*, to whom, in every other respect, they were so superior. The resemblance error bears to truth, when human passions have some interest at stake, deceives many; under deceitful appearances it finds its way to the mind, and then clings to the heart. There is in man an innate desire of tearing asunder the thick veil that hides from him the knowledge of future events. Unable to comprehend the perfect economy of an all-wise Providence in the disposition and management of the affairs of this world, he has recourse to the most absurd means for satiating the cravings of his inordinate curiosity. Hence the prevailing superstition of those days, which induced men to believe that Brahmins, on inspecting the inner part of the hand, could discover certain signs, foreshowing the good or bad destiny of every individual.

the wonderful and unmistakable signs that forced themselves on his view, he exclaimed, "No! this child will not remain long in the society of men; he will free himself from the vicissitudes[3] and miseries attending the existence of all beings, and will finally become a Buddha." As the child was to be the instrument for promoting the welfare and merits of all mortals, they gave him the name of Theiddat.

Seven days after her confinement Maia died, and by the virtue of her merits migrated to the seat of Toocita, and became the daughter of a Nat.* Her death was not the result of her delivery, but she departed this world because the term of her life had come. On their return to their home, the Pounhas assembled their children and said to them. "We are already advanced in years. We dare not promise to ourselves that we will ever see the son of King

---

[3] Metempsychosis, or the transmigration of the soul from one state of existence into another in the same world, is one of the leading dogmas of Buddhism. Many passages of the present work, or rather the Buddhistic system as a whole, can never be understood unless this tenet be always borne in mind. It is by passing through countless existences that a being is slowly purified of his imperfections, and gradually advances in the way of merits and perfection. The sacred writings of Buddhists mention that our Phralaong had to range, during innumerable existences, the whole series of the animal kingdom, from the dove to the elephant, ere he could be born in the state of man, when, in this condition, he, as stated by himself, went often into hell to atone for certain trespassings. Pythagoras had likely borrowed, and received directly or indirectly from the East, this doctrine, which his school re-echoed throughout Greece and Italy. The end of metempsychosis is, according to Buddhists, the state of Neibban. On this point the author of Buddhism has been at variance with other religious schools, which in his own days held and professed the dogma of transmigration.

* Maia was confined in the beginning of the third age. This expression is rather a very loose and general one, and is far from indicating, with any approach to accuracy the period of Maia's age when she was delivered of her son. The age of man is divided into three parts. The first extends from birth to the sixteenth or eighteenth year; the second goes to the forty-fifth year or thereabout; and the third, from the forty-fifth year to the end of life. Phralaong was born on the 68th year of the Eatzana era, on the 6th after the full moon of the month Katsong. Maia was therefore fifty-six years old. The author of this work strives hard to prove this the age, apparently advanced of Maia, was the best fitted for securing the safety and perfection of the fruit of her womb.

Thoodaudana become a Buddha; but to you such a favour is reserved. Listen respectfully to all his instructions, and endeavour to enter the profession of Rahan without delay, and withdraw into solitude. Let us also all join you in that holy vocation." Three Pounhas refused the invitation, and would not enter the profession. The five others cheerfully gave up everything and became distinguished members of the ascetic body.

King Thoodaudana, hearing of the explanation given by the Pounhas, inquired whether his son was really to become a Rahan. Having been assured that all the signs predicted the future destiny of his son to such a calling, he desired to know what those signs were. He was told that the four following things were the very signs foreshowing the future career of his son, viz., an old man, a sick man, a dead man, and a recluse.[4] As soon as his son should

---

[4] The three first allegorical omens or signs which, according to the foretelling of the Pounhas, were to be seen and observed hereafter by Phralaong, are designed to mean and express the compound of all miseries attending human existence, from the moment man crosses the threshold of life to that of death. The view of these objects was intended to make him disgusted with a state necessarily accompanied with such an amount of wretchedness. He was soon induced by reflection to hold in contempt the things of this world, and consequently to seek with ardour some means of estranging himself from all visible and material objects. The fourth sign, that is to say, the view of a Rahan, or a contemner of this world, aspiring to perfect disengagement from the trammels of passion, and shaping his course towards Neibban, was the very pattern he had to imitate and follow for arriving to that state of perfection, which he felt a strong, though as yet somewhat confused, desire of possessing.

The Nats or Dewatas are the ever-ready ministers for affording to Phralaong the assistance he requires to reach in safety the Buddhaship. They rejoice at the news of his approaching conception in the womb of Maia; they watch over the mother who is to give birth to so blessed a child; they receive the newly-born infant, and hand him over to men; they baffle, by their almost supernatural power, the obstacles which the worldly-minded Thoodaudana tries to throw in the way of his son's vocation; in a word, their angelical ministrations are always at hand to help and protect our Phralaong, and enable him to reach that state wherein he shall be fully qualified for announcing to men the law of deliverance. The belief in the agency of angels between heaven and earth, and their being the messengers of God for conveying, on solemn occasions, his mandates to men, is coeval, according to sacred records, with the appearance of man in this world. Innumerable are the instances of angelical ministrations mentioned in the holy writ. We look upon angels as mere

successively remark those four signs, he would immediately come to the conclusion that the state of Rahan alone is worthy of the warm admiration and eager wishes of a wise man.

King Thoodaudana, who ardently wished to see his son become a great monarch, whose sway would extend over the four great islands and the two thousand smaller ones, gave the strictest orders that none of the four omens should ever meet his eyes. Guards were placed in every direction at distances of a mile, charged with but one care, that of keeping out of his son's sight the appearance of these fatal omens.

On that day eighty thousand noblemen, who were present at the great rejoicings, pledged themselves each one to give one of his male children to attend on the royal infant. "If he become," said they, "a mighty monarch, let our sons be ever with him, as a guard of honour to confer additional lustre on his wonderful reign. If he be ever elevated to the sublime dignity of Buddha, let our children enter the holy profession of recluse, and follow him whithersoever he may direct his steps."

Thoodaudana, with the tender solicitude of a vigilant father, procured for his beloved offspring nurses exempt from all corporeal defects, and remarkable for their beautiful and graceful appearance.

---

spiritual substances, assuming a human form, when, by the command of God, they have to bring down to men some divine message. In the system of the Buddhists, Nats are described as having bodies indeed, but of such a pure nature, particularly those inhabiting the superior seats, that they are not only not subjected to the miseries inherent in our nature, but are moreover gifted with such superior attainments as almost to enjoy the perfections and qualifications inherent in the nature of spirits. On this occasion the Nats are endeavouring to make virtue triumph over vice; but, in the course of this legend, we will have several opportunities of remarking a counteraction worked up by evil or wicked Nats for upholding the reign of passion or of sin. In this system the two contending elements of good and evil have each its own advocates and supporters. A Hindu Milton might have found two thousand years ago a ready theme for writing, in Sanscrit or Pali, a poem similar to that more recently composed by the immortal English bard.

The child grew up, surrounded with a brilliant retinue of numerous attendants.

On a certain day happened the joyful feast of the ploughing season. The whole country, by the magnificence of the ornaments that decorated it, resembled one of the seats of Nats. The country people without exception, wearing new dresses, went to the palace. One thousand ploughs and the same number of pairs of bullocks were prepared for the occasion. Eight hundred ploughs, less one, were to be handled and guided by noblemen. The ploughs, as well as the yokes and the horns of the bullocks, were covered with silver leaves. But the one reserved for the monarch was covered with leaves of gold. Accompanied by a countless crowd of his people, King Thoodaudana left the royal city and went into the middle of extensive fields. The royal infant was brought out by his nurses on this joyful occasion. A splendid jambu tree (*Eugenia*), loaded with thick and luxuriant green foliage, offered on that spot a refreshing place under the shade of its far-spreading branches. Here the bed of the child was deposited. A gilt canopy was immediately raised above it, and curtains, embroidered with gold, were disposed round it. Guardians having been appointed to watch over the infant, the king, attended by all his courtiers, directed his steps towards the place where all the ploughs were held in readiness. He instantly put his hands to his own plough; eight hundred noblemen, less one, and the country people followed his example. Pressing forward his bullocks, the king ploughed to and fro through the extent of the fields. All the ploughmen, emulating their royal lord, drove their ploughs in a uniform direction. The scene presented a most animated and stirring spectacle on an immense scale. The applauding multitude filled the air with cries of joy and exultation. The nurses, who kept watch by the side of the infant's cradle, excited by the animated scene, forgot the prince's orders, and ran near to the spot to enjoy the soul-stirring sight displayed before their admiring eyes. Phralaong, casting a glance all round, and seeing no one close by him, rose up instantly, and, sitting in a cross-legged position, remained absorbed as it were in a profound meditation. The other nurses, busy in preparing the prince's meal, had spent more time than was at first contemplated. The shadow of the trees had, by the movement of the sun, turned in an opposite direction. The nurses, reminded by this sight that the infant had been left alone, and that his couch was exposed to the rays of the sun, hastened back to the spot they had so imprudently left. But great was their surprise when they saw that the shadow of the jambu tree had not changed its position, and that the child was quietly sitting on his bed. The news of that wonder was immediately conveyed to King Thoodaudana, who came in all haste to witness it. He forthwith prostrated himself before his son, saying, "This is, beloved child, the second time that I bow to you."

Phralaong[5] having reached his sixteenth year, his father ordered three palaces to be built for each season of the year. Each palace had nine stories; and forty thousand maidens, skilful in playing all sorts of musical instruments, were in continual attendance upon him, and charmed all his moments by uninterrupted dances and music. Phra-

---

[5] From what has been already mentioned of the life of our Phralaong, we may see that many particulars regarding his birth and his childhood have been described with sufficient accuracy; but little or nothing is said of his adolescence, at least until the age of sixteen, when he gets united to the famous and youthful Yathaudara. In common with many other great men, almost all the years of the private life of this celebrated and extraordinary personage are wrapped up in a complete obscurity. We may conclude from his great proficiency in the knowledge of those sciences and attainments befitting his high situation, he was not remiss, since he was enabled to set at defiance the greatest masters of those days. In the midst of pleasures he knew how to devote the best part of his time to study, unless we suppose that science was infused into his mind by no exertion of his own. The Burmese have a regular mania for dividing with a mathematical precision what at first appears to admit of no such division. Virtues, vices, sciences, arts, &c., all, in a word, are subjected to a rigorous division, which, if arbitrary in itself, has the great advantage of conferring a substantial help to the memory.

laong appeared among them with the beauty and dignity of a Nat, surrounded with an immense retinue of daughters of Nats. According to the change of seasons he passed from one palace into another, moving as it were in a circle of ever-renewed pleasures and amusements. It was then that Phralaong was married to the beautiful Yathaudara, his first cousin, and the daughter of Thouppabudha and of Amitau. It was in the eighty-sixth year of his grandfather's era that he was married, and also consecrated Prince royal by the pouring of the blessed water over his head.

Whilst Phralaong was spending his time in the midst of pleasures, his relatives complained to the king of the conduct of his son. They strongly remonstrated against his mode of living, which precluded him from applying himself to the acquisition of those attainments befitting his exalted station. Sensible of these reproaches, Thoodaudana sent for his son, to whom he made known the complaints directed against him by his relatives. Without showing any emotion, the young prince replied, "Let it be announced at the sound of the drum throughout the country, that this day week I will show to my relatives in the presence of the best masters that I am fully conversant with the eighteen sorts of arts and sciences." On the appointed day he displayed before them the extent of his knowledge; they were satisfied, and their doubts and anxieties on his account were entirely removed.

On a certain day Phralaong, desiring to go and enjoy some sports in his garden, ordered his coachman to have his conveyance ready for that purpose. Four horses, richly caparisoned, were put to a beautiful carriage, that resembled the dwelling-place of a Nat. Phralaong having occupied his seat, the coachman drove rapidly towards the garden. The Nats, who knew that the time was near at hand when Phralaong would become a Buddha, resolved to place successively before his eyes the four signs foreshowing his future high dignity. One of them assumed the form of an old man, the body bending forward, with grey hairs, a shrivelled skin, and leaning languidly on a heavy staff. In that attire, he advanced slowly, with trembling steps, towards the prince's conveyance. He was seen and remarked only by Phralaong and his coachman. "Who is that man?" said the prince to his driver; "the hairs of his head, indeed, do not resemble those of other men." "Prince," answered the coachman, "he is an old man. Every born being is doomed to become like him; his appearance must undergo the greatest changes, the skin by the action of time will shrivel, the hairs turn grey, the veins and arteries, losing their suppleness and elasticity, will become stiff and hardened, the flesh will gradually sink and almost disappear, leaving the bare bones covered with dry skin." "What?" said to himself the terrified prince; "birth is indeed a great evil, ushering all beings into a wretched condition, which must be inevitably attended with the disgusting infirmities of old age!" His mind being taken up entirely with such considerations, he ordered his coachman to drive back to the palace. Thoodaudana, having inquired from his courtiers what motive had induced his son to return so soon from the place of amusement, was told that he had seen an old man, and that he entertained the thought of becoming a Rahan.* "Alas!" said he, "they will succeed in

---

* In the course of this work the word Rahan is often used. It is of the greatest importance that the reader should firmly seize the meaning that it is designed to convey. We find it employed to designate, in general, the religious belonging either to the Buddhistic or Brahminical sects. When Buddhists happen to mention their brethren of the opposite creed, who have renounced the world and devoted themselves to the practice of religious duties, they invariably call them Rahans. When they speak of Pounhas or Brahmins, who are living in the world, leading an ordinary secular mode of life, they never style them Rahans. Thence we may safely infer that the individuals to whom this denomination was applied formed a class of devotees quite distinct from the laymen.

That class, it appears, comprised all the individuals who lived either in community under the superintendence and guidance of a spiritual superior, or privately in forests under the protecting shade of trees, and in lonely and solitary places. The

thwarting the high destiny of my son. But let us try now every means to afford him some distraction, so that he may forget the evil idea that has just started up in his mind." He gave orders to bring to his son's palace the prettiest and most accomplished dancing-girls, that, in the midst of ever renewed pleasure, he might lose sight of the thought of ever entering the profession of Rahan. The guard surrounding his palace was doubled, so as to preclude the possibility of his ever seeing the other signs.

On another day, Phralaong, on his way to his garden, met with the same Nat under the form of a sick man, who appeared quite sinking under the weight of the most loathsome disease. Frightened at such a sight, Phralaong, hearing from the mouth of his faithful driver what this disgusting object was, returned in all haste to his palace. His father, more and more disturbed at the news conveyed to him, multiplied the pleasures and enjoyments destined for his son, and doubled the number of guards that had to watch over him. On a third occasion, whilst the prince was taking a walk, the same Nat, assuming the shape of a dead man, offered to the astonished regards of the prince

---

latter religions are, however, generally designated by the appellation of Ascetics and Rathees. They were the forefathers of those fanatics who up to our days have appeared through the breadth and length of the Indian Peninsula, practising penitential deeds of the most cruel and revolting description. They are described by Buddhists as wearing curled and twisted hair, clad in the skins of wild beasts, and not unfrequently quite destitute of any sort of clothing, and in a state of complete nakedness.

The former, who lived in community, did not lead the same course of life. We find some communities, the three, for instance, under the guidance of the three Kathabas, in the Ouroowela forest, not far from Radzagio, whose inmates are called either Rahans or Rathees. This indicates that their mode of life partook both of the common and hermitical life, resembling, to a certain extent, that which was observed by the Christian communities of cenobites established in the desert of Upper Egypt during the first ages of our era.

Those communities appear to have been the centres in which principles were established, opinions discussed, and theories elaborated. The chiefs enjoyed high reputation for learning. Persons desirous to acquire proficiency in science resorted to their abode, and, under their tuition, strove to acquire wisdom. The following pages of this work will afford several striking illustrations of the views just sketched out.

the shocking sight of a corpse. Trembling with fear, the young prince came back forthwith to his residence. Thoodaudana, being soon informed of what had taken place, resorted to fresh precautions, and extended to the distance of one youdzana the immense line of countless guards set all round the palace.

On a fourth occasion, the prince, driving rapidly towards his garden, was met on his way by the same Nat under the meek form of a Rahan. The curiosity of the prince was awakened by the extraordinary sight of that new personage: he asked his coachman what he was. "Prince," answered the coachman, "he is a Rahan." At the same time, though little acquainted with the high dignity and sublime qualifications of a recluse, he was enabled, by the power of the Nats, to praise and extol in dignified language the profession and merits of Rahans. The prince felt instantaneously an almost irresistible inclination to embrace that attractive mode of life. He quietly went as far as his garden.

The whole day was spent in all sorts of rural diversions. Having bathed in a magnificent tank, he went a little before sunset to rest awhile on a large well-polished stone table, overshaded by the far-spread branches of beautiful trees hanging above it, waiting for the time to put on his richest dress. All his attendants were busily engaged in preparing the finest clothes and most elegant ornaments. When all was ready, they stood silent round him, waiting for his orders. Perfumes of every description were disposed in a circular row with the various ornaments on the table whereon the prince was sitting.

At that very moment a chief Thagia was quietly enjoying a delicious and refreshing rest on the famous stone table, called Pantoo Kambala. On a sudden, he felt his seat as it were getting hot. "Lo! what does this mean?" said the astonished Thagia; "am I doomed to lose my happy state?" Having recollected himself, and reflected a while on the cause of such a wonderful occurrence, he soon knew that

Phralaong was preparing to put on for the last time his princely dress. He called to him the son of a Nat, named Withakioon, and said to him, "On this day, at midnight, Prince Theiddat is to leave his palace and withdraw into solitude. Now he is in his garden, preparing to put on his richest attire for the last time. Go, therefore, without a moment's delay to the place where he is sitting, surrounded by his attendants, and perform to him all the required services. Bowing respectfully to the chief of Thagias, Withakioon obeyed, and by the power inherent in the nature of Nats, he was in an instant carried to the presence of Phralaong. He assumed the figure of his barber, and immediately set to work to arrange the turban with as much taste as art round his head. Phralaong soon found out that the skilful hand which disposed the folds of his head-dress was not that of a man, but of a Nat. One fold of the turban appeared like one thousand, and ten folds like ten thousand folds, offering the magical *coup-d'œil* of as many different pieces of cloth, arranged with the most consummate skill. The extremity of the turban, which crossed vertically the whole breadth of the countless folds, appeared covered with a profusion of shining rubies. The head of Phralaong was small, but the folds of the turban seemed numberless. How could that be so? It is a wonder surpassing our understanding; it would be rashness and temerity to allow our mind to dwell too much upon it.

Having completely dressed, Phralaong[6] found himself

---

[6] The triumphant return of Phralaong from his garden to the city, when he is attired with the richest dress, is commemorated by Buddhists, at least in Burmah, on the day a young boy is preparing to enter into a monastery of recluses for the purpose of putting on the yellow robe, and preparing himself to become afterwards a member of the order, if he feel an inclination to enlist in its ranks. Phralaong was bidding a last farewell to the world, its pomps and vanities. So the youthful candidate is doing who is led processionally through the streets, riding a richly-caparisoned horse, or sitting on an elegant palanquin, carried on the shoulders of men. A description of this ceremony will be found in the notice on the Buddhistic monks or Talapoins.

I am obliged to confess that I have

surrounded by all sorts of musicians, singers, and dancers, vieing with each other in their endeavours to increase the rejoicing. The Pounhas sang aloud his praise. "May he

---

found it somewhat difficult to discover any connection between the expressions made use of by Keissa Gautami and the inference drawn therefrom by Phralaong. The explanation of the difficulty may be, however, stated as follows:—Gautami bestows the epithet happy or blessed upon the father and mother as well as on the wife of Prince Theiddat, because she remarked and observed in him those qualities and accomplishments befitting a worthy son and a good husband. The words blessed and happy struck the mind of the future Buddha, attracted his attention, and drew forth his exertions to find out their true import. He asks himself, In what consists true and real happiness? Where is it to be found? By what means can such an invaluable treasure be procured? Can it be conferred upon man by the possession of some exterior object? Can his parents or wife be really happy by the mere accidental ties that connect them with his person? No, answers our young philosopher to himself: Happiness can be procured but by waging war against passions, and carrying it on until their total destruction. Then the victorious soul, sitting calmly on the ruins of her deadly opponents, enjoys in the undisturbed contemplation of truth an indescribable happiness. In this we clearly perceive the unmistakable bearing of Buddhistic morals. It is as it were the embryo of the whole system.

King Thoodandana, influenced by worldly considerations, eagerly wished his son to become a great monarch instead of a poor and humble recluse, even a Buddha. This alone suggests the idea that in those days the *rôle* of a Buddha was not held in so great an esteem and veneration as it was afterwards. Had it been otherwise, the most ambitious father might have remained well satisfied with the certainty of seeing his own son becoming a personage before whom the proudest monarchs would one day lower to the dust their crowned heads.

At that time a Buddha, or the personage honoured with that title, was looked upon as a mere sage, distinguished among his fellow-men by his great wisdom and eminent proficiency in the study of philosophy. It is highly probable that this name had been bestowed upon a great many illustrious individuals who lived before the days of Gaudama. Hence the fabricated genealogy of twenty-eight former Buddhas, supposed to have lived myriads of years and worlds previously, including the three that have preceded him during the continuance of this system of nature. Here a superstitious and ill-judged enthusiasm has raised up heaps of extravagancies, setting up a ridiculous theory, designed to connect the *rôle* of the present Buddha with those of a fabulous antiquity, and give additional lustre to it. There is no doubt that the glowing halo of sacredness and glory, encircling now the name of Buddha, has never adorned that of any former one. It has been created by the extraordinary progress his doctrines made at first in the Indian Peninsula, and next throughout eastern Asia, and kept up by the fervent admiration of his enthusiastic followers.

The means resorted to by Thoodandana to retain his son in the world of passions, and thereby thwart his vocation, could not, we hardly need mention, be approved of by any moralist of even the greatest elasti-

conquer and triumph! May his wishes and desires be ever fulfilled!" The multitude repeated incessantly in his honour stanzas of praises and blessings. In the midst of universal rejoicings, Phralaong ascended his carriage. He had scarcely seated himself on it, when a message, sent by his father, conveyed to him the gladdening tidings that Yathaudara had been delivered of a son. "That child," replied he with great coolness, "is a new and strong tie that I will have to break." The answer having been brought to his father, Thoodaudana could not understand its meaning. He, however, caused his grandson to be named Raoula. Phralaong, sitting in his carriage, surrounded by crowds of people, who rent the air with cries of joy and jubilation, entered into the city of Kapilawot. At that moment a princess, named Keissa Gautami, was contemplating from her apartments the triumphant entrance of Phralaong into the city. She admired the noble and graceful deportment of Prince Theiddat, and exclaimed with feelings of inexpressible delight, "Happy the father and mother who have such an incomparable son! happy the wife who is blest with such an accomplished husband!" On hearing those words, Phralaong desired to understand their meaning and know their bearing. "By what means," said he to himself, "can a heart find peace and happiness?" As his heart was already disentangled from the thraldom of passions, he readily perceived that real happiness could be found but in the extinction of concupiscence, pride, ignorance, and other passions. He resolved henceforth to

city of conscience and principles; but they were eminently fitted to try the soundness of Phralaong's calling, and the strong and tenacious dispositions of his energetic mind. They set out in vivid colours the firmness of purpose and irresistible determination of his soul in following up his vocation to a holier mode of life; and what is yet more wonderful, the very objects that were designed to enslave him became the instruments which helped him in gaining and ascertaining his liberty. Magnificent, indeed, is the spectacle offered by a young prince remaining unmoved in the midst of the most captivating, soul-stirring, and heart-melting attractions; sitting coolly on his couch, and looking with indifference, nay, with disgust, on the crowd of sleeping beauties.

search ardently for the happy state of Neibban, by quitting the world that very night, leaving the society of men, and withdrawing into solitude. Detaching from his neck a collar of pearls of immense value, he sent it to Keissa Gautami, as a token of gratitude for the excellent lesson she had given him by the words which she had uttered in his praise. The young princess received it as a mark of favour which she imagined Prince Theiddat intended to pay her. Without further notice of her, he retired into his own apartment to enjoy some rest.

CHAPTER IV.

Phralaong leaves his palace, the royal city, and retires into solitude, amidst the plaudits of the Nats—He cuts his fine hair with a stroke of his sword, and puts on the habit of Rahan—He begs his food at Radzagio—His interview with the ruler of that place—His studies under two Rathees—His fast and penances in the solitude of Oorouwela during six years.

PHRALAONG had scarcely begun to recline on his couch, when a crowd of young damsels, whose beauty equalled that of the daughters of Nats, executed all sorts of dances to the sound of the most ravishing symphony, and displayed in all their movements the graceful forms of their elegant and well-shaped persons, in order to make some impression upon his heart. But all was in vain; they were foiled in their repeated attempts. Phralaong fell into a deep sleep. The damsels, in their disappointment, ceased their dances, laid aside their musical instruments, and, soon following the example of Phralaong, quietly yielded to the soporific influence caused by their useless and harassing exertions. The lamps, lighted with fragrant oil, continued to pour a flood of bright light throughout the apartments. Phralaong awoke a little before midnight, and sat in a cross-legged position on his couch. Looking all around him, he saw the varied attitudes and uninviting appearance of the sleeping damsels. Some were snoring, others gnashing their teeth, others had their mouths wide open; some tossed heavily from the right to the left side, others stretched one arm upwards and the other downwards; some, seized as it were with a frantic pang, suddenly coiled up their legs for a while, and with the same violent motion again pushed them down. This unexpected exhibition made a strong impression on Phralaong; his heart was set, if possible, freer from the ties of concupiscence, or rather he was confirmed in his contempt for all worldly pleasures. It appeared to him that his magnificent apartments were filled with the most loathsome and putrid carcasses. The seats of passions, those of Rupa and those of Arupa, that is to say, the whole world, seemed, to his eyes, like a house that is a prey to the devouring flames. "All that," said he to himself, "is most disgusting and despicable." At the same time his ardent desires for the profession of Rahan were increasing with an uncontrollable energy. "On this day, at this very moment," said he with an unshaken firmness, "I will retire into a solitary place." He rose instantly and went to the arched door of his apartment. "Who is here watching?" said he to the first person he met. "Your servant," replied instantly the vigilant nobleman Tsanda. "Rise up quickly," replied the prince; "now I am ready to retire from the world and resort to some lonely place. Go to the stable and prepare the fastest of my horses." Tsanda bowed respectfully to his master, and executed his orders with the utmost celerity. The horse Kantika, knowing the intentions of the prince, felt an inexpressible joy at being selected for such a good errand, and he testified his joy by loud neighs; but, by the power of the Nats, the sound of his voice was silenced, so that none heard it.

While Tsanda, in compliance with the orders he had received, was making the necessary preparations, Phralaong desired to see his newly born son Raoula. He opened gently the door of the room where the princess was sleeping, having one of her hands placed over the head of the infant. Phralaong, stopping at the threshold, said to himself:—"If I go farther to contemplate the child, I will have to remove the hand of the mother; she may be awakened by this movement, and then she will prove a great obstacle to my departure. I will see the child after I have become a Buddha." He then instantly shut the door and left the palace. His charger was waiting for him. "To your swiftness," said Phralaong to Kantika, "do I trust for executing my great design. I must become a Buddha, and labour for the deliverance of men and Nats from the miseries of existence, and lead them safely to the peaceful shores of Neibban." In a moment he was on the back of his favourite horse. Kantika was a magnificent animal; his body measured eighteen cubits in length, with which his height and circumference were in perfect proportion. The hair was of a beautiful white, resembling a newly cleaned shell; his swiftness was unrivalled, and his neighings could be heard at a very great distance; but on this occasion the Nats interfered, no sound of his voice was heard, and the noise of his steps was completely silenced. Having reached the gate of the city, Phralaong stopped for a while, uncertain as regarded the course he was to follow. To open the gate, which a thousand men could with difficulty cause to turn upon its hinges, was deemed an impossibility. Whilst he was deliberating with his faithful attendant Tsanda, the huge gate was silently opened by the Nats, and a free passage given to him through it. It was in the year 97 when he left Kapilawot.

Phralaong had scarcely crossed the threshold of the gate when the tempter endeavoured to thwart his pious design. Manh[1] Nat resolved to prevent him from retir-

[1] Phralaong having overcome with uncommon fortitude the numberless obstacles which he had encountered on the part of men, will have now to meet another foe, perhaps more formidable, a wicked Nat, or demon. His name, according to its orthography, is Mar or Mara, but the Burmese call him Manh, which means pride. Manh is, therefore, the evil spirit of pride, or rather personified pride, and the enemy of mankind, ever ready to oppose the benevolent designs and generous efforts of Buddha in carrying on his great undertaking, conceived to benefit humanity, by teaching men the way that leads to deliverance from all miseries. The first plan concocted by Manh for stopping, at the very outset, the progress of Phralaong, was to flatter his ambition by promising him *all the kingdoms of this world and their glory*. From that day the tempter never lost sight of the benevolent Buddha, but followed him everywhere, endeavouring to prevent the immense success that

ing into solitude and becoming a Buddha. Standing in the air, he cried aloud, "Prince Theiddat, do not attempt to lead the life of a recluse; seven days hence you will become a Tsekiawaday; your sway shall extend over the four great islands; return forthwith to your palace." "Who are you?" replied Phralaong. "I am Manh Nat," cried the voice. "I know," said Phralaong, "that I can become a Tsekiawaday, but I feel not the least inclination for earthly dignities; my aim is to arrive at the nature of Buddha." The tempter, urged onward by his three wicked propensities, concupiscence, ignorance, and anger, did not part for a moment from Phralaong; but as the shadow always accompanies the body, he too, from that day, always followed Phralaong, striving to throw every obstacle in his way towards the dignity of Buddha. Trampling down every human and worldly consideration, and despising a power full of vanity and illusion, Phralaong left the city of Kapilawot, at the full moon of July under the constellation Oottarathan. A little while after, he felt a strong desire to turn round his head and cast a last glance at the magnificent city he was leaving behind him; but he soon overcame that inordinate desire and denied himself this gratification. It is said that on the very instant he was combating the rising sense of curiosity the mighty earth turned with great velocity, like a potter's wheel, so that the very object he denied himself the satisfaction of contemplating came of itself under his eyes. Phralaong hesitated a while as to the direction he was to follow, but he resolved instantly to push on straight before him.

His progress through the country resembled a splendid

---

was to attend his future mission. The evil propensities which constitute, as it were, the very essence of Manh's nature, are concupiscence, envy, and an irresistible proneness to do harm. The devil indeed could hardly be made up of worse materials.

It is really interesting through the course of this Legend to read of the uninterrupted efforts made by the personification of evil to thwart Buddha in all his benevolent designs. The antagonism begins now, but it will be maintained with an obstinate and prolonged activity during the whole life of Buddha.

triumphal ovation. Sixty thousand Nats marched in front of him, an equal number followed him, and as many surrounded him on his right and on his left. All of them carried lighted torches, pouring a flood of light in every direction; others again spread perfumes and flowers brought from their own seats. All joined in chorus, singing the praises of Phralaong. The sound of their united voices resembled loud peals of continued thunder, and the resounding of the mighty waves at the foot of the Mount Oogando. Flowers, shedding the most fragrant odour, were seen gracefully undulating in the air, like an immense canopy, extending to the farthest limits of the horizon. During that night, Phralaong, attended with that brilliant retinue, travelled a distance of thirty youdzanas, and arrived on the banks of the river Anauma. Turning his face towards Tsanda, he asked what was the river's name. "Anauma is its name," replied his faithful attendant. "I will not," said Phralaong to himself, "show myself unworthy of the high dignity I aspire to." Spurring his horse, the fierce animal leaped at once to the opposite bank. Phralaong alighted on the ground, which was covered with a fine sand resembling pearls, when the rays of the sun fell upon it in the morning. On that spot he divested himself of his dress, and calling Tsanda to him, he directed him to take charge of his ornaments, and carry them back with the horse Kantika to his palace. For himself, he had made up his mind to become a Rahan. "Your servant too," replied Tsanda, "will become also a recluse in your company." "No," said the prince, "the profession of Rahan does not at present befit you." He reiterated this prohibition three times. When he was handing over to Tsanda his costly ornaments, he said to himself, "These long hairs that cover my head, and my beard too, are superfluities unbecoming the profession of Rahan." Whereupon with one hand unsheathing his sword, and with the other seizing his comely hairs, he cut them with a single stroke. What remained of his hairs on the head measured about one inch and a half in length. In like manner he disposed of his beard. From that time he never needed shaving; the hairs of his beard and those of the head never grew longer during the remainder of his life.[2] Holding his hairs and turban together, he cried aloud, "If I am destined to become a Buddha, let these hairs and turban remain suspended in the air; if not, let them drop down on the ground." Throwing up both to the height of one youdzana, they remained suspended in the air, until a Nat came with a rich basket, put them therein, and carried them to the seat of Tawadeintha. He there erected the Dzedi Dzoulamani, wherein they were religiously deposited. Casting his regards on his own person, Phralaong saw that his rich and shining robe did not answer his purpose, nor appear befitting the poor and humble profession he was about to embrace. While his attention was taken up with this consideration, a great Brahma, named Gatigara, who in the days of the Buddha Kathaba had been an intimate friend of our Phralaong, and who, during the period that elapsed between the manifestation of that Buddha to the present time, had not grown old, discovered at once the perplexity of his friend's mind. "Prince Theiddat," said he, "is preparing to become a Rahan, but he is not supplied with the dress and other implements essentially required for his future calling. I will provide him now with the thinbaing, the kowot, the dugout, the patta, the leathern girdle, the hatchet, the needle, and filter.[3] He took with him all

---

[2] This circumstance explains one peculiarity observable in all the statues representing Buddha. The head is invariably covered with sharp points, resembling those thorns with which the thick envelope of the durian fruit is armed. Often I had inquired as to the motive that induced native sculptors to leave on the head of all statues that sort of inverted nails, without ever being able to obtain any satisfactory answer. It was only after having read this passage of the life of Buddha that I was enabled to account for this apparently singular custom, which is designed to remind all Buddhists of the ever-continued wonder whereby the hairs which remained on Buddha's head never grew longer from the day he cut them with his sword.

[3] Every talapoin or recluse must

these articles, and in an instant arrived in the presence of Phralaong, to whom he presented them. Though unacquainted with the details of that dress, and untrained in the use of those new implements, the prince, like a man who had been a recluse during several existences, put on with a graceful gravity his new dress. He adjusted the thinbaing round his waist, covered his body with the kowot, threw the dugout over his shoulders, and suspended to his neck the bag containing the earthen patta. Assuming the grave, meek, and dignified countenance of a Rahan, he called Tsanda and bade him go back to his father and relate to him all that he had seen. Tsanda, complying with his master's request, prostrated himself three times before him; then, rising up, he wheeled to the right and departed. The spirited horse, hearing the last words of Phralaong, could no more control his grief.[4]

---

be provided with one needle, wherewith he is to sew his dress, one hatchet to cut the wood he may be in need of, either for erecting a shelter for himself or for other purposes, and one filter to strain the water he intends to drink, that it might be cleared from all impurities, but chiefly of insects or any living body that might be in it, which would expose the drinker thereof to the enormous sin of causing the death of some animal.

[4] The various accounts that are given of the horse Kantika, and the grief he feels at parting with his master, grief which reaches so far as to cause his death, may appear somewhat extraordinary, puerile, and ridiculous to every one except to Buddhists. One great principle of that religious system is that man does not differ from animals in nature, but only in relative perfection. In animals there are souls as well as in men, but these souls, on account of the paucity of their merits and the multiplicity of their demerits, are yet in a very imperfect state. When the law of demerits grows weak, and that of merits gathers strength, the soul, though continuing to inhabit the body of animals, has the knowledge of good and evil, and can attain to a certain degree of perfection. Buddhistic writings supply many instances of this belief. Whilst Buddha was in the desert, an elephant ministered to all his wants. As a reward for such a series of services, Buddha preached to him the law, and led him at once to the deliverance, that is to say, to the state of Neibban. When one animal has progressed so far in the way of merits as to be able to discern between good and bad, it is said that he is ripe, or fit to become man. The horse Kantika seems to have reached that state of full ripeness, since, after his death, he passed to the state of Nat. This peculiar tenet of Buddhistic faith accounts for the first of the five great commands, which extends the formal injunction of "thou shalt not kill" to animals. When a candidate is admitted, according to the prescriptions contained in the sacred

"Alas!" said he, "I will see no more my master in this world." His sorrow grew so great that his heart split into two parts, and he died on the spot.

After his death, he became a Nat in the seat of Tawadeintha. The affliction of Tsanda at parting with his good master was increased by the death of Kantika. The tears that streamed down his cheeks resembled drops of liquid silver.

Phralaong, having thus begun the life of a recluse, spent seven days alone in a forest of mango trees, enjoying in that retirement the peace and happiness of soul which solitude alone can confer. The place, in the neighbourhood of which he began his religious life, is called Anupyia, in the country belonging to the Malla princes. He then started for the country of Radzagio, travelling on foot a distance of thirty youdzanas. Arrived near the gate of the royal city, Phralaong stopped for a while, saying within himself, "Peimpathara, the king of this country, will no doubt hear of my arrival in this place. Knowing that the son of King Thoodaudana is actually in his own royal city, he will insist upon my accepting all sorts of presents. But now, in my capacity of Rahan, I must decline accepting them, and by the rules of my profession I am bound to go and beg along the streets, from house to house, the food necessary for my support." He instantly resumed his journey, entered the city through the eastern gate, the patta hanging on his side, and followed the first row of houses, receiving the alms which pious hands offered him. At the moment of his arrival the whole city was shaken by a mighty commotiön, like that which is felt in the seat of Thoora when the Nat Athoorein makes his apparition in it. The inhabitants, terrified at such an ominous sign, ran in all haste to the palace. Admitted into the presence of the

---

Kambawa, into the order of Rahans, he is expressly and solemnly commanded to refrain from committing four sins, which would deprive him *de facto* of the dignity he has been elevated to. The taking away willingly of the life of anything animated is one of these four trespassings.

monarch, they told him that they knew not what sort of being had just arrived in the city, walking through the streets and begging alms. They could not ascertain whether he was a Nat, a man, or a Galong. The king, looking from his apartments over the city, saw Phralaong, whose meek deportment removed all anxiety from his mind. He, however, directed a few of his noblemen to go and watch attentively all the movements of the stranger. "If he be," said he, "a Bilou, he will soon leave the city and vanish away; if a Nat, he will raise himself in the air; if a Naga, he will plunge to the bottom of the earth." Phralaong, having obtained the quantity of rice, vegetables, &c., he thought sufficient for his meal, left the city through the same gate by which he had entered it, sat down at the foot of a small hill, his face turned towards the east, and tried to make his meal with the things he had received. He could not swallow the first mouthful, which he threw out of his mouth in utter disgust. Accustomed to live sumptuously and feed on the most delicate things, his eyes could not bear even the sight of that loathsome mixture of the coarsest articles of food collected at the bottom of his patta. He soon, however, recovered from that shock; and gathered fresh strength to subdue the opposition of nature, overcome its repugnance, and conquer its resistance. Reproaching himself for such an unbecoming weakness:—"Was I not aware," said he, with a feeling of indignation against himself, "that when I took up the dress of a mendicant such would be my food? The moment is come to trample upon nature's appetites." Whereupon he took up his patta, ate cheerfully his meal, and never afterwards did he ever feel any repugnance at what things soever he had to eat.

The king's messengers, having closely watched and attentively observed all that had happened, returned to their master, to whom they related all the particulars that they had witnessed. "Let my carriage be ready," said the king, "and you, follow me to the place where this stranger is resting." He soon perceived Phralaong at a distance, sitting quietly after his refection. Peimpathara alighted from his conveyance, respectfully drew near to Phralaong, and, having occupied a seat in a becoming place, was overwhelmed with contentment and inexpressible joy to such an extent, indeed, that he could scarcely find words to give utterance to his feelings. Having at last recovered from the first impression, he addressed Phralaong in the following manner:—"Venerable Rahan, you seem to be young still, and in the prime of your life; in your person you are gifted with the most attractive and noble qualities, indicating surely your illustrious and royal extraction. I have under my control and in my possession a countless crowd of officers, elephants, horses and chariots, affording every desirable convenience for pleasure and amusement of every description. Please to accept of a numerous retinue of attendants, with whom you may enjoy yourself whilst remaining within my dominions. May I be allowed to ask what country you belong to, who you are, and from what illustrious lineage and descent you are come?" Phralaong said to himself:—"It is evident that the king is unacquainted with both my name and origin; I will, however, satisfy him on the subject of his inquiry." Pointing out with his hand in the direction of the place he had come from, he said:—"I arrive from the country which has been governed by a long succession of the descendants of Prince Kothala. I have, indeed, been born from royal progenitors, but I have abandoned all the prerogatives attached to my position, and embraced the profession of Rahan. From my heart I have rooted up concupiscence, covetousness, and all affections to the things of this world." To this the king replied:—"I have heard that Prince Theiddat, son of King Thoodaudana, had seen four great signs, portending his future destiny for the profession of Rahan, which would be but a step to lead him to the exalted dignity of a Buddha. The first part of the prediction has been already fulfilled. When the second shall have received its accomplishment,

I beg you will show your benevolence to me and my people. I hope my kingdom will be the first country you will direct your steps to, after having acquired the supreme science." To this Phralaong graciously assented.

Phralaong, having left the king, resumed his journey, and fell in with a Rathee,[5] or hermit, named Alara, and

[5] The fact of Buddha placing himself under the tuition of two masters or teachers, leading an ascetic life, to learn from them notions of the most abstruse nature, establishes, beyond all doubt, the high antiquity of the existence in India of a large number of individuals, who, living in some retired spot, far from the tumult of society, endeavoured, by constant application, to dive into the deepest recesses of morals and metaphysics. The fame of the learning of many among them attracted to their solitude crowds of disciples, anxious to study under such eminent masters. Hence we see some of these Rathees at the head of four or five hundred disciples. There is no doubt that the most distinguished Rathees became the founders of many of those philosophico-religious schools for which India was renowned from the remotest antiquity. Like many others who thirsted for knowledge, Phralaong resorted to the schools of the Rathees, as to the then most celebrated seats of learning.

From this fact we may be allowed to draw another inference, which may be considered as a consequence of what has been stated in a foregoing note, regarding the superior antiquity of Brahminism over Buddhism. Phralaong was brought up in the bosom of a society regulated and governed by Brahminical institutions. He must have been imbued from the earliest days of his elementary education with the notions generally taught, viz.: the Brahminical ones. When he grew up and began to think for himself, he was displeased with certain doctrines which did not tally with his own ideas. Following the example of many that had preceded him in the way of innovation, he boldly shaped his course in a new direction, and soon arrived at a final issue on many points, both with his teachers and some of the doctrines generally received in the society in which he had been brought up. We may, therefore, safely conclude that the doctrines supposed to have been preached by the latest Buddha are but an off-shoot of Brahminism. This may serve to account for the great resemblance subsisting between many doctrines of both creeds. The cardinal points on which these two systems essentially differ are the beginning and the end of living beings. Between these two extremes there is a multitude of points on which both systems so perfectly agree that they appear blended together.

The Rathees seem, according to the institutes of Menoo, to have been first in observing two practices, much enforced by the Wini in subsequent times. They were supported by the alms bestowed on them by their disciples and the admirers of their singular mode of life. They were courted and esteemed by the world, in proportion to the contempt they appeared to hold it in. Denying to themselves the pleasures which were opposed to their austere life, they observed, as long as they remained Rathees, the rules of the strictest celibacy.

Phralaong, preparing himself for

inquired about the several Dzans. Alara satisfied him on four kinds of Dzans, but as regards the fifth, he was obliged to refer him to another Rathee, named Oudaka, who gave him the necessary explanations. Having nothing more to learn from these masters, Phralaong said to himself, "The knowledge I have thus acquired is not sufficient to enable me to obtain the dignity of Buddha." Whereupon he resolved to devote himself to the Kamatan[6] or meditation on the instability and nothingness of

---

his future high calling, began to study the science of *Dzan* under distinguished masters. What is meant by Dzan? This Pali word means thought, reflection, meditation. It is often designed by the Burmese to mean a peculiar state of the soul that has already made great progress in the way of perfection. Phralaong intended, by placing himself under the direction of those eminent teachers, to learn the great art of training his mind for the obtaining, by constant and well-directed meditations, of high mental attainments. In the book of Buddhistic metaphysics, I have found the science of Dzan divided into five parts, or rather five steps, which the mind has to ascend successively ere it can enjoy a state of perfect quiescence, the highest point a perfected being can arrive at before reaching the state of Neibban. In the first step the soul searches after what is good and perfect, and having discovered it, turns its attention and the energy of its faculties towards it. In the second, the soul begins to contemplate steadily what it has first discovered, and rivets upon it its attention. In the third stage, the soul fondly relishes, and is, as it were, entirely taken with it. In the fourth, the soul calmly enjoys and quietly feasts on the pure truths it has loved in the former state. In the fifth, the soul, perfectly satiated with the knowledge of truth, remains in a state of complete quietude, perfect fixity, unmoved stability, which nothing can any longer alter or disturb. The Burmese and all Buddhists, always fond of what is wonderful, attribute supernatural perfections to those who have so far advanced in mental attainments. Their bodies become, as it were, half-spiritualised, so that they can, according to their wishes, carry themselves through the air from one place to another, without the least hindrance or difficulty.

[6] Kamatan means the fixing of the attention on one object, so as to investigate thoroughly all its constituent parts, its principle and origin, its existence and its final destruction. It is that part of metaphysics which treats of the beginning, nature, and end of beings. To become proficient in that science, a man must be gifted with a most extensive knowledge and an analysing mind of no common cast. The process of Kamatan is as follows. Let it be supposed that man intends to contemplate one of the four elements, fire, for instance; he abstracts himself from every object which is not fire, and devotes all his attention to the contemplation of that object alone; he examines the nature of fire, and finding it a compound of several distinct parts, he investigates the cause or causes that keep those parts together, and soon discovers that they are but accidental ones, the action whereof may be impeded or destroyed

all that exists. To effectuate thoroughly his purpose, he repaired to the solitude of Oorouwela, where he devoted all his time to the deepest meditation. On a certain day it happened that five Rahans, on their way to a certain place to get their food, arrived at the spot where Phralaong lived and had already entered on the course of his penitential deeds. They soon became impressed with the idea that our hermit was to become a Buddha. They resolved to stay with him and render him all the needful services, such as sweeping the place, cooking rice, &c.

---

by the occurrence of any sudden accident. He concludes that fire has but a fictitious ephemeral existence. The same method is followed in examining the other elements, and gradually all other things he may come in contact with, and his final conclusion is, that all things placed without him are destitute of real existence, being mere illusions, divested of all reality. He infers, again, that all things are subjected to the law of incessant change, without fixity or stability. The wise man, therefore, can feel no attachment to objects which, in his own opinion, are but illusions and deception: his mind can nowhere find rest in the midst of illusions always succeeding to each other. Having surveyed all that is distinct of self, he applies himself to the work of investigating the origin and nature of his body. After a lengthened examination, he arrives, as a matter of course, at the same conclusion. His body is a mere illusion without reality, subjected to changes and destruction. He feels that it is as yet distinct from self. He despises his body, as he does everything else, and has no concern for it. He longs for the state of Neibban, as the only one worthy of the wise man's earnest desire. By such a preliminary step, the student, having estranged himself from this world of illusions, advances towards the study of the excellent works which will pave the way to Neibban. The Burmese reckon forty Kamatans. They are often repeated over by devotees, whose weak intellect is utterly incapable of understanding the meaning they are designed to convey to the mind.

Notwithstanding his singular aptitude in acquiring knowledge, Phralaong devoted six whole years, in the solitude of Oorouwela, busily engaged in mastering the profound science he aimed at acquiring. It was during that time that he received the visits of five Rahans, whose chief was named Koondanha. They were very probably, like so many of their profession, travelling about in search of knowledge. They placed themselves under the direction of Phralaong, and in exchange for the lessons they received from him, they served him as humble and grateful disciples are wont to attend on a highly esteemed teacher. In this, as well as many other circumstances, we see that, previous to Gandama's preachings, there already existed in India an order of devotees or enthusiasts, who lived secluded from the world, devoted to the study of religious doctrines and the practice of virtues of the highest order. The order of Buddhistic monks or talapoins, which was subsequently established by the author of Buddhism, is but a modification of what actually subsisted in full vigour in his own country and in his own time.

The time for the six years of meditation was nearly over, when Phralaong undertook a great fast,[7] which was carried to such a degree of abstemiousness that he scarcely allowed to himself the use of a grain of rice or sesame a day, and finally denied himself even that feeble pittance. But the Nats, who observed his excessive mortification, inserted Nat food through the pores of his skin. Whilst Phralaong was thus undergoing such a severe fasting, his face, which was of a beautiful gold colour, became black; the thirty-two marks indicative of his future dignity disappeared. On a certain day, when he was walking in a much enfeebled state, on a sudden he felt an extreme weakness, similar to that caused by a dire starvation. Unable to stand up any longer, he fainted and fell on the ground. Among the Nats that were present, some said, "The Rahan Gaudama is dead indeed;" some others replied, "He is not dead, but has fainted from want of food." Those who believed he was dead hastened to his father's palace to convey to him the sad message of his son's death. Thoodaudana inquired if his son died previous to his becoming a Buddha. Having been answered in the affirmative, he refused to give credit to the words of the Nats. The reason of his doubting the accuracy of the report was, that

---

[7] In a Buddhistic point of view the only reason that may be assigned for the extraordinary fast of Phralaong is the satisfaction of showing to the world the display of wonderful action. Fastings and other works of mortification have always been much practised by the Indian philosophers of past ages, who thereby attracted the notice, respect, admiration, and veneration of the world. Such rigorous exercises, too, were deemed of great help for enabling the soul to have a more perfect control over the senses, and subjecting them to the empire of reason. They are also conducive towards the calm and undisturbed state in which the soul is better fitted for the arduous task of constant meditation. The fast of Gaudama, preparatory to his obtaining the Buddhaship, recalls to mind that which our Lord underwent ere He began His divine mission. If the writer, in the course of this work, has made once or twice a remark of similar import, he has done so, not with the intention of drawing a parallel as between facts, but to communicate to the reader the feelings of surprise and astonishment he experienced when he thought he met with circumstances respecting the founder of Buddhism which apparently bore great similarity to some connected with the mission of our Saviour.

he had witnessed the great wonders prognosticating his son's future dignity that had taken place, first when Phralaong, then an infant, was placed in the presence of a famous Rathee, and secondly, when he slept under the shade of the tree Tsampoo-thabia. The fainting being over, and Phralaong having recovered his senses, the same Nats went in all haste to Thoodaudana, to inform him of his son's happy recovery. "I knew well," said the king, "that my son could not die ere he had become a Buddha." The fame of Phralaong's having spent six years in solitude, addicted to meditation and mortification, spread abroad like the sound of a great bell,[8] hung in the canopy of the skies.

---

[8] Bells are common in Burmah, and the people of that country are well acquainted with the art of casting them. Most of the bells to be seen in the pagodas are of small dimensions, and differing in shape somewhat from those used in Europe. The inferior part is less widened, and there is a large hole in the centre of the upper part. No tongue is hung in the interior, but the sound is produced by striking with a horn of deer or elk the outward surface of the lower part. No belfry is erected for the bells; they are fixed on a piece of timber, laid horizontally, and supported at its two extremities by two posts, at such a height that the inferior part of the bell is raised about five feet above the ground.

The largest specimens of Burmese art in casting bells of great weight are the two bells to be seen, the one in the large pagoda of Rangoon, called Shway Dagon, and the other at Mingon, about twelve or fifteen miles north of Amerapoura, on the western bank of the Irrawaddy. The first, in the town of Rangoon, was cast in 1842, when King Tharawaddy visited the place, with the intention of founding a new city, more distant from the river, and nearer to the mount upon which rises the splendid Shway Dagon. In its shape and form it exactly resembles the kind of bells above described. Here are some particulars respecting that large piece of metal, collected from the inscription to be seen upon it. It was cast on the fifth day of the full moon of Tabodwai (February), 1203 of the Burmese era. The weight of metal is 94,682 lbs.; its height 9½ cubits; its diameter 5 cubits; its thickness 20 fingers or 15 inches. But during the process of melting, the well-disposed came forward and threw in copper, silver, and gold in great quantities. It is supposed, says the writer of the inscription, that in this way the weight was increased one-fourth.

The bell of Mingon was cast in the beginning of this century. In shape and form it resembles our bells in Europe. It is probable that some foreigner residing at Ava suggested the idea of giving such an unusual form to that monumental bell. Its height is 18 feet, besides 7 feet for hanging apparatus. It has 17 feet in diameter, and from 10 to 12 inches in thickness. Its weight is supposed to exceed two hundred thousand English pounds.

In the interior large yellowish and

Phralaong soon remarked that fasting and mortification were not works of sufficient value for obtaining the dignity of Buddha; he took up his patta and went to the neighbouring village to get his food. Having eaten it, he grew stronger; his beautiful face shone again like gold, and the thirty-two signs reappeared.[9] The five Rahans that had lived with him said to each other—"It is in vain that the Rahan Gaudama has, during six years of mortification and

---

greyish streaks indicate that considerable quantities of gold and silver had been thrown in during the process of melting. No idea can at present be had of the power of the sound of that bell, as its enormous weight has caused the pillars that support it partially to give way. To prevent a fatal disaster, the orifice of the bell has been made to rest on large short posts, sunk in the ground and rising about three feet above it. In no respect can these bells bear any comparison with those of Europe. They are mightily rough and rude attempts at doing works on a scale far surpassing the abilities of native workmen, who otherwise succeed tolerably well in casting the comparatively small bells commonly met with in the courtyards of pagodas.

[9] One of the genuine characters of Buddhism is correctly exhibited in this observation of Phralaong's respecting fasts, mortifications, and other self-inflicted penances. They are not looked upon as the immediate way leading to perfection, nor as *a portion* or a part of perfection itself. Such deeds are but means resorted to for weakening passions and increasing the power of the spiritual principle over the natural one: they are preparatory to the great work of meditation or the study of truth, which is the only high-road to perfection. To the sage that has already begun the laborious task of investigating truth, such practices are of no use, and are nowhere insisted on as necessary, or even useful. In the book of discipline, no mention is made of them. The life of the initiated is one of self-denial; all superfluities and luxuries are strictly interdicted; all that is calculated to minister to passions and pleasure is carefully excluded. But the great austerities and macerations practised by the religious of the Brahminical sect are at once rejected by the Buddhist sages as unprofitable and unnecessary to them. The inmates of the Buddhist monasteries in our days are never seen indulging in those cruel, disgusting, and unnatural practices performed from time immemorial by some of their brethren of the Hindu persuasion. This constitutes one of the principal differences or discrepancies between the two systems. With the founder of Buddhism fasts and penitential deeds are of great concern to him who is as yet in the world, living under the tyrannical yoke of passions and the influence of the senses. By him they are viewed as powerful auxiliaries in the spiritual warfare for obtaining the mastery over passions. This point once gained, the sage can at once dispense with their aid as being no longer required. The follower of the Hindu creed looks upon those practices as *per se* eminently meritorious and capable of leading him to perfection; hence the mania for carrying those observances to a degree revolting to reason, and even to the plain good sense of the people.

sufferings, sought the dignity of Buddha; he is now compelled to go out in search of food; assuredly, if he be obliged to live on such food, when shall he ever become a Buddha? He goes out in quest of food; verily, he aims at enriching himself. As the man that wants drops of dew or water to refresh and wash his forehead, has to look for them, so we have to go somewhere else to learn the way to, and the merit of, Dzan, which we have not been able to obtain from him." Whereupon they left Phralaong, took up their pattas and tsiwarans, went to a distance of eighteen youdzanas, and withdrew into the forest of Migadawon, near Baranathee.

CHAPTER V.

Thoodzata's offering to Phralaong—His five dreams—He shapes his course towards the gniaong tree—Miraculous appearance of a throne—Victory of Phralaong over Manh Nat—His meditations during forty-nine days near the Bodi tree—He at last obtains the perfect science—He overcomes the temptations directed against him by the daughters of Manh—Buddha preaches the law to a Pounha and to two merchants.

AT that time, in the solitude of Oorouwela, there lived in a village a rich man, named Thena. He had a daughter named Thoodzata. Having attained the years of puberty, she repaired to a place where there was a gniaong tree, and made the following prayer to the Nat guardian of the place[1]:—"If I marry a husband that will prove a suitable

[1] The Nats or Dewatas play a conspicuous part in the affairs of this world. Their seats are in the six lower heavens, forming, with the abode of man and the four states of punishment, the eleven seats of passions. But they often quit their respective places, and interfere with the chief events that take place among men. Hence we see them ever attentive in ministering to all the wants of the future Buddha. Besides, they are made to watch over trees, forests, villages, towns, cities, fountains, rivers, &c. These are the good and benevolent Nats. This world is also supposed to be peopled with wicked Nats, whose nature is ever prone to the evil. A good deal of the worship of Buddhists consists in superstitious ceremonies and offerings made for propitiating the wicked Nats, and obtaining favours and temporal advantages from the good ones. Such a worship is universal, and fully countenanced by the talapoins, though in opposition to the real doctrines of genuine Buddhism. All kinds of misfortunes are attributed to the malignant interference of the evil Nats. In cases of severe illness that have resisted the skill of native medical art, the physician gravely tells the patient and his relatives that it is useless to have recourse any longer to medicines, but a conjuror must be sent for to drive out the malignant spirit, who is the author of the complaint. Meanwhile directions are given for the erection of a shed, where offerings intended for the inimical Nat are deposited. A female relative of the patient begins dancing to the sound of musical instruments. The dance goes on, at first in rather a quiet manner, but it gradually grows more animated until it reaches the acme of animal frenzy.

match, and the first fruit of our union be a male child, I will spend annually in alms deeds 100,000 pieces of silver, and make an offering at this spot." Her prayer was heard,

---

At that moment the bodily strength of the dancing lady becomes exhausted; she drops on the ground in a state of apparent faintness. She is then approached by the conjuror, who asks her if the invisible foe has relinquished his hold over the diseased. Being answered in the affirmative, he bids the physician give medicines to the patient, assuring him that his remedies will now act beneficially for restoring the health of the sick, since their action will meet no further opposition from the wicked Nat.

Ignorance brings everywhere superstition in its train. When man is unacquainted with the natural cause that has produced a result, or an effect, which attracts powerfully his mind's attention and affects him to a great degree, he is induced by his own weakness to believe in the agency of some unknown being, to account for the effect that he perceives. He devises the most ridiculous means for expressing his gratitude to his invisible benefactor, if the result be a favourable one; and has recourse to the most extravagant measures to counteract the evil influence of his supposed enemy, if the result be fatal to him. Having once entered into the dark way of superstition, man is hurried on in countless false directions by fear, hope, and other passions, in the midst of the daily occurrence of multifarious and unforeseen events and circumstances. Hence the expression or manifestation of his superstition assumes a variety of forms, and undergoes changes to an extent that baffles every attempt at either counting their numberless kinds or following them up through their ever-changing course. In addition to the stores of superstitions bequeathed by the generation that has preceded him, man has those of his own creation; and the latter, if the thought of his mind and the desires of his heart could be analysed, would be found far exceeding the former in number. Having spent many years in a country where Buddhism has prevailed from time immemorial, and observed the effects of superstition over the people in their daily doings, the writer has come to the conclusion that there is scarcely an action done without the influence of some superstitious motive or consideration. But the most prolific source of superstition is the belief in the existence of countless good and evil Nats, with whom the imagination of Buddhists has peopled this world.

It can scarcely be understood how the followers of an atheistical creed can make, consistently with their opinions, an attempt at prayer. Such an act of devotion implies the belief in a being superior to men, who has a controlling power over them, and in whose hands their destinies are placed. With a believer in God, prayer is a sacred, nay, a natural duty. But such cannot be the case with atheists. Despite the withering and despairing influence of atheism, nothing can possibly obliterate from the conscience and heart of man that inward faith in a supreme being. The pious Thoodzata has in view the attainment of two objects: she prays, without knowing to whom, that by the agency of some one she might obtain the objects of her petition; she is anxious to show her gratitude when she sees that her prayer has been heard. Her faith in the *quasi* omnipotence of the genii makes her address thanks to them. The Nat is

and its twofold object granted. When Phralaong had ended the six years of his fasting and mortification, on the day of the full moon of the month Katson, Thoodzata was preparing to make her grateful offering to the Nat of the place. She had been keeping one thousand cows in a place abounding with sweet vines; the milk of those thousand was given to five hundred cows; these again fed with their own milk two hundred and fifty others, and so on, in a diminishing proportion, until it happened that sixteen cows fed eight others with their milk. So these eight cows gave a milk, rich, sweet, and flavoured beyond all description.

On the day of the full moon of Katson,[2] Thoodzata rose at an early hour to make ready her offering, and disposed everything that the cows should be simultaneously milked. When they were to be milked, the young calves of their own accord kept at a distance; and as soon as the vessels were brought near, the milk began to flow in streams from

---

not the person to whom her prayer appears directed, but he is rather a witness of her petition. The Burmese, in general, under difficult circumstances, unforeseen difficulties, and sudden calamities, use always the cry, *Phra kaiba*—God assist me—to obtain from above assistance and protection. Yet that Phra cannot be their Buddha, though he be in their opinion the Phra *par excellence*, since they openly declare that he in no way interferes in the management of this world's affairs. Whence that involuntary cry for assistance, but from the innate consciousness that above man there is some one ruling over his destinies? An atheistical system may be elaborated in a school of metaphysics, and forced upon ignorant and unreflecting masses, but practice will ever belie theory. Man, in spite of his errors and follies, is naturally a believing being; his own weakness and multiplied wants ever compel him to have recourse to some great being that can help and assist him, and supply, to a certain extent, the deficiency which, in spite of himself, he is compelled to acknowledge existing in him as a stern and humiliating reality.

[2] The Burmese, like all trans-Gangetic nations, divide the year into twelve lunar months of twenty-nine and thirty days alternately. Every third year they add one month, or as they say, double the month of Watso (July). The year begins on, or about, the 12th of April. The days of worship are the days of the four quarters of the moon; but the days of the new and full moon seem to have preference over those of the two other quarters, which latter are scarcely noticed or distinguished from common days. It was on the day of the full moon of April that Thoodzata made her grand offering.

the udders into the vessels. She took the milk and poured it into a large caldron, set on the fire which she had herself kindled. The milk began to boil; bubbles formed on the surface of the liquid, turned on the right and sunk in, not a single drop being spilt out; no smoke arose from the fireplace. Four kings of Nats watched about while the caldron was boiling; the great Brahma kept open an umbrella over it; a Thagia brought fuel and fed the fire. Other Nats, by their supernatural power, infused honey into the milk, and communicated thereto a flavour, such as the like is not to be found in the abode of men. On this occasion alone, and on the day Phralaong entered the state of Neibban, the Nats infused honey into his food. Wondering at the so many extraordinary signs which she saw, Thoodzata called her female slave, named Sounama, related to her all that she had observed, and directed her to go to the gniaong tree, and clear the place where she intended to make her offering. The servant, complying with her mistress' direction, soon arrived at the foot of the tree.

On that very night Phralaong had had five dreams.[3]

---

[3] The Burmese translator, not having given in his remarks the explanation or interpretation of Phralaong's five dreams, it seems rather presumptuous to attempt doing a thing, the neglect of which, on the part of the author, may be attributed either to voluntary omission or to incapacity and inability. Let us try to make up, in part, for the deficiency. The first dream prognosticated the future greatness of Phralaong, whose sway, by the diffusion of his doctrines throughout the world, was to be universal, extending from one sea to the other sea. The grass growing out of his navel and reaching to the sky was indicative of the spreading of his law, not only amongst the beings inhabiting the seat of men, but also amidst those dwelling in the abodes of Nats and Brahmas. The ants covering his legs offer an enigma, the explanation of which is reserved to some future Œdipus. As to the birds of various colours, gathering round him, from the four points of the compass, and on a sudden becoming all white, by their contact with him, they represent the innumerable beings that will come to hear the preaching of the future Buddha with divers dispositions, and different progress in the way of merits, and will all be perfected by their following the true way to merit, that he will point out to them. The fifth dream in which Phralaong thought he was walking on a mountain of filth, without being in the least contaminated by it, foreshowed the incomparable perfection and purity of Buddha, who, though remaining in the world of passions, was no more to be affected by their influence.

1st, It appeared to him that the earth was his sleeping place, with the Himawonta for his pillow. His right hand rested on the western ocean, his left on the eastern ocean, and his feet on the southern ocean. 2d, A kind of grass, named Tyria, appeared to grow out of his navel and reach to the skies. 3d, Ants of a white appearance ascended from his feet to the knee and covered his legs. 4th, Birds of varied colour and size appeared to come from all directions and fall at his feet, when, on a sudden, they all appeared white. 5th, It seemed to him that he was walking on a mountain of filth, and that he passed over it without being in the least contaminated.

Phralaong, awaking from his sleep, said to himself, after having reflected for a while on those five dreams,—"Today I shall certainly become a Buddha." Thereupon he rose instantly, washed his hands and face, put on his dress, and quietly waited the break of day, to go out in quest of his food. The moment being arrived to go out, he took up his patta, and walked in the direction of the gniaong tree. The whole tree was made shining by the rays which issued from his person; he rested there for a while. At that very moment arrived Sounama, to clear, according to her mistress' orders, the place for her offering. As she approached, she saw Phralaong at the foot of the tree. The rays of light which beamed out of his person were reflected on the tree, which exhibited a most splendid and dazzling appearance. On observing this wonder, Sounama said to herself: "Of course the Nat has come down from the tree to receive the offering with his own hands." Overcome with an unutterable joy, she immediately ran to her mistress and related her adventure. Thoodzata was delighted at this occurrence, and wishing to give a substantial proof of her gratitude for such good news, she said to Sounama: "From this moment you are no more my servant; I adopt you for my elder daughter." She gave her instantly all the ornaments suitable to her new position. It is customary for all the Phralaongs to be provided, on the day they are to become Buddha, with a gold cup of an immense value. Thoodzata ordered a golden vessel to be brought, and poured therein the nogana or boiled milk. As the water glides from the leaf of the water-lily without leaving thereon any trace, so the nogana slided from the pot into the golden cup and filled it up. She covered this cup with another of the same precious metal, and wrapped up the whole with a white cloth. She forthwith put on her finest dress, and, becomingly attired, she carried the golden cup over her head; and with a decent gravity walked towards the gniaong tree. Overwhelmed with joy at seeing Phralaong, she reverentially advanced towards him, whom she mistook for a Nat. When near him, she placed gently the golden vessel on the ground, and offered him in a gold basin scented water to wash his hands. At that moment, the earthen patta offered to Phralaong by the Brahma Gatikara disappeared. Perceiving that his patta had disappeared, he stretched forth his right hand, and washed it in the scented water; at the same time Thoodzata presented to him the golden cup containing the nogana. Having observed that she had caught the eyes of Phralaong, she said to him: "My Lord Nat, I beg to offer you this food, together with the vessel that contains it." Having respectfully bowed down to him, she continued: "May your joy and happiness be as great as mine; may you always delight in the happiest rest, ever surrounded by a great and brilliant retinue." Making then the offering of the gold cup, worth 100,000 pieces of silver, with the same disinterestedness as if she had given over only the dry leaf of a tree, she withdrew and returned to her home with a heart overflowing with joy.

Phralaong rising up took with him the golden cup, and having turned to the left of the gniaong tree, went to the bank of the river Neritzara, to a place where more than 100,000 Buddhas had bathed, ere they obtained the supreme intelligence. On the banks of that river is a bathing-place. Having left on that spot his golden cup, he undressed himself, and descended into the river. When he had bathed, he came out and put on his yellow robe, which in shape and form resembled that of his predecessors. He sat down, his face turned towards the east; his face resembled in appearance a well-ripe palm fruit. He divided his exquisite food into forty-nine mouthfuls, which he ate entire, without mixing any water with it. During forty-nine days he spent round the Bodi tree, Buddha never bathed, nor took any food, nor experienced the least want. His appearance and countenance remained unchanged; he spent the whole time absorbed, as it were, in an uninterrupted meditation. Holding up in his hands the empty golden vessel, Phralaong made the following prayer: "If on this day I am to become a Buddha, let this cup float on the water and ascend the stream." Whereupon he flung it into the stream, when, by the power and influence of Phralaong's former good works, the vessel, gently gliding towards the middle of the river, and then beating up the stream, ascended it with the swiftness of a horse to the distance of eighty cubits, when it stopped, sunk into a whirlpool, went down to the country of Naga, and made a noise, on coming in contact with and striking against the three vessels of the three last Buddhas, viz.: Kaukathan, Gaunagong, and Kathaba. On hearing this unusual noise, the chief of Nagas awoke from his sleep, and said: "How is this? yesterday, a Buddha appeared in the world; to-day, again, there is another." And in more than one hundred stanzas he sung praises to Buddha.

On the banks of the river Neritzara there is a grove of Sala trees, whither Phralaong repaired to spend the day under their cooling shade. In the evening he rose up and walked with the dignified and noble bearing of a lion, in a road eight oothabas wide, made by the Nats, and strewed with flowers, towards the gniaong tree. The Nats, Nagas, and Galongs joined in singing praises to him, playing instruments, and making offerings of the finest flowers and most exquisite perfumes, brought from their own seats. The same rejoicings took place in ten thousand other worlds. Whilst on his way towards the tree, he met with a young man, just returning with a grass-load he had cut in the fields. Foreseeing that Phralaong might require some portion of it for his use, he presented him an offering of eight handfuls of grass, which were willingly accepted.

Arrived close to the gniaong tree,[4] Phralaong stopped

---

[4] We have now reached the most interesting episode of Phralaong's life. He is to become a perfected Buddha under the shade of the gniaong or banyan tree (*ficus indica, ficus religiosa*). There are two circumstances attending that great event, deserving peculiar notice. The first is the preference given to the east over the three other points of the compass, and the second, the mighty combat that takes place between Phralaong and the wicked Nat Manh, or Mar. I notice the first circumstance because it agrees with the tradition prevailing amongst most nations previous to or about the coming of our Lord, that from the east there was to come an extraordinary personage, who would confer on the human race the greatest benefits, and cause the return of happy times, like the golden age so much celebrated by poets. The Roman historian Suetonius bears testimony to the existence of that tradition as being universally known in his own days. It is not impossible that the same notion, not unknown in the far east, might have induced Phralaong to look towards the east at the supreme moment when perfect intelligence was to become his happy lot. It may be said in opposition to this supposition, that the splendour and magnificence of the sun, emerging from the bosom of night, and dispelling darkness by pouring a flood of light on the face of the earth, restoring nature to life and action, was a sufficient inducement to Phralaong for giving preference to the east. But to an ascetic like him, who is convinced that this world is a mere illusion, such a consideration would weigh very little on his mind, and would not be a sufficient motive to induce him to give so marked a preference to the east.

The second circumstance remarkable for the time it occurred, is the great combat between Phralaong and Manh. The first is the personification of goodness and benevolence towards all beings; the second is the personification of consummate wickedness. The contest is to take place between the good principle on the one hand, and the evil one on the other. Phralaong, on his becoming Buddha, will preach a law designed to dispel mental darkness, to check vicious passions, to show the right way to perfection, to unloose the ties that keep beings in the wretched state of existence, and enable them to reach safely the peaceful shores of Neibban. Manh, the devil himself, the father of darkness, of lies and deceit, delights in seeing all beings plunged into the abyss of vices, carried out of the right way by the impetuous and irresistible torrent of their passions, and doomed to turn for ever in the whirlpool of endless existences. He looks upon himself as the king of this world, and proudly exults in contemplating all beings bending their neck under his tyrannical yoke, and acknowledging his undisputed power. Now the moment approaches when a

at the south of the tree, his face turned towards the north, when, on a sudden, the southern point of the globe seemed to lower down to the hell Awidzi, the lowest of all, whilst

---

mighty antagonist will contend with him for the empire of the world. His mission will be to labour incessantly for the delivery of all beings from the grasp of their mortal enemy, and set them free from the tyranny of passions. Manh is enraged at the audacious pretensions of Phralaong. Hence the gigantic efforts he makes to maintain his rights, and retain possession of his empire. At the time Phralaong left the world to become a Rahan, Manh endeavoured to dissuade him from attempting such a design. But on this occasion, the tempter summons all his forces to avert, by an irresistible attack, the deadly blow soon to be levelled at him. It is needless to add that the reader, in perusing the detailed account of the attack of Manh against Phralaong, ought to bear in mind that it exhibits throughout but an allegory of the opposition of evil to good. The victory of Phralaong over Manh exemplifies the final triumph of truth over error.

When the contest was nearly over, Phralaong objected to the claims of Manh to the possession of his throne, on the ground that he never had practised the ten great virtues, nor performed works of kindness, charity, and benevolence, which alone can entitle a being to obtain the Buddhaship. It is to be borne in mind that these qualifications form the real characteristics of a Buddha, together with the possession of the supreme intelligence. In this system, they admit that there exist certain beings called Pitzega-Buddhas, who possess all the knowledge and science of a genuine Buddha, but as they are divested of those benevolent feelings, which induce the former to labour earnestly for the benefit and salvation of all beings, they cannot be assimilated to the real Buddhas. The cross-legged position which our Buddha is always taken in preference to any other, whilst he spent forty-nine days at the foot of and in various places round the Bodi tree, is, as every one knows, peculiar to and a favourite with all Asiatics. But with him, it is the fittest position for meditation and contemplation. Hence most of the statues or images of Gaudama exhibit or represent him in the cross-legged position which he occupied when he attained the Buddhaship. As this event is by far the most important of his life, it is but natural that this great occurrence should ever be forced upon the attention and memory of his followers, by objects representing him on that most important stage of his last existence. It is not unusual to meet with statues of Gaudama, sometimes of colossal dimensions, representing him in a reclining position. This is the peculiar situation he occupied when he died. Hence those two most common images of Gaudama are designed to remind his followers of the two greatest circumstances of his life, viz., his becoming Buddha, and his entering the state of Neibban.

Here again one is forcibly compelled to reflect on the singular *rôle* attributed to those Pitzega Buddhas. They possess all the science of a Buddha, but are deficient in that kindness, benevolence, and zeal which prompt the real Buddhas to labour so strenuously for the deliverance of all beings. They appear only in those ages of darkness and ignorance which are not to be brightened and enlightened by the presence of a Buddha. They are like smaller luminaries, shedding a pale light among men, to prevent their sinking into an un-

the northern one appeared to reach the sky. Then he said, "Verily this is not the place where I shall become a Buddha." Thence Phralaong went on his right side towards the east of the tree, and standing up, his face turned towards the west, he said, "This is indeed the place where all the preceding Buddhas have obtained the supreme intelligence. Here, too, is the very spot whereupon I shall become a Buddha, and set up my throne." He took, by one of their extremities, the eight handfuls of grass and scattered them on the ground, when, on a sudden, there appeared emerging, as it were, from the bottom of the earth, a throne fourteen cubits high, adorned with the choicest sculptures and paintings, superior in perfection to all that art could produce. Phralaong, then facing the east, uttered the following imprecation: "If I am not destined to become a Buddha, may my bones, veins, and skin remain on this throne, and my blood and flesh be dried up." He then ascended the throne, with his back turned against the tree, and his face towards the east. He sat down in a cross-legged position, firmly resolved never to vacate the throne, ere he had become a Buddha. Such firmness of purpose, which the combined elements could not shake for a moment, no one ought to think of ever becoming possessed of.

Whilst Phralaong was sitting on the throne in that cross-legged position, Manh Nat said to himself, "I will not suffer Prince Theiddat to overstep the boundaries of my empire." He summoned all his warriors and shouted to them. On hearing their chief's voice, the warriors gathered thick round his person. His countless followers

---

fathomable abyss of ignorance; they maintain on earth some sparks of the knowledge of fundamental truths, which otherwise would be completely obliterated from the memory of men. Not unlike the prophets of old, they prepare men in an indirect manner for the coming of the future deliverer. Their mission being at an end, when a Buddha is to come among men, they disappear, and none of them is to be seen either in the days of Buddha or during all the time his religion is to last.

in front, on his right and on his left, reached to the distance of eighteen youdzanas, and above him to that of nine only. Behind him, they extended to the very limits of the world. The cries of that immense multitude were re-echoed at a distance of ten thousand youdzanas, and resembled the roaring of the mighty sea. Manh Nat rode the elephant Girimegala, measuring in length five youdzanas. Supplied with one thousand right arms, he wielded all sorts of the most deadly weapons. His countless warriors, to avoid confusion, were all disposed in ranks, bearing their respective armour. They appeared like immense clouds, slowly rolling on and converging towards Phralaong.

At that time, Nats surrounded Phralaong, singing praises to him; the chief Thagia was playing on his conch, whereof a single blowing resounds for four entire months; the chief Naga was uttering stanzas in his honour; a chief Brahma held over him the white umbrella. On the approach of Manh Nat's army, they were all seized with an uncontrollable fear, and fled to their respective places. The Naga dived into the bottom of the earth, to a depth of five hundred youdzanas, and covering his face with his two wings, fell into a deep sleep. The Thagia, swinging his conch upon his shoulders, ran to the extremity of the world. The Brahma, holding still the umbrella by the extremity of the handle, went up to his own country. Phralaong was, therefore, left alone. Manh Nat, turning to his followers, cried to them, "There is, indeed, no one equal to the Prince Theiddat; let us not attack him in front, but let us assail him from the north side."

At that moment, Phralaong, lifting his eyes, looked on his right, left, and front, for the crowd of Nats, Brahmas, and Thagias that were paying him their respects. But they had all disappeared. He saw the army of Manh Nat coming thick upon him from the north, like a mighty storm. "What!" said he, "is it against me alone that such a countless crowd of warriors has been assembled? I have no one to help me, no father, no brothers, no sisters, no friends, and no relatives. But I have with me the ten great virtues which I have practised; the merits I have acquired in the practice of these virtues will be my safeguard and protection; these are my offensive and defensive weapons, and with them I will crush down the great army of Manh." Whereupon he quietly remained meditating upon the merits of the ten great virtues.

Whilst Phralaong was thus absorbed in meditation, Manh Nat began his attack upon him. He caused a wind to blow with such an extraordinary violence that it brought down the tops of mountains, though they were one or two youdzanas thick. The trees of the forests were shattered to atoms. But the virtue of Phralaong's merits preserved him from the destructive storm. His tsiwaran itself was not agitated. Perceiving that his first effort was useless, Manh caused a heavy rain to fall with such violence that it tore the earth, and opened it to its very bottom. But not even a single drop touched Phralaong's person. To this succeeded a shower of rocks, accompanied with smoke and fire; but they were changed into immense masses of flowers, which dropped at Buddha's feet. There came afterwards another shower of swords, knives, and all kinds of cutting weapons, emitting smoke and fire. They all fell powerless at the feet of Phralaong. A storm of burning ashes and sand soon darkened the atmosphere, but they fell in front of him like fragrant dust. Clouds of mud succeeded, which fell like perfumes all round and over Phralaong. Manh caused a thick darkness to fill the atmosphere, but to Phralaong it emitted rays of the purest light. The enraged Manh cried to his followers, "Why do you stand looking on? Rush at once upon him and compel him to flee before me." Sitting on his huge elephant, and brandishing his formidable weapons, Manh approached close to Phralaong and said to him, "Theiddat, this throne is not made for you; vacate it forthwith; it is my property." Phralaong calmly answered, "You have not as yet practised the ten great virtues, nor gone through the five acts of self-denial; you have never devoted your life to help others to acquire merits; in a word, you have not yet done all the needful to enable you to obtain the supreme dignity of Phra. This throne, therefore, cannot be yours." Unable to control any longer his passion, Manh threw his formidable weapons at Phralaong; but they were converted into garlands of beautiful flowers, that adapted themselves gracefully round his body. His sword and other weapons, that could cut at once through the hardest rocks, were employed with no better success. The soldiers of Manh, hoping that their united efforts would have a better result, and that they could thrust Phralaong from his throne, made a sudden and simultaneous rush at him, rolling against him, with an irresistible force, huge rocks, as large as mountains; but by the virtue of their opponent's merits, they were converted into fine nosegays, that gently dropped at his feet.

At that time the Nats, from their seats, looked down on the scene of the combat, suspended between hope and fear. Phralaong at that moment said to Manh: "How do you dare to pretend to the possession of this throne? Could you ever prove, by indisputable evidence, that you have ever made offerings enough to be deserving of this throne?" Manh, turning to his followers, answered: "Here are my witnesses; they will all bear evidence in my favour." At the same moment they all shouted aloud, to testify their approval of Manh's words. "As to you, Prince Theiddat, where are the witnesses that will bear evidence in your favour and prove the justness of your claim to the possession of this throne?" Phralaong replied: "My witnesses are not like yours, men or any living beings.[5] The earth

[5] The witness whom Phralaong summoned in support of his claim to the undisturbed possession of the throne was the earth itself. It may be from the example that was set on this occasion that Buddhists have borrowed the habit of calling the earth as a witness of the good works they have done or are doing. I will briefly relate what is done and said

itself will give testimony to me. For, without alluding even to those offerings I have made during several previous existences, I will but mention the forty-seven great ones I made whilst I lived as Prince Wethandra." Stretching out his right hand, which he had kept hitherto under the folds of his garment, and pointing to the earth, he said with a firm voice: "Earth, is it not true that at the time I was Prince Wethandra I made forty great offerings?" The earth replied with a deep and loud roaring, resounding in the midst of Manh's legions, like the sound of countless voices, threatening to spread death and destruction in their ranks. The famous charger of Manh bent his knees, and paid homage to Phralaong. Manh himself, disheartened and discomfited, fled to the country of Wathawatti. His followers were so overpowered by fear that they flung away all that could impede their retreat, and ran away in every direction. Such was the confusion and disorder that prevailed that two warriors could not be seen following the same course in their flight.

Looking from their seats on the defeat of Manh and the

---

on such occasions. During my former residence in Burmah I observed on a certain occasion, when taking my evening walk, about ten or twelve persons of both sexes assembled on a rather retired spot in the vicinity of a pagoda. As they appeared all quite attentive, I came near to them to see what was the cause that had brought them thither, and what occurrence seemed to rivet their attention. As I was known to some of them, they were not frightened by my sudden apparition. On my asking them the motive of their assembling here at a late hour, they said that, having buried yesterday a child two years old, they came to make some offerings of boiled rice, plantains, and other fruits, to propitiate the Nat of the place. Having asked them to repeat the formula they had uttered on the occasion, they kindly complied with my request. Here is the substance of that formula. "Believing in the three precious things, Buddha, the Law, and the Assembly of the perfect, I make this offering, that I may be delivered from all present and future miseries. May all beings existing in the four states of punishment reach the fortunate seats of Nats. I wish all my relatives and all men inhabiting this and other worlds to have a share in this meritorious work. O earth and you Nats, guardians of this place, be witness to the offering I am making." On uttering these last words, the offerer of the present, or a talapoin, sent for this purpose, pours down some water on the ground.

[6] As the Nats and all other beings are to be benefited by the preachings of Buddha, it is but natural that they

glorious victory of Phralaong, the Nats [6] rent the air with shouts of exultation. The Brahmas, Nagas, and Galongs joined the Nats in celebrating his triumph over his enemies. They all hastened from more than ten thousand worlds to pay their respects and offer their felicitations, presenting him with flowers and perfumes, saying: "Victory and glory to Phralaong! Shame and defeat to the infamous Manh!"

It was a little while before sunset when Phralaong had achieved his splendid victory over his proud foe. At that time he was wrapped up, as it were, in the profoundest meditation. The extremities of the branches of the Bodi tree [7] fell gently over him, and, by their undulations,

---

all join in singing his praises and exalting his glorious achievements. The Nagas and Galongs are fabulous animals, which are often mentioned in the course of this Legend. It has been observed in a former note that, according to the Buddhistic notions, animals are beings in a state of punishment, differing from man, not in nature, but in merits. Some of them, having nearly exhausted the sum of their demerits, begin to feel the influence of former merits. They are supposed to have, to a certain extent, the use of reason. No wonder if they rejoice at seeing the triumph of him who is to help them in advancing towards a condition better than their present one.

[7] The banyan tree, at the foot of which Phralaong obtains perfect intelligence, is occasionally called throughout this narrative the Bodi tree. The word Bodi means wisdom, science, or knowledge. The Burmese, in their sacred writings, always mention the tree by that name, because, under its shade, perfect science was communicated to Phralaong. It is supposed to occupy the very centre of the island of Dzampudiba. During all the while Phra or Buddha (let us call him now by that name) remained under that tree his mind was engaged in the most profound meditation, which the gigantic efforts of his enemy could scarcely interrupt. It is not to be inferred from the narrative in the text that supreme intelligence was communicated suddenly or by miraculous process to our Buddha. He was already prepared, by former mental labours, for that grand result; he had previously capacitated himself, by studies and reflection, for the reception of that more than human science; he required but a last and mighty effort of his intelligence to arrive finally at the acme of knowledge, and thereby to become a perfect Buddha. That last effort was made on this occasion, and crowned with the most complete success. He gained the science of the past, present, and future.

It would be somewhat curious to investigate the motives that have determined Buddhists to give to that sacred tree the name of Bodi. At first sight one will infer that such a name was given to the tree because, under its refreshing and cooling shade the Bodi, or Supreme intelligence, was communicated to Phralaong. The occurrence, however extraordinary it be, is scarcely suffi-

seemed caressing, as it were, his tsiwaran; they resembled so many beautiful nosegays of red flowers that were offered to him. At the first watch of the night Phralaong applied all the energies of his powerful mind to ascertain the laws of the causes and effects, in order to account for all that is in existence. He argued in the following manner: "Pain and all sorts of miseries do exist in this world. Why do they exist? Because there is birth. Why is there birth? Because there is conception. Now conception does take place, because there is existence, or that moral state produced by the action or influence of merits and demerits. Existence is brought in by *Upadan*, or the combining of affections calculated to cause the coming into existence. The latter has for its cause the desire. The desire is produced by sensation. The latter is caused by the contact. The contact takes place because there are the six senses. The six senses do exist, because there is name and form, that is to say, the exterior sign of the ideal being and the type of the real being. Name and form owe their existence to erroneous knowledge; the latter in its turn is produced by the imagination, which has for its cause ignorance.[8]

Having followed in his mind the succession of the

---

cient to account for such an appellation. Bearing in mind the numerous and striking instances of certain revealed facts and truths, offered to the attention of the reader of this Legend, in a deformed but yet recognisable shape, it would not be quite out of the limits of probability to suppose that this is also a remnant of the tradition of the tree of knowledge that occupied the centre of the garden of Eden.

[8] The theory of the twelve causes and effects is, in itself, very abstruse, and almost above the comprehension of those uninitiated in the metaphysics of Buddhists. I will attempt to analyse it in as simple and clear a way as possible. This theory is very ancient, probably coeval with the first ages of Buddhism. It forms this basis of its ontology and metaphysics, in the same manner as the four great and transcendent truths are the foundation whereupon rests the system of morals. It is probable that Gaudama, in his preachings, which were very simple, and within the reach of ordinary minds, never formulated his doctrine on this essential point in such a dry and concise manner. But the seed was sown, and the germ deposited here and there in his instructions. His immediate disciples, in endeavouring to give a distinct shape to their master's doc-

twelve causes and effects, and reached the last link of that chain, Phralaong said to himself: "Ignorance, or no science, is the first cause which gives rise to all the phe-

---

trines, gradually framed the formula or theory just stated. It, in fact, presents the very characteristics of a system elaborated in a philosophical school.

In taking our departure from the first cause, which is *Awidza*, or ignorance, or the wanting in science, or no knowledge, we have to follow the different stages and conditions of a being until it reaches decrepitude, old age, and death. When we speak of ignorance, or no science, we must not suppose the material existence of a being that ignores. But we must take ignorance in an abstract sense, deprived of forms, and subsisting in a manner very different from what we are wont to consider ordinary beings. A European has a great difficulty in finding his way through a process of reasoning so extraordinary, and so different from that positivism which he is used to. But with the Buddhist the case is widely different. He can pass from the abstract to the concrete, from the ideal to the real, with the greatest ease. But let us follow the scale of the causes and effects, upon which there are twelve steps.

From ignorance comes *Sangkara*, that is to say conception or imagination, which mistakes for reality what is unreal, which looks on this world as something substantial, whilst it is, indeed, nothing but shadow and emptiness, assuming forms which pass away as quick as the representations of theatrical exhibitions. Sangkara, in its turn, begets *Wignian*, or knowledge, attended with a notion of sentiment, implying that of soul and life, in an abstract sense. From Wignian proceeds *Namrup*, the name and form, because knowledge can have for its object but name and form, &c., or, to speak in the language of Buddhists, things that are external and internal. But let it be borne in mind that what is herein meant is but the individuality of an ideal being.

The name and form give birth to the *Chayatana*, six senses, or seats of the sensible qualities. To our division of the five ordinary senses Buddhists add the sixth sense of Mano, or the heart, the internal sense. Through the senses we are put in communication or contact with all objects; hence the six senses give rise to the sixth cause *Pasa*, which means, properly speaking, contact. From this cause flows the seventh one, called *Wedana*, or sensation, or, more generally still, sensibility. In fact, there can be no contact from which there will not result some sensation, either pleasant or unpleasant. *Wedana* gives infallibly rise to *Tahna*, or passion, or desire, or inclination. From this point the series of causes and effects is comparatively easy, because it presents conditions essentially connected with a material object. By Tahna we ought not to understand only the mere inclination that the sexes have one for the other, but the general propensity created in a being by any contact whatever, or perhaps, as usual with Buddhists, the desire taken in an abstract sense.

The immediate result from Tahna is *Upadan*, the attachment, or the conception. It is that state in which the desire adheres to something, assumes a shape. It is, in fact, the being conceived. From the state of conception the being passes into that of *Bawa*, or existence, or that condition which is created and made by the influence of former good or bad deeds preceding birth, which is but

nomena I have successively reviewed. From it springs the world and all the beings it contains. It is the cause of that universal illusion in which man and all beings are miserably lulled. By what means can this ignorance be done away with? Doubtless by knowledge and true science. By means of the light that science spreads I clearly see the unreality of all that exists, and I am freed from that illusion which makes other beings to believe that such thing exists, when, in reality, it does not exist. The imagination, or the faculty to imagine the existence of things which do not exist, is done away with. The same fate is reserved to the false knowledge resulting therefrom to the name and form, to the six senses, to contact, to sen-

---

the apparition of the being into this world. *Dzati*, or birth, is the eleventh cause. It is the ushering of a being into the world. There are six ways by which a being comes into this world, viz., those of Nat, Man, Assura, Preitta, animal, and the inhabitant of hell. Birth is accomplished in four different manners, by humidity, an egg, a mattrice, and metamorphosis.

The twelfth and last step in the ladder of the causes and effects is decrepitude and death. In fact, every being that is born must grow old, decay, and finally die.

Such is the process followed by Buddhists in attempting to account for all that exists. What effect could such a reasoning have over the mind of the generality of hearers it is difficult to say. But we may rest assured that, though these principles existed, as an embryo, in the discourses of the author of Buddhism, they were never laid before the generality of hearers in that crude scholastic form. Such abstruse ideas, when analysed and commented upon by Buddhist doctors, gave rise to the most opposite conclusions. The materialist school based its revolting doctrines upon that theory; we may add that the opinions of that school are generally held in Burmah, and by the great mass of Buddhists. Some other doctors reasoned in the following manner: Ignorance supposes two things, a being ignoring and a thing ignored, that is to say, man and the world. They admitted the eternity of a soul which had to pass through the series above enumerated. With them metempsychosis was a process exactly similar to that imagined by the Brahmins. As to the world, it was, to them, an unreality. Knowledge enabled them to come to the position of understanding and believing that there is no such thing as what we by mistake call world. The latter opinion, which seems to admit of a principle existing distinct from matter, is opposed to the former and general one, which supposes that spirit is but a modification of matter. We deliberately make use of the doubt, implying expression, at the head of the preceding sentence, respecting the real opinions of the latter school, because, in their way of arguing, it is impossible not to come to the painful conclusion that they ignore, or do not admit, a distinction between spirit and matter.

sation, to desire, to conception, to existence, to birth, and to pain or miseries."

Then Phralaong says to himself: "The knowledge of the four great truths is the true light that can dispel ignorance and procure the real science, whereby the coming out from the whirlpool of existences, or from the state of illusion, can be perfectly effected. These four truths are: 1, The miseries of existence; 2, The cause productive of misery, which is the desire, ever-renewed, of satisfying oneself without being able ever to secure that end; 3, The destruction of that desire, or the estranging oneself from it, is the important affair deserving the most serious attention; 4, The means of obtaining the individual annihilation of that desire is supplied solely by the four Meggas, or highways, leading to perfection. But these Meggas can be followed only by those who have a right intention, a right will, and who, throughout life, exert themselves to regulate their action, conduct, language, thought, and meditations. It was then that the heart of Phralaong acquired an unshakable firmness, a perfect purity or exemption from all passions, an unalterable meekness, and a strong feeling of tender compassion towards all beings.

When these fundamental truths had been known, felt, and relished,[9] Phralaong's mind, casting a glance over the

---

[9] In a work different from that which has been translated is found a more developed exposition of the four great and sublime truths. We think that the reader will like to see in what manner Buddhists themselves understand this important subject, which is, with them, the foundation of their doctrine on morals.

There are four great truths: pain, the production of pain, the destruction of pain, and the way leading to that destruction. What is pain, which is the first of the great truths? It is birth, old age, sickness, death, the coming in contact with what we dislike, the separation from what we feel an attachment for, the illusion which begets false knowledge. All that is pain. What is the production of pain, the second sublime truth? It is the desire which incessantly longs for an illusory satisfaction, which can never be obtained. That desire is a perpetually renewed craving, coveting objects here and there, and never satiated. Such is the cause productive of pain; such is the prolific source of all miseries. What is the destruction of pain, which is

past, was able to discover at once all that had taken place during the countless states of his former existences. He recollected the name he had borne, those of his parents, the places he had seen and visited, the caste he had belonged to, and all the chief events that had marked the course of his progress through the continual migrations. He likewise saw reflected, as in a mirror, the former conditions of existence of all other beings. The immense development and expansion of his mind, which enabled him to fathom the depth of the past, happened during the first watch of the night.

He applied now all the expanded powers of his incomparable mind to take a correct survey of all the beings now in existence. He glanced over all those that were in hell, and the other three states of punishment, those living on earth, and those dwelling in the twenty-six superior seats. He at once understood distinctly their state, condition,

---

the third great truth? It is the doing away with that desire which always shows itself, searches after this or that object, is always attended with feelings of pleasure, or some other sensations. It is the perfect and entire stifling of that craving which always covets, and is never satiated. The estranging oneself from that desire and that craving, the complete destruction of both, constitutes the third great truth. What is the way leading to the destruction of that desire, which is the fourth great truth? The way which one has to follow, in order to obtain that most desirable result, is that which the wise man invariably follows, when he is with an intention, will, diligence, action, life, language, thought, and meditation, always pure and correct.

The four truths are exceedingly praised by Buddhists. They constitute what is emphatically called the law of the wheel, incessantly revolving upon itself, and always présenting successively those four points to the attentive consideration and affectionate piety of the faithful. They are the offensive weapons wherewith passions are attacked and destroyed: they are the sword that cuts asunder the link that retains a being in the circle of existences. The revelation, or manifestation of those truths, is the great work that a Buddha has to perform. When it is made, all beings in their respective seats rejoice in an extraordinary manner. Inanimate nature even partakes in the universal joy. The earth shakes with a great violence, and the greatest prodigies proclaim aloud the fortunate manifestation of a law, which opens to all beings the way leading to deliverance. The preaching of that doctrine took place for the first time in the forest of Migadawon, not far from Baranathee, in the presence and for the benefit of the five Rahans, who had attended on Buddha, during the six years of mortification which he spent to prepare and qualify himself for the Buddhaship.

merits, demerits, and all that appertained to their physical and moral constitutive parts. This labour occupied his mind up to midnight.

Urged by the merciful and compassionate dispositions of his soul, Phralaong often revolved within himself the following: "All is misery and affliction in this world; all beings are miserably detained in the vortex of existences; they float over the whirlpool of desire and concupiscence; they are carried to and fro by the fallacious cravings of a never-obtained satisfaction. They must be taught to put an end to concupiscence by freeing themselves from its influence. Their minds must be imbued with the knowledge of the four great truths. The four ways that I have discovered shall inevitably lead men and Nats to that most desirable end. These ways ought to be pointed out to them, that, by following them, men and Nats may obtain the deliverance."

Whilst these thoughts thronged through his mind, a little before break of day, in the 103d year of the Eatzana era, on the day of the full moon of Katson, the perfect science broke at once over him: he became the Buddha.

When this great wonder took place, ten thousand worlds were shaken twelve times with such a violence as to make hairs stand on one end. These words, "most excellent being," were heard throughout the same series of worlds. Magnificent ornaments decorated all places. Flagstaffs appeared in every direction, adorned with splendid streamers. Of such dimensions were they that the extremities of those in the east reached the opposite side of the west; and those in the north, the southern boundary. Some flags, hanging from the seats of Brahmas, reached the surface of the earth. All the trees of ten thousand worlds shot out branches, loaded with fruits and flowers. The five sorts of lilies bloomed spontaneously. From the clefts of rocks beautiful flowers sprang out. The whole universe appeared like an immense garden, covered with flowers; a vivid light illuminated those places, the darkness of which could not be dispersed by the united rays of seven suns. The water, which fills the immensity of the deep, at a depth of eighty-four thousand youdzanas, became fresh and offered a most agreeable drink. Rivers suspended their course; the blind recovered their sight, the deaf could hear, and the lame were able to walk freely. The captives were freed from their chains and restored to their liberty. Innumerable other wonders took place at the moment Phralaong received the supreme intelligence. He said then to himself, "Previous to my obtaining the supreme knowledge, I have, during countless generations, moved in the circle of ever-renewed existences and borne-up misery. Now I see this distinctly. Again, I perceive how I can emancipate myself from the trammels of existence, and extricate myself from all miseries and wretchedness attending generation; my will is fixed on the most amiable state of Neibban. I have now arrived to that state of perfection that excludes all passions."

It was at the full moon of the month Katson, when these memorable occurrences took place, and it was daylight when Phralaong at last obtained the fulness of the Buddhaship. After this glorious and triumphant achievement, Phralaong, whom from this moment we must call Phra or Buddha, continued to remain on the throne, in a cross-legged position, with a mind absorbed in contemplation during seven days. Mental exertion and labour were at an end. Truth in its effulgent beauty encompassed his mind and shed over it the purest rays. Placed in that luminous centre, Phra saw all beings entangled in the web of passions, tossed over the raging billows of the sea of renewed existences, whirling in the vortex of endless miseries, tormented incessantly and wounded to the quick by the sting of concupiscence, sunk into the dark abyss of ignorance, the wretched victims of an illusory, unsubstantial, and unreal world. He said then to himself: "In all the worlds there is no one but me who knows how to break through the web of passions, to still the waves that waft beings from one state into another, to save them from the whirlpool of miseries, to put an end to concupiscence and break its sting, to dispel the mist of ignorance by the light of truth, to teach all intelligent beings the unreality and non-existence of this world, and thereby lead them to the true state of Neibban." Having thus given vent to the feelings of compassion that pressed on his benevolent heart, Phra, glancing over future events, delighted in contemplating the great number of beings who would avail themselves of his preachings, and labour to free themselves from the slavery of passions. He counted the multitudes who would enter the ways that lead to the deliverance, and would obtain the rewards to be enjoyed by those who will follow one of those ways. The Baranathee country would be favoured first of all with the preaching of the law of the wheel. He reviewed the countries where his religion would be firmly established. He saw that Maheinda, the son of king Asoka, would carry his law to Ceylon, two hundred and thirty-six years after his Neibban.

When these and other subjects were fully exhausted, the most excellent Phra came down from his throne and went to a distance of ten fathoms from the Bodi tree, in a north-east direction. There he stood, his eyes fixedly riveted on the throne, without a single wink, during seven consecutive days, given up to the most intense and undisturbed meditation. The Nats, observing this extraordinary posture, imagined that he regretted the throne he had just vacated, and that he wanted to repossess himself of it. They concluded that, such being the case, Prince Theiddat had not as yet obtained the Buddhaship. When the period of seven days was over, Buddha, who knew the innermost thoughts of the Nats, resolved to put an end to their incredulous thinking respecting his person. For that purpose, he had recourse to the display of miraculous powers.[10] He raised himself high up in the air, and, to

[10] Buddhists allow to their Buddha the power of working wonders and miracles. How is this power conferred upon him? This is a difficulty

their astonished regards, he wrought at once more than a thousand wonders, which had the immediate effect of silencing all their doubts, and convincing them that he was indeed the Buddha.

Having come down to the place which he had started from, for the display of prodigies, Buddha went to the north of the tree Bodi at a distance of only two fathoms from it. He spent this time in walking to and fro from east to west, during seven days, over a road, prepared for that purpose by the Nats. He was engaged all the while in the work of the sublimest contemplation.

He then shaped his course in a north-west direction, at a distance of thirteen fathoms from the sacred tree. There stood a beautiful house, shining like gold, resplendent with precious stones. It was a temporary residence, purposely prepared for him by the Nats. Thither he repaired, and sat down in a cross-legged position during seven days. He devoted all his time to meditating on the Abidamma, or the most excellent science. This science is divided into seven books. Phra had already gone over the six first and fully mastered their contents, but the six glories had not as yet shot forth from his person.

It was only after having mastered the contents of the last division, named Pathan, divided into twenty-four parts, that the six glories appeared. Like the great fishes that delight to sport only in the great ocean, the mind of Buddha expanded itself with undescribable eagerness, and delighted to run unrestrained through the unbounded

---

they cannot explain satisfactorily. The science of Buddha makes him acquainted with all the laws regulating nature, that is to say, the *ensemble* of the animate and inanimate beings constituting a world; but one is at a loss to find the origin of that power which enables him, as often as he likes, to suspend the course of those laws. Be that as it may, certain it is that Buddha resorted always, during the course of his preachings, to miracles, in order to convince those who seemed to listen with rather an incredulous ear to his doctrines. Miracles were used successfully, as powerful and irresistible weapons, against certain heretics, the Brahmins, in particular, who taught doctrines opposed to his own. They often accompanied his preachings, for increasing faith in the heart of his hearers.

field opened before him by the contents of that volume. Brown rays issued from his hairs, beard, and eyelids. Gold-like rays shot forth from his eyes and skin; from his flesh and blood dashed out purple beams, and from his teeth and bones escaped rays, white like the leaves of the lily; from his hands and feet emanated rays of a deep-red colour, which, falling on the surrounding objects, made them appear like so many rubies of the purest water. His forehead sent forth undulating rays, resembling those reflected by cut crystal. The objects which received those rays appeared as mirrors, reflecting the rays of the sun. Those six rays of various hues caused the earth to resemble a globe of the finest gold. Those beams at first penetrated through our globe, which is eighty-two thousand youdzanas thick, and thence illuminated the mass of water which supports our planet. It resembled a sea of gold. That body of water, though four hundred and eighty thousand youdzanas thick, could not stop the elastic projection of those rays, which went forth through a stratum of air nine hundred and sixty thousand youdzanas thick, and were lost in the vacuum. Some beams, following a vertical direction, rushed through the six seats of Nats, the sixteen of Brahmas, and the four superior ones, and thence were lost in vacuum. Other rays following a horizontal direction, penetrated through an infinite series of worlds. The sun, the moon, the stars appeared like opaque bodies, deprived of light. The famous garden of Nats, their splendid palace, the ornaments hanging from the tree Padetha were all cast into the shade and appeared obscure, as if wrapped up in complete darkness. The body of the chief Brahma, which sends forth light through one million of systems, emitted then but the feeble and uncertain light of the glowworm at sunrise. This marvellous light, emanating from the person of Buddha, was not the result of vowing or praying: but all the constituent parts of his body became purified to such an extent by the sublime meditation of the most excellent law that they shone with a matchless brightness.

Having thus spent seven days in that place, close to the Bodi tree, he repaired to the foot of another gniaong tree, called atzapala, or the shepherds' tree, so called because, under its cooling shade, shepherds and their flocks of goats rested during the heat of the day. It was situated at the east of the Bodi, at a distance of thirty fathoms. There he sat in a cross-legged position, during seven days, enjoying the sweetness of self-recollection. It was near to that place that the vile Manh, who, since his great attack on Buddha, had never lost sight of him, but had always secretly followed him with a wicked spirit, was compelled to confess that he had not been able to discover in that Rahan anything blamable, and expressed the fear of seeing him at once pass over the boundaries of his empire. The tempter stooped in the middle of the highway, and across it drew successively sixteen lines, as he went on reflecting on sixteen different subjects. When he had thought over each of the ten great virtues, he drew, first, ten lines, saying: "The great Rahan has indeed practised to a high degree those ten virtues. I cannot presume to compare myself to him." In drawing the eleventh, he confessed that he had not, like that Rahan, the science that enabled to know the inclinations and dispositions of all beings. In drawing the twelfth, he said that he had not as yet acquired the knowledge of all that concerns the nature of the various beings. Drawing the four remaining lines, he confessed successively that he did not feel, like that Rahan, a tender compassion for the beings yet entangled in the miseries of existence, nor could he perform miracles, nor perceive everything, nor attain to the perfect and supreme knowledge of the law. On all these subjects he avowed his decided inferiority to the great Rahan.

Whilst Manh was thus engaged with a sad heart in meditating over those rather humiliating points, he was at last found out by his three daughters, Tahna,[11] Aratee, and Raga, who had for sometime been looking after him. When they saw their father with a downcast countenance, they came to him, and inquired about the motive of his deep affliction. "Beloved daughters," replied Manh, "I see this Rahan escaping from my dominion, and notwithstanding my searching examination, I have not been able to detect in him anything reprehensible. This is the only cause of my inexpressible affliction." "Dear father," replied they, "banish all sorrows from your mind, and be of a good heart; we will very soon find out the weak side of the great Rahan, and triumphantly bring him back within the hitherto unpassed limits of your empire." "Beware of the man you will have to deal with," replied Manh. "I believe that no effort, however great, directed against him, will ever be rewarded with success. He is of a firm mind and unshaken purpose. I fear you shall never succeed in bringing him back within my dominions." "Dear father," said they, "we women know how to manage such affairs; we will catch him like a bird in the net of concupiscence; let fear and anxiety be for ever dispelled from your heart." Having given this assurance, forthwith they went to Buddha, and said to him, "Illustrious Rahan, we approach you respectfully and express the wish of staying with you, that we may minister to all your wants." Without in the least heeding their words, or even casting a glance at them, the most excellent Buddha remained un-

---

11 The great tempter had been foiled in all his attempts to conquer Buddha. In the sadness of his heart he was compelled to acknowledge the superiority of his opponent and confess his defeat. His three daughters came to console him, promising that they would, by their united efforts, overcome the firmness of the great Rahan, by awakening in his heart the fire of concupiscence. The names of those three daughters of Manh denote concupiscence. These new enemies of Buddha, therefore, are mere personifications of the passion of lust. Pride, personified in Manh, had proved powerless against the virtue of Buddha; he is now assailed from a different quarter; the attack is to be directed against the weakest side of human nature. But it is as successless as the former one: it affords to Buddha another occasion for a fresh triumph.

moved, enjoying the happiness of meditation. Knowing that the same appearance, face, and bodily accomplishments might not be equally pleasing, they assumed, one the appearance of a heart-winning young girl, another that of a blooming virgin, and the third that of a fine middle-aged beauty. Having thus made their arrangements, they approached Buddha, and several times expressed to him the desire of staying with him and ministering to his wants. Unmoved by all their allurements, Buddha said to them, "For what purpose do you come to me? You might have some chance of success with those that have not as yet extinguished the fire of passion, and rooted it from their heart; but I, like all the Buddhas, my predecessors, have destroyed in me concupiscence, passion, and ignorance. No effort, on your part, will ever be able to bring me back into the world of passions. I am free from all passions, and have obtained supreme wisdom. By what possible means could you ever succeed in bringing me back into the whirlpool of passions?" The three daughters of Manh, covered with confusion, yet overawed with admiration and astonishment, said to each other, "Our father forsooth had given us a good and wise warning. This great Rahan deserves the praises of men and Nats. Everything in him is perfect: to him it belongs to instruct men in all things they want to know." Saying this, they, with a downcast countenance, returned to their father.

It was in that very same place, at the foot of the adzapala gniaong, that a heretic Pounha, named Mingalika, proud of his caste, came with hasty steps, speaking loudly, and with little respect approached the spot where Buddha was sitting.[12] Having entered into conversation with him,

---

[12] In Burmah the originator of the great Buddhistic system is called Gaudama, and this appellation, according to many, appears to be his family name. When he is called Rahan Gaudama, it means the ascetic belonging to the family of Gaudama. In Nepaul, the same personage is known under the name of Thakiamuni, that is to say, the ascetic of the Thakia family. Those who refused to believe in Buddha and his

the Pounha heard from his mouth instructions worthy of being ever remembered. He said to Buddha, "Lord Gaudama, I have two questions to put to you. Whence comes the name Pounha? What are the duties to be performed in order to become a real Pounha?" Buddha penetrating with the keen eye of wisdom into the innermost soul of

---

doctrines, those who held tenets disagreeing with his own, and professed what, in the opinion of their adversaries, was termed a heretical creed, invariably called Buddha by his family name, placing him on the same level with so many of his contemporaries who led the same mode of life. The Siamese give the appellation of Sammana Khodom to their Buddha, that is to say, Thramana Gaudama, or Gautama. The Sanscrit word Thramana means an ascetic who has conquered his passions and lives on alms. Gaudama belonged to the Kchatria caste. Kings and all royal families in those days came out of the same caste. Hence his father Thoodaudana was king of the country of Kapilawot, anciently a small state, north of Goruckpore.

The young Pounha, not unlike the young man mentioned in the gospel, had, by the preachings of Gaudama, become acquainted with all the laws and practices relating to the general duties and obligations incumbent on men in general. He might have perhaps added that he had observed all those precepts from his youth, or, at least, that he was sure now, with the additional light he had received from his eminent teacher, to observe faithfully all the injunctions mentioned in the course of the lecture: but he was not satisfied with an ordinary proficiency in virtue and observances; he aimed at superior attainments; he wished to obtain the greatest perfection, that is to say, that of Brahmas. In what does such a perfection consist? The book of metaphysics informs us that the five states of Dzan, or contemplations, are enjoyed by the beings located in the sixteen seats of Brahmas, in the following order. The first state, or that of consideration, is shared by all the beings inhabiting the three first seats of Brahmas. Their occupation is to consider the various subjects the mind has to dwell on. The second Dzan, or reflection, is reserved for the beings occupying the next three seats. Those beings have no more to look out for subjects of meditation. Their sole occupation is to dive into truth and fathom its depth and various bearings. The third state of Dzan procures the pleasure which is derived from the contemplation of truth, and belongs to the beings of the three seats, superior to those just alluded to; in the fourth Dzan is enjoyed a placid happiness, which is the result of the possession of truth; it is reserved for the beings of the three next seats. The fifth Dzan, or perfect stability, is the happy lot of the beings living in the five last seats. Those fortunate inmates are so entirely rooted in truth, and so perfectly exempt from all that causes mutability, that they arrive at a state of complete fixity, the whole of their soul being riveted on truth.

Apology is certainly due to the reader, who is but slightly initiated in such abstruse subjects, for laying before him particulars with which he is so unfamiliar; but this trouble must be borne up by him who desires to obtain access into the gloomy sanctuary of Buddhism.

his interlocutor, answered, "The real and genuine Pounha is he who has renounced all passions, put an end to concupiscence, and has entered the ways leading to perfection. But there are others, who are proud of their origin, who walk hastily, speak with a loud voice, and who have not done what is needful to destroy the influence of passions. These are called Pounhas because of their caste and birth. But the true sage avoids everything that is rash, impetuous or noisy: he has conquered all his passions, and put an end to the principle of demerits. His heart loves the repetition of formulas of prayers, and delights in the exercise of meditation. He has reached the last way to perfection. In him there is no longer wavering, or doubt, or pride. This man really deserves the name of Pounha, or pure: he is indeed the true Pounha according to the law." The instruction being finished, the Pounha rose respectfully from his place, wheeled to the right and departed.

Buddha continued the sublime work of contemplating pure truth through the means of intense reflection. Having remained seven days in that position, Buddha arose in an ecstasy and went to the south-eastern side of the Bodi tree, to a distance of an oothaba (1 oothaba = to 20 tas, 1 ta = to 7 cubits), on the sixth day after the full moon of Nayon. On that spot there was a tank called Hidza-lee-dana. On the bank of that tank he sat, under the shade of the Kiin tree, in a cross-legged position during seven days, enjoying the delight of meditation. During those seven days rain fell in abundance, and it was very cold. A Naga, chief of that tank, would have made a building to protect Buddha against the inclemency of the weather, but he preferred, in order to gain greater merits, to coil himself up sevenfold round his person, and to place his head above him, with his large hood extended. When the seven days were over and the rain had ceased, the Naga quitted his position; then assuming the appearance of a young man, he prostrated himself before Buddha and worshipped him. Buddha said: "He who aims at obtaining the state of Neibban ought to possess the knowledge of the four roads leading thereto, as well as that of the four great truths and of all laws. He ought to bear no anger towards other men, nor harm them in any way soever. Happy he who receives such instructions."

Buddha moved from that place, and went to the south of the Bodi tree, to a distance of forty fathoms. At the foot of the linloon tree he sat in a cross-legged position, having his mind deeply engaged in the exercise of the sublimest contemplation. In that position he spent seven entire days, which completed the forty-nine days which were to be devoted to reflection and meditation around the Bodi tree. When this period of days was over, at day-break, on the fifth day after the full moon of Watso, he felt the want of food. This was quickly perceived by a Thagia, who hastened from his seat to the spot where Buddha was staying, and offered him some Thit khia fruits, others say Kia-dzoo fruits, to prepare his system to receive more substantial food. After he had eaten them, the same celestial attendant brought him some water to rinse his mouth, and to wash his face and hands. Buddha continued to remain in the same position, under the cooling and protecting shade of the linloon tree.

To consecrate, as it were, and perpetuate the remembrance of the seven spots occupied by Buddha during the forty-nine days that he spent round the tree Bodi, a Dzedy was erected on each of those seven places. King Pathanadi Kosala surrounded them with a double wall, and subsequently King Dammathoka added two others. There were only three openings, or gates, to penetrate into the enclosed ground, one on the north, another on the east, and the third on the south. The river Neritzara rolls its deep blue waters in a south-eastern direction from the Bodi tree, to a distance of eight oothabas from it. On the eastern bank of that stream another Dzedy has been erected on the spot where, previous to his becoming a Buddha, he had eaten the forty-nine mouthfuls of the delicious Nogana offered to him by the pious Thoodzata.

Whilst Buddha was sitting in a cross-legged position under the linloon tree, two brothers named Tapoosa and Palekat, merchants by profession, arrived with five hundred carts in the Oorouwela forest, at the very place where Buddha was staying. They had sailed from their native town, called [13] Oukkalaba, which lies in a south-eastern direction from the Mitzima country, bound for the port of

---

[13] The episode of these two merchants is well known to the inhabitants of the Irrawaddy valley. In three different manuscripts which the writer has had in his hands, he has found it related with almost the same particulars. Oukkalaba, the place the two young men started from, was situated probably on the spot now occupied by the village of Twaintay, or not far from it. How far that place was from the sea in those remote times it is not possible to ascertain with precision. Certain it is, that it was a port from which vessels sailed across the Bay of Bengal. The port of Eedzeitha has not as yet been identified with any known locality. It was situated in all probability between the mouth of the Krichna and that of the Hoogly. One of the manuscripts mentions that when Gaudama handed over to the two merchants eight hairs of his head, he bade them, on their arrival in their country, deposit the hairs on a small hill called Seingouttara, where the relics of the three former Buddhas of our period had been enshrined. They were twenty-seven days in reaching Maudin or Cape Negrais, rather a long voyage. Having come to their own place, they related to the governor all the particulars of their interesting journey. The latter, without loss of time, assembled the people and set out in search of the Seingouttara mount. All the eminences were cleared of their brushwood, but the mount could not be discovered. Not knowing what to do, they consulted the Nats on that affair. At last, through their assistance, the mount was found out. But when they inquired about the place of the relics of the three former Buddhas, the Nats of Yesapan, Inandra, and Gauveinda confessed that they knew nothing on the subject, but referred the inquirers to other Nats older than they, viz.: those of Deckina, Yauhani, Maubee, Ameisa, and Tsoolay, who at once pointed out the spot which they were so eagerly searching after. This spot is no other than the one over which stands and towers the lofty and massive Shoay Dagon. They erected a Dzedy, in which they enshrined the relics they had brought with them, the eight hairs of Buddha. This story is doubtless the foundation on which rests the popular belief that those very hairs are to this day in the interior of that monument, and the true source from which has originated the profound veneration which, in our own days, Buddhists, from all parts of Burmah, Siam, and the Shan states, pay by their pilgrimages and offerings to the Dagon Pagoda.

Adzeitta. After landing, they hired five hundred carts to carry their goods to a place called Soowama. They were on their way to their destination when they arrived in the Oorouwela forest. Great was their surprise when they saw on a sudden all their carts unable to move, and arrested by some invisible power.

A Nat who had been formerly their relative stopped by his power the wheels of the carriages. Surprised at such a wonder, the merchants prayed to the Nat who was guardian of that place. The Nat, assuming a visible shape, appeared before them and said to them: "The illustrious Buddha who by the knowledge of the four great truths has arrived to the nature of Phra, is now sitting at the foot of the linloon tree. Go now to that place, and offer him some sweet bread and honey; you shall derive therefrom great merits for many days and nights to come." The two brothers, joyfully complying with the Nat's request, prepared the sweet bread and honey, and hastened in the direction that had been indicated to them. Having placed themselves in a suitable position and prostrated themselves before Buddha, they said: "Most glorious Phra, please to accept these offerings; great merits doubtless will be our reward for many days to come." Buddha had no patta to put those offerings in, for the one he had received from the Brahma Gatigara had disappeared when Thoodzata made him her great offerings. Whilst he was thinking on what he had to do, four Nats came and presented him each with one patta, made of nila or sapphire stone. Phra accepted the four pattas, not from motives of covetousness, but to let each Nat have an equal share in such meritorious work. He put the four pattas one in the other, and by the power of his will they on a sudden became but one patta, so that each Nat lost nothing of the merit of his offerings. Buddha received the offerings of the two merchants in that patta, and satisfied his appetite. The two brothers said to Buddha: "We have on this day approached you, worshipped you, and respectfully listened to your instructions; please to consider us as your devoted followers for the remainder of our lives."[14] They obtained the position of Upathaka. They continued addressing Buddha and said: "What shall we henceforth worship?" Buddha, rubbing his hand over his head, gave them a few of the hairs that had adhered to his fingers, bidding them to keep carefully those relics. The two brothers, overjoyed at such a valuable present, most respectfully received it, prostrated themselves before Buddha, and departed.

---

[14] Upasaka is a Pali word which is designed to mean those persons who, having heard the instructions of Buddha, and professed a faith or belief in him and his doctrines, did not enter the profession of Rahans. Hence they are quite distinct from the Bikus or mendicants, who formed the first class of the hearers of Buddha, and renounced the world in imitation of their great master. The Upasakas were therefore people adhering to the doctrines of Buddha, but as yet remaining engaged in the ordinary pursuits of life. The two brothers became disciples of Buddha, but not of the first class, since they did not embrace the more perfect mode of life of the ascetics.

This is the first instance in this legend of an allusion being made to relics, that is to say, to objects supposed to be surrounded with a certain amount of sacredness, and esteemed on that account to be worthy of receiving from devotees respect and veneration. The two young converts, not as yet confirmed in the new faith they had embraced, thought they wanted some exterior object to which they might hereafter direct their homage and offer their respects. They were as yet far from being acquainted with the sublime science of their eminent teacher, who, disregarding matter and all its modifications, could not but feel quite indifferent respecting the pretended value of relics of even the most sacred character. How is it that the stern moralist, the contemner of this illusory world, could think of giving a few hairs of his head to two new young converts, that they might use them as objects of worship? Buddha doubtless knew exactly and appreciated admirably the wants and necessities of human nature as it is, and will very likely ever be to the end of ages. Men are led, actuated, impressioned, and influenced by the senses; in fact, it is through their senses that the knowledge of things is conveyed to their minds. He gave to his imperfectly instructed disciples a thing that would serve to vivify and reanimate in their memory the remembrance of Buddha, and of the instructions they had heard from him. Those grossly-minded hearers asked for an object they might carry about with them and worship. Buddha, out of deference for their weak intellect, gave them a few hairs of his head, the sight of which was designed to maintain in their souls a tender affection for the person of him these things had belonged to. This subject will receive hereafter the further treatment it deserves when we come to examine the nature of the worship paid by Buddhists to the images of Gaudama, and to the relics and Dzedis.

CHAPTER VI.

Buddha hesitates to undertake the task of preaching the law—The great Brahma entreats him to preach the law to all beings—His assent to the entreaties—Journey towards Migadawon—He meets Ouppaka—His first preachings—Conversion of a young nobleman named Ratha, followed by that of his father and other relatives—Conversion of several other noblemen—Instructions to the Rahans—Conversion of the three Kathabas.

HAVING come to the end of his great meditations,[1] Buddha left this spot and returned to the place called Adzapala, where he revolved the following subject in his mind:—"The knowledge," said he, "of the law and of the four great truths, which I alone possess, is very hard to be had.

[1] I have, except on one occasion, always made use of the terms meditation and contemplation to express the inward working of Buddha's mind during the forty-nine days he spent at the foot of the banyan tree. But the Burmese translator most commonly employs a much stronger expression, conveying the idea of trance and ecstasy. Hence after having remained seven days on the same spot, deeply engaged in considering some parts of the law he was soon to preach, it is said of him that he comes out from a state of perfect ecstasy. This expression implies a state of complete mental abstraction, when the soul, disentangled from the trammels of sense, raises itself above this material world, contemplates pure truth and delights in it. All her faculties are taken up with the beauty and perfection of truth; she clings to it with all her might, regardless of all the illusions this world is filled with. This situation of the soul is much esteemed by all fervent Buddhists. It is the lot of but a few privileged Rahans, who have made great progress in perfection, and obtained an almost entire mastery over their passions and senses. This great gift is, as one may well imagine, ardently coveted by many, who, though not possessing it, lay claim to it on false pretences. This being a sin devotees who relish a contemplative life are very liable to, which the framer of the regulations of the Buddhist monks has pronounced as *ipso facto* excluding from the society all those who would falsely claim the possession of uncommon spiritual attainments which they have not. In the book of ordination used for the admission of candidates to the order of Rahans or talapoins, this sin is the last of the four offences which deprive a member of the order of his dignity, and cause his expulsion from the society.

The law is deep; it is difficult to know and understand it; it is very sublime, and can be comprehended only by the means of earnest meditation. It is sweet, filling the soul with joy, and accessible only to the wise. Now all beings are sunk very low by the influence of the five great passions; they cannot free themselves from their baneful operation, which is the source of all mutability. But the law of mutability is the opposite of the law of Neibban or rest. This law is hard to be understood. If I ever preach that law, beings will not be able to understand me, and from my preaching there will result but a useless fatigue and unprofitable weariness. Buddha thus remained almost disinclined to undertake the great duty of preaching the law. The great Brahma, observing what was taking place in Buddha's soul, cried out: "Alas! all mankind are doomed to be lost. He who deserves to be worshipped by all beings now feels no disposition to announce the law to them." He instantly left his seat, and having repaired to the presence of Phra, his cloak over his shoulders with one extremity hanging backward, he bent his knee, lifted up his joined hands to the forehead before the sage, and said to him: "Most illustrious Buddha, who art adorned with the six glories, do condescend to preach the most excellent law; the number of those buried under the weight and filth of passions is comparatively small; if they do not listen to the law there will be no great loss. But there is an immense number of beings who will understand the law. In this world there are beings who are moderately given up to the gratification of sensual appetites; and there are also a great many who are following heretical opinions to whom the knowledge of truth is necessary, and who will easily come to it. Lay now open the way that leads to the perfection of Ariahs; those perfections are the gates to Neibban." Thus he entreated Buddha. This Brahma had been in the time of Buddha Kathaba a Rahan, under the name of Thabaka, and was transferred to the first seat of Brahma for the duration of a world.

On hearing the supplications of that Brahma, Buddha began to feel a tender compassion for all beings. With the keen eyes of a Buddha he glanced over the whole world. He discovered distinctly those beings who were as yet completely sunk in the filth of passions, those who were but partly under the control of passions, and those whose dispositions seemed to be more promising. He then made to the chief of Brahmas the solemn promise that he would preach his law to all beings. Satisfied with the answer he had received, the chief rose up, withdrew respectfully at a proper distance, and turning on the right, left the presence of Buddha and returned to his own seat.

Another thought preoccupied the mind of Buddha. "To whom," said he, "shall I announce the law?" Having pondered a while over this subject, he added: "The Rathee Alara of the Kalama race is gifted with wisdom and an uncommonly penetrating mind; passions have scarcely any influence over him. I will first preach to him the most excellent law." A Nat then said to Phra that Alara had died seven days ago. Buddha, to whom the past is known, had already seen that Alara was dead. He said: "Great indeed is the loss Alara has met with; he would have doubtless been able to understand right well the law I intended to preach to him. To whom shall I go now?" Having paused a while, he added: "The Rathee Oodaka, son of Prince Rama, has a quick perception; he will easily understand my doctrine; to him I will announce the law." But the same Nat told him that Oodaka had died the night before last, at midnight. "O! great is the loss that has come upon Oodaka; he would have easily acquired the knowledge of the perfect law." Buddha considered a third time, and said to himself: "To whom shall I go to preach the law?" After a moment's delay he added: "Many are the services I received in the wilderness from the five Rahans who lived with me.[2] I will repay

[2] The five Rahans alluded to are the very same individuals who met Phralong in the solitude at the time he was undergoing a great fast and

their good offices to me, by preaching to them the law, but where are they now? His penetrating regards soon discovered them in the solitude of Migadawon. Having

---

performing all sorts of works of self-denial and corporal austerities in the most rigorous manner. During all the time he spent in those hard exercises of strict mortification, to conquer his passions and secure the complete triumph of the mind over the senses, he was assisted in all his wants by those five Rahans, who rendered to him the usual services disciples are wont to perform to their teacher. When they saw Phralaong at the end of his mighty efforts in that great struggle resuming the habits of a mendicant, they left him at once, unwilling to believe that he would ever become a Buddha. Our Phra, not unmindful of the good services he had received from them, resolved to impart first to them the blessings of his preachings. Alara and Oodaka, his two first teachers in the science of Dzan, were destined to be the first who would have heard the good news had they not been dead. Gratitude seems to have been the first and main motive that induced him to select as the first objects of his mission the very same persons who had been instrumental in furthering his efforts to acquire the Buddhaship.

The unpleasant epithet of heretic is given to those five Rahans, as well as to another named Upaka, as designed to mean that they held tenets at variance with those of Buddha, and refused to acknowledge him as possessed of the perfect intelligence. Buddhists, in their writings, invariably call their opponents by the name of holders of false doctrines. The Brahmins or Pounhas who refused to seek refuge in Buddha, his law, and the assembly of his disciples, are spoken of as professors of heterodoxical doctrines.

From the narrative of this legend we may conclude, with a probability amounting almost to certitude, that Buddha in his preachings addressed himself first to the Brahmins, as being by their caste the most influential portion of the Hindu community. Those that are called by the name of Pounhas are the Brahmins living in the world and following the ordinary pursuits of life. Those that are mentioned by the names of Rahans and Rathees are probably Brahmins, or at least belong to some other distinguished caste like that of the Kchatrias, but are members of some religious order or ascetics. They were in those days men whom, in imitation of the ancient Greeks, we may call philosophers, and who belonged to one or other of the branches into which the great Indian school was divided. We may conjecture that at that time India exhibited a scene much resembling that which Greece subsequently offered to the eyes of the observer in the days of Socrates and Plato, when schools of philosophy were to be met with in every direction. The Hindu philosophers, favoured by climate and their ardent imagination, carried much farther than the Greek wise men, both in theory and practice, the discussion of dogmas and the fervour of religious practices. If credit is to be given to our Legend in a historical point of view, we may safely conclude that such was the state of India when Buddha began his preachings. His first hearers were Rahans, Rathees, and Pounhas, that is to say, the most learned and wisest men in those days. The latter in particular seemed at first disinclined to offer opposition to Buddha; they listened to him as to a distinguished philosopher; his arguments were examined, discussed, and

enjoyed himself in the place Adzapala, Buddha went on towards the country of Baranathee. All the former Buddhas travelled through the air, but our Buddha, who had merciful designs over Upaka, went on foot. On his way to the village of Gaya, at a distance of three gawots from the Bodi tree, Buddha went to rest, at midday, for a while under the cooling shade of a tree. There he was seen by the heretic Rahan Upaka, who, approaching near him, said, "O Rahan, all your exterior bespeaks the most amiable qualities; your countenance is at once modest and beautiful. Under what teacher have you become a Rahan? To what law or doctrine have you given preference in your arduous studies?" Buddha answered, "Upaka, I have triumphed over all the laws of mutability; I am acquainted with all the laws that rule this universe, and the beings existing therein; from concupiscence and other passions I am wholly disengaged. I have come to preach the most excellent law to all beings, and teach them the four great truths I alone am acquainted with. I will beat

---

answered by them in the best way they could. In that polemical warfare, arguments were at first the only offensive and defensive weapons used and handled by the combatants on both sides. Buddha's two favourite doctrines of Atheism and Neibban, which established the two broad lines of separation between the two systems, begat much discussion and created some animosity between him and his adversaries. But what widened the gap between the two parties, and placed them in a hostile array against each other, was the broad principle of equality amongst men, latent in the bosom of Buddha's doctrines, and levelled at the distinction of castes. Buddha preached to men of all conditions without exception; he opened before all the ways that lead to Neibban; made no distinction between man and man, except that which is drawn by virtue and vice, merits and demerits. He allowed every one to approach him and take rank among his disciples; faith in his doctrine entitled any man to be numbered amidst his followers; the entrance into the order of Rahans or perfect was open to all those who, by their meritorious actions and renouncing the world, qualified themselves for this dignity. This principle which put on a footing of equality men of all castes and nations, and recognised no real superiority but that which is conferred by virtue and merit, could not prove agreeable to the proud Brahmins. It provoked, by its gradual development, the animosity of the opponents of Buddha's doctrines. The battle of arguments, after having raged with various success, was afterwards converted into one of a bloody character, which ended in the total extermination or expulsion of the Buddhists from the Indian peninsula.

the great drum of the law. I have no teacher, and among Nats and men there is none equal to me. Because of my victory, I have been named Zeena. Now I am proceeding to the country of Baranathee, for the sake of preaching the law." Upaka replied, "You are certainly the illustrious Gaudama." He then shook his head, turned away from the road, and went to the village of Wingaha. The instructions, however, germinated as good seed in the soul of Upaka, and were the foundation of his subsequent conversion, which happened as follows :—After this interview with Gaudama, Upaka dwelt as a hermit in the village of Wingaha, where a shed was erected for his dwelling. A hunter brought him support. It happened that the hunter being engaged in a hunting excursion, his daughter went to the hermit's cell, to carry him his food. Upaka was smitten by the beauty of the damsel. He stretched himself on his belly and said to himself, "I will take no food, nor change this position, unless I obtain the object of my wishes." He stayed for several days in that position without uttering a word, or making a single movement, or taking any food. At last the hunter returned and went forthwith to the hermit's cell to inquire about the cause of his strange behaviour. He pulled him by the feet, calling him aloud by the name of hermit; after a while a sepulchral groan was heard, indicating that he was still alive. The good hunter affectionately entreated him to mention to him what he wanted; that he was ready to give him anything that he would ask. The hermit a second time made a prolonged groan, as a man endeavouring to gather strength. He then mentioned to the hunter the passion he had for his daughter, and swore that he would die on the spot if his demand were rejected. The father having given his consent, Upaka rose up, and was soon married to Tsawama, who after due time presented him with a son. It happened that Tsawama soon began to dislike her husband, and poured upon him on every occasion all sorts of abuse. Unable to bear any longer the unpleasant behaviour of his wife, Upaka said to himself, "I have here neither friend nor supporter: I will go to my friend Dzina; he will receive me with kindness." Hereupon he departed, inquiring everywhere about his friend Dzina. At last he arrived at the place where Buddha was staying with his disciples. Some of them, hearing Upaka inquiring with a loud voice about his friend Dzina, took him into the presence of Buddha, who, understanding at once the sad and painful state of the old man, kindly asked what he wanted. Upaka replied that he desired to become a Samanay under his direction. Buddha, to try his disposition, said to him, "You are too old, Upaka, to enter upon the course of the severe life of a Samanay, and conform to the enjoined practices." But the latter renewing his entreaties, he was admitted among the members of the assembly. He became an Anagam, died and migrated to one of the seats of Brahmas. After a short stay up there, he obtained the deliverance. His son was Thoobadda, who became afterwards an illustrious convert. Buddha continued his way towards Baranathee, and soon reached the solitude of Migadawon, a little distant from Baranathee, and went to the place where lived the five unbelieving Rahans. When they saw him coming at a distance, they said to each other, "The Rahan Gaudama is in search after disciples; he has just performed penitential deeds, and he is looking out for alms and clothes. Let us pay no respect to him in the way of going out to meet him, of receiving the tsiwaran from his hands, of presenting him water to wash his feet and preparing a place to sit on; let him sit wherever he pleases." Such was the plan they concerted among themselves. But when Buddha drew near, they could adhere no longer to their resolution. They rose up and went out to welcome his arrival. One took the tsiwaran from his hands, another the patta, a third one brought water for the washing of the feet, and a fourth one prepared a becoming place to rest. Buddha sat in the place that had been prepared for him. They called him by the name of Gaudama and other appellations, usually bestowed on ordinary Rahans. Buddha meekly replied to them, "Do not call me any longer by the name of Gaudama, or any other title bestowed on an ascetic. I have become a Rahanda; I alone am acquainted with the four fundamental truths. Now I am come to preach to you the true law. Listen, O Rahans, to my words; I will lead you to the true state of Neibban. My law will make you acquainted not only with the truths to be known, but at the same time point out to you the duties you have to perform, in order to obtain the state of Arahat. There are four ways leading to perfection. He who steadily follows them will enjoy the rewards and merits gained by his exertions. In that position he will see distinctly his own self; the light of Neibban will break forth upon him. But in order to obtain the great results I set forth before you, he must forsake his house and the world, and become a Rahan."

The unbelieving Rahans persisted in not acknowledging him as a Buddha, and reproached him with going about in search of disciples and in quest of alms. The same preaching was repeated by Buddha, and the same answer was returned by his incredulous hearers. At last Buddha, assuming a lofty and commanding tone, said to them, "I declare unto you that I am a Buddha, knowing the four great truths and showing the way to Neibban." The hitherto unbelieving ascetics humbled themselves, and declared their belief in him and in all that he had taught. From that moment they entered on the four ways of perfection. The day was that of the full moon of Watso. The preaching began at the moment when half the disc of the sun was visible on the western horizon, and half that of the moon was above the eastern horizon. When completed, the sun had just disappeared, and the moon's entire globe was visible on the horizon. The five first converts were named Kautagnya, Baddiha, Wappa, Mahanan, and Asadzi.

The Nats, guardians of the country of Baranathee[3] and Migadawon, hearing the sublime instructions delivered by Buddha on this occasion, cried aloud, "The law which the most excellent Buddha preaches is such as no man, Pounha or Brahma, can teach." Their united voices were heard in the lowest seat of Nats; the inhabitants of that seat, catching their words, repeated them, and they were heard by those of the next seat, and so on, until they reached the seats of Brahmas, and were re-echoed through 10,000 worlds. A mighty commotion was felt all over these worlds.

The five at first unbelieving, but now believing Rahans obtained the perfection of Thautapati. Buddha often repeated to those that approached him, "Come to me; I preach a doctrine which leads to the deliverance from all the miseries attending existence." On that day, being the full moon of Watso, eighteen koodes (18,000,000,000) of Nats and Brahmas who had heard his preachings obtained

---

[3] The mission of Buddha is not, as previously observed, confined to men living on earth, but it extends its beneficial action over all the beings inhabiting the six seats of Nats and sixteen of Brahmas. Those beings, the latter in particular, are much advanced in perfection, but they are not yet ripe for the sublime state of Neibban. Though freed, at least the Brahmas, from the influence of passions, they retain as yet some inclination for matter; they want the help of a Buddha to break at once the few slender ties that retain them in the state of existence.

The first preaching of Buddha was rewarded with the conversion of five Rahans, and of a countless number of Nats and Brahmas. Such a plentiful harvest he could scarcely anticipate to reap; and the beginning of his career, attended with such wonderful success, amply repaid him for the extraordinary exertions he made in order to qualify himself for the Buddhaship. The author of the Legend remarks, with an unfeigned pleasure, that owing to the conversion of the five Rahans, the worlds witnessed the beautiful sight of six Rahandas congregated on the same spot. The Rahanda has attained the summit of perfection; he has arrived at the last existence; his death will relieve him from the burden of existence, and open to him the way leading to perfect rest, to complete abstraction—in a word, to Neibban. The Rahandas rank first among the disciples and hearers of Buddha; they constitute the *élite* of his followers, and form the most distinguished portion of the assembly or congregation of the perfect. We have already stated that the members composing the assembly of the hearers were divided into distinct sections, and formed different degrees, according to the difference of their respective progress on the way of perfection.

the deliverance. The conversion of those five Rahans exhibited to the world the splendid and wonderful sight of six Rahandas assembled in the same place.

At that time, whilst Buddha was in the Migadawon grove, the memorable conversion of a young layman took place. There was in the country of Baranathee the son of a rich man, named Ratha. He was of very gentle and amiable disposition. His father had built for him three palaces for each season of the year. A crowd of young damsels, skilful in the art of playing on all sorts of musical instruments, attended him in each of those palaces. Ratha spent his time in the midst of pleasure and amusements. On a certain day, while surrounded with female dancers and singers, he fell into a deep sleep. The musicians, following his example, laid aside their instruments, and fell asleep too. The lamps, filled with oil, continued to pour a flood of light throughout the apartments. Awaking sooner than usual, Ratha saw the musicians all asleep round him in various and unseemly situations. Some slept with wide-opened mouths, some had dishevelled hair, some were snoring aloud, some had their instruments lying on themselves, and others by their side. The whole exhibited a vast scene of the greatest confusion and disorder. Sitting on his couch in a cross-legged position, the young man silently gazed with amazement and disgust over the unseemly spectacle displayed before him; then he said to himself, "The nature and condition of the body constitute indeed a truly heavy burden; that coarser part of our being affords a great deal of trouble and affliction." Whereupon he instantly arose from his couch, put on his gilt slippers, and came down to the door of his apartment. The Nats, who kept a vigilant watch, lest any one should oppose him in the execution of his holy purpose, kept open the door of the house, as well as the gate of the city. Ratha, free from all impediments, directed his steps towards the solitude of Migadawon. At that time Buddha who had left his sleeping place at a very early hour, was walking in front of the house. He saw at a distance a young man coming in the direction he was in. He instantly stopped his pacing, and going into his own apartment, sat as usual on his seat, awaiting the arrival of the young stranger, who soon made his appearance and stated modestly the object of his visit. Buddha said to him, "O Ratha! the law of Neibban is the only true one: alone it is never attended with misery and affliction. O Ratha! come nearer to me; remain in this place; to you I will make known the most perfect and valuable law." On hearing these kind and inviting expressions, Ratha felt his heart overflow with the purest joy. He instantly put off his slippers, drew nearer to Buddha, bowed down three times before him, withdrew then to a becoming distance, and remained in a respectful attitude. Buddha began to preach the law, unfolding successively the various merits obtained by alms-giving, by a strict performance of all duties and practices of the law, and, above all, by renouncing the pleasures of this world. During all the while the heart of the young visitor expanded in a wonderful manner: he felt the ties that hitherto had bound him as it were to the world gradually relaxing and giving way before the unresisting influence of Buddha's words. The good dispositions of the young hearer were soon remarked by Buddha, who went on explaining all that related to the miseries attending existence, the passions tyrannising over the soul, the means wherewith to become exempt from those passions, and the great ways leading to perfection. After having listened to that series of instructions, Ratha, like a white cloth that easily retains the impressions of various colours printed upon it, felt himself freed from all passions, and reached at once the state of Thautapati.

Ratha's mother, not meeting her son early, went up as usual to his apartment, and, to her great surprise, found him gone; moreover she observed unmistakable marks of his sudden and unexpected departure. She ran forthwith to her husband, and announced to him the sad tidings.

On hearing of such an unlooked-for event, the father sent messengers in the direction of the four points of the compass, with positive orders to search incessantly after his son, and leave no means of inquiry untried. As to himself he resolved to go to the solitude of Migadawon, in the hope of finding out some track of his son's escape. He had scarcely travelled a limited distance, when he observed on the ground the marks of his son's footsteps. He followed them up and soon came in sight of Buddha's resting-place. Ratha was at the time listening with deepest attention to all the words of his great teacher. By the power of Buddha he remained hidden from the eyes of his father, who came up, and, having paid his respects to Gaudama, eagerly asked him if he had not seen his son. Gaudama bade him sit down and rest after the fatigue of his journey. Meanwhile he assured him that he would soon see his son. Rejoiced at such an assurance, Ratha's father complied with the invitation he had received. Buddha announced his law to this distinguished hearer, and soon led him to the perfection of Thautapati. Filled with joy and gratitude, the new convert exclaimed, "O illustrious Phra, your doctrine is a most excellent one; when you preach it, you do like him who replaces on its basis an upset cup; like him, too, who brings to light precious things, which had hitherto remained in darkness; like him who points out the right way to those that have lost it; who kindles a brilliant light in the middle of darkness; who opens the mind's eyes that they might see the pure truth. Henceforth I adhere to you and to your holy law; please to reckon me as one of your disciples and supporters." This was the first layman that became a disciple of Gaudama, in the capacity of Upasaka.[4]

[4] It may be interesting to give an abridgment of an instruction or sermon delivered by Gaudama to a Nat. It will be as a fair specimen of other similar performances. The Nat made his appearance at nightfall, and respectfully entreated Buddha to deliver certain instructions which would enable men to come to the understanding of many points of the law on which they had hitherto fruitlessly meditated. Buddha was then in the

Whilst Buddha was busily engaged in imparting instruction to Ratha's father, the young man had entered into a deep and solemn meditation over some of the high-

---

monastery of Dzetawon, in the country of Thawattie. This sermon is supposed to have been repeated by Ananda, who had heard it from the mouth of Buddha himself. It is, according to the Burmese, the most excellent sermon; it contains thirty-eight points.

"Young Nat," said Buddha, "here are the most excellent things men and Nats ought to attend to, in order to capacitate themselves for the state of Neibban: to shun the company of the foolish; to be always with the wise; to proffer homage to those that are deserving of it; to remain in a place becoming one's condition; to have always with one's self the influence of former good works; steadily to maintain a perfect behaviour; to be delighted to hear and see much, in order to increase knowledge; to study all that is not sinful; to apply one's self to acquire the knowledge of Wini. Let every one's conversation be regulated by righteous principles; let every one minister to the wants of his father and mother; provide all the necessaries for his wife and children; perform no action under the evil influence of temptation; bestow alms; observe the precepts of the law; assist one's relatives and friends; perform no actions but such as are exempt from sin; be ever diligent in such avoiding, and abstain from intoxicating drink. Let no one be remiss in the practice of the law of merits. Let every one bear respect to all men; be ever humble; be easily satisfied and content; gratefully acknowledge favours; listen to the preaching of the law in its proper time; be patient; delight in good conversation; visit the religious from time to time; converse on religious subjects; cultivate the virtue of mortification; practise works of virtue; pay attention always to the four great truths; keep the eyes fixed on Neibban. Finally, let one in the middle of the eight afflictions of this world be, like the Rahanda, firm, without disquietude, fearless, with a perfect composure. O young Nat, whoever observes these perfect laws shall never be overcome by the enemies of the good: he shall enjoy the peace of Ariahs."

Within a narrow compass, Buddha has condensed an abridgment of almost all moral virtues. The first portion of these precepts contains injunctions to shun all that may prove an impediment to the practice of good works. The second part inculcates the necessity of regulating one's mind and intention for a regular discharge of the duties incumbent on each man in his separate station. Then follows a recommendation to bestow assistance on parents, relatives, and all men in general. Next to that, we find recommended the virtues of humility, resignation, gratitude, and patience. After this, the preacher insists on the necessity of studying the law, visiting religious, conversing on religious subjects. When this is done, the hearer is commanded to study with great attention the four great truths, and keep his mind's eye ever fixed on the happy state of Neibban, which, though as yet distant, ought never to be lost sight of. Thus prepared, the hearer must be bent upon acquiring the qualifications befitting the true sage. Like the one mentioned by the Latin poet, who would remain firm, fearless, and unmoved, even in the midst of the ruins of the crumbling universe, the Buddhist sage must ever remain calm, composed, and unshaken among all the

est maxims he had heard from his great teacher. He was calmly surveying, as it were, all the things of this world; the more he progressed in that great work, the more he felt there was in himself no affection whatever for anything. He had not yet become a Rahan, nor put on the Rahan's dress. Phra, who attentively watched all the movements of his pupil's mind, concluded from his present dispositions that there could be no fear of his ever returning into the world of passions. He suddenly caused by his mighty power the son to become visible to his father's eyes. The father, perceiving on a sudden his son sitting close by him, said, "Beloved son, your mother is now bathed in tears, and almost sinking under the weight of affliction caused by your sudden departure; come now to her, and by your presence restore her to life, and infuse into her desolated soul some consolation." Ratha, calm and unmoved, made no reply, but cast a look at his master. Buddha, addressing Ratha's father, said to him, "What will you have to state in reply to what I am about to tell you? Your son knows what you know; he sees what you see; his heart is entirely disentangled from all attachment to worldly objects; passions are dead in him. Who will now ever presume to say that he ought to subject himself again to them and bend his neck under their baneful influence?" "I have spoken rashly," replied the father; "let my son continue to enjoy the favour of your society; let him remain with you for ever and become your disciple. The only favour I request for myself is to have the satisfaction of receiving you in my house with my son attending you, and there to enjoy the happiness of supplying you with your food." Buddha by his silence assented to his request. No sooner had his father departed than Ratha applied for the dignity of Rahan, which was forthwith conferred upon him. At that time there were in the world seven Rahandas.

---

vicissitudes of life. Here is again clearly pointed out the final end to be arrived at, viz., that of perfect mental stability. This state is the foreshadowing of that of Neibban.

On the following morning, Gaudama, putting on his yellow tsiwaran, and carrying the patta under his arm, attended by the Rahan Ratha, sallied from his house, and went, according to his promise, to the place of Ratha's father, to receive his food. He had scarce entered the house and occupied the seat prepared for him, when the mother of the new Rahan and she who was formerly his wife came both to pay him their respects. Buddha preached to them the law, explaining in particular the three [5] principal observances becoming their sex and con-

[5] From the perusal of this legend, it can be remarked that Buddha, in the course of his preachings, withheld from no one the knowledge of his doctrine, but, on the contrary, aimed at popularising it in every possible way. In this respect he widely differed from the Brahmins, who enveloped their tenets in a mysterious obscurity, and even in that state of semi-incomprehensibility, condescended to offer them to the consideration of but a few selected adepts. But Buddha followed quite an opposite course. He preached to all without exception. On this occasion we see him engaged in explaining to the mother and wife of Ratha duties truly becoming their sex and position. He warned them against the danger of speaking too much, or speaking hastily and with a tone of dissatisfaction. He desired them to be always cool and moderate in their conversation, and to take a pleasure in conversing on religious topics, such as the practice of the ten great duties, the merits of almsgiving, and on the other precepts of the law. He showed to them the unbecomingness of inconsistency in speaking, and finally concluded by exhorting them to allow wisdom to guide them in the right use of the faculty of speech. Every one will agree in this that the lecture was a very appropriate one, and would suit women of our days as well as those of Buddha's times.

It is not easy to determine whether these two female converts became Rahanesses by forsaking the world and devoting all their time to religious observances, or simply believed in Buddha's doctrines and continued to live in the world. The Burmese translator makes use of expressions liable to both interpretations. I feel inclined to adopt the second supposition. They became female Upasakas, and continued to live in the world. We shall see, hereafter, that Gaudama's aunt, Patzapati, was the first, after much entreating, who was allowed to become a Rahaness.

The great former of the Buddhistic disciplinary regulations has also laid down rules for the institution and management of an order of female devotees, to match, as it were, with that of talapoins. Hence in almost all countries where Buddhism flourishes, there are to be met houses and monasteries which are the abodes of those pious women, who emulate Rahans in the strict observance of practices of the highest order. Their dress, except the colour, which is white, is quite similar to that of talapoins; their head is shaved; they live in strict continence as long as they continue to wear the dress of their profession. They have certain formulas of prayer to repeat every day several times. Their diet is the same as that of talapoins; they are forbidden to take any food after midday. I am not

dition. The effect of the preaching was immediate and irresistible: they became exempt from all sins, and attained the state of the perfect, of Thautapati, and became, among the persons of their sex, the first Upasakas. They desired to be ranked among his disciples, and devoted themselves to his service. They were the first persons of their sex who took refuge in the three precious things, Buddha, his law, and the assembly of the perfect. Gaudama and his faithful attendant, having eaten the excellent and savoury food prepared for them, departed from the house and returned to the monastery.

Four young men[6] belonging to the most illustrious

---

aware that they render any service to society in the way of keeping schools for the benefit of female children. They live on alms freely bestowed on them by their co-religionists. The Burmese honour them with the title of Mathi-la-shing, which means ladies of the religious duties. The order of those female devotees is now much on the decline; the inmates of houses are but few, enjoying a very small share of public esteem and respect. They are generally looked upon with feelings akin to those entertained towards beggars.

In the Wini, or book of discipline, the relations that are allowed to subsist between the two orders of male and female devotees are minutely described and clearly laid down, so as to prevent the evils that might result from a familiar and unnecessary intercourse. Thoroughly acquainted with the weakest side of human nature, the author of the Wini has legislated on that subject with the utmost circumspection. He allowed rather aged Rahans to be the spiritual advisers of the Rahanesses, but he denies them the leave of ever going to their houses under any pretext whatever. When the latter want to hear preaching or receive some advice from the Rahans, they resort in broad daylight to the monastery, are permitted to stay in a large hall open to the public, at a considerable distance from him whom they desire to consult. Having briefly and with becoming reverence made known the object of their visit, and received some spiritual instructions, they immediately return to their own place.

The same reflection may be applied to the conversion of Ratha's father. It is said that he was the first convert out of the body of laymen. He does not appear to have forsaken the world and become a first-class convert. He became a Thautapati, and at once entered one of the four ways leading to perfection, but remained in the world.

[6] The conversion of Ratha and of his young friends shows to us distinctly the tendency of Buddha's preachings, and their effect over those who believed in him. Ratha is represented as a young worldly-minded man, who, in the midst of riches, has denied himself to no kind of pleasure. He feels that the enjoyments he was so fond of can in no manner satisfy the cravings of his heart: he is disgusted at them, and resolves to withdraw into solitude, with the intention of placing himself under the direction of some eminent teacher, and

families of Baranathee, and formerly connected with Ratha by the ties of intimate friendship, having heard that their friend had shaved his head and beard, had put on a yellow dress and become a Rahan, said among themselves: "Our friend has withdrawn from the society of men, given up all pleasures, and has entered into the society of Rahans. There can be no doubt but the law of Wini[7] is most ex-

---

learn from him the way to happiness. He hopes that the study of philosophy will lead him to true wisdom and the acquirement of the means that may render him happy. He luckily falls in with Buddha, who explains to him that the senses are the instruments through which passions act upon and tyrannise over the soul, by keeping it in a painful subjection to matter. He points out to him the necessity of freeing himself from their control. This principle of Buddhism, which aims at disengaging the soul from matter, isolating it from all that proves a burden to it, and delivering it from the tyrannical yoke of concupiscence, is in itself perfectly correct, but, carried beyond its legitimate consequences, it becomes false and absurd. According to Buddhists, the soul, disentangled from all that exists, finds itself alone without any object it can adhere to; folding itself up into its own being, it remains in a state of internal contemplation, destitute alike of all active feelings of pleasure and pain. This doctrine was known in the time of Buddha, as far as the principle is concerned. The Rathees and other sages in those days upheld it both in theory and practice; but, on the consequences, the originator of Buddhism was at issue with his contemporaries, and struck out a new path in the boundless field of speculative philosophy.

[7] The Wini is one of the great divisions of Buddhistic sacred writings. The Pitagat, or collection of all the Scriptures, is divided into three parts—the Thouts, containing the preachings of Buddha, the Wini, or book of the discipline, and the Abidama, or the book of Metaphysics. That compilation is supposed to embody the doctrines of Buddha in a complete manner. These books have not been written by Buddha himself, since it is said of him that he never wrote down anything. The first Buddhistic compositions were certainly written by the disciples of Phra, or their immediate successors. But there arose some disputes among the followers of Buddha, as to the genuineness of the doctrines contained in the various writings published by the chief disciples. To settle the controversy, an assembly or council of the most influential members of the Buddhistic creed, under the presidency of Kathaba, was held about three months after Gaudama's demise. The writings regarded as spurious were set aside, and those purporting to contain the pure doctrines of Phra were collected into one body, and formed, as it were, the canon of sacred books. The matter so far was settled for the time being, but the human mind, when unrestrained by authority, acted in those days with the same result as it does in our own times. Various and different were the constructions put on the same text by the expounders of the Buddhistic law. All parties admitted the same books, but they dissented from each other in the interpretation. Some of the books hitherto regarded as sacred were

cellent and sublime, and the profession of Rahan most perfect." Whereupon they came to the place their friend resided in, prostrated themselves before him, as usual in such circumstances, and sat down at a respectful and becoming distance. Ratha took them before Buddha, praying him to deliver to those who had been his friends in the world the same instructions he had received from him. Gaudama willingly assented to his request, and forthwith began to explain to them the nature and abundance of merits derived from almsgiving. He initiated them into the knowledge of the chief precepts and observances of the law. These young hearers received with a cheerful heart his instructions, and felt within themselves an unknown power, dissolving gradually all the ties that had hitherto retained them in the world of passions. Delighted at remarking so good dispositions in those young men, Gaudama explained to them the higher doctrine of the four great and fundamental truths which lead to perfection.[8]

---

altered or rejected altogether to make room for the works of new doctors. Confusion prevailed to such an extent, that an hundred years later a second council was assembled for determining the authenticity of the real and genuine writings. A new compilation was made and approved of by the assembly. The evil was remedied; but the same causes that had exercised so baneful an influence previously to the time of the second council soon worked again and produced a similar result. Two hundred and thirty-five years after Gaudama's death a third council was assembled. The books compiled by the second council were revised and apparently much abridged, and with the sanction of the assembled fathers a new canon of scriptures was issued. The Pitagat in its present shape is regarded as the work of this last assembly. All the books are written in the Pali or Magatha language. In the beginning of the fifth century of our era, according to our author's computation, a learned man, named Boudagautha, went to Ceylon, and brought back to Burmah a copy of the collection of the Pitagat. Then he introduced into this country the alphabet now in use, and translated into the vernacular a portion of the scriptures. This important subject shall receive hereafter fuller development.

[8] The four principles or truths so often alluded to in the course of this work ought to be well understood, in order to get a clear insight into the system under consideration. These four truths are as follows:—1. There are afflictions and miseries attending the existence of all beings. 2. There are passions and, in particular, concupiscence, which are the causes of all miseries. 3. There is Neibban, which is the exemption of all passions, and, consequently, the deliver-

When the preaching was over, they applied for and obtained the dignity of Rahans. There were at that time eleven Rahandas in the whole world.

Fifty other young men of good descent, who had been the companions of Ratha while in the world, having heard that their friend had left the world, had put on the yellow

---

ance from all miseries. 4. There are the four ways or high roads leading to Neibban. Here is the summary of the sublime knowledge and transcendent science possessed by a Buddha: these four fundamental truths form the four features or characteristics of his law; they safely guide man in the way to deliverance. The Buddhist sage, who longs to become perfect, must study with attention the position of all beings in this world, survey with a patient regard their diversified conditions, and fathom the depth of the abyss of miseries in which they are miserably sunk. A vague, general and superficial knowledge of these miseries is insufficient to create that perfect acquaintance with human wretchedness. He ought to examine one after the other those series of afflictions, until he feels, as it were, their unbearable weight pressing over his soul. This first step having been made by the means of reflection, meditation, and experience, the sage, standing by the side of all miseries that press upon all beings, as a physician, by the bed of a patient, enquires into the cause of such an awful moral disorder. He soon discovers the generating causes of that universal distemper; they are the passions in general; or rather, to speak more in accordance with Buddhistic expressions, concupiscence, anger, and ignorance are the springs all demerits flow from, are the impure sources wherefrom originate all the miseries and afflictions this world is filled with. The destruction of those passions is the main and great object he has in view. He, therefore, leaves the world and renounces all pleasures and worldly possessions, in order to extinguish concupiscence; he practises patience under the most trying circumstances, that anger may no longer have any power over him; he studies the law, and meditates on all its points, in order to dispel the dark atmosphere of ignorance by the bright light of knowledge.

Having advanced so far, the sage has not yet reached the final object of his desires; he has not yet attained to the end he anxiously wishes to come to. He is just prepared and qualified for going in search of it. Neibban, or the *absolute* exemption and *permanent* deliverance from the four causes productive of existence, or of a state of being, is the only thing he deems worthy to be desired and earnestly longed for. The sage, perceiving such a desirable state, sighs after it with all the powers of his soul. Neibban is to him what the harbour is to the storm-beaten mariner, or deliverance to the worn-out inmate of a dark dungeon. But such a happy state is, as yet, at a great distance; where is the road leading thereto? This is the last truth the sage has to investigate. The four roads to perfection are opened before him. These he must follow with perseverance; they will conduct him to Neibban. They are a perfect belief, a perfect reflection, a perfect use of speech, and a perfect conduct.

garb and become Rahan, said to each other: "The law which our friend listened to may not be a bad one; the profession he has entered into may not be as despicable as many people are wont to assert." They resolved to judge for themselves and to be eye-witnesses to all that had been said on the subject. They set out for the monastery Ratha was living in, came into his presence, paid their respects to him, and stopped at a proper distance in a respectful posture. Ratha led them to his great teacher, humbly craving for his former friends the same favour he had done to him. Buddha graciously assented to the request, and imparted instruction to his young hearers, with such a happy result that they instantly applied for admittance to the dignity of Rahans. This favour was granted to them. The total number of Rahandas was thereby raised to sixty-one.

On a certain day, Gaudama called his disciples into his presence,[9] and said to them: "Beloved Rahans, I am

---

[9] Buddha, having trained up his disciples to the knowledge of his doctrines as well as to the practice of his ordinances, elevates them to the dignity of preachers, or, to be more correct, makes them fellow-labourers in the arduous task of imparting to mankind the wholesome knowledge of saving truths. An unbounded field is opened before him; the number of beings who are designed to partake of the blessings of his doctrines is incalculably great. His own efforts will not prove adequate to the difficulties such a mighty undertaking is encompassed with; he joins to himself fervent disciples that have reached all but the farthest limit of perfection by the thorough control they have obtained over their passions; he considers them as instruments well fitted for carrying into execution his benevolent designs, and entrusts them with the mission he has entered upon. By adopting such a step, the wise founder of Buddhism establishes a regular order of men, whom he commissions to go and preach to all living creatures the doctrines they have learnt from him. The commission he imparted to them was evidently to be handed down to their successors in the same office. He may now die, but he is sure that the work he has begun shall be carried on with zeal and devotedness by men who have renounced the world and given up all sorts of enjoyments, that they might engage in the great undertaking with a heart perfectly disentangled from all ties and impediments of every description.

In entrusting his disciples with the important duty of teaching mankind, Buddha, obeying the impulse of his universal charity, desires them to go all over the world and preach all the truth to all mortals. He distinctly charges them to announce openly and unreservedly all that they have heard

exempt from the five great passions which, like an immense net, encompass men and Nats. You too, owing to the instructions you have received from me, enjoy the same glorious privilege. There is now incumbent on us a great duty, that of labouring effectually in behalf of men and Nats, and procuring to them the invaluable blessing of the deliverance. To the end of securing more effectually the success of such an undertaking, let us part with each other and proceed in various and opposite directions, so that not two of us should follow up the same way. Go ye now and preach the most excellent law, expounding every point thereof, and unfolding it with care and attention in all its bearings and particulars. Explain the beginning, the middle, and the end of the law to all men, without exception; let everything respecting it be made publicly known and brought to the broad daylight. Show now to men and Nats the way leading to the practice of pure and meritorious works. You will meet, doubtless, with a great number of mortals, not as yet hopelessly given up to their passions, and who will avail themselves of your preaching

---

from him. In these instructions the plan of Buddha is clearly laid down, and the features of the mission he assumes distinctly delineated. His object is to spread his doctrines all over the world and to bring all beings under his moral sway. He makes no distinction between man and man, nation and nation. Though belonging by birth to a high caste, he disregards at once those worldly barriers whereby men are separated from each other, and acknowledges no dignity but that which is conferred by virtue. Bold, indeed, was the step that he took in a country where the distinction of caste is so deeply rooted in the habits of the people, that all human efforts have, hitherto, proved abortive in destroying it. It has already been hinted in a foregoing note that Gaudama placed himself on a new ground, in opposition to the Brahminical doctrines. He, doubtless, cautiously avoided to wound directly the feelings of his antagonists; but, at the same time, he adroitly sowed the seed of a mighty revolution, that was to change, if left to grow freely, the face of the Indian peninsula. His doctrine bore two characteristics, that were to distinguish it essentially from that of his adversaries; it was popular and universal, whereas that of his opponents was wrapped up in a mysterious obscurity, and unfolded completely only to a privileged caste. Another great difference between the two systems is this: Buddha paid little attention to the dogmatical portion of religion, but laid the greatest stress on morals. The dogmas are few and little insisted on. He aimed at correcting the vices of the heart, but exerted himself little to redress the errors of the mind.

for reconquering their hitherto forfeited liberty, and freeing themselves from the thraldom of passions. For my own part, I will direct my course towards the village of Thena, situated in the vicinity of the solitude of Ooroowela."

At that time the wicked Nat Manh came into the presence of Buddha, and tempted him in the following manner:—"Men and Nats," said he, "have the five senses; through those five senses passions act upon them, encompass their whole being, and finally keep them bound up with the chains of an unresistible slavery. As to you, Rahan, you are not an exception to that universal condition, and you have not yet outstepped the boundaries of my empire." Phra replied: "O vile and wretched Nat! I am well acquainted with the passions men and Nats are subjected to. But I have freed myself from them all, and have thereby placed myself without the pale of your empire; you are at last vanquished and conquered." Manh, yet undismayed, replied: "O Rahan, you may be possessed of the power of flying through the air; but even in that condition, those passions which are inherent in the nature of mortal beings will accompany you, so that you cannot flatter yourself of living without the boundaries of my empire." Phra retorted, "O wicked Nat, concupiscence and all other passions I have stifled to death in me, so that you are at last conquered." Manh, the most wretched among the wretched, was compelled to confess with a broken heart that Phra had conquered him, and he instantly vanished away.

Full of fervour in preaching the law, the Rahans saw themselves surrounded with crowds of converts, who asked for the dignity of Rahan. They poured in daily from all parts, into the presence of Buddha, to receive at his hands the much-longed-for high dignity.[10] Buddha said to them,

---

[10] In these new instructions delivered to the Rahans, Buddha gives them the power of receiving into the ranks of the assembly those of their converts who should prove foremost in understanding the law and observing its highest practices. He empowers them to confer on others

"Beloved Rahans, it is painful and troublesome both to you and to those who desire to be admitted into our holy brotherhood to come from such a great distance to me. I

---

the dignity of Rahans, and admit them to the various steps that lead to that uppermost one. To observe uniformity in the reception of candidates to the various orders, Buddha laid down a number of regulations embodied in the Kambawa, or book used as a sort of ritual on the days of admission of candidates to the dignity of Patzins and Rahans. The contents of this small but interesting work may be seen in the notice on the order of talapoins, or Buddhist monks, inserted at the end of this volume. That the reader may have now an idea of the general purpose and object of these regulations, I will sketch a slight outline of them. The candidate, who seeks for admission among the members of the order, has to appear before an assembly of Rahans, presided over by a dignitary. He must be provided with the dress of the order, and a patta or the pot of a mendicant. He is presented to the assembly by a Rahan, upon whom devolves the important duty of instructing him in all that regards the profession he is about to embrace, and lead him through the ordeal of the ceremony. He is solemnly interrogated before the assembly on the several defects and impediments which incapacitate an individual for admission into the order. On his declaring that he is free from such impediments, he is, with the consent of the assembled fathers, promoted to the rank of Patzin. But before he is allowed to take his place among his brethren, he is instructed in the four principal duties he will have to observe, and warned against the four capital sins, the commission of which would deprive him of his high and holy character, and cause his expulsion from the society.

It is supposed that the candidate, previous to his making application for obtaining the dignity of Rahan, has qualified himself by study and a good life for admittance among the perfect. By surrounding the admission of candidates into the ranks of the order with a display of ceremonies, the shrewd framer of these regulations intended to encircle the whole body with a halo of dignity and sacredness, and at the same time to provide, as far as human wisdom allows, against the reception of unworthy postulants.

Hitherto Buddha had reserved to himself alone the power of elevating hearers or converts to the dignity of Rahans; now he transfers to his disciples that power and bids them use it as they had seen him do, in behalf of those whom they deem worthy applicants. He has established a society, and striven to infuse into it all the elements necessary for keeping it up hereafter, and securing its existence and permanency. He sets up a kind of ecclesiastical hierarchy, which is to be perpetuated during the ages to come by the same means and power that brought it into existence.

Having put such a power into the hands of his disciples, Buddha very properly exhorts them to emulate him in his efforts to become perfect. He sets himself as a pattern of perfection, and bids them all imitate the examples he places before them. He shows briefly to them by what means he has attained the state of Arahatapho, and stimulates them to the adopting of similar means. The word Arahatapho is composed of two words —arahat, which means perfect, and pho or phola, as the orthography indicates, which means reward, merit. The state of Arahatapho is that in which a man enjoys the merits or

now give to you the power of conferring the dignity of Patzin and Rahan on those whom you may deem worthy to receive it. This is the summary way you will have to follow on such occasions. Every candidate shall have his hair and beard shaved, and shall be provided with the tsiwaran of yellow colour. These preliminaries being arranged, the candidate, with the extremities of the kowot thrown over his shoulders, shall place himself in a squatting position, his joined hands raised to the forehead, repeating three times, 'I adhere to Buddha, to the law, and to the assembly of the perfect.'"

Gaudama, assembling again round him the Rahans, said to them, "Beloved Rahans, it is owing to my wisdom, aided by constant reflection and meditation, that I have at last reached the incomparable state of Arahatapho; endeavour all of you to follow my example, and arrive at last at the same state of excellence and perfection."

The vile and wretched Nat Manh appeared again before Buddha, striving to tempt him in the same manner as before. Buddha, discovering the snares laid down by the tempter, returned the same reply. Finding himself discovered, Manh vanished from his presence.

Having spent his first lent[11] in the solitude of Migada-

---

reward of perfection, which he has reached by the practice of virtue, and particularly the acquirement of wisdom or knowledge of the highest points of the law. It is used often in opposition to the word Arahatamegata, which signifies the ways or roads leading to perfection.

[11] I have translated by *lent* the Burmese expression Watso, which is but the Pali term Wasa, Burmanised. The word "lent," which has been adopted, is designed to express not the real meaning of Wasa, but to convey to the reader's mind the idea of a time devoted to religious observances. Wasa means a season, but it is intended to designate the rainy season, which in those parts of the Peninsula where Buddha was residing begins in July and ends in November. During that period the communications between villages and towns are difficult, if not impossible. The religious mendicants were allowed in former times, very likely from the very days of Buddha, to retire into the houses of friends and supporters, from which they went forth occasionally begging their food. In the beginning, those who were admitted in the society did not live in community, as was afterwards done in those countries where Buddhism has been of a long time in a flourishing condition. They were allowed to with-

won, Phra shaped his course in the direction of the forest of Ooroowela. On his way to that place he stopped for a while in a jungle, and sat under a tree, to enjoy some rest

---

draw into solitude, and lead an ascetic life, or to travel from one place to another to preach the law and make converts. This work could not be well done during the rainy season. Hence the disciples, while as yet few in number, gathered round their master during that period to hear instructions from him, and practise virtue under his immediate superintendence. They lived with him during all the time the rainy season lasted. This was called to spend the season. In the course of this Legend, the same expression is often met with. It is said of Buddha that he spent a season in such a place, another in another place, to indicate that he stayed in one place during the rainy season, which precluded the possibility of doing the duties of an itinerant preacher.

When the religious order became regularly constituted, and the basis it was to stand on was fairly laid down, the ever-increasing number of members made them feel the want of secluded places where they could live in community, and at the same time quite retired from the world. Houses or monasteries were erected for receiving the pious Rahans. The inmates of those dwellings lived under the direction of a superior, devoting their time to study, meditation, and the observances of the law. They were allowed to go out in the morning very early, to beg and collect the food they wanted for the day. Such is the state the religious are living in up to our own time in Burmah, Ceylon, Thibet, Siam, and in the other countries where Buddhism has been firmly established.

The religious season, or lent, lasts three months. It begins in the full moon of Watso (July) and ends at the full moon of Thadinkiout (October). The keeping of the season in Burmah is as follows:—On the days of the new and full moon crowds of people resort to the pagodas, carrying offerings of flowers, small candles, oil, &c. A great many are found to spend the night in the bungalows erected, chiefly for that purpose, in their immediate vicinity. Women occupy bungalows separated from those of men. It must be admitted that there, as in churches, they far outnumber the men. On such occasions, religion appears to be rather the pretext than the real object of such assemblies. With the exception of old men and women, who are heard to converse on religious topics, and repeat some parts of the law, or recite some praises in honour of Buddha, the others seem to care very little for religion. The younger portion of the weaker sex freely indulge in the pleasure of conversation. It is quite a treat to them to have such a fine opportunity of giving full scope to their talkative powers. During that season the pious faithful are charitably inclined to bestow alms on the Rahans. All the necessaries of life pour with abundance and profusion into the monasteries. Besides almsgiving and resorting to the pagodas, some fervent laymen practise abstinence and fastings to a certain extent; these, however, are but few. During that period the Buddhist recluses are often invited to go to certain places, prepared for the purpose, to preach the law to and receive alms from crowds of hearers who are gathered thither on such occasions. Talapoins are generally seated on an elevated platform, facing the congregation; they keep their large fans before the face through modesty, to

under its cool shade. At that time thirty young noblemen had come to the jungle to indulge in sports and diversions. Each of them had brought his wife, with the exception of one, who, having no wife, was accompanied by a harlot. During the night the harlot rose up unperceived, picked up the best articles belonging to the parties, and carrying them with her, took to her heels through the dense forest. In the morning the thirty young noblemen, rising up, soon perceived the havoc made in the richest articles of their dress, and set out in search of her who they suspected had done the mischief. They came by chance to the spot where Gaudama was sitting in a cross-legged position, and inquired from him whether he had seen a woman passing by. Buddha said to them, "Which, in your opinion, is the best and most advantageous thing, either to go in search of yourselves or in search of a woman?" They replied, "Of course it is preferable to look after ourselves." "If so," replied Buddha, "stay with me for a while; I will preach my law to you, and, with its help, you will arrive at the knowledge of self, and thence at perfection." They cheerfully assented to his request, listened attentively to his instructions, and obtained the state of perfect believers, but in various degrees, according to their respective dispositions. They gave up the habit of drunkenness they had hitherto indulged in, and persevered in the observance of the five great precepts.

[It is to be remarked, adds the Burmese translator, that this happy result was secured to the fortunate hearers by

---

save themselves from the danger of looking on some tempting object. They repeat in chorus certain passages of the life of Buddha, enumerate the five great precepts and other observances of the law. The whole preaching generally goes on in Pali, that is to say, in a language unknown to the congregation. When they have done their duty they withdraw, followed by a great number of their disciples, carrying back to the monasteries all the offerings made by the faithful. It happens also, although but seldom in our days, that some fervent recluses withdraw during the whole or a part of the lent season into solitary places, living by themselves, and devoting all their time to reading the books of the law, and meditating on the most important points and maxims of religion.

the influence of good works made during former existences.[12]]

Gaudama, having so happily completed the conversion

---

[12] The remarks of the Burmese translator afford me an opportunity of explaining one of the leading tenets of the Buddhistic creed. All beings in this world are subjected to the double influence of their merits and demerits. The good influence predominates when the sum of merits surpasses that of demerits, and it is superseded by the latter when the contrary takes place. This principle once admitted, Buddhists explain the good or evil that befalls every individual in every conceivable state of existence. Is a man dead, he is attended on his way to another state of being both by his merits and demerits, who, like two inseparable companions, follow him whithersoever he goes. Should the sum of demerits prove greater, he is forced into hell, or into some other state of punishment, to bear sufferings proportionately to his offences, until he has fully paid off his debt, or, to speak the language of Buddhists, until the sum of his demerits be quite exhausted. If, on the contrary, at the moment of his death the influence of merits be the strongest, he is directed into a state of happiness, pleasure, and enjoyment; say in one of the seats of Nats or Brahmas, and remains there as long as the action of the good influence lasts. When it is over he comes again into the abode of man, or in a state of probation, when he has to labour anew for amassing new and greater merits, that will hereafter entitle him to a higher reward than the one he had previously enjoyed. From the foregoing observations it is evident that the idea of a Supreme Being rewarding the good and punishing the wicked is carefully excluded, and all foreign interference on this subject entirely done away with. Another conclusion flowing from the same source is, that there is no eternity of reward or punishment, but both last for a longer or shorter period, in proportion to the sum of merits and demerits, and consequently to the power of each influence respectively.

It may be asked what becomes of the sum of demerits and its consequent evil influence, whilst the superior good influence prevails? The sum of demerits remains all the while entire and undiminished; the operation of the evil influence is suspended, and has no power whatever, its own being checked by a greater one. But the sum of merits being exhausted, and its inherent action at an end, the opposite one is set at liberty, and acts on the individual proportionately to its own strength, and lasts until it is all exhausted. As man can never be without some merits or demerits, good or bad deeds, he must be either in a state of reward or punishment; this is, if I may say so, the mainspring that moves all beings into the whirlpool of countless existences, wherein they meet happiness or unhappiness according to their deserts. The being that tends strongly and perseveringly through his various existences towards perfection, weakens gradually, and finally destroys in himself the law of demerits; he ascends steadily the steps of the ladder of perfection by the practice of the highest virtues. Having reached its summit, there is no more reason for his going through other existences, and he steps at once into the state of Neibban.

On the above principle Buddhists account for all the various phases of human existence. Is a child born from rich, great, and distinguished

of those young noblemen, rose up and continued his journey in the direction of the forest of Ooroowela. At that time there were three distinguished and far-famed teachers who presided over a vast number of Rathees or disciples leading an ascetic life. They were named Ooroowela Kathaba, Nadi Kathaba, and Gaya Kathaba. The first had under him five hundred disciples, the second three hundred, and the third two hundred. Buddha went up to the monastery of Ooroowela Kathaba, and said to him, "I carry but a few articles with me, and need but a small place to rest in; I beg of you to be allowed to spend the night only in your kitchen." Kathaba answered: "Since you have so few things with you, I willingly allow you to accommodate yourself in the best way you can in the cook-room; but I must inform you that the Naga guardian of the place is an animal of a very wicked temper, powerfully strong, and having a most deadly venom." "I fear not the Naga," replied Buddha; "I am well satisfied with your allowing me a place in the cook-room." Whereupon he entered into the kitchen, sat down in a cross-legged position, and, keeping his body in an erect posture, remained absorbed, as it were, in the deepest contemplation. The Naga soon appeared, and irritated at seeing that a stranger presumed to remain in a place committed to his care, resolved to drive out the intruder. He began to vomit a cloud of

---

parents, does he become a wealthy and powerful man, does he become a king or a nobleman, &c.—he is indebted for all that to merits acquired during former existences. Is another child born in a low, poor, and wretched condition, is he born with bodily or intellectual defects and imperfections, &c., &c.—his former demerits are the principle and cause of all his subsequent misfortunes.

The doctrine of merits and demerits, and of their concomitant influences, has been fully illustrated in the person of Buddha himself during his former existences. He said of himself to his disciples that he had passed with various fortune through the range of the animal kingdom, from the dove to the elephant; that being man he had been often in hell, and in various positions of riches and poverty, greatness and meanness, until by his mighty efforts he at last freed himself from all evil influence, and reached his present state of perfection. He is supposed to have recounted to his disciples on different occasions five hundred and ten of his former existences.

smoke, which he directed at the face of the stranger. Buddha said to himself, "I will do no harm to that Naga; I will leave intact his skin, flesh, and bones; but I will conquer him with the very same weapons he uses against me." Whereupon he emitted by his own power such a volume of thick smoke as soon to silence his adversary, and oblige him to have recourse to more effectual means of attack. He vomited out burning flames. Phra opposed flames far more active and destructive than those of the Naga. They shone forth with such an uncommon brightness as to attract a number of Rathees, who stood motionless, admiring the beautiful countenance of Buddha, and wondering at his matchless power. The Naga, vanquished, gave up the contest, and left to Buddha the undisputed possession of the cook-room during the whole night. In the morning opening his patta, Phra thrust in the terrified Naga, and brought it to Ooroowela Kathaba, who, surprised at the power of the stranger, said, "This Rahanda cannot as yet be compared to me." He desired him to stay in his monastery, promising to supply him with food as long as he should be with him. Phra accepted the proffered invitation, and fixed his residence in the midst of a grove little distant from the cell of Kathaba. Whilst he was there, four chiefs of Nats of the seat of Tsadoumaritz came at midnight to the spot where rested Phra. They were very handsome, and a bright hue, encompassing their bodies, filled the grove with a resplendent light. Kathaba, surprised, came to Buddha, and said to him, "Great Rahan, the hour of taking your food is at hand; your rice is ready, come and eat it. How is it that at midnight there was such an uncommon splendour? One would have thought that the whole forest in the neighbourhood was lined with immense fires, spreading a blaze of light." Phra answering said, "This wonder was caused by the presence of four chiefs of Nats that came to visit me and hear my preachings." Kathaba said to himself, "Great indeed must be the virtue of this Rahan, since Nats come to see him and acknowledge him for their teacher. He is not yet, however, my equal." Buddha ate his rice and went back to the same place.

On another occasion, in the middle of the night, the chief of Thagias came to the grove of Buddha, and by his power caused a flood of light similar to that produced by a thousand lighted fires to pour its effulgent rays in every direction. In the morning, Kathaba went to the great Rahan inviting him to come and eat his rice. Meanwhile he asked him the reason of the wonderful light that had been kept up about from midnight until morning, which surpassed in brilliancy that which had been seen on a former occasion. Phra told him that he had been visited by the chief of Thagias, who came for the purpose of hearing his instructions. Kathaba thought within himself: Great indeed is the glory and dignity of this Rahan, but he is not as yet a Rahanda. Phra ate his food, and continued to stay in the same grove.

On another occasion, at the same late hour, Phra received the visit of the chief of the Brahmas. The flood of light that was sent forth by his body surpassed in effulgent splendour all that had been seen. Kathaba came as usual, in the morning, to invite the great Rahan to come and take his food, requesting him at the same time to inform him of the cause of the great wonder that had just taken place. Phra told him that the chief of Brahmas had waited upon him to listen to his preachings. Kathaba wondered the more at the dignity of this great Rahan, who attracted round him so eminent a visitor. But he said within himself: This Rahan is not yet a Rahanda that can be compared to me. Phra partook of his food, and continued his stay in the same grove.

On a certain day, the people of the country had prepared offerings on a large scale to be presented to Kathaba. On hearing this welcome news, the Rathee thought within himself as follows: The people are disposing everything to make large offerings to me. It is as well this Rahan should not be present on the occasion. He might make a display of his power in the presence of the multitude, who, taken up with admiration for his person, would make great offerings to him, whilst I should see my own decrease in a proportion. To-morrow I will contrive in such a way as to prevent the great Rahan from being present. Buddha discovered at a glance all that was going on in Kathaba's mind. Unwilling to offer any annoyance to his host, he conveyed himself to the island of Ootoogara, where he collected his meal, which he came to eat on the banks of the lake Anawadat. He spent the whole day there, and by his miraculous power he was back to his grove at an early hour on the following day. The Rathee came as usual, to invite him to partake of his meal that was ready, and inquired from him why he had not made his appearance on the day previous. Buddha, without the least emotion that could betray an angry feeling, related to Kathaba all that had passed in his mind, and informed him of the place he had been to. Kathaba, astonished at what he heard, said to himself: The knowledge of this Rahan is transcendent indeed, since he is even acquainted with the thoughts of my mind; his power too is wonderfully great; but withal, he is not as yet a Rahanda comparable to me. Buddha, having eaten his meal, withdrew to his grove.

On a certain day Buddha wished to wash his dress. A Thagia, knowing the thought that occupied his mind, dug a small square tank, and approaching him respectfully, invited him to wash his tsiwaran therein. Buddha then thought: Where shall I find a stone to rub it upon? The Thagia, having brought a stone, said to him: "Illustrious Phra, here is a stone to rub your tsiwaran on." He thought again: Where is a proper place to dry it upon? The Nat that watched the tree Yekada caused it to bend its branches, and said: "My lord, here is a fit place to hang up your tsiwaran." He thought again: Where is a fit spot to extend my clothes upon? The chief of Thagias brought a large and well-polished stone, and said: "O illustrious

Phra, here is a fit place to lay your tsiwaran upon." In the morning, Kathaba repaired as usual to his guest's place, to invite him to take his meal. Surprised at what he perceived, he said to Buddha: "O Rahan, formerly there were here neither tank nor stone; how is it that they are here now? How is it, moreover, that the tree Yekadat is now bending down its branches?" Phra related then to the Rathee all that had happened, informing him that the chief of Thagias and one Nat had done all those works for him, and ministered to all his wants. Kathaba wondered more than before at the great virtue and surpassing excellency of the great Rahan; but he persisted in his former opinion, that the great Rahan was not a Rahanda that could equal him. Buddha, having taken his meal, returned to his grove.

On another occasion, the Rathee went to Buddha's place, to invite him to come and partake of his meal. "Very well," said Buddha, "I have a small business to do now; go beforehand, and I will follow you a few moments hence." Whereupon Kathaba went back to his cell. As to Phra, he went to pluck a fruit from the jambu tree, and arrived at the eating place before Kathaba could reach it. The Rathee, on arriving there, was quite surprised to find Phra already waiting for him. "How is this?" said he, with an unfeigned feeling of surprise, "and by what way did you come and contrive to arrive here before me?" Phra said to him: "After your departure, I plucked one fruit from a jambu tree, and yet I have reached this spot sooner than you. Here is the fruit I have brought. It is as full of flavour as it is beautiful; allow me to present you with it, that you may eat it." "O! no, great Rathan," replied the Rathee, "it is not becoming that I should eat it, but rather keep it for yourself." He thought within himself: Wonderful is indeed the power and eminent excellency of that great Rahan; but he is not as yet a Rahan that can be ranked to me. Phra ate his rice, and returned to his grove.

On another day, Phra gave a fresh proof of his miraculous power, by bringing to Kathaba a mango fruit, plucked from a mango-tree growing near the jambu tree, and so went on for several days, bringing fruits that grew at the extremity of the southern island. On another day, Phra ascended to the seat of Tawadeintha, and brought therefrom a beautiful water-lily, and yet arrived at the place where his meal was ready before Kathaba himself. The latter, quite amazed at seeing a flower from the Nat country, thought within himself: Wonderful, indeed, is the power of that great Rahan, who has brought here, from the seats of Nats, a beautiful lily in such a short space of time; but he is not as yet equal to me.

On a certain day, the Rathees were busy splitting firewood. They got a large log of wood upon which their united efforts could make no impression. Kathaba thought within himself: The great Rahan is gifted with mighty power; let us try him on this occasion. He desired Gaudama to split the hard log. Gaudama split it in a moment in five hundred pieces. The Rathees then tried to light up the fuel, but they could not succeed. Kathaba requested his guest to come to their assistance. In an instant, the five hundred pieces were set in a blaze, and presented the terrifying sight of five hundred large fires. The Rathees begged the great Rahan to extinguish those fires which threatened a general conflagration. Their request was instantaneously granted; the five hundred fires were extinguished.

During the cold season in the months of January and February, when a heavy cold dew falls, the Rathees amused themselves with plunging and swimming in the river Neritzara. Phra caused five hundred fires to blaze out on the banks of the river. The Rathees, coming out of the stream, warmed themselves by the side of those fires. They all wondered at the astonishing power of the great Rahan. But Kathaba persisted in saying that he was not a Rahanda like him.

On a certain day, a great rain poured in torrents, so that the water overflowed all the country, but it did not reach the spot Gaudama stood upon. He thought within himself: It is good that I should create a beautiful dry road in the midst of the water. He did so, and walked on the dry road, and clouds of dust rose in the air. Kathaba, much concerned regarding the fate of his guest, took a boat, and, with the assistance of his disciples, pulled in the direction of Buddha's grove; but what was their surprise, when reaching the spot they found, instead of water, a firm dry road, and Buddha calmly walking to and fro. "Is it you, great Rahan," cried Kathaba, "whom we see here?" "Yes," replied Gaudama, "it is I indeed." He had scarcely returned this answer, when he rose in the air and stood for a while above the boat. Kathaba thought again within himself: Great indeed must be the perfections and attainments of the great Rahan, since water even cannot harm him, but he is not yet a Rahanda like me. Phra, who knew what was taking place in Kathaba's mind, said to himself: Long time has this Rathee kept thinking within himself: This Rahan is great, but I am still greater than he; it is time now that I should inspire him with fear and surprise. Addressing Kathaba, he said, "Rathee, you are not a Rahanda, that has arrived to the perfection of Arahat; you have never performed the meritorious actions of the four ways to perfection; you are not, therefore, a Rahanda. But I have, during former existences, carefully attended to those practices which have enabled me to reach perfection, and finally obtain the Buddhaship." Astonished at such an unexpected declaration, Kathaba humbled himself, fell on his knees, and prostrated himself at the feet of Buddha, saying: "Illustrious Phra, I wish to become Rahan under your direction." Phra replied: "Kathaba, you have under you five hundred Rathees, go and inform them of all that has happened." Whereupon Kathaba went to the place where the Rathees had assembled, and said to them: "I wish to place myself under the direction of the great Rahan." The five hundred Rathees told him that they were willing to follow his example, since he had been hitherto to them such an excellent teacher. They rose up, and, collecting their utensils, such as the twisted hairs, the forked staff, the hairy girdle, the honey filtre, &c., flung them into the river; then they came, and prostrating themselves at the feet of Buddha, craved admittance to the dignity of Rahans.

Nadi Kathaba, seeing the utensils floating on the water and carried down by the stream, called his followers and said to them: "Some misfortune must have befallen my elder brother; let us go and see what has happened." They were no sooner arrived, than Kathaba related to them all that had just taken place. Nadi Kathaba went forthwith to Buddha's cell, attended by all his disciples. Falling all at the feet of Phra, they declared their readiness to become his disciples, and applied for the dignity of Rahan. Gaya Kathaba, who lived a little below the place of Nadi Kathaba, seeing on the surface of the water the utensils of the followers of both his brothers floating in the direction of the stream, hastened, with his two hundred disciples, to the place of Ooroowela Kathaba. On his being informed of all that had occurred, he and his followers threw themselves at Gaudama's feet, praying for admittance into the order of Rahans. They were all admitted. The conversion of Ooroowela Kathaba was brought about by the display, on the part of Buddha, of no less than three thousand five hundred and sixty wonders.[1]

---

[1] It has been asserted in a former note that the preachings of Buddha were accompanied with miracles, to impart an additional weight and an irresistible evidence to his doctrines. This assertion is fully corroborated by all the particulars attending the conversion of the three Kathabas and their disciples. On this occasion Buddha met with the greatest amount of stubborn resistance on the part of Ooroowela Kathaba. There is no doubt but our great preacher resorted to every means of persuasion to carry conviction to the mind of his distinguished hearer. He had, however, to deal with a man full of his own merits and excellence, who thought himself far superior to every one else. His best arguments proved powerless before a self-conceited individual, who was used to give and

CHAPTER VII.

Buddha's sermon on the mountain—Interview of Buddha and King Pimpathara in the vicinity of the city of Radzagio—Answer of Kathaba to Buddha's interrogation—Instructions delivered to the king and his attendants—Solemn entry of Buddha into Radzagio—Donation of the Weloowon monastery to Buddha—Conversion of Tharipatra and Maukalan—The Rahans are keenly taunted by the people of Radzagio.

ACCOMPANIED by his thousand followers, Phra went to the village of Gayathitha. This village stands on the bank of the river Gaia. Close to it, there is a mountain resem-

---

not to receive instruction, and enjoyed a far-famed celebrity. Buddha was compelled to resort to his unbounded power of working miracles, and with it overcame at last the obstinate and blind resistance of the proud Rathee. No conquest had ever been so dearly bought; but it proved well worth the extraordinary efforts made to obtain it. Kathaba became one of the most staunch adherents of Buddha, and one of the most fervent disciples, who laboured hard for the propagation of Buddhism. He is the most celebrated of all Buddhistic monks, and to his name is ever prefixed the distinguished epithet of Maha, which means great. After Gaudama's demise, he became the patriarch of the Buddhists. By his care and exertions, a council of five hundred Rahans was assembled at Radzagio, under the reign of King Adzatatha, to condemn the unbecoming language used by some false or imperfectly taught converts, who wished to shake off, on many points, the authority of Buddha.

In the episode of the conversion of the three Kathabas, the attentive reader cannot fail to have observed one particular that throws some light on the position several heads of philosophical schools occupied in the days that saw the origin of Buddhism. Those sages lived in retired places, far from the bustle and tumult of the world. It is probable that at first they were alone, or with but a few other individuals who delighted in the same mode of life. Their time was entirely taken up with study and meditation. The object of their studies and reflections was the boundless field of metaphysics and morals. Their diet was plain, and their abstemiousness carried to a degree Hindu devotees and fanatics are alone capable of reaching. The fame of the proficiency of some of those individuals in science and virtue soon attracted to their solitude numbers of pupils, eager to place themselves under the tuition and discipline of masters so eminent in every respect. The three Kathabas must have been

bling in appearance an elephant's head. On the top of the mountain stands a large rock, wide enough to accommodate Buddha and all his attendants. He ascended the mountain with his disciples, and, having reached its summit, sat down. Summoning all his disciples, he said to them: "Beloved Bickus, all that is to be met with in the three abodes of men, Nats, and Brahmas, is like a burning flame. But why is it so? Because the eyes are a burning flame; the objects perceived by the eyes, the view of those objects, the feeling created by that view, are all like a burning flame. The sensations produced by the eyes cause a succession of pleasant and painful feelings, but these are likewise a burning flame. What are the causes productive of such a burning? It is the fire of concupiscence, of anger, of ignorance, of birth, of death, of old age, and of anxiety. Again, the ear is a burning flame; the sounds, the perception of the sounds, the sensations caused by the sounds, are all a burning flame; the pleasure or pain produced by the sounds are also a burning flame, which is fed by the fire of concupiscence, anger, ignorance, birth, old age, death, anxiety, tears, affliction, and trouble. Again, the sense of smelling is a burning flame; the odours, the perception of odours, the sensations produced by odours, are all a burning flame; the pleasure and pain resulting therefrom are but a burning flame, fed by concupiscence, anger, ignorance, birth, old age, death, disquietude, tears, affliction, and sorrow. Again, the taste is a burning flame; the objects tasted, the perception of those objects, the sensations produced by them, are all a burning flame, kept up by the fire

celebrated throughout the country, since we find them at the head of so many disciples. Humility has never been the *forte* of the heathen sages, either in or out of India. Conceit and self-esteem were fostered in their souls by the consciousness of their own superiority and excellence, by the praises lavished on them by their disciples, and not a little by the seclusion from society to which they voluntarily resigned themselves. Spiritual pride, like a cunning foe, occupied in the heart the place vacated by passions of a coarser nature and less delicate tinge. The conduct of the elder Kathaba fully bears out the truth and correctness of the above assertion.

of concupiscence, anger, ignorance, birth, old age, death, anxiety, tears, affliction, and sorrow. Again, the sense of feeling, the objects felt, the perception of those objects, the sensations produced by them, are a burning flame; the pleasure and pain resulting therefrom are but a burning flame, fostered by concupiscence, anger, ignorance, birth, old age, death, anxiety, tears, affliction, and sorrow. Again, the heart is a burning flame, as well as all the objects perceived by it, and the sensations produced in it; the pleasure and pain caused by the heart are too a burning flame, kept up by the fire of concupiscence, anger, ignorance, birth, old age, death, disquietude, tears, affliction, and sorrow. Beloved Bickus, they who understand the doctrine I have preached, and see through it, are full of wisdom and deserve to be called my disciples. They are displeased with the senses, the objects of the senses, matter, pleasure and pain, as well as with all the affections of the heart. They become free from concupiscence, and therefore exempt from passions. They have acquired the true wisdom that leads to perfection; they are delivered at once from the miseries of another birth. Having practised the most excellent works, nothing more remains to be performed by them. They want no more the guidance of the sixteen laws, for they have reached far beyond them."[1]

---

[1] The philosophical discourse of Buddha on the mountain may be considered as the summary of his theory of morals. It is confessedly very obscure and much above the ordinary level of the human understanding. The hearers whom he addressed were persons already trained up to his teaching, and therefore prepared for understanding such doctrines. Had he spoken in that abstruse style to common people, it is certain he would have missed his aim and exposed himself to the chance of not being understood. But he addressed a select audience, whose minds were fully capable of comprehending his most elevated doctrines. He calls his disciples Bickus, or mendicants, to remind them of the state of voluntary poverty they had embraced when they became his followers, and to impress their minds with contempt for the riches and pleasures of this world.

He lays it down as a great and general principle that all that exists resembles a flame that dazzles the eyes by its brilliancy and torments by its burning effects. Here appears the favourite notion of Buddhism that there is nothing substantial and real in this world, and that the continual

Having thus spoken, Buddha remained silent. His hearers felt themselves wholly disentangled from the trammels of passions, and disengaged from all affections to material objects, and they who had been but Rahans became Rahandas.

---

changes and vicissitudes we are exposed to are the cause of painful sensations. Buddha reviews the six senses (the heart, according to his theory, is the seat of a sixth sense) in succession, and as they are the channels through which affections are produced on the soul, he compares to a burning flame the organs of the senses, the various objects of the action of the senses, the results painful or agreeable produced by them. Hence he fulminates a general and sweeping condemnation against all that exists out of man. The senses, being the means through which matter influences the soul, share in the universal doom. Buddha sets forth the causes productive of that burning flame. They are—first, the three great and general principles of demerits, viz., concupiscence, anger, and ignorance. In the book of Ethics these three principles are explained at great length; they are represented as the springs from which flow all other passions. In a lengthened digression the author aims at simplifying the question, and endeavours to show, by a logical process, that ignorance is the head source from which concupiscence and passion take their rise. It is, therefore, according to Buddhists, into the dark recess of ignorance that metaphysicians must penetrate in order to discover the first cause of all moral disorders. Every being has his mind more or less encompassed by a thick mist that prevents him from seeing truth. He mistakes good for evil, right for wrong; he erroneously clings to material objects that have no reality, no substance, no consistence; his passions are kept alive by his love or hatred of vain illusions. The flame is, moreover, fed by birth, old age, death, afflictions, &c., which are as many *foci* wherefrom radiate out on all surrounding objects fires which keep up the general conflagration. But they play only a secondary action, dependent on the three great causes of all evils just alluded to. What causes birth, old age, and death? inquires the Buddhist. The law of merits and demerits is the immediate answer to the question; it might be added thereto, the necessity of acquiring merits and gravitating towards perfection. A man is born to innumerable succeeding existences by virtue of his imperfections, and that he might acquire fresh merits by the practice of virtue. By birth, a being is ushered into a new existence or into a new state, where the burning flame which is supposed to spread over all that exists exercises its teasing and tormenting influence over him. Old age and death are two periods when a radical change operates upon a being, and places him in a different situation where he experiences the baneful effects of the conflagration. "Blessed are they," says Buddha, "who understand this; they are full of wisdom; they become displeased with all passions and with all the things they act upon. The causes of existences being done away with, they have reached the terminus of all possible existences; one step more and they find themselves placed beyond the influence of the power of attraction that retains forcibly all beings in the vortex of existences, and brings them towards the centre of perfection; they are in fact entering into the state of Neibban."

Whilst the most excellent Phra was enjoying himself in the place of Gayathitha, he recollected that, at the time when he was but a Phralaong, being near the mountain Pantawa, he had received from King Pimpathara an invitation to come to his own country and preach the law. Accompanied with his thousand Rahandas, he set out for the country of Radzagio. Having arrived at a small distance from the royal city he went to the Latti grove, about three gawots from Radzagio, a place planted with palm trees. The king, having heard of his arrival, said to his people: "The descendant of a long succession of illustrious princes, the great Rahan Gaudama, has entered into our country, and is now in the grove of palm-trees, in the garden of Tandiwana." The happy news was soon re-echoed throughout the country. The people said among themselves: The great Gaudama is come indeed. He is perfectly acquainted with all that relates to the three states of men, Nats and Brahmas; he preaches a sublime and lovely law; the morals that he announces are pure, like a shell newly cleansed. Pimpathara, placing himself at the head of 120,000 warriors, surrounded by crowds of nobles and Pounhas, went to the garden of Tandiwana, where Phra was seated in the middle of his disciples. He paid his respects by prostrating himself before him, and then withdrew to a becoming distance. The countless crowd followed the example of their monarch, and seated themselves at a becoming distance. Some of them remained conversing with Buddha, and heard from him words worthy to be ever remembered; some others, having their hands joined to the forehead, remained in a respectful attitude; some were praising his illustrious ancestors; others remained modestly silent. All of them, perceiving the three Kathabas close to the person of Phra, doubted whether Gaudama was their disciple, or they, his disciples. Buddha, seeing at once what thought occupied the mind of the warriors, noblemen, and Pounhas, addressed the elder Kathaba, called Ooroowela Kathaba, and said to him:

"Kathaba, you who lived formerly in the solitude of Ooroowela, answer the question I am now putting to you. You were formerly a teacher of Rathees, who practised works of great mortification, to such an extent that their bodies were emaciated by self-inflicted penances: what has induced you to give up the sacrifices you were wont to make?" "Blessed Buddha," answered Kathaba, "I have observed that exterior objects, the sounds, the taste, the gratification of the senses, are but miserable filth; and, therefore, I take no more delight in the offering of small and great sacrifices." Buddha replied, "Kathaba, if you be no longer pleased with what is beautiful to the eyes, pleasant to the ear, palatable to the taste, and agreeable to the gratification of the senses, in what do you presently find pleasure and delight?" Kathaba answered, "Blessed Buddha, the state of Neibban is a state of rest, but that rest cannot be found as long as we live under the empire of senses and passions. That rest excludes existence, birth, old age, and death; the great mental attainments alone lead thereto. I know and see that happy state. I long for it. I am, therefore, displeased with the making of great and small sacrifices." Having thus spoken, Kathaba rose up, worshipped Buddha by prostrating himself before him, and touching with his forehead the extremities of his feet, and said, "O most excellent Buddha, you are my teacher, and I am your disciple." All the people, seeing what Kathaba had done, knew that he was practising virtue under the direction of Gaudama.[2]

[2] From the purport of Kathaba's reply to Buddha's question, it may be inferred with certainty that the Rathees were in the habit of making sacrifices or burnt-offerings. These sacrifices again were distinguished into two classes; the one, including the small or daily ones, and the other, the great burnt-offerings, made on solemn occasions. That these sacrifices were not performed by the killing and immolating of animals, there can be no doubt, as such an act would have been contrary to the tender regard they always had for the life of animals. The institutes of Menu come to our help to elucidate this point. The Brahmin is enjoined, according to that compilation of laws, to make burnt-offerings of clarified butter and other articles to the manes of his ancestors. Agreeably to this

Phra, who was acquainted with their innermost thoughts, knew that they were longing to hear the preaching of the law. As he had always done, he began to preach to them the virtue of liberality in almsgiving, and then unfolded before them, with matchless eloquence, the advantages of leaving the world, &c. The hearers felt an inward delight in all that was said to them. Observing the favourable impression made upon them, Gaudama continued to instruct them on the four laws, regarding the miseries of this world, the passions, the practice of excellent works, and the ways to perfection. At the conclusion of these instructions, the king and 100,000 of the assembly, like a piece of white cloth which, when plunged into dye, retains the colour it receives, obtained instantly the state of Thautapan.[3] As to the 10,000 remaining hearers, they

---

regulation, Kathaba performed those rites, which, in the opinion of Buddha, were perfectly useless, since they could not be the means of elevating the performer to the knowledge and perfection requisite for obtaining what he always calls *per excellence* the deliverance.

Kathaba is rather obscure in his answer. It seems that he intended to acknowledge that, notwithstanding the sacrifices and burnt-offerings he had made, and upon the value of which he had laid much stress, concupiscence and other vicious propensities were still deeply rooted in him; that, through the channel of his senses, exterior objects continued to make impressions on his soul. He had, therefore, become disgusted with practices which could not free him from the action and influence of passions and matter.

In the opinion of Buddha, the observance of exterior religious rites can never elevate man to the sublime knowledge of pure truth, which alone does confer real perfection to him who has become a true sage, and is deemed worthy of obtaining the deliverance. A serious application of the mind to the meditation of the law and the nature of beings, is the only way leading to the acquirement of true wisdom. As long as Kathaba was contented with material acts of worship, and his mind's attention was engrossed with those vain ceremonials, he had not as yet entered in the way of perfection. He had hitherto missed the true path; he had wandered in the broad road of error, encompassed by mental darkness, and deceived by perpetual illusions. His extensive knowledge had served but to lead him in the wrong direction. He wanted the guidance of Buddha to enable him to retrace his steps and find the right way. He had to become sensible of the truth of the great fundamental maxims of all real wisdom, viz., that in this world all is subjected to change and to pain; and that all beings are mere illusions, destitute of all reality.

[3] To complete what has already been stated respecting the Ariahs or venerables in a foregoing note, the following is added. The reader must bear in mind that the Ariahs are

believed in the three precious things in the capacity of Upathakas.

The ruler of the country of Magataritz, King Pimpathara, having obtained the state of Thautapan, said to Gaudama, "Illustrious Buddha, some years ago, when I was but a crown prince of this country, I entertained five desires, which are all happily accomplished. Here are the five desires—I wished to become king; I desired that the Phra, worthy of receiving the homage of all men, should come into my kingdom; that I might have the privilege

---

divided into four classes, named—Thautapan, Thakadagam, Anagam, and Arahats, and, according to the particular position occupied by the beings of those states, each class is subdivided into two: Thus, for instance, Thautapatti Megata means he who has entered and is walking, as it were, in the way of the perfection of Thautapan; and Thautapatti-pho indicates those who enjoy the merits and blessings of the state of Thautapan; and so with the three superior stages of perfection. To obtain the state of Thautapan, a man must have left the direction followed up by all creatures and entered into the direction or way that leads to deliverance. He will have yet to go through 80,000 kaps or durations of worlds, and must be born seven times more in the state of man and Nat before he be a perfected being, ripe for the state of Neibban. Those who have reached the state of Thakadagam shall have to pass through 60,000 kaps, and be born once in the state of Nat and once in the state of man, before they be perfected. Those who have obtained the third step of Anagam have to travel through 40,000 kaps, and are no more to undergo the process of birth; at the end of that period they are perfected. The fourth stage of perfection, that of Arahat, is the highest a being can ever obtain. The fortunate Arahat is gifted with supernatural powers. At the end of 20,000 kaps he is perfected, and reaches the state of deliverance. Those four states are often called the four great roads leading to deliverance, or to Neibban. It may be asked whether the state of Thautapan is the first step reached by every one that adheres to Buddha's doctrines, or whether it is the one that requires a certain progress in the way of believing and practising? It seems, from the narrative of the conversion of King Pimpathara and his followers, that the state of Thautapan is the reward of those who have shown a more than common proficiency and fervour in adhering to Buddha and his doctrines, but not the first step to enter into the assembly of the faithful and become a member thereof. One may be a simple hearer, or Upathaka, believing in the three precious things, without attaining that of Thautapan. On this occasion, the king and 100,000 of his warriors and noblemen became Thautapans, whereas the remaining 10,000 became believers and members of the assembly without reaching any further. The first entered into the stream or current leading to perfection. The latter were fervent believers, observed the five precepts, but in no way aspired to the attainment of the doctrines of a higher order.

of approaching him; that he might preach his doctrine to me; and, finally, that I might thoroughly understand all his preaching. These five wishes have been fully realised. Your law, O most excellent Buddha, is a most perfect law. To what shall I liken it as regards the happy results it produces? It is like replacing on its proper basis a vase that was bottom upwards, or setting to light objects hitherto buried in deep darkness; it is an excellent guide that shows out the right way; it is like a brilliant light, shining forth and dispelling darkness. Now I take refuge in you, your law, and the assembly of the perfect. Henceforth I will be your supporter, and to-morrow I will supply you and your disciples with all that is necessary for the support of nature." Buddha, by his silence, testified his acceptance of the offered favour. Whereupon the king rose up, prostrated himself before him, and, turning on the right, left the place, and returned to his palace.

Early in the morning Pimpathara ordered all sorts of eatables to be prepared. Meanwhile he sent messengers to Buddha to inform him that his meal was ready. Buddha, rising up, put on his dress, and, carrying his patta, set out for Radzagio, followed by his one thousand disciples. At that time a prince of Thagias, assuming the appearance of a handsome young man, walked a little distance in front of Buddha, singing to his praise several stanzas. "Behold the most excellent is advancing towards Radzagio with his one thousand disciples. In his soul he is full of meekness and amiability; he is exempt from all passions; his face is beautiful, and shines forth like the star Thigi; he has escaped out of the whirlpool of existences, and delivered himself from the miseries of transmigration. He is on his way to the city of Radzagio attended by a thousand Rahandas." (The same stanza is thrice repeated.) "He who has obtained the perfection of Ariahs, who has practised the ten great virtues, who has a universal knowledge, who knows and preaches the law of merits, who discovers at once the sublime attainments, the most perfect being, the most excellent, is entering into the city of Radzagio attended by a thousand Rahandas."

The inhabitants of the city, seeing the beautiful appearance of that young man, and hearing all that he was singing aloud, said to each other, "Who is that young man whose countenance is so lovely, and whose mouth proclaims such wonderful things?" The Thagia, hearing what was said of him, replied, "O children of men! the most excellent Phra whom ye see is gifted with an incomparable wisdom; all perfections are in him; he is free of all passions; no being can ever be compared to him; he is worthy to receive the homage and respect of men and Nats; his unwavering mind is ever fixed in truth; he announces a law extending to all things. As for me, I am but his humble servant."[4]

---

[4] Is not that young man doing the duty of forerunner of Buddha on the occasion of his solemn entry into the city of Radzagio?

The narrative of the donation of the grove or garden of Weloowen by King Pimpathara to Buddha, discloses the manner in which Buddhistic monks have become holders, not as individuals, but as members of society, of landed properties. Buddha and his disciples at first had no place as a body or a society to live in; hitherto he had taken up his quarters in any place where people were willing to receive him. He must have often been put to great inconvenience, particularly after the accession of new disciples, who daily crowded about him. The pious king felt the disadvantage the society was labouring under: he resolved to give them a place where the assembly might live and remain. The donation was as solemn as possible. It transferred to Buddha the property of the garden, without any condition, for ever. The donation, on the other hand, was fully accepted. This is, I believe, the first instance of an act of this description. The grove and monastery of Weloowon is much celebrated in Buddha's life.

In Burmese towns a particular spot is allowed for the building of houses or monasteries for Buddhistic recluses or monks. It is somewhat isolated from all other buildings, and forms, as it were, the quarter of the yellow-dressed personages. Here is a general description of one of these buildings. They are of an oblong-square shape, raised about eight or ten feet above the ground, and supported on wooden posts, and sometimes, though seldom, on brick pillars. The frame of the edifice is of wood, and planks form the wall. Above the first roof rises a second one of smaller dimensions, and a third one, yet smaller than the second. This style of roofing a building is allowed only for pagodas, Talapoins' houses, and royal palaces. The place between the soil and the floor is left open, and never converted to any use. A flight of steps, made of wood or bricks, leads to the entrance of the edifice, the interior whereof is generally divided as follows:—One vast hall designed for the reception of visitors, and used also as a schoolroom for the boys who go to learn

Having reached the king's palace, Buddha was received with every demonstration of respect, and led to the place prepared for him. Pimpathara thought within himself of

---

the rudiments of reading, writing, and sometimes ciphering. Except on grand occasions, the Talapoins generally stay in that hall, doing away with their time in the best way they can, occasionally reading books, counting their beads, chewing betel, and very often sleeping. At the extremity of the hall there is a place raised one or two steps above the level. A portion of that place is left vacant, and reserved for the sittings of the Talapoins, when they receive visitors ; the other portion, which extends to the wall, is occupied by idols or representations of Buddha, raised on pedestals, and sometimes placed on shelves, with the few implements required for exterior worship. There, too, are to be seen a few trunks ornamented with sculptures and gildings, and containing books belonging to the monastery. The hall and the place as far as the walls occupy just one-half of the oblong-square. The other half, parallel to the first, is occupied by rooms intended for the storing of alms, and as dormitories for the inmates of the house. In some monasteries the ceiling is painted and partly gilt. The cook-room, when there is one, is connected with the extremity of the square, opposite to the one occupied by the idols. It is generally on the same level with the floor of the building. Government has nothing to do with the erection, repairs, and maintenance of these edifices. They are erected and kept up by private individuals, who deem it very meritorious to build such places. Those whose piety actuates and prompts them to undertake such an expensive work assume the title of Kiaong Taga, which means supporter of a pagoda or Talapoins' residence. They are proud of such distinction, cause themselves to be called by that title, and always make it to follow their names in signing any paper or document.

The above descriptive sketch of a monastery is rather incomplete, if applied to those found in the large places of Burmah proper, and particularly in the capital. Some of them are laid out on a scale of vastness and magnificence difficult to realise by those who have not examined them. A large open gallery runs all round the building; a second one of a rectangular shape, but protected by the roof, forms, as it were, on the four sides the *vestibulum* to the central portion of the edifice. It is the place where the Phongies spend the greater part of their time, either in talking with the numerous idlers that visit them, or in teaching children. Large shutters separate this from the open verandah ; they may be thrown all open by pushing forward the lower part, the upper one remaining fixed by hinges, and so may be opened to the height required to protect the inmates from the rain and the sun. The central hall, by far the finest and loftiest of the building, is reserved for the idols and all the implements of worship, and the boxes containing the books of the monastery, commonly put together in a very disordered way. The ceiling is gilt and adorned, often with taste and elegance. A partition divides the hall into two equal parts. The one towards the east is for some huge statue of Gaudama, and smaller ones with many articles of worship. The other, facing the south, is used for several purposes ; sometimes as dormitories for the Talapoins. The posts supporting the interior part are six or eight in number, and offer the finest specimens

the thing which could prove acceptable to Phra, in order to offer it to him. He said within himself, My garden, which is situated near the city, would doubtless be a very fit place for Buddha and his followers to live in. As it lies not far from the city, it would be a place of easy resort to all those who should feel inclined to visit Buddha and pay him their respects; it is, moreover, far enough off, so that the noise and cries of the people could not be heard therein. The place is peculiarly fitted for retreat and contemplation; it will assuredly prove agreeable to Buddha. Whereupon he rose up, and, holding in his hand a golden shell like a cup, he made to Phra a solemn offering of that garden which was called Weloowon.[5] Gaudama remained

---

of teak timber I have ever seen, some being fully sixty and seventy feet high. In some of these monasteries the best parts of the interior are gilt, and sometimes the exterior sides; the ornaments of the extremities of the roof and the space between the roofs are covered with gold leaves. In those two places too are displayed carvings, which reflect great credit on the skill of native workmen, and elicit the admiration of foreigners. One of these monasteries called the kioung-dau-gye, near the place where the Arracan idol is, and another close to the place where the supreme head of Talapoins is living, are the finest and largest specimens of monasteries the writer has ever seen in Burmah.

[5] On the occasion of the presentation to Buddha of the Weloowon monastery, and of the lands attached to it, by King Pimpathara, there was observed a curious ceremony, often alluded to in Buddhist writings. He held in his hands a golden pitcher full of water, which he kept pouring down on the ground, whilst he pronounced the formula of donation. This is a ceremony of Indian origin, which, with many others, has been imported into these parts along with the religious doctrines. It is intended to be an exterior sign of, or testimony to, the offering that is made on the occasion. When it is performed, the parties pronounce a certain formula, calling the Nats, guardians of the place, to witness the act of donation, and, in particular, the Nat that is supposed to rule over the earth; and at the same time the offerer, not satisfied with receiving for his own benefit the merits of his pious liberality, expresses the earnest desire that all men, or rather all beings, should share with him in the blessings he expects to reap from his good deed. The generous and liberal disposition of the donor, it may be observed, exhibits the truly pleasing display of an amount of charity and brotherly love scarcely to be expected from the followers of an erroneous creed. The ceremony, therefore, has a twofold object, conferring unreserved and absolute efficiency on the act of donation, and dividing or apportioning the merits of the good work among all beings.

In perusing attentively the contents of this legend, the reader will easily follow the gradual development of the Buddhist religious system, and, in particular, the establishment of most of the disciplinary regulations

silent, in token of his acceptance of the gift. He preached the law and left the palace. At that time he called his disciples and said to them, "Beloved Rahans, I give you permission to receive offerings."

In the country of Radzagio there was a heterodox Rahan named Thindzi, who had under him five hundred and fifty disciples. Thariputra and Maukalan were at that time practising virtue under the guidance of that master. Here is the way they became Rahans. When they were but laymen, under the names of Oopathi and Kaulita, on a certain day, surrounded by two hundred and twenty companions, they went to the top of a lofty mountain to enjoy the sight of countless multitudes of people sporting and playing in the surrounding flat country. While they were gazing over the crowds of human beings they said to each other, "In a hundred years hence all these living beings

---

in full force in our own days in most of the countries where that form of religion has obtained a long standing and a predominating footing. At first the religious that constituted the body of the followers of Buddha were few, and could easily, in the company of their eminent teacher, procure, in accordance with the vow of strict poverty they had made, shelter, food, and raiment. There was no need for them to accept, in the shape of donation, anything beyond what was absolutely necessary for the wants of the day. We may conjecture that their leader watched with a jealous care over his religious on this point, to establish them in the spirit of poverty and of a thorough contempt for the things of this world. But the society or fraternity growing numerous, the dependence on the daily offerings appeared not to meet in sufficient manner the real necessities it felt, particularly as regards shelter. This want was quickly perceived and keenly felt by the pious King Pimpathara, who came to the resolution of presenting Buddha and his followers with a proper place to withdraw to at all times, but particularly during the wet season, when the pouring of the annual rains puts a check of four months to the religious peregrinations of the preachers. The same motives that induced Buddha to accept the proffered royal gift influenced him likewise to grant to his religious the dangerous, it is true, but the absolutely necessary permission of receiving offerings of houses and lands. From that time, the religious communities have made use of the privilege granted to them in all the places where they have been established. In Burmah this favour has not been abused, and the religious body, though never standing in want of anything required for the daily use, cannot be said to be wealthy. Having not to cast in the scales of the political balance the weight of riches, and the preponderance essentially attending the possession of them, their influence in the political affairs is not, at least exteriorly, felt.

shall have fallen a prey to death." Whereupon they rose up and left the place, but their minds were deeply preoccupied with the idea of death. While the two friends were walking silently together, they began at last to communicate to each other the result of their reflections. "If there be," said they, "a principle of death, a universal tendency towards destruction, there must be, too, its opposite principle, that of not dying and escaping destruction." On that very instant they resolved to search ardently for the excellent law that teaches the way of not dying, and obtain the state of perfect fixity and immutability. In those parts there lived six heterodox teachers who were named Mekkali, Gau, Sala, Thindzi, Jani, and Ganti; among them Thindzi was the only one who, with his disciples, wore white clothes. They went to the place where lived the Rahan Thindzi, placed themselves under his direction, and put on the dress of Rahan. Within three days they acquired the science, wisdom, and knowledge of their teacher without having as yet reached the object of their eager pursuit. They said to Thindzi, "Teacher, is this all that you know? And have you no other science to teach us?" "I have indeed," replied the teacher, "taught you all the knowledge I possess." Finding nothing satisfactory in the answer, the two friends said, "Let us continue seeking for the law that has reality in itself; the first that shall have discovered it shall, without delay, communicate it to the other."

On a certain morning one of Gaudama's disciples named Athadzi, having put on his religious habit, and carrying his patta on his left arm, went out to receive his rice. Everything about his person was noble and graceful; his countenance and behaviour were at once gentle and dignified, whether he walked or stopped, looked forward to the right or the left, or sat in a cross-legged position. The false Rahan Oopathi, who became afterwards Tharipputra, perceiving the Rahan Athadzi with such a meek and dignified deportment, said to himself, "Such a Rahan is assuredly worthy to receive offerings; he has doubtless attained perfection. I will go to him and ask him, in case he has had a teacher, who is that distinguished instructor under whom he practises virtue; and in case of his being himself a teacher, what is the doctrine that he teaches. But it is not becoming to put to him any question whilst he is on his way to beg alms. I will follow at a distance." Athadzi, having collected alms, left the city and went to a small dzeat, where he sat down and ate his meal. Oopathi followed him thither. Having entered into the dzeat, he rendered to him the services that a disciple usually pays to his teacher. When the meal of Athadzi was over, he poured water over his hands, and with a heart overflowing with joy, he conversed with him for a while. He withdrew then to a becoming distance, and addressed him as follows, "Great Rahan, your exterior is full of meekness and benevolence; your countenance bespeaks the purity and innocence of your soul; if you be a disciple, pray under what teacher have you become Rahan? Who is your guide in the way to perfection? and what is the doctrine he is preaching to you?" "Young Rahan," replied Athadzi, "have you not heard of the illustrious Buddha, the descendant of a long succession of great monarchs, who has entered the profession of Rahan? I have become Rahan under him; he is my teacher; to his doctrine I cling with all the energy of my soul." "What is the doctrine of that great master?" asked Oopathi. "I am but a novice in the profession," replied modestly Athadzi, "and am as yet imperfectly acquainted with the doctrine of my teacher. The little, however, I know, I will freely communicate to you." Oopathi entreated him to do so. Athadzi replied, "The law which I have learned at the feet of Buddha explains all that relates to matter, to the principles that act upon it, to passions, and to the mind; it makes man despise all that is material, conquer his passions, and regulate his mind." On hearing this doctrine, Oopathi felt the ties of passions gradually relaxing and giving way; his soul became, as it were, disentangled from the influence of the senses. He became enamoured with such a pure and perfect law, and obtained the condition of Thautapan. Convinced that he had at last found what he had hitherto searched after in vain, the law of Neibban, he went without delay to his friend, to make him share in the beneficial result of his fortunate discovery. Kaulita, perceiving his friend coming up to him with a rejoicing countenance, indicative of the happiness his soul was inwardly enjoying, asked him if he had found what he had hitherto vainly looked for. Oopathi related to him all the particulars of his conversation with the Rahan Athadzi. Whereupon Kaulita became instantly a Thautapan. Both resolved to leave their teacher Thindzi, and go immediataly to place themselves under the guidance of Buddha. Three times they applied for permission to execute their design, and three times it was denied them. At last they departed, each with his two hundred and twenty companions. Thindzi, enraged at being left alone, died, vomiting blood from his mouth.

When the two friends and their followers were drawing near to the place of Weloowon, Phra assembled all his disciples and said to them, "Behold these two friends coming up to me; they will become my two beloved disciples; their minds are acute and penetrating; they actually take delight in the law of Neibban; their thoughts are converging towards that great centre of truth; they come to me, and they will become my two most excellent disciples." While he was speaking, the two friends crossed the threshold of the monastery, and prostrated themselves at the feet of Buddha, humbly craving the favour of being admitted among his disciples to practise virtue under his immediate direction. On this occasion Phra uttered the following words: "O Bickus, come to me; I preach the most excellent law: apply yourselves to the practice of the most perfect works, which will put an end to all miseries." A suit of dress and a patta were handed to each of the two friends, that were henceforth to be called Thariputra and Maukalan, and they became members of the assembly. Having put on the new dress, they appeared to the eyes of all with the decent and dignified deportment of Rahans that had sixty years of profession. Their followers became Bickus of the second order. Seven days after, Maukalan became a Rahanda; but it took fifteen days for Thariputra to obtain the same favour. The two new converts were elevated to the dignity of disciples of the right and of the left; that is to say, they obtained precedence over all others.

The distinction thus granted to Thariputra and Maukalan excited a feeling of jealousy among the disciples of Buddha. In their conversations they complained to each other of the preference given to those who had just been admitted among the members of assembly. They went so far as to say that Buddha had acted in this case under the influence of human considerations. These remarks were brought to the notice of Buddha, who assembled his disciples, and said to them, "Beloved Bickus, my conduct in this instance has not been guided by unworthy motives; I have acted as I ought to have done. In the days of the Phra Anaumadathi, the two friends were leading the life of ascetics. They paid the greatest respect and veneration to the then existing Buddha, and entreated him, by repeated supplications, to hold out to them the solemn promise that they would become the disciples of the right and of the left of some future Buddha. Anaumadathi replied to them that the object of their wishes should be granted unto them when the Buddha Gaudama would appear in the world. This is, beloved Bickus, the reason that has influenced me in elevating to the first rank the two new converts." The answer completely satisfied the disciples, and effectually silenced all murmurs. Further particulars regarding the promise that these two illustrious friends received in the time of the Buddha Anaumadathi may be read, with circumstantial details, in the book called Apadan-tera.

The inhabitants of the Magatha country, seeing that so many persons, chiefly belonging to the first families, were embracing the profession of Rahans, said amongst themselves, "Behold how the Rahan Gaudama, by his preachings, causes the depopulation of the country, and forces countless wives to the unwished-for state of widowhood. A thousand Rathees have embraced the profession of Rahans; all the disciples of Thindzi have followed their example; many others will soon tread in their footsteps. What will become of our country?" With these and other expressions, they gave vent to their hatred of the Rahans, and endeavoured to pour over them all kinds of ridicule and abuse. They concluded by saying, "The great Rahan has come to the city of Radzagio, which is like a cow-pen, surrounded by five hills;[6] he has now with him the disciples of Thindzi; who will be the next to go to him?" The Rahans, hearing all that was said against them, went to Buddha and related to him all that they

[6] In his Archæological Survey Report, General Cunningham has supplied us with an accurate description of the position and ruins of the celebrated city of Radzagio. His own measurements of the old ramparts, that are still visible, agree to a surprising degree with those of the two Chinese pilgrims, Fa-Hian and Hwen-Tsan, who visited the same spot in the fourth and sixth century of our era. The city was situated in a valley, surrounded by five hills, which are named Gigakuta, Isigli, Wibhara, Wipula, and Pandawa. It was five miles in circumference. This is meant for the circuit of the inner wall. The exterior one was nearly nine miles. On the southern face of the Wibhara mountain is the famous cave at the entrance of which was held the first Buddhist council, not long after the cremation of Buddha's remains. There is no doubt that the heights were, in the palmy days of Buddhism, covered with Buddhistic monuments. As the place was subsequently occupied by Brahmins and Mussulmans, the Dzedis and monasteries have been mercilessly pulled down to furnish materials for musjids, tombs, and temples. The eminences are now covered with Mussulman tombs, which occupy the places formerly adorned with pagodas. Springs of hot water were numerous in the vicinity of the city. The writer has only met once in Buddhistic compositions an allusion to that natural phenomenon so beneficial to people living in hot climates. The modern Rajghir, both by name and situation, brings to our recollection the celebrated capital of Magatha, so famous in Buddhistic annals. As the extent of Radzagio has been so accurately determined by ancient and modern visitors, one can well afford to laugh at the immensely exaggerated number of houses that are supposed by certain Burmese writers to have composed the city.

had heard. To console them, Buddha said, "Beloved Bickus, the abuses, sarcasms, and ridicule levelled at you shall not last long; seven days hence all shall be over. Here is the reply you will make to the revilers: Like all his predecessors, Buddha is striving to preach a most perfect law; by the means of the truths which he proclaims for the benefit of all, he brings men over to himself. What shall it avail any man to feel envious at the success he obtains by so legitimate a means?" The same torrent of ridicule having been poured on the Rahans, when they went out, they followed the advice of their great teacher, replied in the manner they had been taught to do, and the storm was soon over. The people understood that the great Rahan was preaching a perfect law, and that he never resorted but to fair means to attract disciples round his person. Here ends the narrative of the conversion and vocation of Thariputra and Maukalan.

CHAPTER VIII.

Thoodaudana, desirous to see his son, sends messengers to him—They become converts—Kaludari, a last messenger, prevails on Buddha to go to Kapilawot—His reception—Conversion of the king and of Yathaudara—Nanda and Raoula put on the religious habit—Conversion of Ananda and of several of his relatives—Temptation of Ananda—Conversion of Eggidatta—Story of Tsampooka.

WHILST the most excellent Phra remained in the Weloowon monastery, enjoying himself in the midst of his disciples and the crowds of hearers that daily resorted thither to listen to his preachings, his father Thoodaudana [1] who

[1] In glancing over the episode of Thoodaudana's deputation to his son, to invite him to come and visit his native country, the reader is almost compelled to confess that the motive that influenced the king was only inspired by the natural feeling of beholding once more, before he died, him whose fame, spread far and wide, rendered him an object of universal admiration. Was the monarch induced by considerations of a higher order to send for Buddha? There is no distinct proof in support of this supposition. He was his father, and he but obeyed and followed the impulse of his paternal heart. He entertained a high sense of his son's distinguished qualifications. He had faith in the wonderful signs foretelling his future matchless greatness. He desired, therefore, to honour him in an extraordinary way, on the very spot where he had been born. But he appeared to concern himself very little about the doctrines he was preaching with a success never before equalled. The king exhibited a great amount of worldly-mindedness, until his mind had been enlightened by the oral instructions of the great reformer.

It is difficult, if not impossible, to form an accurate idea of the effect produced on the mass of the people by Buddha's preachings. We see that eminent and zealous reformer surrounded by thousands of distinguished disciples in the country of Radzagio. These converts belonged chiefly to the class of anchorites and philosophers, already alluded to in foregoing notes as existing at the time Buddha began to enter the career of preaching. But the great bulk of the populations of the various places he visited seemed to have received for a long time little or no impressions from his discourses. The opponents of Buddha, the Brahmins in particular, exercised a powerful influence over the public mind. They used it most effectually for retaining their ancient hold over the masses. It required the extraordinary display of

had ever been anxiously and sedulously gathering every possible information respecting his son, from the time he withdrew into solitude, and performed during six years

---

the greatest wonders to break through the almost insuperable barriers raised by his enemies. From that period we see the people following Buddha, crowding round him, and showing unmistakable signs of belief in him.

The only explanation to account for this undeniable result is the philosophical method adopted by Buddha in expounding the principles of his system. His mode of proceeding in the gradual development of his ideas retained the abstruseness peculiar to subjects discussed in schools of philosophy. The technical terms so familiar to scholars prove enigmatical to the uninitiated *vulgus*. It takes a long time before maxims elaborated by scholars are so far popularised as to be understood by the unlearned, which in every age and country have always constituted the great mass of the people. If the mind of the generality of men is unable to comprehend at first a system of doctrines, based on metaphysics, we cannot wonder at the slow progress made by the preachings of the great philosopher: but the working of wonders is a tangible fact operating upon the senses of the multitude, eliciting their applauses, and disposing them to yield an implicit faith to all the instructions imparted by the wonderful being that is gifted with supernatural powers. Feelings, and not reason, become the foundation of a belief which grows stronger in proportion to the mysterious obscurity that encompasses the proposed dogmas, when supported by wonderful deeds.

At the time Thoodaudana sent messengers to his son, the great work of conversion was carried on with a most complete and hitherto unheard-of success. The hall of the Weloowon monastery was too small for the thousands that flocked thither to hear Gaudama. Outside its precincts, crowds stood motionless, listening with unabated attention to the discourses that fell from his lips. So crowded was the audience that the messengers had no chance to make their way to the presence of the preacher. Struck with the intense attention paid to what was said by their master's son, they too wished to make themselves acquainted with the subjects of the instruction. What was listened to from motives of mere curiosity, soon made a deep impression upon their mind. The magic power of the irresistible eloquence of Buddha worked a thorough change almost instantaneously in their dispositions, and they became converts. So perfect was their conversion, that they forgot for the sake of truth the very object of their mission. They became at once members of the Assembly, and took rank among the Rahans. They attained the state of Ariahs, and were foremost among the perfect. The great attainments arrived at by the Ariahs communicate to the material portion of their being such an extraordinary amount of amazing virtues or properties, that it becomes so refined as to partake, to a certain degree, of a spiritual nature. Hence we see the Rahandas going over immense distances through the air, and performing deeds of a supernatural order. The power of working miracles is, therefore, inherent in perfection; and it is greater or smaller in proportion to the degree of perfection possessed by individuals. We find that power expanded in Buddha to an unlimited extent, because his mental attainments were boundless.

the hardest works of bodily mortification, was then informed that his son had already begun to preach the most perfect law, and was actually staying in the city of Radzagio. He felt then an irresistible desire to see him once more before his death. He therefore ordered a nobleman of his court into his presence, and said to him: "Nobleman, take with you a retinue of a thousand followers, and go forthwith to the city of Radzagio. Tell my son that I am now much advanced in years, that I long to see him once more before I die; desire him, therefore, to come over with you to the country of Kapilawot." The nobleman, having received the royal message, took leave from the king, and attended by a thousand followers, set out for Radzagio. When he drew near to the Weloowon monastery, he found it crowded with an innumerable multitude of people, listening with a respectful attention to Buddha's instructions. Unwilling to disturb the audience, the nobleman delayed for a while the delivery of his royal master's message. Halting at the verge of the crowd, he, with his followers, eagerly lent the utmost attention to all that Buddha was saying. They at once obtained the state of Arahat, and applied for admission into the order of Rahans. The favour was granted. To obtain pattas and tsiwarans for so great a number of applicants, Buddha stretched his right arm, when there appeared at once the pattas and dresses required. The new converts put on the dress of their order, when they all appeared with the dignified countenance and meek deportment of Rahans who had had sixty years of profession. Having arrived at the exalted state of Ariahs, they became indifferent and unconcerned about all the things of this material world, and the king's mandate was entirely lost sight of.

The sovereign of Kapilawot, seeing that his nobleman did not return from the country of Magatha,[2] and that no

[2] Magatha is a country in the north of India. It occupied nearly the same extent of territory as that now called North Behar in Bengal. The Pali or

news was heard of him, despatched a second messenger with an equal number of followers on the same errand. They all were taken up with Buddha's preachings and became Rahandas. The same thing happened to seven messengers successively sent to Radzagio for the same

---

sacred language of the southern Buddhists is often called the language of Magatha. Hence we may infer that it was the common language of that country. It is probable that the Pali language was extensively spoken in the days of Gaudama, and it was the channel through which he and his disciples long after him conveyed their religious instructions to the multitude of converts. The Pitagat, or the last amended collection of sacred writings, is written in Pali, which is looked upon in Ceylon, Nepaul, Burmah, and Siam as the language of sacred literature. Except in some old manuscripts, where the old square Pali letters are used, the Burmese employ their common alphabetic characters for writing Pali words. The words, having to pass first through a Burmese ear, and next being expressed by Burmese letters, undergo great changes. To such an extent does the metamorphosis reach, that very often they are scarcely recognisable. The Burmans, however, deserve great credit for having, in very many instances, retained in their orthography of Pali words letters which, though not at all sounded, indicate to the eye the nature of the word, its origin, and its primitive form.

In the southern parts of Burmah the Pali language is learned but not studied, used, but not understood by the inmates of monasteries. They are all obliged to learn certain formulas of prayers to be daily recited in private, and, on great and solemn occasions, to be chanted aloud in the presence of a crowd of pious hearers. The writer, anxious to acquire some knowledge of the sacred language, often visited those monks, who, among their brethren, enjoyed a certain fame for learning, with the express intention of becoming a humble student, under the direction of one of the best informed of the society. He was thoroughly disappointed to find those who proffered their services in great earnest quite ignorant, and utterly incapable of giving him the least assistance.

The Burmese have translated in their vernacular tongue most of the sacred writings. In many instances the translation is not exactly what we call interlineary, but it approaches to it as nearly as possible. Two, three, or four Pali words are written down, and the translation in Burmese follows with a profusion of words which often confuses and perplexes the reader; then come again a few other Pali words, accompanied also with the translation, and so on throughout the whole work. The art of translating well and correctly from one language into another is not so common as many persons may imagine. In a good translator are required many qualifications which are not to be easily met with, particularly in a Burman, to whom we may give credit for knowing well his own tongue, but who, without detracting from his literary attainments, is certainly an indifferent Pali scholar. These translations may convey, perhaps, the general meaning of the original, but, as regards the correct meaning of each term, it is a luxury ever denied to the reader of such crude and imperfect compositions.

purpose. They, with their respective retinues, became converts of the first class.

Disappointed at seeing that none of the messengers had returned to bring him any news regarding his son, King Thoodaudana exclaimed: "Is there no one in my palace that bears any affection unto me? Shall I not be able to get a person who could procure for me some information respecting my son?" He looked among his courtiers and selected one, named Kaludari, as the fittest person for such a difficult errand. Kaludari had been born on the same day as Buddha: with him he had spent the age of his infancy, and lived on terms of the most sincere friendship. The king said to him: "Noble Kaludari, you know how earnestly I long to see my son. Nine messengers have already been sent to the city of Radzagio to invite my son to come over to me, and none of them has as yet come back to me, to bring information respecting the object of my tenderest affections. I am old now, and the end of my existence is quite uncertain; could you not undertake to bring my son over to me? Whether you become Rahan or not, let me have the happiness of contemplating once more my beloved son ere I leave this world." The nobleman promised to the king to comply with his royal order. Attended by a retinue of a thousand followers, he set out for the city of Radzagio. Having reached the Weloowon monastery, he listened to Buddha's preachings, and, like the former messengers, he became at once a Rahanda with all his followers.

Gaudama, having obtained the Buddhaship, spent the first season (Lent) in the solitude of Migadawon. Thence he proceeded to the solitude of Ooroowela, where he remained three months, until he had completed the work of converting the three Kathabas. It was on the full moon of Piatho (January) that he entered into the city of Radzagio, accompanied by his thousand disciples. He had just stayed two months in that place, so that there were five months since he had left the country of Baranathee.

Seven days after Kaludari's arrival, the cold season being nearly over, the new convert addressed Buddha as follows: "Illustrious Phra, the cold season is over, and the warm season has just begun; this is now the proper time to travel through the country; nature wears a green aspect; the trees of the forests are in full blossom; the roads are lined to right and left with trees loaded with fragrant blossoms and delicious fruits; the peacock proudly expands its magnificent tail; birds of every description fill the air with their ravishing and melodious singing. At this season heat and cold are equally temperate, and nature is scattering profusely its choicest gifts." By such and similar allurements Kaludari endeavoured to dispose Buddha to undertake a journey to Kapilawot. Gaudama hearing all these words said: "What means this? To what purpose are uttered so many fine expressions?" Kaludari replied: "Your father, O blessed Buddha, is advanced in years; he has sent me to invite you to come over to Kapilawot, that he might see you before his death. He and your royal parents will be rejoiced at hearing your most excellent law." "Well," said Buddha, "go and tell the Rahans to hold themselves ready for the journey." It was arranged that ten thousand Rahandas from Magatha and ten thousand from Kapilawot would accompany the illustrious traveller. The distance between the two countries is sixty youdzanas.[3] Sixty days were to be employed

[3] It is difficult to ascertain exactly the length of the measure called youdzana, formerly used to indicate land distances. It varies from five to twelve English miles. In measuring the distance from Radzagio to the Brahmin village of Nalanda, the birthplace of Thariputra, which is one youdzana, General Cunningham has found it to be seven miles. This would induce us to hold as certain that at the epoch when Fa-Hian visited the place, the youdzana was equal to seven miles or forty Chinese *li*. But this would not prove that the more ancient youdzana was not shorter than the one used in the time of the Chinese pilgrim. Several authors maintain that such is the case. It appears, likewise, that the length of that measure of distance has varied with localities and places to such an extent that it has been found in some countries to be equal to more than twelve miles. We believe that when that measure of distance is mentioned in this work, one would not be far from the truth in estimating its length six or seven English miles at the utmost.

in going over that distance, so they were to travel at the rate of but one youdzana a day.

Kaludari was anxious to go and inform the king of the happy issue of his negotiation. He flew through the air, and in a short time reached the palace of the lord of Kapilawot. The king, seeing him, was exceedingly glad; he desired the illustrious Rahan to sit in a becoming place, and gave orders that his patta should be filled with the choicest dishes from the royal table. Meanwhile Kaludari related to the king all the circumstances attending his journey. When he had spoken, Thoodaudana desired him to take his meal. Kaludari begged to be excused, saying that he would go and take his meal in the presence of Buddha. "Where is he now?" replied the king. "Mighty lord," answered Kaludari, "Buddha, accompanied by twenty thousand Rahandas, is on his way to this country, to pay a visit to his royal father; on this very day he has left the city of Radzagio." Thoodaudana was exceedingly pleased; he said again to Kaludari, "Eat your meal here, and please to take another meal to my son; I wish to supply him daily with food during his journey." Kaludari acceded to the king's request. When his meal was over, they cleansed his patta with the most exquisite perfumes, and afterwards filled it with the best and choicest eatables. The patta was then respectfully handed to the aërial messenger, who, in the presence of a large crowd of people, rose in the air with the patta under his arm, and in an instant arrived in presence of Gaudama, to whom he offered the vessel containing the delicious food from his father's table. Buddha received the food with pleasure, and ate it. The same thing was daily performed during all the time the journey lasted. Kaludari went every day to the palace through the air, ate his meal there, and brought that of his distinguished instructor, who during all the way partook of no other food but that which was brought over to him from his father's palace. Every day Kaludari carried news of the progress of Buddha's journey. By this means he increased in the heart of all an ardent desire of seeing him, and disposed every one to wait on the great Gaudama with favourable and good dispositions. The services rendered on this occasion by Kaludari were much valued by Buddha himself, who said: "Kaludari is disposing the people to welcome our arrival; he is therefore one of the most excellent among my disciples."

The princes and all the members of the royal family, having heard of Gaudama's arrival, consulted among themselves as to the best means of paying due respect to the noble and illustrious visitor. They selected the grove of Nigraudatha[4] as the fittest place to receive him with his disciples. The place was properly cleared and made ready for the long-expected company. The inhabitants of the country, attended with their richest dress, carrying

---

[4] The attentive reader of this work cannot fail to remark the general tendencies of Buddhism to isolation, retirement, and solitude. In a retired position, the mind is less distracted or dissipated by exterior objects; it possesses a greater share of self-control, and is fitter for the arduous work of attentive reflection and deep meditation. Whenever Buddha, attended by his followers, reaches a place where he is to stay for a while, a grove outside the city is invariably selected. Thither the great preacher retires, as to a beloved solitude. He enjoys it beyond all that can be said. Alone with his spiritual family, unconcerned about the affairs of this world, he breathes at ease the pure atmosphere of a complete calm; his undisturbed soul soars freely in the boundless regions of spiritualism. What he has seen and discovered during his contemplative errands he imparts with a placid countenance and a mild voice to his disciples, endeavouring thereby to make them progress in the way of knowledge and perfection. In those solitary abodes of peace Buddha was willing to receive all those who wished for instruction. They were all, without distinction of rank or caste, admitted into the presence of him who came professedly to point to men the way to happiness, helping them to disentangle themselves from the trammels of passions. He preached to all the most excellent law. The tendency to retreat and withdrawal from worldly tumult is, in our own days, conspicuous in the care taken by Buddhistic monks to have their houses built in some lonely quarter of a town, assigned exclusively for that special purpose, or, as is oftener the case, in fine places at a small distance from the walls. Some of those groves, in the centre of which rise the peaceful abodes of Rahans, the writer has often seen and much admired. In towns or large villages, where the ground is uneven, the small heights are generally crowned with the dwellings of religious.

flowers and perfumes, went out to meet Buddha.[5] Children of both sexes opened the procession; they were followed by the children of the noblest families; next came all the persons belonging to the royal family. All went to the grove of Nigraudatha, where Buddha had just

---

[5] The narrative of Buddha's reception in his father's royal city suggests two reflections. The first is, that the saying *Nemo Propheta in suâ patriâ* was as true in the days of Gaudama as it has been in subsequent ages. The mountains of Kapilawot had often re-echoed the praises of Buddha and the recital of his wonderful doings. The splendid retinue of twenty thousand distinguished converts that attended his person, the hitherto unwitnessed display of miraculous powers, &c.,—all these peculiarly remarkable circumstances seemed more than sufficient to secure for him a distinguished reception among his kinsmen, who ought to have been proud of being connected with him by the ties of relationship. Such, however, was not the case. Actuated by the lowest feelings of base jealousy, his relatives refused to pay him the respect he was so well entitled to. Their wretched obduracy was to be conquered by the awe and fear his miraculous power inspired.

The second reflection suggested by the recital of the ceremonies observed on the occasion of Buddha's reception in his native country is the truly pleasing fact of seeing the weaker sex appearing in public divested of the shackles put upon it by oriental jealousy. In Burmah and Siam the doctrines of Buddhism have produced a striking, and, to the lover of true civilisation, a most interesting result, viz., established the almost complete equality of the condition of women with that of men. In those countries women are not miserably confined in the interior of their houses, without the remotest chance of ever appearing in public. They are seen circulating freely in the streets; they preside at the *comptoirs*, and hold an almost exclusive possession of the bazaars. Their social position is more elevated in every respect than that of the persons of their sex in the regions where Buddhism is not the predominating creed. They may be said to be men's companions, and not their slaves. They are active, industrious, and by their labours and exertions contribute their full share towards the maintenance of the family. The marital rights, however, are fully acknowledged by a respectful behaviour towards their lords. In spite of all that has been said by superficial observers, I feel convinced that manners are less corrupted in those countries where women enjoy liberty, than in those where they are buried alive by a barbarous and despotic custom in the grave of an opprobrious and vice-generating slavery. Buddhism disapproves of polygamy, but it tolerates divorce. In this respect the habits of the people are of a damnable laxity. Polygamy is very rare in Burmah among the people. This nefarious and anti-social practice is left to the magnates of the land, from the king down to a petty myowon, who make a part of their greatness consist in placing themselves above public opinion, above moral and religious precepts, for enjoying the unrestrained gratification of the basest appetite. Though divorce be a thing of common occurrence, it is looked upon as an imperfection, merely tolerated for the sake of human frailty.

arrived with the twenty thousand Rahans that accompanied him.

The princes, secretly influenced by pride, thus thought within themselves: This Prince Theiddat is younger than we all; he is but our nephew, let the young people prostrate themselves before him; as to ourselves, let us remain sitting down behind them. This was quickly perceived by Buddha, who said to himself: My relatives refuse to prostrate themselves before me; I will now even compel them to do so. Whereupon he entered into ecstasy, rose in the air, and standing over the heads of his relatives, as a person shaking dust over them, he exhibited to their astonished regards, on a white mango-tree, wonders of fire and water. Thoodaudana, surprised at such a wonderful display of supernatural power, exclaimed: "Illustrious Buddha, on the day you were born they brought you to the presence of the Rathee Kaladewela, to do homage to him; on that occasion, having seen you placing your two feet on the Rathee's forehead, I prostrated myself before you for the first time. On the day of the ploughing solemn rejoicings, you were placed under the shade of the tree Tsampoothapye. The sun by its daily motion had caused the shadows of all surrounding trees to change their direction; that of the tree under which you were placed alone remaining unmoved. I prostrated myself a second time before you; and now, at the sight of this new wonder, I again bow down to you." The example of the king was instantly imitated by all the princes, who humbly bowed down to Buddha. Satisfied with having humbled his proud relatives, Buddha came down and sat in the place prepared for him. He then caused a shower of red rain to pour down over the assembled multitudes. It had the virtue to wet those who liked it, and not to wet those who disliked it. "This is not," said Buddha, "the only time when such a wonder has happened; the same thing took place once during one of my former existences, when I was Prince Wethandra." He went on, relating the most interesting circumstances of that former state of existence. The whole assembly now delighted at hearing his preachings and witnessing the display of his power. They all withdrew when the preaching was over, and retired to their respective places, without, however, inviting Buddha to come and take his meals in their houses.

On the following morning, Buddha set out with his twenty thousand followers to get his meal. When he had arrived at the gate of the city, he stood for a while, deliberating within himself whether he would go to the palace to receive his meal, or go from street to street to beg for it. He paused for a while, reflecting on the course of conduct that had been followed by all the former Buddhas. Having known that they all, without exception, had been in the habit of going out from house to house in quest of their food, he resolved at once to follow their example. Whereupon he entered the city and began to perambulate the streets in search of his food. The citizens, from the various stories of their houses, were looking out with amazement at such an unusual sight. "How is this?" said they; "we see Prince Raoula and his mother Yathaudara going out attired in the richest dresses, sitting in the most elegant conveyance, and now Prince Theiddat[6] is appearing in the streets with his hair

---

[6] Buddhist monks, out of humility and contempt for all worldly things, do not allow hairs or beard to grow. They walk barefooted, wearing a yellow dress of the simplest make. They are bound to live on the alms that are freely bestowed upon them. The regulations of the Wini are, in this respect, most explicit, and leave no room for false interpretation. A Rahan, having renounced the world, and divested himself of all worldly property, is bound by his professional vows to rely for his daily food on what he may obtain by begging. Hence the appellation of Bickus, or mendicants, always bestowed on them by Gaudama, whenever he addresses them in particular on certain points regarding their profession. In Burmah, as soon as the day begins to dawn, a swarm of yellow-dressed monks sally forth from their abode with the patta under the left arm, and perambulate the streets in quest of food. They never ask for anything; they accept what is voluntarily tendered to them, without uttering a single word of thanks, or even looking at their generous benefactors. This action of bestowing alms on the Rahans is deemed a most meritorious one. The offerer, therefore, becomes liberal, not on account

and beard shaved, and his body covered with a yellow dress befitting a mendicant. Such a thing is unbecoming indeed." Whilst they were holding this language, on a sudden, rays of the purest light shot forth from the body of Buddha, and illuminated all the objects around his person. At this unexpected sight, they all joined in praising and extolling the virtue and glory of Buddha.

King Thoodaudana was soon informed that his son was perambulating the streets of the city in the dress of a mendicant. Startled at such a news, he rose, and seizing the extremity of his outer garment, ran to the encounter of his son. As soon as he saw him he exclaimed: "Illustrious Buddha, why do you expose us to such a shame? Is it necessary to go from door to door to beg your food? Could not a better and more decent mode be resorted to for supplying your wants?" "My noble father," said Buddha, "it is meet and convenient that all Rahans should go out and beg their food." "But," replied the monarch, "are we not the descendants of the illustrious Prince Thamadat? There is not a single person in our illustrious race that has ever acted in such an indecorous manner." Buddha retorted, "My noble father,[7] the descent from the

---

of the person he is assisting, but because of the abundant merits he hopes to derive from the act. This notion agrees very well with the leading tenets of Buddhism.

[7] The answer of Buddha to his royal father is a most remarkable one, and deserves the attention of the observer. The great moralist does away with all the prerogatives man may derive from birth, rank, and riches. Law alone can confer titles of true greatness and genuine nobility. The fervent and zealous observers of the law are alone entitled to the respect of their fellow-men. The begging of alms may be, in the eyes of worldlings, a low and mean action, but it becomes a most dignified one, because it is enforced by the law. This lofty principle boldly establishes the superiority of virtue upon the strongest basis, and sanctions the moral code he was destined to publish to men and saddle on their conscience. The criterion of all that is good, excellent, praiseworthy, and meritorious is no more to depend on the arbitrary and very often erroneous views of men, but must rest upon the immutable tenets of the eternal law, discovered, revived, and published by the omniscient Buddha. This truth, like a flash of light, illuminated the king's mind, and, at this first preaching of his son, he attained the first of the four states of perfection.

The princes Thamadat and Thoodaudana boast to have descended

glorious princes Thamadat is something that belongs both to you and your royal family: the lineage of a Buddha is quite different from that of kings and princes; it bears no resemblance to it. Their ways and manners must essentially differ from those of princes. All former Buddhas have always been in the habit of thus going out in search of their food." Then stopping his course and standing in the street, he uttered the following stanzas, "My noble father, it is not proper that I should ever neglect the duty of receiving alms; it is an action good in itself, tallying with truth, deserving of great merits, and productive of happiness in this and future existences." When he had spoken, his father obtained the state of Thautapan. He went to the palace with his father, saying, "Those who go to beg food according to the injunction and prescription of the law, are doing well, and prepare themselves for a state of happiness both for the present and future: those who do go begging, but without any regard to the ordinances of the law, ought to refrain from doing so." He was speaking in that way when he entered the palace. His aunt Gaudamee became a Thautapan.

---

from are, according to Buddhistic sacred books, the princes who were elected to hold supreme power at the very moment the words *mine* and *thine* began to be heard amongst men, after they had eaten the rice called Tsale, and become subject to passions, that is to say, at the origin of society, in the beginning of the world. The kings of Burmah, down to the present occupant of the throne, who are descended, in their opinion, from the Kapilawot line of kings, lay claim to the same distinction. The writer has heard the present King of Burmah very coolly stating as a matter of fact, which no one could think of contradicting, that he was descended from the Thamadat's royal line.

The Princess Yathaudara, mentioned in this narrative, had been the wife of Buddha, ere he had withdrawn into solitude and renounced the world. A son had just been born to him when he left his father's palace. His name was Raoula. The doctrine of the influence of merits gathered during former existences is forcibly illustrated in the case of Yathaudara, who, unmindful of the position she occupied in former years, did not hesitate to fling herself at Buddha's feet, acknowledging him to be worthy of all honour and veneration. Her former merits disposed her to view in him, who had been her husband, the extraordinary personage who was to lead men through the path of virtue to the deliverance.

His father, after this second preaching, reached the state Thagadagan.

Thoodaudana invited Phra and his followers to ascend to the upper part of the palace and partake of the meal prepared for them. When the meal was over, all the ladies of the palace came to pay their respects to Buddha. Some of them urged the Princess Yathaudara to do the same. But she refused to comply with their request, in the hope that a greater deference would be shown to her, and Buddha would come and visit her in her apartments. Perceiving her studied inattendance, Phra said to his father, "My noble father, I will go and visit the princess, and will, without saying a single word, make her pay obedience to, and prostrate herself before me. King Thoodaudana took up the patta, and accompanied his son to the princess's apartments, together with his two disciples, Thariputra and Maukalan. Buddha had scarcely been seated on the place destined to him, when Yathaudara threw herself at Buddha's feet, and placing her two hands on both ankles, touched repeatedly the upper part with her forehead. Meanwhile Thoodaudana mentioned to his son the respectful and affectionate regard she had ever entertained for his person. "Since she heard," added the king, "that you had put on the yellow robe, she would wear only clothes of that colour; when she knew that you took but one meal a day, that you slept on a small and low couch, and gave up, without regret, the use of perfumes, she instantly followed your example, ate but one meal a day, slept on a low couch, and gave up without grief the use of essences." "Illustrious monarch," replied Buddha, "I do not wonder at the practices of late observed by the Princess Yathaudara; in former times, when her merits were as yet only few and imperfect, she was living at the foot of a certain mountain, and knew, even then, how to behave with becomingness, and attend with a strict regard to all religious duties."

This very day, that is to say, the second day after the full moon of Katson, was fixed as the time for the taking place of five grand ceremonies. Nanda,[8] the younger brother of Buddha, was to have his head washed, to put on the

---

[8] Nanda was Buddha's younger brother, or rather half-brother. His mother was Patzapati, the younger sister of Maia. Since Buddha had renounced the world, Nanda had become the presumptive heir to the crown of Kapilawot. His conversion grieved the king much, who, to prevent the recurrence of such an event, exacted from the great reformer that in after times no one could be admitted into the society of the perfect, without having previously obtained the consent of his parents; failing such a condition, the act of admission should be considered as null and void. Hence, we read in the book of ordination, or admittance to the dignity of Rahan, that the person directed by the president of the assembly to examine the candidate never omits to inquire of him whether he has obtained the consent of his parents.

The conversion of Raoula followed that of Nanda. Of this new and distinguished convert no mention is made afterwards in the course of this work. He must, in all likelihood, have become a celebrated member of the assembly, as he was trained up to the functions and duties of his profession by the greatest and most renowned disciples, such as Maukalan, Thariputra, and Kathaba.

In the history of Buddhism, the Dzetawon monastery is not inferior in celebrity to that of Weloowon. Therein Gaudama announced during a certain night the thirty-six beatitudes of the law to a Nat that had come and requested him to make him acquainted with the most perfect points of his law, In the division of the scriptures called Thoots, or sermons, we see that the most important have been delivered in the hall of that monastery.

Here is another instance of a donation of landed property to a religious corporation. In the first case, the gift had been made to him and to his actual followers. But in this circumstance, Phra desires the rich and pious benefactor to make the donation, not only in behalf of self and the present assembly, but also in that of all future members, who might resort to this place. In a Buddhistic point of view, we may conclude that the advice given to the donor was intended as a means of multiplying the sum of the merits of his liberality, which must be commensurate with the number of the individuals to whom it is designed to be extended.

According to the principle respecting property, which from immemorial time has prevailed under almost all despotic governments in Asia, which recognises the head of the state as the sole, real, and absolute owner of the soil, it is evident that the act of donation was, legally speaking, a declaration or a statement of the disposal an individual made of the rights such as he had them, viz., those of use, in favour of a religious body. The landed property, thus conferred, acquired a kind of sacredness which preserved it from the grasp of even the most rapacious ruler. On the other hand, the religious body had no right or power whatsoever to sell or dispose of that property. In a corporation constituted as the assembly of the disciples of Buddha was, and is in our own days, the society alone could have the possession and management of immovable properties given to monasteries. Donations of this kind must have stood good as long as there were members of the Buddhistic religious family willing and ready to maintain their rights. Nothing short

thingkiit, or royal head ornament, to be raised to the dignity of crown prince, to be put in possession of his own palace, and to be married. When Phra was leaving the palace, he bade the young prince take his patta and follow him. Nanda instantly complied with the request, and departed. He was just leaving the palace, when the young lady he was to marry heard the sound of the steps and of the voice of her lover. She was then busily engaged in combing her beautiful and shining black hair. With the left hand drawing aside her hair, and with the right leaning on the window-frame, she, with a sweet yet tremulous voice, eagerly recommended him soon to return. She then continued to follow him with anxious eyes until he could be seen no longer. Meanwhile, resting against the window-side, she had her heart full of ominous forebodings. Nanda would have gladly given back the patta to his owner; but as he felt backward to hand it over to him, he followed Buddha as far as the monastery. Though he had no intention of becoming Rahan on his way to that place, yet, despite of his former dispositions, he entered into the society of the perfect. So that on the second day after Phra's arrival at Kapilawot, Nanda became a Rahan. Some other writings mention that this happened only on the third day.

---

of a complete revolution in the political state of the country, or the prolonged absence of the individuals vested with the right of occupation, could put an end to the effect of those deeds of donation. In Burmah, the Buddhist monks possess nothing beyond the ground upon which stands the monastery. From certain inscriptions found in the midst of the ruins of the temples at Pagan, it is evident that in the palmy days of that city donations of landed properties, such as paddy-fields, fruit-trees, bullocks, and peasants, were made to monasteries and temples. But for the last three or four hundred years, no vestiges of such deeds have ever been found. So far as I have been able to make inquiries, I am not aware that the order has ever become possessor of lands. In Ceylon such is not the case, at least was not when the English occupied the island. Extensive tracts of valuable lands were in the hands of the Talapoins, who thereby obtained over the people the twofold influence conferred by wealth and religion.

On the seventh day after Phra had entered into the city of Kapilawot, the mother of Raoula, Princess Yathaudara, put on her son the choicest ornaments, and sent him to Phra, saying previously to him: "Dearest son, he whom you see surrounded by twenty thousand Rahandas, whose face resembles gold, and whose body is similar to that of the chief of Brahmas, is indeed your father. He was formerly the owner of the four gold vases which disappeared on the very day he withdrew into solitude; go to him now, and say respectfully, that, being at present crown prince of this kingdom, destined to succeed your grandfather on the throne, you wish to become possessed of the property that will fall to you in right of inheritance." The young prince departed. Having come into the presence of Buddha, he endeavoured, with the simplicity and amiability becoming a young lad, to ingratiate himself in his father's favour, and said how happy he was to be with him, adding many other particulars befitting his age and position. Buddha, having eaten his meal and performed his usual devotions, rose up and departed. Raoula followed behind, saying: "Father, give me my inheritance." Buddha appearing neither displeased nor vexed at such a demand, none of his followers durst tell the young prince to desist from his apparently rude behaviour, and go back to the palace. They all soon reached the monastery. Phra thus thought within himself: Raoula is asking from me perishable things, but I will give him something more excellent and lasting. I will make him partaker of those goods I have gathered at the foot of the Bodi tree, and thereby will provide for him a better inheritance for the future. Whereupon he called Thariputra, and said to him: "Beloved disciple, the young Prince Raoula asks from me a worldly inheritance, which would avail him nothing, but I wish to present him with something more excellent, an imperishable inheritance; let him become a Rahan." Maukalan shaved the head of Raoula and attired him with the tsiwaran. Thariputra gave him the first instructions.

When hereafter he became Patzing, Kathaba trained him up to the duties of his new profession.

King Thoodaudana had seen his first son Prince Theidat leave the palace and all the attracting allurements of a brilliant court; despite of all his precautions, he subsequently witnessed his going into a solitude and becoming a Rahan. Next to him, his younger son Nanda, though assured by the promises of soothsayers of becoming a great and mighty ruler, had joined the society of Rahans. These two events had deeply afflicted him. But, on hearing that his grandson had also become a Rahan, he could no longer keep his affliction within himself. "I had," said he, "hoped that my grandson would succeed me on the throne; this thought consoled me for the loss of my two sons. What will become of my throne? Now the royal succession is at an end, and the line of direct descendants is for ever cut and irrevocably broken asunder."

Thoodaudana obtained the state of Anagam. He said to himself: It is enough that I should have had so much to suffer and endure on the occasion of my two sons and my grandson becoming Rahans; I will spare to other parents a similar affliction. He went to Buddha's place, and having paid him his respects in a becoming manner, asked him to establish a regulation forbidding any son to become Rahan, unless he had the consent of his parents. Buddha assented to his father's wish and preached to him the law. When the instruction was finished, the king bowed to him, rose up, turned on the right, and departed. Buddha, calling immediately the Rahans, said to them: "Beloved Bickus, no one is to be admitted to the profession of Rahan, ere he has obtained the consent of his parents: any one that shall trespass this regulation shall be guilty of a sin."

On a certain day, Phra having eaten his meal at his father's palace, the king related to him the circumstance of a Nat, who, whilst he was undergoing great austerities in the solitude, had come and conveyed the report of his son having succumbed under the hardships of mortification; but he would never give credit to such a rumour, as he was certain that his son could not die ere he had become a Buddha. "My illustrious father," replied Buddha, "you are much advanced in merits; there is no wonder at your not believing a false report; but even in former ages, when your merits were as yet very imperfect, you refused to believe your son was dead, though in proof of this assertion bones were exhibited before you in confirmation of the report." And he went on relating many particulars that are to be found in the history of Maha Damma Pala. It was at the conclusion of this discourse that the king became Anagam. Having thus firmly established his father in the three degrees of perfection, Buddha returned to the country of Radzagio.

During this voyage, the most excellent Phra arrived at the village of Anupya, in the country of the Malla Princes. In the neighbourhood of the village there is a grove of mango-trees. To that place he withdrew with his twenty thousand disciples, and enjoyed himself in that secluded and delightful retreat.

While he dwelt on that spot, the seed of the law that he had planted in his native city was silently taking deep root in the hearts of many. His uncle Thekkaudana had two sons, named Mahanan and Anooroudha. On a certain day Mahanan said to his younger brother: "From among the several families of the royal race, many persons have left the world and embraced the religious profession under the guidance of Buddha. Our family is the only one that has not as yet given any member to the assembly. I will make you a proposal: either you will become an ascetic, and leave me your inheritance; or I will myself take that step, and make over to you all that I possess." Anooroudha at once accepted the proposal.

When the intentions of the two brothers became known, five young princes, their playmates and relatives, named

Bagoo, Kimila, Baddya, Ananda,[9] and Dewadat, desired to join them in their pious design. Having put on their finest dress, they went into the country, having no other attendant but Oopali, their barber. They shaped their course in the direction of Anupya. Being at a small distance from the mango-trees' grove, the young princes stripped themselves of their rich dresses, and gave them all to the barber, as an acknowledgment of his services. The latter at first accepted them, and was preparing to return, when the following thought occurred to his mind: "If I go back to Kapilawot with these fine and rich apparels, the king and the people will believe that I have come by foul means in possession of so many valuables, and I shall certainly be put to death. I will follow my masters, and never leave them." Hereupon he returned in all haste and joined them at the very moment they were disposing themselves to enter into the Anupya mango-trees' grove. Oopali was admitted into their company, and ushered along with them into Buddha's presence. Having paid their respects in the usual manner, they applied for

[9] Ananda, whose conversion is here mentioned, was the son of Amitaudana, a brother of King Thoodaudana, and, therefore, first cousin to Gaudama. He is one of the best known disciples of the celebrated philosopher of Kapilawot. He has gained his well-earned fame, less by the shining attainments of his intellect than by the amiable qualities of a loving heart. He bore to Buddha the most affectionate regard and the warmest attachment from the very beginning of his conversion. The master repaid the love of the disciple by tokens of a sincere esteem and tender affection. Though it was a long period afterwards ere Ananda was officially appointed to minister unto the personal wants of Buddha, yet the good dispositions of his excellent heart prompted him to serve Buddha on all occasions, and in every way that was agreeable to him. He became the medium of intercourse between his beloved master and all those that approached him. When he had to communicate orders or give directions to the religious, or when some visitors desired to wait on him, Ananda was the person who transmitted all orders, and ushered visitors into the presence of the great preacher.

Dewadat was both first cousin to Buddha and his brother-in-law. His father was Thouppabudha, Maia's brother. He was brother of the Princess Yathaudara, who had married our Gaudama, when he was crown prince of Kapilawot. Hereafter, we shall have the opportunity of seeing that his moral dispositions were very different from those of the amiable Ananda.

the dignity of members of the assembly. Their request was granted. But previous to passing through the prescribed ceremonies, the princes said one to another: "Great indeed and deeply rooted is the pride of princes: it is extremely difficult to shake it off, and free oneself of its tyrannical exactions. Let Oopali be first ordained; we will have an opportunity of humbling ourselves by prostrating ourselves before him." Their request was granted. After having paid their respects to the newly ordained convert, they were likewise admitted among the members of the assembly. Their proficiency in spiritual progress was not the same. During the second Lent, which they spent in the Weloowon monastery, Baddya, Bagoo, and Kimila reached the culminating point of perfection by becoming Rahandas. Ananda became Thautapatti. Anooroudha greatly advanced in the higher path of metaphysics. As to Dewadat, he never attained more than the Laukithamabat.

A little while after the conversion of the royal princes, Buddha left Anupya, continued his voyage to Radzagio, and forthwith retired into the Weloowon monastery to spend his second Lent. The time was chiefly employed in training up the new converts in the knowledge of the great truths, and in the practice of virtue. His son Raoula, about eight years old, evinced the greatest dispositions. His attainments were far above his age, and often elicited the admiration of the Rahans. On a certain occasion Buddha overheard them expressing their astonishment at the surprising progress Raoula was making in his studies. Coming among them as if perchance, Phra asked them what was the subject of their conversation. They answered that they were praising and extolling the wonderful abilities of Raoula, and his matchless good dispositions. Thereupon Buddha remarked that this was not to be wondered at. Then he related to them the dzat Miga, by which he showed to them that during former existences Raoula had distinguished himself in a conspicuous manner by his excellent and admirable dispositions. As a reward for his good behaviour and high mental qualifications, he was made Patzin. His mind continuing to expand in an almost miraculous manner, he became a Rahanda with myriads of Nats.

During the same season, Buddha often went to Radzagio to beg his food. There was in that city a flower-seller, who was wont to bring eight bouquets every day to the king, and receive in return from the royal hands eight pieces of silver. On a certain day, as he was coming from the country into the town with his usual supply of flowers for the king, he happened to see Buddha in the streets at a moment when, by a miraculous display of his power, the six glories beamed out of his body. He then said to himself: "I wish to go and offer these flowers to Buddha. But the king will doubtless be much angry with me. He may have me arrested, thrown into prison, and put to death for having failed in offering him the usual present. Despite the great danger that hangs over me, I will go to Buddha and offer him my flowers. Great, indeed, and lasting shall be the merits I will gain; they will follow me during countless existences."

With a heart full of joy, Thoomana, for such is his name, went to the resting-place where Buddha was seated, surrounded by crowds of people, and laid the flowers at his feet. With a marked satisfaction, Gaudama accepted the offer. Thoomana went home and related to his wife what had just happened. The latter, irritated partly by the fear of the king's wrath, and partly by the loss of the money she daily received, began to abuse her husband in the coarsest language. She was so much maddened by passion that she in all haste went to the king, denounced her husband, and instantly sued for a divorce. Pimpathara revolted at such an act of unparalleled audacity, ordered her to withdraw from his presence and go back to her house. Meanwhile he commanded one of his courtiers to order the flower-seller to come to the palace on the following day. As a matter of course, the royal request was punctually complied with. In the presence of the assembled courtiers, the king highly praised the conduct of Thoomana, and instantly rewarded him with great liberality. As Thoomana had offered to Buddha eight bunches of flowers, the king, to acknowledge in a distinct manner such an offering, gave him eight elephants, eight horses, eight slaves, eight bullocks, eight thousand pieces of silver, and the revenue of eight villages. Buddha likewise exceedingly extolled the meritorious behaviour of Thoomana in the presence of the people, and said that during a whole world he would be exempt from the four states of punishment, enjoy happiness in the seat of man and in those of Nats, and finally become a Pitzega-buddha. The value of the offering, though little in itself, became great by the imminent risks he voluntarily exposed himself to. He made his offering, though he was certain of incurring on that account the ruler's displeasure.

When the season of retirement was over, Gaudama travelled through different places. He went to Patzanawonta in the Dzetia country, thence he passed into the Bisakila forest, and returned to Radzagio, in the grove of Yin-daik trees, near the burial-place.

Whilst Buddha was in the splendid Dzetawon monastery, just presented to him, a strong temptation came upon Ananda to renounce his calling and return into the world. He went so far as to tell some of his brethren that he recollected the promise of a prompt return which he made to his young bride Dzanapada-kaliani, and that now he wished to fulfil it by immediately going back into his palace, and resuming his former mode of life. This was soon reported to Gaudama, who resorted to the following expedient to crush in the bud the rising temptation. He took Ananda by the arm, rose with him in the air, and led him in the direction of the Nats' seat of Tawadeintha. On their way, Buddha, by a miraculous process, exhibited to the eyes of his companion the sight of an immense forest in conflagration. On the burnt stump of a tree he showed him a female monkey horribly mutilated, having her tail, ears, and nose cut off. At such a sight the horrified Ananda turned away his eyes in disgust. A little while after this, Buddha exhibited before him the dazzling and heart-captivating sight of a long array of five hundred matchless beauties. They were daughters of Nats going to pay their respects to the great Thagia. Ananda was gazing at them with silent but enraptured feelings. Buddha said to him: "Do you believe those beauties before you to be equal to Dzanapada?" "She is no more to these perfect forms," answered he, "than the bleeding female monkey we have left behind us is to her." "All these celestial damsels," said Buddha, "I shall give to you, provided you agree to remain in the monastery for some years longer." "Willingly do I accept the proposal," replied Ananda; "I will stay cheerfully in the monastery on such favourable terms." Whereupon both returned to the monastery.

The members of the assembly soon became acquainted with what had passed between the master and the disciple, and keenly taunted Ananda with their sarcastic remarks upon the daughters of Nats. Ashamed of himself, Ananda withdrew into solitude. There he devoted himself to reflection and penitential deeds, and finally annihilated the evil desires of his unsubdued passion. When the inward struggle was over and peace had been restored in him, Ananda went to Buddha's presence, and stated his willingness to dwell for ever in a monastery and lead a religious life. Meantime he released him from the promise he had made to him respecting the celestial beauties. Buddha was much pleased at such a happy change. He said to the assembled religious: "Previous to this occurrence, Ananda resembled a badly-roofed house, which lets in the rain of passions; but now it is similar to a well-roofed building, which is so well protected that it is proof against the oozing of passions." Whereupon he related the following story concerning a former existence of Ananda.

A merchant named Kappaka had a donkey which he used to carry goods from place to place. Having one day come near a place covered ,with trees, Kappaka unloaded his animal, to allow him some time to rest and graze. Meanwhile, a female donkey was likewise grazing in the neighbourhood. Its presence was quickly detected by Kappaka's animal. When the moment of departure had come, the latter, attracted by the female, kicked furiously at his master, and would not allow the load to be replaced on its back. The merchant, enraged at this unusual freak, began to threaten the rebellious beast, and then to hit it with the whip as hard as he could. At last the poor animal, unable to bear any longer the blows, mentioned to his master the cause of his unusual behaviour. Kappaka told him that if he would but continue his voyage, he would give him at the end of the journey several fine females, much superior to the one he was now coveting. The proposal was accepted. At the end of the journey Kappaka said to the beast: "I will keep my promise with you: but I must inform you that your daily provender shall not be increased; you will have to share it with your companion. Subsequently you will have little ones to provide for and maintain, but your daily ration shall not be increased in the least; you shall have to work for me as much as you do at present, and also to provide for the maintenance and support of your family." The donkey, after a few moments of reflection, thought it was better to remain as he was; and from that moment he was entirely cured of his inordinate inclination. At the conclusion of the narration, Buddha said: "The male donkey was he who has now become Ananda; the female donkey, Dzanapa-kaliani; and Kappaka is now the most excellent Phra, who is the teacher of men, Nats and Brahmas.

Buddha, whilst at Wethalie, went out through the country, and in all the places that he visited preached to the crowds of hearers. It was during one of his benevolent errands that he met with a celebrated Pounha, named Eggidatta, who with a great many disciples led an ascetic life, after having been formerly, first, the chief Pounha of King Kothala, and next of his son. Buddha earnestly desired the conversion of so distinguished a personage. Maukalan was at first despatched to that famous hermit, to attempt to bring him over to his master; but he utterly failed. The reception he at first met with was anything but pleasant. The work was to be done and perfected only by the irresistible eloquence of the great preacher. Buddha soon came up to the entrance of Eggidatta's cell. He began to upbraid the Rathee for teaching his disciples to worship mountains, trees, rivers, and all that exists in nature. He then initiated him in the knowledge of the four great truths. Eggidatta, seeing the truth, at once became a convert with all his disciples. When this great spiritual conquest was achieved, Buddha returned to Radzagio, and spent the third season in the Weloowon or bamboo-grove monastery. It was during the three months of the rainy season that Buddha imparted, in a more complete manner, to his disciples the knowledge and science which during his peregrinations he had but superficially conveyed to them. At the same time, he carefully trained them up in the practice and observance of those disciplinary regulations which were intended as a means to subdue passions, to estrange them from the world and all its attractions, and to lead a spiritual life.

During his stay in the monastery, among the many instructions that he gave to his disciples, I will relate the particulars that he mentioned respecting the former doings and the final conversion of the Rahanda Tsampooka.[10]

---

[10] The story of Eggidatta gives us an insight into one of the tenets

In the days of the Buddha Kathaba, Thampooka, or rather the being who in the present existence is called by that name, put on the religious dress in the Thawatie country. He lived in a fine monastery, and had for his supporters the best and richest people of the place. One day, a Rahan, belonging to another country, came to his monastery and begged the favour to be allowed to live therein for some time. The heartless Tsampooka denied him admittance into the interior of the building, but tolerated his staying in the verandah during the cold season. The people, however, actuated by better feelings than those

---

which was held by that ascetic. His interlocutor reproached him with worshipping mountains, trees, forests, rivers, and the heavenly bodies. From the expressions made use of by the Burmese translator, the writer is inclined to believe that a direct allusion is made to pantheistic opinions. We know that most of the Indian schools of philosophy have based their various systems of metaphysics upon that most erroneous foundation. According to pantheists, this world is not distinct from the essence of God; all that exists is but a manifestation or a development of the substance of God. This world is not the work of God, existing as distinct from its Maker, but it is God manifesting Himself substantially in all things. Who could, then, wonder at the conduct of Tsampooka? He worshipped God, or rather that portion of the supreme Being he saw in the great and mighty subjects that surrounded him and attracted his notice.

Spinoza, in the seventeenth century, and his unfortunately too numerous followers in this century, have recast into a hundred different moulds the pantheistic ideas of the Hindu philosophers, and offer to the intelligence of their hearers and readers, through an almost unintelligible language, the same deadly food which has finally produced on the Hindu mind the sad results which we witness. If we were better acquainted with the variety of doctrines which the Hindu philosophers have exhibited in the field of metaphysics, we would be soon convinced that the modern metaphysicians, who have placed themselves out of the pale of revelation, have not advanced one step in that science, and that the divergence in their opinions is but a faithful representation of the confusion which for more than two thousand years prevailed on the banks of the Ganges among their predecessors in the same speculative studies.

It appears that Tsampooka was in his days what the Jogies or Hindoo penitents are up to our time. He remained on his rock, in the most difficult position, for the space of fifty-five years, exhibiting himself to the crowd, and aiming at winning their admiration by the incredible sufferings that he voluntarily submitted to. His apparent sanctity was made up of very doubtful materials. He passed himself off for a man who could remain without eating, and who was gifted with supernatural powers. Plain humility, which is nothing but the result of the true knowledge of self, was not the favourite virtue of our spiritual quack.

of their teacher, brought regularly food for the head of the house, as well as for the stranger, for whom they felt great affection. The spiteful Tsampooka could not bear to see the people showing marks of kindness and benevolence towards his hated guest. On one occasion he forgot himself so far as to abuse him, by repeating the following coarse expressions: Eat dirt, go naked, and sleep on the bare ground. Such an inhuman behaviour soon met with a condign punishment. The wretched Tsampooka had at first to endure horrible torments in hell.

On his return to the seat of man on earth, he was born from respectable parents, but he was always prone from his infancy to indulge in the lowest habits. He would secretly steal away, and actually satiate the cravings of hunger by eating the most disgusting things; he would not wear clothing, but ran about in a state of nakedness; he would only sleep on the ground. His parents, after many fruitless attempts to correct him, resolved to make him over to the heterodox ascetics. These received him; but he would not eat in the company of his brethren, nor go to beg with them. He, from the moment they were absent, went to devour the refuse he could find. His eccentric and disgusting habits were soon found out, and his new friends said one to the other: "Let this man be no longer allowed to live with us. Should the disciples of the Rahan Gaudama hear that one of our company is behaving in such a manner, our brotherhood would become a laughing-stock to them." He was, therefore, expelled from this place. Tsampooka went to take his abode on a rock near the place that served as receptacle to the sewers of Radzagio. On that rock he remained in the most fatiguing posture; he leaned on his right hand which rested on the rock, and also on his right knee; the left leg was stretched and the left arm raised up. He kept his mouth opened. When the people asked him why he remained with his mouth wide open, as a man who is incessantly drawing air into his lungs, he answered that, refraining from the use of coarse food, he was feeding on air only: when questioned about the singular position of his two legs, he answered, that, were he to stand on both legs, the earth would instantly shake. He had been during fifty-five years in that sad position, when Gaudama, moved with compassion at his pitiable condition, went in person to convert him. He began to relate to him all that he had done during former existences, mentioning in particular the sin he had been guilty of towards a brother hermit. At this unexpected declaration, Tsampooka humbled himself. Buddha then preached to him his law. The repenting Tsampooka firmly believed in all that was said to him. He then rose up, and, with a heart overflowing with joy, instantly left his place, followed his new master, and soon became a Rahanda. His proficiency in science and virtue was such that he soon occupied a distinguished rank among the members of the assembly.

CHAPTER IX.

A rich man of Thawattie, named Anatapein, becomes a convert—Story of Dzewaka—He cures Buddha of a painful distemper—The people of Wethalie send a deputation to Buddha—Digression on the manner Buddha daily spent his time—Settling of a quarrel between the inhabitants of Kaulia and those of Kapilawot—New converts are strengthened in their faith—Thoodaudana's death in the arms of his son—Queen Patzapati and many noble ladies are elevated to the rank of Rahaness—Conversion of Kema, the first queen of King Pimpathara—Heretics near Thawattie are confounded by the display of miraculous powers—Buddha goes to the seat of Thawadeintha, to preach the law to his mother.

WHEN Buddha was in the country of Radzagio, a certain rich merchant, named Anatapein, came to Radzagio, with five hundred carts loaded with the most precious goods, and took his lodging in the house of an intimate friend. Whilst living with his friend, he heard that Gaudama had become a Buddha. Suddenly, he was seized with an earnest desire of seeing him and hearing his doctrine. On a certain day, he rose at an early hour, and perceived, reflected through the lattices of the window, some rays of an uncommon brightness. He went in the direction of the light to the place where Buddha was preaching the law. He listened to it with great attention, and, at the end of the discourse, he obtained the state of Thautapan. Two days after, he made a great offering to Buddha and to the assembly, and requested him to come to the country of Thawattie. The request was granted. The distance to Thawattie is forty-five youdzanas. Anatapein spent enormous sums that one monastery should be erected at each youdzana distance. When Buddha was approaching, the pious merchant arranged as follows for the reception of the distinguished visitor, and presenting to him a splendid monastery called Dzetawon, which he had made ready for him. He sent first his son, richly attired, with five hundred followers, belonging to the richest families; then followed his two daughters with five hundred girls, all decked with the most costly ornaments. Every one carried flags of five different colours. These were followed by five hundred dames, having the rich man's wife at their head, each carrying a pitcher of water. Last of all, came Anatapein, with five hundred followers, all wearing new dresses. Gaudama let the crowd walk in front, and he followed attended by all the Rahans. When he entered the grove, he appeared as beautiful as the peacock's tail when completely expanded. Anatapein asked Gaudama how he wished the donation should be made and effected? "Let the monastery be offered," said Buddha, "to all the Rahans that may come in future to this place from what quarter soever." Thereupon, the rich man, holding a golden vessel of water, poured its contents on the hands of Buddha, saying: "I present this monastery to Buddha and to all the Rahans that may come hereafter to reside therein." Buddha said prayers and thanks in token of his accepting the offering. Seven days were devoted to making this great offering, and during four months uninterrupted rejoicings went on in commemoration of this great and solemn donation. For the purchase of the place, and the expenses of the ceremony, enormous sums were lavished. During the era of former Buddhas this very place had always been purchased and offered to them and their disciples.

[*N.B.*—Here is found narrated in full the history of a celebrated physician named Dzewaka. As such story has no reference whatever to Buddha's career, I will give but a very succinct account of it.]

At a certain time,[1] when Buddha lived in the city of

[1] It is impossible to a-sign the motive that induced the compiler of

Radzagio, the country of Wethalie was made rich, gay, and attractive by the presence of a famous courtesan. A nobleman of Radzagio, who had just returned from that

---

Buddha's life to insert in his work a long episode on the celebrated physician Dzewaka. The story is in itself uninteresting, and throws no light whatever on the history of the supposed originator or reformer of Buddhism. For this reason it has been thought quite unnecessary to give a complete translation of the whole passage. The name of Dzewaka is quite familiar to the adepts of the medical art in Burmah. Many times the writer has made inquiries respecting the works of the Hippocrates of India, but he has never been able to meet with mention of or allusion to such compositions. Hence he has been led to suppose that the father of medicine in these countries has left behind him no writings to embody the results of his theoretical and practical favourite pursuits. Surgery appears to have been no novelty with our great doctor, since we see him on an occasion extracting from the body of a prince, by means of an incision, a snake that put his life in peril.

The numerous quacks who in Burmah assume the name of physicians, and are ever ready to give medicines in all cases, even the most difficult and complicated, are ignorant of the very elements of the surgical art. They possess a certain number of remedies, made up of plants, which, when applied under proper circumstances and in certain cases, work wonderful cures. But the native physicians, unable in most instances to discern the true symptoms of diseases, prescribe remedies at random, and obtain, in too many cases, results most fatal to the unfortunate patient. In medicine as well as in religion, ignorance begets superstition and recourse to magical practices. We may positively assert that the black art is, with native practitioners, an essential concomitant to the practice of medicine. When a physician has exhausted the limited stock of remedies that he possesses, and he finds, in spite of his exertions, that the disease bids defiance to his skill, he gravely tells the relatives of the patient that some evil spirit is interfering with his remedies, and that he must be expelled ere there can be any chance of relieving the sufferer and obtaining his recovery. Whereupon a shed is erected with the utmost speed on a spot close to the house of the patient. Offerings of rice, fruits, and other articles are made to the pretended evil spirit, who is supposed to have got hold of the sufferer's body. Dances of the most frantic character are carried on by his relatives. Males will only officiate in default of females; preference is always given to the latter. Young girls, say the Burmese, are the fittest persons for the occasion, as it is supposed that the evil Nat is more effectually and easily propitiated by the power of their charms. This exercise lasts until, strength at last failing them, they drop down in a state of complete exhaustion and prostration. They appear as if they had entirely lost their senses. In that state they are supposed to be inspired by the evil spirit. Interrogated by the physician on the nature of the disease, and the proper remedies to be applied for eradicating it, they give answers, or rather they become channels through which the spirit, satisfied with the offerings made in his honour, condescends to declare that he has now left the patient, and that by placing him under a certain treatment, which he fails not to indicate, he will soon

country, narrated to the king all that he had seen at Wethalie, and induced the monarch to set up, in his own kingdom, some famous courtesan, who would be skilful in music and dancing, as well as attractive by the form and accomplishments of her person. Such a person having been procured, she was, by the munificence of the king, placed on a most splendid footing, and one hundred pieces of silver were to be paid for each evening's visit. The king's son being rather assiduous in his visits to her place, she became pregnant. Aware of her state, the courtesan affected to be sick until her confinement. She directed her servant to throw out the newly-born infant, on a heap of rubbish, in some lonely and distant place. The next morning the king's son, going out with some attendants, chanced to pass close to the spot where the infant had been deposited. His attention having been attracted by the noise of crows hovering close by, he went to see what it was. To his great surprise, he saw an infant, yet breathing, half buried in rubbish. Taken with the beauty of this little creature, the prince ordered the child to be carried to the palace, where he was brought up with the greatest care and attention. He was named Dzewaka, which means life, because the prince, when he found him, inquired if he was alive. The young lad, having reached the years of discretion, was unwilling to remain in the palace, not occupied with any business. In order to afford relief and comfort to his fellow-creatures, he resolved to study medicine. He repaired to Benares, placed himself under the direction of a famous physician, and soon became eminent by his extreme proficiency in the profession. Having left his master, and begun practice in his own name and for his own account, Dzewaka worked the most wonderful cures, which soon procured to him unbounded wealth and an extraordinary reputation.

---

recover his health. Occurrences of this nature are exceedingly common. They are called by the natives festivals of the *Nat-pan*, or of the possessing spirit.

Dzewaka was at the height of his fame, when, on a certain day, Buddha happened to be troubled with belly-ache. He called Ananda and said that he wanted some medicine to relieve him from pain. Ananda went to the place where lived the celebrated Dzewaka, and informed him of Buddha's complaint. The doctor ordered first a rubbing of oil, which was to be repeated three days after. This remedy not having a full effect, Dzewaka took three lily flowers, whereupon he spread several powders, and came to Buddha, saying, "Most glorious Phra, here is one lily flower, please to smell it; this will be followed by ten motions. Here is a second one; the smelling thereof will produce a similar effect; and this one will cause the same result." Having handed over the three flowers, the doctor paid his respects to Buddha, turned to the right, and left the monastery.

When he was crossing the gate, he thought within himself, "I have given a medicine calculated to cause thirty motions, but as the complaint is rather of a serious and obstinate character, twenty-nine motions only will take place; a warm bath would be required to produce the thirtieth;" and with this reflection he departed. Buddha, who saw all that passed in the doctor's mind, called Ananda and directed him to prepare a warm bath. A little while after, Dzewaka came back to Buddha, and explained to him his prescription. Buddha was soon restored to his former health, and Dzewaka told him that the people were preparing to make him offerings. Maukalan went to the son of Thauna, a rich man, to get some rice from a field that had been watered with milk. The owner gave rice to Maukalan and urged him to partake of it, assuring him that there was some other in reserve for Buddha; Maukalan assented. After the meal, his patta was cleaned with perfumed water, and filled with the choicest food. Maukalan took it to Buddha, who ate it. Afterwards he preached the law to the king and to an immense crowd; amongst them was Thauna's son. They all obtained the first degree of perfection, but Thauna reached at once the state of Arahat.

Dzewaka came again to Buddha's presence, and requested the favour of presenting him with two splendid pieces of cloth, which he had received in present from a king whom he had cured of a most distressing distemper. Moreover, he wished that the Rahans should be allowed to receive clothes of a better sort than those they were wont to wear. Buddha received the two pieces and preached the law to the donor, who attained the state of Thautapan. Dzewaka, rising from his place, wheeled to the right and departed.

A little while after, Gaudama called the Rahans and said to them, "Beloved Bickus, now I give permission to the faithful to make offerings of cloth for your dress.[2] Whoever is pleased with his present dress, let him wear it; whoever is disposed to receive some other from the people, let him do so. But I must praise you for having hitherto been satisfied with the ancient dress." The people of the city having heard of the permission given to the Rahans,

---

[2] The first followers of Buddha, observing a mode of life much resembling that of the Rathees, had hitherto made use of the dress they had purchased previous to their leaving the world. But when they became professed members of the new society, they were subjected to the observance of the vow of strict poverty, and had to depend entirely on public charity for the obtaining of the required food and raiment. The old clothes brought at the time of their entering the society were worn out and unfit to be put on. Others were to be provided for by some means that would not wound the delicate feeling of absolute poverty. The only one that occurred was the willing and liberal dispositions of the lay members of the Buddhist community. This new source of abundant alms was opened by our Buddha himself, on the occasion of the offering made by Dzewaka. Desiring likewise to do away with the scruples many religious might entertain respecting the lawfulness or unlawfulness of receiving articles of dress, Gaudama laid it down as a regulation that all the religious could lawfully accept all that might be willingly offered them by the faithful. In the foregoing pages we have seen the founder of Buddhism granting to his followers permission to receive houses and landed properties presented to communities. Now the same legislator, adhering to the same principle, gives a fuller development thereto, and extends to articles necessary for dress the leave to receive offerings of this description, proffered by the faithful to the religious. In the book of Buddhist ordinations, or promotion to the degree of Patzin, mention is made of these two sorts of permissions given to the Rahans.

offered at once more than one hundred thousand pieces of cloth. Their example was followed by the people of the country, who made offerings to the same amount.

A little while after this, Buddha received a deputation from the Wethalie people, inviting him to visit their country. Here is the reason of the invitation. The country was very rich and flourishing. The Malla princes governed it each in turn for a certain space of time. On a sudden a terrific pestilence desolated the land, which was in a short time strewed with dead bodies in every direction. In the midst of so great a calamity some advised to propitiate the Nats, by making offerings to them; others said that recourse must be had to the great teachers; a third party insisted upon calling to their aid the great Gaudama, who had appeared in this world for the purpose of saving mankind. The last opinion prevailed. Having ascertained that he lived at Radzagio, a great number of princes, pounhas, and nobles went to Radzagio, with great prèsents for King Pimpathara, to induce him to allow the great teacher to come to their country. The object of their mission having become known, Buddha agreed to go. He sallied forth from the Weloowon monastery, attended by the king as far as the southern bank of the Ganges. Having reached the northern one, he was received with every possible mark of the highest respect and veneration. As soon as he set his feet in the country, a heavy rain fell which almost deluged the land. The water carried away the dead bodies. The atmosphere was purified, the pestilence ceased, and all the sick recovered. On the fifth day after the full moon of Nayon (June), Buddha having conferred such a favour to the people of Wethalie, left that country and returned to Radzagio, which he reached on the full moon of Watso (July), just in time to spend the fourth season in the Weloowon monastery.

Here is inserted a short sketch of the manner in which Buddha spent his days during the rainy season, as the translator has found in one of the manuscripts before him.

Each day was divided into five parts, and a certain occupation was reserved to each part. 1. Buddha generally rose at an early hour, a little after daybreak, washed his face, rinsed his mouth, and dressed. He then retired into a private apartment. With his all-seeing eyes, he glanced over all creatures, carefully examined the amount of their merits and demerits, and the real nature of their dispositions. The reason for his taking a survey of the state and condition of all beings was to ascertain the dispositions of the various beings, and discern those who were prepared to hear the preaching of truth from those who, on account of their demerits, were as yet unprepared for receiving beneficially for themselves such a great favour. When this was done, he put on his full canonical dress, and, with the mendicant's pot under his arm, he sallied forth in quest of his food. He invariably directed his steps towards those places where he knew that his preachings would be heard with beneficial results. Sometimes he went alone; at other times he was attended with a certain number of his disciples. His countenance bespoke an unaffected modesty and an inimitable mildness. Occasionally he allowed a display of wonders to take place. Musical instruments emitted, of themselves, sweet tunes, which, revealing to the people the coming of Buddha, rejoiced their heart and disposed them to bestow abundant alms, and to hear the preaching of the law. Some of the hearers became Upasakas, others Thautapans, &c., &c., agreeably to every one's disposition. Then he returned to his monastery.

2. As soon as he had arrived, he washed his feet, and during the ablution he had his disciples assembled round him, and said to them, "Beloved Bickus, be ever watchful and attentive, with a mind ever prone to reflection. It is exceedingly difficult to obtain the nature of man,[3] to hear

---

[3] It was at that moment that Gaudama delighted to reveal to his disciples the most startling points of his doctrine, and made them familiar with certain tenets upon which he laid much stress. He wished that what he looked upon as subjects of the greatest importance, should be-

the law, to become perfect, to obtain the state of Rahanda, and to arrive to the condition of a Buddha." He then pointed out to them some subjects of meditation. Many of the disciples devoted themselves to mental labour; some combined together manual and mental exertions; others withdrew to lonely places at the foot of certain trees, and into the caves of neighbouring hills. Buddha then took his meal, and retired for awhile alone into his own private apartment. When he arose a little after mid-day, he anew contemplated all beings, and fixed his attention on those that were to come and receive his instructions. He soon came out, and at once began to impart instruction to all those that had arrived, from what place soever. When the instruction was completed, the people withdrew.

3. After the people's departure, Buddha bathed and took a walk in the open verandah of the monastery. His mat, cushion, &c., were spread in a becoming and open place. The Rahans hastened at that hour to come and communicate freely the result of their mental exertions. When they wanted any explanation, they were encouraged to put

---

come familiar to them. No doubt he intended that those favourite topics should become the spiritual food upon which his disciples' minds should feed during the hours devoted to meditation. Those who are uninitiated in the doctrines of Buddhism will not understand the meaning of such an expression. It is difficult to obtain the nature of man. Such language is, however, in perfect accordance with the principles of that system. A being, who is in one of the four states of punishment, that of an animal, for instance, shall have, in many instances, to pass through an immense number of various existences, ere he can escape from the circle of animal existences, and at last emerge into that of man. To give us an idea of the excessive difficulties a being has to encounter, they make use of the following comparison. Let us suppose that a needle be dropped from one of the seats of Brahmas, and at the same time a man on earth be keeping another needle with the point upwards. It will be more easy for the two needles' extremities to come in contact one with the other, than it will be to a being in the condition of animal to reach the state of man. On the same principle one can easily imagine what mighty efforts must be made during countless existences ere a simple man can obtain all the qualifications necessary for enabling him to become a Buddha. The theory of Gaudama, on this point, resembles much that of some modern thinkers who preach the perfectibility of man to an almost infinite degree.

him questions, which were instantly answered; and they received submissively the answers which he condescended to give to them. This exercise lasted until it was dark. The disciples retired from their master's presence.

4. After their departure, the Nats and other celestial beings were admitted. Buddha conversed with and instructed them until nearly midnight.

5. Buddha then walked awhile to relieve his limbs from extreme lassitude, and went into his apartment to take some rest. He rose very early, and began to review the beings who, during the days of former Buddhas, had distinguished themselves by their exertions in the path of virtue and in the high mental attainments.

During one of his usual benevolent errands through the country, Gaudama converted Ouggasena, his wife and companions. Here is an abridged narrative of that event. Ouggasena was the son of a rich man. In the time of his youth a company of comedians came to Radzagio and exhibited during seven days in the presence of King Pimpathara and his court. Our young man, along with many of his companions, attended the exhibition. On a sudden, he became passionately enamoured of a rope dancing-girl, who performed many feats with accomplished grace and uncommon address. Despite his parents' remonstrances and entreaties, he sacrificed to his ungoverned passion all considerations, and he married the damsel. In his new situation, he had no alternative but to learn the art of rope-dancing, tumbling feats, and standing in various attitudes on the extremity of posts or masts, sometimes sixty cubits high. During his noviciate, he had to bear the laughter and taunts of his wife and of his new friends. By dint of exertion he became proficient in the art of performing tumblers' feats with a surprising agility. One day it was announced at the sound of the drum that Ouggasena was to perform on the top of a post sixty cubits high. An immense crowd of citizens went out with great eagerness to see the performance. When the amusements had just begun, Buddha happened to pass by with a number of disciples. He desired Maukalan to go ahead, and begin to preach to Ouggasena. Soon he came up himself in person, and converted the juggler, who forthwith descended from his mast, prostrated himself before Buddha, and asked to be admitted as a member of the assembly. After further instructions he obtained the science of Rahanda. His wife and all the company became likewise converts.[4]

Buddha had now fulfilled the promise he had formerly made to the ruler of Radzagio, to spend three consecutive seasons in his royal city. He went over to the Wethalie country, and fixed his residence in a fine place, in the midst of a forest of sala-trees, called Mahawon. Whilst he enjoyed himself in that place, a quarrel took place between a portion of the people of Kappila and that of Kaulia, who lived on both banks of the little river

---

[4] The conversion of Ouggasena and of his companions, procured by the direct intervention of Buddha himself, is another instance of the truly liberal spirit which animated the great preacher. His law was intended for all without exception. The profession of these individuals whom he so peculiarly selected was far from being a respectable one. The proud Brahmin would not have condescended to take notice of people who, in his opinion, had degraded themselves so low. But the new teacher, though born from parents belonging to a high caste, entirely free from the prejudices inculcated by the narrow spirit of caste, rose himself to such a high position as to look upon man, whatever his condition or position might be, as a fellow-being fully entitled to the benefit of his instructions. This is one of the most striking features of his preachings, its universality as regards persons and places. It enables us to account for the rapid and astonishing diffusion of his doctrines through so many countries. It constitutes the essential and capital difference between the two great systems which, in days long passed by, have contested for the religious supremacy over the Indian peninsula.

In the subsequent story of Thoodaudana's illness, we see Buddha first, then Ananda, Tharipatra, and Maukalan relieving the illustrious patient from his bodily distemper, by invoking, not the interference of a supreme Being, whom they ignore, but a certain power or influence connected with former good deeds. A great, nay, a miraculous, effect is produced by the agency of a cause which no one but a Buddhist can understand. He has recourse to *kan*, or the influence resulting from meritorious actions, as to a mighty agent who has the power to work any desired result whatever. But how a man can by his own will control the influence of his good actions, so as to produce a grand effect in no way short of a miracle, is a thing which can in no rational way be explained or accounted for.

Rauhani. The cause of the dispute was the irrigation of paddy-fields. The small river had been duly barred, but on account of an unusual drought there was not water enough to supply the quantity required for the fields on both banks. One party wanted to have all the water, the other demurred. Hence a dispute arose which, wildfire-like, spread from the banks of the stream all over both countries. A general appeal to arms ensued, and, in a short time, both armies stood facing each other in battle array.

At an early hour Buddha, having risen from his couch, cast, as usual, a glance over all beings. He soon saw the feud that existed between the country of his birth and that of Kaulia. Moved with compassion over the miseries which that people, blinded by a furious passion, were bringing upon themselves, he went through the air, and stood over and above the stream which separated the two armies. Rays of glory, beaming out of his person, soon attracted general attention. Both parties laid down their arms and prostrated themselves, worshipping him. He said to them, "Princes and warriors, hearken to my words. Which is the most valuable, a small quantity of water or the lives of countless beings, and, in particular, the lives of princes?" They answered, "Of course the lives of princes and warriors are most valuable." "If so," retorted Buddha, "lay aside your passion, conquer your anger, throw away your weapons of destruction, love each other, and live in peace." Both parties, by a low and prolonged tone of voice, expressed their deep regret at what they had done, and their sincere desire to follow his instructions. He preached to them the law in such an impressive and convincing manner that on the spot two hundred and fifty noblemen of Kappila and the same number of Kaulia asked for admittance among the members of the assembly.

The instruction they had heard, and which had determined their vocation, had not had time to cast deep roots in their hearts. They soon regretted their home, their families, and their former gay life. Buddha, who saw what was going on in their souls, said to them, "Will you come with me, and enjoy yourselves on the green banks of the beautiful lake Kontala?" They joyfully accepted the proposal. By the power inherent in his nature, Buddha took them through the air, and soon reached the lake. They alighted on its banks. Delighted with the beautiful scenery that surrounded them, and ignorant of the new objects which they saw, they interrogated Buddha about the names of the new plants and fruits which they perceived. Gaudama condescended to answer all their questions. While thus engaged they saw the king of the birds of the lake resting on the branch of a tree. On a sudden five hundred birds of the same kind came crowding round their chief, and, by their cries and various attitudes, testified the happiness which they felt at being in his company.

The new converts wondered at the admirable instinct of those birds, and communicated to each other their mutual surprise. As an accomplished teacher, Buddha availed himself of the opportune moment, and said to them in a mild manner, "Beloved disciples, what you see now and admire is the lively and true image of my family." So effectually was the instruction conveyed that they all at once became Thautapan, and no longer thought of returning into the world. By the virtue inherent in their new position, they were enabled to fly through the air, and they returned with Buddha into the Mahawon residence.

On their arrival, Buddha began his fifth season in that same place. It was in the middle of that season, in the month of Wakhaong (August), that he heard that his father had been seized with a violent distemper, which left him no rest either day or night. Sensible of his approaching end, Thoodaudana ardently wished to see his son for the last time. In the morning, at the hour when Buddha was reviewing all beings, and examining with a compassionate heart their respective condition, he saw the sad and painful position of his royal father. He instantly summoned, by the means of Ananda, a select band of disciples, and flying through the air, alighted with his company in front of the palace. Without a moment's delay he ascended to the upper apartments, and sat on a place prepared for him, near the head of the couch upon which lay the royal patient.

Buddha, recollecting himself awhile, and then laying one of his hands on his father's head, said, "By the virtue of the merits I have acquired during countless existences, by the power of the fruits gathered during forty-nine days round the tree Bodi, let this head be forthwith relieved from all pain." It happened so in the twinkling of an eye. Nan, or Nanda, the younger brother of Buddha, the son of his aunt Patzapati, holding the right hand of his father, said with a fervent earnestness, "By the merits that I have obtained at the feet of Buddha, let this right hand be freed from all pain." And perfect cure instantly followed. Ananda, Phra's first cousin, held the left arm. Thariputra laid his hand on the back, Maukalan grasped the feet. All of them with a similar faith uttered such like prayers, and the same happy result invariably followed. Thoodaudana was delivered from all pain. But he continued to remain very weak.

Buddha, profiting by that favourable opportunity, preached to his father the law of mutability, and gave him many and truly seasonable instructions on that most important subject. With such a persuasive language did he expound this favourite doctrine that his father became at once a Rahanda. At the same time he distinctly informed him that seven days hence the end of his life would inevitably happen. Thoodaudana, perfectly prepared for the new change, that is to say, for death, by his son's instructions, and thoroughly resigned, saw before him the true state of Neibban, and said, "Now I clearly perceive the instability of all things. I am free from all passions. I am completely disentangled from the trammels of existence." Rocking himself in the bosom of these comforting truths, he spent happily the few days he had yet to live. On the last day, and for the last time, he paid his respects to Buddha by worshipping him. Sitting then on his couch, the royal patient humbly asked pardon in the presence of all his attendants for all offences he had committed by thoughts, words, and deeds. Having performed this act of sincere humility, he consoled his wife Patzati, who sat bathed in tears, as well as the other members of the royal family, and several times repeated before them the great truth—that all beings, when they come into existence, have within, inherent in their nature, a principle of death that hurries them to their end and dissolution; that the same principle that has brought near and united beings together is always opposed, and at last overpowered by the opposite one that tends to separate them. He then placidly lay on his couch, and gently breathed his last in the day of the full moon of Wakhaong, on a Saturday, at the rising of the sun, in the year of the Eetzana, era 107, at the advanced age of ninety-seven years.

Gaudama, after his father's demise, when all the Rahans were assembled round the deathbed, said to them: "Beloved Bickus, behold my father's remains. He is no longer what he was a little while ago. He has undergone the change. No one can offer an effectual and lasting resistance to the principle of death, inherent in all beings. Be diligent in the practice of good works: follow steadily the four roads leading to perfection." After this lecture, he consoled his aunt Patzapati and the other ladies of the court, who, with dishevelled hair, were wailing aloud and striking their breasts. He minutely explained to them the consequences resulting from the great principle of mutability, which pervades all beings and infallibly leads them to destruction by the separation of their constitutive parts.

When the instruction was finished, Buddha directed Kathaba to go and prepare the spot on which the funeral and cremation of the corpse were to take place. Aided by Thariputra, he washed the corpse, which was subsequently placed in great state, on a magnificent and lofty catafalco, raised for the purpose. The princes of Thekkara, Thoopawa, and Weritzara, came to attend the royal funeral and offer presents. The corpse was carried processionally through the principal streets of the city at the sound of all musical instruments. Buddha, in person, received the corpse, and laid it on the funeral pile. To no one else would he leave the honourable and pious task of setting fire to it. On that occasion there took place an indescribable outburst of wailings and lamentings. The impassible Buddha preached the law on that occasion. He left aside all praises in behalf of the deceased. He was satisfied with announcing the law; and countless beings, both among men and Nats, obtained the deliverance.

After the loss of her royal husband, Queen Patzapati, profoundly impressed with all that she had seen and heard, desired to renounce the world and embrace a religious mode of life. For that purpose she came to the presence of Buddha, and asked three times the permission to follow her inclination and become Rahaness. Three times the solicited favour was denied her. Buddha then left his own native country and returned to Wethalie, fixing his abode in the Gutagaia-thala monastery, in the Mahawon forest.

Buddha had not been long in this place when he had to grant the request which he at first refused to his aunt Patzapati. The wives of the princes of the Kappila and Kaulia countries, who, to the number of 500, had recently renounced the world, desired also to follow the example set before them by their husbands. They went to the queen's apartments and communicated to her their design, entreating her to help them in obtaining the object of their wishes. Patzapati not only promised them her support, but expressed the determination to join their company. As a token of the sincerity and earnestness of their resolution, all the ladies, without the least hesitation, cut their beautiful black hair, put on a dress in accordance with their pious intentions, and resolutely set out on foot in the direction of the Wethalie country.

Unused to such bodily exertions, the pious pilgrims suffered much during their long journey. At last, worn out with fatigue, covered with dust, they arrived near the Mahawon monastery. They respectfully stopped at the gate, and requested an interview with Ananda. The latter, having ascertained from their own mouth the object of their pious and fatiguing errand, hastened into the presence of Buddha, and entreated him to grant the earnest and praiseworthy demand of his aunt and of the other ladies, her companions. On hearing the request, Buddha, for a while, remained silent, as if deliberating on the answer he had to give. Then he said: "Ananda, it is not expedient to allow women to embrace the religious state; otherwise my institutions shall not last long." Ananda, undismayed by that reply, respectfully reminded Buddha of all the favours he had received from Patzapati, who had nursed and brought him up with the utmost care and tenderness, from the day his mother died, when he was but seven days old, and represented with a fervent earnestness the good dispositions of the pious postulants. Buddha's scruples were overcome by the persuasive language of the faithful Ananda. He asked whether women could observe the eight precepts: and added, that in case they would consent to bind themselves to a correct observance of them, they might be admitted as members of the assembly.

Fully satisfied with the answer he had obtained, the venerable Ananda saluted Buddha, and hastened to the gate of the monastery, where his return was impatiently awaited. On hearing the good news, Patzapati, in the name of her companions, spoke to Ananda: "Venerable Ananda, we all rejoice that the favour so often asked for has been at last granted unto us. As a young maid, who has bathed, and washed her hair, is anxiously desirous to put on her fine ornaments, as she receives with delight the beautiful and fragrant nosegays that are offered to her, so we are longing for the eight precepts, and wish for admittance into the assembly." They all promised to observe the rules of their new profession to the end of their lives. Yathaudara and Dzanapada-kaliani were among these converts. They all, owing to their former meritorious works, became subsequently Rahandas.

One of the new female converts seemed to have retained as yet a certain admiration of and fondness for her handsome features, and secretly prided herself on her beauty. Buddha, who quickly perceived the latent enemy lurking in the folds of her heart, resorted to the following expedient to correct her. On a certain day, when the proud and vain woman was in his presence, he created in an instant a consummate beauty, who as much exceeded her in perfection of form as the snow-white swan surpasses the black crow. Whilst she looked on this suddenly appearing rival with somewhat jealous eyes, Buddha caused the beauty of his creation to appear on a sudden very old, with a wrinkled face and an emaciated frame, and to exhibit on her person all the various and disgusting inroads which the most loathsome diseases make on the human body. The change acted as an electric shock on the young religious woman. When Gaudama perceived the change, and that she was so horrified at such a sight that she was nearly fainting, he said to her: "Behold, my daughter, the faithful foreshowing of what shall inevitably happen to that form you are so proud of." He had scarcely spoken those words, when she was instantly and for ever cured of her vanity.

Buddha left Wethalie and went on the Makula mountain, where he spent his sixth season. During his stay in that place thousands of people were converted and obtained the deliverance. At the end of that season, Buddha went to Radzagio, and stayed in the Weloowon monastery.

It was at that time that Kema, the first queen of King Pimpathara, proud of her rank, youth, and beauty, was at last converted. Up to that time she had obstinately refused to see Buddha and hear his doctrine. On a certain day, the queen went to visit a garden which was in the neighbourhood of the Weloowon grove. By a contrivance of the king, her husband, she was brought, almost against her will, into the presence of Buddha, who worked out the spiritual cure of her foolish vanity by a process similar to the one above mentioned. He caused a beautiful female of his creation to pass successively, in the queen's presence, through the various stages of old age, disease, and death. Her mind having been thus well prepared to hear his instructions, Buddha gave her a lengthened explanation of the miseries attending the body. It had the desirable effect to convert her in so perfect a manner that she entered into the current of perfection, and became Thautapan. After having obtained the consent of her lord, she was, upon her pressing solicitations, admitted into the religious order. She became a Rahanda, and among the female members of the assembly she ranked as the disciple of the right. Such a glorious charge was owing to her former merits.

On a certain day, a rich man of the country of Radzagio went to enjoy himself on the banks of the river Ganges. That man was not a disciple of Buddha, nor did he hold the doctrines of the opposite party. He steered a middle course between both doctrines, with a mind disposed, however, to embrace such opinions as should appear to him based on the best and strongest evidence. Chance offered him a favourable opportunity to acknowledge the superiority of Buddha over his opponents. He saw a log of sandal-wood floating on the stream, took it up, and had a beautiful patta made of it. When finished, he wrote upon it these words, "He who can fly in the air let him take it." The patta was raised on the top of a succession of hampers, tied together, and sixty cubits high. Some heretics living in the neighbourhood asked on successive occasions the rich man to get down the patta for them; he answered them that he would give it only to him who by flight could reach it. The head man of those heretics feigned to prepare himself to fly; but when he was extending his arms, and raising one of his feet, his disciples, according to a preconcerted plan, seized him, saying, "It is not becoming that you should exert yourself for such a trifle." But the wily rich man could not be thus deceived; he persisted in his former resolution, and for six days resisted all their entreaties. On the seventh day Maukalan happened to go to that place in search of his food. He was informed of all that had just happened. He was, moreover, told that the rich man and all his family would become disciples under him who could by flight possess himself of the sandal-wood patta. Maukalan was ready, for the glory of Buddha, to raise himself in the air, but his companion refused to allow him to do it, saying that such an easy work could easily be accomplished by one less advanced in merits. Maukalan agreed to his proposal. Whereupon entering into the fourth state of Dzan, his companion rose in the air, carrying with the toes of one of his feet an enormous rock three-quarters of a youdzana wide. The whole space between him and the bystanders appeared darkened. Every one was half dead with fear, lest, perhaps, it should fall over his head. Maukalan's companion had the rock split into two parts, and his person then appeared to the view of the assembled crowd. After having during a whole day exhibited such a mighty power, he caused the rock to fall on the place he had taken it from. The rich man bade him come down, fully satisfied with the display of such power. The sandal-wood patta was taken down, filled with the best rice, and presented to him. The Rahan received it and went back to his monastery. Many persons living at a distance from the place where the wonder had been exhibited, followed him to the monastery, begging him to show some other signs.

As they approached the monastery, Buddha hearing the noise, inquired what it was. He was informed of all the particulars of the event that had just taken place. He called the Rahan into his presence, took the patta, had it broken into pieces and reduced to dust.[5] He then forbade the Rahan ever to make such a display of his power.

---

[5] The rebuke given by Buddha to the disciple who had, without permission, made such a display of miraculous power, intended though it was for the promotion of his glory, was designed to operate as a salutary check on the pride that might find its way into the heart of even the most privileged beings. Such a lesson was deemed of the greatest importance, since we find in the book of Buddhistic ordinations the sin of boasting of or pretending to the power of working wonders, &c., ranked among the four capital sins, excluding a Rahan for ever from the society of the perfect, and depriving him of his rank and dignity. Buddha, it seems, wished to reserve to himself alone the honour of working miracles, or to give the permission, when circumstances should require it, to some of his disciples to do the same in his name and for the exaltation of his religion.

The following story of Purana and his five associates holds a prominent rank among the events that have rendered Buddha so celebrated. Gaudama, as it has been already mentioned in some foregoing notes, was an ascetic who had studied philosophy under eminent masters who belonged to the Brahminical school. In many of his opinions, as well as in his mode of life, there was no perceptible difference between him and the followers of the Brahmins. The writings of the latter, as well as those of the earliest Buddhists, exhibit to us the sight of a great number of schools, where opinions on ontology, morals, and dogmas, &c., at once various, multifarious, and opposite, were publicly taught. Then the human mind, left to its own resources, launching forth into the boundless field of speculative philosophy, ran in every direction, searching after truth. The mania for arguing, defining, drawing conclusions, &c., in those days, prevailed to an extent scarcely to be credited. Many centuries before Aristotle, wrote the rules of dialectics the Indian philosophers had carried the art of reasoning to a great degree of nicety and shrewdness. Witness the disputes and discussions between the Brahmins and the immediate disciples of Buddha. When our Phra began to attract about his person crowds of hearers and disciples; when his opinions on the end of man were understood and appreciated; when the system of castes received the first shock from the new but rapidly progressing doctrine; when the eyes and hearts of the people were slowly at first, and rapidly afterwards, centred on the new preacher and his disciples; when at last alms, that had hitherto flowed into the abodes of the Brahmins, began to enter into new channels and carry their substantial produce to the door of the followers of the new sect, then jealousy and other passions began to agitate the hearts of those who had hitherto retained an undisputed sway over the credulity of the people. They tried, if credit be given to the works of Buddhists, every effort and devised every means in order to oppose the progress of the new doctrine.

In this instance, Purana and his friends, assisted, as the Buddhists

The heretics soon heard of the prohibition issued by Gaudama to his disciples. They thought that no one would dare to match them in the display of wonders, and that they could easily ascertain their superiority over him. The ruler of Radzagio, hearing of this news, went to Buddha and inquired as to his motive for such a prohibition. Buddha told him that the prohibition regarded his disciples only, but not himself. The heretics, informed of

---

pretend, by the agency of the evil one, wished to enter into discussion with Buddha and to surpass him in the display of miraculous power. The contest was to take place in the country of Thawattie, in the presence of the king and of a countless multitude assembled for the purpose. Purana, as usual with Buddhists in regard to those who held opinions different from their own, is styled a heretic. Of the opinions of the enemies of Buddha nothing is said in the present work, but the writer has had the opportunity of perusing another work where a slight allusion is made to those six holders of heterodox doctrines. Their opinions were at variance on the beginning of this world, the eternity of matter, the existence of the soul, and a first principle, creator of all that exists. We may infer therefrom that they were heads or chiefs of various schools, who, though not agreeing among themselves upon purely speculative doctrines, united and combined against the common enemy. A detailed account of the doctrines held by these six heretics would prove highly interesting, as it would throw some light on the very obscure and imperfectly known history of Indian philosophy, in the days when Buddhism assumed the shape of a religious system. To those who are unacquainted with Indian literature, the great progress made by Hindus in philosophical sciences at such an early period may appear somewhat doubtful: but modern discoveries made all over the Indian peninsula leave not the least doubt respecting this startling assertion. At a period when Greece and the other regions of Europe were sunk in a state of complete ignorance, most of the branches of literature were successfully cultivated on the banks of the Ganges. The study of philosophy always supposes a great intellectual advancement. There would, therefore, be no rashness whatever in asserting that the present state and condition of India, as regards literary progress, are much below the mark that was attained at such a remote period. The epoch of literary decadence began with the devastating expeditions of the fanatical Moslem in the tenth century. It is probable, too, that the religious and sanguinary conflicts between the Buddhists and Brahminists have had their share in bringing about a similar result. The latter, having obtained the ascendancy over their adversaries, became more bigoted. They would no longer tolerate, to the same extent as before, the liberty of elaborating new systems, lest some successful philosopher might hereafter propagate opinions at variance with their own, undermine the mighty fabric of their creed, and endanger the holding of that absolute sway and paramount influence they had recovered, after centuries of a deadly contest with the disciples of the philosopher of Kapilawot.

this, said, "What will become of us? Gaudama himself will show signs." They held a council among themselves as to what was to be done. Gaudama told the king that in four months he would make a grand display of his miraculous power in the country of Thawattie, as it was in that place that all former Buddhas had in former ages showed signs. The heretics from that day never lost sight of Buddha for a moment; they followed him day and night. They gave orders that a large and extensive covered place should be prepared for them, where they might show their power and outshine that of the Rahan Gaudama. Buddha having said that he would select the spot where a white mango-tree stood for the scene of his miracles, the heretics caused the total destruction of all mango-trees in that direction.

On the full moon of Tabaong (February), Gaudama left Radzagio, attended by a large retinue of disciples. He went to preach in different parts. On the seventh of the waxing moon of Watso he entered the country of Thawattie. A gardener gave him by way of present a large mango fruit. Ananda prepared the fruit and Buddha ate it. When this was done, the stone was handed to Ananda with an injunction to plant it in a place prepared to receive it. When planted, Buddha washed his hands over it, and on a sudden there sprang up a beautiful white mango-tree, fifty cubits high, with large branches loaded with blossoms and fruits. To prevent its being destroyed, a guard was set near it by the king's order. Dismayed at such a wonderful sign, the heretics fled in every direction to conceal their shame and confusion. Their head man, named Pourana, took from a husbandman a large jar with a rope, tied up the vessel with one extremity of the rope, passed the other round his neck, and flinging first the jar and next himself into the river, where the water was very deep, he was drowned, and went to the lowest hell, called Awidzi.

Buddha created in the air an immense road, reaching east and west to the extremities of the world. When the sun began to verge towards the west, he thought the time had come to ascend to that road in the presence of an immense crowd, that covered an area of thirty-six youdzanas, and there make a display of his wonderful powers. He was on the point of crossing the threshold of the building that had been erected for him by the care of Nats, when a female convert, named Garamie, who had become an Anagam, came into his presence, and after the usual prostrations said to him, "Glorious Buddha, it is not necessary that you should take the trouble of working wonders; I, your servant, will do it." "What wonder will you work, my daughter, Garamie?" replied Buddha. "I will," said Garamie, "fill up the space with water, and plunging into the water in an eastern direction, I will come back, and reappear in the west like a water-fowl. On my appearance before the crowd they will ask, What is this water-fowl? And I will answer to them, that this water-fowl is Garamie, the daughter of the most excellent Buddha. This is the wonder I will accomplish. The heretics, on seeing it, will say to themselves, If such be the power of Garamie, how much greater and more wonderful must be that of Buddha himself?" "I know," said Buddha, "that you have such a power, but it is not for your sake that these crowds have been gathered together;" and he refused the solicited permission. Garamie said to herself, Buddha would not allow me to work this great wonder, but there is some one else that can do greater things than I; perhaps Buddha will not be so inflexible with them as he is with me. She then withdrew to a becoming place.

Buddha thought within himself, There are many among my disciples who can make a display of great wonders; it is meet that the crowds should be aware of it, and see how, with hearts stout as that of the lion, they are ready to perform the most wonderful feats. He said aloud, "Who are they that can do wonders? let them come forward." Many came into his presence with a lion-like boldness and a thundering voice, craving for the honour of displaying supernatural powers. Among them was a rich man, named Anatapein; a female child, called Tsera; a grown-up woman, and Maukalan. They volunteered their services to perform the most extraordinary wonders, in order both to frighten the heretics, and make them understand that, if such a power belonged to the disciples, what that of Buddha himself must be. But Buddha would not accept their proffered services, and said to them that the people had not been assembled there for their sake, but for his; and that to him alone was reserved the task of enrapturing the crowds by the great wonders he was preparing to show. Addressing Maukalan, he said to him that, being a Buddha, he could not leave to others the trouble of performing his own duty. In a former existence, when he was a bullock, he drew from a muddy place a heavily-laden cart, to save a Brahmin's property and rejoice his heart.

Buddha ascended to the immense road which he had created in the air in the presence of the crowd, that filled a place of eighteen youdzanas in breadth and twenty-four in length. These wonders which he was about to display were the result of his own wisdom, and could not be imitated by any one. He caused a stream of water to issue from the upper part of his body and flames of fire from the lower part, and on a sudden the reverse to take place; again fire issued from his right eye, and streams of water from his left eye, and so on from his nostrils, ears, right and left, in front and behind. The same wonder too happened in such a way that the streams of fire succeeded the streams of water, but without mingling with each other. Each stream in an upward direction reached the seats of Brahmas; each stream in a downward direction penetrated as far as hell; each in a horizontal direction reached the extremities of the world. From each of his hairs the same wonderful display feasted the astonished eyes of the assembled people. The six glories gushed, as it were, from every part of his body, and made it appear resplendent beyond description. Having no one to converse with, he created a personage, who appeared to walk with him. Sometimes he sat down, while his companion was pacing along; and at other times he himself walked, whilst his interlocutor was either standing or sitting. All the while Buddha put to him questions which he readily answered, and in his turn replied to the interrogations that were made to him. At intervals Phra preached to the crowd, who were exceedingly rejoiced, and sung praises to him. According to their good dispositions, he expounded the various points of the law. The people who heard him and saw the wonderful works he performed, obtained the understanding of the four great principles.

Buddha, having completed the twofold work of preaching to the crowds, and exciting their respect and admiration by the most astonishing display of the most extraordinary miracles, began to think within himself as follows: To what place have all former Buddhas resorted after the display of signs, and spent the season? He saw by a stretch of his incomparable foresight that all of them had gone to the seat of Tawadeintha, in the Nats' country, to announce the perfect law to their mothers. He resolved to go thither too. With one step he reached the summit of the mountain Ugando, at a distance of 160,000 youdzanas, and another step carried him to the top of the Mienmo mountain. This was done without any effort on the part of Buddha. Those mountains lowered their summits to the very spot where he was standing, and rose up again to resume their lofty position. Buddha found himself brought almost instantaneously to the seat of Tawadeintha.[6] He took his position on the immense rock

[6] The preachings of Buddha were not to be confined to the narrow limits of man's abode; they were designed to reach much further. All beings living in the six seats of Nats were to share with men the blessings of the publication of the perfect law. It has been already stated at length, in a foregoing note, that the condition of Nats is merely a state of pleasure and enjoyment allotted to those who in former existences had done some meritorious work. The fortunate inhabitants of these celestial regions

Pantukambala. When he lay extended there upon his tsiwaran, the huge mass on a sudden contracted itself to the very narrow dimensions of his dress.

---

remain in those seats until the sum of their respective merits being, as it were, exhausted, they return to the abode of man, the true place of probation for all beings living therein. The condition of Nat, therefore, is not a permanent one; the Nat, after his time of reward is over, has to migrate to our terrestrial abode, begin a new existence, and endeavour to advance himself in the way of perfection by the practice of virtue. He is as yet very far from the state of Neibban. Like man, he has to learn the sublime law, and to become acquainted with the roads leading to the four high perfections. Buddha, who came to announce the law of salvation to all beings, could not but go to the seats of Nats, and teach them the way to free themselves from the turmoil of never-ending existence. The preachings of Buddha for three consecutive months were attended with a success that must have exceeded his most sanguine expectations. Millions of Nats were converted, and forthwith obtained the deliverance. Others less advanced in merits obtained the first, or second, or third state of perfection.

During his stay in the other seats of Nats, Buddha gave a decision on the merits of almsgiving, which is certainly to the advantage of the yellow-dressed Bickus, but appears somewhat opposed to all principles of justice and reason. In his opinion the inward dispositions of him who gives alms has nothing to do with the merits resulting from such a good work. Those merits are strictly proportionate to the degree of sanctity or perfection of him who receives alms. Such doctrine, destructive of the purest and noblest motives that can actuate man to do good, is openly upheld now both in theory and practice by the Buddhist monks. When they receive alms from the admirers of their saintly mode of life, they never think of returning thanks to those who so liberally administer to all their material wants; they content themselves with saying, Thadoo, thadoo; that is to say, Well, well; and the pious offerer withdraws perfectly satisfied and happy, relying on the merits he has gained on this occasion, and longing for another opportunity of doing the like. The liberality of the laity towards the religious is carried to an excess scarcely to be credited. Government do not interfere in the maintenance of the perfect, and yet they are abundantly supplied with all the necessaries, nay, the luxuries, of life. They live on the fat of the land.

That the crowds of people might be better prepared for hearing the sacred law and obtaining a correct understanding of it, Buddha charges Maukalan to a regular fast, or at least abstinence, carried to a considerable degree. A free and copious use of nourishing substances unfits man for mental exertions, occasions in him heaviness and supineness, enervates and weakens the vigour of the intellect, and gives to matter a preponderating influence over the soul. The advice will hold good everywhere, but it becomes particularly pressing and stringent when addressed to an audience of Buddhists, who require the full force of their mind to be able to understand the various bearings of a doctrine resting on the most abstruse principles, the end of which too is to disentangle the soul from the influence of materiality. Up to this day

The people who had seen Buddha, and who could not now descry him, found themselves in a state of bereavement, as if the sun and the moon had disappeared from the sky. They gave full vent to their cries and lamentations, saying: We are now deprived of the blessed presence of him who is the most excellent among the three sorts of beings, men, Nats, and Brahmas. Some said he has gone to this place; some replied, no, he has gone to that place. Many of the people, who had just arrived from different parts of the country, were exceedingly grieved, because they could not see him. They all repaired before Maukalan, to ascertain from him what place Buddha had gone to. Maukalan knew it, but he wished to leave to Anourouda the honour of satisfying their curiosity. The latter said to them that Buddha had gone to the seat of Tawadeintha to preach the law to his mother, and spend there one season on the rock of Pantukambala. He added, that he would be back in three months hence, on the day of the full moon of Thadin-kioot (October). They came to the spontaneous

---

in Burmah there are some remnants of the observance of fast during the three months of Lent, when the law is oftener expounded to and better observed by religious people. The obligation of fasting during the days of the quarters of the moon is generally admitted, and some few observe it, if not always, at least from time to time. The generality of the Burmese people entirely disregard fasting.

Curious but interesting is the reply Buddha gave to Thariputra, who rejoiced exceedingly because men and Nats vied with each other in paying great honours to him. He unhesitatingly states: Blessed are all those who rejoice on his account. By this joy we ought not to understand the transient and momentary affection of the heart, elicited by some pleasing and agreeable occurrence; but the kind of joy alluded to is a rational, philosophical, and religious one, having its origin, first, in a full and perfect knowledge of Buddha's transcendent excellence, rendering his person an object of the highest admiration; and, second, in a lively confidence in his benevolence and goodness towards all beings, which urge him to labour for their deliverance from all miseries and their guidance to a state of peace and rest. Such a joy, diffused over the heart, creates an ardent love for Buddha and his doctrine; that affection rests, not on Buddha, as a mere individual, but on him who is the personification of a saviour of all beings. It implies faith in him and his preachings, as well as a strong confidence in his power and willingness to confer the greatest possible benefits. Hence there is no wonder to hear Buddha declaring all those blessed who on that solemn occasion rejoiced in him.

resolution to remain on that very spot, and not to return to their homes, until they had seen Buddha a second time. They erected temporary sheds; and, though the place was small for such a countless multitude, they managed to accommodate themselves in the best way they could. Previous to his departure, Buddha had enjoined on Maukalan to remain with the people and preach to them the law. Maukalan faithfully complied with the request, and during three consecutive months instructed the people, and answered all their questions. The rich man Anatapein fed the Rahans and the assembly abundantly during the whole time.

CHAPTER X.

Buddha's proceedings in the seat of Tawadeintha—His triumphant return to the seat of men, in the city of Thin-ka-tha—He is calumniated by the heretics of Thawattie—Eighth season spent in the forest of Tesakala—Subsequent preachings—He meets with a bad reception in the Kothamby country—Dissension among the disciples—Reconciliation—Travels of Buddha—Preaching to a Pounha who tilled a field.

WHILE Buddha was in the seat of Tawadeintha all the Nats came from more than ten thousand worlds to his presence; but the glory that always encompasses their bodies disappeared, or was completely outshone by that of Buddha's person. His mother, a daughter of Nats, came from the seat of Toothita to see her son and hear his instructions. She sat on his right. Two sons of Nats stood by the right and left of his mother. The crowd was so great that it covered a surface of eighteen youdzanas. In that immense assembly two Nats were conspicuous by their particular demeanour and position. One of them stood so close to Buddha as to touch almost one of his knees, the other was standing in a respectful position afar off. Buddha asked the latter what he had done to deserve the place he occupied. He answered that, during former existences, he had made abundant alms indeed, but his merits had been comparatively small, because he had not done those good works to persons eminent for their sanctity. The same question was put to the other Nat, who said that he was, in a former existence, living in very narrow circumstances, but that he had had the good fortune of giving alms, according to his limited means, to persons who were much advanced in merits. With a voice that was heard by the crowds on the seat of men, Buddha proclaimed the immense advantage of giving alms to and supporting the Rahans and those advanced in perfection. They were, said he, like good seed sown on a good field, that yields an abundance of good fruits. But alms given to those who are as yet under the tyrannical yoke of passions are like a seed deposited in a bad soil; the passions of the receiver of alms choke, as it were, the growth of merits. At the conclusion, the two Nats obtained the reward of Thautapan. The crowds on earth had also the benefit of hearing his instructions.

Whilst Buddha was in the middle of the Nats, he announced the law of Abidama to his mother. Having to go about to get his food, Buddha created a likeness of another Buddha, whom he commissioned to continue the preaching of the Abidama. As to himself, he went to the mountain of Himawonta, ate the tender branches of a certain tree, washed his face in the lake Anawadat, and partook of the food he received from the Northern Island. Thariputra went thither to render him all necessary services. When he had eaten his meal, he called Thariputra, and desired him to go and preach the law of Abidama to five hundred Rahans, who were present when the display of wonders took place, and were much pleased with it. In the time of the Buddha Kathaba those five hundred Rahans were bats, living in a cave much resorted to by Rahans, who were wont to repeat the Abidama. Those bats contrived to retain a certain number of words, the meaning whereof they could not understand. When they died, they were transferred into one of the seats of Nats; and when they became men anew, they had the good fortune to be born from illustrious parents, in the country of Thawattie, and when Phra showed his powers, they were much pleased. They became Rahans under Thariputra, and were the first to understand perfectly the sublime law of Abidama.

As to Buddha, he returned to the seat of Tawadeintha and continued the instructions, where the Buddha of his creation had left them. At the end of three months' preaching, an innumerable number of Nats knew and understood the four great principles. As to his mother, she obtained the perfection of Thautapan.

The time when Buddha was to return to the seat of men was near at hand. The crowds, eager to know the precise time when Buddha was to come back among them, went to Maukalan to ascertain from him the precise day on which they would be blessed with his presence. "Well," said Maukalan to the people, "in a very short time I will give you an answer on the subject of your inquiry." That very instant he plunged to the bottom of the earth and reappeared, but when he was at the foot of the Mienmo mountain, he ascended, in the view of the crowd whom he had left, and soon arrived in the presence of Buddha, to whom he explained the object of his errand. "My son," answered Buddha, "in what country does your brother Thariputra spend his season?" "In the city of Thin-ka-tha," replied Maukalan. "Well," said Buddha, "seven days hence, at the full moon of Thadin-kioot (October), I will descend near the gate of Thin-ka-tha city; go and tell the people that those who desire to see me must go to that country, distant thirty youdzanas from Thawattie. Let no one take any provision; but by a rigorous abstinence let them dispose themselves to hear the law that I will preach." Maukalan, having paid his respects to Buddha, returned to the place where the assembled multitude anxiously waited for him. He related to them all the particulars regarding his interview with Buddha, and conveyed to them the much-wished-for intelligence of his speedy return on earth.

On the day of the full moon of Thadin-kioot (October), Buddha disposed himself to go down to the seat of men. He called a prince of Thagias and directed him to prepare everything for his descent. Complying with his request, the Thagia prepared three ladders or stairs, one made of precious stones, occupying the middle; one on the right made of gold; and a third, made of silver, on the left. The foot of each ladder rested on the earth, near to the gate of Thin-ka-tha city, and their summits leaned on the top of the Mienmo mountain. The middle ladder was for Buddha, the golden one for the Nats, and that of silver for the Brahmas. Having reached the summit of the steps, Buddha stopped awhile, and resolved to make a fresh display of his power. He looked upwards, and all the superior seats of Brahmas were distinctly descried; on his looking downwards, his eyes could see and plunge into the bottom of the earth to the lowest hell. The Nats of more than a thousand systems could see each other. Men could perceive Nats in their fortunate seats, and Nats saw men in their terrestrial abode. The six glories streamed forth with an incomparable splendour from Buddha's person, which became visible to all the crowds. There was not one who did not praise Buddha. Having the Nats on his right, and the Brahmas on his left, the most glorious Phra began his triumphant coming down. He was preceded by a Nat, holding a harp in his hands and playing the most melodious tunes; another Nat fanned him; a chief of Brahmas held over him a golden umbrella. Surrounded with that brilliant *cortège*, Buddha descended near the gate of Thin-ka-tha city, and stopped there for awhile. Thariputra came forthwith into the presence of Buddha, paid him his respects at a becoming distance, and said, with a heart overflowing with joy: "On this day, O most glorious Buddha, all the Nats and men are showing their love to you." Buddha replied: "Blessed is Thariputra, and blessed are all those who rejoice on my account. Men and Nats love him who is acquainted with the sublime law, who has put an end to his passions, and who has attained to the highest state of contemplation." At the end of his discourse, innumerable beings understood the four great principles, and the five hundred Rahans whom Thariputra was commissioned to instruct reached the state of Arahat. On the spot where all Buddhas set their feet, when coming from the seat of Tawadeintha, a dzedi [1] has always been erected.

Buddha, on leaving Thin-ka-tha, shaped his course

---

[1] The religious edifices that are to be met with in all parts of Burmah deserve a particular notice. They are called dzedis in all the Buddhist writings of the Burmese, but the people generally speak of them under the appellation of Payas or Phras, which, in this instance, is merely a title of honour of a religious character.

Dzedis, in the earliest days of Buddhism, were sacred tumuli raised upon a shrine, wherein relics of Buddha had been deposited. These structures were as so many lofty witnesses, bearing evidence to the presence of sacred and precious objects, intended to revive in the memory of the faithful the remembrance of Buddha, and foster in their hearts tender feelings of devotion and a glowing fervour for his religion.

From the perusal of this legend, it will appear that dzedis were likewise erected on the tombs of individuals who, during their lifetime, had obtained great distinction by their virtues and spiritual attainments among the members of the assembly. Buddha himself ordered that a monument should be built over the shrine containing the relics of the two great disciples, Thariputra and Maukalan. In Burmah, no dzedis of great dimensions and proportions have ever been erected on the ashes of distinguished Phongyies. In some parts, however, particularly in the upper country, there may be seen here and there some small dzedis, a few feet high, erected on the spot where have been deposited the remains of some saintly personages. These monuments are little noticed by the people, though, on certain occasions, a few offerings of flowers, tapers, &c., are made around and in front of them.

Similar kinds of religious edifices have been built sometimes also to become a receptacle of the Pitagat, or collection of the holy scriptures. One of the finest temples of Ceylon was devoted to that purpose. There was also one in the ancient city of Ava, but I am not aware that there is any of this kind at Amarapoora.

Finally, dzedis have been erected for the sole purpose of harbouring statues of Gaudama; but there is every reason to believe that this practice gained ground in subsequent ages. When a fervent Buddhist, impelled by the desire of satisfying the cravings of his piety and devotion, wished to build a religious monument, and could not procure relics, he then remained contented by supplying the deficiency with images of Buddha representing that eminent personage, in attitudes of body that were to remind Buddhists of some of the most striking actions of his life. In many instances, dzedis have been built up, not even for the sake of sheltering statues, but for the pious purpose of reminding the people of the holy relics of Buddha, and, as they used to say, for kindling in the soul a tender feeling of affectionate reverence for the person of Buddha and his religion. If what is put forward as a plea for building pagodas be founded on conviction and truth, we must conclude that the inhabitants of the valley of the Irrawaddy are most devotedly religious, as the mania for building dzedis has been, and even now is, carried to such a pitch as to render almost fabulous the number of religious buildings to be seen on an extent of above seven hundred miles as far as Bhamo.

As Buddhism was imported from India into Eastern Asia there is no

towards Wethalie, and took his abode in the Dzetawon monastery. The fame of the wonders he had performed increased his reputation, and elicited from the people fresh

---

doubt that the style of architecture adopted in the erection of religious edifices came from the same quarter. To the native genius of the Burmese we may allow the merit of ornamental architecture for the great monasteries, and a few details of the exterior decorations of the religious monuments; but no one will take offence at refusing to the tribes that occupy the basin of the Irrawaddy the merit of originating the plan of such monuments as those to be seen in some parts of the country. It is much to their credit that they have been able to raise such mighty fabrics with the imperfect knowledge they possess and the very limited means at their disposal. The resemblance that exists between the much-defaced Buddhist monuments yet to be met with in some parts of India and at Java, and those now studding the banks of the Irrawaddy, leaves no doubt respecting the origin of the shape and form of such monuments.

At first sight, the traveller in Burmah believes that there is a great variety in the shape and architecture of pagodas. He is easily led astray by many fantastical ornaments that have been added by inexperienced natives to religious monuments. After, however, a close examination of those edifices, it seems that they can be arranged into three distinct classes, to which those presenting minor differences may be referred. The first class comprises those which have a cone-like appearance, though much enlarged in the direction of the base. These are without niches, or rather ought to be without niches, as the small ones to be seen added to those monuments indicate that they are no essential appendage of the building, but rather the fanciful and tasteless work of some devotees. The pagodas of Rangoon, Pegu and Prome offer the finest specimens of this order of edifices. The second class includes those of a dome-like shape. They are not common in Burmah. The finest and grandest specimen is that of the Kaong-hmoo-dau, or great meritorious work, situated west of the ancient city of Tsagain. In the third class we may place all the pagodas that approximate to the temple form; that is to say, all those that offer the shape of a more or less considerable rectangle, with a large hall in the centre and several galleries running throughout. Upon this rectangle a conical structure is raised, ending as usual with the tee or umbrella. The most remarkable and perfect specimens of this kind are to be seen at Pagan, which may be aptly styled the City of Pagodas.

The cone-shaped pagoda invariably rests on a quadrangular basis a few feet high. The body of the cone in its lower part is an hexagon or octagon, broad at first, then gradually and regularly decreasing to two-thirds of its height. Upon it rises the regular cone, which ends in a point covered with the gilt umbrella.

The architectural ornaments of such structures are circular, bold and round lines or mouldings; above this, to the place where the cone begins, are sculptures, representing leaves shooting from the middle part, one-half upwards and the other half downwards. That part is often divested of such ornaments, as is the case with the Shoaydagon. On the sides of the cone are horizontal lines grouped together; each group is separated by a considerable distance, then comes a sculptured foliage, different from the one already mentioned, but

tokens of respect and veneration. Alms poured from all quarters into the monastery; the liberality of the people towards his person and that of his disciples expanded in

---

disposed in a like manner. In the middle of the four sides of the base, particularly in the one facing the East, the Burmese have introduced the practice of making small niches for receiving the statues representing Buddha in a cross-legged position. A portico leads to them. On the four angles of the base they likewise place griffins or sometimes fantastic figures of monsters. Small dzedis are often disposed on the lower parts of the hexagon or octagon. This kind of pagoda being naturally destitute of all ornaments, and standing over a tomb or a shrine, as a pillar that has gradually assumed the shape above described, is a very ancient one, and probably coëval with the earliest Buddhist religious monuments.

The second class of religious edifices is that of those that exhibit a dome-like appearance. They are rather uncommon in Burmah. They rest on a square basis. The lower part is adorned with a few mouldings, but the greatest part offers a perfectly even superficies. The umbrella that is placed on them partakes somewhat of the appearance of the monument it is destined to crown. It considerably expands in the horizontal direction, and has a very ungraceful appearance. The Kaong-hmoo-dau in the neighbourhood of Tsagain rests on a basis about 18 or 20 feet high; the dome, according to an inscription, is 153 feet high, the diameter, at the lowest part, is nearly 200 feet. The whole was formerly gilt. The four sides of the square are lined with small niches, each tenanted by a small statue of Gaudama. Separated from the square by an open and well-paved gallery that runs all round the edifice, are disposed in a row eight hundred and two small pillars of sandstone, about 6 feet high, with their upper part perforated, so as to afford room sufficient to receive a lamp on festival days. Splendid must be the effect produced during a dark night by so many lamps, pouring a flood of light that illuminates on all sides the massive edifice. Whether the monument was built about three hundred years ago, as stated to the writer by one of the guardians, or, as it is most probable, only repaired and adorned at that time, certain it is that this kind of religious edifice is very ancient, and very likely not inferior in antiquity to those above referred to. Another of a similar form, but of much smaller dimensions, is to be seen at Bhamo, not far from the eastern gate.

The third class of pagodas comprises all those that are generally of a square form, not made of a solid masonry, but with openings or doors, a room, galleries, &c., for receiving statues of Gaudama. They are all surmounted with the usual conical structure, which is, it seems, the essential appendage to all dzedis. These edifices, in my opinion, are not to be considered as tumuli or topes, but rather as places of worship, and sanctuaries for the reception of the statues of Gaudama. The monuments are, I suspect, of a comparative modern origin; they have not the plainness and simplicity of the tumuli which agree so well with the simplicity of the religious form of worship of primitive Buddhism. They are not made to answer the purpose for which dzedis were primitively raised. They must have been erected at times when Buddhist worship, emerging from its primeval sternness of form, assumed proportions and developments congenial to

a wonderful manner. The heretics, who swarmed in Wethalie and its neighbourhood, became exceedingly jealous of Buddha's successes. The loss which they sustained in the donations of the people added fuel to the inward discontent. They resolved to devise some means to lower the character of Buddha in the opinion of the people. After a long deliberation, they fixed on the following plan:—A certain woman of great beauty, but of a rather doubtful character, was induced to join them in accusing Gaudama of having violated her. She contrived to assume the appearance of a person in a state of pregnancy, and, covering herself with a piece of red cloth, she went about the town spreading evil reports respecting Buddha's character. She had the impudence even to go into the Dzetawon monastery, and ask Buddha to provide a place for her approaching confinement, and likewise maintenance for herself and the child she was by him pregnant with. Such an infamous calumny did not, however, move him in the least. Conscious of his innocence, he lost nothing of his usual composure and serenity. But by the interference of the Thagia the slander was made manifest. Two mice bit the strings that kept tied up on the abdo-

---

the taste and wants of large religious communities. This class of temples offers a great variety of forms as to the size, dimensions, and details of architecture. But they may be all brought to this general outline. From the square body of the temple diverge, in the direction of the four points of the compass, porticoes; the one facing the east is always the largest and best adorned; sometimes there is but one portico, that of the east, and there are only doors in the middle of the three other sides. From these porticoes the galleries converge towards the centre of the temple, where are statues. In the large and magnificent pagodas of Pagan, galleries with vaults in the pointed style run all round the building. Some of those stupendous structures have two stories, and it is only on the second that the conical part rests, which is the essential complement of every religious building. On one of the middle-sized pagodas rises, instead of a cone, an obelisk, with ornaments that appear to resemble hieroglyphic figures. Some of those obelisks swell considerably towards the middle of their height. Great was the surprise and astonishment of the writer, when he observed in the same place, among the prodigious number of pagodas, in a more or less advanced state of decay, one, not considerable by its dimensions, nor in a much-ruined condition, that exhibited the solitary instance of a regular pyramid.

men the apparatus designed to prop up the deceit, and, on a sudden, the whole fell on the ground, proclaiming at once the innocence of the sage and smiting his enemies with confusion.

Every one present on the occasion gave vent to his just indignation at such a base attempt on the part of the heretics. But Buddha meekly replied that what had just happened was a righteous retribution for a misbehaviour of his own during a former existence. At that time, he was on a certain day under the influence of liquor, when he chanced to meet on his way a Pitzegabuddha. Without any reason or provocation, he abused the holy man with the lowest and coarsest expressions, and went so far as to tell him that his whole life was but a series of hypocritical actions. Turning then towards his disciples, he added, with a grave countenance, that what they had now witnessed was the just punishment inflicted on him under the influence of the demerit created and generated by his former evil doing.

The eighth season was spent in the grove or forest of Tesakala, and when the rains were over, the most excellent Phra travelled throughout the country, preaching and teaching the right way to many. Countless converts entered one of the four ways, and many obtained at once the deliverance.

In the town of Santoo-maragiri, he was preaching to the benefactors who had fed him and his disciples. Among the hearers were two persons, Nakoulapita and Nakoulamata, husband and wife, belonging to the pounha race. During a great many successive former existences they had had the good fortune to be father, mother, uncle, aunt, &c., to Buddha. During the present existence the feeling of affection towards him with whom they had been so long and so intimately connected was powerfully awakened and glowed in their hearts. Under the influence of that natural, kindly, and tender feeling, they came forward, and prostrating themselves before Gaudama, said to him:

"Dear son, how is it that you have been away from us for so long a while? We are so happy to see you after so long an absence." Buddha, remaining indifferent to such a scene and language, knew at once what were the real wants of that good couple, and in what manner he could acknowledge the great favours he had during former existences received at their hands. He preached to them the most excellent law. They were thoroughly converted. The next morning they had the happiness to supply their great teacher and his company with the choicest food. Meanwhile they addressed to him the following request: "During many existences we both have always been happily united: not a word of complaint or quarrel has ever passed between us. We pray that in our coming existences the same love and affection may ever unite us together." Their request was affectionately granted, and Buddha, in the presence of a large assembly, pronounced them blessed and happy amongst all men and women.

The son of the ruler of the country where these things happened was, to his great affliction, childless. He invited Buddha to come and partake of his hospitality in his house. The offer was accepted. Great preparations were made for the reception of the illustrious visitor. The prince had some of his own clothes laid on the way that Buddha was to follow, in the hope that by treading over them he might communicate a certain virtue, whereby he would have the object of his earnest desire realised. On his arrival near the entrance of the house, Buddha stopped and refused to proceed farther. Meanwhile, he beckoned Ananda to remove the clothes. This was done accordingly, to the prince's deep disappointment. After the meal, Gaudama explained to him that he and his wife during a former existence had lived on eggs and had killed many birds. Their present barrenness was the just punishment of their former trespassing; but their actual good dispositions having atoned for the past transgressions, they would be blessed with children. Both were overjoyed at this news. They believed in Buddha, obtained the state of Thautapan, and thereby entered into the current of perfection. Their faith in Buddha's word procured for them so happy a result.

During all the time that elapsed after the rain, Buddha travelled through the country, engaged on his usual benevolent errand, and converting many among men and Nats. In the country of Garurit, in a village of pounhas called Magoulia, the head man, one of the richest in the place, had a daughter whose beauty equalled that of a daughter of Nats. She had been in vain asked in marriage by princes, nobles, and pounhas. The proud damsel had rejected every offer. On the day that her father saw Gaudama, he was struck with his manly beauty and meek deportment. He said within himself: "This man shall be a proper match for my daughter." On his return home he communicated his views to his wife. On the following day, the daughter having put on her choicest dress and richest apparels, they all three went with a large retinue to the Dzetawon monastery. Admitted to the presence of Buddha, the father asked for his daughter the favour of being allowed to attend on him. Without returning a word of reply, or giving the least sign of acceptance or refusal, Buddha rose up and withdrew to a small distance, leaving behind him on the floor the print of one of his feet. The pounha's wife, well skilled in the science of interpreting wonderful signs, saw at a glance that the marks on the print indicated a man no longer under the control of passions, but a sage emancipated from the thraldom of concupiscence. She communicated her views to her husband, who had the impudence to go to Buddha's presence and renew the same offer. Buddha meekly replied: "Pounha, I neither accept nor decline your offer; in your turn, listen to what I have to say." He then went on to relate how he had left the world, resisted Manh's temptation, lived in solitude for six years, and freed himself from the net of passions. He concluded by stating that, having become a Buddha, he had for ever conquered all passions. At the conclusion of the instruction, both father and mother became established in the state of Thautapan. The damsel was highly offended at the refusal she experienced, and retained a strong feeling of hatred towards him who had declined her proffered favours. Her father took her into the Kothambi country, where she was offered to the ruler, who, smitten with her charms, elevated her to the rank of first queen.

In the country of Kothambi, there lived three rich men. These three men fed during the rainy season every year five hundred hermits, who came from the Himalaya range for the purpose of obtaining their maintenance. These charitable laymen went over to Wethalie for the purpose of trade. There they met Buddha, and earnestly pressed him to come to their country and preach the law. The invitation was accepted. They returned home, and built for the accommodation of the illustrious visitor each of them one monastery. When all was ready, Buddha went to Kothambi, attended by five hundred disciples. He spent there the ninth season. During his stay he dwelt by turns in each of the three monasteries, and was abundantly supported by the rich man in whose monastery he took his abode.

In the country of Kothambi there were as yet few disciples or believers in Buddha; but the number of holders of false doctrines was exceedingly great. Secretly supported by the first queen, and actuated by jealousy against the new-comer, they reviled him and his disciples in every possible way, and did their utmost to destroy in public opinion his rising fame. Whenever they met Buddha's disciples, they abused them with the coarsest language. Unable to bear any longer so many insults, Ananda, in the name of his brethren, went to Buddha, and asked him to remove to some other place, where they would receive a becoming treatment. "But," said Buddha, "if we be ill-treated in the new place we go to, what is to be done?"

"We shall proceed to some other place," replied Ananda. "But," retorted Buddha, "if in that new place we be likewise reviled, what then?" "We shall," replied Ananda, "remove to some other place." Buddha remained silent for awhile, and, casting a gentle glance on Ananda, said to him: "A little patience will save us the trouble of so many travels, and certainly procure for us here what we may perhaps vainly look for anywhere else. By patience and endurance the wise man conquers all his enemies. Behold the war-elephant; he plunges into the thickest of the raging conflict, regardless of the darts and arrows flying in every direction, and carries all before him. I, too, the most excellent Buddha, shall certainly stay here, diligently preach the most excellent law, and perseveringly labour to disentangle men from the net of passions. In no way shall I care for the abuses they may pour on me and my disciples."

Not long after this a trifling accident kindled the fire of dissension among the members of the assembly. The subject was, as usual, of a trifling nature. It was concerning a point of discipline of scarcely any importance, infringed unintentionally by a Rahan. He was accused by one of his brethren of having committed a sin. But he replied that, having done an act in which his will had not participated, he did not consider himself guilty. Each disputant attracted to his party some religious who supported his view of the case. The Kothambi Rahans seem to have been the cause of the disunion which prevailed in the community, and soon, like a devouring flame, extended to the female portion of the assembly. In vain Gaudama interfered, and exhorted the two parties to patience, union, and charity. In his presence the parties were silent, but in his absence the quarrel grew worse. At last his entreaties were unheeded, and discord continued to rend asunder the bond of unity. Disgusted with such a state of things, Buddha preached to the most distinguished members of the assembly the blessings of peace and concord. Such men as Baddia, Kimila, and Anourouddha, treasured up in their heart the instructions of their great master. But others continued the dispute. Meanwhile he resolved to separate himself for a time from all company, and to go to a lonely spot to enjoy the happiness of peace and meditation. He shaped his course towards the village of Palelayaka, where he received his food, and went into a grove of sala-trees, to fix his residence at the foot of one of those trees. The villagers, hearing of his intention, hastened to the spot, and built a hermit's hut for his use, and promised to supply him daily with his food.

It was in this place that, delighting in the contemplation of unclouded truth, Gaudama spent the tenth season alone. The rich men of the Kothambi country, hearing that Buddha had departed because of the dissension that took place among the Rahans, became indignant. They openly declared their fixed intent of refusing to give anything for the maintenance of the Rahans, until they agreed among themselves, and became reconciled with their teacher. The timely threat had the desired effect. The disputants felt the unpleasant seriousness of their uneasy position. They could hold on no longer. The Rahans came to an agreement among themselves, and promised that after the season they would go to Buddha and solicit his pardon. In the forest of Paleliaka there lived a certain elephant, much advanced in merits, which went to Buddha, and, during three months, ministered to all his wants, as a most affectionate and devoted disciple would do towards a beloved master.

The three months of Lent being completed, the rich man Anatapein made earnest inquiries with Ananda, respecting the place Buddha had withdrawn to, and charged him to invite the great preacher to come back to Thawattie, and live as usual in the Dzetawon monastery. Complying with the pious wishes of the rich man, Ananda took with himself five hundred Rahans, and went to the solitude of Paleliaka. He was likewise followed by the five hundred refractory Rahans of Kothambi, who had come to Wethalie. The ruler of the country and Anatapein had refused at first to receive them. But the prohibition had been removed on account of their repentance. He approached alone the place where Buddha was living. After the usual prostrations, Gaudama inquired whether he had come alone. He replied that there were with him many of his faithful disciples and the Kothambi Rahans. The latter came with the express purpose of asking his pardon, and a firm resolution to yield henceforward a perfect obedience to all his commands. Buddha desired them to appear in his presence. They came, were there well received, and their misbehaviour was forgiven. Gaudama explained to them the great advantage of shunning bad company and of living in retirement. The hearers were fully converted and established in the state of Thautapan. Buddha, on his return to Wethalie, continued preaching in every direction, and led to the deliverance a great number of men, Nats, and Brahmas. The stay in the Dzetawon monastery was not very long. Buddha went into the Magatha country, to a pounha village, named Nala. Not far from that village there is the Deckinagiri, or southern mountain, with a monastery. In that place Buddha spent the eleventh season.[2] His supporters were

[2] The few particulars that have been gathered respecting the mode that Buddha followed in disseminating his doctrines, exhibit him in the light of a zealous and indefatigable preacher. We see him passing from one place to another with the sole purpose of instructing the ignorant and pointing out to them the way leading to the deliverance. Behar and Oude appear to have been the seat of his labours, and the scene on which he acted in behalf of all, without any distinction of condition, caste, or sex. Individuals in the humblest walks of life, men engaged in wicked practices, women of an abandoned character, were all, to an equal degree, the object of his tender solicitude. They were all summoned to come to his feet and partake in the blessings that he had in store for them. Gaudama was to an eminent degree an earnest and fervent propagandist. This is a striking feature in his character, which distinguishes him not only from all his contemporaries, but also from all the philosophers that have appeared throughout the Indian peninsula. All these sages aimed at becoming the heads of schools, but none of them thought of promulgating a code of morals intended for the whole human race.

the pounhas of the village. The chief occupation of those men was the tillage of the fields. Gaudama took a particular pleasure during his daily walks in conversing with them, when he met them engaged in their daily labours.

One day Buddha went into the fields, where he met a pounha, with whom he began to converse, in the intention of ultimately preaching to him the holy law. He spoke at first on the subject of his daily labour, his bullocks, his plough, the seed, and the harvest, which supplied the pounha and his family with their daily food during the year. He added: "I, too, am a labourer, provided with the seed and all the implements necessary for carrying on tillage." The pounha, surprised at what he heard, asked Buddha in what place he had left his bullocks, the seed, the plough, &c. The latter coolly replied: "All these things are with me at present. Hearken, O pounha, to what I am about to state. The seed is that fervent desire, that benevolent disposition, which prompted me at the feet of the Buddha Deipinkara to ask for the Buddhaship: it is the science which I have gathered under the tree Bodi. The rain water is that uninterrupted series of good works performed by me, until I have become a Buddha. They

---

Gandama has the honour of being the first who, with enlarged views, looked upon his fellow-men as equally entitled to the benefit of his instructions. His love of all men prompted him to undergo all sorts of fatigue, to procure for them what he imagined to be a great boon. In making this statement we have no intention to pass an opinion on the doctrines of the founder of Buddhism; we merely bring forward to the notice of the reader a peculiar characteristic of that sage, which, in our humble opinion, helps to account for the extraordinary spread of Buddhism from the banks of the Oxus to the Japanese archipelago. The tenets of that creed have become popular, because they were intended for all. False though they be, particularly in what has a reference to dogmas, they were accepted by the masses, because there were no other proffered to them. The disciples of Gaudama must have been well received in the various places they went to, for they showed a disposition of mind quite unknown in those days, viz., a lively interest in the welfare of all. This zeal, which appeared so conspicuously in Gaudama and during the first ages of Buddhism, has become all but totally extinct. There is no desire on the part of those who in our days follow that creed to propagate its tenets among other nations or tribes.

have been as the means of watering the good seed which was in me. The knowledge, or science, and wisdom are as the yoke, as well as the plough-shaft. The heart, or the knowing principle which is in me, represents the reins that serve to guide the bullocks. The teeth of the plough represent the diligence that must be used in attending to the eradicating of the principle of demerits and of bad works. The plough-handle represents the guiding principle of the law, which enables me to remove all that is bad, and promote what is good. The food which you, O pounha, derive from your exertions, represents the pure relish which is tasted by him who is bent on avoiding evil and doing good. When you make use of the plough, you cut or uproot all bad weeds. So it is with him who is penetrated with the full meaning of the four great truths; he cuts and uproots from himself the wicked inclinations and low propensities that are in him. When the labour of the field is over, you unyoke your bullocks and leave them to go whithersoever they please; so it is with the wise man. By application to invigorating the principle of good that leads to perfection, he lets go the opposite principle which gives rise to all imperfections. The bullocks have to work hard to complete the work of tillage. So the sage has to struggle hard, to till perfectly and cultivate thoroughly the soil of his own being, and reach the happy state of Neibban. The husbandman who labours so much for bringing his field into a position to receive the seed, and in every way to favour its growth, is imitated by the true sage who endeavours to free himself from the miseries attending existence, to advance in the way of merits by the practice of good works, and who thirsts after the happy condition of the perfect. He who works in the field is sometimes disappointed, and feels occasionally the pangs of hunger. He who works in the field of wisdom is exempt from all miseries and afflictions. He eats the fruit of his labour. He is fully satiated when he beholds Neibban. It is in this manner, O pounha, that I am a true husbandman, and am always provided with all the implements necessary for the tillage of man's soul." The pounha, delighted with such doctrine, became a convert, and professed his belief in Buddha, the law, and the assembly. Subsequently he applied for admittance into the assembly, and by energetic efforts in the arduous work of meditation, he became at last a Rahanda.

When the rains were over, Buddha travelled through the country, preaching the most excellent law, with the happiest results. He went to the town of Satiabia, in the Kosala country. There he received from a pounha of Waritzaba an invitation to go to that place. The invitation was graciously accepted. In that town he spent the twelfth season. A great many pounhas were enlightened and converted by professing their firm adherence to the three precious things. The vile Manh Nat did his utmost to thwart the beneficial results of Buddha's preachings. A great dearth prevailing in the country, he did all that he could to starve the most excellent Buddha and all his followers. But he was frustrated in his iniquitous design by the charity of five hundred horse merchants, who had come from Outharapata, and were then staying in Waritzaba.

Buddha, leaving this country, shaped his course through the great Mantala country; he travelled by the shortest route, a distance of 500 youdzanas. He started on the day after the full moon of Tabodway, and spent nearly five months in this voyage. He reached the banks of the Ganges at Gayagati, where he crossed the mighty stream and went to Benares. He had not been long in that city, when he recrossed the Ganges and went to Wethalie, dwelling in the Gootagarathala monastery. Thence he went into Thawattie, preaching through all the places he visited. When he was in the Dzetawon monastery, he delivered the Maha Rahula instruction for the benefit of his son Rahula, who then was eighteen years old.

CHAPTER XI.

Voyage to Tsalia—Instructions to Meggia—Raoula is made a professed religious—Manahan's questions to Buddha—Misbehaviour of Thouppabuda—Questions proposed by Nats in the Dzetawon monastery—Conversion of a Biloo—Episode of Thirima at Radzagio—Attention paid to a poor pounha and to a weaver's daughter on account of their faith—In the twentieth season, appointment of Ananda to the stewardship—Conversion of a famous robber.

AFTER a rather short stay in Thawattie, Buddha went to the town of Tsalia. The inhabitants built for him a monastery on a hill not far from the town, and liberally supplied him with all that he wanted. Pleased with the good reception the people gave him, Gaudama spent on that spot the thirteenth season. He went to receive his food in the village of Dzantoo. Thence travelling through the country, he reached the banks of the river Kimikila and enjoyed himself in a beautiful grove of mango-trees. The disciple Meggia, being too much taken up with the beauty of the place, eagerly wished to remain here for some time. As a punishment for such an inordinate attachment to a particular spot, he who had renounced the world and the gratification of passions, felt on a sudden a strange change pass over him. A flood of concupiscence inundated his soul. Buddha, who saw what was taking place in Meggia, gave him an instruction on contempt for the things of this world, and entirely cured him of his great spiritual distemper.

Thence he proceeded to Thawattie into the Dzetawon monastery, where he spent the fourteenth season. The great disciple Thariputra, with five hundred religious, was spending the season in a neighbouring village. The people were so much pleased with him and his company, that they offered to each of them a piece of yellow silk. Some religious, jealous of the great disciple, came to Buddha and accused him of covetousness. Buddha fully justified his great companion and commended the liberality of the donors, who had thus an opportunity of gratifying their liberality and gaining merits.

The Thamane Raoula was then twenty years old. Having reached the canonical age, he was elevated to the dignity of Patzin. The young religious could scarcely defend himself from a certain feeling of vanity on account of his father's dignity and his own personal mien and bearing, which he was very fond of admiring. Buddha was intimately acquainted with what was going on in Raoula's soul. He preached to him the contempt of self and of all varieties of form. The instruction was so impressive that it led the young hearer to the state of Rahanda. On a certain night when Raoula was sleeping near the door of Gaudama's private apartment, Manh Nat, wishing to frighten the young Rahanda, created the likeness of an elephant, which, keeping his trunk over his head, suddenly made a frightful noise. Buddha, who was inside, saw clearly that this was only a temptation of the vile Manh. He said to him, "O wretched one, are you not aware that fear is no longer to be found in him who has become a Rahanda?" Manh, being discovered, vanished away, covered with shame and confusion at the abortiveness of his malicious attempt.

In the same year, Buddha went to Kapilawot, which is in the Thekka country, and took up his residence in the Nigranda monastery, situated close to the banks of the river Rohani. At that place he spent the fifteenth season. On a certain day, his cousin Mahanan, the son of Thoodaudana, came to the monastery, and having paid his respects to his illustrious relative, took the liberty to propose to him the four following questions:—1. In what consists the fulfilment of the religious duties? 2. What is meant by the religious disposition? 3. What is the real renouncing? 4. What is the true knowledge?

Buddha replied in the following manner: "The fulfilment of the religious duties consists in observing carefully the five precepts obligatory on all men. The religious disposition is but a loving inclination and affection for all that refers to Buddha and the law that he has published. He who possesses it experiences a continual longing for the acquisition of merits. The renouncing is that disposition a man is habitually in when he finds his pleasure in parting with his riches for the purpose of relieving the needy and bestowing alms on the members of the assembly. Finally, wisdom consists in making one's self perfectly acquainted with what can procure merits for the present and the future; under its influence man acts up to that knowledge, and also attends with the utmost diligence to what may put an end to the law of miseries."

Even among his nearest relatives, Buddha was doomed to meet with the bitterest enemies. Thouppabuda, who was at once his uncle and his father-in-law, bore to him a deadly hatred, and secretly harboured in his heart a sentiment of revenge, for two principal reasons, because his daughter Yathaudara had been abandoned by Gaudama, when he left his palace and began the life of an ascetic; and also for having admitted his own son Dewadat among the members of the assembly. Having been informed that on the following day Buddha would direct his steps towards a certain quarter of the town to beg his food Thouppabuda partook largely of intoxicating liquor, to nerve himself for the execution of the design he had in his mind, and went out in the direction in which Gaudama was expected to come. As soon as he saw him drawing near, he planted himself in the middle of the road, barring the passage, and loading his great relative with abuses. Buddha stopped awhile without showing the least sign of emotion. Then turning to Ananda, he said, "Great is the crime of my uncle; seven days hence he shall be swallowed up alive by the earth at the foot of the great staircase of his palace." On this fearful prediction being reported to Thouppabuda, he laughed and stated that he would stay during eight days in the upper story of his palace, and belie his nephew's prediction. Despite the precautions that he took, the fatal prediction was literally fulfilled. The unfortunate unrepenting prince saw the earth burst open under his feet, and he was precipitated to the very bottom of the Awidzi hell. Buddha took advantage of the awful punishment that had befallen a prince of his family to exhort Mahanan to seek a firm asylum in the three precious things, to bear a sincere love and an affectionate fondness to all that related to the law and its practices.

Up to the present period of his life, Buddha had reserved to himself the right of preaching the law to and extolling the merits of those who had brought him his food, after having partaken of their liberal donation. This instruction may be properly called the sermon of thanksgiving. It is called Anou-mau-dana. Now he allowed his disciples to do the like, and repay the generosity of their benefactors by distributing unto them the knowledge of truth.

At that time Buddha preached the four laws of A-sawau, or the four bands that retain a being in the vortex of existences. From Kapilawot Buddha returned to Thawattie in the Dzetawon monastery. At that time a Nat had proposed four questions to his companions which they had not been able to answer. They were subsequently communicated to all the denizens of the six seats of Nats, but no one had been able to solve the difficulty. Not knowing what to do, they agreed to refer the particulars to the most excellent Buddha, then in the Dzetawon monastery. A deputation was forthwith sent to him with the view of proposing to him the puzzle, and entreating him to condescend to give the much-desired solution. The members of the deputation having duly paid their respects, said to him, "O most excellent Phra, which is the best thing to be bestowed in alms? Which is the most savoury and relishing of all things? Which is the most pleasurable? Which is the best and the fittest thing to put an end to passions?" To these four questions Buddha answered by one word—"The law." Addressing himself both to the Nats and to his assembled disciples, he added, "The giving of alms, though good in itself, cannot introduce a being into the path that leads to the deliverance. The law alone can afford such a benefit. The preaching of the law, and the exertions in communicating its knowledge to others, are therefore the most excellent alms. All that in this world confers pleasure to the senses is but a means to plunge man into the vortex of existences, and thereby into all miseries. On the contrary, the hearing of the law rejoices the heart to such an extent as often to open a spring of joyful tears; it destroys concupiscence, and leads gradually out of the whirlpool of existences. It establishes man in the state of Arahat, which is the end of all passions. The law, therefore, is the most savoury, the most pleasing thing, leading beings to the cessation of all miseries. You, my beloved disciples, exert yourselves in making known by your preaching the said law to all beings. This is the most excellent alms that you can bestow on the beings that inhabit the three different states of men, Nats, and Brahmas."

Buddha soon left Thawattie and went to Alawee. A Biloo was in the habit of eating every day some children of that place. Owing to the ravenous and horrible appetite of the monster, all the children had been eaten up; there remained only the child of the king, who was on the following day to be given over to him. Buddha reviewed, as usual, on a certain morning the condition of all beings. He saw the sad position of the king of Alawee and of his son. He resolved to proffer assistance to both, and also to convert the Biloo. He arrived in the country of Alawee, where he was received with every mark of respect. He forthwith went into the forest where the monster lived. At first he met with a most determined and violent opposition. But, opposing to his enraged antagonist meekness, patience, and kindness, Buddha gradually softened that terrible nature. Concealing affectedly the change which was taking place in him, almost against his perverse inclination, the Biloo said to Buddha, "I have put certain questions to many famous ascetics, but they have not been able to answer them. On seeing their utter incapacity, I have seized them, torn their bodies in pieces, and flung their quivering limbs into the Ganges. Such shall be your fate, O Gaudama, if your science fails you on this occasion. By what means can a man get out of the stream or current of passions? How can he cross over the sea of existences? How can he free himself from the evil influence? How shall he be able to purify himself from the smallest stain of concupiscence?" Buddha replied: "Listen, O Biloo, to my words; my answer shall fully satisfy you. By faith in and affection for the three precious things, man escapes from the current of passions. He who applies himself with a diligent earnestness to the study of the law of merits passes over the sea of existences. He who strives to practise the works that procure merits frees himself from evil influence, and from the attending miseries. Finally, the knowledge of the four meggas or ways to perfection procures perfect exemption from the least remnant of concupiscence. The Biloo, delighted with what he had heard, believed in Buddha, and soon was firmly established in the state of Thautapan. On that spot, where so glorious and unexpected a conversion had taken place, a monastery was erected. Buddha spent herein the sixteenth season. As usual, myriads of Nats and men who had heard his preachings obtained the deliverance.

From Alawee Buddha went to Radzagio, and spent the seventeenth season in the Weloowon monastery. During that season a famous courtesan, named Thirima, sister of the celebrated physician Dzewaka, renowned all over the country for her wit and the incomparable charms of her person, wished to show her liberality to the disciples of Buddha. Every day a certain number of them went to her dwelling to receive, along with their food, abundant alms. One of the pious mendicants, in an unguarded moment, moved by an unholy curiosity, looked at her, and was instantly smitten by her charms. The mortal wound was widened and deepened by a fortuitous occurrence. On a certain day Thirima fell sick. But she did not relax in her daily work of charity. Weak though she was, and in her *negligée*, she insisted on the mendicants being introduced into her room, that she might pay her respects to them. The unfortunate lover was among the company. Her incomparable charms were heightened by her plain dress and drooping attitude. The poor lover went back with his brethren to the monastery. The arrow had penetrated to the core of the heart. He refused to take any food, and during some days completely estranged himself from the society of his brethren. While the intestine war raged in his bosom, Thirima died. Buddha, desirous to cure the moral distemper of the poor religious, invited King Pimpasara to be present when he should go with his disciples to see the remains of Thirima. On the fourth day after Thirima's death he went to her house with his disciples. There her body was laid before them, with a livid appearance, and all swollen. Countless worms already issuing out through the apertures, rendered the sight loathsome, whilst a horrible stench almost forbade a standing close to it. Buddha coolly asked the king, "What is that object which is stretched before us?" "Thirima's body," replied the king. "When she was alive," retorted Buddha, "people paid a thousand pieces of silver to enjoy her for a day. Would any one take her now for half that sum?" "No," replied the king; "in all my kingdom there is not one man who would offer the smallest sum to have her remains; nay, no one could be found who would be willing to carry her to any distance, unless compelled to do so." Buddha, addressing the assembly, said, "Behold all that remains of Thirima, who was so famous for her personal attractions! What has become of that form which deceived and enslaved so many? All is subjected to mutability; there is nothing real in this world." On hearing the instruction, eighty-two thousand persons obtained the knowledge of the four truths. The Rahan who, because of his passion, would not eat his food, was entirely cured of his moral distemper, and firmly established in the state of Thautapan. All this happened whilst Buddha spent his seventeenth season in the bamboo-grove monastery.

When the season was over, he went, as usual, to preach in every direction, and returned to Thawattie, to the Dzetawon monastery. His stay in that place was not long. He undertook another voyage to Alawee. He was received with the greatest demonstrations of joy by the people, who gladly ministered to all his wants. On a certain day, when he was to receive large offerings from the people and preach to them, it happened on that occasion that a poor pounha, who was very desirous to hear his instructions, was informed at an early hour of that very day that one of his cows had gone astray from the herd and could not be found. Hereupon he felt greatly aggrieved. He was afraid to let go the golden opportunity to hear the instruction. However, he trusted that by making the utmost diligence he would be back in time. He ran in all haste until he found the strayed animal and brought it back. It was nearly midday when he returned to the town. Though pressed with the pangs of hunger and overwhelmed with fatigue, he went straight forward to the place where the congregation was assembled. The offerings had been brought a long while ago; the people out of respect stood motionless, with their hands joined, in the presence of Buddha, who, contrary to the general expectation, remained perfectly silent. With his supernatural vision he had seen the perfect dispositions of the poor pounha. He would have him to share in the blessing of his instruction. As soon as the pounha had taken his place among the hearers, Buddha, casting a benevolent glance towards him, beckoned him to come near his person. Meantime, he ordered some of his disciples to bring the poor man some food, because he was very hungry; and he would not condescend to begin the instruction till the man had been relieved from the pangs of hunger by a good meal. When the preaching was over, several Rahans ridiculed the attention paid by their master to a common man. Buddha, knowing their innermost thoughts, spoke to them by way of an instructive rebuke: "Beloved sons, you seem to be surprised at my behaviour towards that poor pounha. But I had perceived at once the super-excellent dispositions of that man, his craving for the holy law, and his lively and strong faith in me, which prompted him to lay no stress on hunger, nor on fatigue, and to make no account of his personal discomforts, in order to satisfy his earnest longings for the law." On that occasion an immense number of hearers were converted.

Buddha went to a monastery built on a hill, near the town of Tsalia, where he spent the eighteenth season. In that town there was a weaver, who had one daughter, who followed the same profession as her father. The damsel was very desirous to hear Buddha's preachings; but on the day when Buddha was to come into the town to deliver instructions to the people, it happened she had to finish the weaving of a piece of cloth that was urgently required by the owner. She then said to herself: I will exert myself with so much diligence that I will be enabled both to finish my work and listen to my teacher's preaching. She set instantly to work, wound up the thread on the quill, and took it with her, to carry it to the shed where her father's loom was. On her way to the shed, she had to pass near the place where a motionless congregation stood before Buddha, eagerly waiting for the words that were to fall from his mouth. She laid aside her quill, loaded with thread, and squatted timidly behind the last rank of the congregation. Buddha had seen at a glance the perfect dispositions of the young girl. It was chiefly for her benefit that he had undertaken a long journey and come over to that place. As soon as he saw her, he made her draw nearer to him. The injunction was joyfully complied with. With an encouraging tone of voice, Buddha asked her whence she came and whither she was going. The damsel modestly answered that she knew whence she came, and also whither she was going; at the same time, she added that she was ignorant of the place she came from, and of the place she was going to. On hearing this apparently contradictory answer, many of the hearers could scarcely refrain from giving vent to indignant feelings. But Buddha, who had fathomed the girl's wisdom, prayed them to be silent. Then, turning towards his young interlocutor, he desired her to explain the meaning of her answer. She said: "I know that I come from my father's house, and that I go to our loom-shed; but what existence I have come from to this present one, this I am entirely ignorant of. I am likewise uncertain about the existence that shall follow this one. About these two points I am completely ignorant; my mind can discover neither the one nor the other." Buddha extolled the wisdom of the damsel, and forthwith began his instruction. At the conclusion, she was firmly grounded in the state of Thautapan. She withdrew immediately, took up her quill, and went to the shed. It happened that her father was asleep, with his hand on the loom's handle. She approached the loom, and began to arrange the thread. Her father, awaking suddenly, pushed inadvertently the part of the loom his hand was laid upon, and struck his daughter in the chest. She fell down and instantly expired. Overwhelmed with grief, the unfortunate father poured a flood of tears over the lifeless corpse of his daughter. Unable to console himself, he rose up and went to Buddha, in the hope of receiving some comfort at his feet. Buddha affectionately received him, and, by his good instructions, relieved him from the load that pressed on his heart, and gradually enlightening his mind by the preaching of the four great truths, he gently infused into his heart and his soul that sweet joy which wisdom alone can impart. The weaver resolved to abandon the world, asked for admittance into the assembly, and not long after became a Rahanda. This conversion was followed by that of a great many others.

Buddha returned to Radzagio, and spent the nineteenth season in the Weloowon monastery. The season being over, Buddha went into the districts of Magatha, preaching in all places. Previous to that time, there lived at Radzagio a rich man who had an only daughter, who was brought up with the greatest care and the utmost fondness. She lived in the upper apartments of a splendid dwelling. On a certain day, at an early hour in the morning, she was looking on the people that flocked from the country into the town. She saw among many a young hunter driving a cart loaded with venison. She much admired his fine, energetic appearance. She was instantly enamoured of him, and made all the necessary arrangements to elope with him. She succeeded, married the hunter, and had by him a large family. Passing on one day through a forest, the most excellent Buddha chanced to meet with a deer which was caught in the net of a hunter. Moved with feelings of commiseration, he helped the poor beast to get out of the meshes. After this benevolent action, he went to rest under a tree. The hunter soon made his appearance, and to his great dismay at once discovered that some one had deprived him of his prey. Whilst he was looking about, he saw Buddha, in his yellow dress, calmly resting under the shade of a large tree. "This," said the hunter to himself, "is the man who has done the mischief; I will make him pay dear for his undue interference." Hereupon he hastily took up an arrow and placed it on the bow, with the intention of shooting dead the evildoer. But despite his exertions, heightened by the thirst for revenge, he could not succeed; both his hands were seized with a sudden quivering, and his feet appeared as if nailed to the ground. He stood motionless in that attitude. Absorbed in meditation, Buddha was not aware what was going on so close to him.

The sons of the hunter as well as their wives grew very much troubled that their father did not return at the usual hour from visiting his nets. They feared that some untoward accident had overtaken him. They armed themselves and went in search of him. They soon came to the spot where they saw the sad position of their father. At the same moment, perceiving a yellow-dressed individual, they hastily concluded, that, by the power of some charms, he had brought their father into this miserable condition. They made up their mind to kill him. But whilst they were preparing to put their cruel design into execution, their hands, suddenly benumbed, could not grasp the weapons, and they all stood motionless and speechless. Awaking at last from contemplation, Buddha saw the hunter and all his family standing before him. Taking compassion on them, he restored them to their ordinary condition, and preached to them. They all fell at his knees, craved his pardon, believed in him, and became fervent Upasakas.

Buddha returned to Thawattie to spend the twentieth season in the Dzetawon monastery. It was at that period that there happened a remarkable change in the management of the domestic affairs of Gaudama. Up to the present time, no one among the religious had been specially appointed to attend on Buddha and minister to his wants. But some of them, as circumstances occurred, undertook the agreeable and honourable duty of serving him. However human nature will occasionally let appear, even in the best of men, some marks of its innate imperfections. On two occasions, the Rahans who followed Buddha and carried his mendicant's pot and a portion of his dress wished to go in one direction, whilst Buddha desired them to follow in another. They had the imprudence to part company with him. Both paid dearly for their disobedience. They fell into the hands of robbers, who took away all that they had, and beat them severely on the head. This twofold act of insubordination painfully affected Buddha. He summoned all the religious into his presence, and declared that, being old, he wished to appoint one of them to the permanent office of personal attendant on himself. Thariputra and Maukalan immediately tendered their services with a pious and loving earnestness. But Buddha declined to accept their offer, as well as that of the eighty principal disciples. The reason was, that their services were required for preaching to the people, and labouring with him for the dissemination of the true science among men. Some of the disciples urged Ananda to volunteer his services; but out of modesty he remained silent. Then he added that, should Buddha be willing to accept his humble services, he knew his heart's dispositions and his willingness to attend on him on all occasions; he had but to signify his good pleasure. As to him, he would be too happy to accept the office. Buddha expressed his readiness to confer on him the honourable employment. He was formally appointed and nominated Phra's attendant, and, during the twenty-five remaining seasons, he acted as the beloved and devoted attendant on Buddha's person. Through him alone visitors were ushered into Buddha's presence, and orders were communicated to the members of the assembly. Gaudama was then fifty-five years old.

On a certain day he went to the village of Dzantoo for the purpose of collecting alms. Manh Nat, his inveterate foe, entered into the heart of all the villagers to prevent them from giving alms to the mendicant. He succeeded so well in his wicked design that no one noticed Gaudama's passage through the street, nor gave him alms. When he drew near to the gate, Manh stood by the side of the street, and asked him, with a sarcastic tone, how he felt under the pangs of hunger. Buddha replied to him, that he could, by entering into the state of perfect trance, remain, like the great Brahma, without using material food, feeding only, as it were, on the inward happiness created by the immediate sight of unclouded truth. Five hundred young virgins, who happened to return from the country into the place, prostrated themselves before Buddha, listened to his instructions, and reached the state of Thautapan.

On leaving the place, Buddha happened to travel through a forest, which had become an object of terror to all the people of Kothala, as being the favourite haunt of Ougalimala, a notorious robber and murderer. The ruler of the country, Pasenadi, had heard from the windows of his palace the cries of his alarmed subjects. Despite the many remonstrances that were made concerning the dangers of such an attempt, Buddha went straight forward to the den of the formidable man, who, enraged at such presumptuous boldness, was preparing to make him pay dear for his intrusion. But he had to deal with an opponent that could not easily be frightened. To his threats and attempts to inflict harm Gaudama opposed the meekest composure, the mildest expressions, and an invincible patience. Softened by the kindness of his opponent, Ougalimala altered the tone of his voice, and showed signs of respect to Buddha. The latter, quickly perceiving the change that had taken place in the robber's soul, preached to him the law, and made of him a sincere convert. Coming out from the forest which had been the scene of so many crimes, he followed Buddha, with the behaviour of an humble disciple. The people of Kosala could scarcely give credit to the change that had taken place in Ougalimala. In a short time he became a Rahanda, and died not long after he had become perfect. The members of the assembly were, on a certain day, talking among themselves about the place he had probably migrated to. Buddha, who had overheard their conversation on this subject, said to them: "Beloved Bickus, the Rahan Ougalimala, who died a little while after his conversion, has reached the deliverance. His conversion was at once prompt and perfect. He was very wicked previous to his conversion, because he never cohabited except with wicked and perverse associates, the company of whom led him into all sorts of disorders. But he no sooner had the good fortune to meet me, hear my instructions, and converse with you, than he, at once believed in my doctrine, adhered to me with all his might, and entered into the way leading to perfection. He laboured strenuously to destroy in himself the law of demerits, and thus rapidly reached the summit of perfection."

CHAPTER XII.

Buddha is slandered in Thawattie—Questions put to him by a pounha—Story of Anatapein's daughter—Conversion of a pounha whose navel emitted rays of light—Blank in a great part of Buddha's life—Story of Dewadat—His jealousy towards Buddha—His friendship with Prince Adzatathat—His ambition—His attempt to kill Buddha—His miserable end.

WHILE the most excellent Buddha was in the Dzetawon monastery, the heretics of Thawattie made another attempt to lower, nay, to destroy his reputation. They prevailed upon Thondarie, a woman entirely devoted to their interests, to spread the rumour that she had spent a night in the apartments of Buddha. When the calumny had been noised abroad, they suborned a gang of drunkards, to whom they promised a large sum of money, if they would do away with the instrument of the slander. They accordingly selected a favourable opportunity, killed Thondarie, and threw her body into a cluster of bushes close to the monastery. When the crime had been perpetrated, the heretics raised a cry all over the country inquiring about Thondarie. She could nowhere be found. Search was made in every direction, until at last, by the secret directions of their emissaries, the body was found on the spot where it had been apparently concealed. The party hostile to Buddha laid the crime at his door. The king of the country, urged on by them, ordered a strict inquiry to be made. The infamous trick was at last discovered in the following manner. The perpetrators of the deed happened to go into a drinking-place. Heated by the liquor they had taken, they began to accuse each other of having killed Thondarie. Their conversation was overheard by one of the king's servants, who had them arrested and led to the palace. The king said to them, "Wicked men, is it true that you have killed the woman Thondarie?" They answered, "It is true we have killed her." "Who advised you to commit the murder?" "The Deitty teachers, who have paid us one thousand pieces of silver." Indignant at such a horrible deed, the king ordered the murderers and their advisers to be put to death. Their punishment consisted in their being buried in the earth up to their waist. They were subsequently covered with a heap of straw, which being set fire to, they were burnt to death. Buddha told his disciples that what had happened on this melancholy occasion was but a just retribution for his having in a former existence been drunk, and in that state abused and slandered a holy personage.

In one of his preaching excursions, Gaudama converted a distinguished pounha, who asked him, "Illustrious Buddha, what has the great Brahma done to merit the extraordinary glory that encompasses his person and the unsurpassed felicity that he enjoys?" To whom he answered, "The great Brahma, during several existences, has bestowed abundant alms on the needy, delivered many people from great perils, and delighted in giving instruction to the ignorant. Such meritorious deeds have procured for him the transcendent rank that he occupies, and secured to him for an immense period of time the matchless happiness that he possesses."

Two rich men, one of Thawattie, and the other a denizen of the Ougga city, had in their youth, when engaged in their studies, promised each other that he who should have a daughter would give her in marriage to the son of the other. When they had grown up, the rich man of Thawattie became a disciple of Buddha, but his friend followed the teachings of the heretics. In due time Anatapein, for such was the name of the former, had a beautiful daughter. His friend Ougga had also a fine grown-up son. It came to pass that Ougga on a certain day arrived from his place with five hundred carts of goods to Thawattie, for the purpose of trading. He lodged, as a matter of course, in his friend's house. During the conversation Ougga reminded his host of their former promise, and declared that he would be too happy to have it fulfilled without delay. Anatapein, having consulted his wife and daughter, and secured their consent, agreed to the proposal that was made to him. The pious rich man, however, was somewhat concerned respecting the dangers of his daughter's position in the midst of upholders of false doctrines. He gave her a retinue of female attendants, who could, by their advice and conversation, maintain intact in her the faith in Buddha. When the bride arrived, after a long journey, to Ougga's city, she was desired by her father-in-law to go in the company of his wife to pay her respects to his teachers, who were sitting quite naked, with dishevelled hairs, in the midst of the most disgusting uncleanness, under a shed prepared for them. Unused to such an unsightly and revolting display, the modest girl recoiled back with a becoming horror, refusing even to cast a look at them. Enraged at the contempt shown to his teachers, the unnatural father-in-law threatened to send her away from his house, as being an unsuitable match for his son. Firm in her faith, she withstood all the efforts that were made to induce her to alter her resolution and pay attention to such individuals. She went back into her apartments. Having somewhat recovered her spirits, and regained her usual calm and serene composure, the pious young lady began, in the presence of her mother-in-law and other ladies of the town, to praise and extol the glory, modesty, meekness, and all the other qualifications which adorned her great teacher and his disciples. The hearers were delighted at all that they heard, and expressed an eager desire to see them and hear their instructions.

On that very day the compassionate Buddha was at an early hour, as usual, reviewing the beings dwelling on the island of Dzampoudipa, endeavouring to discover those that were well disposed to hear the truth. His searching glance soon discovered what was going on in the house of the rich man Ougga, and the good dispositions of many of its inmates. "Thither," said he, "I shall hasten to preach the law, for many shall be converted." Hereupon he summoned five hundred disciples to attend him. They all took their pattas and other articles. With his company he flew through the air, and soon alighted in the courtyard of the rich man's house. All were rejoiced to see Buddha and his disciples. They lent a most attentive ear to his instructions. The rich man, his household, and a great number of the people of the town were converted. Anouroudha was left at Ougga to complete, perfect, and extend the good work so happily begun. Buddha in all haste returned to Thawattie.

At that time a great noise was made throughout the country on account of a certain pounha whose navel emitted a sort of light in the shape of a moon. He belonged to the party of unbelievers. He was led by them into every village and town, as a living proof of the power they possessed. At last his friends introduced him into the Dzetawon monastery. He was no sooner introduced into Buddha's presence, when the prodigy suddenly ceased. He went away somewhat annoyed at his misfortune; but he had scarcely crossed the threshold of the monastery when the light reappeared. Three times he came before the great preacher, and three times the light was completely eclipsed. No doubt could be entertained that there was in Buddha some secret power superior to the one he possessed. The pounha was at once disconcerted and bewildered. In his ignorance he attributed the accident to some superior magical formula possessed by Buddha, and asked him to teach him the said formula. Buddha said to him, "O pounha! I possess no charm; I ignore all magical formulas. There is in me but one virtue; it is that which I have gathered at the foot of the Bodi tree during the forty-nine days that I have spent there in the deepest meditation.

As to what attracts now the attention of the people in your person, your are indebted for it to the offering of a gold coronet, in the shape of a moon, you made to a Buddha during a former existence. The reward bestowed on you for such a good work is but a transient one. It can afford you no real, substantial, and lasting happiness. Hearken to my doctrine; it will confer on you a never-ending recompense." He went on explaining to him many points of the law. The pounha believed in Buddha; nay, he applied for the dignity of Rahan, and finally became a Rahanda.

N.B.—The history of Buddha offers an almost complete blank as to what regards his doings and preachings during a period of nearly twenty-three years,[1] beginning with the twenty-first season, when he was fifty-six years old, and ending with the forty-fourth season, having reached the patriarchal age of seventy-nine years. So entirely are we kept in ignorance of the important transactions that took place during so long a portion of Buddha's life, that the

---

[1] This short summary of Buddha's life, indicating but little more than the names of the places where he had spent twenty seasons, and leaving us in the dark as to all the particulars regarding the twenty-three other seasons, is another illustration of the assertion, made in some foregoing passages, that the present compilation is very concise and imperfect, supplying us with but an outline of Buddha's proceedings during the course of his preachings. He reached the age of eighty. According to the authority of this legend, Buddha lived forty-five years after he had obtained the Buddhaship. He was therefore thirty-five when he began his public life and entered the career of preaching the law. It is not in my power to say anything positive respecting the antiquity of this work, but the statement of the main facts is borne out by the united testimony of the Buddhistic works existing in various parts and in different languages of Eastern Asia. If it be true that our Buddha lived so long, we must believe that his time during the last twenty-five years was employed in the same benevolent undertaking, viz., to preach the sacred law and point out to beings the way that shall lead them to the deliverance. Many volumes are full of the disputes on religious subjects between Buddha and the heretics, that is to say, his opponents. We may conclude that those controversies took place during the latter part of Buddha's life, as it cannot be doubted that they increased in proportion to the progress the new doctrines made among the people. If, however, we are in great part kept in the dark respecting the doings of the great reformer during a long period of his public life, we are amply compensated by the account of many interesting circumstances that occurred chiefly during the last year of his earthly career.

writer, after having vainly consulted several manuscripts, is reluctantly obliged to come to the same conclusion as that which the Burmese authors have arrived at, viz., that there is a complete disagreement as to even the names of the places where Buddha spent the twenty-three remaining seasons. Out of regard for the rich man Anatapein, who for so many years had been one of his most liberal supporters, Buddha spent the greatest part of the remaining seasons in the Dzetawon monastery. During the few others he seems to have stayed at or near Radzagio, chiefly in the Weloowon monastery. The amount of seasons spent by our Phra from the time he obtained the Buddhaship till his death is forty-five.

I find related, as a fact worthy of notice, the donation by a rich widow of Wethalie, named Wisaka, of the celebrated Pouppayon monastery. It was situated not far from the Dzetawon, in an eastern direction from that famous place. It is mentioned that when Phra sallied from the Dzetawon monastery by the eastern gate, the people of the country knew that he was going to dwell for awhile in the Pouppayon monastery; when, on the other hand, he was observed to leave it by the northern gate, all the people understood that he was undertaking a journey through the country for the purpose of preaching. The epoch of this donation is not certain. It appears from some particulars indirectly alluded to that it must have taken place when Buddha was sixty years old.

In following our manuscript, we find inserted in this place the detailed accounts respecting Dewadat, related by Buddha himself in the Dzetawon monastery, in the presence of a large party of his disciples. The fact of Buddha mentioning the name of Adzatathat as king of Radzagio, leaves no doubt respecting the time when the awful punishment is supposed to have been meted out to Dewadat, on account of the many heinous sins laid to his charge. Adzatathat, having murdered his father Pimpathara, by starving him to death in a prison, became king of Radzagio, and succeeded him when Buddha was nearly seventy-two years old. He was already king, as the sequel will show, when Dewadat was as yet his spiritual adviser. It is probable that the following narrative was made not more than two years after the above date.

When the most excellent Buddha was in the Dzetawon monastery, alluding to the sad fate that had fallen Dewadat, he related the causes that had brought on this dreadful occurrence.

At a certain time, when Buddha was spending a season in the Kosamby country, the people came in great numbers every day to the monastery to bring abundant alms, and pay their respects to him and the assembly. On certain occasions they made inquiries about the most distinguished members of the assembly, such as Thariputra, Maukalan, Anouroudda, Ananda, Bagoo, Kimila, and others, giving utterance to the feelings of admiration and love they entertained towards them. But they never took the least notice of Dewadat. The latter keenly resented the studied slight; the more so, because he thought that in his capacity of member of the assembly and of his royal descent, he was entitled to as much consideration as many others, who in this twofold respect were greatly his inferiors. He resolved to leave the company of Buddha and go to some other place. He went to Radzagio and ingratiated himself in the favours of the young Prince Adzatathat, son of King Pimpathara. The young prince, taken up with the grave manners of the new-comer, acknowledged him as his teacher, and built for him a monastery on the Yanthitha hill, close to the city.

Some years afterwards Buddha came to Radzagio to spend a season in the Weloowon monastery. Dewadat went to his monastery. Having paid his respects in the usual manner and occupied a becoming place, he three times requested the permission of having an assembly or thinga of his own, quite distinct from the other, which was under the immediate management of Buddha. On this point he three times received a direct refusal to his demand. From that day the jealousy he entertained towards Buddha waxed to a base envy, which soon generated in his soul a deadly hatred against him. He made up his mind to break with Buddha all ties of spiritual relationship, and to become the chief of a new religious body. To succeed in his impious design he required the support of the secular arm. The king of Magatha was in favour of Buddha, but his son had warmly espoused the cause of Dewadat. In such a position, the evil-disposed Dewadat advised Prince Adzatathat to compass the destruction of his father, in order to become king. The ambitious son followed the detestable advice, and put an end to his father's life by starving him to death in a prison, in spite of his own mother's exertions to save her royal husband's life.

It was in the thirty-seventh season of Buddha's public mission that Adzatathat ascended the throne of Magatha. Under the new king's auspices, Dewadat carried everything before him with a high hand. Assured of the new king's support, he hired thirty bowmen and promised them an ample reward if they killed Buddha. The ruffians gladly agreed to the proposal. But when they were on the point of committing the crime, they felt themselves overawed by the presence of Buddha. Instead of executing the order they had received, they fell at his feet, craved his pardon, listened to his preaching, and were converted one after the other. Disappointed on this point, Dewadat designed another plan to rid himself of the great preacher. He watched the moment when Buddha was walking at the foot of a hill, named Weitsa-gout. From the summit he rolled a large stone that was to crush his enemy. Fortunately on its way down the hill's side it met with a small obstacle, on which it split into several parts. One splinter alone hurt the toe of one of Buddha's feet, and severely bruised it. On hearing of such a nefarious and cowardly attempt, the disciples hastened to the spot and conveyed their beloved master to his monastery. They offered to keep guard round his person, to prevent the repetition of other attempts on his life. But Buddha said to them that no mortal had the power to hurt him so far as to cause his death. He thanked them for this new token of their affectionate regard towards him, and bade them return to their respective places. The celebrated physician Dzewaka, having been sent for, applied a bandage, which, being removed on the following morning, it was found, to the surprise and joy of all present, that the injured toe was perfectly cured. On another occasion Dewadat made a last attempt on Buddha's life, in the suburbs of Radzagio, by the means of an elephant, infuriated and maddened by strong liquor forced into his throat. The animal was let loose in one of the streets which Gaudama was perambulating gathering alms in his mendicant's pot. But far from doing any injury to Buddha, the elephant, having come into his presence, stood for awhile, and then knelt before him in token of respect. In this manner Dewadat signally failed in this last wicked attempt.

Dewadat differed from his cousin on some points of discipline; and this difference occasioned the schism that he meditated to establish.[2] He had proposed to Buddha to

[2] Dewadat, in insisting upon the adoption of regulations of a more rigid character, intended to imitate, to a certain extent, the conduct of the mendicants of the opposite party. He aimed at rivalling them in the practice of austere observances. It does not appear that he innovated in the dogmas that he had learned at the school of his great teacher. As his royal pupil, Adzatathat, had hitherto supported the party of the pounhas, it is not improbable that Dewadat wished to lessen the differences between the practices and observances of the two parties, to render them less perceptible, and by doing so, to prepare the way, by gradual approximation, for a complete fusion. He exhibited himself in the character of a rigid reformer, who was displeased with the too lenient tenor of the disciplinary regulations instituted by Buddha. Be that as it may, it is certain that jealousy in the beginning inspired him with the idea of separating from the assembly. This first step led him farther than he at first contemplated. He wished to set up an assembly, or things of his own, and thereby to place himself on a footing of equality and rivalry with his cousin. Meeting with greater resistance than he expected, and being convinced that he could not succeed so long as Buddha should be alive, he did not shrink from making several attempts on his life. It is a fact worthy of notice that the disturbances which took place subsequently

make it obligatory on all Rahans to live in forests at the foot of certain trees; not to receive food from the people in their own places, but to use only as articles of food such things as they could procure by their exertions; to use robes made up of rags collected in the dust of public thoroughfares, and not such as might be offered by pious laymen; to abstain from fish and meat; and to dwell in unroofed places. Gaudama positively refused to accede to his demands. Meanwhile he meekly warned him against the sin of schism, telling him that the commission of such an offence would throw the perpetrator into the hell Awidz for a whole revolution of nature. Deaf to such a salutary warning, Dewadat precipitated himself into schism. He gained over to his party five hundred inexperienced Rahans of the Witzi country, and with them dwelt in the monastery of Gayathitha. He signally failed in his attempt to draw Ananda to his side. Thariputra, by the advice of Buddha, went to Dewadat's place. Profiting from the time he was asleep at a distance, he prevailed upon the five hundred Rahans to abandon schism and return to Buddha, the centre of unity, who was then in the Dzetawon monastery in Wethalie. Rising from his sleep, Dewadat fell into a paroxysm of rage at the trick played on him. He instantly resolved to start for the Dzetawon monastery, to have his revenge on Buddha for the injury done unto him. He was carried in a litter. Messenger after messenger informed Buddha of the approach of his antagonist. But he calmly said to his disciples: "Beloved sons, do not trouble yourselves. Dewadat shall not see my face nor enter the precincts of this place." Information was, in haste, conveyed that Dewadat had actually reached the

---

in the Buddhist society had their origin, in most instances, in points of discipline of a trivial importance, which were altered or rejected by a fraction of the assembly, whilst they were upheld with the utmost tenacity by the greater portion of the Rahans, as having been established by Gaudama. This observation will be fully corroborated by the particulars that we shall relate on the subject of the councils or meetings held after Gaudama's death.

tank close to the monastery, and was resting a while under the shade of a tree. Gaudama calmly gave the same assurance to his trembling disciples. But the moment of a terrible punishment was at hand. Dewadat, quitting his couch, stood up for a while, to refresh his wearied limbs. But he was seen by his astonished and bewildered companions gradually sinking into the earth, first up to his knees, then to his navel, and finally to his shoulders. At that moment he humbled himself, confessed his fault, acknowledged and proclaimed the glory of Buddha. He then disappeared, wrapt in flame, and fell to the bottom of the hell Awidzi. His punishment consists in having his feet sunk ankle-deep in a burning ground; his head is covered with a red-hot pan, that caps his head down to he lobe of the ears; two huge red-hot iron bars transfixt him horizontally from right to left, two from back to front, and one impales him from top to bottom. He shall have to suffer in that frightful position during a revolution of nature. But, for his tardy and sincere repentance, he shall be delivered, and, by his exertions in practising virtue, he shall become a Pitzegabuddha, under the name of Atisara.

Adzatathat ruled over the two countries of Enga and Magatha. His mother was Waydahi, the sister of King Pathenadi, who ruled over the two countries of Kaci and Kosala. Adzatathat, who was of a bellicose temper, quarrelled with his uncle on account of some districts in Kaci, which he seized by force of arms. Unable to resist the army of his nephew, Pathenadi offered to the invader the hand of his daughter Watzera-komma. The offer was accepted, and a reconciliation followed. Three years afterwards, Pathenadi lost his throne, which was seized by Meittadoubba, a son he had had by a concubine. Pathenadi went to Radzagio to ask assistance against the usurper from his son-in-law. But he died on his way to that place.

It was under the rule of Meittadoubba, in the forty-fourth season, that occurred the total destruction of the

Thagiwi princes of Kosala and Kapilawot by the ambitious Adzatathat.

Buddha spent the forty-fourth season in the Dzetawon monastery. When the season was over, he went to dwell in the Weitzagout monastery, near Radzagio. While he was in that place, there was spread a rumour that Adzatathat entertained hostile feelings towards Wethalie. Buddha then foretold that as long as the princes of Wethalie would be united and avoid internal strife and contention, they would be more than a match for their enemy; but should quarrel take place among them, they and their country would fall an easy prey to the invader. These words, which fell from Buddha's mouth, were not forgotten by a pounha who was one of Adzatathat's ministers. He planned, with his royal mother's consent and secret encouragement, the destruction of the rulers of Wethalie, and the conquest of that country, by contriving to sow the seed of dissension among the Letziwi princes. His plan met with complete success some years later, about three years after Gaudama's Neibban, as we shall have the opportunity of relating.

END OF VOL. I.

THE
LIFE OR LEGEND
OF
GAUDAMA

THE LIFE OR LEGEND OF GAUDAMA

THE BUDDHA OF THE BURMESE.

WITH ANNOTATIONS.

THE WAYS TO NEIBBAN, AND NOTICE ON THE PHONGYIES OR BURMESE MONKS.

BY THE

RIGHT REVEREND P. BIGANDET,

BISHOP OF RAMATHA,
VICAR APOSTOLIC OF AVA AND PEGU.

IN TWO VOLUMES
VOL. II.

Fourth Edition

GYAN

Published by

Gyan Publishing House
5, Ansari Road
Daryaganj, New Delhi-110002
Phone: 011-47034999, 9811692060
E-mail: books@gyanbooks.com

Distribution Network
gyanbooks.com
India, USA, Canada, UK, Australia, France

ISBN : 978-81-212-2810-7 (Set)
ISBN : 978-81-212-2812-1 (HB)
First Published, 1912

2nd Impression 2021

Printed at: Gyan Press, Delhi.

The
Life or Legend of Gaudama Vol. II
Author: P. Bigandet

THE LIFE OR LEGEND

OF

GAUDAMA

THE BUDDHA OF THE BURMESE.

With Annotations.

THE WAYS TO NEIBBAN, AND NOTICE ON THE PHONGYIES OR BURMESE MONKS.

BY THE

RIGHT REVEREND P. BIGANDET,

BISHOP OF RAMATHA,

VICAR APOSTOLIC OF AVA AND PEGU.

IN TWO VOLUMES.

VOL. II.

Fourth Editio

LONDON:

KEGAN PAUL, TRENCH, TRÜBNER & CO. LTD.

BROADWAY HOUSE, CARTER LANE, E.C.

1912.

CONTENTS.

LEGEND OR LIFE OF THE BURMESE BUDDHA, CALLED GAUDAMA.

CHAPTER I.

CHAPTER II.

CHAPTER III.

CHAPTER IV.

CHAPTER V.

LEGEND OF THE BURMESE BUDDHA

CALLED

GAUDAMA.

CHAPTER I.

Buddha, being seventy-nine years old, delivers instructions to the Rahans—Preachings in the village of Patalie—Miraculous crossing of the Ganges—Conversion of a courtesan—Sickness of Buddha—His instructions to Ananda—Last moments and death of Tharipatra—His eulogium by Buddha—Death of Maukalan—Reflections of Buddha on that event.

DURING all this time Buddha was travelling about the country, preaching the law to those that were worthy to obtain the deliverance. He had reached his seventy-ninth year.[1] At that time there were eighteen monasteries in

[1] The first particular related at length by the compiler of this work is one of peculiar interest. Buddha summons the Rahans to his presence, through the ever faithful and dutiful Ananda, and addresses to them instructions which form the basis of the duties and obligations of all true disciples. He styles them Bickus—that is to say, mendicants—to remind them of the spirit of poverty and of the contempt of worldly things which must ever be dear to them. The epithet "beloved" is always prefixed to the word Bickus, as conveying an idea of the true and pure affection the master bore to his disciples, or rather his spiritual children. Buddha charges them at first to be always diligent in holding assemblies, where religious subjects should be discussed, controversies settled, and unity of faith secured. This obligation has long been held as a binding one by the primitive Buddhists, as mention is always made in their books of the three great assemblies held during the three first centuries of the Buddhistic era, when the sacred writings were carefully revised, amended, and, as it were, purged of all spurious doctrines. It was during the last council that the canon of scriptures was adopted,

the neighbourhood of Radzagio, peopled by a great number of religious. On a certain day, Buddha said to Ananda, "Invite all the Rahans to assemble in the Gny-Moora hall." When they had gathered together in that place, Buddha repaired thither, and spoke to them as follows: "Beloved Bickus, as long as you shall remain united, and continue to hold regular meetings, you shall certainly prosper and flourish—as long as you shall agree together, and come unitedly to a decision on all principal affairs, so that you will impose no obligation where there is no pre-

---

which has ever since been maintained by orthodox Buddhists. Nothing can be wiser than the desire he so strongly expresses that no one should ever presume to alter the true and genuine nature of the precepts, by making, according to his whim, light what is heavy, or obligatory what is but a matter of counsel. He expresses the strongest wish to see them always united among themselves, and fervent in the observance of the precepts of the law. He establishes as a fundamental principle the obedience to superiors. There is no society of a religious character among heathens where the various steps of the hierarchy are so well marked and defined as in the Buddhistic institution. The whole body of religious has a general superior in each province, exercising a thorough control over all the houses within the limits of the province; he may be looked upon as a regular diocesan. In each house of the order there is a superior, having power and jurisdiction over all the inmates of the place. Under him we find the professed members of the society, then those who may be called novices, and last of all the postulants and disciples allowed to wear the clerical dress, or yellow garb, without any power or authority, and being looked upon merely as students in the way of probation. In his charge to his disciples, Buddha lays much stress upon the necessity of destroying in themselves the principle of passion, and in particular concupiscence. The general tendency of all his preachings is to teach men the means of freeing themselves from the tyrannical yoke of passions. No one, indeed, can obtain the state of perfect quiescence or Neibban unless he has annihilated in himself all passions, and thereby qualified himself for the practice of all virtues. The character of the great body of religious Buddhists is clearly set forth in the exhortations their great master directs to them to love retreat and solitude. The noise, tumult, and bustle necessarily attending the position of a man living in the world are entirely opposed to the acquirement of self-knowledge, self-possession, and self-control, so much required in a religious. As long, concludes Buddha, as you shall remain faithful to your regulations you will prosper, and secure to yourselves and your order the respect and admiration of all. He winds up his speech by exhorting them to act in a manner ever becoming their sacred calling. The greatest moralist, possessing the most consummate and perfect knowledge of human nature, could not lay down wiser regulations for setting on a firm and lasting foundation a great and mighty institution, destined to spread itself far and wide amidst nations and tribes, and subsist during an unlimited period.

cept, and that you will fervently observe all the commands, strictly adhering to all the rules of your profession, you will ever be in a prosperous condition. It is required that you should behave respectfully towards your superiors, yielding due obedience to their injunctions. Beware of passions, and particularly of concupiscence, lest you should ever be brought under their tyrannical yoke. Love retreat and solitude; endeavour to observe your regulations, as well as all the ordinances and ceremonies of the law. Let it be a pleasure to you to receive kindly good religious who may come to your monasteries, and converse with them. Avoid carefully to take pleasure in what you do or say, or pride yourselves in the number of your attendants. Shun bad company; apply yourselves diligently to acquire knowledge and wisdom; meditate on the great truths, mutability, pain, and unreality. As long as you observe those important points and adhere to them, you shall prosper and be ever respected by all. Moreover, you will be thereby enabled to avoid all that which is base and unbecoming in your sacred calling."

When the instruction was over, Buddha called Ananda and bade him inform the Rahans to hold themselves ready for going to Ampaladaka.

Whilst staying in a dzeat or bungalow, Thariputra approached Buddha, and having paid him his respects, said to him, "O most illustrious Buddha, there is no one that surpasses, or that is even equal to you in the knowledge of the law. There has never been, nor will ever be, a being that can be compared to you. This is what elicits my admiration towards and love for your person." Buddha replied, "You are not mistaken, Thariputra; blessed are they who, like you, know the value and the science of a Buddha." Desiring to try the wisdom of his great disciple, he added, "Beloved son, how do you know that no one can be compared to me, and that my knowledge of the law is unrivalled?" Thariputra answered, "I have not the knowledge of the present, nor of the past and future, but I understand the law; through you, O most glorious Buddha, I have come to that understanding; you have said that you have infinite wisdom, hence I conclude that you know the present, the past, and the future—you are to be ever praised; you are most excellent, ever glorious, and free from all passions, and therefore to you I attribute all the qualities inherent in him who is invested with the Buddhaship." From Ampaladaka Buddha went to the large village of Nalanda, where he was well received by the inhabitants. He preached to them and made a short stay with them.

Phra summoned again Ananda to his presence, and directed him to tell the Rahans to be ready for a voyage, as he desired to go to the village of Patalie. When he arrived at that place, the people prepared for him the dzeat[2] or hall, which had been erected by the order of

---

[2] A dzeat is a building erected by the piety of Buddhists for the purpose of affording shelter and a place of rest to devotees, travellers, and strangers. These buildings are to be found at the entrance of towns, in villages, and often in the neighbourhood of pagodas. Those of Burmah are erected in the plainest manner. A verandah in front extends to the full length of the building, a spacious hall running parallel to the verandah occupies the remaining place. There is no partition between the hall and the verandah. It happens sometimes that a space at one of the hall's corners, screened by mats or dry leaves, offers an asylum to him who does not like to mix with the *vulgus*. The carelessness of Government in all that relates to the comfort of the people is amply compensated by the zeal of pious laymen, who readily undertake the erection of those works of public utility in the hope of securing to themselves the attainment of merits to be enjoyed perhaps in this, but certainly in some future existences.

In Burmah proper some of the dzeats are, for the country, beautiful buildings. The edge of the roof and the front part are covered with a profusion of sculptures and carvings that vie with those that adorn the finest monasteries. This fact, among many, indicates the truly beneficent and philanthropic influence exercised by some tenets of Buddhism over the followers of that creed. Pride and vain-glory may have their share in the erection of those monuments of benevolence, but it is not the less certain that those who build them yield first and principally to the strong influence of religious feeling.

On this occasion Buddha preached to the crowd, when we see a line of distinction well drawn between the assembly of the disciples of Buddha and those we may merely style hearers. The latter are addressed by the name of darakas, meaning laymen that hear the preaching. A daraka is not as yet a perfect convert, and therefore not a member of the assembly of the perfect. The daraka differs from the Upasaka. The latter is not only a mere hearer of the law; he is a firm believer, and fervently

King Adzatathat, for receiving the Letziwy princes of Wethalie, who had come to a conference for settling some affairs with him. Everything being ready, they invited Phra, who by his silence testified his acceptance of their invitation. Water to drink, rinse the mouth, and wash his hands and feet, was ready. Buddha sat leaning against the central post of the hall, facing the east. His disciples remained behind in a humble posture, whereas the people sat opposite to him, having their faces turned towards the west. Phra began to explain to the numerous hearers the demerits and punishments attending the trespassing of the precepts of the law, and the advantages reserved to those who religiously observe them. "Darakas," said he, "whoever trespasses the moral precepts, or is remiss in observing them, will see his happiness and fortune gradually decreasing, and his good character falling away. He will ever live in a sad state of doubt and uncertainty,

---

practises the precepts: he is among laymen a pious Buddhist; the former is not so forward: he begins to hear and believe the doctrines preached to him. He has already some faith in Buddha; he is under instruction, but he cannot be called a professed disciple. The rewards of faith are both of a natural and supernatural order. Riches, happiness, an honourable reputation, are promised to the faithful observer of the law. He is to be ever free from doubts, since faith makes him adhere firmly to all the instructions of Buddha; and after his death he is to migrate to some of the seats of Nats. The trespassing of the law is to be attended with poverty, shame, and misery, doubts in an unsettled mind, and at last punishment in hell. That place of suffering is minutely described in Buddhistic works. Such a description appears, in the opinion of the writer, of no importance to those who desire to understand not the superficial portion of Buddhism, but its fundamental and constitutive parts. Hell is a place of punishment and torment, as the Nats' seats are places of reward and happiness. There is no eternity of sufferings; the unfortunate inhabitant of those dark regions is doomed to remain there, until the sum of his offences has been fully atoned for by sufferings. When the evil influence created by sin is exhausted, punishment ceases too, and the wretched sufferer is allowed to migrate to the seat of man in order to acquire merits and prepare himself for happier future existences.

In recording the account of the conversion of a courtesan named Apapalika, her liberality and gifts to Buddha and his disciples, and the preference designedly given to her over princes and nobles, who, humanly speaking, seemed in every respect better entitled to attentions, one is almost reminded of the conversion of the woman that was a sinner mentioned in the Gospel.

and at last, when death shall have put an end to his present existence, he will fall into hell. But the lot of the faithful observer of the great precepts shall be widely different. He will obtain riches and pleasures, and gain an honourable reputation. He will be welcome in the assemblies of princes, pounhas, and Rahans; doubt shall never enter his mind, and his death will open before him the way to the pleasant seats of Nats." The people were so much taken up with the preaching that they remained in the dzeat until a very late hour. At last they paid their homage to Buddha, rose up, turned on the right, and departed.

It is in the following year that the same king built the city of Patalibot or Pataliputra, on that same spot. In anticipation of that event, Buddha foretold that the village would become a great city, which would obtain a renowned celebrity among all other cities. Thither countless merchants would resort from all parts of Dzampoodipa. At the same time he predicted the great calamities that would befall it. Internal discords, fire, and inundation of the Ganges would gradually work out its total destruction.

In the morning Buddha went to the southern bank of the Ganges, and preached the law to some pounhas, who, in return, made him offerings and paid him much respect. He stood on that place as if waiting for some boat to cross the mighty stream. Some of the people were looking out for boats, others were busily engaged in preparing rafts. Whilst they were making all the necessary arrangements, Buddha stretched both arms and found himself, with all his Rahans, on the opposite bank. Turning his face in the direction of those who were in search of boats and rafts, he said: "He who has crossed the sea of passions is an Ariah. The practice of the great duties are the boats and rafts whereupon he contrives to cross the sea of passions. He who desires to pass a river wants the aid of rafts and boats, which are made up of different pieces of wood joined together; but he who has become an Ariah by the knowledge of the great roads that lead to perfection, weakens all passions and extricates himself from the whirlpool of concupiscence: he can also, without the help of boats or rafts, cross rivers."

Phra informed Ananda that he intended to go to the village of Kantikama. Having reached that place, he explained to the Rahans the glorious and sublime prerogatives of Ariahs. Thence he passed over to the village of Nadika. It was in that place that Ananda asked him what had become of a certain Rahan, named Thamula, and of a certain Rahaness, named Anaunda, who had both just died. "The Rahan," answered Buddha, "has conquered all his passions and obtained the state of Neibban. As to the Rahaness, she has gone to one of the seats of Brahmas: thence she will migrate to Neibban without reappearing in the world of passions."

Buddha went to the country of Wethalie with his disciples, and dwelt in a beautiful grove of mango-trees. There he earnestly recommended his disciples to have their minds always attentive and ready to engage in serious reflections and meditations. In Wethalie lived a famous courtesan, named Apapalika. She had her dwelling in a beautiful place, near to an extensive and delightful grove, planted with mango-trees. She went along with others to hear the preaching of Gaudama, which had the good effect of disposing her to make a great offering to the distinguished preacher and his followers. Buddha was submissively requested to come on the following day with all the Rahans to receive his food. The invitation was graciously accepted. The courtesan hastened to prepare the meal for Buddha and his followers. On the same day he preached the law to a number of young princes who had offered to supply him with his meal on the following day. He refused to accept the invitation, because he had already promised to Apapalika to go to her place for the same purpose. The princes had come in their finest and richest dress; in their deportment they vied in beauty with the Nats. But foreseeing the ruin and misery that was soon to come upon them all, Buddha exhorted his disciples to entertain a thorough contempt for things that are dazzling to the eyes, but essentially perishable and unreal in their nature. The princes were greatly disappointed at the preference given to the courtesan. On the following day, Gaudama went to the grove of mango-trees, attended by all his Rahans. After the meal, Apapalika presented the grove to Gaudama, who readily accepted the pious gift.

Having remained a while on this spot, Buddha went to the village of Weluwa, where he spent the forty-fifth and the last season. There he assembled the Rahans and said to them: "I intend to spend the season in this place, but you have my permission to go and remain in the neighbouring districts." The reason that induced him to part for a while with his disciples was the smallness of the place and the difficulty of procuring rice, whilst in the contiguous districts there were many monasteries and an abundance of all the necessaries of life. He would not, however, allow them to withdraw to too great a distance, for two reasons: first, because he knew that in ten months hence he would attain the state of Neibban; and, second, because he desired to see them assembled in his place several times every month, that he might have opportunity to preach the law, and deliver to them his final instructions.

Whilst he was living in that place Buddha was visited with a most painful distemper, which threw him into a state of prolonged agony. But owing to the absence of his disciples, and knowing besides that this was not the spot he was to select for his last moments, he overcame, by his incomparable power, the evil influence of the illness, and entering soon into a state of absolute trance, he remained therein for a while. Awakening from that situation, he appeared anew with his strength and usual vigour. When he came out from the monastery to take his wonted walk, Ananda went into his presence, and expressed to him the profound grief felt by all those who had heard of his illness. "When I saw you ill, O illustrious Buddha," said the faithful Ananda, "I was so deeply affected that I could scarcely hold up my head or draw my breath. I always cherished the hope that you would not go to Neibban ere you had preached once more the law to us all." "Ananda," replied Buddha, "why are the Rahans so much concerned about my person? What I have preached has no reference to what is within me or without me. Besides me there is no one else to preach the law. Were they not looking upon me as such, it would be perfectly useless to attempt to preach to them. I am now very old; my years number eighty. I am like an old cart, the iron wheels and wood of which are kept together by constant repairing; my earthly frame is kept entire and whole by the force and power of trance. O Ananda, I feel truly happy whenever I consider the state of Arahat, which is the deliverance from all the miseries of this world, whilst at the same time it sets a being free and disentangled from all visible and material objects. As to my disciples, as long as my religion shall last they ought to rely on themselves, and take refuge in the law, for there is no other refuge. They will truly rely on themselves when, by a careful attention, profound reflection, and true wisdom, they will be bent upon the destruction of concupiscence and anger, and engaged on meditating upon the constituent elements of this body." Such were the instructions he gave to Ananda.

Having spent the season in the village of Welouwa, the most excellent Buddha desired to return by the same way he had previously followed to the country of Thawattie. Having arrived there, he took up his residence in the monastery of Dzetawon.[3] The great disciple Thariputra,

---

[3] The duties performed by Thariputra on this occasion exhibit more fully than language can express the profound veneration he entertained for Buddha. He was with Maukalan the most distinguished member of

having just returned from begging his rice, hastened to render to Buddha the usual services. He swept the place, spread the mat, and washed his feet. These duties being

---

the assembly; he occupied the first rank among the disciples; in point of intellectual and spiritual attainments and transcendent qualifications, he stood second to none but to Buddha. Notwithstanding his exalted position, he did not hesitate to render to his superior the lowest services. The high opinion he had of Buddha's supereminent excellencies prompted him to overlook his own merit, and to admire without reserve that matchless pattern of wisdom and knowledge. Hence the inward satisfaction he sweetly enjoyed in serving as an humble disciple him whose unutterable perfections cast in the shade his far-famed and much-praised acquirements. The unaffected humility of the disciple does the greatest credit to the sterling worth of his inward dispositions, and conveys the highest idea of the respect and veneration entertained for the master's person.

In the houses where Buddhist monks are living it is a fixed rule that the superior and elders of the institution should be attended in the minutest services by the youngest members wearing the canonical dress. The framer of the disciplinary regulations, intending, on the one hand, to confer dignity on the assembly, and, on the other, to oppose a strong barrier to covetousness and to all inordinate worldly affections, wisely laid down a stringent order to all the members of the society never to touch or make use of any article of food, dress, &c., unless it had previously been presented to them by some attendant, layman or clerical. Hence when water is needed for washing the head, hands, and feet, or for rinsing the mouth, when meals are served up, when offerings are made, a young postulant, holding a vessel of water on the board whereupon are placed the dishes, or the articles intended to be offered, respectfully approaches the elder, kneels before him, squatting on his heels, lays before him the object to be presented, bows down with the joined hands raised to the forehead, resumes then the article with his two hands, presents it, with the upper part of the body bent in token of respect. Before accepting it the elder asks, Is it lawful? The answer, It is lawful, having been duly returned, the article is either taken from the hand of the offerer, or he is directed to place it within the reach of the elder. Any infraction of this ceremonial is considered as a sin. In the presence of the people the monks never fail to submit to that somewhat annoying etiquette. Their countenance on such occasions assumes a dignified and grave appearance, that has always much amused the writer whenever he had the opportunity of witnessing this ceremony, which is called Akat. There is no doubt but this custom is a very ancient one. We find it blended to a certain extent with the manners of the nations inhabiting eastern Asia. It is minutely described in the Wini, and carefully observed by the inmates of the Buddhistic monasteries. It agrees remarkably well with the spirit that has originated, promulgated, and sanctioned the disciplinary regulations. He who in this instance would look at the mere skeleton of the rule without any reference to the object aimed at by the legislator would show himself in the light of a very superficial observer. This, unfortunately, is too often the case when we scorn and laugh at customs, the demerit of which consists simply in not being similar to ours, whereas the com-

performed, he sat in a cross-legged position, entered into a state of trance for a while, whence having awakened, he thought within himself as follows: Has it been the custom in former ages for the Buddhas to arrive first at the state of Neibban, or for their great disciples to precede them in that way? Having ascertained that the latter alternative always happened, Thariputra examined his own existence, and found that the period of his life was not to extend beyond seven days. He next considered what place was the fittest for him to depart from and go to Neibban. The remembrance of his mother occurred to his mind, and he said to himself, My mother has given birth to seven Rahandas, and she has not as yet taken refuge in the three precious things—Buddha, the law, and the assembly of the perfect. Is she capable of understanding and knowing the four ways to perfection? Yes, she is indeed. But

---

monest sense tells us that we ought to judge them in connection with the institutions they have sprung from, and the end aimed at by him who has established them.

The narrative of Thariputra's departure for his birthplace and of his last moments suggests to the mind several reflections. He is certain of the last day of his existence; he foresees with a prophetic glance that his mother is well prepared for hearing profitably the preaching of the most perfect law. By the incomparable powers of his memory he relates to Buddha that 100,000 revolutions of nature ago he was possessed with the strong desire of seeing him and hearing his instructions, &c. How can these particulars be accounted for, according to Buddhistic notions? The spring all evils or demerits flow from is ignorance. A being is imperfect in proportion to his being sunk deeper in the bosom of ignorance. On the contrary, a being perfects himself in proportion to the efforts he makes for dispelling the thick cloud of ignorance that encompasses his mind. The more a man grows in the knowledge of truth the farther he removes the horizon of darkness. He who has made the greatest and most persevering efforts in fervently prosecuting the work of searching truth by studying the law that teaches the way of reaching it, contemplates and enjoys a portion of truth commensurate to his efforts and success. A Buddha, who has reached the last boundaries of knowledge, has therefore triumphed over ignorance and indefinitely enlarged the sphere of truth. He enjoys, in fact, a cloudless sight of all that exists; his science is unlimited, extending over all the countless series of worlds, which, in the opinion of the Buddhists, are supposed to form a system of nature. Thariputra, though much advanced in perfection, had not as yet reached its acme. His knowledge, however, was wonderfully great and extensive; it enabled him to obtain a clear insight into the darkness of the past and a distinct foresight of the future.

who is destined to preach to her? I am the person who ought to perform such a good office to her. I will go, teach her, and, by my instructions, make her renounce her false belief and embrace the true one. The very room I was born in shall be the spot wherefrom I shall depart for the rest of Neibban. On this day I will ask Buddha's leave to go to my birthplace. Having come to this resolution, he called the faithful Tsanda, and said to him, "Go and summon my five hundred Rahans to attend at my place." Tsanda departed forthwith, and said to the Rahans, "The great Thariputra desires to go to the village of Nalanda; be ready to accompany him; arrange everything in your own place, take up your pattas and tsiwarans." The five hundred Rahans immediately complied with the request, and were ready to follow their master. Thariputra, having disposed everything in his own cell, rose up, and casting an attentive and serious look upon the place he was wont to sit on during the day, he said, "This is the last time I will ever see this place; never will I any more enter into this cell." Thereupon he left the spot followed by the five hundred Rahans, went to the presence of Gaudama, and humbly requested permission to go and quietly enter into the state of Neibban, and thereby be delivered from the whirlpool of endless existences. Gaudama asked him in what place he intended to obtain Neibban? Thariputra replied: "In the country of Magatha, in the village of Nalanda,[4] in the very room where I was born." "You

---

[4] The village of Nalanda, the site of which is at present occupied by that of Baragaon, was the birthplace of the great disciple Thariputra. His illustrious companion in religion, Maukalan, was born in the village of Kaulita, about one and a half miles southwest of that place. Nalanda, says Fa-Hian, the Chinese traveller, lies one youdzana north of Radzagio, that is to say, seven English miles according to Cunningham's measurement, and is seven youdzanas or forty-nine miles distant from the tree Bodi. It was the great seat of Buddhistic learning, renowned all over India. Now the whole site is covered with ancient tanks and mounds of ruins on an immense scale, offering fine specimens of sculpture. The great monastery and five smaller ones were all within one enclosure. A row of lofty conical mounds, running north and south, 1600 feet by 400, indicates the place

alone, O Thariputra," said Buddha, "know the time of your entering the state of Neibban. As it is difficult, if not impossible, ever to find among all my disciples one like unto you, I desire you to preach once more to the assembly of Rahans." Thariputra, knowing that Buddha wished him at the same time to show a display of his power, prostrated himself before him, then rose up in the air to the height of one palm-tree, and came down to worship Buddha. He rose seven times in succession, each

---

and extent of those religious buildings. Outside of the enclosure there were several temples. General Cunningham fixes the era of the construction of those edifices between A.D. 425 and 625. Among the several proofs adduced in support of his opinion there is one that appears conclusive. Fa-Hian, who visited all the places famous in the history of Buddhism, and describes them with a minute attention, simply alludes to Nalanda as the birthplace of Thariputra, without saying a word about monasteries or temples, whilst Hwe-Thsang, who visited the same spot in the beginning of the seventh century, describes the splendid temples and monasteries which he saw, and from his statement we infer that the principal edifices were not inferior to those of Buddha Gaya in size and height. Some of them reached to a height of 170 and 200 feet. The greatest was 300 feet high. The number and extent of the tanks is truly surprising. Two of them, in the north-east, were nearly a mile in length, while another in the south was half a mile.

The inference to be drawn from the above is, that during the fifth and the sixth century of our era, Buddhism was in a flourishing condition in the country of Magatha or South Behar, since the finest and loftiest structures in the shape of monasteries and temples have been raised within that period, both at Nalanda and Buddha Gaya. It appears that, during the three first centuries of the Christian era, its fortune alternated, and met with varied results, agreeably to the favourable or unfavourable dispositions of the rulers of the country towards the followers of the philosopher of Kapilawot. This succession of successes and reverses reveals the important fact that Buddhism had not struck deep root in the heart of the inhabitants of Central India, since its fate depended from the will and opinions of the monarch, and was almost at the mercy of his caprices. Moreover, in the country north of the Ganges, such as Wethalie, Thawattie, Kapilawot, places which had been favoured with Buddha's incessant preachings, religion was on its decline at the time of Fa-Hian's visit, that is to say, in the beginning of the fifth century; monasteries were deserted and emptied, dzedies were crumbling down and fast decaying. In some instances, heretics, that is to say, pounhas, occupied the dwellings formerly tenanted by holders of the *genuine* doctrines. This unexpected sight very much grieved the heart of the good Chinese pilgrim. It must be regretted that we have not the written journals of some other Chinese travellers in the eighth or ninth century to reveal to us the state and condition in which they found the magnificent temples of Nalanda and Buddha Gaya when they visited them.

time higher by the length of a palm-tree than the preceding one. On the last time he stood in the air for a while, and announced the law to the multitude of Rahans and people; then coming down, he submissively requested Buddha to withdraw into the interior of the monastery. Buddha, complying with his wishes, entered into a hall studded with diamonds. Thariputra, having bowed towards the four points of the compass, said: "O most glorious Buddha, a hundred thousands of worlds ago I was prostrated at the feet of Buddha Anaumadathi, and earnestly prayed that I might enjoy the happiness of seeing all successive Buddhas that would appear during the period of my countless existences. My prayer has been heard, and now I contemplate you, O most glorious Buddha, and it is the last time that I will ever enjoy your presence. Now, O Buddha, worthy to be adored by all rational beings, I will soon be free from the thraldom of existences, and this existence shall be the last; this my prostration before you shall be the last. The end of my life is near at hand: seven days hence, like a man who rids himself of a heavy load, I will be freed from the heavy burden of my body." He raised his joined hands to his forehead, and from the extremities of his ten fingers rays of glory shot forth, In this position he bowed to Buddha, and withdrawing slowly, with his face towards Buddha, he continued bowing down as long as he could see him, because it was for the last time. When Buddha was out of sight he took his departure. At the same time the earth trembled with a tremendous shake. Buddha said to the Rahans that surrounded Thariputra: "Beloved children, your elder brother is departing; accompany him for a while." The people, too, hearing that Thariputra was going away, came forward, and gathering in large crowds, said to each other: "The great Thariputra, having obtained leave from Buddha, is going to prepare himself for the state of Neibban; let us follow him, that we may still enjoy his presence." Whereupon taking flowers and perfumes in their hands, they ran in the direction he had taken, with dishevelled hair, crying aloud, with tears and lamentations, "Where is Thariputra?" Having come up to him, they said: "Illustrious Rahan, you have left Buddha; whom do you now intend to join?" Thariputra, full of the most affectionate feelings towards the people, mildly desired them not to accompany him farther, and he added a few last words, enjoining upon them ever to remember Buddha and the Rahans. During the seven days that his journey lasted, Thariputra never ceased to praise and exalt the affection and kindness the people bore to him.

It was a little before dark when the great Rahan arrived at the entrance of the Nalanda village. He went to rest at the foot of a banyan-tree close to that spot. At that time there came a young man, his nephew, named Ooparewata, who, perceiving Thariputra, bowed down before him, and stood in that place. The great Rahan said to him: "Is your grandmother at home?" Having been answered in the affirmative, he continued addressing him: "Go now to her, and tell her to prepare for me the room wherein I was born, and a place for these five hundred Rahans that accompany me. I will stay for awhile in the village, and will go to her house somewhat later." The lad went in all haste to his grandmother's house, and said to her: "My uncle is come, and is staying at the entrance of the village." "Is he alone?" inquired the grandmother, "or has he with him a numerous retinue? For what purpose is he coming here?" The young man related to her all the particulars of his interview with his uncle. Noopathari, the mother of Thariputra, thought within herself, Perhaps my son, who has been a Rahan from his youth, desires in his old age to leave his profession. She, however, gave orders to have the desired room cleaned, and a place prepared for all his attendants.

In the evening, the great disciple went to his mother's house with all his followers. He ascended to the room prepared for him and rested therein. He bade all the Rahans withdraw and leave him alone. They had scarcely departed, when a most violent disease seized Thariputra, which caused an abundant vomiting of blood, so great, indeed, that the vessel into which it flowed could not hold it. His mother, at the sight of such an awful distemper, did not dare to approach, but retired, with a broken heart, into her own room, and leaned against the door. At that time, four great Nats, a Thagia their chief, and four Brahmas, came to see him, and to minister to him during his painful illness; but he bade them retire. His mother, seeing the coming and going of so many distinguished visitors, and the respect they paid to her son, drew near to the door of his room, and calling the faithful Tsanda, inquired of him wherefore so many distinguished individuals had come. Tsanda explained to her that the great Nats and a chief Thagia had come to visit and assist her son, and enjoy the presence of the great Rahan. Meanwhile he informed the patient that his mother wished to see him. Thariputra replied, that the moment was not a proper one, and he asked his mother the motive of her untimely visit. "Beloved son," said she, "I am come here to contemplate your ever dear countenance. But who are they that have just come to see you?" Thariputra explained to her how he had been visited by Nats, Thagias, and Brahmas. His mother inquiring of him if he were greater than any one of these, he unhesitatingly replied, that he was more excellent than any of them. His mother thought within herself: If my son be so exalted, how much more must Buddha be! Her heart then overflowed with the purest joy.

Thariputra rightly understood that the moment had come to preach the law to his mother. He said to her, "Woman, at the time my great teacher was born, when he obtained the supreme intelligence, and preached the most excellent law, a great earthquake was felt throughout ten thousand worlds. No one has ever equalled him in the practice of virtue, in understanding, wisdom, and in the knowledge of and affection for the transcendent excellencies of the state of Arahat." He then went on explaining to her the law, and many particulars relating to the person of Buddha. "Beloved son," said his mother, delighted with all that she heard, "why have you been so late in acquainting me with such a perfect law?" At the conclusion of the instruction, she attained the state of Thautapan. Thariputra replied, "Now, woman, I have repaid you for all the labours you have bestowed on me in bearing, nursing, and educating me; depart from me and leave me alone."[5]

---

[5] The conduct of Thariputra on this occasion wears an appearance of rudeness towards his aged mother, which at first hurts the feelings of human nature. But a close examination of all the circumstances connected with this last episode of the great disciple's life, shows that he was far from being divested of filial piety. He leaves his beloved master, undertakes a long and fatiguing journey for the sole purpose of preaching the law to his mother, and conferring upon her a boon of greater value than that he had received from her. In return for all the favours bestowed upon him by his mother, he initiates her in the knowledge of truth, and enables her to enter into the great ways that lead to the deliverance, that is to say, to the state of Neibban. It cannot be denied that his language on this occasion partook of an austere tone, sounding harsh to the ears of worldly men, but it must be borne in mind that Thariputra was an old ascetic, dead to all affections of nature, looking upon truth alone in an abstractively pure form, without any regard to material objects. He loved the law of truth, which he had learned from Buddha, and afterwards preached to others with an unparalleled zeal and fervour. The spirit of Buddha lived in him: he desired to see all beings availing themselves of the means of salvation which he had it in his power to impart unto them; he loved them all with an equal affection; the state of ignorance they were sunk in deeply affected his compassionate soul, and he had but one desire, that of dispelling the thick mist of ignorance by the pure light of truth.

When the instruction to his mother was over, Thariputra desired to be left alone with his disciples. His last words to them bespeak the humble sentiments of his mind. Though the first member of the assembly of the perfect, he begs pardon of his inferiors for the causes of offence he may have unwillingly given them during the period they had lived together: regardless of all the good he had done unto them, he feels that he could not well part with them ere he had atoned to them for any wrong, however involuntary, he might have done to some of them.

For those uninitiated in Buddhistic metaphysics it is not easy to understand and distinctly to appreciate the situation of Thariputra at his last moments. It is stated that he fell into ecstasy or trance, though his soul remained as yet connected with this

Thariputra inquired of the devoted Tsanda whether the moment had come. Having been informed that it was nearly daylight, he requested to be set up. By his order all the Rahans were called to his presence, and he said to them, "For the last forty-four years you have ever been with me; if I have offended any one of you during all that time, I beg to be pardoned." The Rahans answered him: "Great teacher, we have lived with you during the last forty-four years, and have been your inseparable attendants, following you everywhere, as the shadow follows the body. We have never experienced the least dissatisfaction with you, but we have to request your forbearance with us and pardon for ourselves."

It was on the evening of the full moon Tatsaongmon (November), when Thariputra went to his mother's place,

---

world by slender and almost invisible ties. This was the last and mighty struggle of a being to disengage himself from the trammels of existence and become free from all exterior influence. Soaring above all that exists, Thariputra's soul passed successively through the four stages he had so often visited, whilst engaged in the arduous effort of investigating truth, preparing to enter the fifth and last one, where she was to stay finally and perpetually, without any further change, in a state of quiescence. When the sage, during his meditations, has brought his mind to bear upon some object, he wishes to contemplate attentively and thoroughly to comprehend, he at first gets hold of that object by his thought, he then examines it by means of reflection: the knowledge he thus acquires never fails to create a pleasurable sensation; this pleasure or satisfaction conveys to the soul enjoyment and happiness; he loves the truth he has discovered, and he rests fixedly in it. This is the last stage he ever can or wish to reach. What has human mind, indeed, to do, after having found truth, but to cling to it, and remain ever attached to it? During the last trance, Thariputra, with his almost immensely developed mental faculties, knew comprehensively truth, reflected on it, felt a pleasure in considering it, enjoyed it, or rather fed upon it, and at last adhered so perfectly to it, that he became, as it were, merged into it. He then had reached the state of Neibban, where he was for ever exempt from the influences created and put in motion and activity by matter and passions in every state of existence. Buddhists, in Burmah, at least, owing to their very limited and imperfect education, are unable to give any satisfactory or even intelligible account of the state of Neibban or perfection. What is here but superficially stated, has been found in one of the last Buddhistic compositions on this and other metaphysical subjects. Fuller particulars shall, hereafter, be given as to the state of Neibban, when the death of one greater than Thariputra shall be related.

and lay down in the room wherein he had been born. During the night he was attacked with the most distressing distemper. In the morning, at daylight, he was habited with his tsiwaran and made to lie on his right side. He entered into a sort of ecstasy, passed successively from the first state of Dzan to the second, third, and fourth, and thence dived into the bottomless state of Neibban, which is the complete exemption from the influence of passions and matter.

Noopathari, bathed in her tears, gave full vent to her grief and desolation. "Alas!" exclaimed she, looking on the lifeless body, "is this my beloved son? His mouth can no more utter a sound." Rising up, she flung herself at his feet, and with a voice ever interrupted by sobs and lamentations, said, "Alas! beloved son, too late have I known the treasure of perfections and excellencies that was in you. Had I been aware of it, I would have invited to my house more than ten thousand Rahans, fed them, and made a present of three suits of dresses to each of them. I would have built a hundred monasteries to receive them." Day[6] having dawned, she sent for the most

[6] In Burmah, when a person has just given up the ghost, the inmates of the house send for musicians, who soon make their appearance with their respective instruments. They forthwith set to work, and keep up an incessant noise during the twenty-four hours that elapse before the corpse is removed to the place where it is to be burnt. Relatives, friends, and elders resort to the deceased's house for the ostensible purpose of condoling with those who have lost their kinsman, but in reality for sharing in the mirth and amusements that go on in such occasions. Strange to say, the thought of death strikes no one's mind; the fate of the deceased is scarcely pitied, nay, remembered. Were it not for the presence of the corpse, and the perhaps conventional cries and lamentations of some old women at certain intervals, no one could imagine, still less find out, the real motive that has induced such a crowd to assemble on that spot.

If the departed belong to a respectable family in tolerably good circumstances, the funeral ceremony is arranged in the following manner: Presents, intended as offerings for the Buddhist monks, having been made ready, they are invited for the occasion, and their presence is expected in numbers proportionate to the amount of offerings. The procession starts from the deceased's house, and directs its course towards the place of burning or the cemetery. It is headed by the yellow-dressed monks, carrying their broad, palm-leaf fans on the shoulder, and at-

skilful goldsmiths, opened her chests, and gave them a great quantity of gold. By her command, five hundred small piathats and as many dzedis were prepared: the

---

tended by their disciples. Next follow the bearers of the offerings in two lines. They are partly men and partly women, but walk separately and apart from each other. The coffin appears next, laid on thick poles, and carried by six or eight men. In front of the coffin, and sometimes at the sides, are arranged the musicians, who perform all the way without an instant's interruption. Behind the coffin are grouped the male relatives, friends, &c., and lastly the procession is closed by crowds of women, attired in their finest dress. The coffin is beautifully decorated, and carried on the shoulders of six or eight stout young men by means of bamboos or poles. An unnatural merriment is allowed, and generally kept up all the way to the cemetery, and fantastic gestures and dances are performed by the bearers and their friends to the imminent danger of upsetting the coffin. The burning place is generally without the precincts of the town, and in the vicinity of some large pagodas. The funeral pile is of a very simple structure; its shape is that of an oblong square of a moderate size. Two large pieces of wood are at first laid parallel, at a distance of eight feet; other logs of wood, disposed at about six or eight inches from each other, are laid across the two first mentioned, so that their extremities are supported on these two pieces. A second set of logs is laid at right angles with the first; a third one placed across the second, and so on, until the pile is three, four, or five feet high. The coffin is deposited upon it. Fire is set below the pile by means of inflammable materials, which soon communicate fire to the logs the pile is made of. The whole is soon in a blaze and rapidly consumed by the devouring flames. The bystanders talk, laugh, or busy themselves in stirring the fire. As to the Talapoins, they sometimes take position under a neighbouring shed, repeat a few passages of Buddha's law, and when they are tired they give orders to their disciples to take up the offerings and then go back to their peaceable abodes. Very often they do not take the trouble of muttering prayers; they depart forthwith, followed by the offerings intended for them.

The fire being extinguished, the ashes, charcoal, &c., are carefully searched, and the particles of bones discovered are piously collected by the nearest relatives, and then buried in a hole dug for that purpose near some pagoda.

Persons in good circumstances keep up for seven days in their houses a sort of solemnisation of the funeral. Every day, in the evening particularly, musicians are kept up playing until a very late hour at night. The house is all the while crowded with people, who come for the purpose of enjoyment. Some play at various games; others drink tea; all chew betel-leaves' tobacco in profusion. Sometimes stories relating to Gaudama's former existences are read and listened to by the elders of the party. This mode, intended either to do honour to the deceased's memory or to afford relief to the grief of relatives, is rather expensive, and might often prove a heavy drain on the limited means of most of the families. But the spirit of mutual assistance on this occasion removes the difficulty. Every visitor, according to his means, makes a present of some money to the master of the house. Though the present of the

outsides were all covered with gold leaves. The great Thagia sent down on the spot a number of Nats, who made also the same number of religious ornaments. In the middle of the city a high square tower was erected; from its centre a tall spire rose to an immense height. This principal one was surrounded by a great number of smaller ones. Men and Nats mingled together, uniting in their endeavours to do honour to the deceased. The whole place was lined with countless beings, vieing with each other in their efforts to show the utmost respect, joy, and exultation on this extraordinary occasion.

The nurse of Thariputra, named Rewati, came and deposited round the mortal remains three golden flowers. At that very moment the great Thagia made his appearance, surrounded with myriads of Nats. As soon as the multitudes perceived him, they withdrew hastily to make room for him. In the midst of the confusion, Rewati fell down, was trampled upon, and died. She migrated to the fortunate seat of Tawadeintha, became a daughter of Nats, and inhabited a niche made with the most consummate skill, and adorned with the richest materials. Her body shone like a beautiful statue of gold, and was three gawoots tall. Her dress exceeded in richness, variety, and beauty all that had ever been hitherto seen.

On the following day, Rewati came from her glorious seat to the spot where crowds of people surrounded the body of the deceased. She approached with the dignified countenance and majestic bearing of a queen of Nats.

---

greatest numbers of visitors is comparatively small, yet, when added together, there is a considerable sum, which is generally more than sufficient to defray all expense that may be incurred. This custom or system of voluntary contributions burdens no one in particular, whilst it enables a family to make a show of liberality which, otherwise, would almost prove ruinous in many instances. The custom of burning the dead prevails amongst the Hindus, the Cingalese, Nepaulese, Burmese, Siamese and Cambodians. Though holding the tenets of Buddhism, the Chinese have never adopted this usage. The Mahomedans, living in Hindustan and the countries of eastern Asia, retain the custom of burying the dead. Buddhists have doubtless received that practice from the Hindus.

No one recognised her, though the eyes of all were riveted on her person, encompassed with the splendour of Nats. While all the spectators, overawed by the presence of that celestial being, remained motionless with a silent admiration, Rewati said to them, "How is it that none of you recognise me? I am Rewati, the nurse of the great Thariputra. To the offering of the three golden flowers made by me and placed at the feet of the mortal remains of the great Rahan, I am indebted for the glory and splendour of my present position." She explained at great length the advantages procured by doing meritorious actions. Having stood for awhile above the cenotaph, whereupon they had deposited the body of the deceased, she came down, turned three times round it, bowing down each time, and then returned to the blissful seat of Tawadeintha.

During seven consecutive days, rejoicings, dancings, and amusements of every description were uninterruptedly kept up in honour of the illustrious deceased. The funeral pile was made of scented wood; upon it they scattered profusely the most rare and fragrant perfumes. The pile was ninety-nine cubits high. The corpse having been placed upon it, fire was set to it by means of strings made of flowers and combustibles. During the whole night that the ceremony lasted, there was a constant preaching of the law. Anoorouda extinguished the fire with perfumed water. Tsanda carefully and piously collected the remaining relics, which were placed in a filter. "Now," said he, "I will go to Buddha with these relics, and lay them in his presence." With his companion Anoorouda, he took, together with the relics, the patta and tsiwaran of the deceased, and returned to Buddha to relate to him all the particulars concerning the last moments of his great disciple.

Tsanda was the younger brother of the great Thariputra. It was to him that the honour belonged of being the person selected to convey to Buddha the precious relics.

When, however, he had come to the monastery, he was unwilling to go alone into Buddha's presence. He went first to Ananda, his intimate friend, and said to him, "My brother Thariputra has obtained the state of Neibban. Here are the patta, tsiwaran, and relics," exhibiting before him, one after the other, those precious articles. Both went together to Buddha's place, and laid at his feet the patta, tsiwaran, and relics of the great disciple. Buddha, placing the relics on the palm of his right hand, called all the Rahans and said to them, "Beloved Rahans, this is all that remains of one who, a few days ago, was performing wonders in your presence, and has now reached the state of Neibban, something resembling a pure white shell. During an a thingie and hundred thousands of worlds, he has perfected himself by the practice of virtue. Beloved children, he could preach the law like another Buddha. He knew how to gain friends; crowds of people followed him to hear his instructions. Excepting me, no one in ten thousand worlds was equal to him. His wisdom was at once great and cheerful, his mind quick and penetrating. He knew how to restrain his desires, and to be easily satisfied with little. He loved retirement. He severely rebuked evil-doers. Beloved children, Thariputra renounced all pleasures and gratifications to become a Rahan; he always shunned strifes and contentions, as well as long and idle conversations. His patient zeal for the diffusion of my religion equalled the thickness of the globe. He was like a bull, the horns of which have been broken. My beloved Rahans, look once more at the relics of my wise son, Thariputra." Buddha in this manner eulogised the virtues of the illustrious deceased in five hundred stanzas.[7]

---

[7] The custom of making funeral orations for the purpose of eulogising distinguished individuals after their demise is of the highest antiquity. The sacred records bear witness to its existence amongst the Jews. The present legend offers repeated instances of *eulogia* made to honour the memory of the dead. On this occasion Buddha would not leave to another the honour of extolling the extraordinary merits and transcen-

On hearing all that Buddha had said to honour the memory of Thariputra, Ananda was filled with sentiments of the tenderest emotion. He could not refrain from shedding abundant tears. Buddha quickly remarked all that was taking place in his faithful and loving attendant, and said to him, "Ananda, on former occasions I have, in

---

dent excellencies of the illustrious Thariputra. But he had a higher object in view when he exhibited to the eyes of the assembled Rahans the relics of the deceased, which were all that remained of so celebrated a disciple, who had lived with them for so many years, and had just parted from them. It was impossible to give them a more forcible illustration of the truth he had so often announced to them, that there is nothing permanently subsisting in this world, but that all things are liable to a perpetual and never-ending change. The stern Buddha gently rebuked the amiable Ananda for the signs of inordinate grief he gave on this occasion; because, said he, the law of mutability acting upon all that surrounds us, we must ever be prepared to be separated from what is dearest to our affections; grief on such occasions is useless, and quite inconsistent with the principles of a wise man.

To honour the memory of Thariputra, and perpetuate the remembrance of his virtues, Buddha directed that a dzedi should be erected on the very spot where he had heard the news of his death. A dzedi is a religious monument very common in Burmah, and to be seen on all rising grounds in the neighbourhood of towns. Within the enclosure of all monasteries, a dzedi is invariably erected; it is the only purely religious building to be found in Burmah. The traveller in that country is always delighted, and experiences the most pleasurable sensations on approaching some town or village, when he sees several dzedis of various heights raising their white cones capped with the gilt crown from the bosom of beautiful groves of tall cocoa-nut trees, graceful areca palms, and massive tamarind, mango, and jack trees, all loaded with a green and luxuriant foliage. When the monument is on a grand scale, niches are made in the middle of each side of the square, facing the four points of the compass. In those niches are placed statues of Buddha, exhibiting him in the usual cross-legged position. The size of those religious monuments varies much in dimensions. They range from the height of a few feet to the colossal proportions of the tall Dagon Pagoda at Rangoon.

The custom of raising monuments over the ashes of religious distinguished by their virtues and extraordinary attainments, is a very ancient one, coeval in all probability with the first ages of Buddhism. They were real tumuli, surmounted with some ornaments in the shape of a cone. Such ornaments are seen towering over nearly all the religious monuments in Burmah. Royalty, in its head paraphernalia, and in its abode, has appropriated them to its own uses. We may at once infer that they are of a Hindu origin. The great monarchs who are called Tsekiawade kings, because they ruled over the whole of the Dzampoudipa island, were, according to Buddha's opinion, entitled to the honour of a dzedi after their demise.

my preachings, endeavoured to shelter your soul from the impressions caused by such and like emotions. Two things can alone keep us separated from father, mother, brothers, sisters, &c.,—in a word, from all that we most cherish, viz., death and distance. I, though a Buddha, have been exposed to all those changes brought on by distance when I practised the great virtues in the solitude, when I displayed wonders and spent a season in the seat of Tawadeintha. In those circumstances, distance kept me far from all those that were dearest to me. Would it not have been considered as useless, if not unbecoming, to shed tears either on my account or that of others? Can there ever be a time when any, how painful soever, occurrence may warrant wailing and lamenting?" With these and other considerations, Buddha soothed the affliction of Ananda, and filled his soul with consolations.

Buddha, to complete, as it were, the work of praises in favour of his great disciple, caused a dzedi to be erected in his honour near the entrance of the Dzetawon monastery. Having satisfied the sacred duty of gratitude towards the greatest of his disciples, Gaudama resolved to leave the monastery of Dzetawon for the country of Radzagio. Ananda was, as usual, directed to inform the Rahans to hold themselves ready for immediate departure.

The most excellent Phra having reached Radzagio, which he was to visit for the last time, took his abode into the Weloowon monastery. He had not stayed long in that place when the other great disciple, Maukalan, went to Neibban. Here are the particulars respecting the last moments of the illustrious companion of Thariputra. The heterodox Rahans, who lived in a state of complete nakedness, were extremely jealous of the popularity of Buddha, and coveted the abundant alms that were offered to him and his disciples. Maukalan, who was living on the Isigili mountain, in the cave of the dark rock, was supposed, on account of his great attainments and profound science, to be the cause of the great respect the people paid to his master. They resolved to kill him. For that purpose they armed five hundred robbers, and gave them one thousand pieces of silver to perpetrate the horrible crime. The assassins went twice to the cave; but their victim twice escaped their fury. At last, owing to the influence of a former bad deed, Maukalan resigned himself into the hands of the ruffians, who put him to death. They beat him so severely, that his lifeless remains were no more than a heap of mangled flesh, which they threw into the midst of bushes. The news of the appalling murder spread rapidly through the country. King Adzatathat had the murderers arrested. Having known from their own confession that the naked Rahans were the instigators of the murder, he had them likewise arrested. In front of his palace he ordered one thousand holes to be dug; in each hole a criminal was sunk up to his navel. All the ground was then overspread with straw, which being set fire to, all the wretches soon perished.

On hearing such news the disciples were greatly grieved, and asked each other what might have been the cause which had brought the aged Maukalan to such a cruel end. Buddha, appearing suddenly among them, said, "Beloved sons, what is the subject of your conversation?" They replied that they were conversing on the tragical death of their great companion. "I declare unto you," retorted Buddha, "that Maukalan has met a well-merited death. In one of his former existences, my beloved son, at the instigation of his wife, misled his aged and blind parents into a forest, where, leaving them alone, he went away for awhile. On his return, affecting the manners and voice of a highwayman, he killed his parents, and threw their bodies into a thicket. For this crime he has suffered the torments of hell during one thousand years, and has had to undergo the cruel death that has put an end to his last existence." Having thus spoken, he ordered that a dzedi should be erected in honour of Maukalan near the gate of the Weloowon monastery.

CHAPTER II.

Voyage to Wethalie—Last temptation of Manh—Causes of earthquake—New instructions to the Rahans—Last meal of Buddha—His painful distemper—His conversation with one of the Malla princes—Sign foreshowing Buddha's coming death—Arrival in the Kootheinaron forest—Buddha lays himself on his couch—Wonders attending that event—Instructions to Ananda—Eulogium of Ananda by Buddha—Conversion of Thoubat—Last words of Buddha to the Rahans—His death.

HAVING left Radzagio, Buddha intimated to Ananda that he wished to return to Wethalie. On his way to the right bank of the Ganges, he arrived at a place called Oukkatsela, where he preached on the death of his two greatest disciples. Thence he crossed the mighty stream and shaped his course towards Wethalie. On the day that he entered the city he went in quest of his food. Having partaken of what he had received, he called Ananda, bade him take his mat and cushion, and follow him to the Tsapala dzedi, where he intended to spend a part of the day. Complying with the command, Ananda followed Buddha, and with him went to the beautiful site of Tsapala, to the place prepared for his master. Ananda approached Phra, and, respectfully prostrated, said to him, "This is, indeed, a very agreeable place." Whereupon Buddha, rejoicing, praised the different sites of that country which were in the neighbourhood of the Wethalie city, as well as the dzedis that adorned them, and added, "Ananda, every wise person ought to be earnest in perfecting himself in the four laws of edeipat. Having advanced in the practice of these laws, he can, if he choose to do so, remain in a state of fixity during a whole revolution of nature, and even more. I, the Buddha, have become perfect in those laws, and I may remain as I am now during an innumerable number of years." Three times the same words were repeated. But Ananda, entangled as yet in the meshes of the tempter Manh Nat, remained prostrated before Buddha. It never came to his mind to entreat him to remain longer on earth for the benefit of mortals, who would derive the greatest advantages from his presence.

At that time Ananda rose up, with his mind troubled by the influence of the evil one, withdrew from Buddha's presence and went to the foot of a tree at a small distance. He had scarcely left Buddha alone when the Nat Manh, perceiving that Buddha remained alone for awhile, approached near his person, and keeping at a respectful distance, said to him, "Great, illustrious, and glorious Phra, who preachest an excellent law, it is now time for you to enter into the state of Neibban. You said in former times, that as long as your disciples were not much advanced in knowledge, as long as they had not obtained a thorough command over their heart, mouth, and senses, as long as they were still wanting in firmness and diligence for hearing and understanding the law, or unequal to the task of preaching the law, you would not go to Neibban. Now the Rahans, members of the assembly and your disciples, both males and females, are thoroughly instructed in all the parts of the law; they are firm in controlling their passions; they can preach the law to the other mortals; the Nats and Brahmas have heard your preachings, and countless numbers among them have obtained the deliverance; the time, therefore, is come for you to enter into the state of Neibban." Buddha knowing the wicked one, with his evil dispositions, replied, "Ha! wretched Manh, do not concern yourself about me. Ere long I will go to Neibban."

Whilst he was near the dzedi of Tsapala, Buddha, in a moment of perfect calmness of mind, entered into a sort of extraordinary state of contemplation, in which, for the first time, he mastered completely the principles of life, and appeared as if he had abandoned life. But it ought not to be understood that he parted with life, as a man lets go a stone that he has in his hands; but he estranged himself from the material life, renounced it, and placed himself beyond the reach of the influence that produces reward in the material or immaterial seats, and above that other influence which, procuring merits or demerits, keeps a being in the whirlpool of transmigration. As a mighty warrior on the battle-field throws down every barrier or obstacle that he meets, so Buddha broke down all the ties that had hitherto linked him to the state of existence.[1] At that very instant the earth trembled with

---

[1] It is very difficult to understand the extraordinary state in which Buddha placed himself on this occasion. It must have been a remarkable occurrence, since it caused a violent commotion which shook our planet. The only interpretation that can be put on the terms used to describe this particular action of Buddha is this: He renounced existence, that is to say, not only the actual existence that he enjoyed, but also all other forms of existence. He severed connection with this and other worlds; he broke the ties that had hitherto retained him linked to a form of existence. He had come now to the end of all transmigrations. By the power of his will, he placed himself in the state of complete isolation from all that exists, even from self, that is to say, into Neibban, a state which death was soon to realise and render visible to the eyes of his disciples. It is not death that causes a being to reach the state or condition of Neibban, but it is the abstraction from all conceivable forms of existence that constitutes its very essence. The expression made use of by our author to designate the particular condition in which Gaudama brought himself, and which caused a terrific shake of the earth, is this: He parted with the life of change, of mutability, that is to say, he had nothing more to do with existences, which, in the opinion of Buddhists, are produced by the principle of mutability. Buddha called himself Zina, or conqueror, after he had obtained the perfect mastery over his passions. We may give him the same title on the occasion when he has obtained the mastery over existence itself. This last achievement is the greatest of all: the first one was only preparatory to securing the second one. The writer is well aware that such a language is at variance with the notions that the reader is familiar with. To understand its true and correct meaning one must be initiated into the doctrines of Buddhism.

The preaching of the law of the wheel, which is mentioned as one cause that produces the phenomena of earthquake, took place, as above related, in the Migadawon forest, or the Deer's grove, near Benares, in the very beginning of Buddha's public life, after he had left the Bodi tree.

such violence that it caused the hairs of one's head to stand on end. Then he said to all present, "I am delivered from the influence of the world of matter, of the world of passions, and from every influence that causes the migration from one existence to another. I enjoy now a perfect calm of mind; like the mighty warrior who on the field of battle has conquered all his enemies, I have triumphed over all passions. I have mastered existence itself by destroying the principle that causes it." These words were uttered by Phra, lest perhaps some people might infer that he entered into the extraordinary state on which he mastered the elements of life, from fear caused by the language of the tempter, inviting him to go forthwith to Neibban.

Ananda, having felt the earthquake, respectfully approached Buddha and prostrated himself before him. Withdrawing then to a becoming distance, he asked him the causes that produce the extraordinary and terrifying phenomenon of earthquakes. "My son," answered Buddha, "eight causes make the earth tremble: 1st. The earth lies on a mass of water, which rests on the air, and the air on space; when the air is set in motion, it shakes the water, which in its turn shakes the earth; 2d, any being gifted with extraordinary powers; 3d, the conception of Phralaong for his last existence; 4th, his birth; 5th, his becoming a Buddha; 6th, his preaching the law of the wheel; 7th, his mastering and renouncing existence; 8th, his obtaining the state of Neibban. These are the eight causes of earthquakes. Ananda, a little while after having become a Buddha, I was in the solitude of Ouroowela, on the banks of the river Neritzara, under the shade of a banyan-tree planted by some shepherds. The wicked Nat came into my presence and requested me to go forthwith to Neibban. I refused then to comply with

---

The preaching of the law of the wheel is nothing else than the manifestation of the four sublime and transcendent truths, which, as mentioned in foregoing pages, constitute the essence of Buddha's doctrines.

his demand, and said to him, 'Wretched Manh, my disciples, members of the assembly, either males or females, the believers, either men or women, have not yet acquired sufficient knowledge, prudence, and penetration, courage, and resolution. They have not been as yet properly instructed in the most essential and highest articles of the law; they are unable to teach others: my religion is not yet resting on a strong foundation. The time, therefore, is not yet come for me to enter into the state of Neibban. Now, near this very dzedi of Tsapala, he has come anew and told me the same thing. Do not trouble yourself, miserable wretch, have I said to him; three months hence, I will obtain the state of Neibban. On this occasion I have fallen into the state in which I have mastered the principles of life by the means of the four laws of edeipat."[2]

[2] The particulars of the apparition of the evil one, or the tempter, related by Buddha himself to the faithful and amiable Ananda, show the incessant efforts made by Manh to render abortive, to a certain extent, the benevolent mission undertaken by Buddha to procure deliverance to numberless beings, and supply others with adequate means for entering into, and steadily following, the way that leads to it. He had been defeated in his endeavours to prevent Phra from leaving the world and obtaining the Buddhaship. He had been thwarted in his wicked designs to weaken the effects of Buddha's preachings. Heretics of all sorts had been summoned to his standard, to carry on a most active warfare against his opponents, but he had failed in all his attempts. Buddha had now almost completed the great and beneficial work he had undertaken: his religious institutions, known over a vast extent of territory, and zealously propagated by fervent and devoted disciples, seemed to be now firmly established. The edifice, indeed, was raised, but it required the action of a finishing hand; the keystone was yet wanting in the vault to render it complete and durable. Manh was aware of all that; hence his last and wily effort for impeding the finishing and perfecting of a work he had vainly] opposed in its beginning and during its progress.

The line of distinction between the members of the assembly and the mass of those who merely believed in the doctrines of Buddha, without leaving the world, is plainly drawn by Buddha himself; therefore, there can be no doubt that, from the origin of Buddhism, there existed a marked difference between the body of laymen and that of Rahans. Again, the body of the perfect, or those who formed what may emphatically be termed the assembly, was composed of men and women, living, as a matter of course, separately, in a state of continence, and subjected to the disciplinary regulations which we find embodied in the Wini. In Bur-

Ananda said to Phra: "Illustrious Buddha, please to remain during a whole Kalpa in this world for the benefit of men, Nats, and Brahmas." "Ananda," replied Phra, "your present request is too late and cannot be granted." Three times the faithful disciple begged of his great teacher this favour, and three times he received the same refusal. "Do you believe, O Ananda, that I know the four ways that lead to science and wisdom, and that I am perfect in the four laws of edeipat?" "I do believe it," answered Ananda. "Do you recollect, O Ananda, that a little while ago I said to you three times that he who was perfect in the laws of edeipat could remain, if he chose, during an entire Kalpa in this world? I added that I was thoroughly acquainted with these four laws; but you remained silent, and made no demand of me to remain longer in this world. The time for making this request is now irrevocably past. The term of my life is for ever fixedly determined. Now, Ananda, let us go to Mahawon Kootagara in the forest of the sala-trees." Having reached the place and stayed therein for a few days, he desired his faithful attendant to go to Wethalie and assemble all the Rahans in the Gnyipoora hall. When they had all assembled in that place, Ananda informed

mah, vestiges of female devotees, living secluded from the world, are to be met with in many places, but, as already noticed in a foregoing remark, the order of religious females has much fallen off. Its professed members are few in number, and the exterior observance of the regulations is much neglected. The comprehensiveness of Buddhism, its tendency to bring all men to the same level, and allow of no difference between man and man but that which is established by superiority in virtue, its expansive properties, all those striking characteristics have mightily worked in elevating the character of the woman, and raising it to a level with that of man. Who could think of looking upon the woman as a somewhat inferior being, when we see her ranking, according to the degrees of her spiritual attainments, among the perfect and foremost followers of Buddha? Hence in those countries where Buddhism has struck a deep root and exercised a great influence over the manners of nations, the condition of the woman has been much improved and placed on a footing far superior to what she occupies in those countries where that religious system is not the prevalent one, or where it has not formed or considerably influenced the customs and habits of the people.

Buddha that his order had been duly executed. Phra went to the hall, and sat in the place prepared for him. He then, addressing the assembly, said: "My beloved children, the law which my supreme wisdom has discovered, I have announced for your benefit and advantage. You have attentively and perseveringly listened to it, firmly adhered to its tenets, and zealously propagated them. Now my religion shall last for a long period, and prove the source of great blessings to all Nats. But to the end that my religion may last long, shine forth with splendour, and be productive of incalculable benefits, it is necessary that great attention should be paid to the thirty-seven laws from which all good works proceed.[3] These laws you have been acquainted with by my preachings; it is

[3] The Buddhists of these parts, following the track of their ancestors, or rather copying their writings, are fond of arbitrary divisions in all that concerns the different parts of their metaphysics. Buddha, on this occasion, alludes to thirty-seven articles, which may be considered as the foundation whereon rests philosophical and moral wisdom. They are called *Bodi-pek-kera;* meaning, I believe, points or articles of wisdom. They are subdivided into seven classes. In the first are enumerated the four subjects most deserving of attention, viz., the body, the heart, the sensations, and the law. In the second are described four objects extremely worthy of our efforts, viz., preventing the law of demerits to come into existence; preventing its developments, when it exists; causing the law of merits to come into existence, and furthering its progress when it is already existing. In the third are found likewise four points meriting control, viz., one's will, one's heart, one's efforts, and one's exertions. In the fourth class we find enumerated five pre-eminently necessary dispositions or inclinations; that is to say, disposition to benevolence, to diligence, to attention, to steady direction towards what is excellent, and to considerate wisdom.

The fifth class comprises the *pola*, or rewards or good effects resulting from the above inclination, viz., perfect benevolence, diligence, attention, steadiness in what is excellent, and considerate wisdom.

The sixth class comprehends the seven following virtues, which enable man to raise himself very high in the scale of perfection:—Attention, consideration of the law, diligence, equanimity of the soul, constancy in good, fixity, and delight.

The seventh class comprises the ways that lead to good and perfection. They are eight in number:—Perfect doctrine, intention, language, actions, regular mode of life, diligence, attention, and fixity in good.

A volume might be written upon these thirty-seven principles or points of moral philosophy, by way of comment and explanation; but we think it better to leave the reader to make his own reflections, and run at liberty over this broad field of metaphysics.

to you to announce them to all beings. Meditate with unremitting attention on the principles of change and mutability. As to me, ere long I will go to Neibban; three months more, and this last drama shall be over."

In the morning Buddha, putting on his dress, went out to beg his food, carrying the patta on his left arm. When he had eaten his meal, he looked with the steadiness of an elephant over the whole country. The reason why he cast a look like an elephant over Wethalie is, as he explained it to Ananda, the following:—The neck-bone of all Buddhas is not like the links of a chain, but consists of one single solid bone: hence when they wish to consider some object lying behind they cannot turn their heads backwards, but the whole body, like that of the elephant, must follow the same motion. On this and other occasions of this kind, our Buddha had not to make any effort, but the earth turning round, like the wheel of the potter, brought the object to be looked at before him. The great city of Wethalie was within three years to be destroyed by King Adzatathat. As Buddha had always received many marks of respect and attention from the inhabitants of that city, he felt the greatest commiseration for them. His last glance was a sorrowful farewell he bade to the devoted city. This is the motive that induced Buddha to cast a last look over it.

Buddha went to a place called Pantoogama. He passed successively through Hatti, Tsampou, and Appara, and thence to Bauga. In the latter place he preached the four laws of Padesa. Summoning Ananda to his presence, he desired him to inform the Rahans to hold themselves ready to go to the Pawa country. Having reached that district, he went with all his Rahans to live in a monastery built in a grove of mango-trees erected by Tsonda, the son of a wealthy goldsmith. Tsonda had previously seen Buddha, and obtained the state of Thautapan. His gratitude induced him to build a monastery, which, together with the grove, he had given over to Buddha. His arrival at that place happened on the 14th of the waxing moon of Katson.

Informed that Phra had come to the monastery, Tsonda repaired hastily thither, prostrated himself before him, and having taken a seat at a becoming distance, requested Buddha to accept the meal he would prepare for him and all the Rahans. Buddha by his silence acquiesced in the request. Tsonda rose up, bowed down, and turning to the right, left the monastery. During the whole night, all sorts of the choicest dishes were prepared. He had a young pig, neither fat nor lean, killed, and the flesh dressed with rice in the most exquisite manner. The Nats infused into it the most delicious flavour. At daybreak, everything being ready, Tsonda went to the monastery, and invited Buddha and all the Rahans to come and partake of the meal that was ready for them. Buddha rose up, and, carrying his patta, went to Tsonda's house, where he sat in the place prepared for his reception. He took for himself the pork and rice, but his attendants feasted upon the other dishes. When he had eaten, he desired Tsonda to bury in the earth the remains of the pork and rice, because no one in the Nats' or Brahmas' seats but himself could digest such a food. A little while after, Buddha was seized with a violent attack of dysentery, the pain whereof he bore with the greatest patience and composure. He suffered so much, not because of the food he had taken, as he would otherwise have been exposed to the same distemper. The pain was rather alleviated by the eating of the pork and rice, because the Nats had infused therein the choicest flavour.

Buddha desired Ananda to be ready to go to the town of Koutheinaron. While on the way he felt very weak, and retired under the shade of a tree, commanding Ananda to fold his dugout to sit upon. When he had rested a little, he called Ananda and said to him: "Ananda, I am very thirsty; bring me some water." Ananda replied: "One of the Malla princes, named Poukatha, has just passed through the Kakouda river with five hundred carts, and the water is quite muddy." The Malla princes ruled by turn over the country. When the time for ruling had not yet come, or had passed, many of them devoted their time to the pursuit of trade. Notwithstanding this objection, Buddha repeated three times the injunction. Ananda at last took up Phra's patta and went to the stream to fetch water. How great was his surprise when he found the water clear and limpid. He said to himself: "Great indeed is the power of Buddha, who has worked such a wonderful change in this stream." He filled the patta with water and brought it to his great teacher, who drank of it.

Prince Poukatha had been a disciple of the Rathee Alara. He came to Buddha, and said to him, whilst he was under the shade of the tree: "Great indeed is the peace and calm composure of mind of the Rahans. On a former occasion," added he, "whilst the Rathee Alara was travelling, he went to rest under the shade of a tree, at a small distance, by the wayside. A merchant with five hundred carts happened to pass by. A man that followed at a distance came to the place where Alara was resting, and inquired of him if he had seen the five hundred carts that had just passed by. Alara replied that he was not aware that any cart had come in sight. The man at first suspected that Alara was unsound in his mind, but he was soon convinced that what he was at first inclined to attribute to mental derangement was caused by the sublime abstraction of the Rathee from all that was taking place."

Buddha having heard this story, rejoined: "Which is, in your opinion, the more wonderful occurrence, to see a man in his senses and awake not to notice the passing of five hundred carts or even of one thousand, or to see another man, equally awake and in the enjoyment of his mental faculties, who did not hear the violence of a storm, a heavy fall of rain, accompanied with loud peals of thunder and uninterrupted flashes of lightning? In former times, I, the Buddha, was sitting under a small shed. A most violent storm came on; peals of thunder resounded more awfully than the roaring of the sea, and lightnings seemed to rend the atmosphere in every direction. At that time two brothers were ploughing in a field with four bullocks. They were all killed, men and bullocks, by lightning. A man came to me whilst I was walking in front of the shed, and told me that he came to see the accident that had just happened, and asked me some particulars concerning it. I answered him that I was not aware that any storm had raged near this place, nor any accident attended it. The stranger inquired of me whether I was asleep; or if not, whether I was in possession of my senses. I answered him that I was not asleep, and that I was in the perfect enjoyment of my mental and physical faculties. My answer made a powerful impression upon him: he thought within himself that great and wonderful is the power of Thamabat, which procures to the Rahans such an imperturbable calm of mind, which cannot be disturbed by the mightiest convulsions of nature. Now, Prince Poukatha, in whom do you think that the greatest calm of mind has prevailed?" "Most excellent Phra," replied the prince, "the great respect I bore formerly unto the Rathee Alara has disappeared like the chaff before the wind, and run out like the water of a rapid stream. I am now like a man to whom the true road has been pointed out, who has discovered hidden things, and who has a shining light before him. You have announced to me the true law, which has dispelled the cloud of ignorance and brought happiness and calm to my hitherto disturbed soul. From this moment I believe in Buddha, the law, and the assembly, and to the end of my life I will ever remain a believer." The prince called a young man, and directed him to go and bring two beautiful and rich pieces of cloth having the colour of pure gold thread. When they had been brought over, the prince, holding them in his hand, said: "O most glorious Buddha, these pieces of cloth I have occasionally worn: they are in colour like gold, and the tissue is of the finest description; please to accept them as an offering I make to you." Phra desired him to present one of the pieces to himself, and the other to Ananda, that his merits might be greater, since the offering would be made to Buddha and to the assembly in the person of Ananda. This attention in favour of Ananda was also intended to reward him for his unremitting exertions during the twenty-five years he had served Buddha with the utmost respect, care, and affection, without having received any adequate return for his services. Buddha preached afterwards the law to the prince. When the instruction was over, Poukatha believed in, and firmly adhered to, the three precious things, and became a sincere convert. He rose up, prostrated himself before Buddha, turned on the right, and departed.

Ananda, after the prince's departure, brought the two dresses to the great Phra, who put one on his shoulders, whilst the other was girded round his waist. His body appeared shining like a flame. Ananda was exceedingly surprised. Nothing of this kind had as yet happened. "Your exterior appearance," said he to Buddha, "is at once white, shining, and beautiful above all expression." "What you say, O Ananda, is perfectly true. There are two occasions when my body becomes extraordinarily beautiful and shining: the first was on the night I obtained the supreme intelligence; and the second now, when I am about to enter into the state of Neibban. Doubtless, O Ananda, on the morning after this very night, in a corner, near the Koutheinaron city, that belongs to the princes Malla, in the forest of sala-trees, I will go to Neibban. The shining light emanating from my body is the certain forerunner of this great event."

Ananda, summoned by Buddha to his presence, received the order to move to the banks of the Kakouda stream.[4] Having reached the place, Buddha descended

[4] The Kakouda stream was one of the arms or channels of the little Gundak. It is at present dried up, but up to this day are to be seen

into the stream, bathed, and drank some water. Thence he directed his steps towards a grove of mango-trees. Ananda had remained to dry the bathing-robes of his

---

several marks indicating the ancient bed of that stream.

The river Hiranyawati is one of the channels of the little Gundak, which was flowing a little west of the city of Koutheinaron. The Gundak being very winding in its course, and the mass of water being sometimes very considerable, there is to be seen a great number of old channels, now dried up, or occasionally filled in the time when inundation is prevailing. For this reason, it becomes difficult in some instances to follow the Chinese pilgrim, Hwen Thsang, through his minute and accurate description of the places he has visited. The mounds of ruins which stud the ground may not be always correctly identified, because they are not at present, relatively to the river, in the same position as that mentioned in his interesting itinerary. However, there are here and there some remnants of the old channels which are sufficient to guide safely the sure and patient Government Archæological Surveyor, who now does so much, with the assistance derived from the books of the two Chinese pilgrims, to find out and identify on the spot most of the places and localities mentioned in the Buddhist writings. It is not a little surprising that we should have to acknowledge the fact that the voyages of two Chinese travellers, undertaken in the fifth and seventh centuries of our era, have done more to elucidate the history and geography of Buddhism in India, than all that has hitherto been found in the Sanscrit and Pali books of India and the neighbouring countries.

The young religious who is called Tsanda was the younger brother of Thariputra. He seems to have shared with Ananda the honour of attending on Buddha's person.

The forest which was close to the vicinity of Koutheinaron was planted with trees which the Burmans call ingien, the Bengalies, sal. The latter name is evidently the Sanscrit and Pali appellation of the tree, which the Burmese author has retained but once or twice throughout the course of his work, and wrote Sala. It is the *Shorea robusta.*

The four laws of edeipat, which, in the opinion of Buddha, can confer to him who knows and possesses them the extraordinary privilege of an indefinitely prolonged existence, are, absolute power over the will, absolute power over the mind, absolute power of exertion, absolute power over the means to attain any object. How can a man, in the present state of existence, obtain the possession of such a power? The only way that a Buddhist has to account for it is the following:—A perfected being, having estranged himself from all passions, from matter and its concomitant influences, solely by the power and energy of his will, acquires a freedom from all impediments, an unbounded liberty of motion, and a lightness and swiftness which enable him to do all that he pleases. He is independent of the elements of this world, which can no more offer obstacles and resistance to his wishes. Several instances of something approaching to those wonderful attainments have been mentioned in the course of this work. We have seen how those much advanced in perfection could raise themselves very high, and travel through the air with an almost incredible velocity. This was but the beginning of far superior and transcendent qualifications obtained only by those that had made greater progress in science, in virtue, and in the renouncing of all things; in a

master. Phra called the Rahan Tsanda, and directed him to fold in four his dugout, because he wished to rest. The order having been complied with, Buddha sat down, lying on his right side, with the solemn and fearless appearance of a lion. During his short sleep Tsanda watched by his side. Ananda soon came up. Buddha called him, and said, "The meal which the goldsmith's son has prepared for me, which I have eaten, is my last meal. He is, forsooth, much grieved because of the illness that has come upon me after having eaten at his place.[5] Go now to him,

---

word, by those who had mastered the four laws of edeipat.

Mahawon Kootagara means the hall of the upper story in the great forest. Not far from Wethalie there was a monastery of great celebrity, situated in a forest of sala-trees. It had, at least, an upper story, in which was the hall where Gaudama often preached to his disciples and to the people.

[5] The meal Buddha partook of in company with his disciples at Tsonda's residence is the last repast he ever made. The violent distemper which followed immediately is not, says the author of the legend, to be attributed to the food he took on this occasion. On the contrary, that very food, owing to the virtue infused therein by the agency of Nats and Brahmas, was rather an antidote against the illness that was to come inevitably upon Phra's person. Previous to the dissolution of his bodily frame, it was decreed that Buddha should suffer. No occurrence could ever cause or avert this tragical circumstance. He had foreseen it, and with perfect resignation submitted to what was absolutely to happen. In the early days of Buddhism, when a deadly antagonism with Brahminism began to fill the peninsula of Hindustan with endless disputes between the supporters of the rival systems, Brahmins, with a cutting sneer, insulted their opponents by reminding them that the founder of their creed, whom they so much revered and exalted, had died from the effects of his having indulged too much in pork. About twenty-two years ago, when the writer was in Burmah, he chanced to meet with a shrewd old Christian, who, by the way, was fonder of disputing about religion than paying regard to the practice thereof. He boasted of having at his command deadly weapons against Buddhists, and unanswerable arguments to bear with an irresistible force on the vital parts of their creed. The chief one, which he always brought forward with a Brahminical scorn and laugh, was that Gaudama had died from his having eaten pork. He always did it with so much mirth and wit that his poor ignorant adversaries were completely overawed and effectually silenced by his bold and positive assertion, and left to him uncontested the field of battle, and allowed him to carry away undisputed the palm of victory. This way of arguing may prove a very amusing one, but it can never be approved of, as error is never to be combated by another error or a false supposition. The Burmese translator was doubtless aware of the weak side offered to the attacks of malignant opponents by the unpleasant distemper that followed the last meal of Buddha. He strenuously labours to defend the

and make him acquainted with the merits he has gained in making an offering to me. Two meals that I have taken during this existence are equally deserving of the greatest rewards. The first was the Nogana, served up to me a little while before I obtained first the Neibban of Kiletha, or the destruction of passions, and subsequently the supreme intelligence; the second is the one just offered

---

character of his hero by proving, in the best way he can, that such a bodily disorder was necessarily to take place, in order to set in relief the patience, composure, and other sterling virtues of the founder of Buddhism. The text of the legend has been read over several times with the greatest attention, for the purpose of ascertaining the reasons put forward to account for such an occurrence, but the result has proved unsatisfactory. A thick veil wraps in complete obscurity this curious episode of Buddha's life. All that can be said is this: it was preordained that Buddha should be visited with a most painful distemper ere he attained Neibban; and so it happened.

To prove that the eating of pork had nothing to do with the distemper that followed, we have the authority of Gaudama himself, who commended the delicacy and flavour of that dish, and placed it on the same footing with the delicious Nogana he ate on the morning of the day previous to his obtaining the Buddhaship. He desired his ever-faithful attendant, Ananda, to repair to Tsonda's place, and explain to him the great rewards reserved to him for having made the offering of such an excellent food.

The practical working of the Buddhistic system relatively to almsgiving deserves some notice. A man bestows alms on the Rahans, or spends money towards promoting some religious purpose; he does so with the belief that what he bestows now in the way of alms will secure to him countless advantages in future existences. Those favours, which he anticipates to enjoy hereafter, are all of a temporal nature, relating only to health, pleasures, riches, honours, and a long life either in the seat of man or in the seats of Nats. Such is the opinion generally entertained by all Buddhists in our days. Talapoins make the preaching of the law consist chiefly in enumerating the merits and rewards attending the bestowing of alms on persons devoted to a religious mode of life. In this respect the practical result of their sermons is certainly most beneficial to themselves. The spiritually-minded Buddha seems to have levelled a blow at concupiscence and covetousness by openly stating that alms have not the power to stem the current of demerits, to give rise and energy to the principle of merits, or to lead to wisdom, which enables man to weaken gradually concupiscence, anger, and ignorance, and to open and prepare the path to Neibban. True knowledge, attended by the practice of the virtues peculiar to those who have entered into the current of perfection by following the four Meggas, can alone enable a man to reach Neibban. Many excellent practices enforced by Buddhism have, so to speak, been reduced to a mere lifeless skeleton by ignorance and passions, but they would appear in a very different light were they animated with the spirit that has brought them into existence.

to me by the goldsmith's son, when I ate the dish of rice and pork. That is the last food I will ever take until I attain the state of Neibban, that is to say, the Neibban of Khandas, or the destruction of all the supports of existence. Both these meals were excellent, and are deserving of an equal reward; viz., beauty, a long life, happiness, a large crowd of attendants, the happiness of the Nats' seats, and all sorts of honours and distinction. Such are the merits reserved to Tsonda, the son of the goldsmith; go and mention them to him, that his sorrow may be assuaged." Gaudama uttered on this occasion the following stanzas:[6]

---

[6] The observance of the five precepts incumbent upon all Buddhists is the foundation whereupon is to be erected the spiritual edifice; it is the first step towards the great ways leading to perfection; it is preparatory for the great exercise of meditation, by which true wisdom may be acquired. The faithful who observe the five precepts and the three additional counsels show that faith is living in their hearts, and give unmistakable marks of their zeal in the practice of religion. They are real Upasakas, or laymen, fervently adhering to and taking refuge in Buddha, the law, and the assembly; but they cannot take rank among the members of the assembly or Thanga. Practice of and progress in meditation can alone usher an Upasaka into the sanctuary of the perfect.

The rewards destined to the faithful after their death are exactly proportionate to their merits and the real worth of their deeds. The seats of Nats, placed immediately above the seat of men, but under the sixteen seats reserved to the perfect, are opened to the pious Upasaka who migrates from the seat of probation and trial. The nature of the pleasures enjoyed in the Nats' seats are all referable to the senses. All that can be imagined best fitted for the delectation of the five senses is accumulated in those blissful regions, and proffered with an ever-renewed profusion to their fortunate inhabitants. The vivid imagination of Asiatics has, one would say, exhausted its stores in picturing with an amazing variety the riches to be possessed there. It would be of no utility to attempt to give a compendious narrative of what we meet with in Buddhistic compositions respecting those regions. Suffice it for our purpose to say that the distinction of sexes remains in the Nats' countries. In the two lowest seats connection takes between the two sexes, but no procreation ever results from it; in the third seats the Nats of different sexes are fully gratified by a simple kiss; in the fourth, by the touch of the hand; in the fifth, by merely looking at each other; and in the sixth, by the mere fact of their being in the same place, upon which we may make two observations. The first is that pleasures therein enjoyed lose their coarseness, and become more refined and more perfect in proportion as the seats are more elevated. The greater are the merits of the Upasaka in this life, the higher is the seat he is destined to occupy, and the more refined are the pleasures and enjoyments allotted to him. Hence our Gaudama having, during the existence preceding this last one, practised moral virtues of the highest order,

"Alms-deeds can defend from and protect against the influence and the sources of demerits, which are man's true enemies. He alone who is full of merits and wisdom shuns evil doings, puts an end to concupiscence, anger, and ignorance, and reaches Neibban." Buddha, calling Ananda, said to him, "Let us now go to the bank of the river Hignarawati, in the forest of sala-trees belonging to the Malla princes." Attended by a crowd of Rahans, he went to the bank of the stream. The forest was on a tongue of land, encircled on three sides by the river. "Ananda," said Buddha, "you see those two lofty trees on the skirt of the wood; go and prepare a resting-place for me between those two trees, in such a way that, when reclining thereupon, my head should be turned towards the north. The couch must be arranged in such a manner that one extremity may be near one tree, and the other extremity close to the opposite tree. Ananda, I am much fatigued, and desire to rest." Though Buddha's strength was equal to that of a thousand koudes of black elephants, it forsook him almost entirely from the time he had eaten the dish of Tsonda's rice and pork. Though the distance from the place of Pawa to the forest of sala-trees in the district of Koutheinaron is but three gawots, he was compelled to rest in traversing it twenty-five times, and it was by dint of

---

migrated to Toocita, the fourth seat of Nats. The second observation is, that the duration of the enjoyments in the Nats' seats increases in an arithmetical progression; that is to say, the pleasures of the second seat last twice as long as those of the first or lowest seat. Those of the third seat last twice as long as those of the second, and so on to the last or highest seat.

In the sermons that the Talapoins address to the people for stirring up their zeal chiefly in making alms to them, they are most fluent and abundant in the promises of rewards in the Nats' seats, as a powerful inducement held out to them for keeping up their zeal in bestowing alms. They admirably succeed in obtaining their object with most of their hearers. It cannot be denied that those poor deluded followers of Buddha are fully convinced of all that is narrated to them by Talapoins respecting the Nats' seats. Such is the implicit faith of the mass of the Buddhists. One may occasionally meet with a few individuals who laugh at those fables, but these are looked upon in no better light than that of rationalists or freethinkers by the orthodox portion of the community.

great exertions that he reached the place after sunset. Four places along the road from Pawa to Koutheinaron became subsequently celebrated by the resort of many pilgrims who visited them.

[*Remarks of the Burmese Translator.*—It has been often asked why Phra allowed his body to experience fatigue. The reason of his conduct was to convey instruction to all men, and to make them fully prepared to bear pain and sickness. Should any one ask why Buddha exerted himself so much to go to Neibban in that particular place, it should be answered that Buddha saw three reasons for acting in the manner he did. 1st. To preach the great Soodathana. (This is the story of a prince called Maha Soudana, who ruled over the country of Kousawatti. At the conclusion Buddha declares that in that great prince the law of mutability has acted throughout his life with an irresistible force; while, as for himself, he now delights at being emancipated from its thraldom, and longs to be freed from the prison of his body.) 2d. To instruct Thoubat and lead him to perfection. 3d. To secure that the disputes that were to arise on account of the division and possession of his relics should be quieted by the Pounha Dauna, who would fairly and peaceably effectuate the partition of those sacred remains.]

Phra, having reached the couch, lay down on his right side with the noble composure and undaunted fearlessness of a lion.[7] The left leg was lying directly on the right

---

[7] The posture assumed by Buddha at this last stage of his life has supplied the subject of an artistic composition to the Southern Buddhist sculptors. A statue representing Phra in that reclining position is to be seen in almost every pagoda. Some of these statues are made on truly gigantic proportions. I have measured one that was forty-five feet long. If we take such rough works as exhibiting the amount of skill possessed by natives in the art of carving, we must confess that that art is with them yet in its infancy. The huge idols I have met with are never made of wood or hewed stones, but are built up with bricks. The artist, having made in this way the principal parts of the statue, covers the whole with a thick coat of mortar, the softness of which enables him without much labour to put the finishing hand to his work. These statues are invariably made after a certain pattern belonging to the antiquity, and to an

one; but in order to avoid pain and the accompanying trouble, the situation of the two legs was such as to prevent the immediate contact of the two ankles and knees. The forest of sala-trees lies at the south-west of the city of Koutheinaron. Should any one wish to go to the city from the forest, he must first go due east, and then turn north. The place, therefore, where Phra stood was a tongue of land, surrounded on three sides by the river.

When Buddha was reclining on the couch, the two sala-trees became suddenly loaded with fragrant blossoms, which gently dropped above and all round his person, so as almost to cover it. Not only these two trees, but all those of that forest, and also those in ten thousand worlds, exhibited the same wonderful and graceful appearance. All the fruit-trees yielded out of season the best fruits they had ever produced; their beauty and flavour exceeded all that had ever been seen. The five kinds of lilies shot forth from the bosom of the earth, and from every plant and tree; they displayed to the astonished eyes the most ravishing sight. The mighty mountain of Hymawonta, which is three thousand youdzanas in extent, shone with all the richness of the colours of the peacock's tail. The Nats, who watched over the two ingien or sala-trees, showered down without interruption the most fragrant

epoch when the art was yet in its very infancy: they are, in an artistic point of view, the worst, rudest, and coarsest attempts at statuary I have ever seen. Gold is, however, profusely lavished on those shapeless and formless works. The big idol above referred to was covered with gold, that is to say, gilt from head to feet.

Idols of smaller dimensions, those in particular representing Buddha sitting in a cross-legged position, in the attitude of meditation, are likewise wretched specimens of art. A great many are made of a soft stone, almost white, resembling marble in appearance, and capable of receiving a most perfect polish. About three miles west of the old and ruined city of Tsagain is a place where the manufacturing of marble idols is carried on to a great extent. The stone used by the carvers is brought from a place north of Amerapoora, where it is abundant. It is soft, transparent, white, and sometimes, when polished, exhibits a slightly bluish appearance. The instruments used by the artists are simple and few. Were it not for the custom which obliges them to follow always the same patterns, the Burmese workmen would much improve in that branch of the fine arts.

flowers. From the seats of Nats, the flower Mandarawan, which grows on the banks of the lake Mandawan, and glitters like the purest gold, with leaves expanding like an umbrella, was showered down by the Nats, together with powder of sandal-wood and other odoriferous plants. The Nagas and Galongs, joining the Nats, brought from their respective seats all kinds of flowers and perfumes, which they let drop like dew over and about Buddha's sacred person. Phra, seeing the wonderful display performed by men, Nats, Nagas, and Galongs, to do him honour, and hearing the sweet accents of Nats' voices, singing his praises, called Ananda and said to him, "You witness all that display[8] which is intended to do me

---

[8] If Buddha ever deserved the surname of sage, it was assuredly on this occasion that he entitled himself to such an honourable distinction. All nature reversed its course on his account: wonders of the most extraordinary character loudly proclaimed his supereminent excellencies: the most exalted beings united their voices in extolling his transcendent merits, and showing their unbounded respect for his person; all that could dazzle the eye, please the ear, and flatter the heart, was displayed on an unparalleled scale to do honour to him who was about to leave this terrestrial abode. Buddha, however, solemnly declares, and unhesitatingly says to Ananda, that such a display is infinitely below his merits and perfections, and can bear no comparison with his fathomless wisdom and boundless knowledge of truth. Such things, in his opinion, are mere externals, quite destitute of substantial worth; they confer no real honour to him. They, adds he, who truly do honour to me are those who practise all that is enjoined by the most excellent law; nothing short of the observance of the law can please me; the practice of the virtues leading to perfection alone give the right to be called my disciple. My religion can rest firmly only on such solid foundation.

These expressions make every reader understand that, in Buddha's opinion, religion is not a mere theory, teaching fine moral precepts, destined to excite a vain admiration in the mind, or elicit useless applauses; but it is a moral and practical system, making man acquainted with the duties he has to perform in order to shun vice and practise virtue. Nothing can be more explicit and positive than the notions he entertains of religion. They are worthy of the founder of a religious system now believed and admitted, with more or less considerable variety, by nearly one-fourth, or at least one-fifth, of the great human family. It must be admitted that the high religious sense entertained by Buddha, and communicated in all its purity to his immediate disciples, has almost vanished away in all Buddhist countries. With the people religion consists in certain exterior observances, such as giving alms to the Talapoins, building pagodas, and making offerings during the three months especially consecrated to religious duties. The influence of religious teachers, owing to ignorance

honour; it is not as yet worthy of me, who possess the knowledge of the most sublime law. No one can be my true follower, or accomplish the commands of the law, by such a vain and outward homage. Every Rahan or Rahaness, every believer, man or woman, who practises the excellent works leading to perfect happiness, these are the persons that render me a true homage, and present to me a most agreeable offering. The observance of the law alone entitles to the right of belonging to my religion. Ever remember this, O Ananda, and let every believer in my religion act up to it."

Why did Buddha, on this last occasion, lay little stress on the offerings that were made, whilst on former occasions he had much extolled the innumerable merits to be derived from the making of offerings? The reason of his conduct was to give every one to understand that religion could not subsist unless by the practice of all the duties it commands, and that it would soon disappear were it supported only by alms-deeds, offerings, and other outward ceremonies. Alms-deeds are productive of great rewards, but the practice of virtue alone secures to religion a prolonged existence.

At that time an illustrious Rahaness, named Oupala-

---

and want of zeal, may be thought by many to be almost null, and scarcely felt by the masses of nominal Budhists. Two causes, however, seem to be the generators and supporters of the religious sentiment that influences the people,—education, and the political institutions. The male portion of the community is brought up in the monasteries by the Phongyies. All the books that are put into their hands, and most of those that they subsequently read, are treatises on religious subjects. This system keeps up, in a wonderful manner, the knowledge of religion, which exercises a great control over the actions of individuals, and regulates their conduct. But, besides, the religious element almost predominates in the body of the civil laws; it acts indirectly upon the people, and must be allowed a great share of influence in all that regards their morals. It is, therefore, to political institutions that Buddhism owes much for the continuation of its existence in these regions. Were it deprived of such a powerful support, there is every reason to believe that it could not perhaps long retain its hold over the masses, when regularly and extensively attacked by the followers of another system. But the first cause is by far the weightier and the more influential.

wana,[9] at a single word from Buddha, lowered her fan and went to sit at a certain distance. Ananda, who had seen this Rahaness attending assiduously on Buddha's person during more than twenty seasons, was surprised at seeing that, without any apparent reason, she had been desired on that occasion to withdraw to a distance. Phra, reading in the soul of Ananda his innermost thoughts, said to him, "Ananda, I am not displeased with Oupalawana; but her body being of a very large size, it prevents the myriads of Nats that have come from ten thousand worlds to see and contemplate me on this supreme moment. The Nats can see through the bodies of the generality of men, but this

[9] In the first edition of this work the writer had made an error in supposing Oupalawana to have been a male religious. Another palm-leaf manuscript that he has consulted leaves no doubt about her real character. She was, among the female body of religious, the disciple of the left; and Kema, who had been for many years the first wife of King Pimpathara, was the disciple of the right. Oupalawana belonged to a distinguished family of Kapilawot. The female portion of the Thanga or assembly was constituted after the mode of the Rahans. Thariputra and Maukalan were respectively the disciples of the right and of the left. One of the duties of the Rahaness of the left was to fan Buddha on certain occasions, and render to him such services as were compatible with her sex. The order of nuns in Burmah in our days has fallen very low. Instead of the yellow colour, they have adopted the white one for their dress, which, in other respects, resembles that of the Phongyies. Their head is shaved. They are to be seen in the neighbourhood of pagodas, and in the streets, going about to beg the food required for their maintenance. The only large convent of those nuns which I have ever met is one on the right bank of the Irrawaddy, about five miles north of Tsagain. It contains about forty or fifty inmates. Some of them belong to good families, and reside in the house for a few years, after which they return into their home. That house is under the special protection of the king, who supplies the nuns with all the necessaries of life. In the valley of Tavoy a small convent also has been pointed out to the writer. It was situated on a beautiful spot, west of the river. When he went to see it, he was surprised to meet with two or three old women, habited in the canonical dress, who appeared to be wretchedly poor and slovenly in their habits. The house was in every respect in keeping with the exterior appearance of the tenants. The nuns do absolutely no work, except in certain localities where they try to do away with a portion of their time in clearing the weeds which grow so luxuriantly in the enclosure of some famous pagoda. They have no schools to teach girls the rudiments of reading and writing. They are on this head greatly behind the Buddhist monks, who have assumed to themselves the great and important task of teaching boys in the towns and villages.

power falls short with persons much advanced in merits. I therefore desired her to remove a little far, that the Nats might not be angry at not seeing my person."

Ananda put a great many questions to Buddha, which are related at full length in the Parinibana Thoots.

He asked him, among other topics, how the Rahans were to behave when women should resort to their monasteries.[10] "Ananda," answered Buddha, "a Rahan, desirous

[10] The founder of Buddhism shows himself on this particular subject a consummate moralist. He who could have spoken as he did on this truly delicate point must have been deeply versed in the knowledge of human nature, and thoroughly acquainted with its frailties and weaknesses. Buddha desired to maintain the members of the assembly in a state of spotless purity. To attain that desirable object he raised the strongest barrier against the wildest passion of the heart. No virtue, in his opinion, can withstand the incessant assaults directed against it by daily and familiar intercourse with persons of another sex. He would have, if possible, the inmate of a cell in a monastery out of the reach of temptation itself; he knows that the best tactics against such an enemy do not consist in boldly meeting the adversary, but rather in carefully avoiding encounter with him, manœuvring in such a way as to keep far from him. Hence idle conversations with female visitors are not only forbidden in a most positive manner, but the very sight of women is to be, if possible, avoided. When duty shall oblige a recluse to come face to face with the enemy, it is his bounden obligation to keep at as great a distance from female visitors as practicable. The subject of the conversation ought to be of a purely religious character; some portions of the law may be expounded, doubts of conscience may be proposed, and a solution given to them, &c. On such occasions the spiritual adviser is never to be left alone, but he must be surrounded by some of his brethren or disciples, at all times very numerous in the monasteries.

It is not without interest to place one's self in the centre of the Buddhistic system, and examine therefrom the motives that have induced Buddha to enjoin celibacy on all the members of the assembly, and enforce it with the utmost rigour by all the means that the profoundest moralist could devise.

The philosophy of Buddhism has for its primary object to lead man into the way of freeing himself from the influence produced upon the soul by exterior objects, through the medium or channel of the senses. That influence sets in motion the various passions which darken the intellect and trouble the heart, opposing an insuperable barrier to the acquirement and intuition of truth, and to the progress towards the state of quiescence, so ardently coveted and longed for by every true Buddhist. No one is ripe for the state of Neibban as long as he retains affection for things without self. The last and greatest effort of wisdom is the emancipation of self from every possible influence created and produced by objects or things distinct from self. Concupiscence, as the meaning of the word implies, is that disposition of the soul to search after, long for, and cleave to things placed without self.

to free himself from the sting of concupiscence and keep his heart firm and steady, ought to have his door shut, and never look at the women coming to the monastery or

---

Such a disposition is diametrically opposed to the perfect independence aimed at by a perfect Buddhist, and leads to results the very reverse of those to be arrived at; it retains man in the vortex of never-ending existences, and precludes him from the possibility of ever reaching the state of Neibban. Concupiscence, taken in a more restricted and limited meaning, signifying the propensity to the indulgence of sensual pleasures by the union of sexes, must ever prove the greatest obstacle in the way leading to perfection, inasmuch as it fosters in men the strongest affection to external objects.

Buddha is great, in his own opinion, because he has conquered all passions, not by curbing them under the yoke of reason, but by rooting them out of his very being. When he wished to become an ascetic, he practised at first self-renouncing, not merely by giving up riches, palaces, dignities and honours, but chiefly and principally by denying to himself and for ever the enjoyment of sensual pleasures. A firm and unshaken resolution of parting for ever with his wife and concubines, and living in a perpetual celibacy, was considered as a preliminary and essential step for entering upon the course of life of a sincere searcher after truth and perfection. During the six years he spent in solitude, he laboured with unremitting zeal for securing to the spiritual principle an undisputed control over the material one, by stifling the vehemence and ardour of his passions. His austerities and mortifications during that long period had no other object than that of first weakening and then finally destroying passions, and in particular concupiscence. When he is praised in the writings, he is much extolled for having come out from the net of passions. His victory over concupiscence is repeatedly alluded to as the greatest of all achievements. The master, therefore, having laid such stress on this favourite and important maxim, could not but preach and enjoin it on all his future imitators and disciples. The earliest records of Buddhism bear testimony to the paramount importance attached to the practice of chastity. It has ever been considered as an essential requirement in all those that have desired to follow the footsteps of Buddha and imitate his mode of life. No qualification, ever so great and shining, could be admitted as a substitute for chastity. Science, talent, zeal, and fervour could never entitle an individual to the distinction of member of the assembly of the perfect without having previously given up the gratification of sensual pleasures. Independently of what is found written on this subject in the Wini, or book of discipline, the opinion of the Buddhist public is on this subject positive, universal, and absolute. He who leaves the condition of layman to become a religious must live in a state of perfect continence. An infraction of the regulations on this point is looked upon with horror and indignation by the people at large. The guilty individual is inexorably expelled from the religious house, after having been previously stripped of his religious dress and subjected to a humiliating degradation in the presence of the assembled members of the community. Nothing short of such a severe treatment could satisfy a public so deeply hurt and offended in their religious feelings. How is it that the practice of perfect continence is not merely a desideratum in an in-

standing at the entrance; because through the eyes concupiscence finds its way into the heart, and shakes its firmest purposes." "But," replied Ananda, "what is to be done when they come over to bring food to the inmates of the monastery?" "Ananda," said Buddhā, "in such a case no conversation is to take place with them. Much safer and better it would be to hold conversation with a man who, sword in hand, would threaten to cut off our head, or with a female Biloo ready to devour us the moment we open the mouth to speak. By conversing with women, one becomes acquainted with them; acquaintance begets familiarity, kindles passion, leads to the loss of virtue, and precipitates into the four states of punishment. It is, therefore, most prudent not to have any conversation with them." "What is to be done, O Buddha, in cases when women come to the monastery to hear religious instructions, to expose their doubts, to seek for spiritual advice, to learn the practice of religious duties, and render becomingly certain services to the Rahans? Should a Rahan be silent on such occasions, they will ridicule him and say, 'This Rahan, forsooth, is deaf or too well fed; he therefore cannot speak.'" "Ananda," replied Buddha, "when on such occasions a Rahan is obliged to speak, let him consider as mothers those who are old enough to be mothers, as elder sisters those who appear a little older than he, as younger sisters or children those that are younger than he. Never, O Ananda, forget these instructions."

---

dividual consecrated to religion, but an absolutely required qualification, which can never be equivalently supplied by any other moral or scientific attainment? How is it that such a notion is universally adhered to by nations noted for the undoubted laxity of their morals? Can a notion so generally believed and so tenaciously retained, in spite of its direct opposition to the wildest and the dearest passion of the heart, be ever called a prejudice? Is it possible to trace its connection with some of the noblest feelings of our nature and the most refined ideas of our mind? To a superficial and biassed observer, many things appear contradictory and irreconcilable, which a serious, acute, and dispassionate inquirer after truth readily comprehends, easily connects and accounts for, and satisfactorily reconciles one with the other.

Ananda inquired of Buddha what ceremonies were to be performed on his mortal remains after his demise. "Ananda," replied Buddha, "do not be much concerned about what shall remain of me after my Neibban, but be rather earnest to practise the works that lead to perfection. Be not over solicitous concerning the affairs of this life, where the principle of change is ever entire; put on those inward dispositions which will enable you to reach the undisturbed rest of Neibban. There are many among the princes, rich men and pounhas who are well disposed towards me, and who will gladly perform all the usual ceremonies on my remains." "They will," replied Ananda, "no doubt come to me, and ask advice as to the most suitable mode of arranging everything in a becoming manner." "Ananda," answered Buddha, "here are the funeral ceremonies performed after the death of a Tsekiawaday king. When such a monarch is dead, they wrap his body with a new fine cloth of Kathicaritz, surround it with a thick layer of the whitest cotton, wrap it again with a second cloth of the same country, place over it another layer of cotton, and repeat the same process five hundred times. The body, thus prepared, is deposited in an open coffin, gilt outside, and rubbed inside with fragrant oil. Another coffin, also gilt, is turned over it as a covering. The pile is made of sandal and other odoriferous woods; flowers, perfumes, and scented water are profusely spread over it. The coffin having been placed on the pile, fire is set to it. Similar ceremonies shall be performed on my body after my death. On the spot where four roads meet, a dzedi is to be erected. Whoever shall come to that place and make offerings of flags, umbrellas, flowers, and perfumes, shall thereby perform an act of religion, and give a token of his respect and affection for my person."[11] He shall gain many merits; among

[11] It is curious to investigate the origin and the real nature of the worship and honour paid by Buddhists to Gaudama, to his relics, to his statues, as well as to monuments erected for enshrining and sheltering those

others, a complete exemption from all troubles and disquietudes during a long period. Ananda, four sorts of persons are deserving of the honour of having dzedis

---

objects of devotion. The attempt at elucidating this point is beset with difficulties. The more we attentively reflect on the inward operations of the soul in all that relates to religion, the more we find ourselves puzzled and hesitating in qualifying and selecting the appellation most befitting them.

All the simple terms of our language intended to express the several sorts of acts of worship and adoration paid to objects partaking of a religious nature, are inadequate to represent to us, by sounds, the nature of the inward workings of the soul when she carries on a pious intercourse with the object of her devotion. The terms that are used merely express to us the exterior acts of worship, as manifested by peculiar attitudes of the body (which vary according to the habits and customs of various nations), or singing, making offerings, and other visible signs. They may be, in fact they are, used with equal fitness all over the world by the worshippers of the true God as well as by the adorers of idols. The difference between the true and false worship does not consist, therefore, in the externals, nor in the ceremonies or exterior signs that make impression on the ear and the eye, but it is to be found in reality in the objects that the adorers have in view. Here lies the essential difference between the true and false worship.

This being premised, we have naturally to ask: What is Gaudama, the great and principal object of worship to all Buddhists? Gaudama, in their opinion, is a mere man, that has attained, by the practice of virtue, and principally by his almost infinite science, the highest point of perfection a being can ever reach. The first qualification entitles him to the unbounded admiration of his followers; it inspires them with expressions the best calculated to eulogise him, and represent him as the first and greatest of all beings. Again, Gaudama is represented to them full of benevolence and compassion for all beings, whom he earnestly wishes to deliver from their miseries, and help to obtain that state in which they come for ever to a perfect rest from all transmigrations, or to what they emphatically call the deliverance. The second qualification is much insisted upon by Buddhists, and from it originate those feelings of love and tender affection for him who has laboured so much for enlightening all beings, and showing to them the way that leads to the deliverance. Buddhists on this subject are very eloquent. The writer has often admired many fine thoughts and truly beautiful expressions he has met in some writings devoted to the praises of Buddha.

It may be asked whether the followers of Gaudama in the worship they pay the author of their religion expect any aid or assistance from him. The answer is an easy one. Gaudama to them is no more. His interference with the affairs of this world or of his religion absolutely ceased with his existence. He sees no one; he hears no prayer; he can afford no help neither here on earth nor in any other state of existence. In fact, to the Buddhists there is no Providence, and, consequently, there can be no real prayer, none of the feelings that constitute its essence. All the worship of Gaudama may be summed up in a few words: he is admired as the greatest, wisest, and

erected after their death: 1. The Buddha who possesses the infinite science; 2. A semi-Buddha; 3. A Rahanda; 4. The Tsekiawaday king. He who builds a dzedi in

most benevolent of all beings; he is praised, eulogised as much as language can express; he is the object of a tender affection for the good that he has done. No idea whatever of a supreme being is to be met in the genuine worship paid to Gaudama by his most enthusiastic adherents. It cannot be denied that, in practice, Buddhists of these parts betray often without perceiving it that they have some vague idea about a supreme being, who has a controlling power in the affairs of this world and the destiny of man. But such an idea does not come from their religious creed; it is the offspring of that innate sentiment adherent in our nature, as is maintained by some philosophers: or it is a remnant of a primitive tradition, which error has never been able entirely to obliterate, as asserted by others.

The worship paid to Buddha does not extend further than it has been above stated, since it is always placed on a footing of equality with the one due to the law and to the assembly. These three *precious things* are always enumerated together; no distinction is made between them; they are equally entitled to the veneration of all believers.

Let us come now to the veneration offered to the statues and relics of Gaudama, and to the religious monuments called dzedis. In the foregoing pages we have seen Buddha giving to two brothers who had requested him to supply them with some object of worship eight hairs of his head. After his death and the combustion of his body, the remaining bones, or parts of bones, even the very ashes and charcoals, were piously coveted, with an eagerness that indicated the high value people set on these articles. According to several Buddhist authors, Gaudama, previous to his death, intimated to his disciples that his religion was to last five thousand years; that, as he would be no longer among his believers in a visible manner, he wished that they would keep up his statues as his representatives, and pay to them the same honour they would pay to his own person. Relying upon this positive injunction, the Buddhist looks on the statues of Buddha as objects destined to remind him of Buddha: they are the visible mementoes of him who is infinitely dear to his affections; they put him, by their variety of shapes and form, in remembrance of the principal events connected with his existence. The princes that have been most remarkable for their religious zeal and piety, such as Adzatathat and Athoka, were anxious to multiply the statues of Buddha and the religious monuments, to nourish in the soul of all the faithful, as says our Burmese author, a feeling of tender affection, of lovely disposition for the person of Buddha and his holy religion. The relics being articles that have been most intimately connected with Buddha's person, are designed to act on the religious feelings of the people even more powerfully than the statues. They are treasured up with the greatest care, worshipped with the profoundest respect, looked upon with a most affectionate regard. No earthly treasure can be compared with them. As Buddha's sacred person is more valuable in their eyes than the whole world, his relics partake of that invaluable estimation. It becomes evident that the statues and relics are so much valued, esteemed, and worshipped because of the intimate connection they have with the person of Buddha, and the great help they afford in

honour of Buddha, shall, after his death, migrate to a place of rest in the seats of Nats. To him that shall build a dzedi in honour of a semi-Buddha, an inferior honour shall be awarded in a lower seat of Nats, and a similar reward shall be enjoyed by those who erect dzedis in honour of Rahandas and Tsekiawaday kings. It may be asked why the honour of a dzedi is conferred on a king who lives in the world, enjoys its pleasures, &c., whilst it

---

keeping alive a religious spirit and a tender affection for him.

In the worship of statues and relics, superstition has had its share too in giving an undue extension and development to the religious *sentiment*. This development has brought into existence the belief in prodigies and miracles wrought by the virtue of the relics. This popular error has always found a powerful support among the ignorant masses; it has been much propagated by that inordinate and irrational tendency towards all that is new and extraordinary. Man wants but a pretext, even a very futile one, to give credit to the most incredible occurrences, when they have a reference to a deeply cherished, and, as it were, favourite object. But in no way do we find genuine Buddhism countenancing such spiritual eccentricities or extravagances, which have their origin in ignorance and an inordinate fondness for the marvellous.

The articles of worship offered to or placed before the statues of Buddha, and the shrines supposed to contain some of his relics, are few and remarkable for their simplicity. They consist in flowers arranged in fine bouquets, in flags and streamers made of cloth, sometimes of paper, and cut into a great variety of figures, with considerable taste and skill. There are to be seen also small wax candles, little earthen lamps, and sometimes incense and scented wood, which are consumed in large burners, placed on pedestals made of masonry. The worshippers are generally in a squatting position, the back resting on the heels, the body slightly bending forward, the joined hands raised to the forehead. Ordinarily a string of flowers, or little bits of wood adorned each with a small paper flag, are held on these occasions. On the days of worship, particularly during the three months of Lent, the crowd of people of every age, sex, and condition, resorting to the most venerated pagoda of the place, is truly extraordinary. Men and women of a certain age have in their hands a string of beads, upon which they repeat the formula Aneitsa, Duka, Anatta, or some other.

Since the Buddhist knows that his Buddha is no more, and, therefore, can afford him no assistance whatever, that there is no virtue inherent in his relics or images, in fact, that there is no Providence, it is difficult to account for the zeal that he often displays in honouring the great founder of his religion, and all that has a reference to him. To account satisfactorily for such a moral phenomenon, we must bear in mind the belief that he has in the intrinsic worth of the devotional practices he performs. Those works are good *per se;* they give rise, power, and energy to the law of merits, or to the good influence which will procure to him abundant rewards in future existences, and gradually lead him to the harbour of deliverance, the object of his most ardent wishes. That hope is, as it were, the great feeder of his devotion.

is denied to a Rahan, who has renounced the world, and practised the excellent works. Formerly, in Ceylon, the dzedis erected in honour of deceased Rahans became so numerous that they threatened to cover the superficies of the whole country. It was then resolved that none should be built for Rahans, though it is acknowledged that they deserve such distinction. The same reason does not exist for a Tsekiawaday king, who is alone, and appears in the world at but distant intervals. But all the Rahans that are full of merits are deserving, after their demise, of all honours, except that of a dzedi."

When Buddha had finished his instruction, Ananda thought within himself: Phra, the most excellent among all beings, has just taught me how to honour dzedis and other religious monuments raised to the glory of religion; he has pointed out to me the source of merits; he has indicated to me the sure way to deal with women, when they resort to our monasteries for the purpose of hearing the preaching of the law, and, finally, he has declared that there were but four sorts of persons deserving of the honour of a dzedi after their death. From the tenor of these instructions, I know with certainty that on this very day Buddha is to enter the state of Neibban. Unwilling to show his profound affliction in the presence of his illustrious master, he retired into the hall of the Malla princes close by, and leaning on the door-bolt, wept bitterly, and said, "Alas! the most excellent Buddha soon shall be no more. By what means shall I obtain the three last degrees of perfection? Who shall be my teacher? To whom shall I henceforth bring water in the morning to wash the face? Whose feet shall I have to wipe dry? For whom shall I prepare the place for sitting, and the couch for sleeping? Whose patta and tsiwaran shall I have to hold ready, and to whom shall I render the ordinary services?" In the midst of sobs and wailings, he was giving vent to his deep affliction.

It was not long ere Buddha, not observing the faithful

Ananda among the Rahans, said, "My dear Rahans, where is Ananda?" Having been informed of all that was taking place, he desired a Rahan to go and call Ananda. The message having been conveyed rapidly to Ananda, he hastened to come back into the presence of Buddha, whom he saluted as usual, and then took his seat. Buddha, addressing him, said, "O Ananda, your tears and lamentations are to no purpose; do not give yourself up to disquietude; cease to shed tears. Have I not previously said to you that distance or death must separate us from the dearest objects? In the body there is a principle which causes its existence and its preservation as long as the opposite principle of destruction does not prevail. It is true you have ministered unto me for many years with all your strength and the most perfect devotedness. But you shall reap the reward due for so many good offices. Apply yourself to the exercise of Kamatan, and soon you shall be freed from the world of passions and the influence of mutability."

Addressing then with a gentle voice all the Rahans present, Buddha began to praise Ananda, saying, "Beloved Rahans, Ananda[12] has been during many years my

---

[12] On a former occasion, Buddha had raised his voice to bestow praises on the memory of the great Thariputra, whose relics he was holding on the palm of one of his hands in the presence of the assembled Rahans. Now, a short time before he yields up the ghost, he summons all his strength, and at great length passes the highest encomium on his amiable and ever-devoted attendant, the truly kind-hearted Ananda. These are the only two instances mentioned in this compilation, when Buddha has condescended to eulogise the great virtues and eminent merits of two disciples. In Thariputra, Buddha extolled the transcendent mental attainments, the heroic achievements in the practice of virtue, the fervour and zeal for the propagation of religion, which had ever distinguished the illustrious friend of Maukalan. In Ananda, the searching and keen eye of Buddha discovered excellencies of a less shining and bright hue, but, in point of sterling worth, second to none. Ananda is a matchless pattern of gentleness, amiability, devotedness, and placid religious zeal. He loves all his brethren, and he is, in return, beloved by them all. His superior goodness of heart and placidity of temper secure to him an almost undisputed precedence over the other members of the assembly. Tearing the veil that conceals futurity from our eager regards, Buddha foretells the future conquests to be made by the mild and persuasive eloquence

faithful and devoted attendant. He has served him who is worthy to receive all offerings, and is, moreover, acquainted with all the laws of the physical and moral world. Ananda is a true sage; he is well versed in all that relates to my person; he can show to the male Rahans and female Rahans, as well as to the crowds, the time, the moment, and the place to approach my person and pay the honours due to me. Ananda is graceful and full of amiability amidst all other Rahans. He has heard and seen much; he shines in the midst of the assembly. Rahans will come from a distance, on hearing all that is said of his graces, to see and admire him; and

---

of his ever dearly beloved disciple. The far-spread fame of Ananda shall in days to come attract crowds of visitors, eager to see and hear him. The sight of his graceful and lovely appearance shall rivet to his person the attention and affection of all. Enraptured at the flow of this tender, touching, and heart-moving eloquence, visitors shall eagerly listen to him; they will experience sadness only when his silence shall deprive them of that food which their mind and heart were feasting on.

The eulogium of Ananda by Buddha is unquestionably one of the finest passages of the legend. Divested of its original beauties by having passed through several translations, it retains, however, something that charms and pleases. The reader is involuntarily reminded of similar specimens, found here and there in the earliest records of antiquity.

In the instructions that Ananda is to give to laymen, it is somewhat curious to see Buddha distinctly stating that Ananda will exhort the people to make offerings both to Rahans and to pounhas; that is to say, to the members of the assembly, and to the Brahmins. From this passage, it becomes evident that, in the days of our Buddha, the two sects that were subsequently to struggle during many ages for superiority over the Indian Peninsula, subsisted free from inimical feelings towards each other. It might be said that no line of separation kept them apart, indicating or pointing out their respective limits. The wide gap that was during succeeding centuries to intervene between those two great religious sects was not perceptibly felt. The levelling results of Buddhism had not yet awakened the susceptibilities of the proud Brahmins. Buddhists and Brahminists lived on friendly terms, and looked upon each other as brethren. The discrepancies in the respective creeds were regarded with indifference, as involving only philosophical subtleties, well suited to afford occupation to ideologists, and give to disputants the opportunity of displaying their abilities in arguing, reasoning, and defining. It is not easy to determine whether the conduct of Buddha was regulated by a well-calculated policy, intended to calm the suspicious scruples of his opponents, or whether he was actuated by plain and straightforward principles. It is probable that at that time many Brahmins followed a mode of life almost similar to that of the disciples of Buddha; they were, therefore, entitled to the same honours and support.

all will agree in saying that what they observe surpasses all that they had heard. Ananda will make inquiries regarding their health; they, on hearing his words, will be filled with joy. He will then keep silent, and they will retire with an increased desire to listen to him. He will say to the female Rahans that will come to see him, 'Sisters, observe the eight precepts.' On hearing Ananda, they will be exceedingly glad. He will then remain silent, and his silence will grieve them. The laymen and laywomen on hearing all that is said of Ananda shall come to contemplate him. He will say to them, 'Adhere to the three precious things; observe the five great commands; keep the four days of worship of each month; pay honour and respect to your father and mother; feed the Rahans and pounhas that observe strictly the law.' They will all be delighted at hearing his instructions. His silence will leave them earnestly wishing to hear something else from him. Beloved Rahans, Ananda much resembles a Tsekiawaday king. Like him, he is exceedingly beautiful, amiable, and lovely; he can fly through the air; he can teach the people and justly administer the law."

When Buddha had finished his discourse, Ananda said: "O illustrious Buddha, it is not becoming your dignity that you should go to Neibban near such a small city, and in a place almost surrounded by forests. We are in the neighbourhood of the great countries of Tsampa, Thawattie, Thakila, and Baranathee. The kings, pounhas, noblemen, and people of those countries are full of love and reverence for your person. They could render greater honours to your mortal remains." "Ananda," replied Buddha, "do not call the country of Koutheinaron a small country. I have on former occasions often been to this place and extolled its riches and crowded population. This is the place where it is most becoming I should enter into the state of Neibban. Go now to the city and inform the Malla princes that to-morrow morning, at the break of the day, the most excellent Buddha shall go to Neibban. Let them not have reason to complain hereafter that they have not received a timely information of this event, nor say that they had not had a last opportunity to come and see me." Ananda, putting on his dress and carrying his patta, went alone to the city. At that moment the princes were assembled in the hall to deliberate upon some important affair. As soon as the message was delivered, the princes, with their wives, their sons, and daughters, began to cry aloud, "Alas! the most excellent Buddha is too soon going to Neibban." Some appeared with dishevelled hair; some lifted their hands to their foreheads; some, crying out and wailing, threw themselves on the ground, rolling and tossing about, as persons whose hands and feet had been cut off. They all set out in haste with Ananda at their head towards the place where Buddha was lying on his couch. All of them were admitted into the presence of Buddha and paid their respects to him.

In the city of Koutheinaron lived a certain personage holding heretical opinions.[13] His name was Thoubat, a

[13] Buddha had so much at heart the conversion of the heretic Thoubat, that the earnest desire of performing this great and meritorious action was one of the three motives that induced him to select the comparatively insignificant city of Koutheinaron for the last stage of his existence. Particulars regarding that personage would prove interesting, because he is the last convert Buddha made. From what has been alluded to in some Buddhistic writings regarding Thoubat, it is certain that he was of the caste of pounhas or Brahmins. He had studied in some of the numerous schools of philosophy, at that time so common in India. From his way of addressing Buddha, there is no doubt but he was acquainted with the principal theories upheld by the most renowned masters in those days. It is related of Thoubat that, in a former existence, he was tilling a field with one of his brothers, when some Rahans happened to pass by. His brother gave abundant alms to the holy personages, whilst Thoubat showed less liberal dispositions. When, then, Buddha appeared, the law was announced to the generous donor, and in company with eighteen koudes of Brahmas he obtained the state of Thautapan. The rather parsimonious Thoubat obtained the favour of conversion at the eleventh hour. He must have, however, subsequently atoned for this offence, as his dispositions seem to have been of the highest order when he came into Buddha's presence. In a few hours he had gone over the four ways leading to perfection, and had become a Rahanda.

In the days of Buddha, the philosophical schools of India seem to have

pounha of the Oudeitsa race, who wore a white dress. His mind, hitherto uncertain and unfixed, hesitated between the belief in Buddha's doctrines and his former opinions.

---

had six eminent teachers, whose doctrines exhibited on some points a considerable variance. In a book of religious controversy between a Christian and a Buddhist, composed more than a hundred years ago by a Catholic priest at Ava, the writer had the chance of meeting with a faint outline of the leading tenets maintained by the six teachers, so often alluded to in this compilation. One of them maintained the existence and agency of numberless genii, who, at their will, could favour man with fortune and every possible temporal benefits, as well as visit him with their displeasure, by depriving him of all happiness and heaping misery and all sorts of calamities over his head. Geniolatry was the necessary consequence flowing from such a principle. A second teacher denied at once the dogma of metempsychosis, and maintained that every being had the innate power of reproducing by way of generation, &c., another being of similar nature. A third one had singular notions regarding the nature of man. He said that he had his beginning in the womb of his mother, and that death was the end and destruction of his being: such a destruction he called Neibban. A fourth teacher taught that all beings were without beginning and ending, and that there existed no influence of good and bad deeds. A fifth doctor defined Neibban, a long life like that of Nats and Brahmas. He saw no harm in the killing of animals, and he asserted the existence of a state of reward and punishment. The last teacher boldly asserted the existence of a Supreme Being, creator of all that exists, and alone worthy of receiving adorations.

Thoubat's mind was rather perplexed by so many contradictory and opposite opinions and doctrines. He had lived, it appears, in a state of doubt and uncertainty, fluctuating, as it were, between conflicting theories which could not carry conviction to his soul. He had heard of Buddha and wished to see him, hoping that perhaps he might fall in with the truth he was so ardently panting after. With these dispositions, he came to the spot where Buddha was lying on his couch, in the hope of easing his mind from the state of doubt and fixing it in truth. Like a man of consummate abilities in the way of arguing and convincing his adversary, Buddha sets aside all that was put forward by his antagonist, and, coming at once to the point, preaches to him the true doctrine. As light dispels darkness, so truth disperses the mist of error. Thoubat, seeing truth, at once embraced it, gladly ridding himself of the burden of errors that had hitherto weighed down his soul. All his doubts vanished away, and he found himself, on a sudden, safely anchored in the calm and never-agitated harbour of perfect truth.

Next to the conversion of Thoubat, follows an interesting instruction delivered to Ananda and the assembled Rahans. Here Buddha displays the superiority of his lofty mind. Clinging to the principles of abstract truth, he has no regard for persons or things. This material world, man included, is, in his opinion, a mere illusion, exhibiting nothing real, but only an uninterrupted succession of changes, which exclude the idea of immutable fixity. He apparently has no wish to infuse consolation into the afflicted souls of his disciples. He supposes that, being all initiated in

Having been informed that there was a Buddha in the neighbourhood, and that he was soon to go to Neibban, he desired to see him, and, in his conversation, to clear up his doubts. His age was not great, but he enjoyed such a renown for learning that he was called the master of masters. Thoubat went at first to Ananda, stated to him that he felt irresistibly a strong attachment to, and a sincere affection for, the great Buddha, that his mind was preyed upon by doubts and uncertainties, and that he hoped a short conversation with the great Gaudama would relieve his mind from its present painful situation. Ananda, fearing that such a conversation might be much protracted, refused to admit Thoubat into the presence of Buddha, representing his extreme weakness and inability to speak much. Thoubat made several entreaties, but with no better success. Ananda persisted in his refusal to introduce him. Buddha, hearing some noise, inquired from Ananda what was the cause of the noise he heard. Ananda related to him all that had taken place between him and Thoubat. "Allow him to come," said Buddha; "I wish to hear him. Soon he shall be enlightened and convinced. I have come to this spot for the very purpose of preaching to him the most perfect law." Ananda returned to Thoubat, and said to him, "The most excellent

---

the knowledge of truth, and having entered in the ways of perfection, they must know that the person of a Buddha is subjected to the law of mutability, and, therefore, to destruction or to death. He says plainly to them that his absence from among them is a circumstance scarcely worth noticing: by his doctrines contained in the Abidama, the Thoots and the Wini, he will ever be present among them. In these sacred writings they will possess something more valuable than his material being: they will have and enjoy the truth that was in him, and that he has communicated to them by his oral instructions. He earnestly invites them to lay stress only on that doctrine which they have received from him.

It is hardly necessary to notice a serious anachronism made by the unskilful compiler of this legend on this occasion. We know that Buddha wrote nothing, and that the compilation of his doctrines with its division in three distinct portions was the work of the three great councils held after Gaudama's death or Neibban. How could the dying originator of Buddhism speak of compilations of his doctrines, which were not as yet existing?

Buddha desires to see you." Thoubat, full of joy, arrived in the presence of Buddha, saluted him, and, sitting at a becoming distance, said to him, "Do the six celebrated teachers, who are always attended by a great number of disciples, who are famous amidst other doctors, know all laws? Are there some laws they are unacquainted with? or do they teach some doctrines which they but partially understand?" Buddha having gently reminded Thoubat that such questions were not suitable and unprofitable, said, "O Thoubat, I will preach to you the law; listen with attention to my words, and treasure them in your heart. No heretic has ever known the right ways that lead to perfection, and, in the religion of heretics, no one can obtain the state of Thautapan, and become a Rahanda. But in my religion there are found persons that have become Thautapan, Anagam, &c., and finally Rahandas. Except in my religion, the twelve great disciples who practise the highest virtues, and stir up the world to free it from its state of indifference, are not to be met with. They are not to be found among heretics. O Thoubat, from the age of twenty-nine years up to this moment, I have striven to obtain the supreme and perfect science, and I have spent to that end fifty-one years, following the ways of Ariahs, that lead to Neibban." On hearing these words, Thoubat, overwhelmed with joy, endeavoured, by several similitudes, to express to his great instructor the pleasure he had derived from his preaching. "O most illustrious Buddha," added he, "now I believe in you, and adhere to all your doctrines; I wish to become a Rahan. But it is a custom with you, not to admit to the dignity of Rahan a heretic who is newly converted, except after a four months' probation. I wish to remain during that period as a probationer, and beg afterwards to be admitted among the Rahans." Buddha, who knew the fervour of the new convert, desired to dispense in his case with the four months' probation. He called Ananda and commanded him to admit Thoubat to the dignity of Rahan.

Ananda forthwith led Thoubat into a becoming place, poured water over his head, whilst repeating certain forms of prayer, shaved his head and beard, put on him the tsiwaran, and taught him to repeat the formulas whereby he professed to take refuge in Buddha, the law, and the assembly. When this was done, Thoubat was conducted into the presence of Phra, who desired he should be promoted to the dignity of Patzin, and instructed in the knowledge of Kamatan. Thoubat went into the garden, walked for a while, and soon learnt the forty Kamatans. He was the last convert Buddha made, before he entered the state of Neibban.

Buddha, calling Ananda and all the Rahans, said to them: "When I shall have disappeared from the state of existence, and be no longer with you, do not believe that the Buddha has left you, and ceased to dwell among you. You have the Thoots and Abidama which I have preached to you; you have the discipline and regulations of the Wini. The law, contained in those sacred instructions, shall be your teacher after my demise. By the means of the doctrines which I have delivered to you, I will continue to remain amongst you. Do not, therefore, think or believe that the Buddha has disappeared or is no more with you."

A little while after, Buddha, addressing the Rahans, gave them some instructions regarding the attention and respect the Rahans were to pay to each other. "As long," said he, "as I have been with you, you have called one another by the name of Awoothau, but after my demise you will no more make use of such a title. Let those who are more advanced in dignity and in years of profession call those that are their inferiors by their names, that of their family, or some other suitable appellation; let the inferiors give to their superiors the title of Bante. Ananda, let a Rahan Hauna be visited with the punishment of Brahma." "But what is this punishment?" replied Ananda. "The Rahan Hauna is indiscreet in his speech; he says indiscriminately all that comes into his head. Let the other Rahans avoid speaking with him, or even rebuking him. This is the punishment of Brahma."

Addressing again all the assembled Rahans, Buddha said to them [14]: "My beloved Bickus, if among you there

---

[14] Buddha's zeal is not chilled in the least by the cold of approaching death. His boundless knowledge enabled him at a glance to obtain the most intimate acquaintance with the inward dispositions of his disciples' minds. If, therefore, he asked them three successive times whether they entertained doubts on any doctrinal points, it was not to satisfy himself that their faith was firm and unshaken. He wished to make them conscious of a fact which was felt and clearly understood by every one in particular, but was not as yet fully appreciated by the universality of his disciples. Every individual in particular was well aware of the unwavering dispositions of his mind respecting Buddha's teachings, but no one ever had the opportunity of ascertaining that all his brethren had the same firmness of belief. On this solemn occasion they witnessed the most comforting sight of a perfect unity of faith in all the members of the assembly. Buddha revealed then one great truth which no one but himself could be acquainted with. A true Rahan, says he, has entered at last in the first way that leads to perfection; he is, therefore, no more exposed to the danger of wavering in his belief; he knows enough of truth to adhere firmly to it, and is enabled to prosecute safely his researches after what is still unknown to him. Every member of the assembly is a true believer, more or less advanced in the knowledge of the law, it is true, but at least he is conscious of his being in the right way. On this subject no doubt subsists in his mind; he adheres to Buddha and his doctrines as to the centre of truth, and never thinks for a moment to question the veracity of his doctor, or to call in doubt any portion of his instructions.

The last words of Buddha to the assembled Bickus are designed to remind them of the great and vital principle he has endeavoured to inculcate in their minds during the forty-five years of his preaching, viz., that change and mutability are acting upon all that exists, and are inherent in all parts of nature. This world, therefore, offering but an endless vicissitude of forms, that appear and disappear, has no real existence. It is an illusion from beginning to end. As long as man remains tied up, so to speak, to nature, he is carried away by the ever-acting principle of change: nowhere can he find any rest or fixity; he quits one existence to pass into another; he leaves one form to assume a different one. What happens to man befalls all other parts of nature. From this notion, Buddha infers that there is nothing existing but *name* and *form*. There is no substance in nature, and therefore no reality. So much stress was laid by Buddha on this capital principle that he bequeathed it, as his last Will, to his disciples: he wished that they should ever bear in their minds and remember that he came among them for the purpose of making them thoroughly acquainted with it. From this cardinal point he inferred the chief conclusions that form his religious system, viz., metempsychosis, the contempt of the world, and Neibban. By the law of endless changes, man is hurried from one state into

be one that has any doubt respecting Buddha, the law, the assembly, the ways of perfection, and the practice of virtues, let him come forward and make known his doubts, that I may clear them up." The Rahans remained all silent. The same question was three times repeated, and three times the Rahans continued silent. Then he added: "My beloved Bickus, if you have any respect for my memory, communicate your dispositions towards my person and doctrines to the other Rahans whom you shall hereafter meet with." The Rahans still remained silent. Ananda then said to Buddha: "O most exalted Buddha, is it not truly surprising that among so many not one should be found entertaining any doubt respecting your doctrine, but all should feel so strong an attachment to it?" "Ananda," replied Buddha, "I knew well that doubt and false doctrine could never be harboured in the

---

another, or from one form of being into another form. Where is the wise man that could love a world, or an existence therein, when he finds no substance, no reality in it? Is he not induced, or rather compelled, to search after a state in which he can find fixity, reality, and truth, or at least an exemption from the harassing condition of perpetual migration from one state into another?

The reader who has been almost born with and educated in theistic notions, and who sees in the world nothing but what has been created by a supreme and all-wise Being, is at a loss to understand how a grave philosopher, as undoubtedly Buddha was, gifted with great powers for observing, arguing, discussing, and inferring conclusions, could have fallen into errors so glaring and so contrary to his reason. That we might properly appreciate the efforts of such a genius, and have some correct ideas about his process of arguing, we must divest ourselves of the knowledge supplied to us by revelation, and descend to the level occupied by the founder of Buddhism. Unacquainted with a first cause, or with the existence of a Supreme Being, he studies nature as he finds it. What does he see in it? Perpetual changes, endless vicissitudes. The form that he perceives to-day has undergone some change on the following day. Everything about him grows, reaches a certain point, and then falls into decay. He finds nothing that stands always in the same condition. Hence he proclaims the great law of mutability pervading all nature, and concludes that all that we feel, see, or hear, is illusion and deception, &c.; deprived of all reality, fixity, and substance. His philosophical mind is not satisfied with such a discovery. He pants after truth and reality, which are not to be found here. He feels that he must disentangle himself from the condition of illusion and deception. But where is reality and fixity to be found? Beyond all, that exists in Neibban.

soul of a true Rahan. Supposing a number of five hundred Rahans, and taking the one who is the last in merits, he is at least a Thautapan, and as such there is no demerit in him that could lead him to one of the four states of punishment; his heart is fixed upon the first way that leads to perfection, and he constantly strives to advance to the three superior ways of perfection. No doubt, therefore, and no false doctrine can ever be found in a true Rahan."

After a short pause, Buddha, addressing the Rahans, said: "Beloved Bickus, the principle of existence and mutability carries along with it the principle of destruction. Never forget this; let your minds be filled with this truth; to make it known to you, I have assembled you."

These are the last words Buddha ever uttered. As a man who is about to undertake a long journey takes an affectionate farewell of every one of his relatives and friends, and fondly embraces successively all of them, Buddha likewise wished to visit for the last time the abodes wherein his soul had so amorously dwelt during his long and lofty mental peregrinations. He entered into the first state of dzan, then the second, the third, and the fourth: he ascended therefrom successively to the first, second, third, and fourth immaterial seats. When he had reached the fourth state, which is the farthest boundary of existence, Ananda asked the Rahan Anoorouda whether Phra had completed his Neibban. "Not as yet," answered Anoorouda, "but he has reached the last stage of existence." A little while after, Buddha had entered into the perfect state of Neibban.[15]

[15] The epoch of Gaudama's death is a point on which the various nations professing Buddhism do not agree. The Cingalese, Burmese, and Siamese annals place that event somewhat before the middle of the sixth century before the Christian era. The difference of dates is but of a few years, and is so inconsiderable as not to be worth notice. The Thibetans, and, as a consequence, the Mongolians with the Chinese, place that event several hundred years previous to the epoch just mentioned. Notwith-

Thus in the first watch of the night he had preached the law to the Malla princes; at midnight he had converted the heretic Thoubat; and in the morning watch he had instructed the Rahans. It was not quite full dawn of the day when he entered the state of Neibban, in the 148th year of the Eetzana era, on the full moon of Katson, on a Tuesday, a little before daybreak.[16]

---

standing this discrepancy, it seems difficult not to adopt the chronology of the southern Buddhists. The *savans* in Europe, who have bestowed a considerable degree of attention on this interesting subject, give a decided preference to the opinion of the former.

We have not to depend solely on the chronological tables of kings, supplied by the Hindus, for settling this point, but fortunately we are put indirectly by Greek writers in possession of a fixed and well-established epoch, from which we can take with a sufficient degree of certainty our departure for arriving at a satisfactory conclusion. After the death of Alexander the Great, Seleucus, one of his lieutenants, obtained for his share all the provinces situated east of the Euphrates, in which the Indian conquered territories were included. Seleucus, at first in person, and next by an ambassador, came in contact with a powerful Indian king, named Chandragupta, who had the seat of his empire at Palibotra or Pataliputra. This intercourse took place about 310 B.C. The Hindu chronological tables mention the name of this prince as well as that of his grandson, called Athoka, who, according to the testimony of the Burmese authors, ascended the throne of Palibotra two hundred and eighteen years after Gaudama's death. We may suppose that Athoka reigned in or about 270 or 280 B.C. These two periods added together will give but a sum of five hundred years. There will remain a difference of only forty years, for which it is not easy to account with sufficient precision, unless we suppose that the reign of Athoka began earlier than is generally admitted. Cunningham has given very strong reasons for fixing the period of Gaudama's death sixty-six years later than the usual one, hitherto generally admitted, 543; that is to say, in the year 477 B.C. This new epoch enables us to adhere at once with perfect safety to the computation above related, and does away with the small discrepancy of a few years that has been mentioned. Tradition and ancient inscriptions leave almost no doubt upon this important point.

Our legend is positive in stating that Gaudama died under the reign of Adzatathat, as will hereafter be seen. But the Hindu chronologists place the reign of that monarch about 250 or 260 years before that of Chandragupta, who, as stated, was a contemporary of Seleucus Nicator. We have, therefore, the combined authority of both foreigners and natives for admitting the chronology of the southern Buddhists respecting the epoch of Gaudama's death, in preference to that of the northern Buddhists, and for fixing that event during the first part of the sixth century before the Christian era, or rather sixty-six years later, in the beginning of the fourth part of the fifth century.

[16] What is Neibban, the end a true Buddhist ever longs for throughout his great struggles in the practice of virtue and his constant efforts for

Not to leave out a single particular connected with the epochs of Gaudama's life, the Burmese author sums up all that has already been related on this subject, by stating

---

attaining the knowledge of truth, which he finally reaches when he has become perfect? The writer confesses at once his inability to answer satisfactorily this question, because Buddhists do not agree among themselves in explaining the nature of the state of Neibban. From the earliest period of their religion we see the Brahmins keenly taunting their opponents for the discordance of their opinions on a subject of the utmost importance—a subject which had ever been prominent in Buddha's teachings, and held up as the only one worthy of the most earnest and ardent desires, the fittest reward of the generous and extraordinary exertions of a perfected being, and the final state in which his soul, wearied after such a prolonged spiritual warfare, longed to rest for ever. A certain school of Buddhists has maintained that Neibban implied the destruction of the state of being, and consequently complete annihilation. This opinion is at once practically rejected by the portion of the southern Buddhists, who are not so well acquainted with the more philosophical part of their creed. They assert that a perfected being, after having reached Neibban, or having arrived at the end of his last existence, retains his individuality, but they utterly fail in their attempts at explaining the situation and condition of a being in Neibban. At a later period the opinion about a supreme Buddha, uncreated, eternal, and infinite, began to gain ground, and modified to a considerable extent on many points the views of the earlier Buddhists. Neibban, according to the comparatively modern school, is but an absorption into the supreme and infinite Buddha. This opinion so much approximates to that of the Brahmins that we may say it is almost the same. The means of obtaining perfection are somewhat different in both systems, but the end to be obtained is precisely the same.

Setting aside idle speculations, let us try to form some idea of Neibban by explaining the meaning of the term, and the definition such as we find it in the Burmese writings.

The word Neibban, in Sanscrit Nirvana, according to its etymology, means what is no more agitated, what is in a state of perfect calm. It is composed of the negative prefix *nir* and *va*, which means to be set in motion, as the wind. It implies the idea of rest in opposition to that of motion or existence. To be in the state of Neibban is therefore to be carried beyond the range of existence, as understood by Buddhists; there can be no longer migration from one state of being to another. This point is admitted by all sects of Buddhists. To the idea of Neibban is often attached that of extinction, as a lamp which ceases to burn and whose light becomes extinct when the oil is exhausted. The sum of existence being exhausted, a being ceases to be or to move within the range of existence; he becomes extinct relatively, at least to all kind of existences we have a notion of. In conversing with the Buddhists of Burmah, the writer has observed that the ideas of rest and extinction are invariably coupled with the notion of Neibban. In their rough attempt at explaining the inexplicable nature of that state they had recourse to several comparisons intended to convey to the mind that they believed Neibban to be a state of undisturbed calm and a never-ending cessation of

that he was conceived in his mother's womb, in the year 67 of the Eetzana era, under the constellation Outtarathan, and born in 68, under the constellation Withaka, on a

existence, at least such as we have an idea of in this world. When questioned on the situation of Buddha in Neibban, they answer that they believe him to be in a boundless space or vacuum beyond the boundaries ever reached by other beings, alone by himself, enjoying, if the expression be correct, a perfect rest, unconcerned about this world, having no further relation with all existing beings. They assert that he is to remain for ever a stranger to all sensations of either pain or pleasure. But it must be borne in mind that this is the popular opinion rather than the philosophical one. Talking one evening with a well-informed Burman on Neibban, the light of a lamp that was burning on the writer's table happened to die away for want of oil. The Buddhist, with an exulting tone of voice, exclaimed, "Do not ask any more what Neibban is; what has happened to the lamp just now, tells you what Neibban is. The lamp is extinct because there is no more oil in the glass. A man is in Neibban at the very moment that the principle or cause of existence is at an end or entirely exhausted." How far such an answer can satisfy a superficial mind like that of a half-civilised Burman, it is difficult to say; but it appears certain that he does not carry his researches nor pursue his inquiries beyond these narrow boundaries. Any further attempt to penetrate deeper into the darkness of Neibban is, in his opinion, presumptuous and rash.

Buddhist metaphysicians in India, in their foolish efforts to survey that *terra incognita*, have originated several opinions that have had their supporters in the various schools of philosophy. The more ancient philosophers or heads of schools, in attempting to give an analysis of a thing they knew nothing about, approximated to the opinion that Neibban is nothing more or less than a complete or entire annihilation. Following the course of arguments, and admitting their premises, one is reluctantly compelled to come to the awful conclusion that the final end of a perfected Buddha is the destruction of his being, or annihilation. This opinion is still further corroborated by the short exposition of Buddhist metaphysics at the end of this volume. The crudest materialism is openly and distinctly professed. There is nothing in man distinct from the six senses. The faculty of perceiving the object they come in contact with is inherent in their nature. The sixth sense, that is to say, the heart, has the power of perceiving ideas, that is to say, things that have no form or shape. But this power is not distinct from the living sense; it disappears when the life of that sense is extinct, or, in other terms, when the heart is destroyed. To the holders of such an opinion the cessation of existence, the going out of the circle of existences, by the destruction of kan, or the influence of merits and demerits, must be and cannot but be complete annihilation.

From a long period the plain sense of the masses of believers, unprejudiced by sophistical bias, revolted against such a doctrine, and at once rejected the horrible conclusion arrived at by former disputants. No one in practice openly admits that Neibban and annihilation are synonymous terms. If their views can be properly understood, we may infer from what they say that a being in Neibban retains his individuality, though isolated from all that is dis-

Friday. He went into the solitude in the year 96, on a Monday. He became a Buddha in the year 103, on a

---

tinct from self. He sees the abstract truth, or truth as it is in itself, divested of the material forms under which we in our present state of existence but imperfectly see it. Passions and affections are not to be found in such a being; his position, in truth, can scarcely be understood and still less expressed by us, who can never come in communication with an object but through our passions and affections. We know that there exists a spiritual substance, but we can have no distinct idea of it. We vouch for its existence by what we observe of its operations, but it is impossible for us to explain its nature. It is not, therefore, surprising that Buddhists should be at a loss to account for the state in which a perfected being is when in Neibban. The idea of a state of apathy or rest must be understood as expressing simply a situation quite opposite to that of motion, in which all beings are as long as they are within the pale of existences. If it be admitted that the perfected being retains in Neibban his individuality, it must be inferred that he becomes, as it were, merged into the abstract truth in which he lives and rests for ever. But we must distinctly state anew that this view is in opposition to the doctrines of the earliest Buddhists, and the philosophical principles and inferences maintained as genuine. This contradiction illustrates the truth of a remark made above, that error can never entirely obliterate from man's mind the knowledge of certain fundamental truths, which are almost constitutive of his moral being.

Let us come now to a definition of Neibban translated from Pali by the Burmans. Neibban is the end of all existences, the exemption from the action of *kan, i.e.*, the good or bad influence produced by merits or demerits; of *Tsit, i.e.*, the principle of all volitions, desires, and passions; of the seasons, and of taste or sensations. What means this rather curious, not to say almost unintelligible, definition? To understand it the reader must be aware that *kan* is the principle which causes all beings to move incessantly from one existence into another, from a state of happiness to one of unhappiness, from a position where merits are acquired into another where further merits are to be obtained and greater proficiency in perfection secured, from a state of punishment or demerits into a worse one, &c. *Kan* may be called the soul of transmigration, the hidden spring of all the changes experienced by an existing being. In Neibban the law of *kan* is destroyed, and therefore there are no more changes or transmigrations.

By *Tsit* is understood the principle of all volitions and desires. Buddhist metaphysicians, always fond of divisions and classifications, reckon one hundred and twenty *Tsits*. Some are the root of all demerits, and their opposites are the principles of merits. Some have for object matter this material world; others have for object the immaterial world, or, as I believe, ideas and things that have no form. The last of tsits, and of course the most perfect, is entire fixity. This is the last stage ever to be reached by a perfected being in the world of existences. One step further, and he has reached the undisturbed shores of Neibban. In that latter state there is no more operation of the mind or of the heart; or at least there is no intellectual working, such as we conceive it in our actual condition.

Wednesday (Withaka). In the year 148, on the full moon of Katson, on a Tuesday (Withaka), he expired; on the

---

The word *Udoo*, or season, is evidently used for designating a revolution of nature. The meaning is obvious, and affords no difficulty. In Neibban* there is neither nature nor revolutions of nature. Neibban, if a state it be, lies in vacuum or space far beyond the extensive horizon that encircles the world or worlds, or systems of nature.

The word *Ahara*, which literally means taste, is intended to designate all sensations acquired through the senses. By means of the senses, indeed, we obtain perceptions and acquire knowledge; but the perfected being having come to the possession of universal science, no further knowledge is needed; the senses are, therefore, useless. The senses, moreover, are the appendage of our nature, as it is during its existences. Neibban putting an end to further existences, it destroys also the constituent parts or portions of our being.

Admitting that the above definition of Neibban is a correct one, and that it has been understood in a purely Buddhistic sense, we may conclude that in that state there is no more *influence*, and consequently no transmigration, no volition of the mind, no desires of the heart, no materiality, and no sensations. The difficulty as to whether Neibban is annihilation seems all but entirely and completely solved. There is another way of arriving at a similar conclusion. Let us ascertain what are the constituent parts of an intelligent being, and then inquire whether these parts are entirely destroyed and annihilated in Neibban. In an intelligent being, according to all doctors, we find materiality, sensations, perceptions, consciousness, and intellect. These five aggregates constitute a thinking being. These, assert the same doctors, do not exist in Neibban; they are destroyed. One word more and the question would be settled; but that word has not been, at least to my knowledge, ever distinctly uttered. It is probable that these five aggregates or component parts are, in the opinion of many, the conditions of existence such as we now understand it. But it would be too hasty to conclude that a being under different conditions of existence could not retain his individuality though deprived of these five component parts. Buddhists, as already said, have very imperfect notions of a spiritual substance. It is not surprising, therefore, that they cannot express themselves in a manner more distinct, precise, and intelligible when they treat of subjects so abstruse and difficult. In practice they admit the existence of something distinct from matter, and surviving in man after the destruction of the material portion of his being; but their attempts at giving a satisfactory explanation of the nature of that surviving individuality have always proved abortive. In their process of arguing the learned reject such an admission.

The question, as may be inferred from the foregoing lines, if considered in the light of purely theoretical notions, is philosophically left little open to discussion, though it will probably ever remain without a perfect solution. But the logical inferences to be deduced from the principles of genuine Buddhism inevitably lead to the dark, cold, and horrifying abyss of annihilation. If examined from a practical point of view, that is to say, taking into account the opinions of the masses of Buddhists, the difficulty may be considered as resolved too, but in an opposite sense.

12th, after the full moon of the same month, his corpse was laid on the funeral pile.

At the very moment he had yielded up the ghost, a tremendous earthquake was felt throughout the whole world; it took place with such a violence that it filled every one with fear and trembling, and caused their hair to stand on end.

CHAPTER III.

Stanzas uttered after Buddha's death—Ananda informs the Malla princes of Buddha's demise—Preparations for the funeral—Arrival of Kathaba at the spot where the body was exposed to public veneration—He worships the body—Wonder on that occasion—The burning of the corpse—Partition of the relics made by a pounha called Dauna—Extraordinary honours paid to the relics by King Adzatathat—Death of that king and of Kathaba.

On the occasion of the Buddha's Neibban, the chief of Brahmas uttered the following stanzas:—"O Rahans, the great Buddha who has appeared in this world, who knew everything, who was the teacher of Nats and men, who stood without an equal, who was mighty and knew all laws and all the great principles, the most excellent and glorious Buddha, is gone to Neibban. Where is the being who shall ever escape death? All beings in this world must be divested of their terrestrial and mortal frame."

The chief Thagia, on the same occasion, repeated aloud the following words:—"O Rahans, the principle of mutability is opposed to the principle of fixity. It carries with it the elements of creation and destruction. There is no happiness but in the state of Neibban, which puts an end to all changes."

The great Anoorouda said in his turn: "O Rahans, the most excellent Buddha, free from all passions, has entered, by this death, into the state of Neibban. He whose soul, ever firm and unshaken, was a stranger to impatience and fear, has gone out from the whirlpool of existences, and is no longer subject to the coming into existence and to the going out therefrom. Passions have no more influence upon him. He is disengaged from the trammels of mutability, and has ended like the light of a lamp, the oil of which is exhausted."

Ananda added: "O Rahans, when the great Buddha, full of the most transcendent excellencies, attained the state of Neibban, the earth quaked with that violence which fills the soul with fear, and causes the hair of the head to stand on an end."

After the demise of Buddha, the Rahans that had reached the two states of Thautapan and Thakadagan, lifting to the forehead their joined hands, began to wail and loudly lament. Men threw themselves down on the ground, bitterly lamenting the loss the world had sustained. They all exclaimed, "The glorious and illustrious Buddha has too soon gone to Neibban. He who never spoke but good and instructive words, he who has been the light of the world, has gone too soon to Neibban." In these and other words they gave utterance to their grief and affliction, with tears and lamentations. The Rahans who had reached the two last states of perfection, the Anagans and Rahandas, more calm and steady in their mind, were satisfied with repeating in solemn tones, "There is nothing fixed in the principle of mutability. Buddha, entering in the current of change, could not but die; his body was to be destroyed." They remained meditating on this great truth, retaining an unchangeable and calm composure.

Anoorouda, assembling together all the Rahans, said to them, "Cease now to weep and lament; banish sorrow and affliction from your hearts; remember presently what the most excellent Buddha has told us, that all that exists is liable to destruction, which it can never escape. What will become of Nats and men? What will they say when they see the Rahans delivered up to grief, and giving vent to it in loud wailings?"

Ananda inquired from Anoorouda what actually took place among the Nats on the occasion of the death of the great Buddha. He was told that some of them, lifting up the joined hands to the forehead, loudly wept and lamented; but others more wise, bearing in mind what Buddha had said on the subject of the principle of mutability, remained wrapt up in a solemn and resigned composure of mind. Anoorouda spent the remainder of the night in preaching the law. He said to Añanda, "Go now to the city of Kootheinaron, say to the Malla princes that the great Buddha is gone to Neibban; that they ought to dispose everything for the funeral." At daybreak Ananda put on his tsiwaran, and, taking his patta, went alone to the city. He met the princes assembled in the public hall, deliberating on what was to be done when Phra should have gone to Neibban. He said to them, "O princes of the Wathita race, the great Buddha has gone to Neibban; the moment is come for you to go to the spot where are his mortal remains." When the princes heard this sad news from the mouth of Ananda, they, with their wives and children, began to wail and lament, and give all the marks of the deepest grief, unceasingly repeating, "The most excellent Buddha, who was infinitely wise and knew all laws, has too soon gone to Neibban." The princes, now selecting one of their family, directed him to go throughout the city and collect all the richest and rarest perfumes, to keep in readiness the drums, harps, flutes, and all other musical instruments, and have them carried to the place where the remains of Buddha were lying. Having reached the spot, the princes began to make offerings of flowers and perfumes with the greatest profusion, in the midst of dancings, rejoicings, and the uninterrupted sounds of all the musical instruments. A temporary canopy was erected with the finest pieces of cloth, and they remained under it during seven consecutive days. After this lapse of time, eight of the youngest and strongest princes, having washed their heads and put on their finest and best dresses, prepared to carry the corpse to a place situated in the south of the city, where they intended to have it burned. In spite of their united efforts, they could not remove it from the place it was laid on. Anoorouda, consulted on the subject of this extraordinary and unexpected occurrence, said, "O princes, your intent does not agree with that of the Nats. You wish, after having performed all ceremonies about the corpse, to carry it to a certain place in the south of the city; but the Nats will not agree to this; they intend to accompany the corpse with music, dancings, singings, and offerings of flowers and perfumes. They desire that the corpse should be carried to the western side of the city, thence to the northern one, afterwards to re-enter through the northern gate, and go to the middle square; thence to sally forth, through the eastern one, and take the body to the place called Makula-bandan, where the Malla princes are wont to assemble for their festivals and rejoicings." "Let it be done," answered all the princes, "according to the wishes of the Nats."

The funeral procession then set out.[1] The Nats in

---

[1] The lengthened description of Buddha's funeral has suggested the idea of laying before the reader a brief account of the ceremonies observed by Buddhists in Burmah, when funeral rites are performed on the mortal remains of Talapoins, who have been eminent in the profession and have spent their whole lives in monasteries. By comparing the following account with the narrative of the legend, we will see that the rubrics of the funeral service, in our days, are nearly the same as those existing at the origin of Buddhism.

When a Buddhist recluse has given up the ghost, the corpse is carefully and diligently washed by laymen, or the younger inmates of the monastery. A large incision is made in the abdomen; its contents are taken out and buried in the earth without any ceremony being observed on the occasion. The empty cavity is filled up with ashes, bran, or some other desiccative substances for preventing putrefaction. The corpse is then tightly wrapt with bands or swathes of a white colour from head to foot, and then covered with the yellow habit of the profession. Sometimes a coat of black varnish is put over and then leaves of gold, so that the whole body is gilt. It is afterwards bound all over with ropes tightened as much as possible, so as to bring it within the narrowest dimensions. When thus prepared, the corpse is placed in an open coffin. The coffin is made of the trunk of a tree, rudely hollowed, and often so imperfectly scooped out as not to afford sufficient room for the corpse. In the middle of the interior part of the coffin, an opening, about two inches in diameter, has been made, to afford issue to the humours that may ooze out through the swathes. The coffin is unceremoniously laid on the floor of the monastery. A bam-

the air honoured the corpse with their music, singing, and the showering down of flowers and perfumes. Men did the same all round the corpse. The way which the

boo, 7 or 8 feet long is procured; one of its ends is inserted in the hole made in the coffin, and the other is sunk into the ground below; it is the channel through which the humours flow into the earth. After a lapse of ten or twelve days, the body is supposed to be quite dry; they set about putting a covering over the coffin and effectually shutting it.

Whilst residing at Tavoy, I wished, on a certain day, to go and witness all the particulars observed on such occasions. A most opportune event favoured the prosecution of my wishes. A Talapoin of my acquaintance had died a fortnight before, after thirty years of profession. His body, laid in the coffin, was to be for ever concealed from human sight. I went into the monastery, where I met a large party of the brethren of the deceased, who had assembled for the ceremony. Most of them were known to me. My reception was at once kind and cordial. Great was my surprise at seeing, instead of the grief and mourning which the circumstance seemed to demand, laughing, talking, and amusement, going on at a rate which is to be called scandalous. No one appeared to take the least notice of the deceased, whose corpse was lying at our feet. A momentary stop was put to the indecorous behaviour of the assistants by the appearance of two stout carpenters bringing a board four or five inches thick, designed for the cover. They vainly tried to fit it in its place; the hollow of the coffin was neither broad nor deep enough for holding the corpse, though reduced to the smallest proportions. The operation was not a very easy one to bring the board in contact with the sides of the coffin, despite the resistance that was to be offered by the corpse. The carpenters were determined not to be disappointed. At the two ends and in the middle of the coffin, ropes were passed several times round it with the utmost tension, in such a manner as to have six or seven coils in the same place. Enormous wooden wedges were inserted right and left in three places between the sides and the coils. On these wedges the workmen hammered with their whole strength during about twenty minutes, to the great amusement of all the bystanders. Each blow of the hammer lessened the distance between the cover and the brim of the coffin. Every perceptible success, gained over the latent resisting power, elicited a burst of applause, and a cheer to the persevering workmen. At last all resistance being overcome, the cover rested fixedly in its place. It is needless to add that the corpse inside was but a hideous mass of mangled flesh and broken bones.

According to the custom observed on such occasions, a rude building was erected for the purpose of placing therein the mortal remains of the deceased, until preparations on a grand scale should have been made for doing honour to the illustrious departed individual. That building, as well as those made for a similar purpose, is but a temporary edifice raised for the occasion, and made of bamboos with an attap roof. In the centre of that large bungalow was erected a kind of estrade, about twelve feet high, well decorated. The upper part is often gilt, but always plated with thin metal leaves and tinsels of various colours. From the sides hang rough drawings, representing animals, monsters of various kinds, religious subjects, and others, but rarely of

procession slowly moved through was strewed with the finest and choicest flowers. When the *cortège* had reached the centre of the city, the widow of General Bandoola, named Mallika, hearing of the approach of the funeral

---

great indecency. Around this estrade are disposed posts, from the top of which are suspended small flags and streamers of different forms and shapes. On the summit is arranged a place for the coffin, but the four sides at that place are about two or three feet higher than the level whereupon rests the coffin, so that it is concealed entirely from the sight of the visitors.

Things remained in that state for four months, that is to say, until all the arrangements had been made for the grand ceremony, the expense of which is commonly defrayed by voluntary contributions. The arrangements being all complete, a day was appointed at the sound of gongs, for burning the corpse of the pious recluse. At noon of that day, the whole population of the town flocked to a vast and extensive plain beyond the old wall and ditch in the north. Men and women, dressed in their finest attire, swarmed in every direction, selecting the most suitable and convenient situations for enjoying a commanding view of the *fête*. The funeral pile occupied nearly the centre of the plain; it was about fifteen feet high, of a square shape, encased with planks, which gave to it a neat appearance. It was large at the base, and went on diminishing in size in the upper part, terminating in a square platform where the coffin was to be deposited. A small roof, supported on four bamboo posts, elegantly adorned, overshaded the platform. A huge four-wheeled cart, decorated in the most fantastic manner, was descried at a distance; it was drawn by a great number of men, and brought to the foot of the pile. Upon it was the coffin. Immense cheers, shouts of thousands, had announced the progress of the cart with its precious relics, as it passed through the crowd. The coffin was forthwith hoisted on the platform. Mats were then spread round the pile, whereupon sat numbers of Talapoins, reciting aloud long formulas in Pali. The devotions being performed, they rose up and prepared to depart, attended with a retinue of their disciples, who loaded themselves with the offerings made on the occasion. These offerings consisted of plantains, cocoa-nuts, sugar-canes, rice, pillows, mats, mattresses, &c. Masters and disciples returned to their monasteries with their valuable collections.

The place being cleared, the eyes were all riveted on two large rockets, placed horizontally, each between two ropes, to which they were connected by two side rings. One of the ends of the ropes was strongly fixed at posts behind the rockets, and the other was made as tight as possible at the foot of the pile. At a given signal, the rockets, emitting smoke, rushed forward with a loud, hissing, and irregular noise, tremulously gliding along the ropes, and in an instant penetrating into the interior of the pile, and setting fire to a heap of inflammable materials, amassed beforehand for that purpose. In a short while the whole pile was in a blaze, and soon entirely consumed with the coffin and the corpse. The bones or half-burnt bits of bones that remained, were carefully collected, to be subsequently interred in a becoming place.

procession, took a magnificent piece of cloth, called Mahalatta, which she had never worn since her husband's death. She perfumed it with the choicest essences, and, holding it in her hands until the procession reached the front of her house, she desired the bearers to wait for a while, that she might offer to the body her beautiful piece of cloth, and extend it over it. Her request was granted. By a very happy chance, the cloth had the desired dimensions in breadth and length. Nothing could equal the magnificent sight of the body; it looked beautiful, like a statue of gold, when covered with that splendid cloth, finely worked and adorned with the richest embroidery. The *cortège* having reached the place Matulabandana, where the funeral pile was erected, the corpse was lowered down. The princes inquired from Ananda what was to be done to perform in a becoming manner the last rites over Buddha's remains. Faithful to the last request of Buddha, Ananda said to them that on this occasion they were to observe the same ceremonies as were prescribed for the funerals of a Tsekiawade prince. The body was forthwith wrapt up with a fine cloth, covered with a thick layer of cotton; to which a second succeeded, and then another layer of cloth, and so on, until the same process was repeated five hundred successive times. When this was done, the corpse was placed in a golden coffin, and another of the same form and size was turned over it as a covering. A funeral pile, made with fragrant wood and sprinkled with the choicest perfumes, was prepared. Upon it the coffin was pompously deposited.

At that time, the great Kathaba, attended by five hundred Rahans, was going from the city of Pawa to the city of Kootheinaron. On their way, at noon, the heat was so excessive that the soil appeared to burn like fire under their feet. The Rahans, extremely fatigued, desired to rest during the remainder of the day, intending to enter the city of Kootheinaron during the cool of the night. Kathaba withdrew to a small distance from the road, and, having extended his dugout under the shade of a large tree, rested upon it, refreshing himself by washing his hands and feet with water poured from a vessel. The Rahans followed the example of their chief, and sat down under the trees of the forest, conversing among themselves upon the blessings and advantages of the three precious things. Whilst they were resting, a heretic Rahan appeared, coming from the city of Kootheinaron, on his way to that of Pawa, carrying in his hand a stick, at the extremity of which there was a large flower, round like a broad cupboard, forming as it were an umbrella over his head. Kathaba perceiving the man at a distance with that extraordinary flower, the Mandawara, *Erithrina fulgens*, thought within himself, "It is very rare ever to see such a kind of flower; it appears only through the miraculous power of some extraordinary personage and on great and rare occasions. It shot forth when my illustrious teacher entered his mother's womb, when he was born, when he became Buddha, wrought miracles at Thawattie, and came down from the seat of Tawadeintha. Now that my great master is very old, the appearance of this flower indicates that he has gone to Neibban." Whereupon he rose from his place, wishing to question the traveller; but he desired to do it in such a way as to show his great respect for the person of Buddha. He put on his cloak, and, with his joined hands raised over his forehead, went to the traveller and asked him whether he knew his great teacher, the most excellent Buddha. The ascetic answered that he knew him well; but that seven days ago he had reached the state of Neibban, and it was from the place where this occurrence happened that he had brought the Mandawara flower. He had scarcely said this word, when those among the Rahans who had but entered into the two first ways of perfection began to wail and loudly lament over this untimely occurrence, exhibiting every sign of the deepest grief and greatest desolation. The others that were more advanced in perfection remained calm and composed, remembering the great maxim of Buddha, that everything that has come into existence must also come to an end.

The name of this heretic was Thoubat.[2] He had been previous to his apparent conversion a hermit, leading an ascetic's life. Subsequently he became a disciple of Gaudama, but retained in his heart an ill feeling towards his spiritual master, which revealed itself in the manner he communicated the sad news to Kathaba and his companions. Seeing them penetrated with the deepest affliction, and exhibiting in an unfeigned manner the grief which weighed on their heart, he said to them: "Why do you weep and cry? You have no reason for doing so; we are now freed from the control of the great Rahan. He was always telling us: Do this, or do not do that. In every way he annoyed and vexed us. Now every one can act as he pleases."

---

[2] In the course of this work, allusion is often made to pounhas who appear to have led a mode of life not altogether the same, but varying considerably according to circumstances. All the pounhas were doubtless religious, who practised certain duties not regarded as obligatory by ordinary people, and lived under certain regulations, which separated them more or less from society, and distinguished them from those who followed the ordinary pursuits of life. The difference among them originated in a sort of religious enthusiasm, which impelled many to perform penitential deeds of the most cruel and sometimes revolting nature.

Some of the pounhas are described as living in villages or towns, and wearing a white dress. In many of their practices they appear to have approximated to the Buddhist monks, except that in many instances they married. Others are mentioned as living in a state of complete nakedness, staying in the midst of filth and dirt. It seems that those whom Alexander the Great met in some parts of the Punjaub, belonged to this class. Many of these disgusting fanatics delivered themselves up to cruel tortures, much in the same way as we see some fakhirs and jogies do even in our days, and under our eyes. A third class of pounhas affected to live in lonely places, on high mountains, in small huts made of branches of trees, and sometimes at the foot of trees, exposed to the inclemency of the weather. They were hermits. They clothed themselves in the skins of wild beasts, allowed the hairs of the head to grow to the greatest length, divided them into several parts which they twisted separately like a rope, so that, when looking at them, one would have thought that, instead of hairs, several small ropes were hanging down on the back and the shoulders, giving to them the wildest and most fantastic appearance. Some of those hermits, famous for their science, attracted round their persons many pupils eager to acquire science and discipline under them. Such were the three Kathabas, whom Gaudama converted during the first year of his public life. Others travelled through the country, exhibiting themselves in the capacity of preachers and mendicants.

The Rahan Thoubat bore envy and revenge towards Buddha for the following reason. Formerly he was a barber in the village of Atooma, where he then became a Rahan. At the time we speak of, Buddha was coming to that place, attended by twelve hundred Rahans. Thoubat wished to make an offering to Buddha and his followers and give them food. For this purpose he resorted to the following very questionable expedient for obtaining from the villagers rice and other eatables, and preparing them for the great occasion. Thoubat had two sons who wore the dress of Samane. He gave to each of them a pair of scissors, and desired them to go through the street of the village and shave the head of all the children they might meet with, as a token of their entering into religion. The order was punctually executed. The parents of the lads were then told, that on such an occasion it was customary to make considerable offerings. The offered articles, however, would be on this occasion employed for feeding the great Gaudama, who was expected in the place with a great number of disciples. All the people brought in large offerings of various articles of food, such as rice, oil, butter, and other comestibles. In this manner, by means of such an expedient, the cunning Thoubat, without any cost to himself, was able to make a great display of the choicest dishes to be laid before Gaudama and his disciples on their arrival to Atooma, and earn for himself the reputation of a very liberal and generous man. Buddha, acquainted with his conduct on the occasion, refused to accept the offering, and forbade all his followers to eat of the food prepared by Thoubat. From that time the latter ever entertained ill-feelings towards Buddha, though he did not dare openly to give vent to his passion.

Kathaba was thunderstruck at hearing such an unbecoming language [3] from the mouth of the Rahan Thoubat.

---

[3] The virtuous and zealous Kathaba was at once convinced of the absolute necessity of soon holding a meeting of the wisest members of the assembly, for the purpose of ascertaining, and authoritatively deter-

He said to himself: "If at this time, when there are only seven days since Buddha entered Neibban, there are to be found people holding such a language, what will

---

mining, the genuineness of Buddha's doctrines. Human passions were already at work, deforming more or less in various ways the instructions of the great preacher. Many, laying more stress on their talents than on the authority of their departed instructor, began to entertain on certain questions views and opinions evidently at variance with those of Buddha. The enemies of truth were numerous even during his lifetime, when as yet overawed by his presence and matchless wisdom. Kathaba sagaciously foresees that their number and boldness would soon increase to a fearful extent and threaten the very existence of religion. He was roused to exertions by such considerations, and on that very moment he resolved to assemble the elders of the assembly, as soon as convenient after Buddha's funeral. He was, it appears, acknowledged by common consent the first of the disciples. He was entitled to that distinction by the renown of his abilities before his conversion, and by his great proficiency under Buddha's teachings subsequently to that event. But a circumstance related by Kathaba clearly indicates the intimate familiarity existing between the master and the disciple, and the unbounded confidence the former placed in the latter. During a walk, the two friends, if such an expression be allowed, had entered into a more than usual intimate communion of thoughts and feelings; the soul of the one had passed into the person of the other, or rather both souls were blended together, and united so as to become one in the bosom of a virtuous, high, refined, sublime, and philosophic friendship. They made an exchange of their cloaks. Kathaba, by putting on Buddha's cloak, inherited as it were his spirit and his authority. Hence his legitimate right to be appointed president or head of the first council, assembled a little while after Gaudama's Neibban.

Our author maintains that the first council was held three months after Gaudama's demise. This important step was taken at Radzagio, the capital of the kingdom of King Adzatathat, who doubtless made use of his royal power to secure tranquillity during the deliberations of this assembly, under the presidency of Kathaba. The number of religious that formed the council is reckoned at five hundred. Its object was, as mentioned by Kathaba himself, to silence the voice of many who wished to innovate in religious matters, and follow their own views, instead of the doctrines of Buddha. They wished to shake off the yoke of authority, and arrange all things in their own way.

The second general assembly of the Buddhist religious was held one hundred years later at Wethalie, in the tenth year of the reign of King Kalathoka, under the presidency of Ratha, who was assisted by seven hundred religious. The object of this assembly was to regulate several matters of discipline. It is probable that a spirit of innovation had reappeared and begun to undermine the strictness of the disciplinary institutions, threatening to weaken the ties that kept together the members of the religious body, and deprive it of that halo of sacredness that had hitherto rendered it an object of so profound and general esteem, respect and veneration. The council, moreover, revised the canon of sacred books, and purified it from all the

happen hereafter? These persons will soon have followers who will embrace the profession of Rahans, and then the true religion shall be totally subverted: the excellent law shall be in the hands of such persons like a heap of unstrung flowers that are scattered by the wind. The only remedy to such an impending misfortune is to as-

---

imperfections and spurious writings that had been embodied in it.

Two hundred and eighteen years after Gaudama's death, King Damathoka or Athoka ascended the throne of Palibotra, which was the capital of a vast and powerful empire. It was in the seventeenth year of that monarch's reign that the third and last general assembly was held at Palibotra, under the presidency of Maugalipata. The last and final revision of the sacred scriptures was made with the greatest care and labour. The pious Athoka lent to the decisions of the assembly the influence of the secular power. The Pittagat, or the collection of the religious books, such as it now exists, is supposed to be the work of that council. In the two following chapters, the subject of the councils shall receive the attention it deserves.

There is a most important fact to be noticed here, which must be considered as a most remarkable result of the third assembly. It forms the grandest era in the history of Buddhism, and it is carefully noted down by our Burmese author. I mean the extraordinary zeal and fervour which seemed at that time to have simultaneously and powerfully acted for the bringing about of this mighty but peaceful religious commotion, that was to be felt, not only in the Indian Peninsula, but far beyond the valley of Cashmere, the country of Guzerat in the west and north-west, beyond the snowy ranges of the Himalaya in the north, and the territories and kingdoms in an eastern direction. King Athoka was then at the height of his power. His religious zeal induced him to make use of all the vast resources at his command to favour the development of the comparatively new religion. During the holding of the council, the religious tempered, as it were, their zeal, fervour, devotion, and ardour for their religious creed, in the middle of their conferences. They resolved to propagate with unremitting zeal the tenets of the holy religion, and extend it all over the world. The spirit of Gaudama seemed to have been infused into the soul of every individual religious. His ardent fervour glowed in the soul of all, who from that period had but one desire, that of extending the boundaries of their spiritual empire.

This is certainly one of those extraordinary epochs, when the indolent and apathetic mind of the Hindus, after centuries of a profound slumbering, seems on a sudden to awake, and, with an unexpected vigour and youthful energy, bursting forth as a terrific hurricane, brings about the most astounding revolutions, or commotions, that sweep away with irresistible power the old political and religious forms, to establish new ones on the ruins of the former. The religious zeal that seized on the Buddhists of those days, and impelled them with an unheard-of resolution to disseminate their doctrines, coupled with the astonishing success that attended their preachings, forms one of the most prominent periods in the religious history of the world.

semble a council composed of all the true disciples, who, by their decisions, shall insure stability to religion, and fix the meaning of every portion of the law, contained in the Wini, the Thoots, and the Abidama. I am, as it were, bound to watch over the religion of Buddha because of the peculiar predilection he has ever shown to me. On one occasion I walked with Buddha the distance of three gawots; during that time he preached to me, and at the end of the instruction we made an exchange of our tsiwarans, and I put on his own. He said: 'Kathaba is like the moon: three times he has obtained the inheritance of the law. His affection to my person, his zeal for my religion, have never been equalled. After my demise, it will behove him to stem the current of evil, to humble the wicked, and condemn their false teachings as subversive of the genuine doctrine. With such energetic means, my religion shall remain pure and undefiled, and its tenets shall not be lost and drowned in the midst of the raging waves of errors.' Therefore," said the great disciple, "I will hold an assembly of all the disciples, for the promotion and exaltation of the holy religion." This design Kathaba kept perfectly secret, and made known to no one.

At that time, four of the ablest Malla princes, having washed their heads, and each put on a fine new dress, tried to set fire to the funeral pile, made of sandal and other odoriferous woods, and one hundred and twenty cubits high. Their efforts proving useless, all the other princes joined them, in the hope that, by their united exertions, they would be able to set fire to the pile. Fans, made of palm-leaves were vigorously agitated over the heap of coals; bellows made of leather blew in the same direction; but all the efforts were of no avail. The princes, surprised and disheartened, consulted Anoorouda as to the cause of such a disappointment. Anoorouda said to them, that the Nats did not approve of their proceedings; they wished that the great Kathaba should arrive and venerate the corpse, ere it be consumed by fire.

No fire could be lighted before the great Rahan had made his appearance.

The people, hearing the answer of Anoorouda, wondered at the transcendent merit of the great Kathaba, and anxiously waited for his arrival. They said to each other, "Who is this distinguished Rahan? Is he white or black, short or tall?" They took perfumes, flowers, and flags, and went out to meet him and honour him in a becoming manner.

When the great Kathaba arrived in the city of Kootheinaron, he without delay repaired to the place where the funeral pile was erected. He adjusted his clothes in the most becoming manner, and, with his hands joined to the forehead, three times turned round the pile, saying at each turn, "This is the place of the head; that is the place of the feet." Standing then on the spot opposite to the feet, he entered into the fourth state of dzan for a while. His mind having emerged therefrom, he made the following prayer:—"I wish to see the feet of Buddha, whereupon are imprinted the marks that formerly prognosticated his future glorious destiny. May the cloth and cotton they are wrapped with be unloosened, and the coffin, as well as the pile, be laid open, and the sacred feet appear out and extend so far as to lie on my head." He had scarcely uttered his prayer, when the whole was suddenly opened, and there came out the beautiful feet, like the full moon emerging from the bosom of a dark cloud. The whole assembly burst into loud applauses and continued cheers on seeing this matchless prodigy. Kathaba, stretching his two hands, that resembled two lilies just blooming, held both feet firmly by the heels, placed them on his head, and worshipped. All his disciples followed his example, and worshipped. Perfumes and flowers were profusely offered by the crowd. When this was done, the feet slowly withdrew into their place, the pile and coffin resumed their natural position. As the sun and the moon disappeared below the horizon, so the feet of Buddha disappeared, buried as it were, in the folds of cloth and cotton. The people, at this moment, wept and loudly wailed: their affection for Buddha was evinced on this occasion more forcibly than when he entered the state of Neibban.

The feet had hardly been concealed from the sight of the people, when, without the interference of any one, fire caught the pile, and soon set it in a blaze of flames. The skin, the flesh, the muscles, the entrails, and liver of the body were all consumed, without leaving any trace of ashes and charcoal; as butter or oil, poured on a great fire, burn and are consumed without anything remaining. Of the body all had disappeared except the relics. All the pieces of cloth that served to wrap up the body, except the outermost and innermost, were also consumed. The relics of former Buddhas, whose lives were very long, resembled a lump of gold. Our Buddha, whose life had been comparatively of a short duration, had said whilst yet alive: "During my lifetime, religion has not been sufficiently diffused; those, therefore, who, after my Neibban, shall obtain of my relics a small portion, be it but of the size of a mustard-seed, and build a dzedi to place them in, and worship and make offerings to them, shall obtain a place of happiness in one of the seats of Nats." Among the relics were the four canine teeth, the two bones that connect the shoulders with the neck-bone, and the frontal bone. These are the seven great relics. They were in a state of perfect preservation, not at all damaged by fire, and are called Athambinana. Besides these relics there were some others of a smaller dimension, in sufficient quantity to fill up seven tsarouts. Here is the size and shape of those sacred remains: the smallest were of the size of a mustard-seed, and resembled the bud of the Hingkow; the middle ones equalled the size of a rice-grain, divided into two parts, and looked like pearls; the largest were of the size of a pea, and appeared like gold.

When the pile was consumed by fire, water came down

from the sky, as thick as the arm, which soon extinguished the fire. The Malla princes poured also upon it an immense quantity of scented water. During all the while the pile was burning, streams of flames issued from the leaves and branches of the trees, shining forth with uncommon brightness, without burning the trees; insects of every description were seen flying in swarms on those trees, without receiving the least injury.

In the place where the corpse had been exposed during seven days, the relics were deposited during the same length of time, and offerings of perfumes and flowers were incessantly made. Above them, a canopy bespangled with gold and silver stars was raised, and bouquets of flowers and perfumes were hanging therefrom. From that place to the one where the ornaments were deposited, the road was lined on both sides with fine cloth; the road itself was covered with the finest mats. Above the road was spread a splendid canopy bespangled with golden stars and flowers. The interior of the building was richly decorated; perfumes and flowers were seen hanging from the canopy. Around the building, masts were planted, and adorned with the five sorts of flags. Plantain-trees were planted on both sides of the road, and jars of cool water were laid down at a very short distance one from the other. From posts of well-polished wood were suspended lamps to be lighted day and night. The box, containing the relics, was placed on the back of a richly-caparisoned elephant, and the precious remains were honoured in every possible way by offerings of flowers and perfumes; by dancing, singing, music, rejoicings, and loud acclamations. The Malla princes, to insure the safety of the relics, had a line of elephants drawn round the place, then a second line of horses, then a third of chariots, then a fourth of warriors. Such precautions were taken both for insuring the safety of the relics, and allowing time to everybody to come and do honour to them.

At that time the courtiers of King Adzatathat,[4] knowing well the tender affection their royal master bore to Buddha's person, were reluctant to convey to him the sad

---

[4] It is not easy to determine with precision in what year occurred the conversion of King Adzatathat to Buddhism. Though his father Pimpathara was a zealous Buddhist from the very beginning of the preaching of Gaudama, his son seems to have kept aloof from the religious movement that took place in the royal city of Radzagio, within the precincts of the royal palace, and continued to adhere to the tenets of the ancient creed. His faith, however, in the hitherto national religion, that is to say, Brahminism, does not appear to have been deeply seated in his soul. He was a shrewd, ambitious, and crafty politician; and from what we know of the beginning of his reign, his political principles were of the most elastic nature. Even after his conversion to Buddhism, he does not appear to have scrupled in the least to resort to the most questionable means for satisfying his ambition. The disputes between the upholders of the contending systems had, as is often the case, shaken his former convictions without imparting new ones. Perhaps he remained in that ambiguous position for a political object. He was glad to place himself at the head of the malcontents, who, on account of the king's religious innovations, must have been numerous. Be that as it may, we see the Crown Prince of Radzagio receiving with open arms Dewadat, the enemy of Buddha, espousing his party, and looking upon him as his spiritual adviser. This occurred about ten or twelve years before Buddha's death. With the advice of his new friend, he compassed and effected the destruction of his father three or four years afterwards, and became king in the seventh year before Phra's Neibban. His conversion probably took place after the death of Dewadat, four or five years subsequent to that event; but it appears to have been sincere and earnest. His love for Buddha's person was so intense that it atoned fully for the harm which, under his name and protection, Dewadat had endeavoured to inflict on his great relative.

Adzatathat reigned thirty-two years, that is to say, twenty-five years after Gaudama's death. Under his reign, the first council was held with his consent, and a promise to make the decisions of the assembly be received with respect and strictly attended to. This is the first direct interference of the secular power in matters of a purely ecclesiastical nature. Adzatathat was, however, too prudent in his policy to persecute directly the holders of anti-Buddhistic opinions, who as yet formed the great mass of the people. He zealously supported the new creed he had adopted, but he left full liberty to the followers of the pounhas. By the advice of Kathaba, Adzatathat fixed the beginning of the religious era in the year of Buddha's demise. It is the one which is followed by all the southern Buddhists. It was not the necessity of correcting certain errors in the calendar which induced the king to adopt that measure, since a correction had been made a hundred and forty-eight years ago by King Eetzana with the assistance of a celebrated hermit. A religious motive alone induced the king to obtemper the solicitations of Kathaba on this subject, and lay, as the point of departure for the reckoning of years, the great event of the death of the founder of religion.

The two names of Pimpathara and

intelligence of his demise, for fear of causing in him too great an affliction. They took every possible precaution, and devised various means for preparing the king's mind to bear with composure the loss he had sustained. As soon as the monarch understood what the courtiers intended to say, he fainted three times in succession. Each time steam baths and an abundant pouring of water over the head restored him to consciousness. When he became sensible, he wailed and lamented for a long time. Recovering from the shock of his deep affliction, he desired to assuage the grief caused by Buddha's death by procuring some of his relics. For that purpose a messenger was despatched to the Malla princes with the following request: "You are the descendants of the great Thamadat; I too, who rule over the Magatha country, boast of the same noble origin. For this reason, I put forward my claim for obtaining the possession of some of Buddha's relics, which are now his representatives. I will give directions for the erection of a beautiful and tall dzedi wherein they shall be deposited. I and my people shall have thus an object of worship." The princes of Wethalie and of the neighbouring states sent a similar request. Those of Kapilawot and Alekapa followed their example. The kings of Rama and Pawa, the pounhas of Withadipa also sent in their reclamations, with a threat of having

---

of his son Adzatathat are indissolubly connected with the origin of Buddhism and its spread through the Magatha country. To the first, Gaudama owed much for the extraordinary success that attended his preachings and the conversion of remarkable personages. In a country like India, the example of the king must have exerted an extraordinary influence over the courtiers and the wealthy and powerful persons. The second rendered no less important services to the cause of religion, by supporting openly the great Kathaba, the patriarch of Buddhism, and countenancing the decisions of the first council, which secured unity among the members of the assembly at the very time that evil-minded individuals endeavoured to sow the seeds of dissension among the religious, and upset the fabric which Buddha's genius and zeal had just set up. Under the reign of those two sovereigns religion gained a firm footing in Magatha, and secured for itself an ascendancy which it retained with various successes for many centuries.

recourse to the force of arms, if their demands should be disregarded. They soon followed their messengers at the head of their troops.

The Malla princes, on receiving those messages, consulted among themselves as to what was to be done. They agreed that, the relics of Buddha being the most valuable possessions in the world, they would not part with them. Many angry words were exchanged among contending parties. They were almost ready to draw the sword when a celebrated pounha, named Dauna, made his appearance. He stood on an elevated spot, and making a sign with his hand, began to speak in a language calculated to soothe the irritation of the parties. Great was his influence over all, since there was scarcely a man in the island of Dzampoudipa who did not acknowledge Dauna as his teacher. "O kings and princes," said he, "hear one word that I have to say to you. Our most excellent Buddha always extolled the virtue of forbearance; but you are ready to fight for the possession of his relics. This is not good. Let all of you be now of one mind, with cheerful dispositions. I will divide the relics into eight equal portions. Let every one be ever solicitous to multiply in all directions dzedis in honour of him, who was possessed of the five visions, that many may feel affection for the most excellent one." Dauna went on explaining more fully the two stanzas he had recited, saying: "O kings and princes, our most excellent Buddha, previous to his obtaining the Buddhaship, whilst he was even an animal, still more a man and a Nat, practised the virtue of patience; he always recommended it in all his subsequent preachings. How could you have recourse to open violence, to warlike weapons, for his relics? You are kings of eight countries; come to a quiet and peaceable arrangement on this subject: speak to each other words of peace and good-will. I will have the relics divided into eight equal parts. You are all equally worthy to receive your share."

The kings, on hearing the words of Dauna, came to the

place where he stood, and entreated him to make eight equal portions of the relics. Dauna assented to their request. They went with him to the place of the relics. The golden coffin that contained them was opened, and there appeared to their regards all the relics beautiful like gold. The princes seeing them said: "We have seen the most excellent Buddha gifted with the six glories, and all the bodily qualifications of the most accomplished person: who could believe that these are the only things that remain of him?" They all wept and lamented. Whilst they were overwhelmed with grief, Dauna abstracted one of the canine teeth and concealed it in the folds of his turban. All the relics were duly apportioned to all the kings. A Thagia, who had seen the doing of Dauna, took adroitly the tooth, and without being perceived carried it into the Nats' seats, and placed it in the Dzoolamani dzedi. When the partition was over, Dauna was surprised not to find the tooth he had stolen: he did not, however, dare to complain, as his pious fraud would have been discovered. To console himself for such a loss, he asked for the possession of the golden vessel wherein the relics had been kept. His demand was favourably received, and the golden vessel was given to him.

The Maurya princes, who ruled over the country of Pipilawana, hearing what had been done by Adzatathat and other kings, went also with a great retinue to the city of Kootheinaron. The Malla princes informed them that the relics had already been divided, and that there remained nothing but the coals of the funeral pile. They took them away, built a large pagoda over them, and worshipped. The places where the relics were deposited are Radzagio, Kootheinaron, Wethalie, Kapilawot, Allakapata, Rama, Pawa, and Witadipakka.

King Adzatathat ordered a beautiful and well-levelled road, eight oothabas broad, to be made from the city of Kootheinaron to that of Radzagio. The distance is twenty-five youdzanas. He wished to adorn it, in all its length, in the same manner as the Malla princes had done the road leading from the place where the cremation of the corpse had taken place to that where the relics had been deposited. At fixed and proper distances houses were built for resting and spending the night. The king, attended by a countless crowd of people, went to take the relics and carry them into his country. During the journey, singing, dancing, and playing of musical instruments were uninterrupted. Offerings of perfumes and flowers were incessantly made by the people. At certain intervals they stopped during seven days, when fresh honours were paid to the relics in the midst of the greatest rejoicings. In this manner seven months and seven days were employed in going over the distance between the two countries. At Radzagio the relics were deposited in a place prepared for that purpose, and a dzedi was erected over them. The seven other kings built also dzedis over the relics they had obtained. Dauna built one, too, over the golden vessel, and the Maurya princes erected likewise one religious monument over the coals. Thus there were at that time ten dzedis, situated respectively in Radzagio, Kootheinaron, Wethalie, Kapilawot, Allakapata, Witadipaka, Rama, Pawa, the Dauna village, and Papilawana. The partition of the relics happened on the fifth of the waxing moon of Nayon (June). There were altogether eight tsarouts of relics; that is to say, a basketful. Each prince had one tsarout; that is to say, two pyis. The upper right canine tooth was taken to the Nats' seats; the lower right tooth was carried to the Gandala country; the upper left tooth was removed to Kalingga, and the lower left tooth to the Naga seat. The other teeth and hairs of the head and body were distributed by the Nats in a great number of other worlds.

When the funeral ceremonies were completed, and the distribution of the relics effected in a manner satisfactory to all parties, Kathaba, who was the acknowledged head of the assembly, advised King Adzatathat to do away with the Eetzana era, and establish a new one, that would be called the era of religion, beginning with the year of Buddha's Neibban, that is to say, on the year 148 of the Eetzana era. The king joyfully assented to the pious request of the Buddhist patriarch, and was exceedingly rejoiced to have this opportunity of affording a fresh token of the great esteem he had for Buddha's person.

Many years afterwards, the great Kathaba entertained some fear in his mind respecting the safety of the relics, distributed over eight distinct places, viz., Kootheinaron, Radzagio, Kappila, Allakabat, Watadipaka, Rama, Pawa, and Wethalie.[5] He wished to have them all put together in a safe and secure place, where they could be preserved until better circumstances would afford an opportunity to bring them forth, and expose them to the respect and veneration of the true believers all over the Dzampoudipa

---

[5] We are without any direct information concerning the history of Buddhism during the twenty years that elapsed after Gaudama's death. But we have allusions made in several places which clearly indicate that the new religion had to struggle with many difficulties before it could gain a firm footing in the places lying north of the Ganges. Though they had been the seat of Buddha's preachings, though the people had been intimately acquainted with all his doings, it appears that the pounhas contrived to thwart to a great extent the results of his labours. At Kootheinaron, on the very spot rendered illustrious by his death, we have seen an individual rejoicing at Buddha's demise, because he would be now at liberty to act according to his wishes. He was not a solitary instance of open insubordination, since Kathaba felt that it was necessary, in order to check the growing evil, to assemble a council three months after the death of Gaudama. This step does not appear to have produced all the good effects that were anticipated. The patriarch of the Buddhistic Church is represented to us as trembling for the safety of the relics. What could have caused this great anxiety? Doubtless there was a strong party, either within or without the assembly, which was inimical to the worship paid to the remains of Buddha, and aimed at procuring their total destruction. In the relation of Hwen-Thsang the writer has met with a passage in which mention is made of a period of time when the pure doctrine alone was held, and of a subsequent period when the worship of relics would be prevailing. It is not improbable that in this passage allusion is made to the time when the relics were buried secretly, by the care of Kathaba, in the neighbourhood of Radzagio, and remained concealed during two hundred years. The conduct of Kathaba in securing the safety of the relics reveals an important fact, viz., that there existed from the earliest days of Buddhism a great antipathy, in a fraction of the community, against keeping and venerating Buddha's remains. It created a schism among the disciples which was never healed up, as the sequel will show.

island. For this purpose, in the year of religion 20, he went to King Adzatathat and said to him that precautions were to be taken for securing the preservation of the relics. The king asked him by what means all the relics could be had from those who now possessed them. Kathaba replied that he would know how to manage such a delicate affair. He went to the seven kings, who gave to him all the principal relics, keeping beside themselves only what was strictly necessary to be deemed an object of worship and goodwill towards Buddha's person. One exception was made in favour of the relics deposited in the village of Rama, because they were in future times to be carried to Ceylon and placed in the great wihara or pagoda. All the relics having been brought to Radzagio, Kathaba took with him those pious articles, and went out of the city. He directed his steps in a south-eastern direction, loaded with this precious burden, which he carried all the way. Having reached a certain spot, he made the following prayer:—"May all the rocks and stones of this place disappear, and there be, in place thereof, a fine sandy soil; may water never issue from this spot." Adzatathat ordered the soil to be dug very deep. With the earth bricks were made, and eight dzedis were built. This was done for the express purpose of preventing people suspecting the real object that both Kathaba and the king had in view. The depth of the hole was eighty cubits. Its bottom was lined with iron bars. To that bottom was lowered a chapel monastery made of brass, similar in shape and proportions to the great wihara of Ceylon. Six gold boxes containing the precious relics were placed in this chapel monastery. Each box was enclosed in one of silver, the latter in one adorned with precious stones, and so on, until eight boxes were placed one within the other. There were also arranged 550 statues, representing Buddha in 550 preceding existences described in the sacred writings, the statues of the eighty great disciples, with those of Thoodaudana and Maia. There also were arranged 500 lamps of gold and 500 lamps of silver, filled with the most fragrant oil, with wicks made of the richest cloth. The great Kathaba, taking a leaf of gold, wrote upon it the following words:—"In aftertimes a young man, named Piadatha, shall ascend the throne, and become a great and renowned monarch under the name of Athoka. Through him the relics shall be spread all over the island of Dzampoodipa." King Adzatathat made new offerings of flowers and perfumes. All the doors of the monastery were shut, and fastened with an iron bolt. Near the last door he placed a large ruby, upon which the following words were written: "Let the poor king who shall find this ruby present it to the relics." A Thagia ordered a Nat to watch over the precious deposit. The Nat disposed around it the most hideous and terrifying figures, armed with swords. The whole was encompassed by six walls made of stone and brick; a large slab of stone covered the upper part, and upon it he built a small dzedi.

Five years afterwards, that is to say, in the twenty-fifth year of the religious era,[6] King Adzatathat died; and,

---

[6] In the previous note on Neibban, the writer, having forgotten to mention the application which the Burmese make of this term to three distinct objects, supplies here the omission, in the hope that what follows may enable the reader to come nearer to the true Buddhistic meaning of Neibban.

There are, say the Buddhist doctors, three kinds of Neibban respecting the person of Gaudama—the Neibban of *Kiletha*, or passions: the Neibban of *Khandas*, or supports of the existence of a living being; and the Neibban of *Datou*, or of the relics.

The first took place at the foot of the gniaong or bodi-tree, when Gaudama became Buddha. Then, to make use of the language of Buddhists at that moment, the fifteen hundred passions—that is to say, all passions—were quieted, extinguished, and for ever put an end to.

The second kind of Neibban happened near the town of Kootheinaron, when the five Khandas, or the constitutive parts of Gaudama's being, were quieted, that is to say, ceased to act, and were absolutely destroyed.

The third kind will take place at the end of the period of five thousand years, reckoning from the death of Gaudama. This is the period which he has assigned to the duration of his religion. Then all the relics of Buddha that will be still existing will be miraculously congregated on the spot where stood the tree Bodi. After

likewise, all those that had been present on this occasion disappeared one after the other from the scene of this world. A small dzedi indicated the place where the sacred relics had been religiously deposited. But in due course of time, the place, being no longer heeded by the people, soon became overgrown with bushes, which screened from sight the modest monument itself. The relics remained buried in that manner in the bosom of the earth, until after a long period of time there was to appear at last a

---

having been the centre of the display of several extraordinary wonders, they will be consumed by a fire that is to come out of them. They will disappear and vanish for ever, as the flame that has consumed them.

The idea suggested to us by the application of the word Neibban to these three objects is that of a cessation of action, cessation of existence, and cessation of being. Indeed, it is impossible not to see in the meaning of this word the horrifying idea of absolute annihilation. The writer frankly avows that he has been, during many years, unwilling to adopt a conclusion which the obvious meaning of the words point out in a clear manner. He hoped that a deeper insight into the system of Buddhism would lead him to a conclusion more consonant with reason. But he has been completely disappointed in his expectations. By what process of arguing has the founder of Buddhism arrived to such a despairing terminus? How has he been led into that horrible abyss? How has he contrived to silence the voice of conscience, and set aside the clearest innate notions of the human mind? Gaudama took his departure from a true principle, viz.: that there are miseries in this world, attending the condition of all beings moving within the circle of existences. But ignorant of the real cause that has imported miseries into this world, he never could discover the way by which man can convert them to a useful and beneficial result. He declared that all the efforts of a wise man ought to converge towards one point, that of freeing himself from all the states of existence. The four meggas or ways to perfection lead to that great result. By science, connected with the practice of virtue, the wise man frees himself from all passions, which are the real causes which make a being move in the circle of existences. When they are not subdued but exterminated, there is no longer a cause that impels man into another existence. The end of a being has come. When we speak of the end of a being, we understand its complete and entire destruction, or, in other terms, its Neibban. Nothing remains of him. The materialistic principles of genuine Buddhism forbid us to think of a soul or spiritual substance surviving the destruction of the terrestrial portion of man's being. When Gaudama unfolds his precepts and maxims for guiding man in the acquisition of science and the destruction of his passions, he elicits the admiration, nay, the astonishment of the reader, at the sight of the profound knowledge of human nature which he displays. But this feeling soon gives place to another of pity, sadness, and horror, when one sees that he has been led to the brink of Neibban.

mighty ruler, full of zeal for the promotion of religion, who would be worthy to render a becoming honour to the relics, and to distribute them throughout the length and breadth of the island of Dzampoodipa. This great event shall be narrated in a following chapter.

CHAPTER IV.

After Buddha's death, zeal of Kathaba in upholding genuine doctrines—He selects five hundred elders to become members of a council or assembly—Radzagio is fixed upon for the holding of the council—He repairs thither with a portion of the appointed members—Behaviour of the amiable Ananda previous to his departure for Radzagio—King Adzatathat supports Kathaba in his views—The hall for holding the council is prepared by his orders—Ananda is qualified in a miraculous manner for sitting as a member of the council—Holding of the council under the presidency of Kathaba—Establishment of the religious era—Destruction of Wethalie by Adzatathat—The successors of that prince—In the days of King Kalathauka a second council is held at Pataliputra, under the presidency of Ratha—Causes that provoked the holding of a second assembly.

HAVING completed the narrative of all that relates to the relics, we have to trace back our steps, and give an account of the development and spread of Buddhism into various countries.

After the cremation of Buddha's mortal remains and the distribution of the relics, peaceably managed by the Pounha Dauna, Kathaba, on account of the high esteem Buddha ever had for him—esteem which he had manifested in a striking manner when he invested him with his one robe—considered himself as having been thereby especially appointed to provide effectual means for placing the law on an unshaken foundation. As a monarch before his death appoints his son to succeed him, to wield the supreme power and keep it in his family, in a like manner Buddha had appointed his eldest spiritual son to take his place. Being, therefore, the acknowledged head of the assembly, he had but one object in view, the maintenance of the doctrines and institutions of his great master in their original purity, and the establishment of religion on a firm basis. When on his way from the town of Pawa to that of Kootheinaron, to be present at the funeral of Buddha, he had met with a Rahan, who had given him particulars respecting the last moments and death of Gaudama, and at the same time had dared to express feelings of satisfaction on that mournful occasion in the following manner: "Now that our master has gone to Neibban, he will be no longer amongst us, to tell us, 'You must do this, you have to shun that; such a regulation ought to be observed; such a duty is to be performed.' We shall hear no longer the reproaches he was wont to address to us. At present we are at liberty to do what we like, and to follow our own inclinations." Such unbecoming, nay, impious language, stung to the quick the ardent soul of the venerable Kathaba. From that moment he was daily engaged in revolving in his mind, and examining within himself, what would be the best course to be entered upon, in order to keep intact the doctrines he had heard from the mouth of Buddha himself, and establish upon a firm basis the religious institutions he so much valued. "As soon," said he within himself, "as the funeral of the most excellent Phra shall have been performed with a becoming solemnity, I shall congregate together the most zealous and learned members of the assembly, and, with their united efforts and energy, I will oppose the spreading of false doctrines, which obscure the true ones. I will put down the newly-invented erroneous disciplinary regulations, by setting in a strong light the genuine ones. To prevent, in future, the re-occurrence of similar evils so detrimental to religion, all the preachings of Buddha as well as the disciplinary rules shall be arranged under several heads, and committed to writing. The books containing the above shall be held up as sacred." [1]

[1] Kathaba speaks of the Pitagat or collection of the scriptures as of a compilation that was to be put in writing for better securing its fixity and permanency, and preventing, as far as human wisdom could reach, the introduction of new and heterodox doctrines. I feel inclined to be-

Agreeably to the plan he had fixed upon twenty days after Buddha's demise, the great Kathaba, profiting by the circumstance that had brought together so many Rahans from all parts to the town of Kootheinaron, communicated his views to all the Rahans congregated in that place. Having received from all his brethren a suitable encouragement, Kathaba selected from among them four hundred and ninety-nine of the most learned. They were all Rahandas, that is to say, they had all reached the last degree of perfection, with the exception of Ananda, who was but a Thautapan, and, therefore, had only entered into the current that was to drift him to perfection.

It may be asked why Ananda was selected as a member of the future council, since, in point of spiritual attainments, he was very inferior to all his brethren upon whom Kathaba's selection had fallen. Let it not be believed that he owed this distinction to his royal extraction, or to his being first cousin to Buddha and the friend of Kathaba, or to the venerable appearance which grey hairs imparted to his person. His brethren were full of love and esteem for him. They had the greatest regard for all that he said, because, having always attended on Buddha's person during

---

lieve that this expression is put into the mouth of the patriarch, and that in all likelihood he never uttered it. It is probable that, during the first ages of Buddhism, the doctrines were not put in writing, but orally transmitted. For supporting this apparently incredible assertion, we have the testimony of the authors of the Cingalese collection, who distinctly state that, during more than two hundred years after the introduction of the religion in Ceylon, tradition was the only vehicle for transmitting the contents of the Pitagat. Moreover, it is by no means certain that the inhabitants of the Irrawaddy valley possessed a copy of the sacred scriptures previous to the voyage of Budhagosa from Thaton to Ceylon in the beginning of the fifth century of our era. He went to that island for the express purpose of making a copy of the Pitagat, and bringing it over to his countrymen. Be that as it may, the question on this subject is far from being settled. It well deserves the attention of the learned. A satisfactory solution may throw a much wanted light upon the history of early Buddhism. When we consider that Maheinda, the son of the mighty and pious Athoka, was the head of the mission, which, after the termination of the third council, went to preach religion in Ceylon, it is impossible not to suppose that he would have brought over with him a copy of the collection of the sacred scriptures, had that collection been put in writing at the time that he left Pataliputra on his pious errand.

twenty-five years, lived with him in the greatest intimacy, and followed him as the shadow does the body, he was perfectly conversant with the doctrines of Gaudama, which he had heard expounded on all occasions and to all sorts of people. All the religious were unanimous in declaring him worthy to be associated with those who were to compose the synod. Kathaba was delighted at such an opinion, which agreed so well with his own.

Kathaba examined afterwards what was the most befitting place for holding the council. Having reviewed successively the various cities situated in the neighbourhood of Kootheinaron, he was pleased with none of them. Radzagio appeared to him in every respect the best place that could be selected. The city and its suburbs were very populous; the people lived in affluent circumstances; alms could easily be procured even for a large assembly during any period of time; monasteries about the city were both numerous and of great extent. All these advantages combined together induced Kathaba to give the preference to that city. To this his brethren unanimously assented.

When these preliminaries had been settled, Kathaba, on the fifth of the waxing moon of Nayon, spoke as follows to the members of the future council: "Brethren, you have before you forty days to prepare yourselves, and dispose everything to hold yourselves ready for beginning the great and important affair for which we have to assemble at Radzagio. Let none of you bring forward any pretext for postponing his going to the place that has been fixed upon, such as sickness, or the consideration of parents, friends, relatives, or even teacher. Every one of us must be prepared to forsake everything to promote the great object we have in view, the exaltation of religion."

When he had spoken in this manner he took with himself two hundred and fifty religious, and shaped his course in the direction of Radzagio. Some while afterwards Anoorouda, attended by nearly a similar number of brethren, went to the same place by following another road. The venerable pounha remained in Kootheinaron with seven hundred brethren. The other religious, not designated by Kathaba, withdrew into various other localities.

Whilst these things were taking place, the ever kind-hearted and affectionate Ananda availed himself of a portion of the forty days allowed by Kathaba to proceed to Radzagio, to give full scope to the feelings of love he entertained for the person of Buddha. He employed a part of that time in revisiting the various places that had been the favourite resorts of his beloved departed master, the Dzetawon monastery in particular. Full of love for the memory of Buddha, he was seen entering into the monasteries where he was wont to serve him daily with a most affectionate regard, his eyes bathed in tears, and doing, out of respect for him, the same humble but devoted services. He swept the room, made the bed, brought the water in the same way as if Buddha had been present. With a low tone of voice, often interrupted by sobs, he was heard repeating, with the accent of deep sadness, tempered by love, "This is the place where the most excellent Phra sat down; this is the bed upon which he slept; this is the verandah through which he paced to and fro; this is the place where he bathed;" and on each spot he stood a while and shed abundant tears. At such a sight the people felt their love towards Buddha's person increasing tenfold. They accompanied his loving disciple, joined him in his pious offices, and with him wept as bitterly, in remembering the person of the great teacher, his manners and his preachings, as they did when they heard of his death. Having performed all these pious duties, Ananda left that place, and hastened to the city of Radzagio.

When all the religious had congregated, the occupants of the eighteen monasteries that were spread in the neighbourhood of Radzagio had to leave them, and make them over to the new-comers. All the five hundred religious spent the festival day of the full moon of Watso together with the occupants of those places. After the performance of the usual devotions they were left alone in the undisturbed possession of the above-named monasteries. But the buildings were found in such a bad order that they required important and immediate repairs. Moreover, they were in a state of unbearable uncleanness, and it was deemed necessary to have them well rubbed and washed. The cause of this disordered state was this: when the occupants of those places heard of the approaching death of their great teacher, they had hastened to Kootheinaron, and there was no one left to take care of the dwellings and keep them in good order. To have the evil remedied, Kathaba, accompanied by a large retinue of his most remarkable brethren, went on the second day after the full moon of Watso to the palace of King Adzatathat, who received him with every mark of respect, and immediately inquired about the object of his visit. Kathaba explained to the monarch the purpose of his coming to Radzagio with five hundred of the most distinguished religious. "I desire," said he, "to confute error and to proclaim truth. My greatest wish is to promote the sacred cause of our holy religion. For that purpose I have, with the concurrence of all my brethren, resolved to hold a synod composed of the principal members of the assembly. We ask from you, O King, the favour of causing the eighteen monasteries of Radzagio to be repaired for our dwelling, and also to give orders for the erection of a spacious hall, which shall be the place of our meetings for discussing various subjects relating to religion."

Adzatathat joyfully assented to the proposal and demands of the Buddhist patriarch. He gave full liberty for the holding of the council, saying, "My power and that of the law are now at your command." He gave immediate orders for putting in perfect order the dwelling-place of the Rahans. On the southern face of Mount Webhara there was a cave which had been a favourite place of resort with Buddha during the seasons that he spent at

Radzagio in the Weloowon or bamboo-grove monastery. That spot was fixed upon as the fittest for the holding of the assembly. Adzatathat summoned to his presence the most skilful workmen, and commanded them to exert all their skill and talents in erecting a hall worthy of the assembly that was to meet within its precincts. The ground was first encircled with a fence. A fine flight of steps, made with the utmost care, led from the bottom of the hill to the spot where was built the magnificent hall, decorated with a profusion of the choicest ornaments, and surpassing in beauty and elaborate work the stately dwellings of princes. Five hundred mats for the accommodation of the religious were disposed in the south of the hall. The seat of the president was placed opposite, in the northern part. In the centre, but facing the east, a seat resembling a pulpit was raised; upon it was laid a beautiful fan, made of ivory. When the work was finished, Adzatathat informed Kathaba that the work was completed, and the hall ready for the projected meetings.

It was on the full moon of the Wakhaong (August) that the first conference was to take place and the council to be opened. On the day previous some Rahans made a remark on the circumstance of Ananda being allowed to become a member of the council, though he was but a Thautapan, and had still to ascend the three other steps of Thakadagan, Anagan, and Rahanda before he became an Arahat. This remark, made with very little moderation, greatly affected and grieved the tender heart of Ananda. No time was to be lost; he knew that on the following day the council would be opened, and he could scarcely hope to be tolerated as an exception in the midst of his brethren. He withdrew to a quiet and retired place, and resolved to do his utmost to obtain that which he felt he was in need of. He began to meditate with much attention; but the desired object of his wishes was as yet far from him. He thought of Buddha. Whilst he was continuing his mental labour until midnight, he heard a voice telling him to apply himself to the labour of a higher order, to Kamatan. This was a flash of light that illuminated his mind. The exercise lasted until a little before daybreak. At that time Ananda left the walking place, and went to his room to take a little rest. He sat on his bed. Between the short time that it took to raise his feet from the ground and lay the head over the pillow, Ananda was delivered from the bands that keep a being in the whirlpool of existences, and he became a Rahanda.

On the fifth of the waxing moon of Wakhaong the 499 venerable members, attired in their cloaks and carrying the mendicants' pots, assembled in the hall at the entrance of the Webhara cave. Each member occupied his own place; Ananda's alone was without its occupant. On a sudden, by the power of the virtue now inherent in his person, Ananda appeared among his brethren. The appearance of his face resembled a ripe palm fruit. It was beautiful as the moon at its full emerging from the bosom of a cloud; as a newly polished precious stone on a piece of fine cloth; as the water-lily blooming in the rays of the morning sun. It reflected the inward perfection which had just been communicated to him, and exhibited it in unmistakable signs to the assembled religious.

Every arrangement being completed, and the members occupying in silence their respective seats, Kathaba three times praised Buddha. He then asked the fathers of the assembly which of the three parts—the instructions, the discipline, or the metaphysics—deserved the priority in the discussions that were to begin. They answered that the discipline, being the soul and ornament of religion, deserved the preference. He asked them to appoint him whom they thought the fittest to occupy the pulpit. They were unanimous in selecting Oopali, though Ananda was worthy of such a distinction. The reason of the selection is the following: On one occasion Buddha had openly declared that among all the religious, or the members of the assembly, Oopali was the most fervent in observing the regulations of the Wini. Then Kathaba said, "Brethren, since you have given the preference to the venerable Oopali, let him have it." The venerable Oopali said in his turn, "Brethren, hearken to my words: having been selected by the assembly to answer all the questions relating to the Wini, I accept the honourable task thus imposed upon me." When he had spoken he rose from his place, threw a part of his cloak upon one shoulder, bowed to the members of the assembly, went to the pulpit, sat down, and held the ivory fan in his hand.

Kathaba, from his own seat, addressed Oopali, and said, "Venerable Oopali, in what place has the most excellent Phra enacted the commandment respecting the first of the four sins, called Paradzika?" Oopali answered, "In the country of Wethalie." "To whom was allusion made when this commandment was published?" "Allusion was made to Thoudein, the son of Tananda Pounha." "What was the cause of such an enactment?" "The sin of fornication he had committed." The president, addressing the assembled fathers, said, "Brethren, you have all heard what regards the circumstances connected with the first Paradzika. Let this article be noted down, and its admission and sanction be proclaimed aloud." It was done so. All the members accepted it. At that moment an earthquake was felt. The same method was observed as regards the three other Paradzika. They were unanimously accepted by the members of the assembly. Oopali was successively questioned by the president upon the other regulations of the Wini, viz., the 13 Thingaditheit, the 2 Donay-a-niga, the 30 Niseggi Padzeit, the 92 Padzeit, the 4 Walidathani, the 75 Theikkabot, which are named Adikarana-thama; in all, 227 regulations. Moreover, there were added the 80 (Banawara) Khandaca and the 25 Parawira. These several divisions form the collection called Wini Pitagat. When the final sanction had been given to all those points a mighty earthquake was felt a second time. The venerable Oopali laid down the ivory fan, rose up, came down from the pulpit, reverentially saluted all the brethren, and returned to his own seat.

The president, addressing the company, said, "Brethren, hearken to my words. If it be your good pleasure, we shall discuss at present the thoots or the instructions orally delivered unto us by our most excellent master. Whom shall we appoint to answer the questions I shall put him on this subject?" They unanimously elected Ananda, who, having always and on all occasions accompanied Buddha, was better acquainted with his preachings than any other religious. Then the president added, "Brethren, if it be agreeable to you, I will duly question the venerable Ananda." The latter likewise said, "Brethren, hearken to my words. Since it is acceptable to you, I will answer all the questions on the thoots which our venerable president shall put to me." Then he rose from his seat, arranged his cloak on one of his shoulders, respectfully bowed to the assembly, and, ascending the steps of the pulpit, he sat down, and held in his hand the ivory fan.

The president, addressing the assembly, said, "Brethren, in the thoots there are several parts or divisions. There is the division called Thingiti, which has also subdivisions. Which shall I fix upon to begin our session?" They answered, "Let us begin with the Diga-thingiti, which contains thirty-five thoots, and out of this the Silakhanda, which includes thirteen sermons or thoots." It was on the first, called Bhramadzala, that the questions were put. The president put the following questions to the venerable Ananda: "In what place was the Bhramadzala thoot preached?" He answered, "In the Mingoon hall, situated in the middle of a grove of mango-trees half-way between Radzagio and the village of Nalanda." "To whom was allusion made?" "To Thouppya, a holder of false doctrines, and to a young man named Bramada." "For what reason was such allusion made?" "Because both had been ungrateful to Buddha." Similar questions were put for each thoot of this division, and suitable answers were given in a like manner. The same mode of proceeding was observed for each sermon or thoot of the following divisions. When all the explanations had been given by the speaker, all the assembled brethren, with a perfect unanimity, assented to all that had been said.

When the work on the thoots was completed, the whole collection was called the Pitagat Thoots. Ananda rose from the pulpit, placed the ivory fan upon the table, respectfully bowed to the assembly, and returned to his own place.

The president, addressing again the assembly, requested them to designate him who, in their opinion, appeared to be best fitted for answering all questions on the third part of the sacred scriptures, the Abidama. They unanimously selected the venerable Anooroudha. When the choice had been fixed upon and agreed to, Anooroudha accepted the honour conferred on him, rose from his seat and saluted his brethren. He then gravely ascended the pulpit, sat down, and held the ivory fan in his hand.

The president questioned him on the seven divisions of the Abidama, following the same order he had observed previously in treating of the two first parts called Pitagat. The occupant of the pulpit having returned due answers, and the assembly having testified their approbation in a unanimous manner, the council was brought to a close. It had lasted seven months, from the full moon of Wakhaong to the full moon of Tabaong.[2]

---

[2] The collection of the Buddhist scriptures is divided into three parts, called the three Pitagats, or the three baskets, respectively named the Wini Pitagat, the Thoots Pitagat, and the Abidama Pitagat. The manuscript that the writer has had for his use, though correct in the main, is certainly defective in the enumeration of the divisions and subdivisions of the three great collections. He will, however, mention them, such as they are enumerated by the Burmese author; the few errors that may be detected can easily be corrected by those who have in their possession the Ceylonese collection, as there is no doubt that the work now under consideration is an abridgment of a more voluminous compilation to be found in Ceylon.

The divisions of the Wini are: Bikoo Patimouk, Bikoonee Patimouk, Bikoo Witin (probably Bikoo Win), Bikooni Win, twelve Kandaka, and sixteen Pariwara.

The thoots are considered as the instructions orally delivered by Gaudama himself, either to his disciples in private, or to the assembled mul-

The first council is called Pitzasatika Sangarana, because it was composed of five hundred religious. It is also named Terika-sangarana, because it was composed of religious of

---

titudes, during the forty-five years of his public mission. In this collection the disciples have learned the doctrines of the master, and found all the elements necessary to compose all the treaties, which subsequently have formed the collections called Wini Pitagat and Abidama Pitagat. No one could ever believe that the author of Buddhism could have busied himself in writing treatises on metaphysics, or minutely and elaborately publishing the regulations under which the body of his followers, called the Sanga, were to live and spend their time. In his instructions Gaudama gave utterance to certain principles, which, being appropriated by his disciples and their successors, were enlarged, developed, and reduced to the shape of a treatise. In fact, he sowed the seed which, being let into the soil of the mind of enthusiastic disciples, grew up and multiplied into the voluminous above-named collections. Genuine Buddhism must be found in the thoots of the oldest stamp. Anywhere else we meet with the Buddhism such as it has been developed by doctors and commentators.

There are four collections of the thoots, named Nidia Nike, Midzima Nike, Thangoutta Nike, and Engouttara Nike. They are likewise arranged under fifteen heads, called: Koudakapata, Dammapata, Oodana, Ithi, Wouthaka, Thouttanibat, Wi, Mama-wouttoo, Pita-wouttoo, Terakatta, Terikatta, Dzattakani, Pitisambika, Apadana, Buddha-wattoo.

The Abidamma has seven divisions, viz., Dammathingakani, Wittin, Datoogatta, Pouggala-pignia, Kathawattoo, Yamaik, Patan.

The attentive reader cannot be but surprised to see how the three great divisions of the Buddhistic scriptures are mentioned by the members of the first council as things already existing and arranged with the same method as they have been disposed during succeeding ages. It is certain that such divisions of Gaudama's doctrines did not then exist at that time. Are we to conclude therefrom that the fact of the holding of the first council is to be rejected as a mere invention, because the mode of relating some particulars concerning that great assembly is liable to be seriously objected to? It seems that such a conclusion would be a too hasty one.

For establishing the fact of the holding of the first council, we have the evidence supplied to us by all the Buddhistic writings, found in the various countries where that religion has been established. Moreover, several monuments of great antiquity allude to that first assembly. We can scarcely raise a doubt upon the existence of the fact. But how are we to account for the manner in which mention is made of compilations which undoubtedly were not existing at that time? The redaction of all the particulars connected with the first assembly must have been made a considerable time after the holding of the said assembly, at an epoch when the Buddhistic scriptures had already been arranged under three distinct heads. The author, familiar with the division or compilation into three parts, called Pitagats, has arranged his narration in such a way as to give to it a sort of agreement with a form which he thought must have been as familiar to others as it was to himself. It is probable that most of the points of discussion, such as we find them in

the first order. The soul of Kathaba, at the happy conclusion of this important undertaking, overflowed with the purest joy. He felt that with such a work the religious institutions rested on a strong basis, and would last the whole period of 5000 years assigned to the duration of religion by Gaudama himself.

It was at the conclusion of the council that King Adzatathat, with the concurrence of the Buddhist patriarch, did away with the Eetzana era, and substituted the religious era beginning in the year 148 of the said era; that is to say, on the year of Gaudama's death, on a Monday, the first of the waxing moon of Tabaong.

Here is inserted, as a genealogical link, the names of the kings who reigned at Pataliputra, from Adzatathat to Kalathoka, under whose reign the second council was held.

Agreeably to the prediction of Gaudama respecting the calamities that were to befall Wethalie on the third year of the religious era, Adzatathat, having contrived to sow, through the instrumentality of a famous pounha, the seed of dissension among the princes of that city, flung himself on a sudden with a large force on the devoted city, possessed himself of it, and totally destroyed it. On his return to his own territories, the conqueror carried away

---

the narrative, were actually brought forward before the assembly, but in a shape more simple and general, and less technical and positive. This is what can be said in the present imperfect knowledge of the history of Buddhism, for extenuating the charge of wilful forgery, which might be brought against the author of the redaction. On the other hand, whilst prudent discretion commands us not to be too hasty in passing a sweeping condemnation upon the compilation, we must be very cautious in not admitting at once, and not giving an absolute credit to all that is found in writings which do convey to us many things of great antiquity, but evidently mixed with multifarious details of a comparatively modern origin. This last remark ought to be ever present to the mind of him who peruses some portions of the Pitagats. The huge mass of rubbish which constitutes the largest portion of the scriptures is the production of the various Buddhistic schools which flourished eight and ten centuries after the first council.

as captives three hundred of the princes and nobles of the conquered state. His reign lasted altogether thirty-five years. He died in the year 25 of the religious era. He was slain by his own son Oudaia-badda, who succeeded him and reigned until the year 40. He was in his turn murdered by his son Anoorouda, who also fell after a short reign by the hand of his son and successor, Manta. This prince reigned until the year 49. He met with a similar tragical end. His son Nagata-saka killed him and ascended the throne. He reigned until the year 53. The people of Pataliputra, justly shocked at the horrible and barbarous murders which incessantly sullied the very steps of the throne, revolted against the race of these bloody princes, and put an end to the line of kings who are aptly called the parricide kings.

Among the three hundred princes and nobles whom Adzatathat had brought over from Wethalie, one of them had a daughter remarkable for the attractions of her person and the accomplishments of her mind. She was by the order of the king raised to the position of a courtezan in Radzagio. Whilst engaged in that course she had a male child, whom, with unnatural feelings, she ordered to be thrown during the night into the midst of bushes, outside the city. A Naga guardian of the place watched over the infant and carefully protected him. On the following morning, the king, happening to pass by, heard the sound thoo-thoo many times repeated. It was the Naga who made this noise in order to attract his attention. The king having sent one of his officers to the spot the sound was coming from, was informed that an infant still alive was lying there under the guard of a Naga. Moved with compassion, he ordered the child to be forwarded to his palace and had him carefully brought up. On account of the sound thoo-thoo which had been heard, and of the Naga that had been met on the spot, the child was named Thoo-thoo-naga. He grew up and became an accomplished prince. The people, who had rid themselves of the line of parricide kings, unanimously proclaimed him king in 63.

That monarch, not unmindful of his mother's origin, re-established the city of Wethalie, and fixed in it the royal residence. From that time Radzagio lost her rank of royal city, which she never after recovered. He died in 81, and was succeeded by his son Kalathoka, who, as we shall see subsequently, had a long reign of twenty-eight years.

We must show now how there has ever been a regular and uninterrupted succession of eminent doctors, who have successively communicated to each other the genuine doctrine, from Buddha down to the time of the third council, that is to say, during more than two hundred years. The venerable Oopali had learned the Wini at the feet of Buddha himself, and had for his chief pupil the venerable Dantaka, who in his turn became the teacher of the venerable Thaunaka. The latter was the instructor of the venerable Seiggiwa, who also brought up in the knowledge of the true doctrine the venerable and renowned Mauggali-patta. Dantaka belonged, by birth, to the pounha race of Wethalie. Having become a patzin, he attained to so great a proficiency in the religious science, that Oopali appointed him the instructor of a thousand religious in the three Pitagats. Thaunaka was the son of a rich merchant. He became a convert to Buddhism, and entered as a religious at Radzagio. His remarkable mental attainments induced his superior to give him the charge of initiating others into the knowledge of the sacred doctrines. Seiggiwa was the son of a nobleman of Pataliputra. On a certain day he went with many companions into the monastery of Thaunaka, and found him in a state of trance. The young visitor wondered at what he saw. From admiration he passed to respect and love, and wished to become a disciple under him. He succeeded so well in his studies that he merited to become the master of the most celebrated of all, Mauggalipatta. Previous to his present existence, the latter was in one of the seats of Brahmas. He was incarnated in the womb of a pounha woman. When he was born, he grew up and showed a decided inclination to become a Buddhist, and tread in the footsteps of Gaudama. It was in 163 that the future president of the third council became a patzin.

In the 20th year of the reign of Kalathoka, in the year 100, there happened a sort of schism amongst the Rahans of Wethalie. Those of the Weitzi district, little regarding the positive injunctions of the Wini, indulged in certain practices openly at variance with them. This occasioned strong remonstrance on the part of the Rahans living in the western district, called Pawera. The dispute among the religious was soon noised abroad and caused some scandal. It was the following incident which revealed all the peril.

The venerable Ratha was then living in the monastery, situated in the Mahawon, in the district of Wethalie. Chancing to travel through the Weitzi district, he heard that on festival days the Rahans were wont to place near the entrance of their monasteries certain vessels half full of water, and advised the people to put therein, each of them, a piece of silver, saying that the produce would be employed in purchasing dresses and the other utensils required by the Rahans. They also allowed as lawful the use of spirits, and were not very particular respecting the observance of the law of celibacy. Ratha was greatly scandalised at all that he saw. He boldly told the people that it was not good to make offerings of money, because it was unlawful for religious to possess any. He made similar observations respecting the other trespassings.

On the following festival day no money was offered. The Rahans were much incensed at such a neglect. Ratha said to the people: "Laymen, because of such irregularities, the beauty of the days of worship is fading, the glory of religion is darkened. Buddha in his days forbade the offering of money, the use of liquors, and several other practices which are now introduced in this place. By the innovators I am held up as a reviler of the Rahans, and as one deficient in benevolence towards you. I, as well as the Rahans of the royal race, attend only to the prescriptions of the Wini, such as they have been laid down and published by Buddha. The people replied to him: "Venerable Ratha, you are a true Rahan, and you follow the right way. Pray stay with us and be our teacher; we will abundantly supply you with the necessaries of life." Ratha, going on his way, was always followed by the people, who, in token of their respect and love, accompanied him to the Kootagara monastery, in the midst of the forest of sala trees.

The guilty Rahans, hearing of all that had been said, and fearing the paramount influence of the venerable Ratha over the people, said to them: "We shall not join with the Rahans of the royal race. We shall hold no intercourse with them. We shall expel Ratha from this district." With these dispositions they encouraged each other in the determination to offer a most decided opposition and maintain their newly invented practices.

On his side, the venerable Ratha, anxious for the safety of the genuine practices, and zealous for the exaltation of religion, hastened to Kothambi to warn the religious of that and the neighbouring districts against the evil practices of the Weitzi Rahans. To those whom he could not meet in person he sent letters and messengers to say to them: "Brethren, before the evil-doers succeed in their iniquitous efforts to subvert religion, and render doubtful and uncertain the genuine regulations of the Wini, ere they have time to set up false tenets, let us assemble, and with our united efforts give strength and confidence to the good and righteous, and crush the wicked and the impious."

At that time there lived on a mountain, in the Upper Ganges, a celebrated religious, named Samputa-kami. He was 120 years old, and had been a disciple of Ananda. To him the zealous Ratha applied in order to have the questions at issue with the Weitzi Rahans finally settled.

He minutely explained to him the ten points of discipline on which they were at variance with the Wini. Samputakami fully agreed with the proposal, and was of opinion that there should be held a general assembly, in which the points in dispute should be examined and the schism put an end to.

Some religious, about sixty in number, appeared to have a leaning towards the schismatical party. They resolved to go to Thaurya, where lived the celebrated Rewati, whose extraordinary wisdom equalled the quickness and flash of the lightning. The venerable Rewati, hearing of their wicked design, would not, in his abhorrence for their opinions, meet them on any account. He left his own place, and went from Thaurya to the town of Sankasa. When he had heard that they were following him, and were already close to the place he lived in, he removed to Kaiinna-goutra, then to Oudampara, subsequently to Eggalamoura and to Tharaudzati.

At the same time, it happened that Ratha, with the venerable Tsamputa, wished to go and have a meeting with Rewati, in order to place him on his guard and to bring him over to their party. They met him at Tharaudzati in the evening, and during the whole night made him acquainted with all the doings of the Weitzi Rahans, and begged him to declare openly which of the two parties was in the right. Rewati at once pronounced in favour of the Pawera Rahans, and condemned the opposite party on each of the ten points in dispute, and looked upon them as innovators and schismatics.

During that time the schismatic Rahans were not idle. They wished also to draw Rewati to their party. Having ascertained that he lived in Tharaudzati, they went by boat and ascended the river as far as that place. They carried with them many presents suitable for religious. Having landed, they took their quarters under a large tree. Rewati, knowing their wicked intent, would not receive their presents, nor hold communion with them.

Undismayed by this first check which they had received, they tried to obtain access to the master by means of the disciple. They offered him some presents, which in his simplicity he accepted. Meanwhile they urged him to prevail upon his teacher to give them a favourable hearing. He only once made the attempt to introduce the subject with the greatest caution. Rewati, however, was on his guard: he administered to his imprudent disciple such a rebuke as to deter him from making any further attempt. His name was Outtara. He and all the Rahans went to Wethalie.

To calm the heat of discussion, and bring the question at issue to a complete settlement, the Walikarama monastery in Wethalie was selected as the fittest place for holding a general assembly, where both parties would attend, and endeavour to come to a mutual understanding. Out of an immense number of religious, 700, the most conspicuous for their learning were selected by Ratha and Rewati to be members of the assembly. But to render the discussion clearer and easier, it was agreed that each of the ten points should be first discussed by eight Rahans, four from each party. Rewati, Samputa, Ratha, and Thoumana represented the western or orthodox party: Samputa-kami, Thala, Koudyabantaka, and Wathakami acted for the opposite party.

It is evident that in this dispute the question was not about the Pitagat itself; this was admitted by both parties. The difficulty affected certain points of discipline, ten in number, which were to be settled by the authority of the Kambawa and Patimauk. The eight delegates having met in a private hall of the monastery, Rewati was desired to question the venerable Samputa-kami on the ten points on which there was disagreement. He said: "Is it lawful to add to the food that is received some salt or other condiments?" Samputa-kami answered: "It is not lawful." "In what place was that point settled?" "In Wethalie, as being contrary to the spirit of the Wini."

"What sin is entailed on him who does such a thing?" "The sin of Patzeit." Questions of a similar import were put as regards the drinking of milk in the afternoon, the use of waters half-fermented, the drinking of spirits, the receiving of gold and silver. Answers were given agreeably to the tenor of the Wini regulations.

When the eight delegates had come to a decision upon the ten points of discipline, they went into the great hall where the 700 Rahans were assembled. Ratha was the president of the assembly. Samputa-kami was desired to ascend the pulpit and hold the fan. The president said to the assembled Rahans: "Brethren, if it be pleasing to you, I will interrogate the venerable Samputa-kami on the Wini, and on the ten points in discussion." He followed the same order that had been observed in the first meeting of the eight Rahans. The answers were unanimously received and approved of by the whole assembly. Then the president said: "All discussion concerning the ten points is now over; let every one accept the decisions of the assembly and act agreeably to them."

This second council is called Thattasakita, or the assembly of the 700 Rahans. It was held in 102, under the reign of Kalathoka. That prince appears to have favoured the party of the Weitzi Rahans. The assembly lasted eight months. The canon of scriptures was likewise arranged and determined as it had been done by Kathaba in the first council.

Among the principal members of the assembly were Samputa-kami, Thala, Koudzasambita, Rewati, Thauna, and Samputa, who had been disciples of Ananda. Thoumana and Wauthabakami had been disciples of the venerable Anoorouda.

Partly from the countenance given by the king to the condemned party, and partly from the obstinacy shown by the easterners in resisting the decisions of the council, the Buddhistic society was divided into two great factions. The latter, that is to say the Weitzi Rahans, established the great school called the Maha Thingika. The Terathaka was that of the orthodox; it never changed in doctrine or in discipline. Until the third council, that is to say, during the space of more than a century, eighteen different schools branched off.[3] Of these, seventeen offered

---

[3] The few and meagre particulars which we possess respecting the causes that have occasioned the holding of the second council, disclose a curious state of things as existing in the Buddhist community. The disciplinary regulations appear to have occupied a conspicuous part in the discussions that took place during the period of the first century. Some of those regulations were of trifling importance. We wonder how the religious could lay so much stress upon such a trifle as this, "Is it lawful to put salt or other condiments into articles of food, that would have been offered without such requisites?" The activity displayed by both parties in the controversy indicates the gradual working of opinions which in those parts had been always inimical to genuine Buddhism. In Wethalie and Thawattie, the holders of false tenets had been at all times bold and numerous. In the days of Buddha, heretics were swarming in those places. In the beginning of the fifth century of our era, Fa-hian, when he visited those places, says that he found that religion had almost disappeared, and that heretics were prevailing in every direction. We must conclude from these two circumstances that Buddhism never flourished in those places, or, at least, that it was never the prevailing creed of the mass of the people.

The disputes that took place in those days were not looked upon as of serious moment, since we see several religious of eminence supporting the anti-orthodox party. King Kalathoka himself was in favour of those whose opinions were condemned by the council. We may also infer from this state of things, that the disciplinary regulations were far from being settled at that time. It required the experience of succeeding generations to determine exactly what was best fitted for promoting the well-being of the religious body, and causing its members to live agreeably to the spirit which Gaudama desired to infuse into the souls of his followers. It cannot therefore be a matter of surprise to see the assembly striving, in the midst of discussions, to elaborate the framing of the rules destined to guide the religious in the details of their daily duties. Under such circumstances there could not but be a great variety of opinions, supported with that heat and ardour so peculiar to individuals who live estranged from the world. Moreover, the conflicting opinions were maintained by the various schools, which, from the early period of the existence of Buddhism, sprung up and divided the members of the religious body. Circumstantial details respecting the various schools we allude to, would prove of the greatest advantage for elucidating the state of the great religious system under consideration, for enabling us to enter into the history of its internal development, and witnessing the various incidents that have marked its progress through ages, down to the period when it gradually lost its footing in the Indian Peninsula.

The eighteen different schools which have obtained celebrity throughout the Buddhist world are mentioned in the Cingalese collection, and in that of all the northern Buddhists, includ-

the sad spectacle of important changes in points of discipline and of doctrine. But the Terawada never changed: it retained both doctrine and discipline in their original purity. All the different schools received their denomination from their respective founders.

---

ing the Chinese. In the manuscript which the writer possesses nothing is mentioned respecting these schools but their respective names. Had the chief opinions held out by each school been given out, they would have been expounded here at great length and with a scrupulous correctness. Such not being the case, the author has thought that it was useless to the reader to lay before him a dry and uninteresting array of names.

CHAPTER V.

Kalathoka is succeeded by his eldest son, Baddasena—And finally by the youngest, Pitzamuka—This prince is killed and succeeded by a chief of robbers, named Ouggasena-nanda—King Tsanda-gutta—King Bandasura—Miraculous dreams of Athoka's mother—King Athoka—His conversion—His zeal for Buddhism—Finding of the relics—Distribution of them—Third council held under the presidency of Mauggalipata—Preaching of religion in various countries, and particularly in Thaton—Voyage of Budhagosa to Ceylon—Establishment of religion in Pagan—Various particulars relating to the importation of the scriptures in Burmah.

At the conclusion of the synod, Samputa-kami and several of the most distinguished members of the Buddhistic assembly, astonished at the progress of schism and dissension which the united voices of seven hundred religious had not been able entirely to root up, endeavoured to divine, as far as human wisdom could reach, what would be in after times the fate of religion. They foresaw that one hundred and twenty years hence there would be at Pataliputra a mighty ruler full of love for religion, and zealous for its propagation, who would do much to promote its exaltation. But before the reign of that pious monarch they saw distinctly that there would appear many heretics, fond of their own will, coining doctrines of their own invention, and that they would thereby inflict the most serious harm on religion. They had, however, the consolation to know that this was to come to pass after their death. But who was the fortunate being who was destined to check effectually the coming evil? They saw him in one of the seats of Brahmas. His name was Teissa. In due time he would come down to the seat of man, operate his incarnation in the womb of a pounha female, named Maugali, and would afterwards become a famous religious under the name Mauggalipatta. This vision filled their souls with the purest joy, which was increased by the view of the expansion and development which religion would receive through the zeal of that great personage.

After a reign of twenty-eight years, King Kalathoka died, leaving nine sons, the eldest of whom was named Baddasena. They all reigned one after the other through a period of thirty-three years. The last of them, Pitzamuka, was the youngest. During his reign a gang of robbers desolated the country of Magatha. On a certain day a man named Ouggasena, having fallen in with that gang, inquired of them what pursuit they followed in order to obtain their livelihood. They plainly told him that they knew nothing about the tillage of the fields, and were unacquainted with the business of trade; they had no other way left for maintaining themselves but to seize by force whatever they chanced to meet. Ouggasena, taken up with the boldness of these desperadoes, offered to join their company with his eight brothers. The offer was gladly accepted. It happened afterwards that in one of their depredatory expeditions their chief was slain. Ouggasena was appointed by common consent to take his place. Being of a bold and lofty daring, he said to his associates: "Friends, it does not suit brave and enterprising men as you are to confine your attacks to petty villages and small towns: you ought to aim higher." He then represented to them in forcible language that King Pitzamuka was deficient in courage, and neglected entirely the duties of a king. "The moment is favourable," added he, "to attack Pataliputra itself." His opinion was universally accepted. The king, fonder of pleasure than of business, offered little resistance. He was killed at the taking of his capital, and Ouggasena sat on the throne, under the name of Ouggasena-nanda.

He was succeeded by his eight brothers. They reigned successively during the short period of twenty-two years. The last of them was called Dzananda. These princes were not followers of Buddha, but they supported the party of the pounhas, to which they adhered. Their generosity towards the pounhas was very great. They fed daily a great number of them in their own palace.

Among the pounhas who were maintained by the king's liberality, there was one named Dzanecka, who was much versed in the science of astrology. Being once in the country, he saw in himself certain signs indicating that one day he would become a king. Having communicated this intelligence to his mother, she wisely advised him to ignore such dangerous signs, which would inevitably bring the king's anger upon him, and expose him to great perils. Dzanecka was wise enough to comply with his mother's wishes.

On a certain day Dzanecka returned to Pataliputra, from the country place where his mother lived. On his arrival, he, in company with his brethren, went to the palace to receive alms, that were to be distributed in the king's presence in a large hall, fitted for that special purpose. He occupied the foremost rank. The king, who saw him, could not help remarking something extraordinary in his person. Suspicions arose in his bosom respecting the fidelity of that pounha. He instantly felt angry with him. Unable to control his passions, he ordered one of his officers to turn him out of the palace without giving him anything. The pounha had but to obey the unwelcome summons. Stung to the quick by shame and rage, he rose from his place. When he was just crossing the threshold of the hall's entrance, he took off his caste's string, and cut it in pieces; he likewise broke his mendicant's pot, and flung all against one post of the door of the hall, uttering at the same time imprecations, and praying that the king might never from that day enjoy rest. He ran away as far as he could, and under a disguise he eluded the pursuit of those that had been sent to arrest him. He escaped into Tekkaso. There he plotted the destruction of the king.

In one of his rambles through the country, Dzanecka met by chance a child, whom he knew to belong to a royal race. He at once adopted him, and brought him up with the greatest care and attention. It was not long, however, ere he found out that the signs prognosticating promotion to royalty were rather doubtful and somewhat insufficient. He could not rely on him for the execution of the important and long-cherished design he had in his heart. He had now to look out for some other one, who could afford him a greater subject for hope and confidence. Chance soon served him admirably well, to the utmost of his wishes.

After the destruction of Wethalie by Adzatathat, the princes that had escaped from the massacre had fled in an eastern direction, and built a city called Maurya. New misfortunes having befallen them, they were obliged to search for safety in precipitate flight. One of the wives of those princes, being in the family way, was led to the city of Pouppaya. Having been delivered of a son, she had the barbarity to order the little creature to be put into a jar, which was cast in a neighbouring cow-pen. The Nats watched over the child, and the bull of the herd, stationing itself near the infant, kept, with his horns and feet, at a distance any animal that came near. The cow-keeper, observing what was taking place, took the child and gave it to his wife Tsanda to bring him up as if he were their own child. He was called from the name of his adopted parents, Tsanda-gutta.

When the lad had come to the age to play the cowherd, he assumed among his fellow-herdsmen all the ways and manners and deportment of a king. He appointed some of them his ministers; others were invested with other mock dignities. He would sit on a tribunal, decide small cases, and strictly enforce the execution of his sentences.

The Pounha Dzanecka, who was living in the neighbourhood, hearing all this, wished to see the extraordinary boy. He recognised at a glance in the lad the sure signs foreshadowing his coming greatness. He purchased him for the sum of one thousand pieces of silver, and brought him up along with his other adopted son. Each of the boys had a splendid necklace of gold. On a certain day, Dzanecka ordered Pouppata, for such was the name of the first adopted son, to take a sword and go to Tsanda-gutta whilst asleep, and take from him his necklace of gold, without, however, cutting the thread, or even unloosing it. Pouppata, agreeably to his father's order, went near the place where his brother was sleeping. He stood over him, and examined attentively by what means he could execute his father's order. After many fruitless combinations, finding it impossible to do so, he went back to his father and related his disappointment. Dzanecka, without addressing him a word of blame, remained silent.

A few days afterwards, Dzanecka called Tsanda-gutta, and commissioned him to take a sword, and during his brother's sleep to steal away from him his gold necklace, carefully avoiding either to cut the string or to untie it. Tsanda-gutta went to the place where his brother was sleeping. After a few moments of reflection, seeing but one way to obey his father's order, he cut off at once his brother's head, and brought entire the necklace of gold, which he placed at his father's feet. The latter, without giving a sign of approbation or displeasure, remained silent.

Dzanecka gave all his treasures to Tsanda-gutta. Having pointed out to him and minutely explained the course he had to follow for obtaining the high station he was destined to, the pounha repaired to some other place, bidding him remember him after he became a king. With the treasures left at his disposal, Tsanda-gutta levied men, and went on from success to success, until he possessed himself of Pataliputra and killed Dananda. He received the water of consecration, and began his reign in 163. That monarch seems to have been accustomed to the use of poisons. For it happened that, on a certain day, his first queen, belonging to the Maurya race, tasted a mouthful of a dish prepared for the king. This caused her death. At the time of that fatal occurrence she was far advanced in pregnancy. The king, without a moment's delay, ordered her belly to be opened; the infant was taken out and put in the belly of a goat freshly slain. The child lived, and was called Bandusara.

Tsanda-gutta, after a reign of twenty-four years, died in 187, and was succeeded by his son Bandasura, only sixteen years old. Both the father and the son were supporters of the pounhas, and fed daily an immense number of them in their palace. Bandasura reigned twenty-seven years, that is to say, until the year 214. He had altogether 101 sons. His first queen, called Damma, had become the mother of two sons, called Athoka and Teissa. When she was pregnant of the first, she had five dreams: First, she thought she was stretching her two feet, one resting on the sun, and the other on the moon; second, it appeared to her that she was devouring the stars; third, she fancied she was eating the clouds; fourth, she imagined she was eating the worms' dunghills; fifth and finally, she imagined she was eating the leaves of all the trees. According to the prediction of the soothsayers, the five dreams meant that the son whom she had in her womb would rule over the whole of the island of Tsampoudipa; that he would destroy all his brothers, who would unite to dispute the throne with him; that he would disperse all the heretics or upholders of false tenets, who, like clouds, obscure the glory of religion; that he would possess all above the earth to the height of one youdzana, and all below the earth to an equal depth.

When Athoka was sixteen years old, his father sent him to Outzeni to govern that city, and the territories annexed to it. On his way to that city, Athoka had to pass through Wedika, distant fifty youdzanas from Pataliputra, in an eastern direction. The town had been founded by the princes of Kapilawot, when that city had been almost destroyed in the days of Buddha. In that place he married the daughter of a rich man, named Dewa. After his arrival at Outzeni, Athoka's wife presented him first with a son, who was named Maheinda, and subsequently with a daughter, called Seingamitta. Athoka remained nine years at Outzeni. At the end of that period, hearing that his father lay dangerously ill, he hastened to Pataliputra, to assist him and render all the services dictated by filial love. On his return, having to pass through Wedika, he left in that place his wife and his two children. A little while after his arrival at his father's capital, the king breathed his last, and Athoka was proclaimed king.

The new monarch, however, found himself soon surrounded by many enemies. With the exception of Teissa, who was born from the same mother, all his brothers conspired against him. The oldest of all, named Thoumana, was the originator and leader of the rebellion. After a protracted struggle, Athoka's good fortune prevailed. His rebellious brother Thoumana was overcome and made a prisoner; soon after, he was put to death. The same sad and cruel fate befel the other ninety-eight brothers. But it took three years before Athoka could free himself from all his enemies. On the fourth year after his accession to the throne, that is to say, in 218, he received the royal consecration, and in honour of his mother took the name of Dammathoka. He obtained a universal sway all over Dzampoudipa.

Up to the period of his consecration, Athoka had always favoured the pounhas. In imitation of his father's conduct, he fed daily an immense number of them in his palace. They all dressed in white clothes. It was only after he had received the royal consecration that he became a convert to Buddhism, through the instrumentality of his own nephew, the Rahan Nigrauda. A few particulars respecting this celebrated religious may not be unacceptable to the reader.

After Thoumana's death, his wife Thoumana-dewi was near the moment of her confinement. Under disguise, she contrived to baffle the snares of her husband's enemies and elude their pursuit. She went to the neighbourhood of the village of Dountsanka, a little distant from Pataliputra in an eastern direction, and rested under a banyan tree. A small shed was provided for her, and the head man of the village, who looked upon her as his daughter, supplied her with food. She was delivered of a son, whom she named Nigrauda. When he was about seven years old he was confided to the care of the venerable Varuna, who instructed him in his monastery, and taught him the Kamatan. He became a religious, and was made a patzin. The monastery of the venerable Varuna was not very distant from the southern gate of the city.

On a certain day the young religious Nigrauda rose up at an early hour, and having paid his respects to his great instructor, put on his cloak, and, taking under his arm the mendicant's pot, left his monastery, entered the city by the southern gate, and shaped his course towards the eastern one, with the intention of going to visit his mother. At that very moment King Athoka was standing over the lion's gate of his palace enjoying the cool of the morning breeze. He saw the young religious passing with a grave and steady step. All was graceful and dignified in his deportment. A placid joy, a serene modesty, and a majestic appearance beautified his countenance to such an extent that, at the first look, the king felt an irresistible affection for the young Samane. Without a moment's delay he despatched an officer to call him. With a kind and affectionate tone the king invited him to ascend the steps of his palace, and insisted on serving him with his meal. When the repast was over, Athoka said: "Young Samane, do you know well all the doctrines taught by your instructor?" "I am somewhat acquainted with them," replied Nigrauda modestly. "If such be the case, will you be pleased to explain them to me?" He then said in reply: "He who is diligent in practising the duties that procure merits, enjoys true happiness; he shall be exempt from death. He who neglects the duties that procure merits is unhappy, and is in a state of death." The king, delighted with the instruction delivered to him by the young Samane, offered him several presents suitable to the religious profession. But Nigrauda would not accept them, except in the name and for the benefit of his instructor; because it was he who had the charge of teaching people to avoid evil, to do good, and to practise the religious duties. As to him, he was but a disciple. Athoka was greatly pleased with the modesty and disinterestedness of the young Samane.

On other occasions the king sent for Nigrauda, and heard his instructions with such a good result that he gradually became a perfect convert. By the advice of his spiritual guide, Athoka made daily presents to a certain number of religious of the Buddhistic persuasion. The number of the religious who every day attended the court to receive presents gradually swelled to the amount of 60,000. Nigrauda instructed his royal pupil on the three Saranans and the five precepts. He infused into his soul a tender love for Buddha and his religion. The great change in the king's dispositions happened on the fourth year after his coronation. Up to that time he had favoured the party of the pounhas, as his father and grandfather had done. He was in the habit of daily affording food and maintenance to sixty thousand pounhas wearing the white dress.

Not satisfied with the liberal offerings of every day, the king said to the Rahans: "My intention is to build a great number of dzedis in all the cities of Dzampoudipa.

But where are to be found the relics of the most excellent Buddha, that they may be divided and enshrined in the principal dzedis?" By his order the relics were searched for in every direction. The dzedis already built in Wethalie, Kapilawot, Allakappa, Pawa, and Koutheinaron were all demolished. An exception was made in favour of the dzedi in the village of Rama. The Nagas, guardians of the place, would not allow that monument to be touched. In vain did the workmen strive with pickaxes to demolish the dzedi. Their instruments broke in pieces as soon as they came in contact with the building. But in none of them could the precious deposit be found. The king commanded that the demolished sacred monuments should be rebuilt precisely in the same shape and form as they stood previously. Athoka, disappointed but undismayed by his want of success, directed his steps towards Radzagio, and resolved not to relax in his exertions until he had found the precious object of his eager desires. Having arrived at that place, he assembled all the Rahans and people, and inquired if there was no person who could lead him in the way to discover the relics. In the crowd there was a Rahan one hundred and twenty years old, who said that when he was a Samane about seven years old, his superior directed him to take some flowers and perfumes, and, leading him to a retired place, said to him, "You see that dark bush in the middle of which there is a small stone dzedi; let us prostrate ourselves before it and make our offering." When this was done he added with a solemn tone of voice, "Young Samane, observe well this spot, and ever remember it." He said nothing more, and we returned to our home. "This is doubtless," said the king, "the very spot I am searching after, without having ever been able hitherto to discover it." The king and his people hastened to the indicated place. Great offerings were made to the guardian Nat in order to propitiate him. The Nat, assuming the shape of a young man, removed all the obstacles that obstructed the way to the place. When the king was near the first door, he discovered the ruby whereupon was seen the above-related inscription. On touching the bolt the door was suddenly opened, when, to the great surprise of all present, the lamps that had been lighted two hundred and eighteen years ago were found burning and full of oil; the flowers, without the least sign of withering, were as fresh and beautiful as those in the gardens; the smell of the perfumes seemed to be even more exquisite than that of new ones. The king, taking the gold leaf, read the inscription concerning him. He took all the relics, except a few that he left therein, replaced and arranged everything as he had found it. The finding out of the relics happened in 218.[1]

---

[1] It has been thought of some importance to mention in a particular note all the principal epochs named in the course of this work, and to show how they stand relatively to the Christian era. As a matter of course, the starting-point for the reckoning and computing of years is the epoch of Gaudama's death, which is fixed by the southern Buddhists in the year 543 B.C. The exactness of this epoch has been contested by A. Cunningham, one of the greatest authorities in such matters. In his opinion, the epoch of Gaudama's Neibban ought to be placed seventy years later. But as his views on this subject have not as yet been universally received by the learned in Europe, we will remain satisfied with the hitherto generally accepted data.

The first era is that of King Eetzana, the grandfather of Gaudama by his mother's side. It was made by the help and under the guidance of a famous hermit, named Deweela, who is mentioned as highly versed in the science of astronomy, such as it existed in those days. The king's object was to correct the glaring errors that had crept into the calendar. It is said that he did away with the era 8640 on a Saturday, on the day of the new moon of Tabaong (March), and fixed the beginning of the new era on the following day, that is to say, on a Sunday, the first day after the new moon of the same month. This happened in the year 691 B.C. This new reckoning of years lasted only a hundred and forty-eight years, the epoch of Gaudama's Neibban, 543 B.C.

The second era, the most celebrated of all, is the religious one. King Adzatathat and the venerable Kathaba, actuated by the desire of rendering ever memorable the death of the founder of their religion, and paying to him a homage that would be re-echoed by succeeding generations, came to the resolution of doing away with the Eetzana computation, and fixed a new reckoning of years, from the annual revolution which witnessed that event, which, in the opinion of Buddhists, is the greatest of all. In the year 148, the first day of the month of Tagoo (April), which fell on a Sunday, was fixed as the beginning of the new computation, emphatically called the era of religion, 543 B.C. It is adopted by all the southern Buddhists.

In addition to this general era, each

All that has been herein above related respecting the partition of the relics by Dauna, &c., has been extracted from the book called Nibana Thoot. But he who wishes

---

Buddhist nation has had, for one reason or for another, particular periods, from which they have reckoned time and computed years. It is probable that the reform in the calendar, necessitated by the errors introduced into it owing to incorrect computations, have given rise to several eras, which are generally known by the name of the kings under whose reign they have taken place, and by whose authority they have been introduced and brought into common use.

The Burmans have the era called Dandoratha. It was introduced by Thamugdara, or, as spelt by others, Thamugdaritz, king of Prome, in the year of religion 625 = to 81 A.D. That monarch is represented as well informed and skilled in the knowledge of the astronomical calculations. The months were no longer in unison with the seasons. What did the royal reformer of the calendar do to remedy the evil? No other particular is mentioned in the manuscript which the writer has in his possession, except that the king did away with 622, and began the reformed computation with two, so that its beginning must be made to agree with the year 79 A.D.

That era lasted only 562 years. The reformer on this occasion was Pouppa-dzau, king of Pagan, who is represented to us as well versed in the science of astronomical computations. This monarch imitated in this reform the conduct of the king of Prome. He did away with 560 years, and had his new era to begin with two. This happened in the year of religion 1182 = to 639 A.D. This is the common era used by the Burmese up to this day, and is known as the Pagan or Pouppa-dzau era.

We find also mentioned occasionally the Thaton era. It is made to begin with the year of the arrival of the two Buddhist missionaries, Thauna and Outtara, in the great place of Thaton, in the year of religion 237 = to 306 B.C. Thirimathoka was, at that time, king of that country. That period of years has lasted 1362 years. It ended in the year of religion 1599 = to 1156 A.D., when the king of Pagan, Naurata-dzan, invaded the country, possessed himself of Thaton, and carried away captive the last king, Mein-hnit.

It is perhaps as well to mention here an epoch which has been, at all times, famous in the history of Buddhism in Burmah. I allude to the voyage which a religious of Thaton, named Buddhagosa, made to Ceylon in the year of religion 943 = to 400 A.D. The object of this voyage was to procure a copy of the scriptures. He succeeded in his undertaking. He made use of the Burmese or rather Talaing characters, in transcribing the manuscripts, which were written with the characters of Magatha. The Burmans lay much stress upon that voyage, and always carefully note down the year in which it took place. In fact, it is to Buddhagosa that the people living on the shores of the Gulf of Martaban owe the possession of the Buddhist scriptures. From Thaton, the collection made by Buddhagosa was transferred to Pagan, 656 years after it had been imported from Ceylon.

Without the knowledge of those various epochs, it is difficult to understand with anything approaching to clearness and exactness the datas that we find alluded to and mentioned in the Burmese literary compositions. The foregoing particulars appear to be sufficient for all practical purposes.

to know all the particulars concerning the places where the relics have been deposited, &c., must have recourse to the books called Data Win and Nalatadata Win.

On a certain day a likeness of Buddha was placed before the eyes of Athoka. The king was delighted with it. He wished to multiply the number of statues, so that they could be seen in every part of his dominions. He gave orders for the building of monasteries in the 84,000 towns of his immense dominions. This happened in 220 of the religious era. It was but three years afterwards, that is to say, in 223, that the dedication or consecration of the dzedis took place, in which portions of the relics were to be enshrined. Throughout his realm the king issued a proclamation inviting all the people to attend to the observance of the eight precepts. The royal mandate was duly attended to, and the religious festival celebrated with the greatest solemnity. On that occasion the king made abundant donations to the religious, and strove to display his zeal for the promotion of religion.

Delighted with all that he had done, the king said to the venerable Mauggalipata: "I have endeavoured to labour for the exaltation of religion by every means in my power. I have built religious monuments through the length and breadth of my dominions; I have made offerings on the grandest scale. May I now consider myself as entitled to the inheritance of religion?" The venerable Mauggalipata replied: "Great prince, you have indeed done much towards the advancement of the good cause. But something else more excellent still is to be performed that you may acquire a right to the inheritance of religion." "What is that?" asked the king. "It is most perfect and meritorious," replied Mauggalipata, "that you should consecrate your son Maheinda and your daughter Singameitta to the service of religion." Athoka immediately asked his son, who was eighteen years old, whether he would like to become a religious. Maheinda answered in the affirmative. He was forthwith ordained Samane.

Mauggalipata acted on the occasion as president, and Mahadewana as master of the ceremonies. Singameitta was similarly ordained. The president was Dammapata, and the person acting in the ceremony was Oopali. This happened in 223. Maheinda learned the Pitagat under the immediate superintendence and tuition of Mauggalipata himself. His proficiency both in the study of religious science and in the practice of virtue was so great that his teacher placed him at the head of a thousand Rahans, whom he was commissioned to instruct.

The great liberality of the king towards the Buddhists, the efforts that he made for the promotion of the new religion he had embraced, alarmed those who belonged to the opposite party. The pounhas saw themselves without support, and unable to provide for their maintenance. They had recourse to the following expedient to secure their livelihood, and also a well-concerted plan to weaken their enemies. They all assumed the yellow dress, entered into the Buddhistic monasteries, and affected to be converts, without being so in reality. They retained their own opinions, and even as regards regulations they refused to comply with some of the ordinances of the Wini. Some of them fed large fires; others exposed themselves to various degrees of excessive heat; others affected the mania of fixing their eyes upon the sun in the morning, and following it in its course during the whole day.[2] Many appeared to lay little stress on several portions of the Pitagat. As a matter of course, the true religious

[2] From this passage we see that, in those days of remote antiquity, there existed in the Indian Peninsula individuals who, led away by a fanaticism still existing in our own days, devoted themselves to rigorous and extravagant penances, often in a state of complete nakedness. In the days of Alexander the Great, the same fanatics were met with in the Punjaub. Such ridiculous and unnatural exhibitions, far from being approved of and countenanced by the founder of Buddhism, were positively prohibited. Though he aimed at subduing passions, and elevating the spiritual principle above the material one, he recommended in the spiritual warfare a line of conduct more consonant with reason, and supplied his disciples with weapons of a far better quality and a superior description.

were much scandalised at such a conduct, and refused to hold communion with them on the days of worship. This state of things, after having lasted seven years, produced an irritation that could be no longer tolerated. Maugga-lipata, disgusted at such a perturbation, left Maheinda at the head of the community, and withdrew to the Ahan Ginga mountain to enjoy some tranquillity.

King Athoka was informed of the prevailing disorder. With the view of pacifying the inmates of the monasteries, he sent an officer of his household with stringent orders to oblige the two parties to come to an understanding, to communicate with each other, and to worship in common on the festival days. The officer went to one of the monasteries, explained the royal order, and drew his sword, threatening to cut off the head of the first Rahan who would dare to offer opposition. One of the orthodox party came forward, and having explained the true state of things, concluded by firmly stating that he would not hold communion with heretics. The officer in vain expostulated, and entreated the religious not to be so tenacious in his views, but rather to show a willingness to obey the king's orders, for the sake of peace. The latter persisted in his refusal. The officer, carried away by passion, struck off the head of the refractory Rahan. An immense uproar followed this tragical occurrence. All hopes of bringing about a pacification were then at an end. The officer withdrew from the monastery, and related to the king all the particulars as they had occurred.

Athoka bitterly deplored the murder that had been committed on a saintly personage, and reproached the officer with having outstepped the orders he had received. His religious feelings were grievously hurt, and his conscience greatly alarmed. He sent for several religious, and consulted them as to whether he was responsible for the murder committed by his officer. The spiritual advisers did not agree in their decision. Some of them were of opinion that the king was answerable for the doing of his messenger; others declared that the king, having given no order to the effect of using violence, the officer alone was responsible for the murder. Such conflicting opinions increased the king's perplexities, and threw him in a state of great anxiety and uneasiness.

Some courtiers, grieved at the sadness which overspread their master's mind, advised him to send for the celebrated Mauggalipata, and abide by the decision of that eminent man, whose knowledge was unsurpassed. The king gladly accepted the proposal. A messenger with a great retinue was at first sent to the place of Mauggalipata. The king's desires were respectfully explained. But the old ascetic refused to quit his abode of peace. A second messenger was despatched, but with no better success. At last a third one was sent on the same errand, with several religious. The latter, who knew the great zeal of Mauggalipata for promoting the cause of religion, represented to him the imminent dangers religion was threatened with, and entreated him to come, and by his presence save it from an approaching ruin. On hearing this sad news the old man no longer hesitated. He immediately left his abode, went in the boat prepared for him, and gently sailed down the mighty stream to Pataliputra. The news of his coming down was spread in a moment. When the boat was reported to be near the city, the king, with his whole court, hastened to the banks of the Ganges. On her nearing the bank, Athoka went knee-deep into the stream, and helping the venerable Mauggalipata with his royal hand out of the boat, led him into a garden, where a suitable place had been prepared for his residence. There he sat at his feet, and rendered to him the same humble services which a disciple is wont to tender to his teacher.

The king, anxious to alleviate his scruples and relieve his much-troubled conscience, related the particulars of the case of the Rahan's murder, and concluded by asking whether he was to be considered as responsible for the death of the religious. Mauggalipata said, "O king, had you, when you despatched the officer, the intention of having any refractory Rahan put to death?" "No," replied the king. "Since you gave no such order to your officer, and you had no intention that any disobedience to your orders should be visited with capital punishment, the murder of the religious can in no way be imputed into you, because intention is the thing that makes actions good or bad, and entails merits or sin on the perpetrator." Athoka recovered at once his peace and tranquillity of mind. Meanwhile he entreated the venerable Mauggalipata to labour for the extinction of schism and the exaltation of religion.

Seven days after the arrival of the great religious, a vast hall was erected in the grove where Mauggalipata was living. At the end of it a fine pavilion made of cloth of various and bright colours was prepared for the accommodation of the monarch. Each religious had then to be examined separately in the presence of Mauggalipata on the doctrines and practices he held as genuine and good. Those whose doctrines and observances were found to be at variance with the Pitagat were expelled from the assembly, stripped of the canonical robe, and compelled to resume the white dress, that is to say, the one befitting the pounhas. The presence of the king silenced all murmurs, and rendered any attempt at resistance impossible. In this manner the orthodox Rahans were separated from the heterodox ones.

To heal the wounds inflicted on religion by schism, to restore purity of doctrine, and confirm the genuineness of the canon of scriptures, such as had been done by Kathaba in the first council, and by Ratha in the second one, Mauggalipata, with the concurrence of the pious Dammathoka, resolved to hold a third council. From the Rahans then present at Palibotra he selected a thousand, and with them he regulated the Pitagat. The council was opened in the year 235, and ended in 236 = to 307 B.C. It was presided over by Mauggalipata, who was seventy-two years old.[3]

At the conclusion of the council, the president, who

---

[3] It is much to be regretted that no details concerning the third assembly of the Buddhists in Patalipootra could be found by the writer in the manuscript he has in his possession. The cause that occasioned the holding of the council was the desire to establish a perfect unity in the practices of discipline among the religious, and to come to an agreement on the subject of the genuineness of the scriptures.

During the period of 236 years that elapsed from the death of Gaudama, Buddhism seems to have remained confined within the limits of Magatha, that is to say, north and south Behar. Its hold over the mind of the people within those limits appears to have been very imperfect and uncertain, particularly in the parts north of the Ganges. It is from the reign of King Athoka that the propagation of Buddhism in every direction dates. The uninterrupted successes which attended his arms enabled him to afford a powerful support to the propagators of the new religion in the remotest parts which they visited. But we have no reason to suspect that he had recourse to violence in order to gain proselytes. No doubt he protected them, and supplied all their wants on a liberal scale. He does not appear to have extended farther the effects of the countenance he lent to the heralds of the new religion. He built monasteries and dzedis throughout the length and breadth of his immense dominions; he erected stone pillars, which he covered with inscriptions commemorative of his piety and zeal, a few of which exist up to this day. Athoka may be looked upon as a monarch who did more for the propagation of Buddhism in foreign parts than any of those who preceded him or came after him.

The establishment of Buddhism in Ceylon is mentioned at great length in the writer's manuscript, but he has thought it unnecessary to relate all that he has found on this subject, as being foreign to the purpose he has had in view in the publication of this book. In a foregoing note it has been stated how extraordinary is the fact that during more than two hundred years Buddhism was propagated in Ceylon solely by means of oral tradition without writing. The Cingalese authors are so unanimous on this point that it cannot be doubted. But in the Burmese manuscript we have found stated, in unmistakable expressions, that the religious who assembled in the village of Malliya wrote the Pitagat in Sanscrit, and with the Sanscrit characters. The word made use of is *Sanskarain*, which surely is designed to mean Sanscrit. How can this be reconciled with the undoubted fact that all the southern Buddhists have the scriptures in Pali and not in Sanscrit, whilst the northern nations that have embraced Buddhism possess the scriptures in Sanscrit? Until we can obtain further information on the subject, I have no hesitation in stating that the Burmans, ignorant of the existence of the two distinct languages—the Pali and the Sanscrit—are very apt to mistake the one for the other, and that in their opinion what they call the language of Magatha, Pali, and Sanscrit are but one and the same language, to which different names have been given by ancient authors. As the translator of a manuscript, the writer was bound to render into English what he has found written in Burmese. This is the reason why

was acknowledged the head of the Buddhists, thought of extending the sway of the new religion through the whole of Dzampoudipa. Hitherto it had been confined within the limits of Magatha. Now the time had come to extend it far and wide among the nations and tribes of the whole world. To carry out such a bold and comprehensive plan, Mauggalipata made an appeal to the ablest and most zealous members of the council, and charged a certain number of them to go and preach the true law in the countries beyond the boundaries of Magatha. The venerable Mitzaganti, with four companions, was directed to proceed to the country of Kashmera-gandara. Rewati was ordered to go to Mahithakan-pantala. Gaunaka-damma Reckita went to Aparanta. Maha-damma Reckita was sent to the Mahrata country. Damma Reckita received a mission to proceed to Yaunaka, which is the country inhabited by the Pantsays. The venerable Mitzi directed his steps, in company with several brethren, towards some parts in the Himalayas. Thauna and Outtara proceeded in a south-eastern direction to the country of Souwana-boumi. Finally Maheinda, Ittia, Outtia, Thamala, and Baddathala went to establish religion into the island of Tappapani (Ceylon).[4]

Great success attended the preachings of the Buddhist heralds. If credit can be given to all that is related in the books on this subject, religion must have taken deep root in the heart of the people dwelling in those distant lands.

As regards Ceylon, there is an important fact to be stated. It appears that until the year of religion 454, the knowledge of the Pitagat was transmitted by means of oral tradition. The heads of monasteries required from

---

he has, against his intimate conviction, made use of the word Sanscrit, applied to the first compilation of scriptures made in Ceylon under the reign of King Watakamani.

[4] The island of Ceylon was called, says the Burmese author, in former times, by different names—Audzadipa, Waradipa, Mautadipa, Singgadipa, Sihala, and Tappapani. There is no doubt but the last name was corrupted by the Greeks into Tapobrane.

their pupils to know the whole collection by heart. It is probable that one portion of the scriptures was learned by one section of the community, and another by another. In this manner the whole Pitagat was known in each monastery, and could be rehearsed in full by the inmates. This state of things lasted two hundred years. The great inconvenience necessarily attending it was soon felt so keenly that some means had to be devised in order to render the study of the sacred books surer and easier. In the reign of King Watakamani five hundred religious assembled in the village of Mallaya, and wrote the whole Pitagat in Sanscrit, and with the Sanscrit characters. Under the reign of that monarch a great dearth prevailed all over the island. Numerous Buddhist religious crossed over to the continent, and established religion in many parts of the southern portion of the peninsula. That prince also built the famous Bayagiri monastery. With the Mahawihara already existing, and the Dzetawon monastery subsequently erected, there sprung up three distinct schools. The latter was erected in 811, in the time of King Mathena of Ceylon. But the teaching of the Mahawihara was the only one truly orthodox. After a protracted existence, they were all merged in the Mahawihara school, under the reign of Thiri Singa-bodiparanna-maba, in the year of the Pouppa-dzau era (Pagan era), 522; of religion, 1714 = to 1161 A.D.

The venerable Thauna and Outtara of the pounha race, came to the district of Thaton,[5] which is called Souwana-

[5] The Burmans have, from the time of their conversion to Buddhism, or at least from the period they became familiar with the scriptures, had the mania of giving Pali names to countries, large towns, and new places that were settled by the authority of the rulers, in addition to the ordinary and common names. What has been the result of such a measure? The people have continued to designate such places by the vulgar names, whilst in most of the public documents and in the court they have always used the scientific and uncommon names. Hence has arisen a confusion in the minds of the people to such an extent that in many instances they believe that two names given to the same place indicate two distinct towns and localities.

The position of Thaton is well

boumi, in the country of Ramagnia, for the purpose of establishing religion in that distant land, which lies south-east of Mitzima. Thirimathauka was the king who at that time reigned at Thaton. Previous to the arrival of the Buddhist messengers of peace, the town was desolated by the ravages of Biloos, who, coming from the sea, devoured all the newly-born infants. A great consternation and panic had seized the inhabitants when they saw

---

known, and is between the mouths of the Salween and the Tsitang rivers. Its actual distance from the sea is about eight or nine miles. In the days of Buddhagosa, that is to say, in the beginning of the fifth century of our era, it was a sea-port. The Burmese writers invariably call Thaton, not by the name of city, but by that of country. They add the epithet of Souwana-boumi, the land of gold. According to the same writers, Thaton was situated in the state or kingdom of Ramagnia. From what is found mentioned about Ramagnia, it appears that it comprised three distinct parts or districts ; that of Kouthein, which is the present Pouthein or Bassein, including the territory situated between the Irrawaddy and the mountains of Arracan ; that of Henthawati, between the Irrawaddy and the Tsitang river; and that of Mouttama, or Martaban, between the Tsitang and the Salween. It seems that the kingdom of Ramagnia extended in the north as far as Akaouk-taong, south of Prome. The limits that are assigned must have undergone considerable changes, on account of the continual wars that have raged in those parts, but they are those assigned by several native authors.

The people that dwelt in Ramagnia are called Moun. They are the Talaings or Peguans of modern times. They had attained a considerable degree of civilisation at a time when the Burmans were in a state of barbarism. The proximity of the sea afforded them opportunities of coming in contact with other nations—the Hindus in particular, who appear to have settled at Thaton in great numbers. The Rahan Buddhagosa is said to have belonged to the pounha race, though he was a fervent Buddhist.

The town which was the capital of the territory called Henzawati cannot, we believe, be the town which is called at present Pegu, but another one, much more ancient, the ruins of which are still visible close to the eastern side of Pegu.

The language of the Talaings is totally different from that of the Burmans, but the characters for writing are somewhat the same. It is from them that the latter have received their religion, the scriptures, and the characters used in writing.

Since the final conquest of Pegu by Alaong-phra in the middle of the last century, and the extermination of a great number of its inhabitants, the remaining Peguans have gradually amalgamated with the Burmans. With their nationality they have lost also their language to such an extent that it is now spoken only in a few isolated places. It is not unusual to meet with descendants of Peguans whose aged parents still speak their native language, whilst they know and speak only Burmese.

the two strangers, clothed in yellow robes, setting their feet upon the shore. They mistook them for monsters of a new description, who were coming to increase their misfortune. They ran to arms, and were preparing to attack the two religious. The latter, perceiving the danger that threatened them, said with a meek tone of voice to the infuriated mob, "Why do you attack us? We are not Biloos, nor are we come hither with any hostile intention. Know ye that we profess a religion which forbids us to take away intentionally the life of even the smallest insect, to rob, to commit adultery, and to use spirituous and intoxicating liquors. By our regulations we are allowed to eat rice but once in a day." On hearing the explanations given by the two strangers, the people of Thaton were quieted. They received them with kindness, and treated them with great respect. By the power inherent in the two religious, the sea-Biloo was put to flight, and was seen no longer. The king and the people, grateful for the service they had received, and delighted with the new doctrine preached to them, accepted joyfully the five precepts, and promised to observe them. An immense number of men and women were converted. Among the new converts, a great many embraced the religious life.

King Thiri-mathauka was informed that, a little while after Gaudama's death, a Rahan, named Gambawatti, had brought thirty-three teeth of Buddha, and deposited them in a dzedi upon the mount Inda-danoo, which lies north-east of Thaton. Moreover, he had heard that after the eighth season, Gaudama had gone to Mitila. Whilst he dwelt into that place, it happened that a certain Rahan came to remember of some of his relatives whom he had known during a former existence. He saw them living in Thaton. He then earnestly supplicated his great master to condescend to go to that place and preach the law to his relatives. Gaudama, complying with the request, resorted thither through the air, attended by a great retinue. He preached the law, and previous to his departure, gave to the ruler of Thaton eight hairs of his head. Relying on the accuracy of the information, Thirimathauka felt a great desire to find out the precious relics, in order to have them distributed in eleven towns of Henzawatti, in eleven towns of Kouthein, and in eleven towns of Mouttama. These three countries constitute what is called Ramagnia. All happened agreeably to his wishes. The relics were duly found on mount Indadanoo, in the very dzedi in which they had been enshrined, and were distributed in the various towns, as above mentioned. It is probable that there occurred at Thaton the same curious fact which we know to have taken place in Ceylon, viz.: Religion was propagated at first by the means of oral tradition.

The first one who made an attempt to possess himself of a copy of the sacred scriptures was Buddhagosa, a religious of Thaton, of the pounha race. That man embarked at Thaton, which was then on or near the sea. That place is in the Ramagnia country, and is inhabited by a people called Moun. He sailed to Ceylon in the year of religion 943,[6] under the reign of King Mahanama. He resided three years on that island, wrote the Pitagat on palm leaves with the Burmese characters which was found written in the language and characters of Ceylon. In another manuscript we read that he translated into Pali the scriptures which were in the language of Ceylon. Buddhagosa remained three years in Ceylon, in order to complete the work he had undertaken. During his stay in that island the people were so much pleased with him that they made him many and costly presents on his leaving their country. He brought over with him to Souwana-boumi, which is in the Ramagnia country, a complete collection of the scriptures.

In or about the year of the Pagan era 419,[7] the forty-second, some say, the forty-fourth king of Pagan, named

---

[6] = to 400 A.D. [7] = to 1058 A.D.

Anaurata, having invaded the Ramagnia country, possessed himself of the Moun's territories and entered triumphant into the venerable city of Thaton. He took away from that place the collection of scriptures brought over from Ceylon by Buddhagosa, as well as the most learned among the Rahans. With the aid of these distinguished Rahans, religion was then firmly established in Pagan. He became master of the whole of the Ramagnia country, which includes Henzawatti, Mouttama, and Kouthein.

We have alluded briefly to the reconciliation that has taken place in Ceylon between the three great schools. Two of them the Bayagiri and the Dzetawon merged into the great Mahawihara school, which had always held up the orthodox doctrines. In the year that followed that event—that is to say, in the year of religion 1714 of the Pagan's era 522[8]—many Rahans, natives of Thaton, Pagan and other places in Ramagnia, attended by a large retinue, crossed over to Ceylon for the express purpose of worshipping the relics and the Bodi tree, and making themselves perfectly acquainted with the genuine doctrine and discipline. As a matter of course, they joined the Mahawihara school. They remained on that island during nearly one year. One of the party, named Tsapada, who was but a young Samane, was raised to the dignity of Patzin, according to the rules and regulations adopted by the Mahawihara. The party, having performed their devotions, and penetrated themselves with the spirit of the community in which they had spent a year, returned to their countries. The young religious, who had been but recently ordained, applied to his superior and obtained permission to remain behind in Ceylon for the purpose of studying the Pitagat and mastering its contents.

---

[8] = to 1161 A.D.

After ten years of unwearied application he went back with four companions, named Maheinda, Thiwali, Ananda, and Rahula. After their landing in the neighbourhood of Cape Negrais, they spent a year in Kouthein, and finally reached Pagan in the eighth year of the reign of King Narapati-sisoo of the Pagan era 534 = to 1173 A.D. In this manner, by the exertions of those five religious, the religion of Ceylon was firmly established and set up in Pagan. In this manner the doctrines and institutions preached and set up in Ceylon by Maheinda and his companions were blended with the doctrines and institutions which the venerable Thauna and Outtara had established in Thaton. Both flourished in Pagan and were much extended.[9]

The brilliant and glorious reign of Narapati-sisoo was soon followed by a series of misfortunes, which contributed to the weakening of his great empire, and finally brought on its total overthrow. Pagan was taken by foreign invaders. In the midst of such calamities three noblemen, named Radzasingian, Asinkara, and Sihasoo, set themselves up as kings, the first in Miyntsain, the second in Pekkara, and the third in Pinlay, in the year 662 = to 1301 A.D. The King of Miyntsain, having treacherously enticed Kiantza, the king of Pagan, to visit him in his new capital, detained him under various pretexts, and finally had him murdered. Thaunit, the son of Kiantza, hearing of his father's detention, ascended the throne of

[9] It is obvious from the testimony of Burmese writers that they acknowledge the fact that the scriptures brought from Ceylon by Buddhagosa, and the institutions flourishing in Thaton, found their way to Pagan in the reign of King Naurata-dzau. They likewise affirm that under the reign of Narapati-sisoo the religious who came from Ceylon, imbued with the spirit of the Mahawihara school, set up practices which were little, if at all, observed in Pagan at that time.

There was no doubt a great revival of Buddhism in Pagan, from the days of King Naurata-dzau to those of Narapati-sisoo. Most of the great monuments which excite the admiration of the travellers who visit Pagan were raised during that period.

Pagan, and reigned twenty-two years. He was succeeded by his brother Mou-hnit, who reigned forty-three years. With him ended the line of Pagan kings in 730 = to 1369 A.D.

Sihasoo, the King of Pinlay, reigned in that place twelve years, and in 684 removed the seat of royalty to Panya. In that place there were successively five kings, whose aggregate number of years on the throne amounts to fifteen.

One son of Sihasoo, named Athinkara-dzau-goun, established royalty in Tsitkain in 684 = to 1323 A.D. Under the reign of his son and successor, named Thirimega, a canine tooth of Gaudama was brought to Tsitkain. The king had the precious relic placed in a golden casket, and enshrined in a turret of his palace. He daily worshipped it.

Thirimega having died, his two sons Dzeta and Tissa quarrelled about the crown. Neither of them ever had the title of king; both of them oppressed the country during nine years. The son of Dzeta, named Budadasa, became king, and reigned during twenty-nine years. It was under the reign of that monarch that five venerable religious, who were well versed in the science of the Pitagat, translated the whole compilation, which was in Sanscrit, into the language of Ceylon (Pali).[10]

Tsitkain ceased to be a royal residence in 725=to 1364 A.D., and in the following year the city of Ava was founded on the sixth of the waxing moon of Tabaong, on a Tuesday at noon, under the constellation Pounnapha-shou.

On the following year, Mouhnit, king of Pagan, died at the age of sixty-four, after a reign of forty-three years, with whom ended the line of the Pagan monarchs. In the great city of Ava religion greatly flourished, and in 1134

---

[10] It is probable that our Burmese author makes here a mistake similar to the one alluded to in a foregoing note.

=to 1773 A.D., this book was composed[11] in the province of Dybayen.

---

[11] When the writer set at work to publish the second edition of this book he had at his disposal a Burmese palm-leaf manuscript, in which he found a vast amount of information respecting the history of Buddha, which was wanting in the work called Malla-linkara-wouttoo, the translation of which has afforded matter for the first edition of the legend of Gaudama. The work is named Tathagatha-oudana, the meaning of which is, Praises of him who has come like all his predecessors. This is one of Buddha's titles of honour. He is sometimes called Bagawat, the blessed or benevolent; Sugatha, he who has happily come; Dzina, the conqueror. From what is stated at the end of the work, it appears that it was composed in the town of Dibayen, sometimes called Tabayin, lying west of the river Mu, at a distance of about fifteen miles. The place is at present in a ruinous condition. Though the province continues to bear the name of Tabayin, the residence of the governor is in the town of Ye-ou, on the right bank of the Mu.

The compiler of the work was a Phongyie, who, according to his own testimony, finished his task on the thirty-eighth year after he had become a Patzin, ninety-three years ago. He was, therefore, at least fifty-eight years old, as he could not become a Patzin before he had reached his twentieth year. The compilation contains 636 pages of ten lines each, is written on palm leaves, and forms two huge volumes. We may well say that the narration begins at the beginning. The author informs us of the origin, not of Gaudama, since he has obtained the Buddhaship, but of the being who was indeed hereafter to become a Buddha, but who had to move into the circle of countless existences, slowly gravitating towards that perfected state in which he was to be fitted for discharging the duties of a deliverer. He presents us with a sketch of the origin of the country of Kapilawot, and of the kings from whom Gaudama's father descended. The above particulars were not to be found in the Malla-linkara. In all that relates to the birth, boyhood, &c., of Gaudama, both compilations agree in the main. The variations are few and unimportant. The author of the Tathagatha-oudana is immensely diffuse when he relates all that took place in Buddha's mind during the forty-nine days that he spent around the tree Bodi. Besides the important theory of the twelve Nidanas, or causes and effects, he supplies us with a complete exposition of the whole Buddhistic system of metaphysics, ontology, geography, and cosmography, the various seats in which all rational beings are placed, from the lowest hell to the last or the highest of the immaterial seats. All these details are purposely omitted by the compiler of the Malla-linkara. Finally, the author supplies us with a few particulars respecting Buddha, during the twenty first seasons or years of his public life. The story of Dewadat is presented at great length. But what is more important, we possess in the compilation of the Tathagatha-oudana a concise account of the three great assemblies or councils held in Radzagio, Wethalie, and Pataliputra, with the names of the sovereigns who have ruled over Magatha from Adzatathat, under whose reign Gaudama died, to Athoka, who promoted religion more than any of his predecessors, and who by his royal influence supported the decisions of the last council. He likewise mentions the names of the religious, who,

For the purpose of creating and increasing feelings of affection towards the most excellent Buddha,[12] who is

---

after the third council, were commissioned to go and preach religion in various countries *out of Magatha.* From this last expression we learn that Buddhism, until 236 after Gaudama's death, had not extended its influence beyond the boundaries of Magatha. As a matter of course, our author dwells more particularly on the two missions that were sent, the one to Ceylon and the other to Thaton. He enables us to follow the development of Buddhism in Pegu and Burmah, by informing us that King Naurata-dzau of Pagan, after the conquest of Thaton, took the king prisoner, seized upon the collection of the scriptures, and therewith carried to his capital all the best informed of the Phongyies, in 1056 A. D. Our author brings his narration to the time of the foundation of Ava, in 1365 A.D.

In imitation of all other compilers, our author ends his narrative with the following pious wishes. As a fit reward of the good work that I have happily brought to a close, I desire to become in some future existence a true Buddha, possessing all the science which will enable me to know all beings, their state and condition, and all the relations subsisting between them, and likewise to be gifted with a true compassion for and benevolence towards all beings, which will prompt me to labour for their deliverance. I desire that during the existences which are to precede the last one, I may continually practise the ten great and principal virtues. May my father, mother, relatives, teachers, and friends, have their share in this my good work!

Though far more comprehensive than that of the author of Mallalinkara, the compilation of the Tathagatha-oudana is very inferior to it as regards the drawing up of the subject and the disposition of its parts. Both are made by Burmans. We do not mean to say that the Burmans have made works of an original character. The authors have extracted from various parts of the scriptures all the materials they wanted for composing a work which might be considered as the history of the founder of their religion.

[12] The Burmese translator of the Malla-linkara finishes his work by candidly stating the motives that have induced him to undertake it. He desires to create, promote, and propagate, in the heart of future generations, religious sentiments, and feelings of the tenderest affection for the person of Buddha and his doctrine, that is to say, the law and the assembly of the perfect. Such are the lofty objects he had in view when he began to write. He was encouraged in his difficult task by purely religious considerations, viz., the promotion and triumph of Buddhism. For securing the attainment of what he considered to be a most desirable end, he summoned all his abilities with a most praiseworthy energy and perseverance.

With a somewhat different object in view, the Burmese work has been translated into a European language. The translation has been accompanied with notes intended to explain the text, which would otherwise prove, in many parts, almost unintelligible to the generality of readers. The principles of Buddhism, such as they are held and professed by Buddhists in general, but in particular by those inhabiting Burmah, have received a certain degree of attention, and have been examined as carefully as possible from a Buddhistic point of view. That great religious system has been

greater than the three rational beings, towards his glorious perfections, as well as the law and the assembly, I have, to the best of my abilities, endeavoured to translate from the Pali into Burmese the sacred book called Mallalinkara wouttoo, or history of the most excellent flower.

---

considered, as it is in itself, without any regard to its intrinsic merits or demerits. The notes are not designed to be an apology or a confutation of Buddhism, but an exposition of its doctrines, such as they are found in the best writings and believed by its votaries. When certain tenets or practices were to be accounted for, recourse has always been had to the general principles of Buddhism and to the notions certainly prevailing at various periods in Buddhist countries. It is needless to add that the notes, having been hurriedly written in the midst of almost uninterrupted and time-absorbing occupations, are destitute of pretension either to deep research or scientific merit. In former years, the writer bestowed a certain amount of time and efforts on the study of Buddhism in Burmah, where it has been for centuries the only religious creed. A portion of the knowledge thus acquired has been embodied in the foregoing notes, with the intention of compressing within a narrow compass the elementary principles and general notions of Buddhism, affording thereby to the readers, who cannot have access to the voluminous writings of the French and German Orientalist *savans*, on the great religious system of Eastern Asia, comparatively easy means to obtain some information on a religion, which, false as it is, deserves to be known and understood, since in point of antiquity it is second to none except to Brahminism, and as regards diffusion extends its sway over probably one-fifth of the human race.

AN ABSTRACT

OF

A FEW SMALL DZATS, AND OF TWO PRINCIPAL ONES, CALLED

NEMI AND DZANECKA.

THE writer has thought that it would not be without interest to the reader to make a few remarks respecting the five hundred and ten Dzats so famous amongst the Burmese, and to give as a specimen of those compositions the abbreviated translation of some of those fabulous accounts. We will begin with a few of the small Dzats, and end with the compendious summaries of two of the great ones, known under the names of Nemi and Dzanecka. The Buddhists of these parts maintain that all the Dzats contain a short and concise narrative of some of the circumstances attending certain existences of Gaudama, when he was born in the state of animal, man, prince, nobleman, poor, rich, Nat, &c. The narrator is no other than Gaudama himself, who is supposed to have condescended to make his disciples and the crowds of hearers acquainted with certain particulars relating to his person whilst he was passing through the slow process of metempsychosis and gradually gravitating towards the perfection he had at last reached. In fact, each of these pieces is prefaced with these words: When the most excellent

Buddha was in such a monastery, surrounded with his disciples, he spoke as follows, &c.

It is not improbable that some of these stories may have been told by Gaudama for the two following purposes: First, to impress his hearers with a profound respect for his incomparable wisdom, which enabled him to penetrate into the deep recesses of the past, and to bring to light some events hitherto buried in its dark bosom. The second and principal object he had in view was to give some important lessons to his disciples, to correct some of their defects, and stir up others to the practice of the highest deeds which he had himself performed during former existences. On his respect Gaudama followed the practice of all Eastern sages, who had recourse to the use of parables, similitudes, apologues,&c.,in order to convey, under a gentle, amiable, graceful, and interesting form, the most important instructions, designed to enlighten the mind and correct the heart.

The collection or compilation comprises most of those fables that are to be met with amongst most of the Asiatic nations, whence they have found their way to Europe, first among the Greeks, and next the Western nations. The writer has been not a little surprised to find in that collection a number of fables the very same as those so inimitably narrated by the great French fabulist, the good La Fontaine. This is another confirmation to the old adage, There is nothing new under the sun.

These stories have certainly an Indian origin; at least the Burmans have received them, as almost all the things that are connected with their religion, from that quarter. Under despotic governments, the plain and naked truth cannot show itself, or make its voice to be heard, without exposing its friends to the most imminent dangers on the part of those tyrants who practically maintain that their will must ever stand above truth and reason. Stories nicely told were the pleasing and innocent but necessary dress which that sacred goddess was obliged to wear in order to make her presence supportable to the despots, and help her friends to find favour with those whose absolute and uncontrollable sway made everybody bow the head in their awful though detested presence.

The first five hundred stories have, it seems, no historical value whatever. They are most of them short and concise. But the last ten may very likely contain many facts or allusions to individuals and places that might afford a clue to some parts of the history and geography of India in days of a remote antiquity. A complete translation of the ten Dzats might not be without interest, provided such a work be accompanied with copious notes, made by a competent person, well acquainted with the ancient history of India.

All the stories end with a most important disclosure made by Gaudama himself. The personage that has played the most important and praiseworthy *rôle* is, as a matter of course, our Buddha himself. Those who befriended him, assisted him, and rendered him any services, are those who subsequently became his favourite and most distinguished disciples and hearers; whilst those who acted in any reprehensible manner, who opposed him and did him harm, afterwards became the individuals who were in his days heretics or holders of false doctrines, and in particular his arch enemy, the notoriously wicked Dewadat.

The compilation of all these stories is prefaced as follows:—In the country of Amarawadi lived a pounha named Thoumeda. After the death of his father he became the owner of a considerable estate. Having enjoyed it during many years, he began to reflect on the many and various accidents attending human life, and came to the resolution of leaving the world. He therefore distributed in alms all his riches, and withdrew into solitude, to lead an ascetic life. He soon reached a high degree of perfection. At that time Deipinkara, one in the series of the twenty-eight Buddhas, came to that country, attended by 400,000 Rahans, to beg his food. Our Rathee

Thoumeda, having nothing to offer to the great Buddha and the assembly, came, threw himself at his feet, and delivered himself up soul and body to his service. In another compilation it is stated that Thoumeda had volunteered his services to level a portion of a road that Deipinkara was to follow. The work was finished, with the exception of a small gap that was not yet filled, when the Buddha made his appearance. The hermit, without a moment's hesitation, flung himself on the ground, and bridged the place with his own body.

It was at the sight of such a perfect abnegation of self that Buddha gave to Thoumeda the assurance that one day he would become a Buddha. On that occasion great wonders took place.

From that time he began to practise with a fervent earnestness the great virtues and perfections prescribed by the law. The whole period of time that elapsed from the time Gaudama was the pounha Thoumeda to the time he became Prince Wethandara—that is to say, reached that existence which immediately preceded the last one, when he became Buddha—is of four thingies and one hundred thousand worlds or revolutions of nature. A detailed account of the most meritorious and interesting actions performed by him during several existences that illustrated that almost incalculable period is to be found in the great dzedi of Ceylon.

The accounts must be short and concise, otherwise the dzedi above referred to, how large soever we may suppose it to have been, could never have held them.

THE FOX AND THE LION.

1. When the most excellent Buddha was in the Dzetawon monastery, surrounded by his disciples, desiring to correct a religious who was in the habit of keeping bad company, he narrated the following story: At the time that the Princes Bramanas reigned at Baranathee, Phralaong was then a lion, father to two little ones, one male and the other female. The first was named Menandza. The lion's household, when Menandza was grown up and had married, was composed in all of five individuals. Menandza, strong and bold, went out every day in quest of prey for the support of his four relations that remained in the den. One day, in the middle of one of his predatory excursions, he happened to meet with a fox, which was lying on his belly, in a most respectful posture. On being asked by the proud lion, with a terrific voice, heightened by a threatening glance, what he was doing, the fox respectfully answered: "I am humbly prostrated here to do homage and pay my respects to your majesty." "Well," said Menandza; and he took him alive to his den. As soon as the father saw the fox, he said to his son: "My son, the fox is an animal full of cunning and deceit, faithless, without honour, addicted to all wicked practices, and always engaged and embroiled in some bad affairs; be on your guard; beware of such a companion, and forthwith send him away." Unheeding his father's wise advice, Menandza persisted in his resolution, and kept his new friend with him.

On a certain day the fox intimated to Menandza that he longed to eat the flesh of a young colt. "Where is the place these animals are wont to graze?" asked Menandza. "On the banks of the river of Baranathee," replied the fox. Both started immediately for the indicated spot. They saw there a great number of horses bathing in the river. Menandza, in an instant, pounced upon a young one, and carried it to his den. "It is not prudent," said the old father, "to eat those animals which belong to the king. One day he will cause you to be shot from a distance with arrows, and kill you. No lion that eats horse-flesh has ever lived long. From this day cease to attack those animals." Deaf to such wholesome warnings, Menandza continued to carry destruction among the horses. News was soon conveyed to the king that a lion and a fox were making great havoc among his horses. He ordered the animals to be kept within the town. The lion, however, contrived to seize some and carry them away. Orders were given to keep them in an enclosure. Despite this precaution, some horses disappeared. Enraged at this, the king called a bowman and asked him whether he could transfix a lion with his arrows. The bowman said that he could do it. Hereupon, leaving the king, he went and hid himself behind a post, waiting for the offender. It was not long ere he made his appearance; but the cautious fox had remained somewhat to the rear, hidden in a drain. In one start, the lion, with the quickness of lightning, was on the wall, and straightway he went to the stable. The bowman said within himself: "The lion's movements are very quick; I will wait until he come back loaded with his prey." He had scarcely revolved this thought in his mind, when the lion was already on his way back carrying a horse. The bowman, all ready, shot an arrow that transfixed the fierce animal. The lion made a start, crying with a terrific voice, "I am wounded." The fox, hearing his friend's accents, and the sharp whistling of the bow-string, knew at once what had happened. He said to himself, shaking his head: "There is no friendship, forsooth, with the dead; my friend has fallen under the bowman's arrow; my life is safe; I will go back to my former place."

The wounded lion, making a last effort, went back to his den, and dropped dead at its entrance.

Menandza's relatives, perceiving the wound and the blood gushing out of it, understood at once that he had been shot through with an arrow, and that the fox was the cause of his miserable and untimely end. His mother gave vent to her grief as follows: "Whoever associates with the wicked shall not live long; behold my Menandza is no more, because he followed the fox's advice." The father, in his turn, bewailed the loss of his son: "He who goes in company with the wicked shall meet with some evil fate; witness my son, whom his desolate mother sees weltering in the very blood she gave him." His sister cried aloud: "He who does not follow the advice of the good shall repent of it; he is mad, and, like my brother, shall come to an untimely and cruel end." Menandza's wife exclaimed: "He who belongs to a superior rank ought to beware to associate with those of a rank inferior to his own, otherwise he soon becomes as despicable as those he associates with. He loses his position, and becomes the laughing-stock of all."

Buddha concluded his discourse with this reflection, that no one ought to keep company with those that are wicked and of an inferior position. The religious profited so well by the lecture that he broke at once with his former friends, and soon reached the state of Thautapan. The fox has been since Dewadat, Menandza, the religious, the object of the lecture, Menandza's sister, Oopalawon; his wife, Kema; his mother, Yathaudara; his father, Phralaong.

THE JACKAL AND THE HUNTER.

2. When the most excellent Phra was in the Weloowon monastery, alluding to Dewadat, who aimed at harming him, he spoke as follows: "At the time the Princes

Bramanas reigned at Baranathee, Phralaong was then a jackal, presiding over 500 other jackals of his own tribe. His dwelling-place was in a cemetery. One day it happened that the inhabitants of Radzagio made a great feast, where every one ate and drank as much as he liked. The repast was nearly over when some one asked for a last piece of meat, to give the finishing-stroke to his appetite. He was told that not the smallest morsel remained. On hearing this unwelcome news, he rose up, laying hold of a wooden club, and went straight to the cemetery. Then stretching himself on the ground, he lay down as if dead. Phralaong, cautiously drawing near to the pretended dead body, smelt it from a becoming distance, and soon discovered the snare laid for him. Coming up close to him, he suddenly seized the club with his teeth, pulling it with all his might. The young man did not let go his hold. The animal, withdrawing, said to the hunter: "Young man, I perceive now that you are not dead." The hunter, goaded with shame and anger, rose up, and with more energy than dexterity flung his club at the jackal; but he missed him. "Go away," said he, "wretched beast; you may boast that you have escaped this time." "Yes," mildly replied the jackal; "I have been saved from your club; but no one shall ever be able to preserve you from the punishments in the eight great hells." Having thus spoken, he soon disappeared. The young man, having washed away in the ditch the dust that covered him, walked back, quite disappointed, into the town. The hunter was the same that subsequently became Dewadat. As to the jackal, he is the same that has since become Buddha.

THE PIGEON AND THE HUNTER.

3. When Phra was in the Dzetawon monastery, desiring to give instruction to the young son of a nobleman, named Ootara, he spoke as follows. At the time the Princes Bra-

manas reigned at Baranathee, Phralaong was a pigeon. There was then a man in that country who was wont to catch pigeons, bring them to his house, and carefully feed them until they became fat, when he then sold them at a high rate. Together with other pigeons, Phralaong was caught and brought over to the house. But he would not peck the grain that was spread before him. "Should I eat," said he to himself, "I will soon get fat, and then be sold like others." He soon became wretchedly thin. Surprised at this, the hunter took the pigeon out of the cage, placed it on the palm of his hand to examine it more closely and find the cause of its great leanness. Phralaong, watching the opportunity of a favourable moment when the attention of his guardian was called to some other object, flew away to his own old place, leaving the hunter quite vexed at and ashamed of his confiding simplicity. The hunter is in these days Dewadat; and the pigeon is now Buddha himself.

Here is the abridgment of two stories, well known to the readers of fables.

4. When Phralaong was a deer, he became intimate friend with the bird khaoukshia and a turtle. On a certain night it happened that a hunter having laid down his net, the deer was caught. A tortoise that was near to the place came and bit the net; the deer then soon made his escape from the dangerous position he was in. Whilst this was going on the friendly khaoukshia, perceiving the danger his friend was in, amused the hunter by flying right and left close to him, to retard his progress towards the place where the net was laid. Mad at the escape of the deer, he seized the turtle and thrust her into his bag. But the wily bird contrived by its peckings to make a large hole in the bag, and the tortoise too made her escape.

5. One day Phralaong, being then a husbandman, observed once, to his great surprise, that a lion of an uncommon size paid frequent visits to his rice field, and

ate and destroyed many of the young plants. On a certain occasion he examined closely the intruder, and perceiving the extremities of his feet, he discovered that the pretended lion was but a colt that had clothed himself in a lion's skin.

NEMI.

When the most excellent Buddha was in the country of Mitila, he went, attended by a great many Rahans, to the monastery of Meggadawa, situated in the middle of a beautiful grove of mango trees. He spoke as follows to the assembly: "Beloved Bickus, in former times I lived in this very place where we are now congregated, and was the ruler of the country of Mitila." He then remained silent. Ananda respectfully entreated him to condescend to narrate to them some of the principal events that happened at that time. Buddha assented to the request, and said: "Formerly there reigned at Mitila a prince named Minggadewa. During 82,000 years he remained a prince, and spent all his time in the enjoyment of all sorts of pleasure; he was crown prince of that country during the same space of time, and reigned as king during a similar period."

On a certain day the barber of the king having detected a grey hair on the royal head, exhibited it to his astonished regards. The king, struck at such a sight, soon understood that this object was the forerunner of death. He gave up the throne, and resolved to become a Rahan. Having put into execution his resolve, he practised with the greatest zeal the highest virtues, and after his death migrated to one of the fortunate seats of Brahmas. The 82,000 princes who succeeded him followed his footsteps, inherited his virtues, and after their demise obtained a place in the same seat.

Prince Mingga-dewa, who had opened the way to such a succession of pious monarchs, perceiving that his race was near being extinct, left the seat of Brahmas and took flesh in the womb of the queen of the king who then governed Mitila. On the tenth month the queen was delivered of a son, who received the name of Nemi. The pounhas who were invited to the palace to tell the horoscope of the royal child, assured the king that this child would follow the example of all his predecessors who had left the throne and embraced the profession of Rahans.

From his tender age the young prince displayed the most liberal and pious dispositions in making abundant alms, and fervently observing all the religious practices. All the inhabitants of that kingdom followed his example, and when some one died, he migrated to one of the Nats' seats. During those happy times, hell seemed to have become quite unnecessary.

On a certain day Nemi appeared to be most anxious to know which was the most excellent practice, the bestowing of alms, or the observance of the precepts. The great Thagia came down from his glorious seat, encompassed with an incomparably shining brightness, and went to the place where the prince was busy revolving this thought in his mind. The angelical visitor told him that the bestowing of alms could only procure an admittance into the seats of Nats, but that a perfect compliance with the ordinances of the law opened the way to the seats of Brahmas. As soon as he had given his decision, he returned to his blissful seat. On his arrival he found crowds of Nats given up to rejoicings. The Thagia gave them a detailed narrative of all that he had seen on earth during his errand, and in particular eulogised at great length the religious dispositions of Prince Nemi. Enraptured with the heart-moving description they heard, all the Nats at once exclaimed that they wished to see in their seats so accomplished and virtuous a prince. The Thagia commanded a young Nat, named Matali, to have his carriage ready, depart for the country of Mitila, and bring to this fortunate seat the ruler of that country. Matali, bowing before the Thagia, forthwith left the seat of Nats in a magnificent chariot. It was then the day of the full moon, when all the inhabitants of Mitila were busily engaged in discharging their prescribed religious duties. On a sudden there appeared, issuing from the east, the magnificent and bright equipage of the Nat, splendidly emerging from the bosom of clouds at the same time as the moon in its full. Surprised at such an unexpected sight, all wondered, and believed that two moons were miraculously rising on that occasion. They were soon undeceived by the nearer approach of Matali's carriage. The messenger went to the king, and conveyed to him the intelligence that the Nats were exceedingly anxious to see him. Without a moment's hesitation the king stepped into the carriage, and abandoned himself to the guidance of his heavenly guide. "Two roads are now opened before us," said Matali, "the one through the dismal dungeons, where the wicked are consigned to undergo punishment for their offences, and the other through the blissful seats, where the good are enjoying the rewards allotted to them for their virtues. Which of the two do you wish to follow?" The prince said that he wished to visit both places. Matali answered in a mild tone of voice that his request should be complied with.

The celestial guide directed his rapid course through the regions of desolation, where dwells an eternal horror. The first object they met with was a broad and deep river, filled with frightful whirlpools, where the water seemed as if boiling. It was glowing like a flame, and the whole mass of water appeared like a lake of fire. The river is called Wattoorani. On the banks of that river stand the infernal ministers, armed with all sorts of sharp-edged instruments, cutting, wounding, piercing the unfortunate wretches, who try to get out of that horrible and burning water. They are forcibly pushed again into the same place of torments, and tumble over pointed darts, whence they are taken up and roasted on living coals. Nothing is heard but the horrifying howlings and yells of those unfortunate beings, who are waiting with the greatest impatience the moment of their deliverance. "What are the crimes," asked the terrified prince, "that have committed the unfortunate inhabitants of this place to undergo such unheard-of sufferings?" "They are," replied Matali, "the persecutors of the weak, the heartless oppressors of the poor, &c., who are doomed to undergo such punishments." Thence the guide drove rapidly to another place, where dogs, each with five hideous heads, famished eagles, and devouring crows, fed with a ravenous hunger on the bodies of unfortunate victims, the flesh of which is incessantly reproduced to afford a continual prey to these never-satiated ferocious animals. "These," said Matali, "suffer for having done no good to their fellow-creatures, for preventing others to do some, and for having borne envy to their neighbours."

Here follows a long description of the other places of hell, given to Nemi by his celestial guide. We omit it, lest its tedious and revolting particulars tire and disgust the reader. Suffice it to mention that the torments of Tantalus are described here with a horrifying correctness, such as almost casts into the shade the description given to us by the Latin poet.

Having ranged the various regions of hell, and heard all the particulars given to him by Matali, Nemi was suddenly brought over to the beautiful, smiling, and blissful seats of the blessed. He soon descried at a distance the celebrated palace, made of diamonds, disposed in an immense square of twelve youdzanas on each side, and five stories high; then the garden, the tank, and the padetha tree. In that palace Biranee occupied a splendid apartment; she was then lying on a soft sofa, surrounded by more than a thousand beauties. "What good works," asked Nemi, "has Biranee practised, to deserve such a magnificent reward?" Matali replied, "This daughter of

Nats was formerly a slave in the house of a pounha. She was always very attentive to all the duties of her position, and at the same time regularly observed the precepts of the law. On a certain day her mistress, who was wont to feed eight Rahans daily, fell into a fit of anger, and said that she was unable to bear any longer the fatigue attending the maintenance of these religious. But the young slave, full of religious zeal, took upon herself the labour of feeding the Rahans. For this good and meritorious work she is enjoying the happiness of her present position."

Nemi was successively led into the various seats of the inhabitants of those blissful regions, and his guide explained at great length the good works that had procured to each of them the respective happy situation which they enjoyed, and occasionally mentioned the period of time they were allowed to dwell in those abodes of unparalleled happiness. He was finally introduced to the presence of the great Thagia, who is the chief of all Nats. Having finished the survey of all the seats of Nats, Nemi was brought back to the seat of men in his own capital by the same celestial guide.

On his return Nemi saw himself surrounded by his pious subjects, who eagerly inquired of him all the particulars respecting his journey. He minutely explained to them all that he had seen both in the region of hell and in those of Nats, and concluded by exhorting his people to be liberal in bestowing alms, that they might hereafter be admitted to share in the enjoyment of the Nats' happiness.

Nemi, perceiving that his hairs were turning grey, became still more zealous in the practice of alms-deeds, and resolved to embrace the profession of Rahans. But previous to his taking such a step he had his son Ralaradzana appointed to succeed him. With that prince terminated the long succession of kings who in the decline of their lives became Rahans.

DZANECKA.

This is one of the best written Dzats possessed by the Burmese. The writer has translated it from beginning to end; but he will give here only an outline of its contents. The narrator, as usual, is our Buddha himself, when he was in the Weloowon monastery, surrounded by the members of the assembly and a crowd of hearers.

In the country of Mitila there reigned a king named Dzanecka, who had two sons called Arita Dzanecka and Paula Dzanecka. After a long and prosperous reign he passed to another existence. Arita Dzanecka, having celebrated his father's obsequies and made the usual purifications, ascended the throne. He confirmed his younger brother in the situation of commander-in-chief, which he had hitherto held.

On a certain day a vile courtier, by a false report, awakened in the king's breast sentiments of jealousy and suspicion against his brother's fidelity. The innocent prince was cast into a dungeon; but in the virtue of his innocence he found means to make his escape, went to a part of the country where he had powerful supporters, and soon found himself in a condition to bid defiance to his brother. The king assembled his troops; a battle ensued, in which the king was slain, and Paula Dzanecka ascended the throne.

The queen, who was with child, on hearing the news of such a disaster, went to the treasury, took some ornaments of the purest gold and the most valuable precious stones, and placed the whole in a basket. She then spread out rice so as to cover the treasure, and extended an old and dirty cloth over the opening of the basket. Putting on the dress of one of the meanest women, she went out of the town, carrying the basket over her head. She left the city through the southern gate and passed into the country without being noticed by the guards.

Having gone to a certain distance from the place, the queen did not know which way to direct her steps. She sat in a dzeat during the heat of the day. Whilst in the dzeat she thought of the country of Tsampa, where some of her relatives lived, and resolved to go thither. She began to make inquiries at the people that were passing by respecting the route she would have to follow.

During this time the attention of a Nat was suddenly attracted by the inspiration of Phralaong, who was in the queen's womb, to the sad position his mother was in. He, leaving forthwith his blissful seat, assumed the appearance of an old man guiding a carriage along the road. He came close to the dzeat and invited the queen to ascend his carriage, assuring her that he would convey her safely to Tsampa. The offer was accepted. As the queen was far advanced with child, she had some difficulty in getting into the conveyance, when that portion of the earth which she was standing upon suddenly swelled and rose to the level of the carriage. The queen stepped into the chariot and they departed. During the night they arrived at a beautiful place close to the neighbourhood of Tsampa. The queen alighted in a dzeat. Her celestial guide bade her to wait until daybreak before she ventured into the city, and returned to the seat of Tawadeintha.

During that very night a famous pounha, attended by five hundred of his disciples, had left the town at a late hour, to take a walk by moonlight and enjoy the cool of the night and a bath in the river. Pamaouka, for such is the name of the pounha, came by chance to the very place where the queen was seated. His disciples continued their walk and went on the bank of the river. She appeared full of youth and beauty. But by the virtue of Phralaong the pounha knew that she was in the family way, and that the child she bore was a Phralaong. Pamaouka alone approached close to the queen and entreated her to entertain no fear whatever; that he looked upon her as his sister. The queen related to him all the particulars of her misfortune. The great pounha, moved with compassion, resolved to become her supporter and protector. At the same time he recommended her to say that he was her brother, and when his disciples should come back, to shed tears in token of the tender emotion she felt at meeting with him. Everything having been arranged, Pamaouka called his disciples, told them how happy he was at having found his sister, from whom he had parted many years ago. Meanwhile he directed them to take her to his house, and recommended her to the special care of his wife. As for him, he would be back soon after having performed the usual ablutions. The queen was welcome in the pounha's house, and treated with the greatest care and tenderest affection. A little while after she was delivered of a beautiful child, resembling a statue of gold. They gave him the name of Dzanecka.

Having reached the years of boyhood, he was one day playing with boys of his own age, when, by way of teazing, they called him the son of the widow. These keen tauntings made him urge his mother to reveal to him the name of his father. It was then that he knew the author of his birth. Pamaouka taught him all the sciences known in those days, such as medicine, mathematics, &c. At the age of sixteen years young Dzanecka had completed all his studies.

Dzanecka resolved to devote himself to trade, and acquire thereby ample means to reconquer one day the throne of his ancestors. With a part of the treasure his mother had brought with her, he was in a position to fit out a ship in company with several other merchants. He resolved to sail for a place called Caumawatoura. He had scarcely been at sea two days when a mighty storm came on. The vessel, after having held out some time against the roaring and raging billows, at last gave way, and was broken in pieces. All the crew and passengers, amounting to 700, miserably perished in the sea, without making the least effort to save themselves. Our Phralaong, on the contrary, seizing the extremity of a log of wood, swam with all his strength, resolved to struggle to the last against adversity. Mighty were his efforts for several days. At last a daughter of Nats, whose duty it was to watch over the sea, saw his generous and courageous behaviour, took pity on him, and came to his assistance. There followed a sort of dialogue between her and Dzanecka. The latter displayed his undaunted courage and firm purpose. The former admired the more his determined resolution. She resolved to save him from the dangerous position. Taking him in her arms, she carried him, according to his wishes, to the country of Mitila, in the garden of mango-trees, and placed him on the very table-stone where his ancestors were wont to enjoy themselves with a numerous retinue. Phralaong immediately fell asleep. The daughter of Nats, having enjoined the Nat, guardian of the place, to watch over the prince, returned to her blissful seat.

On the very day that the vessel was wrecked the ruler of Mitila died, leaving one daughter, named Thiwalee. Previous to his giving up the ghost and ascending to the seats of Nats, the king had ordered his ministers into his presence, and enjoined on them to select for the husband of his daughter a man remarkable for the beauty and strength of his body, as well as by the acuteness and penetration of his mind. He was to be able to bend and unbend an enormous bow, a feat which the united efforts of a thousand soldiers could scarcely achieve, and find the place where he had concealed sixteen golden cups. On the seventh day after his death, the ministers and pounhas began to deliberate among themselves about the choice of a match worthy of the princess. Several competitors offered themselves for the hand of Thiwalee, but they were all rejected. At last, not knowing what to do, they resolved to leave to chance the solution of the difficulty. They sent out a charmed chariot, convinced that by the virtue inherent in it they would find out the fortunate man whose destinies were to be united to those of the princess. The chariot was sent out attended by soldiers, musicians, pounhas, and noblemen. It came straight forward to the mango-trees garden, and stopped by the side of the table-stone Phralaong was sleeping upon. The pounhas, on inspecting the hands and feet of the stranger, saw unmistakable signs foreshowing his elevation to the royal dignity. They awakened him by the sound of musical instruments, saluted him king, and begged of him to put on the royal dress, mount on the chariot, and proceed triumphantly to the royal city. He entered the palace through the eastern gate. Having been informed of the king's last intentions, he forthwith bent and unbent the bow, found out the sixteen golden cups, and was duly united to the beautiful and youthful Thiwalee. All the people showed signs of the greatest rejoicings; the rich made him all sorts of offerings; the pounhas in white costume, holding the sacred white shell, adorned with flowers and filled with water, with their bodies bent forward, poured respectfully the water, imploring blessings on the new monarch.

When the rejoicings were over, the king rewarded the pounha Pamaouka, who had been as a father to him during his exile. He applied himself to do as much good as he could in relieving the poor, and promoting the welfare of all. He delighted in mentioning to his courtiers his misfortune, and the great efforts he had made to extricate himself from difficulties. He praised the reward which attended generous efforts, and exhorted them never to flinch under difficulties, but always to exhibit a strong and unconquerable resolution under all trials, because it must sooner or later be crowned with success.

During the 7000 years that he reigned over Mitila with the queen Thiwalee, he faithfully practised the observances of the law, governed justly, fed the Rahans and Pitzega-buddhas, and gave abundant alms to the poor.

On the 10th month Thiwalee was delivered of a son,

whom they called Digaout. On a certain day, the king, having received from his gardener some mangoes full of flavour and beauty, wished to go to the garden to see the tree that yielded such delicious fruits. When he arrived at the place, he saw two mango-trees, one with a luxuriant foliage, but without fruits, the other loaded with fruits. The monarch approached the tree, riding his elephant, and plucked some mangoes, which he ate and found delicious. Thence he proceeded further to inspect the other parts of the extensive garden. The courtiers and the people that followed plucked fruits from the same tree, and did it with such eagerness that they left neither fruits nor leaves on the tree.

On his return the king was surprised to see the fruitful tree destitute of both leaves and fruits, whilst the barren one had a beautiful appearance. The monarch, after a lengthened dialogue with his courtiers, concluded as follows: "The riches of this world are never without enemies; he who possesses them resembles the fruitful mango-tree. We must look out for goods that excite neither envy, jealousy, nor other passions. The Rahans and Pitzega-buddhas alone possess such riches. I will take a lesson from the barren mango-tree. That I may cut off and eradicate the troubles, vexations, and anxieties of life, I will renounce everything and embrace the profession of Rahan."

With this idea strongly impressed on his mind, Dzanecka came back to his palace. He forthwith sent for the general of his troops, and directed him to place a strong guard in front of his apartment, and allow no one for four consecutive months to come into his presence, not even the queen, but only him who would bring his daily meal. He gave orders to his ministers to judge with impartiality, agreeably to the law. Having thus arranged everything, he withdrew alone to the upper apartment of his palace. Here follows a stanza in praise of the prince, who had separated from his queen, concubines, and all the pleasures and honours attending royalty.

Dzanecka alone began to meditate on the happiness of the life of pounhas and Pitzega-buddhas; he admired their poor diet, their zeal in practising the observances of the law, their earnest longings after the happiness of Neibban, their disengagement from the ties of passions, the state of inward peace and fixity which their souls enjoyed. In his enthusiasm he venerated them with a holy fervour, called them his masters and preceptors, and exclaimed: "Who will teach me to imitate their lives, and help me to become similar to them?" In ten stanzas Dzanecka reviews successively all that had belonged to him, his capital with its stately edifices, fine gates, the three walls and ditches, the beautiful and fertile country of Wintzearitz, the palace with its lofty domes and massive towers, the beautifully ornamented throne, the rich and magnificent royal dresses, the royal garden and tank, the elephants, horses, and chariots, the soldiers, the pounhas, the princes, his queen and concubines. He then concludes each stanza with the following words: "When shall I leave all these things, become poor, put on the humble habit of Rahans, and follow the same mode of a perfectly retired life?" With these and similar reflections Dzanecka endeavoured to sunder one after the other many threads of passions, to pull down successively the branches of the impure tree, until he could give a final stroke to the roots.

At the conclusion of four months' retirement, Dzanecka sent for a faithful servant, and directed him to procure for him the various articles of the dress of a Rahan. He had his head and beard shaved; put on the cherished habit, and placing a staff in his hand walked out of his apartments, and directed his course towards the gate, with the dignified deportment of a Rahan of sixty years profession.

Queen Thiwalee was tired of having been so long deprived of her husband's company. She summoned seven hundred of the handsomest damsels of the palace to go with her to the king, and by the efforts of their united charms entrap him in the net of passion and prevail upon him to come back to their society. When they ascended the stair-case, they met with Dzanecka in his new attire. None recognised him; but all paid him due reverence as some holy personage that had come to give instructions to the king. Having reached the apartment and seen the royal dress set aside, and the beautiful and long black hairs laid on one of the sofas, the queen and her attendants soon understood the sad and heart-rending intimation which these objects were designed to convey. She ran in all haste with all her retinue down the stairs and overtook the new Rahan at the moment he was crossing the outer gate of the palace. Every means that could be devised to make impression on the king's heart were resorted to by the queen and the damsels, in order to prevail upon him to forego his resolution. Tears, cries, wailings, striking of the breast, display of the most graceful and seducing forms, supplications, entreaties, were all used in vain; the new Rahan, unmoved and firm, continued his course, protesting that passions and concupiscence were dead in him, and that what could be said or done to engage him to change his resolution was in vain. During his progress towards the solitude of Himawonta, he was comforted and encouraged by the advice and instruction of two Rathees, who from their solitude flew through the air to witness the beautiful struggle between passions and virtue, and help him not to flinch before the repeated obstacles the queen put in his way, to retard, impede, and prevent the execution of his holy design. The names of these two instructors were Narada and Migalzein; they were clothed in the skins of panthers. They instructed him in the duties of his new calling, and exhorted him to root out of his heart with perseverance all passions, and in particular concupiscence and pride.

Comforted with such timely instructions, the new Rahan felt himself more than ever fixed in his resolution. On his way to the solitude, Dzanecka arrived one evening at the gates of a town called Daunu. He passed the night under a tree, at a distance from the queen and the crowd that followed her. On the morning he entered the town, and went, as usual, along the streets to beg his food. He happened to stop for a while at the shop of a man that was fabricating arrows. Dzanecka, seeing the workman shutting one eye and looking with the other to see if the shaft of the arrow was straight, asked him the reason of his doing so, as he would see better with both eyes than with one. The workman told him that it was not always good that each object in this world should have a match. "Should I," said he, "look on this shaft with both eyes, my sight, distracted by several objects, could not perceive the defects of the wood, &c., but by looking on it with only one eye the least irregularity is easily detected. When we have a work to perform, if there be two opposite wills in us, it cannot be regularly made. You have put on the habit of Rahan; you have apparently renounced the world; how is it that you are followed by such a large retinue of women and other attendants? It is impossible to attend well to the duties of your profession, and at the same time keep such a company." This cutting remark made a deep impression on Dzanecka. He had gone over a little distance, when he met a number of little girls playing together. One of them had a silver bangle on each hand, with one of gold on the right hand. When she agitated the right hand, the two bangles hitting each other produced a sound. Dzanecka, willing to try the wit of the little creature, asked her the reason why the movement of one hand produced a sound, whilst that of the other did not. She replied, "My left hand, that has but one bangle, is the image of the Rahans who ought to be alone. In this world, when an object has its match, some collision and noise inevitably result. How is it that you, who have put on the habit of Rahan, allow yourself to be followed by that woman who is still full of freshness and beauty? Is she your wife or sister? Should she be only your sister, it is not good that she should be with you. It is dangerous for Rahans to keep the company of women."

This sharp lecture, from the mouth of a little girl, produced a deep impression on our Rahan. He left the city. A large forest was in the vicinity: he resolved to part company with the queen at once. At the entrance he stopped awhile, and paused for a moment. There, on a sudden, stretching his arm, he broke the small branch of a tree, and showing it to Thiwalee he said, "Princess, you see this small branch; it can never be reunited to the stem it has been taken from. In like manner, it is impossible that I should ever go back with you." On hearing the fatal words the queen fainted. All her attendants crowded round her, to afford her some relief. Dzanecka himself, in the tumult and confusion that was going on, stole away with rapidity and disappeared in the forest. The queen was then carried back to Daunu by her attendants, whence they all returned to Mitila. Alone in the solitude, Phralaong enjoyed the sweets of perfect contemplation during a period of three thousand years. Thiwalee, on her part, resolved to renounce the world and follow the example of her husband. She became a Rahaness, in one of the royal gardens, during the same period of years, and subsequently migrated to one of the seats of Brahmas, called Brahma-parithitsa.

At the conclusion of the narrative Buddha added: "Mani-megala, the daughter of Nats, who saved me in the midst of the sea, is now my beloved fair disciple of the left, Oopalawon. The little girl who gave me such a wholesome instruction, at the gate of the town of Daunu, is now Kema, my fair disciple of the right. The Rathee Narada has since become my great disciple Thariputra, whose wisdom is second only to my own. The other Rathee Miga-dzein is now my disciple Maukalan, whose power for displaying wonders yields only to mine. The arrow-maker has since become Ananda, my faithful and dutiful attendant. Queen Thiwalee has become the Princess Yathaudara. As to Prince Dzanecka, he is now the Phra who is before you and addresses you, who is perfectly acquainted with all the laws and principles, and who is the teacher of men, Nats, and Brahmas."

REMARKS

ON

THE SITES AND NAMES OF THE PRINCIPAL PLACES MENTIONED IN THE LEGEND.

THE identification of the places mentioned in the course of the Life of Gaudama is certainly a great desideratum. This difficult and laborious task has been boldly undertaken by several government servants of both services. Great and important successes have attended their efforts. One of the most successful among them has been Major-General Cunningham, the archæological surveyor to the government of India. The sphere of his laborious and scientific researches has extended over north and south Behar, the cradle of Buddhism, and some parts of the Punjaub and Peshawar. Under his direction excavations have been made, inscriptions found and deciphered, the nature and dimensions of old ruined monuments correctly ascertained. In his valuable reports may be found important elements for reconstructing the history and geography of ancient India. He has been greatly assisted by the history of the voyages of the Chinese pilgrim, Hwen Thsang, who spent sixteen years in travelling throughout India, and visiting all the places rendered famous by the actions connected with the life of Buddha, and the spread of his doctrines and institutions. The voyage began in 629 and ended in 645 of the Christian era. The itinerary begins with the starting of the traveller from a city on the banks of the Hoang-ho. He shaped his course through the centre of Tartary, entered by the northern extremity of the plateau of Panin into what is called now Independent Tartary, visited Samarcand, where there were no Buddhists, but only fire worshippers. Thence he passed over to Balk, where he found religion in a flourishing condition. He ascended the mighty Hindu Kush mountains, penetrated into Cabul and Peshawar, crossed the Indus at Attock, and turning abruptly to the north, visited Oudiana, where he found dzedis and monasteries on the grandest and most magnificent scale, and came back to Attock, following the western bank of the Indus. He then proceeded through the Punjaub to Mathura, and minutely examined all the Buddhistic monuments to be found in the territories situated between the Ganges, the Gunduck, and Nepaul. He went to Benares, Pataliputra, and all the places in Magatha, or south Behar, where his religious curiosity could be satisfied. Thence he shaped his course in an eastern direction, and visited the whole of Bengal. He passed to Orissa, visited many places in Central India and a portion of the Upper Deccan. He went to Molwa and Guzerat, returned to Magatha, and began his homeward voyage. He recrossed the Indus at Attock, followed up the valley of the Cabul river, and with unheard-of difficulties and dangers passed over the Hindu Kush range. His route across Chinese Tartary led him back through Kashgar, Yarkand, and Khotan, to his native place.

It is a matter of surprise to see how acute in his observations, correct in his descriptions, and exact in his measurements, our pilgrim has been. With his book in hand, the above-named eminent archæologist was enabled, in many instances, to identify at once mere mounds of ruins, and satisfy himself that they were the remnants of the monuments described by our pilgrim. When he entertained any doubts in his mind, he had recourse to excavations, which, in most instances, demonstrated the perfect accuracy of Hwen Thsang.

Nearly two hundred years previous to the voyage of Hwen Thsang, another Chinese pilgrim named Fa-hian had undertaken a similar journey. Impelled by a purely religious zeal, he came to India for the sole purpose of visiting the places rendered famous and venerable by the birth, life, doings, and death of Foe, the same personage who is known in these parts under the name Buddha Gaudama. His object was also to make a complete collection of all the religious books acknowledged as genuine in India, and carry them with him to China. The errand of Hwen Thsang had a similar object.

Our worthy traveller, according to his account, passed through Southern Thibet, Little Tartary, and visited successively Cabul, Cashmere, Candaḥar, and the Punjaub. Following a nearly south-eastern direction, he reached Mathura on the Upper Jumna, crossed the Ganges at Kanouj, at the confluence of the Kali with that river, travelled almost in an eastern direction through Oude, and crossed the Gogra near the Fyzabad. Keeping close to the eastern bank of that stream, he struck in a slightly northern direction, passing the Rapti south of Goruckpore, and followed the same course, nearly to the western bank of the Gunduck. From thence he shaped his course in a south-easterly direction, parallel to the course of that river, which he crossed a little higher up the place where it empties into the Ganges. Following then a southern direction, he crossed the Ganges near the place where the city of Patna is now. From thence our pilgrim travelled in a south-easterly direction, crossed successively the Morhar and the Fulgo, examined all the places in the neighbourhood, south and south-west of Behar, which are so celebrated in Buddhistic annals. After having spent three years in India, busy in mastering the Pali language and collecting copies of the religious works, he then embarked on the Ganges. Near its mouth he went on board of a ship bound to Ceylon. After having visited that celebrated island, Fa-hian sailed in the direction of the Malayan Archipelago, called at Java, and safely arrived at his country, after having performed one of the most extraordinary and difficult journeys any man could have undertaken in those ancient times. It was in the beginning of the fifth century that this feat was performed in the space of more than seven years. He spent three years in India, and two at Ceylon.

The Chinese original of Fa-Hian has been translated into French by A. Remusat. The English version from the French is accompanied by the annotations of Remusat and those of other celebrated Orientalists. The book of Hwen Thsang has been translated by M. Julien. For the loan of these two works the writer is indebted to the ever-obliging kindness of the worthy and learned Chief Commissioner of British Burma, Col. A. P. Phayre. From these works we have extracted the above and following particulars.

1. The name given by northern Buddhists to Buddha is Thakiamuni, which means the religious of the Thakia family. He belonged to the Kshatria, or the warriors' caste. The name Gaudama, according to the opinion of the late E. Burnouf, is the name of the religious instructor of his family, which members of families of that caste often adopted. This instructor might have been a descendant of the celebrated philosopher Gotama, mentioned in certain writings, but distinct from our Buddha.

2. Kapila, or Kapilawot, the birthplace of Buddha, was situated on the left bank of the Gogra, straight north of Benares.

It was a heap of ruins when Fa-Hian visited it, and the country almost a desert. Some are of opinion that it was situated near the mountains that separate Nepaul from Goruckpore, on the river Rohini, a mountain stream, feeder of the Rapti. But this assertion has very few supporters, and appears improbable.

3. The river Anauma cannot be the Amanat in Behar, south of Patna. It is probably one of the feeders of the Gogra, and to be met with half-way between Kapila and Radzagio, the site of which city, as will be subsequently seen, lies close to modern Behar. The legend bears out this supposition. Buddha travelled thirty youdzanas from Kapila to the river Anauma, thence thirty to Radzagio. The youdzana of those times in Magatha is supposed to have been equal probably to seven miles.

4. Oorouwela was one of the mountains famous for the number of the hermits that withdrew thither for the purpose of meditation. It is not far from Gaya Buddha.

5. The river Neritzara, in Mongol, Nirandzara, is a considerable stream flowing from the south-west. It unites with the Monah and forms the Fulgo.

6. Baranathee is beyond doubt the famous city of Benares. The Burmans call it by name of Baranathee, or rather Varanasi. The town is so named from its situation between the small river Varana and the Asi, a mere brook. The solitude of Migadawon, whither Buddha went to preach the law to the five Rahans that had served him during the six years of mortification which he spent in the forest of Oorouwela, lies in its vicinity. Benares is famous in the Buddhistic annals, because in its neighbourhood the law of the wheel, or rather the super-excellent law of the four sublime truths, was announced for the first time. Migadawon means the deer-forest. It lies three and a half miles from Benares in a northern direction. It is said that, after having travelled nine miles from the Bodi tree, Buddha had to go over a distance of eighteen youdzanas ere he reached Benares, making a total of about 120 miles.

7. Radzagio, or Radzagihra, was the capital of Magatha or South Behar. Its situation is well ascertained. Its ruins have been minutely described by several travellers. It was situated on the left bank of the same small river as Behar, but a few miles south of that place. The mountains or peaks surrounding that ancient city are full of

caves, tenanted in former ages by Buddhist ascetics. The mountain Gayathitha, where Buddha preached his famous sermon, lies in the neighbourhood. It is perhaps the same as the Gridrakuta, or the Vulture's Peak.

8. The Buddhist annals often mention the country of the middle or Mitzima-desa. It comprised the countries of Mathura, Kosala, Kapila, Wethalee, and Magatha; that is to say, the provinces of Agra, Delhi, Oude, and South Behar.

Magatha, south of the Ganges, had for capital at first Radzagio, until Kalathoka, a hundred years after the death of Gaudama, transferred the seat of his empire to Patali-putra, or Palibothra. The celebrated Weloowon monastery was situated in the neighbourhood of Radzagio, and was offered to Buddha by King Pimpathara, the ruler of that country.

9. Kosala is the same as the kingdom of Ayodya, now called Oude. Thawattie, or Crawastu, was the capital of a district of that country. It was situated nearly at the same place where at present stands the modern town of Fyzabad. According to the legend, the distance from Radzagio to Thawattie is forty-five youdzanas of about seven miles. Twelve hundred paces from that city was to be met the renowned monastery of Dzetawon, or the grove of the victorious. Many ruins that have been visited and examined leave no doubt regarding the certain position of Thawattie.

10. Thing-ka-tha, or Tsam-pa-tha, lies in an eastern direction between Mathura and Kanouj, near the site occupied by the town of Ferruckabad. Captain A. Cunningham has met with the ruins of that place in the village of Samkassa, on the left bank of the Kalinadi, twelve cos from Ferrukabad. According to a popular tradition, it was destroyed in 1183 by the King of Kanouj, at the instigation of the Brahmins, who endeavoured by every means in their power to sweep all the remnants of Buddhism from those parts of the peninsula. It was in that

place that Buddha arrived on his return from the seats of Nats, whither he had gone to preach the law to his mother. According to the legend, the distance from Thawattie to Thing-ka-tha is thirty youdzanas in a westerly direction. Fa-Hian says that he saw in one of the temples of that place the ladder Buddha had used when he came down from the seats of Nats.

11. The village of Patali is the very place where was subsequently established the renowned city of Patalibothra, capital of Magatha. The place had reached the height of its glory when Megasthenes, the ambassador of Seleucus, visited it in the reign of Chandragupta. In the time of Buddha it was but an insignificant place. There was, however, a sort of fort to arrest the inroads of some troublesome neighbours. Buddha, when he passed through that place, predicted that it would become a flourishing town. The prediction begun to have its accomplishment one hundred years after his death, when King Kalathoka left Radzagio, and removed the seat of his empire to Palibothra, near the place where the modern city of Patna stands.

12. The town of Wethalie is supposed to have stood north of Patna on the Gunduck, not far from the place where that river joins the Ganges. The large village of Besarh, twenty miles north of Hajipur, occupies a portion of the place on which stood Wethalie. In the seventh century Buddhism was there on its decline; false doctrines, as says one of the Chinese pilgrims, were much prevailing. Nothing was to be seen at that time but a ruined town and many monasteries, almost deserted, and also falling into decay. Many signs of ancient ruins are also to be met with between Besarh and Bakra; they belong to the same city, which was both populous and wealthy. Its circumference was about twelve miles, including the two modern places of Bakra and Besarh. All the mounds of ruins have been carefully searched and described by A. Cunningham, and the sites of ancient tanks exactly laid down. There

is a curious episode in the legend connected with the name of Wethalie. A courtezan, who, despite her dishonourable calling, occupied a brilliant position in the country, courted the favour of feeding Buddha with all his followers. The latter accepted her invitation, and received a beautiful grove, which she presented to him and to the assembly. It does not appear that her avocation was looked upon as a disgraceful one. It is probable that persons of this description were as much for the intellectual as for the sensual enjoyments of their visitors. There existed in Greece and at Rome something similar to what is here alluded to. According to Plutarch, Aspasia at Athens was courted by Pericles on account of her high literary attainments and political abilities. Socrates visited her sometimes in company with his disciples. Visitors took occasionally their wives to her place, for the purpose of enjoying the charms of her highly refined and instructive conversation. The same philosophical biographer does not scruple to quote sometimes the sayings of the celebrated Roman courtesan, named Flora.

13. Nala or Nalanda was a Brahmin village about seven miles north of Radzagio. It was the birthplace of the great disciple Thariputra. It seems that there was there a sort of Academia, whither the learned of Radzagio resorted to discourse on moral and philosophical subjects. The magnificent ruins, which subsist up to this day in that locality, have been minutely examined, measured, and described by several visitors. The great temple must, in the opinion of A. Cunningham, have been built in the sixth century of our era.

14. Kootheinaron is the place in the neighbourhood of which Buddha entered into the state of Neibban, or died. Some antiquarians, laying much stress on the name of a village up to this day called Kushia, have placed the position of Kootheinaron on the road between Betiah and Goruckpore. On that spot is to be seen a pyramidical-looking mound of bricks, over which spreads a large banyan

tree. But, from the narrative of the legend, we must look for the site of Kootheinaron nearer to the river Higniarati or Gunduck, since the spot where Gaudama died was near to the city, and is described as surrounded on three sides by the river. Kootheinaron was situated a little north or north-west of Betiah, on or near the banks of the Gunduck. There too ruins are to be seen, which doubtless will prove to be those of Kootheinaron. The name may have subsequently migrated to the locality above mentioned.

15. Papilawana, the capital of the Mauria princes, was situated between the Rapti and the Gunduck, nearly east of Goruckpore. South of that place Fa-Hian visited the dzedi of the coals. The Mauria princes, agreeably to the text of the legend, having come too late for sharing in the partition of the relics, took with them the coals that remained after the cremation of Buddha's remains, carried them into their country, and built a dzedi over them. It was not far from that place that the Brahmin Dauna built another dzedi over the vessel that had contained Buddha's relics.

16. The village of Rama is the same as the Ramaganio of the Cingalese collection. The two Chinese pilgrims in their relations call that place Lan-mo. Can it be that the modern Ramnagar is indicative of the ancient Ramaganio? At all events we would not be far from the truth if we place it between the Gogra and the Rapti, but nearer to the latter, almost due west of Goruckpore.

17. The Pawa town is supposed by A. Cunningham to have occupied the same site as the large village of Padarawana, twelve miles to the west of the river Gunduck, and forty miles north-north-east of Goruckpore. A large mound of more than 200 feet in length by 120 in breadth exists in that locality. From the excavations made on the place, it is supposed that there was a courtyard, with cells for monks, on each side, the centre being, as was often the case, occupied by a dzedi. The people of Pawa obtained one-eighth of the relics, after the cremation of Buddha's remains, and built one dzedi over them.

18. Kapilawot, or Kapilawastu, was situated between Fyzabad and Goruckpore, but a little nearer to the latter place. It was on or near the banks of the Gogra. The small river Rohini formed the boundary between the territory of Ḳapilawot and that of Kaulia.

19. Gaya and Buddha-Gaya are two distinct places. The first is well known as the town of Gaya. The second lies six miles southward, and is famous as the locality of the Pipal or Bodi tree, under which Gaudama obtained the Buddhahood. A tree of the same description is still to be seen on the same spot. The present one was in full vigour in 1811, when Dr. Buchanan saw it. He describes it as not being more than a hundred years old. A. Cunningham says that it is now much decayed. One large stem with three branches on the westward side are still green; but the other branches are barkless and rotten. Hwen Thsang, in his itinerary, speaks of an early renewal of that tree by King Purna Varmma, after its destruction by King Sasangka, who, with a true Brahminical and inimical feeling, dug up the very ground on which it had stood, and moistened the earth with sugar-cane juice, to prevent its renewal. The same eminent archæologist describes a massive brick temple, standing east of the Bodi tree, and with great plausibility maintains that it is the same which has been described by the above-named Chinese pilgrim. As Fa-Hian is silent respecting that temple, A. Cunningham concludes that it was erected during the sixth century of the Christian era, when Buddhism, under the favour of King Amara-sinha and some of his successors regained a vigorous ascendancy at least in Magatha. It is probable that all the temples, the ruins of which have been examined at Buddha-Gaya, Nalanda, and Behar, having a similarity in architectural plans and ornaments, were erected during the sixth and a part of the seventh century of our era. The inference therefrom is that Buddhism was flourishing in Magatha at that period. Hwen Thsang, who has visited and described those monu-

ments in or about 625, speaks of them in the highest terms. How long lasted the prosperous days of Buddhism in those parts? It is difficult to state with any degree of accuracy. But it seems probable that it maintained itself in a satisfactory condition until the beginning of the tenth century. It had then to give way before the irresistible and triumphant ascendancy of Brahminism.

To the south-east of the great temple is a small tank which is probably that of the Naga, who protected Buddha during one of the several stations that he made round the Bodi tree.

20. Anawadat is the name of a lake famous in Buddhist sacred history. Its etymological meaning is, agreeably to some savans, exempt of tumult, and, according to others, not brightened. This last appellation is owing probably to the high peaks that surround it and prevent its being brightened by the rays of the sun. This is certainly the famous and extensive lake, which covers a portion of the high table-land of Pamir. It has been visited and described by Lieutenant Wood. What he states from a careful observation on the spot agrees well with what is found in the itineraries of the Chinese travellers. From that high plateau which embosoms the lake flows in an eastern direction one of those small streams that form the river Ganges; whilst, in an opposite direction, the Oxus, issuing from the western slope, shapes its course nearly towards the west.

21. Udiana is a country the position of which is fixed on the banks of the Indus, between Cabul and Cashmere, west of the latter country. Gandara is, it appears, the country called Candahar by the Mussulmans, lying between the Swat and the Indus. The Burmese author mentions always Kashmera along with Gandara. This would indicate that the two places are in the vicinity of each other, and that they formed primitively one and the same state. Yaunaka is perhaps the peninsula of Guzerat. But the writer entertains serious doubts on this subject.

It might be the countries situated west of the Hindu Kush, that is to say, the ancient Bactriana. The Burmese author states that Yaunaka was inhabited by a people call Pantsays. What people were they? Is it an allusion to the Greeks that had settled in Bactriana? It is not without interest to hear our Chinese traveller stating that religion was flourishing in the above-mentioned countries, whilst in the Punjaub he met with religious with whom he declined holding intercourse, and of whom he speaks in rather unfavourable terms. Hence we may conclude that heretical opinions were then prevailing in that country, and that doctrines at variance with those of Buddha had already taken a deep root, and in their growth almost choked genuine Buddhism, if it had ever been the prevailing creed in the land of the five rivers.

22. On his way down the Ganges, our pilgrim does not appear to have left his boat for any considerable time; he contents himself with mentioning a fact that to some may appear somewhat doubtful, viz., the flourishing condition of the Buddhist religion as far as the neighbourhood of the present metropolis of India. He speaks of the kingdom of Champa. Campapuri, or Karnapura, was the capital of that state. It was situated on the site of the present Bhagulpore, or not far from it. Thence Fa-Hian came to the state of Tamaralipti. The town which bore that name, is the modern Tumlook, on the right bank of the Hoogly, not far from Calcutta. It was at that port that he embarked on board of a ship bound to Ceylon. Tamaralipti must have been a famous sea-port several centuries before Fa-Hian's days. We are informed that Maheinda and his companions, who were appointed to proceed to Ceylon to preach Buddhism to the people of that island, embarked at the same place.

THE SEVEN WAYS TO NEIBBAN.

THIS is an abridgment of all the principles that constitute the system of Buddhism. In the LEGEND OF BUDDHA the reader has become acquainted with the life of the founder of Buddhism, the establishment of his religion, and the promulgation of his chief doctrine. In the following pages he will find compressed within narrow limits the several observances to be attended to in order to reach the goal of quiescence. As it is chiefly and principally by the help of meditation and contemplation that such a point can ever be attained, the reader must be prepared to wade up to his very chin in the somewhat muddy waters of metaphysics if he has a wish to penetrate into the very sanctuary of Buddhism.

To encourage the reader, and console him in the midst of his fatiguing journey through such dreary tracts, the writer would remind him that he has first borne up the fatigues of such a journey, and that, impelled by friendly feelings, he has endeavoured to smooth the rugged path in behalf of those that would follow him on the same errand. How far he has succeeded in his well-meant efforts he will not presume to state. But he will say this much, that if his success be commensurate with his exertions he may entertain a well-founded hope that he will not be altogether disappointed in his anticipation, and feel somewhat confident that he has afforded to the uninitiated some help to go over the difficult ground of metaphysics.

Following, in this instance, the line of conduct he has adopted through the foregoing pages of this book, the writer will allow the Buddhist author to speak for himself and explain his own views on the different subjects under consideration. His sole aim will ever be to convey as faithfully and as succinctly as possible the meaning of the original he has under his eyes. The task, however simple it may appear, is far from being an easy one, as the Burmese are utterly incapable of fully understanding the metaphysical portion of their religious system. Their ignorance is calculated to render even more obscure what is *per se* almost beyond the range of comprehension, because they must have frequently put an erroneous interpretation on many Pali words, the meaning of which is far from being accurately determined.

Our Buddhist doctor begins his work with enumerating the advantages to be derived from a serious and constant application to the earnest study of these seven ways. "Such an exercise," says he, "has the virtue to free us from all evils; it expands the intelligence in the highest degree, and leads straight to Neibban. Man, through it, is delivered from all errors, is happy, and becomes during his life an honour to the holy religion of Buddha."

The various subjects he intends to treat of in this work are arranged under seven heads, which are laid down in his own original way as follows:—The observance of the precepts and the practice of meditation are the twofold foundation of the spiritual edifice. The consideration of the nature and form of matter shall be the right foot of the sage; the investigation about the causes and principles of living beings shall be as his left foot; the application of the mind to find out the four high-roads to perfection, and the obtaining the freedom from all passions, shall be as his right and left hands; and the possession of the perfect science or knowledge shall be as his head. The happy man who shall have reached so far will be certain to obtain the deliverance.

This summary is thus divided by our guide into seven distinct parts, which will be condensed into six articles.

It is as well to add that this work, an abridged translation of which is now set before the reader, was composed at first in the Siamese language at Bangkok, and has been subsequently translated into Burmese. We find, therefore, that all the principles expounded throughout are received as genuine on the banks of the Irrawaddy as well as on those of the Meinam, and may be looked upon as a faithful exposition of the highest tenets of Buddhism, such as they are held in both countries. This observation confirms a notion which has been denied by many, viz., that the chief doctrines of Buddhism are pretty nearly the same in all the places where it has become the dominant creed. The discrepancies to be met here and there relate principally to practices and observances which present to the eyes of the observer an infinite variety of hues and forms. When Buddhism was established in several countries, it did not destroy many observances and practices that were found deeply engrafted on the customs and manners of the people; it tolerated them, and made with them a tacit compromise. As, for instance, the worship of Nats existed among the tribes of the Irrawaddy valley long before the introduction of Buddhism. Most of the superstitious rites now prevailing in Burmah originate from that belief. With the Chinese the worship of ancestors continues to subsist side by side with Buddhism, though the latter creed has nothing to do with it. In Nepaul and at Ceylon, Hindu superstitions obtrude themselves on the view of the observer to such an extent that it is not easy to state which of the two creeds obtains the preference.

ARTICLE I.

OF THE PRECEPTS.

Our author, in a truly philosophical spirit, at first puts to himself the three following questions: What is the origin of the law? What is man, the subject of the law? What is the individual who is the promulgator of the law? The three questions he answers in the following manner: 1st. All that exists is divided into two distinct parts, the things which are liable to change and obey the principle of mutability, such as matter, its modifications, and all beings which have a cause;[1] and those which are eternal and immutable, that is to say, the precepts of the law and Neibban. These have neither author nor cause; they are self-existing, eternal, and placed far beyond the reach of

---

[1] The distinction alluded to by our author is a most important one. What does he mean when he states that all things in this world obey the principle of mutability, and are liable to perpetual changes and modifications, and that they have a cause? One would be tempted to believe that the Buddhists admit of a first cause. But such is not the case. To understand such a language coming from a Buddhist's mouth, we must bear in mind the theory of the twelve Nidanas, or causes and effects. Each of the Nidanas is an effect relatively to the preceding one, and a cause to the following one. All existing beings are, relatively to each other, effects and causes. All undergo the irresistible influence of mutability and change. The beings that reside in the seats of Brahma are not beyond the reach of that influence, not even those who dwell in the four immaterial seats.

Are there things which are fixedly and everlastingly the same, upon which no change, no vicissitude can ever act? There is the law, there is the state of Neibban. The law is the expression of truth, which is reality, in contradistinction to the unreality of the visible world. The essence of the law is contained in the four sublime truths, which are emphatically called the Law of the Wheel. They are the declaration of the true state and condition of all beings; they proclaim the necessity of putting an end to such a miserable state of things, and point out the sure means of freeing oneself from the miseries attending existence. These truths are eternal, insomuch that what they proclaim has ever been true in all the worlds that have preceded the present one, since they always resemble each other, and will ever be equally true during the endless series of worlds that will follow. In this sense the law, in the opinion of Buddhists, being the declaration of truth, or of what is, must be eternal, as truth itself is everlasting. The state of Neibban, in contradistinction to that of existence such as we comprehend it, is likewise a thing which never changes, since it is the end of changes. It remains always the same; it is the opposite of existence. What is then called here everlasting, or eternal, is, in the opinion of Buddhists, but the things that are conceived as subsisting abstractively *per se*, and never affected by the great principle of mutability that pervades all beings. To sum up the whole in a few words, the science which points out the means of coming out of the whirlpool of existences, and the being out of that circle, such are the two things which are always the same, never undergo any change, and are eternal.

the influence that causes mutability. 2d. As to the publisher of the law, Buddha, he is a mere man, who during myriads of centuries has accumulated merits on merits, until he has obtained the Neibban of Kiletha, or the deliverance from all passions. From that moment till his death this eminent personage is constituted the master of religion and the doctor of the law. Owing to his perfect science he finds out and discovers all the precepts that constitute the body of the law. Impelled by his matchless benevolence towards all beings, he promulgates them for the salvation of all. He is not the inventor of those precepts; he merely discovers them by the power of the supreme intelligence, in the same manner as we perceive clearly during the night, by the help of a light, objects hitherto wrapped in utter darkness. 3d. Man, who is to be subjected to the observance of the law, is distinguished by the following characteristics. He possesses more knowledge than the animals and other beings, except the Nats and Brahmas; his intelligence and thoughts reach farther than those of other beings; he is capable of reflecting, comparing, drawing inferences, and observing freely the rules of life;[2] despite the allurement of his passions, he can free himself from the three great passions, concupiscence, anger, and ignorance; finally, he is a descendant from those Brahmas who, in the beginning of this world, came from their seat,

[2] In the definition of man which is given by the Buddhist author, we find the words intelligence, capacity for reflecting, comparing and drawing inferences, &c. He who is not familiar with the revolting materialist doctrines of Buddhism would be tempted to believe that they admit of a soul or spiritual principle subsisting in man. But such is not the case. The faculty for performing all the functions which we rightly attribute to the soul resides in the sixth sense, called *mano*, or the heart, or the knowing principle. But this sense, in their opinion, is as material as the eye, the ear, and the other senses. It is delightful to the Christian reader to find in the midst of a heap of rubbish and fables a few fragments of the primitive revelation. We see man coming from a noble origin, appearing in this world with the most glorious privileges, which he forfeits by eating the rice called Tsale, which produced on his being the same destructive effects which the eating of the forbidden fruit caused on our first parents in the garden of Eden.

lived on earth, and, by their eating the rice *Tsale*, lost all their glorious privileges, and became beings similar to those who are known to us under the denomination of men.

The great end to be aimed at in the observance of the precepts of the law and the exercise of meditation, is the obtaining of a state of complete indifference to all things. The state of indifference alluded to does not consist in a stupid carelessness about the things of this world. It is the result of a knowledge acquired with much labour and pain. The wise man who has possessed himself of such science is no longer liable to the influence of that vulgar illusion which makes people believe in the real existence of things that have no reality about them, but subsist only on an ephemeral basis, which incessantly changes and finally vanishes away. He sees things as they truly are. He is full of contempt for things which are at best a mere illusion. This contempt generates a complete indifference for all that exists, even for his own being. He longs for the moment when it shall be given to him to cast away his own body, that he may no longer move within the circle of endless and miserable forms of existence. In this sense must be understood the state of perfect quietism or indifference, which is the last stage the wise man may reach by the help of the science he possesses. The religious of the Brahminical creed have professed the same indifference for all the accidents of life. Hence our Buddha, when he became a perfected being, looked on the wicked Dewadat with the same feelings as he did on the great Maia, his mother. Numberless Rathees or anchorites have ever been eulogised for having allowed themselves to be devoured by ferocious beasts or bit by venomous snakes, rather than offer the least resistance that could exhibit a sign of non-indifference. Entire was their unconcern towards their very body, which they knew well is, as everything else, a compound of the four elements, a mere illusion, totally distinct from self.

Five commandments constitute the very basis whereupon stand all morals, and are obligatory on all men without exception. They include five prohibitions. (It is not a little surprising that the five precepts obligatory on all men, are merely five prohibitions designed not to teach men what they have to do, but warning them not to do such things as are interdicted to them. This supposes that man is prone to do certain acts which are sinful. The Buddhist law of the five precepts forbids him to yield to such propensities, but it does not teach him particular duties to perform. It does not elevate man above his original level, but it aims at preventing him from falling lower.) The five prohibitions are: Not to destroy the life of any being; not to steal; not to commit adultery; not to tell lies; not to drink any intoxicating liquors or beverages.

Our author seems to be a perfect master in casuistry, as he shows the greatest nicety and exactness in explaining all the requisite conditions that constitute a trespassing of those precepts. We will give here but a few samples of his uncommon proficiency in this science. As regards the first prohibition, he says, five things are necessary to constitute an offence against the first commandment, viz., a being that has life, the intention and will of killing that being, an act which is capable of inflicting death, and the loss of life of that being consequent on the inflicting of that action. Should but one of these conditions be wanting, the sin could not be said to have taken place, and therefore no complete trespassing of the first prohibition.

Again, as regards the second precept, five circumstances or conditions are necessary to constitute a trespassing, viz., an object belonging to another person, who neither by words nor signs showed any intention to part with it; the knowing that the owner intends to keep possession of it; having the actual intention to take away secretly or forcibly that object; an effort to become possessed of the thing by deceiving, injuring, or by mal-practices causing the owner or keeper of the thing to fall asleep; and, finally, removing the thing from its place, however short may be the distance, should it be but that of the length of a hair of the head.

For the infraction of the third precept the following conditions are required : the intention and will of sinning with any person of another sex, which comes within the denomination of Akamani-jathan, that is to say, persons whom it is forbidden to touch ; acting up to that intention and the consummating of such an act. Women that fall under the above denomination are divided into twenty classes. The eight first classes include those that are under the guardianship of their parents or relatives ; the ninth class comprises those affianced before they be of age ; the tenth, those reserved for the king. Within the ten other classes come all those who, owing to their having been slaves, or from any other cause, have become concubines to their masters, or married their seducers, &c.

The fourth prohibition extends not only to lies, but likewise to slander, coarse and abusive expressions, and vain and useless words. The four following conditions constitute a lie, viz., saying a thing that is untrue ; the intention of saying such a thing ; making manifest such an intention by saying the thing ; and some one's hearing and clearly understanding the thing that is uttered. That the sin of medisance may be said to exist, it is required that the author of it should speak with the intention of causing parties to hate each other or quarrel with each other, and that the words spoken to that end should be heard and understood by the parties alluded to.

The fifth precept forbids the drinking of Sura and Meria, that is to say, of distilled liquors and of intoxicating juices extracted from fruits and flowers. The mere act of putting the liquor in the mouth does not constitute a sin ; the swallowing of it is implied.

Besides these five general precepts, obligatory on all the faithful without exception, there are three other precepts, or rather counsels, that are strongly recommended to the

Upasakas, or pious laymen. They are designed as barriers against the great propensity inherent in nature which causes men to exceed in all that is used, through the senses of taste, hearing, seeing, smelling, and feeling. They are so many means that help to obtain a sober moderation in the daily use of the things of the world.

The first counsel regulates all that regards eating. It forbids using any comestible from noon to daybreak of the following morning. The second interdicts the assisting at plays, comedies, and the use of flowers and essences with the intention of fondly handling and smelling them. The third prescribes the form and size of beds, which ought never to be more than one cubit high, plain and without ornaments. The use of mattresses and pillows, filled with cotton or other soft substances, is positively prohibited. The very intention of lying upon these enervating superfluities, and *a fortiori* reclining on them, constitutes the breaking of such a command.

These three latter precepts are to be observed chiefly in the following days, on the 5th, 8th, 14th, and 15th of the waxing moon, and on the 5th, 8th, and 14th of the waning moon, as well as on the new moon. The pious Upasakas sometimes observe them during the three consecutive months of the season of Lent.

In the opinion of our author those men and women are deserving of the respectable title of Upasakas who have the greatest respect for and entertain a pious affection towards the three precious things, Buddha, the law, and the assembly of the perfect. They must ever view them as the haven of salvation and the securest asylums. They must be ready to sacrifice everything, their very life, for the sake of these three perfect things. During their lifetime, under all circumstances, they must aim at following scrupulously the instructions of Buddha, such as they are embodied in the law and preached by the Rahans.

Five offences disqualify a man for the honourable title of Upasaka, viz., the want of belief and confidence in the three precious things, the non-observance of the eight precepts, the believing in lucky and unlucky days,[3] or in good and bad fortune, the belief in omens and signs, and keeping company with the impious, who have no faith in Buddha.

We now come to the rules which are prescribed to all the Buddhist religious. They are 227 in number, and are found in a book called Patimauk. This book is the *vade mecum* of all religious. They study it and often learn it by heart. On certain days of each month the religious assemble in the Thein. The Patimauk is then read, explained, and commented upon by one of the elders of the fraternity. It is an abridgment of the Wini, the great book of discipline. It teaches the various rules respecting the four articles offered by the faithful to the religious; that is to say, vestments, food, mats, and the ingredients for mastication. These rules likewise regulate all that relates to the mode of making prayers, devotions, walking, sitting, reclining, travelling, &c. Everything is described with a minute particularity.

Here, if any interest could be awakened, would be the place to enter into the system of casuistry carried by Buddhist religious to a point of nicety and refinement

---

[3] Buddhists lay the greatest stress on the belief in the three precious things. It is the foundation on which rests the whole spiritual edifice. But it is somewhat extraordinary to see that the superstition of believing in lucky and unlucky days, in good and bad luck, is openly condemned, and entails upon him who is addicted to it the severest penalty. Though such childish belief is so exceedingly common in Burmah that it influences man in his daily and hourly affairs, yet we must admit that it is opposed to the tenets of strict Buddhism. There can never be any good or bad luck in the opinion of him who has faith in the influence of merits and demerits. There is no other agent in this world but that one; it is it alone that brings in and regulates all the accidents which attend the life of man. Such is indeed the theory of the true Buddhist. But how widely differs the practice from the theory? He who has lived for some time in a Buddhist country, and made himself acquainted with the intimate habits of the people, will soon discover that superstitious ideas, and, as a necessary consequence, superstitious practices, are the spring and prime mover of all actions from morning to night. In this respect, Buddhist monks differ not from the laity; nay, they are often seen as the leaders of the people in the performance of rites at variance with the tenets of their creed.

truly astonishing. Suffice it to state that they have gone over the boundless field of speculative conjectures respecting all the possible ways of fulfilling or trespassing the precepts and regulations that concern the body of religious.

Every law and precept must have a sanction. This essential requisite is not wanting in the Buddhist system. Let us examine in what consists the reward attending a regular and correct observance of the precepts, and what is the punishment inflicted on the transgressors of these ordinances. As usual, we will follow our author and allow him to make known his own opinions on this important subject. It is often inquired of us, says he, why some individuals live here during many years, whilst others appear but for a short time on the scene of this world. The reason of the difference in the respective condition of these persons is obvious and evident. The first, during their former existence, have faithfully observed the first command and refrained from killing beings, hence their long life; the second, on the contrary, have been guilty of some trespassings of this precept, and therefore the influence of their former crimes causes the shortness of their life. In a similar manner we account for all the differences that exist in the conditions of all beings. The observance or trespassing of one or several precepts creates the positions of happiness and unhappiness, of riches and poverty, of beauty and. ugliness, that chequer the lives and positions of mortals in this world.

In addition to the rewards bestowed immediately in this world, there are the six seats of Nats, where all sorts of recompenses are allotted, during immense periods, to those who have correctly attended to the ordinances of the law. There are likewise places of punishment in the several hells, reserved to the transgressors of the precepts. The conditions of animal, Athoorikes and Preittas, are other states of punishment.

A lengthened account of all that relates to the blissful

regions of Nats and the gloomy abodes of hell is found in one of the great Dzats, or accounts of the former existences of Gaudama, given by himself to his disciples, when he was a prince under the name of Nemi. The writer has read and partly translated this work, which delightfully reminded him of the fine episodes on similar subjects he had read in the sixth book of the Æneid. The wildest, most fertile, and inventive imagination seems to have exhausted its descriptive powers, on the one hand, in multiplying the pleasures enjoyed in the seats of Nats, and beautifying and adorning those delightful regions; and, on the other, in representing with a dark and bloody pencil the frightful picture of the numberless and horrid torments of the regions of desolation, despair, and agony.

All that is so abundantly related of the fortunate abodes of Nats in their sacred writings supplies the Buddhist religious with agreeable and inexhaustible topics of sermons which they deliver to their hearers, to excite them more effectually to bestow on them abundant alms. The credulous hearers are always told that the most conspicuous places in those regions are allotted to those who have distinguished themselves by their great liberalities. We think it idle and superfluous, uninteresting and fatiguing to repeat those fabulous accounts of the seats of Nats and abodes of hell, as given at great length by Buddhist authors. The only particulars deserving to be attended to are these: the reward is always proportionate to the sum of merits, and punishment to that of demerit. There is no eternity of reward or of punishment.[4]

[4] This is a consequence of the axiom established by our author, viz., that the principle of mutability pervades all the beings which reside in the thirty-one seats allotted to them. It cannot be supposed for a moment, according to Buddhists, that a being, whatever may be the amount of his merits and demerits, can ever be placed without the pale of the influence of his good or bad deeds. It accompanies him in all positions, and causes the vicissitudes that attend his existence. It works upon him in hell, as well as on earth, and in the seats of Nats and Brahmas. Fixity is to be found nowhere except in going out of the circle of existences, that is to say in Neibban. When we speak of existence in a Buddhistic

This first article shall be concluded by an important remark bearing upon the system under consideration. The seats of happiness, as already mentioned, are divided into two great classes; the one including the superior, and the other the inferior seats. The latter are the six seats of Nats, and are tenanted by beings as yet under the influence of concupiscence and other passions. Those who observe the five general precepts have placed, and, as it were, established themselves on the basis whereupon stands perfection, but not yet in perfection itself; they have just crossed the threshold thereof. They are as yet imperfect; but they have prepared themselves for entering the way that leads towards perfection; that is to say, meditation, or the science of Dzan. The very reward enjoyed in those seats is, therefore, as yet an imperfection. The superior seats can only be reached by those who apply themselves to mental exercises. These exercises are the real foundation of the lofty structure of perfection and the high-road to it.

---

sense, we mean *a state of being* in any conceivable form or situation or place. Fixity in the enjoyment of reward or in the undergoing of punishment is a contradiction with the first principle of Buddhism. The awarder of reward or punishment is the above-named influence, which proceeds from the actions performed, and in its turn allots good or evil in exact proportion with the cause that has created it.

Gaudama, having wilfully and unwilfully ignored a first cause from which all the things that exist draw their being and life, has been forced to allow to an imaginary agent the very same attributes which belong exclusively to the supreme being. On the rock of atheism he has made a sad shipwreck. Apart from this capital error it is surprising to see him maintaining with an admirable acuteness the existence of many fundamental truths; such, for instance, as the reward of good actions and the punishment of bad ones. With him the doing of evil is ever attended with consequences fatal to the perpetrator, whilst the performance of good is always accompanied with beneficial results. One would be inclined to believe that Gaudama has appropriated to himself with a great tact all the truths emanating from the belief in a supreme being; and whilst he has, with a barefaced and impious audacity, denied to the eternal author of all things the very existence, he has been placed under the necessity of accounting, in a most unlogical manner, for the existence of this world.

ARTICLE II.

OF MEDITATION AND ITS VARIOUS DEGREES.

This and the following articles contain subjects of so abstruse and refined a nature, that it would require one to possess the science of a Buddha to come to a right understanding of them. The difficulties arising from this study are due to the confused and very unsatisfactory ideas of the Buddhist philosophers respecting the soul and its spirituality, and perhaps to the inability of the writer to understand the vague and undefined terms employed to convey their ideas on these matters. The field of Buddhist metaphysics is, to a European, in a great measure a new one; the meaning of the terms is half-understood by the Burmese translators; definitions of terms do not convey explanations such as we anticipate, and ideas seem to run in a new channel; they assume, if we may say so, strange forms: divisions and subdivisions of the various topics have no resemblance to what a European is used to in the study of philosophy. The student feels himself ushered into a new region; he is doomed to find his way by groping. Finally, the false position assumed by the Indian philosophers, and the false conclusions they arrive at, contribute to render more complicated the task of elucidating this portion of the Buddhist system. That the difficulties may be somewhat lessened, and the pathway rendered less rugged and a little smooth, the writer proposes to avoid as much as it is in his power overcharging with Pali terms the explanations he is about to afford, under the guidance of the Buddhist author.

In the preceding article we have treated of meritorious actions that are purely exterior, and briefly alluded to the nature of the rewards bestowed on earth and in the six seats of Nats upon those who have performed these good actions. Now we leave behind all the exterior good deeds, and turn the attention of our mind to something more excellent, to those acts that are purely interior, and are performed solely by the soul and the right exercise of its faculties; that is to say, by meditation and contemplation.

The root of all human miseries is ignorance. It is the generating principle of concupiscence and other passions. It is the dark but lofty barrier that encircles all beings and retains them within the vortex of endless existences; it is the cause of all existences, and of all those illusions to which beings are miserably subjected; it causes those continual changes which take place in the production of all beings. This great cause once found and proclaimed by Buddha, it was necessary to procure a remedy to counteract the action of ignorance, and successfully oppose its progress. Another antagonistic and opposite principle had to be found, adequate to resist the baneful agency of ignorance and stem its sad and misfortune-creating influence. That principle is science or knowledge. Ignorance is but a negative agent: it is only the absence of science. Let knowledge be, and ignorance shall vanish away in the same manner as darkness is noiselessly but irresistibly dissipated by the presence of light.

All beings in this universe, says our author, are doomed to be born and die. We quit this place to go and live in another; we die here to be born elsewhere. We can never be freed from pain, old age, and death. Whether we like it or not, we must suffer and always suffer. But why is it so? Because we do not possess the perfect science. Were we blessed with it, we would infallibly look towards Neibban, and then, escaping from the pursuit of pain and miseries, we would infallibly obtain the deliverance from those evils which now incessantly press upon us. It rests with us only to perfect our intelligence, so that we might gradually attain to the perfect science, the source of all good. But by what means is so desirable an end to be obtained? By the exercise of meditation, answers, with a decided tone, our philosopher. This word implies, besides, other intellectual operations of a superior order, such as contemplation, visions, ecstasy, union, &c., which are the more or less complete results of that intellectual exercise.

The act of meditating can take place but in the heart, where resides the *mano*, or the faculty of knowing. Its object can never be but the *nam-damma*, literally the name of the thing; or, in other terms, the things of a purely intellectual nature. But it can by no means happen in the seats of the other senses or organs, such as the eyes, the ears, &c., which are only channels to communicate impressions to the faculty of *mano*.

The constitutive parts of meditation are five in number. *Witteka*, the action of raising the mind to an object; *Witzara*, the attentive consideration of that object; *Piti*, the bringing of the soul and body to a state of satisfaction; *Suka*, the pleasure enjoyed in the thing considered; *Ekatta*, the perseverance or stability of the mind in that object. There is also *Upekka*, which implies a greater and more intense degree of fixity of the mind, extending not only to one object in particular, but to all things.

It may be called the absolute quietism of the soul, and the net result of a complete course of general meditation on the universality of things. It is the last and highest point that can ever be reached.

To explain more fully the nature and definitions of the two first parts, our philosopher has recourse to the following comparison. Let us suppose a man that has to cleanse a rusty copper vessel. With one hand he grasps the vessel, and with the other he rubs it up and down, right and left. This is exactly what is dône by the means of Witteka and Witzara. The first gets hold of the object of meditation, and the second causes the mind to pass and repass over it, until it has perfectly seen it in all its particulars.

The third stage in the exercise of meditation is that of Piti, which consists in a sort of transitory delectation, experienced by him who has reached that third step of mental labour. It produces on the whole frame the following effects:—It seems to him that is engaged in that exercise that the hairs of his head stand on an end, so strong is the sensation he then feels; at other times it produces in the soul sensations similar to that of the lightning that rends the atmosphere. Sometimes it is in a commotion resembling that of mighty waves breaking on the shore; at other times the subject is, as it were, carried through the air, or only raised above the ground, and occasionally it causes a chill running throughout all the limbs. When these results have been, through persevering efforts, repeatedly experienced with an ever-increasing degree of intensity, the following effects are attained:—The body and the soul are completely restrained, subdued, and composed; they are almost beyond the influence of concupiscence. Both acquire a remarkable lightness, so that the exercise of meditation offers no further trouble or labour; the natural repugnance or opposition to self-recollection is done away with, then the exercise of meditation becomes pleasing from the pleasurable state of the soul and body, and finally both parts are in a true and genuine condition, so that what there was previously in them either vicious or opposed to truth disappears at once and vanishes away. Such are the various effects experienced by the soul that has reached the degree of Piti, or mental satisfaction.

When the soul and body have thus been perfectly subdued, and freed from all that could wrongly affect them, the soul then reaches the state of *Suka,* that is to say, of perfect and permanent pleasure and inward delight. The effects or results thereof are called *Samati,* or peace or quiescence of the soul. As a matter of course, that state of inward peace has several degrees both as regards the time it lasts and the intensity of the affection. It lasts sometimes for a moment, or for a period of uncertain duration, as it happens when we reflect on some subject, or we listen to a sermon. At other times its duration is longer; when, for instance, we are about to enter into contemplation or ecstasy, and it lasts as long as we are in one of these states.

From *Piti* originates the *Samati-tseit,* the idea or consciousness of inward quiescence. It is the secondary cause of the real joy and delight, and is followed by an unshaken resolution to adhere to all the precepts of the law. It produces in the soul a certain freshness, expansion, and ravishment in the practice of virtue. Such a state is illustrated by the following comparison. A traveller has to go over a very difficult road; he is exposed to an intense heat, and tormented with a burning thirst. Let us imagine the intensity of his delight when he finds himself on the brink of a rivulet of clear and cool water; such is precisely the state of the soul under the influence of *Piti.* The state of *Suka* follows it very soon. It is exemplified by the condition of the traveller who has been perfectly refreshed and relieved from thirst and fatigue, and enjoys the delightful and pleasurable effects resulting therefrom.

The last state or the crowning point to be arrived at by the means of meditation is that of *Upekka,* or perfect fixity, whence originates an entire indifference to love or hatred, pleasure or pain. Passions can no more affect the soul in that happy condition. But in this, as well in the preceding states, there are several degrees, according to the various objects it refers to. In the *Upekka,* relating to the five senses, man is no more affected by beautiful or unseemly objects, by harsh or melodious sounds, &c. As to what refers to creatures, man has neither love nor dislike for them. Man obtains the state of *Upekka,* relating to science or knowledge, by examining and considering all things through the medium of the three great principles, *aneitsa, duka, anatta,* that is to say, change, pain, and illusion. There is also the *uirya upekka;* as when a man, after great struggles and efforts to obtain a certain object, sees that he cannot reach it, he becomes indifferent to it, and without trouble or the least disquiet gives up the undertaking. There are many other effects of the Upekka mentioned by our author, the enumeration of which would prove tedious. What has been just stated is sufficient to afford a correct idea of the nature of the highest state of meditation that the human mind can ever reach. The last and most transcendent result of the condition of Upekka is this: when an individual, by successful exertions, has ascended to the top of the spiritual ladder, there is a certain virtue that attracts everything to him. He becomes a centre to which all appear to converge. He is like the central point of our planet, that ever remains distinct from the bodies it incessantly draws to itself. Seated in the centre of the most complete quietism, the sage contemplates, without the least effort, the unclouded truth that indefinitely unfolds itself before him. Hence, as our author observes, the sage that has reached the state of Upekka has no more to pass successively through the four preceding stages to be enabled to meditate; that is to say, he no more requires the help of thought, reflection, satisfaction, and pleasure. He is in the middle of the cloudless atmosphere of truth which he enjoys, and therein remains as unmoved as truth itself.

As stated in the previous article, the observance of the precepts, or the performance of exterior good actions, draws abundant rewards upon those who faithfully comply with them. These rewards are bestowed either in the seat of man or in the six abodes of Nats, which we will agree to call the six inferior heavens, where concupiscence as yet holds its empire.

The inward good deeds produced by the operation of the intellectual faculties of the soul being of an incomparably greater value than the external ones, the recompense of the former is of a higher order than that of the latter. Hence there are twenty superior heavens reserved to the sages that have made progress in meditation.[5] The

---

[5] It will perhaps be of some interest to a few of our readers to men-

accounts of the Buddhists respecting the extent of these seats, their respective distance in a perpendicular direction, the myriads of centuries to stay in each of them, &c., are puerilities not worth attending to, and in no way belonging to the genuine and original Buddhism. They are the inventions in subsequent ages of individuals who wished to emulate their neighbours and rivals, the Hindus, at a time when the latter substituted the gross and revolting idolatry of the Puranas for the purer doctrines of the Vedas. But what is directly to our purpose is the distinction of these twenty seats into two classes. The

---

tion the names of the thirty-one seats in which Buddhists have located all beings. Let us begin with the lowest step of that immense ladder. The four first steps are the four states of punishment. In them are to be found living the unfortunate beings who, pursued by the inflexible law of their demerits, are doomed to atone in different ways for the evil that they have done. The lowest seat is Nga-yai or hell. It is placed in the centre of our planet, and subdivided into eight principal quarters, the last of which is called Awidzi. The second step of the ladder is occupied by the seat of Animals; the third by certain monsters called Preittas; and the fourth by another kind of inferior beings named Athourikes. These four seats are tenanted by beings who undergo punishment for the evil deeds they have performed.

The fifth seat is that of Manusa, or men. The beings that occupy it are in a state in which they can merit or demerit. It may be called a position of probation.

Above the seat of man are the six seats of Nats called Tsadoomaritz, Tawadeintha, Yama, Toocita, Nimanarati, Pare-neimittawasawati. The denizens of those seats enjoy the reward awarded to them for the performance of good and meritorious exterior works.

The three places above those of Nats, called Brahma-parisitsa, Brahmah-parau-hita, Maha-Brahma, are occupied by the contemplatives who have reached the first step of Dzan, or meditation. The three following, Pareitta-ba, Appa-ma-naba, Appasara, are tenanted by the beings who have attained the second degree of contemplation. The three next to those just enumerated are: Paweitta-sou-ba, Appa-mana-sou-ba, Soubakannaka. They are the abodes of the contemplatives who have ascended to the third step of meditation. The two following steps of the ladder, Wa-happala, A-sou-gna-sat, are tenanted by the contemplatives of the fourth degree; and the five that follow, viz., Awiha, Atabpa, Sou-dasa, Sou-dasi, Agga-nita, are occupied by the contemplatives of the fifth degree; that is to say, by the beings who have entered the Thoda, or current of perfection, and who have qualified themselves for obtaining the state of deliverance, or Neibban.

Above those seats we find the four and last abodes of Arupa, without form. They are called: Akasanitza-yatana, Wigniana-witza-yatana, Akeitsignia-yatana, Newa-thagnia-nathagnia-yatana.

first comprises sixteen seats, under the designation of *Rupa*, or matter; the second includes four seats, called *Arupa*, or immaterial abodes or conditions. Here are located on a grand and immense scale, according to their respective proficiency in science and meditation, the beings that have striven to advance in knowledge by the exertion of the mental faculties. The general appellation given to each class bears a great meaning, and therefore deserves explanation. In the sixteen seats of *Rupa* are placed the contemplatives who have as yet a body, and have not been hitherto able to disengage themselves from some affection to matter. The subjects of their meditations are still the beings inhabiting this material world, together with some of the *Kathain*, or coarser portion of their being. But in the four seats called *Arupa*, which terminate the series of Buddhist heavens, the contemplatives are destitute of shape and body; they are almost brought to the condition of pure spirits. In their sublime and lofty flight in the regions of spiritualism, they seem to have bid a last farewell to this world, and to be no longer concerned with material things.

Let us glance rapidly over these various seats, and pay a visit to the beings that have been rewarded with a place in them, owing to their great proficiency in the mental exercise of meditation. We will begin with the lowest seat, and from it successively ascend to the loftiest. We must bear in remembrance that there are, as above stated, five degrees of meditation or five parts, viz., perception, reflection, satisfaction, happiness, and fixity. He who has been much exercised in the first degree shall inhabit one of the three first seats of Rupa. Those who, leaving aside the first degree, shall delight in the second and third, shall inhabit, according to their respective progress, one of the three following seats. Those who take delight only in the fourth degree, having no further aid of the three first parts, perception, consideration, and satisfaction, shall be located in the seventh, eighth, and ninth seats. When the fifth degree of Dzan, or meditation, has been attained, that is to say, when a privileged contemplative is able to meditate and contemplate, without having recourse to the representation and consideration of the object, without allowing himself to be influenced by pleasures or joy, then he has attained to the state of fixity and indifference; he occupies the tenth and eleventh seats. The five remaining seats bear the collective name of *Thoodawata*, or abodes of the pure or perfect, that is to say, the dwelling-place of those who have entered into the current of perfection. They are inhabited by the Kaliana Putadzans, and the four sorts of contemplatives called Thautapan, Thakadagan, Anagan, and Rahandas. The latter have entered into the *Thoda*, or current of perfection. The Thautapans and Thakadagans are pure and exempt from all influence of demerits; the Anagans are delivered from the five concupiscences. The Rahandas are enjoying a perfect indifference for all. They are strangers to such language as this: I am great, I am greater, I am greatest. Such terms of comparison are but mere illusions; they are deceitful sounds that confuse, distract, and bewilder the ignorant.

Above the *Thoodawata* seats are the four called *Arupa*, or immaterial. The denizens of these places first recognise that the miseries attending man in this world have their origin in the body. They then conceive the utmost disgust and horror for it; they long for the dissolution of this agent to all wickedness. So great is their horror for bodies and matter, that they no longer select them for subjects of meditation; they endeavour to cross beyond the limits of materiality, and launch forth into the boundless space, where this material world does not seem to reach. The inhabitants of the first seat have assumed for their subject of meditation the *Akasa*, the air, the fluid of the atmosphere, or the space. Those of the second meditate on the *Winiana*, or the spirit, or life of beings, taken in an abstract sense; those of the third contemplate the

Akintzi, or immensity; those of the fourth, *Newathagnia*, lose themselves in the infinity.

By what mental process has the sage to pass in order to reach the first degree of sublime contemplation? He will have to begin with the consideration of the form of some material object, say one of the four elements. Let him afterwards set aside those *Kathain*, or material portions of the element brought under consideration, and occupy his mind with the ether, or fluid, or space; the former, that is to say, the kathain, shall disappear to give place to something divested of all those coarser forms, and the mind shall be fixed only on the *akatha*. The sage then shall repeat ten hundred thousand times these words,—The space or air is infinite, until there will appear at last the first *tseit*, or idea of *arupa*. In a similar manner, the *tseit akan*, or the idea of conformity with purpose, disappears; then begins the science of *upekka*, or indifference, with its four degrees; the idea that then succeeds is precisely that of *akasa ananda*, or infinite ether, or space. This unintelligible mental process is explained by a comparison. If they shut with a white cloth the opening of a window, the persons inside the room, turning their eyes in the direction of the opening, see nothing but the white cloth. Should the cloth be suddenly removed, they perceive nothing but that portion of the space corresponding with the extent of the window. The piece of cloth represents the material forms, that are the subjects of meditation, or contemplation, of those living in the seats of *Rupa;* the free opening of the window exemplifies the subjects of contemplation reserved to the first class of *arupa*. Having reached so far, the contemplative soon feels the utmost disgust for all material forms, and is entirely delivered from the three *Thagnia*, or false persuasions, supplied by matter, by the action of the senses, and by the result of merits and demerits. He is displeased with all the coarser forms of beings. The action of the contemplative has its sphere in the *mano*, or seat of knowledge. The ideas originating from the action of the senses have no share in that purely intellectual labour. In that state, the sage has fallen into a condition of so perfect abstraction, that all the accidents on the part of the elements can produce no effect over him. The action of the senses is completely suspended during all the time that the contemplation lasts. In fact this is nothing else but *thamabat*, or ecstasy.

The same course of meditation must be followed by the sages inhabiting the other three seats; only the object to be contemplated will be different.

Having explained the important subject of meditation, endeavoured to show the different parts or degrees of that intellectual exercise, and given a faint outline of the recompenses bestowed on those that have distinguished themselves by proficiency in that exercise, we have now to follow our author, and, with him, make ourselves acquainted with the principal subjects that attract the attention of the contemplative.

ARTICLE III.

OF THE NATURE OF BEINGS.

The Buddhist philosopher, in his earnest prosecution after the antidote of ignorance, that is, science, rightly states that all beings, and man, in particular, must ever be the first and most interesting subject the sage has to study. The knowledge of man in particular constitutes a most important portion of the science he must acquire, ere he can become a perfect being, and be deemed worthy to be admitted to the state of Neibban. In the very limited sketch of this part of the work under consideration, the attention of the reader will be directed on man as the most interesting of all beings. With our Buddhist author, therefore, he will take human beings as the subject of his investigations. Provided with the philosophical dissecting knife, he will anatomise all the component parts of that extraordinary being, whose nature has ever presented an insoluble problem to ancient sages. What is to be said on this subject will be sufficient to convey a correct idea of the mode of reasoning and arguing followed by Buddhist philosophers, when they analyse other beings and select them for the subjects of their meditations.

At the very beginning, our author proclaims this great maxim: All beings living in the three worlds, heaven, earth, and hell, have in themselves but two things or attributes, *Rupa* and *Nam*, form and name. Accustomed as we are to a language that expresses clear and distinct notions, we would like to hear him say, in nature there are but two things, matter and spirit. But such is not the language of Buddhists, and I apprehend that were we giving up their somewhat extraordinary, and, to us, unusual way of expressing their ideas, we could not come to a correct knowledge of the notions they entertain respecting the nature of man. Let us allow our author to speak for himself, and, as much as possible, express himself in his own way. By *rupa*, we understand form and matter; that is to say, all that is liable *per se* to be destroyed by the agency of secondary causes. *Nam*, or *nama*, is the thing, the nature of which is known to the mind by the instrumentality of *mano*, or the knowing principle. In the five aggregates constituting man, viz., materiality or form, the organs of sensation, of perception, of consciousness, and those of intellect, there is nothing else to be found but form and name. We are at once brought to this materialist conclusion, that in man we can discover no other element but that of form and that of name.

To convey a sort of explanation of this subject, our author gives here a few notions respecting the six senses. I say six senses, because with him, besides the five ordinary senses, he mentions the *mano*, or the knowing principle that resides in the heart, as one of the senses. The organs or faculties of seeing, hearing, feeling, tasting, smelling, and knowing, he calls the inward senses. These same organs, as they come in contact with exterior objects, are called exterior senses. The faculty inherent in each of the senses whereby is operated the action between the organ and its object, is designated by the appellation of the life of the senses, as, for instance, the eye seeing, the ear hearing, &c. In this treble mode of considering the senses, what do we meet with but form and name, ideas and matter? Supposing the organ of seeing to exist, and an object to be seen, there will necessarily result, as an essential consequence, the perception or idea of such a thing. Even as regards the *mano*, where there exists the heart on one side, and truth on the other, there will follow immediately the idea or perception of truth.

This materialist doctrine, if the meaning of our author be accurately understood, is further confirmed by the method he proposes for carrying on the investigation respecting the nature of things. He who desires to penetrate deeply into such a sublime science, must have recourse to the help of meditation. Having selected an object, he considers it by the means of *witekka*. He passes successively through the ideas and impressions he derives from the contemplation of such an object. He then says to himself: the ideas obtained by the means of *witekka*, or the first degree of dzan, or meditation, are nothing but *nam-damma*, since their nature is to offer themselves to the *arom*, as the thought to its object. But where is the seat of that *arom?* It resides in the substance of the heart, which, in reality, affords asylum both to it and to the *nam-damma*. It is nowhere else to be found. But what is the heart? Whence does it come? By what is it formed? To these three questions we answer, that the heart is composed of the four elements. It is but one and the same thing with them. This startling doctrine is explicit, and excludes at once the idea of a spiritual substance.

Our author has now reached the elements or the parts

constituting all that exists with a form. He boldly asserts that all that has an existence is but an aggregate of earth, water, fire, and air; all the forms are but modifications and combinations of the four elements. The bare enumeration of this general principle is not sufficient to satisfy our philosopher. He wishes to know and explain the reason of everything. Here begins an analysis entirely unknown to our chemists and philosophers of the west. The body is divided into thirty-two parts, which are often enumerated in formulas of prayer by pious Buddhists. Each of these thirty-two parts is subdivided into forty-four. The hair, how slender soever it appears, is submitted to that minute analysis. The result of this subtle division is to show what is the proportion of each element that enters into the formation of these atomical parts. We have not the patience to write down these uninteresting details, nor do we believe that the reader will be displeased if we spare him the trouble of going over such worthless nomenclature. There is another division of matter, or body, into forty-two parts, called *akan.* This is based upon the distinction of the four elements that enter unequally into the formation of the body; twenty parts belong to the earth, twelve to water, six to fire, and six to wind. Then again the body is divided into sixty parts; the division is based upon the distinction of the ten constitutive parts belonging to each of the senses, as it will be hereafter explained. The object which Buddhist philosophers have in view in entering into so many divisions and subdivisions of the forms of the body, is to prove, in their opinion to demonstration, that, by the nicest analysis of every part of the body, we find in the end nothing but the primary elements that are called the supports of all that exist.

We have now to follow our author through a path more difficult than the preceding one, and hear him explain the theory of ideas and their various modifications. These, says he, are known, not by their forms, since they have none, but only by their name. Through the practice of reflection and meditation we become acquainted with them. We call them *arupa damma*, things without a form or shape. They are designated under the name of *tseit* and *tsedathit*,[6] that is to say, ideas and the result of ideas. Where are these ideas to be met? Where have they their seat? In the six senses and nowhere else, is the answer. Having already become acquainted with the organs of the senses, it will be easy to find out the ideas that are as the tenants of the senses.

All the *tseits* inhabiting the organs of sense are called

---

[6] The number of tseits or ideas is one hundred and twenty, divided as follows:—

1. The tseits or ideas of the beings as yet under the influence of passion; they are named Kama-watsara-tseits.

2. The tseits or ideas peculiar to beings who have not as yet been able to raise themselves entirely above materiality; they are called Rupa-watzara-tseits.

3. There are four tseits peculiar to those beings, who, setting aside the coarser portions of this world, launch forth into abstract truth, and delight in the contemplation of the highest, purest, and most boundless things the mind may imagine. They are known as the ideas working on what may be called immaterial, impalpable objects.

The ideas of the first series belong to all the beings located in the four states of punishment, in the seat of man, and in the six seats of Nats, that is to say, in the eleven seats where is the reign of passions.

Those of the second series belong to the beings located in the sixteen seats of the Brahmas, including those who have entered into the current of perfection, by following the four Meggas, and enjoying the merits and rewards connected with the condition of the perfect.

The ideas of the third series are the happy lot of those superior beings who soar high in the regions of pure spiritualism, leaving below them all the things that have a reference to this world, such as we see it.

The Tsedathits, or results essentially connected with ideas, are fifty-two in number. The seven enumerated at the end of this article are: contact, sensation, perception, inclination, fixity, command over self, and remembrance: they are inherent in all ideas. Six Tsedathits are connected with the act of perception, viz., thought, reflection, decision, energy, pleasure, and liberty. Fourteen others are connected with the ideas of demerits, viz., impudence, audacity in evil, unsteadiness, concupiscence, pride, boasting, grievous offence, envy, anxiety, want of respect, lowness of feelings, doubt or indecision, covetousness.

The Tsedathits connected with merits are: affection for all that refers to religion, remembrance of all that is good, shame of all that is bad, fear of evil, exemption from concupiscence and from anger, serenity of soul, freedom from evil inclinations and evil thoughts, swiftness of the body and of the mind, good habits of the body and of the soul, uprightness in the feelings and the thoughts, good words, good actions, good behaviour, compassion, joy at the prosperity of others, wisdom, or the acquirement of the knowledge of truth by reflection.

loki tseit, that is to say, ideas of the world, because they are to be met with in all the beings as yet subjected to concupiscence. They are distinct from *lokoudra tseits*, which belong properly to the beings free from passions, and who have entered into the four *megga*, or ways to perfection. The *tseits* of this world are eighty-one in number, classified as follows: the perception of each of the five organs, and the perception of the respective faculties of those organs. This gives ten tseits. There are three for the sense of the heart, the perception of the substance of the heart, of its faculty of knowing, and of the object of its knowledge.

Each of the six senses has ten constitutive forms or parts, viz.: earth, water, fire, air, colour, odour, taste, fluid, life, and the body attached primitively thereto. Now there is an action from each of these forms upon the subject. Thence ten *tseits* to each of the six senses.

There are no words so ill defined and so ill understood by our philosopher as the two words Tseit and Tsedathit. The first in a moral sense means idea, thought, perception, &c.; in a physical sense it means that secondary cause created by *kan*, producing the living being, the senses wherein reside the moral *tseit*. Tsedathit, being the result of ideas, must, of course, have likewise two meanings. In the first place it will designate the impressions made upon us by ideas; in the second, it will mean the secondary cause or life in the body, or the modifications of the principles of corporeal life.

This being premised, we may a little understand our author when he says: There are seven *tsedathits* existing at the same time as the eighty-one above-mentioned *tseits*, viz.: *pasa tsedathit*, so called because it is the real effect of the tsedathit to attain its object, and, as it were, to touch it. We may call it the agreement between the idea and its object. *Wedana tsedathit*, the feeling of the impression of an idea; *thagnia tsedathit*, the comprehension of the object; *dzetana tsedathit*, the inclination for the object;

eketa tsedathit, the fixity on the object; *dziwi-teindre tsedathit*, the observance of what relates to form and name; and *mana sikaramana tsedathit*, consciousness. It is evident, therefore, that the tsedathit is neither the idea nor the object of the idea, but the result from the idea that has come in contact with an object. These seven results are, if we may say so, the third part of the idea. They do not give occasion to modifications of ideas. But those which really give rise to the greatest variety of results are the *akuso tsedathit*, or the results of evil thoughts and ideas, and their opposite, or *kuso tsedathit*, or the consequence of good and virtuous thoughts. To mention here all the *kuso* and *akuso tsedathit* would be but a dry exposition of the nomenclature of the vices and virtues, such as is met with in the catalogues of Buddhist moralists. They are all enumerated in the preceding note.

ARTICLE IV.

OF THE CAUSE OF THE FORM[7] AND OF THE NAME, OR OF MATTER AND SPIRIT.

The duty of our intelligence is to investigate the cause of all the modifications of forms and names. This being effected, we are delivered from all doubts and disquietude.

---

[7] Having in two previous notes explained what regards the ideas, and the results from or the things connected with ideas, we must come to the third great principle, viz., *Rupa*, or form, or matter, and state further the curious divisions of our Burmese metaphysicians. 1. The form of all that is visible is found in the four elements: earth, water, fire, and air. 2. The form for coming in contact are the five senses, the eyes, the ear, the nose, the tongue, and the body, or rather the skin of the body. 3. The form of the objects of the senses is likewise divided into five parts, essentially connected with the five above-enumerated senses. 4. The forms peculiar to the living beings are the male and female sexes. 5. The forms of life taken abstractedly are the life of the body and the life of language or uttered words. 6. The forms in which appearance exhibits itself are swiftness, softness, and acting. 7. The forms of the signs of being are: the appearance of being, or coming into being, the remaining

When we perceive such a form, such an idea, &c., we are able forthwith to account for its causes. In this study we must copy the conduct of the physician, who, when attending a patient, sits by his bedside, closely examines the nature of the distemper and the causes that have given rise to it, in order to find out counteracting agents or remedies to check its progress at first, and gradually to

---

into being, the fulness of the state of being, and the destruction of being.

The last great principle is Neibban, that is to say, the exemption from the action of the influence originating from merits and demerits, from the volitions of the mind, from the seasons or time, and from nourishment, which are the causes of mutability: it is the end of existence.

As regards the state of man and that of other rational beings, there are several notions which are arranged in a curious manner under several heads, which it is thought necessary to notice as briefly as possible. 1. The five *Khandas*, or supports of man's being: materiality, sensation, perception, mutability, and intellect or thought. 2. The inward five *Ayatana*, or seats of the senses of seeing, of hearing, of smelling, of tasting, and of feeling. 3. The outward five *Ayatana*, or seats of what is perceived by the senses, viz., appearance or form, sound, odour, taste, tangibility, and idea. 4. The ten *Dat*, or constitutive parts of the five senses, and of the five results of the perception of the five senses, as above enumerated. 5. The four *Thitsa*, or truths: the truth of the miseries attending existence; the truth of concupiscence or passions, the cause of all miseries; the truth of the Neibban of passions, or the destruction of passions, the summit of which is Neibban, the truth of the Megga or ways to Neibban. 6. The twenty-two *Indray*, or dispositions or capacities for acting, viz., the capacity of seeing, hearing, smelling, tasting, feeling, of uniting one sex with the other, of thinking, of enjoying peace, of bearing pain, of yielding to anger, of enjoying pleasure, of remaining indifferent, of using exertions, of being attentive, of adhering to true doctrine, of putting on sentiments of benevolence, of searching after wisdom, of using meekness, of entering the four ways of perfection, and of enjoying the happiness resulting from following those ways. 7. The nine *Phola*, or rewards resulting from walking in the path of perfection are: intensity of benevolence, of diligence, of attention, of fixity of wisdom, of shame of all that is bad, of fear for all that is bad, of diligence in avoiding evil, and the fear of hardness in sin. 8. The *Megga*, or ways, are: good doctrine, good thinking, good language, and good actions. What follows is but a completive of the above, viz., good conduct, good diligence, good attention, and good fixity. 9. The *Dzan*, or meditation, have five parts, viz., thought of the object, reflection on the object, satisfaction resulting therefrom, affectionate inclination for the object, fixity in the object.

The writer craves the reader's indulgence in setting before him such a dry nomenclature; but no one can understand the language of Buddhist metaphysicians, unless he has made himself familiar with the terms they use, and the arbitrary distinctions they have adopted.

uproot it from the constitution. In the moral order, the philosopher too has to examine the nature of all moral distempers, ascertain the principles or causes they spring from, and thereby become qualified to cure those disorders.

The beings that inhabit the three worlds, says our author, must have a cause. To say that they exist of themselves and without a cause, is an absurdity. The very dissimilarity we observe among them indicates that their mode of existence results from certain causes. We, however, cannot agree with our antagonists, the Brahmins, who maintain that Maha Brahma is the cause of all that exists. This being is not out of the circle of Rupa and Nam; he is himself a compound of Nam and Rupa, that is to say, effect but not cause. In vain our opponents will add that all that is distinct of Maha Brahma is subjected to a cause, but that the Rupa and Nam, constituting his essence, are without a cause. This is removing the difficulty a little further, without advancing a step towards its solution; our answer must ever be the same.

Before expounding the opinions of our philosopher on this important subject, it is necessary to state the views entertained by that class of philosophers whose doctrines appear to have taken root in these parts. It is easy to perceive that they are modifications of the opinion of the Hindus on the same subject, and akin to that respecting the Adi Buddha, or supreme Buddha.

Some doctors maintain that there is a first cause or being that has made matter and spirit. Others, admitting the eternal co-existence of matter and of the supreme being, say that he is the remote cause of the organisation of matter, as we at present see it. But all agree in this, that no one can ever come to the knowledge of that first cause, and it is impossible ever to have an idea of it. Hence it is the height of folly and rash presumption to attempt to come to the knowledge of what is placed beyond the range of human investigation. It behoves us to apply all the powers of the mind to discover the immediate cause that certainly produces existence.

The sage, to be worthy of his sublime calling, must remain satisfied with striving to find out that immediate cause which brings into action the form and name, and causes the appearance of all those modifications which we call beings or forms of existence. He ought to strive to account for the organisation of matter and all its modifications, by discovering the hidden spring that effectually sets all in motion, in action, in combination of existences.

Now, our author puts this important question: What thing is to be considered as the mover of the forms and ideas? We know, says he, that the human body has its beginning in the womb of the mother; we are acquainted with its position in that fœtid and narrow prison; its being surrounded with nerves, veins, &c., having above it the new elements, and under it the old ones. The manner in which the body originates in the womb much resembles the process by which worms and insects are formed in rotten substances, and in putrid and stagnant water. But this is not accounting for the real cause of living bodies. The real causes, according to some doctors, are five in number, viz., ignorance, concupiscence, desire, *kan* (the influence of merits and demerits), and *ahan* (the aliments). They concur together in the formation of the living body in the following manner. Ignorance, concupiscence, and desire give asylum to the body, as the mother supplies the infant with a refuge in her womb. Kan, like the father, is the cause productive of the body. Ahan affords nourishment to the body.

The ideas are but the result of the formation of the organs of senses. Let us suppose, for instance, the organ of seeing. The *Tsekkou Wignian*, that is to say, the life of the eyes, or the ideas connected with the use of that sense, presupposes two things, the organ and a form or an object on which the organ acts. These existing, there necessarily result the idea of vision, the perception, &c.,

in a word, all the ideas arising from the action of the eyes upon various objects. The same mode of arguing is employed relatively to the other five senses.

Other philosophers argue in the following way. The primary causes of all ideas and thoughts are disposed under two heads, that of ideas which have a fixed place, and that of those that have no fixed place. Under the first head are comprised the six *Ayatana*, or seats of senses, and the six *Arom*, or the objects of senses. Thence flow all the ideas and consequences that relate to merit and demerit. Under the second head are placed the causes or agents that produce ideas and thoughts, the exercise of the intellect holding the first rank. He who applies his mind to the meditation of what is good, such as the commands and other parts of the most excellent law, and labours to find out that all that is in this world is subjected to change, pain, and illusion, opens at once the door to the coming in of the *tseit*, or ideas connected with merit. On the other hand, the application of the mind to things bad and erroneous, contrary to the prescriptions of the holy law, generates the idea of demerit. Such are the causes of the ideas and thoughts. As to the cause of form, they assert that *kan*, *tseit*, fire, and *ahan* are the sole agents in the formation of the living body. Kan, as the workman, makes the body and sets in it all that relates to its good and bad qualities. The *tseit*, seventy-five in number, are also principles of the existence of the body, of which forty-four are called Kamawatzara tseit; they relate to the demerit and merit of those who are still under the influence of concupiscence; fifteen *rupa* watzara tseit, relating to beings in the seats of rupa; eight *arupa* watzara tseit, relating to those in the seats of arupa; eight *lokoudara* tseit, relating to the beings that have entered on the four ways of perfection. The *Tedzo-dat*, or the element of fire, contributes its share by the head and rays of light, and *ahan* by supplying the required aliments.

Some other philosophers account for the causes of form

and ideas following this course of argument. The form and ideas that constitute all beings are liable to miseries, old age, and death, because there is generation and death. Generation exists because there are worlds, worlds exist because there is desire, desire exists because there are organs, organs exist because there are form and name, form and name exist because there are concepts, concepts exist because there is merit and demerit, merit and demerit exist because there is ignorance. The latter is, indeed, the real cause of all forms and ideas. There is no doubt but this latter opinion is the favourite one with our author. It is based upon the theory of the twelve Nidanas, or causes and effects, and appears to be the orthodox opinion, and bears the stamp of great antiquity.

Having thus accounted in the best way he could for the existence of all that relates to the beings in the three worlds, our author fondly dwells on the benefits that accrue from the knowledge of causes. It dissipates all the doubts that had previously darkened the mind; it quiets all the anxieties of the heart, and affords perfect peace. For want of it, the impious fall from one error into another; the disciples of Buddha are chiefly perfected by its help.

We read in the Buddhist scriptures that a Brahmin went to consult Buddha on some points that much perplexed his mind. He said to him, "I am beset with doubts respecting the past, the present, and the future. Respecting the past, I ask myself, Have I passed through former generations or not? What was my condition during those existences? My answer is, I am ignorant on all those points. What was my position previous to those generations? I know it not. As to the present, is it true that I exist? or is my existence but an illusion? Shall I have to be born again or not? What are those living beings that surround me at present? Are they but so many illusions which deceive me by their appearance of reality? On these points I am sunk in complete ignorance. The future is likewise full of doubts and most perplexing uncertainties. Shall I have other generations or not? What shall be my condition during these coming existences? A thick veil hides from my eyes all that concerns my future destiny. What are the means to clear up all those doubts that encompass me on all sides?"

Buddha said to him, "Reflect first on this main point, that what we are wont to call self, or *moi*, is nothing but name and form—that is to say, a compound of the four elements, which undergoes perpetual changes under the action or influence of *Kan*. Having acquired the conviction of the truth of this principle, it remains with you to investigate carefully the causes which produce both name and form. This simple examination will lead you at once to the perfect solution of all your doubts. Behold the difference that exists between the holders of false doctrines and the true believers. The former, whom we may almost call animals, never take the trouble to examine the nature of beings or the causes of their existence. They are stubbornly attached to their false theories, and persist in saying that what the ignorant, delivered up to illusion, are used to call an animal, a king, a subject, a foot, and a hand, &c., is really an animal, a king, a subject, a foot, and a hand, &c.; whilst all living beings and their component parts are nothing else but name and form—that is to say, a compound made up of the four elements. Those impious are delivered up to error; hence it happens that they follow all different ways. We reckon among them more than sixty different sects, all at variance among themselves, but all uniting in a common obstinacy to reject the true doctrine of Buddha. They are doomed to move incessantly within the circle of endless and wretched existences.

"How different is the condition of the true believers, our followers! They know that the living beings inhabiting the world have a beginning. But they are sensible of the folly of attempting to reach this beginning or first cause. This is above the capacity of the loftiest intelligence. It is evident, for instance, that the seeds of plants and trees, which are continually in a state of reproduction, have a beginning; but what that beginning is, no one presumes to determine. So it is with man and all living beings. They know well, too, that what is vulgarly called man, woman, eyes, mouth, are all illusory distinctions, vanishing away in the presence of the sage, who sees nothing in all that but name and form, the production of Kan and Wibek, that is to say, of the first and second causes. These two things are not the man and the woman, &c., but they are the efficient causes of both. What we say respecting man and woman may be applied to animals and to all other beings. They are all the productions or results of Kan and Wibek, quite as distinct from these two agents as effect is distinct from its cause. To explain this doctrine, Buddhists have recourse to the comparison of a burning-glass. When there is such an instrument in one hand, and the rays of the sun pass through it to the other, fire is then produced; but fire is quite distinct from the two causes that have concurred jointly in producing it. Our disciples, too, are aware that the five *khandas*, or aggregates constituting a living being, succeed each other at each generation, but in such a way that the second generation partakes or retains nothing of the *khandas* of the first. But the causes producing them—such as Kan and Wibek—never change; they ever remain the same. Let us suppose lamps lighted up. If they burn always, it is owing to the action of individuals that supply them with oil, and light them as soon as they are extinguished. Such is the condition of the *khandas*. Those which belong to one existence have no more in common with those of the following one than the fire of the lamp just lighted anew has with that of the fire of the lamp that has just died away. As to the way beings are reproduced, we say that when a man is dying, the last *tseit* having appeared and soon disappeared, it is succeeded forthwith by the *patti* tseit or the tseit of the new existence; the interval between both is so short that it can scarcely be appreciated. This first *tseit* has nothing in common with the last one. It is, let it be well remembered, the production of *kan*, or of the influence of merits and demerits, as well as the *khandas* above alluded to.

This article is by far the most important of all. The latter part, in particular, elucidates in a distinct manner the genuine opinions of Buddhism on points of the greatest concern. We may sum up the whole as follows:—

1. There is a first cause that has acted in bringing into being all that exists; but that first cause is unknown, nor can we ever come to the knowledge of it.

2. The immediate causes of all the modifications of beings, or states of being, are ignorance and *kan*.

3. All beings are but compounds of the four elements. The intellectual operations are carried on by the instrumentality of the heart, in the same manner as vision is obtained by the means of the eye and of an object to act upon.

4. Each succeeding existence is brought on and modified by the action of Kan, or the influence of merits and demerits.

5. The component parts of a new being are in no way connected with those of the previous being. This is the key to the difficulty many persons find in accounting, in a Buddhistic sense, for the process of metempsychosis. A new term ought to be coined to express that doctrine.

6. The question respecting Neibban may be theoretically resolved without difficulty, by application of the principles contained in this and the preceding article. There is no doubt that the solution forced upon the mind from what has been above stated is that the end of the perfected being is annihilation. Horrifying as this conclusion is, it is not, after all, worse than that which is the terminus of the theories of some modern schools. What an abyss is the poor human mind liable to fall into when it ceases to be guided by Revelation!

ARTICLE V.

OF THE TRUE MEGGAS OR WAYS TO PERFECTION.

The subject under consideration is a very important one. It comprehends and comprises a summary of many particulars already alluded to in the foregoing two articles. The reader will find the path he has to follow less rugged, and the ground he will have to go over not so arid.

Our author seems to lay great stress on this special point. The sage, says he, who is desirous to arrive at the supreme perfection, must apply all the powers of his mind to discern the true ways from the false ones. Many are deceived in the midst of their researches after wisdom. The real criterion between the true and false ways is this: when, in considering an object, and making a philosophical analysis of it, the sage finds it somehow connected with concupiscence and other passions so far that he cannot, as it were, dissolve it by the application of the three principles of aneitsa, duka, and anatta—that is to say, change, pain, and illusion, then he must conclude that he is out of the right ways; the high road to perfection is barred before him. But on the contrary, whenever, by the appliance of the three great principles, he sees that all the objects brought under his consideration are nothing more or less than the mere compound of the four elements, divested of these illusory appearances which deceive so many, then he may be certain that he is in the right position, and is sure of making progress in the way to perfection.

To facilitate the study of the *Meggas*, Buddhists have classified all real and imaginary beings under a certain number of heads. The sage, to complete his laborious task, has to examine separately each of these subjects and submit them to the following lengthened, difficult, and complicated process. He takes up one subject, attentively considers its exterior and interior compound parts, its connection and relation with other things, its tendency to adhere to or part with surrounding objects. Pursuing his inquiries into the past, he endeavours to make himself acquainted with the state and condition of that object during several periods that have elapsed; when his mind is satisfied on this point he follows up in future the same object, and calculates from the experience of the past what change it may hereafter become subjected to. This study enables him to perceive distinctly that it is subjected to the three great laws of mutability, pain, and illusion. This conviction once deeply seated in his soul, the sage holds that object in supreme contempt; far from having any affection for or attachment to it, he feels an intense disgust at it, and longs for the possession of Neibban, which is the exemption from the influence of mutability, pain, and illusion.

What we have now stated is tolerably clear and intelligible; but what follows is less evident. It partakes of that obscurity and complication so peculiar to Buddhist metaphysics. This state of things is created and maintained chiefly by a mania for divisions and subdivisions that would have puzzled even the schoolmen of the middle ages. We have to listen to what our author says respecting the method to be observed in carrying on the great examination of all subjects of investigation. If that labour be patiently and perseveringly prosecuted until all the objects of inquiry be exhausted, ample and magnificent shall be the reward for such labours. The sage will be in possession of the perfect science; Neibban will appear to him; he will long for it, and unremittingly shape his course in its direction: in a word, he shall have reached the acme of perfection. Seated on that lofty position, enjoying a perfect calm in the bosom of absolute quietism, the sage is beyond the reach of passions; there is no illusion for him; he has cut the last thread of future generations by the destruction of the influence of merits and demerits; he has obtained the deliverance from all miseries; he has reached the peaceful shores of Neibban. But such a prize is not easily obtained; it is to be purchased only at the expense of an immense amount of lasting and strenuous mental exertion.

The sage, agreeably to the old and always true saying, Know thyself, very properly begins his mightily difficult task with the examination of the five aggregates constituting a living being, the organs of the six senses, and all that relates to them. Then he applies himself to the studies of the five Dzan, or the parts of meditation and contemplation, and to all that is connected with the seats of Rupa and Arupa. All the objects of examination ranged on that scale are '600 in number. We shall rapidly glance over this table, indicating but the heads of the principal divisions.

We ought not to forget that the five aggregate, or *khandas*, constituting a living being, are form, sensation, perception, consciousness, and intellect. Supposing that we take the first of those attributes as subject of examination. We must represent it to the mind, carefully examine it in all its bearings and properties, respecting the past, the present, and the future. We must proceed on and bring it in contact with the three great principles of aneitsa, duka, and anatta, and inquire whether form be changeable or not, passive or impassive, transient or permanent. We thereby acquire the knowledge of the following great truth; viz., form is essentially liable to change, pain, and illusion. The examination of each of the four other attributes is proceeded on in a like manner, and a similar result ensues.

The six organs of the senses come next under consideration. These are the eyes, the ears, the nose, the tongue, the body, or rather the skin that envelops it, and the heart in a physical sense, and *mano* in a moral one. Each of the six senses partakes of the eleven conditions or attributes we are about to describe; and each of these eleven attributes being brought successively into relation with each of the six senses, must be considered, as above stated, under the treble relation to mutability, pain, and illusion. This will supply the inquirer with a good amount of information. But to shorten this long enumeration, we will mention now successively those eleven attributes the senses may be affected by, and make the application of all to one of the senses, the eye. The same process may be easily repeated for each of the other senses. Nothing is to be changed but the name of the sense that has become the subject of examination.

1. *Ayatana*, the door, the opening of each of the senses. Applied to the eye, it is the opening through which exterior sensations are communicated to the heart by the organ of seeing.

2. *Arom*, the object of each of the senses. With regard to the eye, it is the appearance or form perceived by the eye; with respect to the ear, it is the sound.

3. *Winian*, the action of perceiving and knowing. Applied to the eyes, it is the eye seeing and perceiving, or the sight.

4. *Phasa*, literally the feeling or coming in contact with objects, applied to each of the senses. With the eye, it is the passive and active impression it derives from the objects it considers, and which it conveys to the heart. With the ear it is the impression it receives, and similarly communicates to the heart.

5. *Wedana*, the sensation of pain or pleasure obtained through the senses. With the eye it is the sensation created by the sight of objects perceived by the eye, and communicated to the heart.

6. *Thangia*, the idea or persuasion resulting from the six senses, or, according to some doctors, the identity of the appearance with reality. With the eye, it is the conviction we have that such an object, perceived by the eyes, is round or square, &c., according to the impressions received by that organ.

7. *Dzetana*, the inclination or rather adhesion to good or bad, consequently to the impressions received from each of the six senses.

8. *Tahna*, concupiscence originating from the impressions of agreeableness communicated by the six senses.

9. *Witeka*, the idea or representation of objects to the mind through the agency of the senses.

10. *Witzara*, the consideration of the objects offered to the mind by the instrumentality of the senses.

11. *Dat*, the matter or elements of the six senses, or, to speak the language of our author, that on which the organs rest, that which supports them.

After the examination of the senses and of the eleven subjects just related, we find the almost boundless field of inquiry to expand in proportion as we appear to make rapid progress. Then come successively for examination: 1. The ten *Kasaings*, or the ten parts or elements to be found in each part of a living being, viz., earth, water, fire, colour, odour, flavour, and grease, to which we add the *Dziwa* or life, and that of the organ to which belongs the part under consideration. 2. The thirty-two *Akan*, or thirty-two parts of the living body, of which the first are the hairs, the beard, the nails, the teeth, &c. 3. The twelve *Ayatana*, or seats of the six senses. Each sense is double, as far as it is considered in a double capacity, that of receiving and that of transmitting the impressions. 4. The eighteen *Dat*, or matter of the six senses. The organs afford six *Dat;* the objects that act upon the organs supply six other *Dat;* and the last six are afforded by the objects submitted to the action of the senses. 5. The twenty-two *indre*, or faculties or capabilities of the organs. Each organ has three. The eye, for instance, is capable of receiving an impression and of transmitting it; the eye really receives and transmits impressions. The *mano*, or heart, being a double organ, has six faculties; three if it be considered physically, and three if morally or intellectually. 6. The nine *Bon*, or seats occupied by the Brahmas. 7. The five *Rupa Dzan*, or degrees of contemplation proper to the Brahmas who have a form. 8. The four *Megga*, or ways that lead near to Neibban. They are followed by the Brahmas occupying the four superior seats of *Rupa*. 9. The *Arupa Dzan*, or contemplation proper to those who inhabit the four immaterial seats. 10. The nineteen *Damma*. This word means what we know as certain by the use of our mental faculties. When the *mano*, by a right use of its three faculties, has freed itself from the principle of illusion and error, then there will be the sixteen virtues or good qualities, known by the name of *Phola* and *Megga*. 11. Finally, the twelve *Patan*, or elements that are in the *mano*, which constitute the memory, and enable man to remember, and silently repeat the impressions transmitted by the senses.

Such is the immense extent of observations the sage has to range for obtaining the perfect science. This task is truly an Herculean one; very few can perform it.

Before coming to the last article, the writer will make a remark tending to show that there is more of the analytic spirit in all what is told us by Buddhist philosophers respecting those abstruse subjects than one may be tempted to give them credit for. We have seen that the number of precepts and counsels is almost countless, yet it is agreed by all doctors that the five general precepts are the basis of all, and that he who observes them in all their bearings is as much advanced in the path of righteousness as can be expected. Again, Buddhists can never exhaust the stores of all that they have to say about the mental operations and meditation. Yet all is summed up in the comparatively short doctrine of *tseit* and *tsedathit*. The living beings are by them infinitely modified, yet after all we find everything condensed in two words, Nama and Rupa. The theory respecting the generation of beings and their mutual dependence upon each other, is a boundless field. We find, however, that, after all, *kan*, or the influence of merits and demerits, is the sole cause of and agent in the existence and modification of all beings. Mental operations are numbered by hundreds, but the six senses are, after all, the foundation on which that enumeration is raised. The general principles and primary ideas of all these metaphysical theories doubtless belong to genuine and early Buddhism. But such plain and elementary principles having been got hold of by heads of philosophical schools, and worked upon in their intellectual laboratory, there have come out therefrom at various periods those theories which have given to the doctrines of Buddhism so many different hues, and at the same time contributed so much to puzzle and torment the European student.

ARTICLE VI.

OF THE PROGRESS IN PERFECT SCIENCE.

In the preceding article we have reviewed the whole scale of beings, and analysed summarily some of them, merely to show the way to the general analysis of all others. The ultimate result of such an investigation is to acquire the conviction that all beings are subjected to mutability, pain, and illusion. This conviction, once seated in the soul,generates a generous contempt for such miserable objects. In this article we must see by what means this philosophical sentiment may be firmly rooted in the soul, and man may finally entertain a thorough disgust for all creatures, even for his own body. This loathsomeness for all that exists is immediately followed up byan ardent desire of becoming free and disentangled from all the ties and trammels that encompass other beings. When a man has become familiar with such a conviction to the extent that his thoughts, desires, and actions are entirely regulated by its immediate influence, he is free from the errors that deceive almost all other beings; he sees things as they are in their nature, and appreciates them by their real value.

He estranges himself from them. He is in mind in the state of Neibban, until death will complete outwardly what was already existing inwardly in his mind.

We are all aware, says our author, that the principle of instability pervades all that exists in hell, on earth, and in the superior seats. But this important science is with many too superficially and but imperfectly understood. Our great object is to root it deeply in our mind, so that we might ever be preserved from those false impressions which too often tempt us to believe that mutability and changes are not affecting all beings. What are the obstacles that oppose in us the progress to true science? There are three. The first is *Santi,* or duration of existence. We allow ourselves to be lulled into the opinion that our life shall be much longer prolonged; that we have as yet many days, months, and years to spend in this world. This groundless supposition prevents us from attending to the principle of mutability. To counteract this dangerous impression, let us examine how all things are born only soon to die, and therefore let us have always death present to our mind. Let us consider the short duration and vanity of our being, then we will soon be convinced that the form of the body is like the waves of the sea, that swell for a moment and soon disappear; that sensation is produced like froth from the dashing of the waves; that the *Thangia,* or persuasion we acquire, has no more stability or reality than lightning; that the *Sangkara,* or concept, or production, is like the plantain-tree without strength, and that the view of objects through our senses deserves no more credit than the words of a quack. Let us reason in a similar manner on the ephemeral existence of all the beings that are in this world; we will easily come to a similar conclusion, that they are the victims of mutability, incessantly tossed about as a piece of wood by the billows of the sea.

A second obstacle to our perceiving the great principle that pain is heavily weighing on all creatures is the *iriabot,* or the four situations or positions which the body assumes, viz., sitting, standing, lying, and walking. If a man enjoys good health, he owes it chiefly to the change of situation. Were he doomed to occupy always the same place, or remain in the same situation, he would feel quite miserable. He momentarily relieves himself from his temporary afflictions by a change of situation. This relief makes him forgetful of the great principle of *duka.* But in truth our body is like a patient that requires the constant attendance of the physician. We must feed it, refresh it, wash it, clothe it, &c., to save it from hunger, thirst, dirt, and cold. What is all that but a sad and constant proof that we are slaves to pain? There is nothing but pain and affliction in this wretched world. The same fate awaits all other beings; they are all in a state of endurance and suffering, proclaiming aloud the irresistible action of duka.

A third obstacle to our being convinced that all is illusion in this world is that false persuasion which makes us to say, This is a foot, a hand, a woman, &c.; whilst these things have no reality, no consistence, but are mere shades, ready at any moment to vanish and disappear. These and like expressions being always used, impart at last a sort of conviction that they are true; but, after all, what are all these things but a compound of the four elements, or more simply nama and rupa?

In addition to this examination, the sage considers also our ideas and the operations of our mental faculties. Here he sees these ideas appearing for a moment and then disappearing; he concludes that ideas are likewise subjected to the great law of mutability. He finds as much misery in his own mind as he has met with in the exterior objects; all around his mind is only illusion. When he has reached this point, he is delivered at once of the three *Nimeit* that make one believe that there is something real in birth, existence, and action. The destruction of all beings, of all things, is ever present to his mind. In such a state, the sage is free from all erroneous doctrines; he is disgusted with life; the exercise of meditation is easy to him, and almost uninterrupted. He is free from all passions.

Our author has another chapter devoted to the consideration of the miseries attending all living beings. To make us better informed on this subject, he desires the sage to meditate upon the miseries attending birth, existence, old age, and death; he wishes him to examine attentively the condition of all creatures, that he might never be seduced by the dazzling appearance that encompasses them. He insists at great length upon the dangers surrounding the wise man, as yet compelled to remain in contact with this material world. To make us better understand this subject, he makes use of the following similitude. A man worn out with fatigue enters a cave wherein he longs to enjoy a refreshing rest. He is just lying down in the hope of abandoning himself to the sweet delight of undisturbed repose, when, on a sudden, he perceives close by him an infuriated tiger. At that moment all idea of rest, of sleep, of happiness, vanishes away; he is taken up solely with the imminent danger of his position. Such is the position of the sage who, living among creatures, may be tempted to allow himself to look on them with an idea of enjoyment. But when he has come to that state, to be disgusted with all the modifications matter is subjected to, he is likened to the pure swan who never sets his feet in low and dirty places, but delights to rest on the bosom of a beautiful lake, of limpid and clear water. Our sage, who has in abhorrence all the filth of this miserable world, is delighted only in the consideration of truth. He is displeased with the world and all things that are therein. His mind is busily engaged in finding out the most effectual means to break with this world, and rend asunder the ties that retain him linked to it. He is like a fish caught in the net, or a frog seized by a snake, or a man shut up in a dungeon. All three strive, to their utmost, to escape the danger that threatens them and regain their liberty. Such is the condition of the perfect who has attentively considered the many snares that are around them. He, too, has but one object in view, that of freeing himself from them and obtaining the deliverance.

The best and surest means to save himself from the dangers attending existence is a profound and unremitting meditation on the three great principles: aneitsa, duka, and anatta. We will select among many reflections supplied by our author, a few on each of these principles, to convey to the reader some ideas respecting the subjects that engross much of the attention of the Buddhist sage. Most of these reflections are strikingly true, and could as well find place in the mind of a Christian as in that of a Buddhist.

Speaking of *aneitsa*, our author says: Let us reflect on this, that there is nothing permanent or stable in this world. We hold all things as a sort of borrowed property, or on tenure; we are by no means proprietors of what we possess. We acquire goods but to lose them very soon. All in nature is subjected to pain, old age, and death; everything comes to an end, either by virtue of its own condition, or by the agency of some external cause. Shall we ever be able to find in this world anything stable? No; we leave one place, but only to go and occupy another, which, in its turn, is soon vacated. No one is able to enumerate the countless changes that incessantly take place. What exists to-day disappears to-morrow. In fact, all nature is pervaded from beginning to end by the principle of mutability, which incessantly works upon it.

On the miseries of this world our philosopher speaks as follows: Pain is the essential appendage of this world. Survey, if you can, the whole of this universe, and everywhere you will find a heavy load of pain and afflictions, so harassing and oppressing that we can scarcely bear them with a tolerable amount of patience. Look at birth, examine existence during its duration, consider senses, the organs of our life. In every direction our eyes will meet with an accumulation of pain, sufferings, and miseries; on every side we are beset with dangers, difficulties, and calamities; nowhere lasting joy or permanent rest is to be found. In vain we may go in quest of health and happiness; both are chimerical objects nowhere to be met with. Everywhere we meet with afflictions.

In speaking of the *anatta,* or illusion in which we are miserably rocked as long as we stay in this world, our philosopher is equally eloquent. If we consider with some attention this world, we will never be able to discover in it anything else but name and form; and, as a necessary consequence, all that exists is but illusion. Here is the manner we must carry on our reasoning. The things that I see and know are not myself, nor from myself, nor to myself. What seems to be myself is in reality neither myself nor belongs to myself. What appears to me to be another is neither myself nor from myself. The organs of senses, such as the eyes, the ears, &c., are neither myself nor to myself. They are but illusions, or as nothing relatively to me. The form is not a form; the attributes of a living being are not attributes; beings are not beings. All that is an aggregate of the four elements, and these again are but form and name, and these two are but an illusion, destitute of reality. In a being, then, there are two attributes, form and sensation, that appear to have some more consistency than other things. Yet they have no reality; their nature and condition is to be destitute of all reality and stability.[8] Penetrated with the truth of

---

[8] In this latter part our author clearly explains his opinion on this world, that is to say, on all that exists. He states at first, in general terms, that what we see and perceive by means of our senses, possesses no reality; it is a mere illusion. Our ignorance of the real state of things deceives us, by making us believe in the reality of objects that have nothing but an ephemeral and illusory existence. He proceeds a little farther, and treats our senses in like manner. They are the instruments that procure unto us a general illusion. But the senses, what are they? They are distinct from us. By a strict analysis we find them to be but a compound of the four elements, liable to dissolution and destruction. A living being has certain attributes which are the supports of his existence; but those attributes are equally a compound of the elements, subjected to the same

these and like considerations, the sage declares at once that all things are neither himself nor belong to himself. Nothing, therefore, appears worthy his notice. He at once divorces himself from the world and all the things that are therein. He would fain have nothing to do with it; he holds it in supreme contempt and utter disgust.

He who has reached this lofty point of sublime science is at once secure from the snares of seduction and the path of error. He will escape from the whirlpool of human miseries, and infallibly reach the state of Neibban. The most perfect among the perfect are so much taken upon with and deeply affected by the view of Neibban, that they tend in that direction without effort. Others, somewhat less advanced in the sublime science, discover, it is true, the state of Neibban at a distance, but its sight is as yet dimmed and somewhat obscured. They want as yet to train up their mind to and perfect it in the exercise of that meditation of which we have given an abbreviated analysis.

---

modifications of reproduction and destruction and deprived of consistence. The attributes of the living beings being disposed of in this manner, the being itself vanishes away. There remain but name and form. But does what we call form possess a real existence? Undoubtedly not. It is a mere phantom, an illusion. Our author comes to the necessary and final consequence that there is no world really existing. In fact, he denies the existence of matter and spirit. With such an abuse of the powers of reasoning, there is no wonder that he looks upon Neibban, or annihilation, as the only end to be arrived at. Man in his opinion being but a compound of the four elements, which have no real existence, cannot be himself but an illusion without a reality. Gracious Heavens! what an excess of mental aberration will man reach when he is left to himself, deprived of the light from above! Never has the writer witnessed such a total eclipse of human intellect.

NOTICE ON THE PHONGYIES, OR BUDDHIST MONKS,

SOMETIMES CALLED TALAPOINS.[1]

IN the foregoing pages we have first given a sketch of the life of the founder of Buddhism, and in the accompanying notes endeavoured to explain the more important particulars respecting the extraordinary religious system he has established. Subsequently, in the way to Neibban, we have laid down, in as few words as possible, the great metaphysical principles upon which is raised the great structure of Buddhism, and pointed out the way leading to the pretended perfection, or rather the end of perfection, Neibban. It seems to be necessary to devote a particular notice to the religious Order which forms the most striking feature of that religion, which has extended its sway over so many nations. This association of devotees holds the first rank among the followers of Buddha; it comprises the *élite* of that immense body. The system of

[1] The word Talapoin, imported into Europe by the writings of early Portuguese authors in the East Indies, derives its origin probably from two Pali words, Tala-pat, meaning the leaf of the palm-tree. These two words, coupled together, are used by the Siamese to designate the large fan made of palm-leaves, set in a slender wooden frame, which Talapoins carry with them on certain occasions when they go abroad.

In the course of this notice we will indiscriminately make use of the words Phongyies, Talapoins, and Rahans to designate the Buddhist religious.

discipline to which the Buddhist religious are subjected, is the highest practical illustration of the doctrines and practices of Buddhism. We may see reflected in that corporation the greatest results that the working of these religious institutions can ever produce. All that Buddha, in his efforts, has been able to devise as most fit to lead man to the perfection, such as he understood it, will be found in the constitutions of that order. It is a living mirror in which we may contemplate the masterpiece of his creation. The Buddhist religious constitute the thanga, or assembly of the perfect, that is to say, of the disciples who have left the world, conformed their life to that of their teacher, and striven to acquire the science that will qualify them for entering into the way leading to perfection. They are the strict followers of Buddha, who, like him, have renounced the world, to devote themselves to the two-fold object of mastering their passions and acquiring the true wisdom which alone can lead to the deliverance.

The best method for obtaining correct information respecting the Buddhist religious is not, it seems, to consider their order from an abstract point of view, but rather in connection with the religion it has sprung from, as affording a perfect exemplification of its highest practices, maxims, and tendencies, as well as of the real nature and true spirit of that creed.

Buddhism is evidently an off-shoot of Brahminism. We find it replete with principles, practices, observances, and dogmas belonging to the great Hindu system. Gaudama, being himself a Hindu, reared in a Hindu society, trained up in the Hindu schools of philosophy, could not but imbibe, to a great extent, the opinions and observances of his contemporaries. He dissented from them, it is true, in many important points, but in the generality of his teachings he seems to have agreed with them. He found existing in his times a body of religious and philosophers, whose mode of life was peculiar and quite distinct from that of the people. When he laid the plan for the religious institution he contemplated to establish, he found around him most of the elements he required for that work. He had but to improve on what he saw existing, and make his new order agree with the religious tenets he innovated.

In the hope of tracing up the ties of relationship that must have existed between the religious of the Brahminical order, and those of the Buddhist one, the writer will begin this notice with establishing a short parallel between the former, such as they are described in the Institutes of Menoo, and the institution of the latter, such as it is explained in the Wini, or Book of discipline. Afterwards the nature of the Buddhist order and the object its members have in view in embracing it will be examined; next to that, the constituent parts of that body and its hierarchy shall receive a due share of attention. We will describe at the same time the ceremonies observed on the solemn occasion of admitting individuals into the religious society, and expound briefly the rules that direct and regulate the whole life of a professed member as long as he remains in the brotherhood. It will not be found amiss to inquire into the cause and nature of the great religious influence undoubtedly possessed by the members of the order, and examine the motives that induce the votaries of Buddhism to show the greatest respect and give unfeigned marks of the deepest veneration to the Talapoins or Phongyies. This will be concluded with a short account of the low and degraded state into which the society has fallen in these parts, particularly in what has reference to knowledge and information.

ARTICLE I.

A SHORT PARALLEL BETWEEN THE BRAHMINICAL AND THE BUDDHISTIC RELIGIOUS ORDERS.

It has been stated, on apparently incontrovertible grounds, in the foregoing pages, that Buddhism has originated to a considerable extent from Brahminism. The following remarks will corroborate the statement, and give an additional weight to the reasons already brought forward. In fact, both systems have the same objects in view, viz., the disentangling of the soul from passions and the influence of the material world, and its perfect liberation from metempsychosis and the action of matter. The final end to be arrived at is, however, widely different. The perfected Brahmin longs for his absorption in the infinite being; the perfect Buddhist thirsts after a state of complete isolation, which is nothing short of total annihilation. But the means for obtaining the ardently coveted perfection are in many respects the same. The moral observances enforced by both creeds differ so little from each other that they appear to be almost identical. In both systems, moreover, we find a body of individuals who aim at a complete and perfect observance of the highest injunctions, striving to reach the very summit of that perfection pointed out by the founders of their respective institutions: these are the Brahminical and Buddhist religious. To glance over the regulations enjoined on the Brahmins, such as we find them in the Institutes of Menoo, and those prescribed by the Wini to the Talapoins, cannot fail to be truly interesting. A summary comparison will enable the reader to perceive at once how closely allied are the two creeds, and how great is the resemblance between them both. He will see on the clearest evidence that to Buddha is not to be ascribed the merit of having originated so many fine moral precepts and admirable disciplinary regulations, but that he found in his own country, in the schools where he studied wisdom, already well-known, pure moral precepts, actually discussed, studied, and by many strictly observed, together with the disciplinary regulations. He was brought up in a society which beheld with astonishment and admiration a body of religious men entirely devoted to the great work of securing the triumph of the spiritual principle over the material one, and endeavouring by dint of the greatest and severest austerities, the most rigorous penances, and the most entire renouncing of all this material world, to break down the material barriers that had hitherto kept the soul captive, and prevented her from taking her flight into regions of blissful freedom and perfect quiescence. There is, however, a remarkable difference between the sacerdotal caste of Brahmins and the members of the Buddhist monkish institution. The position of the former is hereditary; he is rendered illustrious by his lineage and descent. That of the second is personal, and ends with him; it is the result of his own free choice; he derives all the glory that shines round him from his virtuous life and a strict adherence to the institutions of the Wini. The Brahmin owes everything to religion and to birth. The Buddhist religious is indebted for all that he is solely to religion; the monk's title to distinction is the holy mode of the saintly life that he has embraced. Both are the greatest and most distinguished in their respective societies; but merit and intrinsic worth alone elicit veneration and respect in behalf of the humble religious, whilst the casual birth of the Brahmin from individuals belonging to the highest caste centres upon his person the reluctant homage of men belonging to inferior castes, who, in virtue of the prejudices in which they are reared, consider themselves obliged to do homage to him. The person of both is sacred and looked upon with awe and veneration, but from somewhat opposite and different motives.

Notwithstanding these and many other differences and

discrepancies, it is not the less striking to find in the Brahminical body, such as it is constituted by the regulations of the Vedas, the germ of all the principal observances enjoined on the Buddhist that leaves the world, to follow the path leading to perfection.

The life of a Brahmin, not as it is now, but as it originally was, and now ought to be, if the regulations of the Vedas had not been partly set aside, is one of laborious study, austerity, self-denial, and retirement. The first quarter of his life is spent in the capacity of student. His great and sole object is the study of the Vedas, and the mastering of their contents. Worldly studies are not to be thought of. He is entirely under the control of his preceptor, to whom he has to yield obedience, respect, and service in all that relates to his daily wants. He must, moreover, daily beg his food from door to door. The Buddhist novice likewise withdraws from his family, enters the monastery, lives under the discipline of the head of the house, whom he obeys and serves in his daily necessities, and devotes all his undivided attention to the study of religious books. He pays no regard to worldly knowledge. He has likewise to go out every morning to beg the food that he will use during the day.

The second quarter of the Brahmin's life is thus employed. He marries and lives with his family, but he must consider his chief employment to be the teaching of the Vedas and a zealous discharge of the religious observances and of all that relates to public worship. He must sedulously abstain from too sensual and worldly enjoyments, even from music, dancing, and other amusements calculated to lead to dissipation. The Buddhist monkish institution being not hereditary, and its continuance and development having not to depend upon generation, its members are bound to a strict celibacy, and to an absolute and entire abstinence from all sensual and worldly enjoyments inconsistent with gravity, self-recollection, and self-denial. Their chief occupation is teaching to children the rudiments of reading and writing, that they might read religious books, which are the only ones used in schools. He must pay a strict regard to devotional practices, and take care that the religious observances and ceremonies be regularly attended to in his monastery.

The third quarter of his life is spent by the Brahmin in solitude as an anchorite. He dwells in the forests, where he must procure what is necessary for food and raiment. The latter article is looked after when he thinks it to be a requisite to cover his nakedness. With many of them fanaticism has so far prevailed over reason and the sense of decency that they live in a state of disgusting nakedness. The roots of plants, the fruits and leaves of wild trees, will supply the needful for the support of nature. That time too must be devoted to the infliction of the severest penances and to the practice of the hardest deeds of mortification. To the Buddhist monk solitude and retirement must ever be dear. Ascetic life is much recommended, and praised as most excellent. It was formerly much in use among religious Buddhists. In Burmah several places are pointed out with respect as having been sanctified by the residence of holy anchorites. Now in our days a few zealots, to bear, as it were, witness to this ancient observance, retire into solitude during a portion of the three months of Lent. The spirit of mortification and self-renouncing is eminently Buddhist; but from the very days of Gaudama we remark a positive tendency on the part of his religious to give up and renounce those unnatural and ultra-rigorous penances regularly observed by their brethren of the opposite creed. The principle is cherished by them, but the mode of carrying it into practice is more mild, and more consonant with reason and modesty.

The last portion of the Brahmin's life is devoted likewise to meditation and contemplation. He is no more subjected to the ordeal of rigorous penances; nature has been subdued; passions silenced and destroyed; the soul has obtained the mastery over the body and the material world. She is free from all the trammels and obstacles that impeded her contemplation of truth. She is ready to quit this world, as the bird leaves the branch of the tree when it pleases him. The Buddhist religious, having likewise crushed his passions and disentangled his soul from affection to matter, delights only in the contemplation of truth. As the mighty whale sports in the bosom of the boundless ocean, so the perfected Buddhist launches forth into abstract and infinite truth, delights in it, completely estranged from this world, which meditation has taught him to consider as a mere illusion, as destitute of reality. He is then ripe for the so ardently coveted state of Neibban.

When Buddha originated the plan of a society of religious, and framed the regulations whereby it was to be governed, he had but to look around him for patterns of a religious life. The country where he had been born, the society in which he had been brought up, swarmed with religious following the different systems of philosophy prevailing in those days. He saw them, conversed with them, and for some time lived in their company under the same disciplinary institutions. He was, therefore, thoroughly conversant with all that in his days constituted a religious life. But the same bold and enterprising spirit which made him dissent from his masters and contemporaries on many important questions of morals and metaphysics, and induced him to improve, as he thought, and perfect theories in speculative and practical philosophy, impelled him also to do something similar respecting the disciplinary regulations to which his religious were to be hereafter subjected. We freely confess that on this latter point he was eminently successful. The body of Buddhist religious is infinitely superior in most respects to the other societies of Indian religious. The regulations of the former breathe a spirit of modesty, mildness, and unaffectation, which in a striking manner contrasts with those disgusting exhibitions of self-inflicted penances so fondly courted by Brahmins, where immodesty seems to dispute the palm with cruelty. Buddha opened the door of his society to all men without any distinction or exception, implicitly pulling down the barriers raised by the prejudices of caste. Did he in the beginning of his public career lay down the plan of destroying all vestiges of caste, and proclaiming the principle of equality amongst men? It is, to say the least, very doubtful. The equalising principle itself was never distinctly mentioned in his discourses. But he had sown all the elements constitutive of that principle in his instructions. Every member put on the religious dress of his own free choice, and set it aside at his pleasure; no hereditary right, therefore, could be thought of; the dying religious could bequeath to his brethren but the example of his virtues. His complete separation from the world had broken all the ties of relationship. The double vow of strict poverty and of celibacy, cutting the root of cupidity and sensual enjoyments, precluded him from aiming at the influence and power which is conferred by wealth and rank. With the Brahminical religious the case is the very reverse. His sacerdotal caste, exclusive of his personal merits, confers on him an almost divine sacredness, which is to be propagated by generation. He may possess riches and have a numerous posterity. He is, therefore, almost irresistibly impelled to seize on a power which is forced on him by the treble influence of birth, religion, and wealth.

The subject of the comparison between the two societies of religious might receive further developments, but what has been briefly stated appears sufficient to bear out the point it was intended to establish, viz., the close resemblance subsisting between the two religious orders in both systems, and the necessary inference that the order of Buddhist religious is an improvement on the orders of religious subsisting in India in the days of Gaudama.

There is another characteristic of the religious order of

Buddhists which has favourably operated in its behalf, and powerfully contributed to maintain it for so many centuries in so compact and solid a body that it seems to bid defiance to the destructive action of revolutions. We allude to its regularly constituted hierarchy, which is as perfect as it can be expected, particularly in Burmah and Siam. The power and influence of him whom we may call the general of the order in Burmah, and who is known under the appellation of Tha-thana-paing, when, as was very often the case, backed by the temporal power, was felt throughout the whole country, and much contributed to maintain good order and discipline in the great body of religious. The action of the provincial or superior of the religious houses of a province is more directly and immediately felt by all the subordinates. It does not appear that the religious of the Hindu schools, at least in our days, possess such an advantage that they may well envy their brethren of the Buddhist sect. The members of the Brahminical body are not kept together by the power and government of superiors, but by regulations that are so deeply rooted and firmly seated in the mind of individuals that they are faithfully observed. The superiority of caste, connected too with a certain amount of spiritual pride, has been hitherto sufficient to maintain that body distinct and separate from all that is without itself. The religious spirit that pervades that body in our days seems to have abated from its original fervour and energy. The Brahmin has maintained with the utmost jealousy the superiority that caste confers upon him, but appears not to have been so particular in keeping up the genuine spiritual supremacy, which a strict adherence to the prescriptions of the Vedas must have ever firmly secured to him.

ARTICLE II.

NATURE OF THE RELIGIOUS ORDER OF PHONGYIES.

He who has not seriously studied the religious system of Buddhism, nor acquired accurate notions of its doctrinal principles, is scarcely capable of forming a correct opinion of the religious order of those austere recluses, whom Europeans, with a mind biassed by educational influence, denominate priests of Buddha. Were we to apply to the members of that order the notions generally entertained of a priesthood, we would form a very erroneous conception of the real character of their institution. For in every religious system admitting of one or several beings superior to man, whose providential action influences his destinies either in this or the next world, persons invested with a sacerdotal character have always been considered as mediators between men and the acknowledged deity, offering to the supreme being on all public occasions the prayers and sacrifices of the people, and soliciting in return his gracious protection. When in the early ages of the world the sacerdotal dignity was coupled with the patriarchal or regal ones, when in the succeeding ages there existed a regular and distinct priesthood, such as subsisted under the Mosaic dispensation, or among the Greeks, Romans, Gauls, &c., the priests were looked upon as delegates of the people in all that related to national worship, carrying on in the name of the Deity the mysterious intercourse that links heaven to earth. Priesthood, therefore, necessarily implies the belief in a being superior to man and controlling his destinies. The moment such a belief is disregarded, the very idea of priesthood vanishes. Buddhism, such at least as it is found existing in Ceylon, Burmah, Siam, and other places, is a purely atheistical religious system, and presents the solitary instance, at least as far as my information goes, of a religious creed, admitted by various nations, the doctrines of which are not based upon the notion of a supreme being controlling more or less the affairs of this world. In support of an assertion that may appear to many somewhat hazardous, we will briefly lay down the leading tenets of the Buddhistic doctrine.

According to that system, matter is eternal. The existence of a world, its duration, destruction, and reproduction, all the various combinations and modifications matter is liable to, are the immediate results of the action of eternal and self-existing laws. Through life man is subjected to the continual but successive influences of his good and bad deeds. This double influence always attends him through his numberless existences, and inevitably awards him happiness or misfortune, according as the respective sum of good or evil predominates. There exists an eternal law, which, when obliterated from the memory of men, can be known again, and, as it were, recovered only and thoroughly understood by the incomparable genius and matchless wisdom of certain extraordinary personages, called Buddhas, who appear successively and at intervals during the various series or successions of worlds. These Buddhas announce that law to all the then existing rational beings. The great object of that doctrine is to point out to those beings the means of freeing themselves from the influence of passions, and becoming abstracted from all that exists. Being thereby delivered from the action of good or evil influence, which causes mortals to turn incessantly in the whirlpool of never-ending existences, men can obtain the state of Neibban, or rest, that is to say, according to the popular opinion, a situation wherein the soul, disentangled from all that exists, alone with herself, indifferent to pain as well as to pleasure, folded, as it were, upon herself, remains for ever in an incomprehensible state of complete abstraction and absolute rest. I say that such is the popular opinion, fortunately unbiassed by scholastic theories. But the opinion of the Buddhist doctors respecting Neibban is that it means the negation of all states of being; that is to say, a desolating and horrifying annihilation. A Buddha is a being who, during myriads of existences, slowly and gradually gravitates towards this centre of an imaginary perfection by the practice of the highest virtues. Having attained thereto, he becomes on a sudden gifted with a boundless genius, wherewith he at once discovers the wretched state of beings and the means of delivering them from it. He thoroughly understands the eternal law which alone can lead mortals in the right way, and enable them to come out of the circle of existences, wherein they have been unceasingly turning and moving in a state of perpetual agitation, opposite to that of fixity or rest. He preaches that law whereby man is taught the practice of those virtues which destroy gradually in him all evil influences, together with every affection for all that exists, and brings him at last to the end of existence, the possession of Neibban. His task fulfilled, Buddha dies, or rather, to use the language of Buddhists, he enters into the state Neibban. In that situation, which is truly inexplicable, he knows nothing of and enters no wise into the affairs of this world. He is as if he was not or had never been. He is indeed annihilated.

Buddhists venerate three precious things—Buddha, his law, and the assembly of the just or perfect—in the same sense as we venerate and admire what is morally good and beautiful, such as virtue considered abstractedly, and the acts originating from it. The statues of the last Buddha Gaudama are honoured by his followers, not with the idea that certain powers or virtues are inherent in them, but solely because they are the visible representations of Buddha, who, according to Buddhists, desired that the same honours should be paid to them as would be offered to his person, were he yet living among them. This faint outline of the Buddhistic creed is sufficient to bear out the above assertion, that it is in no wise based on the belief in a supreme being, but that it is strictly atheistical, and therefore that no real priesthood can ever be found existing under such a system. It may prove, too, of some assistance for better understanding what is to be said regarding the subjects of this notice.

The Talapoins are called by the Burmese Phongyies, which term means great glory; or Rahans, which means perfect. They are known in Ceylon, Siam, Thibet, under different names, conveying nearly the same meaning and expressing either the nature or the object of their profession.

What induces a follower of Buddha to embrace the Talapoinic state? What is the object of his pursuit in entering on such a peculiar and extraordinary course of life? The answer to these questions will supply us with accurate notions of the real nature of this singular order of devotees. A Buddhist on becoming a member of the holy society proposes to keep the law of Buddha in a more perfect manner than his other co-religionists. He intends to observe not only its general ordinances obligatory on every individual, but also its prescriptions of a higher excellency, leading to an uncommon sanctity and perfection, which can be the lot of but a comparatively small number of fervent and resolute persons. He aims at weakening within himself all the evil propensities that give origin and strength to the principle of demerits. By the practice and observance of the highest and sublimest precepts and counsels of the law, he establishes, confirms, and consolidates in his own soul the principle of merits, which is to work upon him during the various existences he has as yet to go through, and gradually lead him to that perfection which will qualify him for and entitle him to the state of Neibban, the object of the ardent desires and earnest pursuit of every true and genuine disciple of Buddha. The life of the last Buddha Gaudama, his doctrines as well as his examples, he proposes to copy with a scrupulous fidelity and to follow with unremitting ardour. Such is the great model that he proposes to himself for imitation. Gaudama withdrew from the world, renounced its seducing pleasures and dazzling vanities, curbed his passions under the yoke of restraint, and strove to practise the highest virtues, particularly self-denial, in order to arrive at a state of complete indifference to all that is within or without self; which is, as it were, the threshold of Neibban.

The Talapoin, fixing his regards on that matchless pattern of perfection, would fain reproduce, as far as it lies in his power, all its features in his own person. Like Buddha himself, he parts with his family, relatives, and friends, and seeks for admission into the society of the perfect; he abandons and leaves his home, to enter into the asylum of peace and retirement; he forsakes the riches of this world to practise the strictest poverty; he renounces the pleasures of this world, even the lawful ones, to live according to the rules of the severest abstinence and purest chastity; he exchanges his secular dress for that of the new profession he enters on; he gives up his own will, and fetters his own liberty, to attend, through every act and all the particulars of life, to the regulations of the brotherhood. He is a Talapoin for himself and for his own benefit, to acquire merits which he shares with nobody else. On the occasion of certain offerings or alms being presented to him by some benevolent admirers of his holy mode of life, he will repay his benefactors by repeating to them certain precepts, commands, and points of the law; but he is not bound by his professional character to expound the law to the people. Separated from the world by his dress and his peculiar way of living, he remains a stranger to all that takes place without the walls of his monastery. He is not charged with the care of souls, and therefore never presumes to rebuke any one that trespasses the law, or to censure the conduct of the profligate.

The ceremonies of the Buddhistic worship are simple and few. The Talapoin is not considered as a minister whose presence is an essential requisite when they are to be performed. Pagodas are erected, statues of Buddha are inaugurated, offerings of flowers, tapers, and small ornaments are made, particularly on the days of the new and full moon, but on all those solemn occasions the interference of the Phongyie is in no way considered as necessary, so that the whole worship exists independently of him. He is not to be seen on the particular occasions of births and marriages. He is, it is true, occasionally asked to attend funerals; but he then acts, not as a minister performing a ceremony, but as a private person. He is present for the sake of receiving alms that are profusely bestowed upon him by the relatives of the defunct.

The Buddhists have three months of the year, from the full moon of July to the full moon of October, particularly devoted to a stricter observance of the practices and ceremonies of the law. Crowds of people of both sexes resort to the pagodas, and often spend whole nights in the buildings erected close to those places. The most fervent among them fast and abstain from profane amusements during that period; they devote more time to the reading of their sacred books and the repetition of certain formulas calculated to remind them of certain important truths, or intended to praise the last Buddha Gaudama and the law he has published. Alms pour more abundantly into the peaceable dwellings of the pious recluses. During all the time the Talapoin quietly remains in his place, without altering his mode of life, or deviating in the least from his never-changing usages and ordinary habits. By the rules of his profession he is directed to pay, during that time, a particular regard to religious observances, to join his brethren from time to time in the recital of certain formulas, and in the reading of the book embodying the regulations of the profession. He enjoys, as usual, the good things which his liberal co-religionists take pleasure in proffering to him. On two occasions the writer has seen, and on many has heard of Talapoins withdrawing during the three months of Lent to some lonely place, living alone in small huts, shunning the company of men, and leading an eremitical life, to remain at liberty to devote all their time to meditations on the most excellent points of the law of Buddha, combating their passions, and enjoying in that retired situation a foretaste of the never-troubled rest of Neibban.

In many respects the Talapoinic institutions may be likened to those of some religious orders that appeared successively in almost every Christian country previous to the era of the Reformation, and that are, up to this day, to be met with amidst the Churches of the Latin and Greek rites. Like the monk, the Talapoin bids a farewell to the world, wears a particular dress, leads a life of community, abstracts himself from all that gives strength to his passions, by embracing a state of voluntary poverty and absolute renunciation of all sensual gratifications. He aims at obtaining, by a stricter observance of the law's most sublime precepts, an uncommon degree of sanctity and perfection. All his time is regulated by the rules of his profession, and devoted to repeating certain formulas of prayers, reading the sacred scriptures, begging alms for his support, &c.

These features of exterior resemblance, common to institutions of creeds so opposite to each other, have induced several writers, little favourable to Christianity, to pronounce without further inquiry that Catholicism has borrowed from Buddhism many ceremonies, institutions, and disciplinary regulations. Some of them have gone so far as to pretend to find in it the very origin of Christianity. They have, however, been ably confuted by Abel Remusat, in his *Memoir* entitled "Chronological Researches into the Lamaic Hierarchy of Thibet." Without entertaining in the least the presumptuous idea of entering into a controversy entirely foreign to his purpose, the writer will confine himself to making one or two remarks calculated to show that the first conclusion is, to say the least of it, a premature one. When in two religious creeds, entirely opposed to each other in their ultimate object, there are several minor objects equally set forth by both, it will necessarily happen that, in many instances, means nearly similar will be prescribed on both sides for effectually obtaining them, independent of any previously concerted plan or imitation. The Christian system and the Buddhistic one, though differing from each other in their respective objects and ends, as much as truth from error, have, it must be confessed, many striking features of an astonishing resemblance. There are many moral precepts equally commanded and enforced in common by both creeds. It will not be deemed rash to assert that most of the moral truths prescribed by the Gospel are to be met with in the Buddhistic scriptures. The essential, vital, and capital discrepancy lies in the difference of the ends to which the two creeds lead, but not in the variance of the means they prescribe for the attainment of them. The Gospel tends to reunite man to his Maker, points out to him the way he must follow for arriving at the possession and enjoyment of Him who is the great principle and end of all things, and teaches him, as a paramount duty, to conform his will and inclinations to His commands. Buddhism tends to abstract man from all that is without self, and makes self his own and sole centre. It exhorts him to the practice of many eminent virtues, which are to help him to rise to an imaginary perfection, the summit of which is the incomprehensible state of Neibban. It is the mildest expression which the writer can command when he has to speak of so sad a subject, the final end of a Buddhist. It would be more correct to say at once that the pretended perfect being is led, by the principles of his creed, into the dark and fathomless abyss of annihilation.

If the end aimed at by the followers of Buddha is widely different from that which the disciples of Christ strive to obtain, the means prescribed for the attainment of these two ends are, in many respects, very much similar to each other. Both creeds teach man to combat, control, and master the passions of his heart, to make reason predominate over sense, mind over matter, to root up from his heart every affection for the things of this world, and to practise the virtues required for the attainment of these great objects. Is there anything surprising that persons, having, in many respects, views nearly similar, resort to means or expedients nearly alike for securing the object of their pursuit, without having ever seen or consulted each other? He who intends to practise absolute poverty must of course abandon all his earthly property. He who proposes renouncing the world ought to withdraw from it. He who will lead a contemplative life must look out for a retired place, far from the gaze and agitation of the world. To control passions, and particularly the fiercest of all, the sensual appetite, it is required that one should keep himself separate from all that is calculated to kindle its fires and feed its violence. Every profession has its distinctive marks and peculiar characteristics. Hence peculiarity of dress, manners, and habits in those who have adopted a mode of life differing from that of the rest of the community. He who has bound himself to the daily recitation of certain prayers or devotional formulas a certain number of times, will have recourse to some instrument, or devise some means for ascertaining the number of times he has complied with his regulation in this respect. He too who is eager to acquire self-knowledge and to carry on a successful war with himself, will apply to a guide to whom he will lay open his whole soul, and ask spiritual advice that will enable him to overcome the obstacles he meets on his way to perfection.

These and many other points are common to all those that intend to observe not only the precepts but also the mere counsels of their respective creeds. Causes being the same, in many instances, in both systems, consequences almost analogous must inevitably result therefrom. Religious institutions always bear the stamp of the religious ideas that have given rise to them. They, together with their rules and regulations, are not the principle, but the immediate consequence or offspring of religion, such as it is understood by the people professing it. They exemplify and illustrate religious notions already entertained, but they never create such as are not yet in existence. When the learned shall have collected sufficient materials for giving an accurate history of the origin, progress, spread, and dogmatical revolutions of Buddhism, it will not be uninteresting to inquire into the causes that have operated in communicating to two religious systems essentially differing in their respective tendencies so many points of resemblance. But that study is yet to be made. We know very little on all those points. The best informed are compelled to acknowledge that in the present state of information we are still in the dark, the thickness of which is occasionally relieved by a few transient and uncertain glimpses which are insufficient to enlighten the mind, and enable the searcher after truth to guide safely his steps. In reading the particulars of the life of the last Buddha Gaudama, it is impossible not to feel reminded of many circumstances relating to our Saviour's life, such as it has been sketched out by the evangelists. The origin of the close affinity between many doctrinal points and maxims common both to Christianity and Buddhism having been ascertained, it will not be difficult to find out and explain how the votaries of both have come to adopt so many practices, ceremonies, observances, and institutions nearly similar.

Having endeavoured to explain the nature of the institution of the Talapoins, and the object aimed at by its professed members, we will now proceed to examine its systematical organisation, or sacred hierarchy.

ARTICLE III.

HIERARCHY OF THE ORDER.

It is somewhat surprising to find in the middle of half-civilised nations, such as the Burmese, Siamese, Cingalese, and Thibetans a religious order, with a distinct and well-marked hierarchy, constitutions and regulations, providing for the admission of members, determining their occupations, duties, obligations, and their mode of life, and forming, as it were, a compact, solid, and perfect body, that has subsisted, almost without change, during several centuries, and survived the destruction of kingdoms, the fall of royal dynasties, and all the confusion and agitation produced by political commotions and revolutions. It is in Thibet that the order is found existing in the greatest perfection, under the fostering care of the Grand Lama, or High Priest, who combines in his own person the regal as well as the sacerdotal dignity and power. In the city of Lassa, a pontifical court, an elective sacerdotal chief, and a college of superior Lamas impart to the order dignity, decency, respectability, and stability, which insure its continued existence, and more or less extend its influence over its members living in distant countries. The period of the introduction of Buddhism from India into Thibet is very uncertain, if not quite unknown. Buddhist annals mention that after the holding of the third council, 236 years after Gaudama's death, some missionaries were deputed by the president of that assembly to go and preach religion in some parts of the Himalayan range. We may suppose that this had reference to the southern slopes of the mountains. Be that as it may, it appears certain that the establishment of a pontifical chief or sovereign, with royal prerogatives, was set up by one of the grandsons of the great Tartar warrior Gengis in or about the middle of the thirteenth century. In other countries, where the order has no connection whatever with the civil power, we can scarcely expect to see it surrounded with an equal splendour, or subsisting in the same state of splendour and regularity. Though this is the case in Burmah, it is impossible not to acknowledge the fact that the regulations of the Wini are more carefully attended to in this country than in Thibet. The conduct of the monks here is incomparably more regular. The public could not bear an open dereliction of the duties imposed by the vows of poverty and chastity. But, if credit be given to the narratives of travellers, the Thibetan monks do not scruple to forsake occasionally those duties, without appearing to fear the rising of a popular cry of indignation, on account of their misbehaviour in points considered of such vast importance. Extraordinary, indeed, would be its vital energies, were the remotest parts of this great and far-spread body to receive the same impulse and exhibit the same symptoms of vitality as those nearest to the heart or principle of life. Having never met with any detailed particulars regarding the Thibetan monks, we must remain satisfied with laying before the reader an account of all that relates to the constituent parts of the order, such as they are found existing in Burmah and developed in the sacred writings.

The whole fraternity is composed, 1st, of young men who have put on the Talapoinic dress without being considered professed members of the fraternity, or having hitherto passed through a certain ordeal somewhat resembling an ordinary; they are called *Shyins;* 2d, of those who, having lived for a while in the community in a probationary state, are admitted professed members with the ceremonies usually observed on such occasions, whereby the title and character of Phongyie are solemnly conferred; they are denominated *Patzins;* 3d, of the heads of each house or community, who have the power to control all the inmates of the house; 4th, of a provincial, whose jurisdiction extends over all the communities spread in the towns and villages of the province or district; 5th, of a superior general, residing in the capital or its suburbs, called *Tsaia-dau*, or great master, having the general management and direction of all the affairs of the order throughout the empire. He is emphatically called by the name of Tha-thana-paing, which means that he has the power over religion. Let us say something upon each of these five degrees of the Buddhistic hierarchy.

It is an almost universal custom among the Burmese and Siamese to cause boys who have attained the age of puberty, or even before that time, to enter for a year or two one of the many Talapoinic houses, to put on the yellow dress, for the double purpose of learning to read and write, and of acquiring merits for future existences. On the occasion of the death of certain persons, it happens sometimes that a member of the family will enter the community for six months or a year. When a young lad is to make his first entrance into a house of the order, he is led thereto, riding on a richly caparisoned pony, or sitting in a fine palanquin carried on the shoulders of four or more men. He is allowed to use one or several gold umbrellas, which are held opened over his head. During the triumphal march he is preceded by a long line of men and women, attired in their richest dresses, carrying a large quantity of presents destined for the use of the inmates of the *Kiaong* (such is the general name given to all the houses of the brotherhood in Burmah) which the young postulant is to reside in. In this stately order the procession, attended with a band playing on various musical instruments, moves on slowly and circuitously through the principal streets of the town towards the monastery that has been fixed upon. This display of an ostentatious pomp is, on the part of the parents and relatives, an honour paid to the postulant who generously consecrates himself to so exalted a calling, and on the part of the youth a last farewell to worldly vanities. He has no sooner descended from his splendid conveyance and crossed the threshold of the kiaong than he is delivered by his parents into the hands of the superior, and placed under his care. His head is instantly shaved; he is stripped of his fine secular dress, and habited in the plain and humble yellow garb; he must lay aside every sort of ornament, and remain contented with the unassuming simplicity becoming his new position. The kiaong is to become his home, and its inmates are substituted in the room of his father and mother, brothers and sisters.

The duty of the young shyin is to minister to the wants of the elders of the house, to bring and place before them at fixed times the usual supply of water, the betel-box, and the daily food; to attend them on some pious errand through the town or the country. A portion of his time is devoted to acquiring the art of reading and writing, and occasionally the elements of arithmetic. There are five general precepts obligatory on all men; but the shyin is bound to the observance of five additional ones, making ten altogether, by which he is forbidden—1st, to kill animals; 2d, to steal; 3d, to give himself up to carnal pleasures; 4th, to tell lies; 5th, to drink wine or other intoxicating liquors; 6th, to eat after mid-day; 7th, to dance, sing, or play on any musical instrument; 8th, to colour his face; 9th, to stand on elevated places, not proper for him; 10th, to touch or handle gold or silver.[1]

---

[1] In glancing over the latter part of Buddha's life, the reader has seen that the less important points of discipline have been the subject of much discussion in the early days of Buddhism. Among those points of dispute and contention were the last five articles above enumerated. The second council was assembled for the purpose of settling warm disputes which distracted the Buddhist Thanga, or Assembly, and caused great disturbances. The venerable Rasa, who lived in Wethalie, a city situated on the Gunduck, north of Hajipoor, undertook a long journey, as far as Kosambi, for the express purpose of warning the religious of that country against the dangerous innovations which were introduced by a considerable body of rahans belonging to the eastern districts of Wethalie.

The journey was certainly a long one in a western direction. The ruins of the famous city of Kosambi have been discovered at a place called Kosam, thirty miles above Allahabad, on the Jumna. They are most extensive, and at once indicate the import

The trespassing of the five first precepts is visited with expulsion from the kiaong; but that of the five last may be expiated by a proper penance.

The young shyins, as before observed, do not remain in the kiaong beyond the period of one or two years; they generally leave it and return to a secular life. There are, however, some of them, who, fond of the easy and quiet life of Talapoins, or actuated by other motives, prefer remaining longer in those places of retirement. They betake themselves to the study of the duties, rules, and obligations of the professed members of the society; they pay more attention to the reading of religious books, and endeavour to obtain the required qualifications. Being sufficiently instructed on all these points, and having attained the age of twenty years, they are solemnly admitted among the professed members of the brotherhood under the name of Patzin. The interesting ceremonies observed on the occasion will hereafter be fully described. The state of Patzin is, therefore, properly speaking, that of Phongyie, though that name is sometimes reserved for him who is the head of a monastery. Every other step or promotion in the hierarchy is purely honorary, in so far that it does not impose upon him who

---

ance that place must have had in the days of its prosperity. A broken pillar, the polished shaft of which must have measured 34 feet, is covered with inscriptions; it is one of the most important Buddhist relics. It is probably one of those pillars erected by Athoka in every part of his extensive dominions. It bears no inscription more ancient than the second and third century of the Christian era. A similar one was erected at Prayag, an ancient city mentioned by Hwen Thsang as being situated at the confluence of the Ganges and the Jumna, and finally destroyed by the gradual encroachments of the rivers. The place remained abandoned until the days of the Emperor Akhbar, who built a fort called Illahabas. The new city received the name of Allahabad from the Emperor Shah Jehan. The famous pillar called the Allahabad Pillar bears three inscriptions. The first is that of Asoka, 240 years B.C., recording his edicts for the propagation of Buddhism; the second is that of Samudra Gupta, in the second century of our era, commemorative of his extensive dominions; the third is that of Jehangir, mentioning his accession to the throne. The last resetting up of this famous pillar took place in 1838.

is so promoted any new duty or obligation different from what is obligatory on every professed member; but it confers a power or jurisdiction for commanding, controlling, and governing all the brethren under his care. In virtue of such distinctions, a superior, how high soever his rank may be, is bound to the observance of the same rules, duties, and obligations as the last Patzin; his sacred character is not enlarged or altered; he is only entrusted with a certain amount of jurisdiction over some of his brethren.

The Talapoin is bound to his community, so that in every kiaong or house of the order there are ordinarily to be met several Patzins and a good number of shyins. Each kiaong has a chief who presides over the community, under the appellation of Tsaya, or, as is more often the case, under that of Phongyie. He is, in most instances, the nominee of the individual who has built the monastery, and who is vested with a kind of right of patronage to appoint whom he likes to be the head of the house he has erected. He who is the head of the house has power over all the inmates, and every one acknowledges him as his immediate superior. He has the management of all the little affairs of the community, enforces the regular observance of the rules and duties of the profession, corrects abuses, rebukes the trespassers, spurs the lazy, excites the lukewarm, keeps peace and maintains good understanding amongst his subordinates. He receives, in his official character, the pious visitors who resort to his monastery, either for the sake of making voluntary offerings in token of their respect for and admiration of his eminent sanctity, or for conversing with him on some religious subjects, which, let it be said quietly, out of deference to human frailty, sometimes make room for those of a worldly character. If the alms-givers or advice-seekers belong, as often happens, to the fair and devout sex, they must remain at a distance of six or twelve cubits, as the place may allow, from their pious adviser.

It is supposed that a nearer proximity might endanger the virtue of the holy recluse.

In every town a considerable number of kiaongs are found, either in the suburbs or within the walls, in a quarter reserved for the purpose. In every village the kiaong is to be met with, as the parson's house in our villages of Europe. The poorest place is not without a small and often very humble house for the Phongyie who resides there, if not during the whole year, at least during the rainy season. One or several dzedis, a sort of flagstaff painted, and with some of its parts gilt, bearing the emblem of the sacred bird henza, or Brahminical duck, at three-fourths of its height, from which hang down gracefully several streamers, amid a grove of fruit trees, indicate to the traveller the habitation—sometimes humble, sometimes stately—with its superposed three roofs, where the Rahans dwell. The kiaong is also a place where the traveller is well received, and can stay for a day or two. During the dry season, when there are few boys remaining with the Phongyies, it is a place much safer than the dzeats. The inmates are generally very glad to receive strangers, who by their conversation afford them some moments of pleasant diversion which relieve the habitual monotony of their life. These various communities are placed under the jurisdiction of a general superior, or a provincial named Tsaia-dau, or great master; they form, under his authority, a province of the order; a division much similar to that of several religious orders in Europe. He enjoys a large share of public respect and veneration. His kiaong outshines the others in splendour and decorations. The first and wealthiest inhabitants of the place are proud to call themselves his disciples and supporters, and to supply him liberally with all that he may require. His chief duty is to settle disputes that not unfrequently arise between rival communities. The demon of discord often haunts these abodes of peace and retirement. The authority of the provincial interferes to put down feuds and contentions, which envy and jealousy, the two great enemies of devotees, not unfrequently excite. When a Talapoin is accused of incontinence or other serious infringement of the vital rules of the profession, he is summoned to the tribunal of the Tsaya-dau, who, assisted and advised by some elders, examines the case and pronounces the sentence. Superior intellectual attainments do not appear to be the essential qualifications for obtaining this high dignity. The writer has met with two or three of these dignitaries who, in his opinion, were vastly inferior to many of their subordinates in talents and capacity. They were old and good-natured men, who had spent almost all their lives within the precincts of the monastery. Their dress, manners, and habits were entirely similar to those of their brethren of inferior grade.

In the capital, or its suburbs, of the kingdom of Ava, where is the keystone of the Talapoinic fabric, the *superlatively* great master resides. His jurisdiction extends over all the fraternity within the realm of his Burmese majesty. His position near the seat of government, and his capacity of king's master or teacher, must have at all times conferred upon him a very great degree of influence over all his subordinates. He is honoured with the eminent title of *Tha-thana-paing,* meaning that he has power and control over all that appertains to religion. It does not appear that peculiarly shining qualifications or high attainments are required in him who is honoured with such a dignity. The mere accidental circumstance of having been the king's instructor when he was as yet a youth, is a sufficient, nay, the only necessary recommendation for the promotion to such a high position. Hence it generally happens that each king, at his accession to the throne, confers the highest dignity of the order on his favourite Phongyie. In that case the actual incumbent has to resign the place to his more influential brother, and becomes an ordinary member of the fraternity, unless he prefers leaving the society altogether, and re-entering the lay condition. Great indeed is the respect paid by the king to the head Phongyie. When on certain days of worship he is invited to go to the palace and deliver some instructions to his majesty, the proud monarch quits the somewhat elevated place he occupies, and takes one almost on a level with that of the courtiers, whilst the venerable personage goes to sit on the very same carpet just vacated by the king. When he happens to go out and visit some monasteries or places of worship, he is generally carried on a gilt litter, in great state, attended by a large number of his brethren and a considerable retinue of laymen. During the passage, marks of the greatest respect are given by the people. The monastery he lives in is on a scale of splendour truly surprising. Its form and appearance are similar to that of other religious houses, but in variety and richness of decorations it surpasses them all. It is entirely gilt both inside and out; not only are the posts covered with gold leaves, but often they are inlaid with rubies, which I suppose are of the commonest description and of little value.

To confer an additional sacredness to his person and position, the *Tha-thana-paing* lives by himself, with but one or two Phongyies, whom we may consider as his secretaries or major-domos, who remain in an apartment near to the entrance, to receive visitors and usher them into the presence of the great personage. Besides, there are lay guardians who take good care that not the least noise should ever disturb the silence of the place.

When the writer first visited that dignitary, he was much amused, on his approach to the place, to meet with those mute guardians, who by all sorts of signs and gestures were endeavouring to make him understand that he must walk slowly and noiselessly, and beware to speak aloud. When admitted to the presence of the Tsaya-dau, he was not a little surprised to find a man exceedingly self-conceited, who thought that to him alone belonged the right of speaking. His language was that of a master to whom no one was expected to presume to offer the least contradiction. He appeared quite offended when his visitor was compelled to dissent from him on certain points brought forward during the conversation. He was then about fifty years old. He was, for a Burman, of a tall stature, with regular and handsome features. The face was a little emaciated, as becomes a monk. His spiritual pride cast a darkish and unpleasant appearance on his person. He spoke quickly and sententiously; appearing all the while scarcely to notice his interlocutor. Admiration of self and vanity pierced through the thin veil which his affected humility spread over his countenance. The writer left him with an impression very different from that which a worthy English envoy, in the end of the last century, entertained of a similar personage, whose mild, benign, and pious exterior captivated him to such an extent as to elicit from him a request to be remembered in his prayers.

In our days, the power of the Tha-thana-paing is merely nominal; the effects of his jurisdiction are scarcely felt beyond his own neighbourhood. Such, however, was not the case in former times. Spiritual commissioners were sent yearly by him, to examine into and report on the state of the communities throughout the provinces. They had to inquire particularly whether the rules were regularly observed or not, whether the professed members were really well qualified for their holy calling or not. They were empowered to repress abuses, and whenever some unworthy brother, or *black sheep*, was found within the enclosure of a monastery, he was forthwith degraded, stripped of the yellow garb, and compelled to resume a secular course of life. Unfortunately for the welfare of the order, those salutary visits no more take place; the wholesome check is done away with. Left without a superior control, the order has fallen into a low degree of abjectness and degradation. The situation of Talapoins is often looked upon now as one fit for lazy, ignorant, and idle people, who, being anxious to live well and do nothing, put on the sacred dress for a certain time, until, tired of the duties and obligations of their new profession, they retire and betake themselves anew to a secular life. This practice, as far as my observation goes, is pretty general, if not almost universal. There are, however, a few exceptions. Though labouring under many serious disadvantages, the society continues to subsist with all its exterior characteristics; the various steps of its hierarchy are as well marked and defined now as they were before under more favourable circumstances. Its framework remains entire, but the materials composing it are somewhat imperfect and unsound.

There is in that religious body a latent principle of vitality, that keeps it up and communicates to it an amount of strength and energy that have hitherto maintained it in the midst of wars, revolutions, and political convulsions of all descriptions. Whether supported or not by the ruling power, it has remained always firm and unchanged. It is impossible to account satisfactorily for such a phenomenon, unless we find a clear and evident cause of such an extraordinary vitality; a cause independent of ordinary occurrences, time, and circumstances; a cause deeply rooted in the very soul of the populations, that exhibit before the observer this great and striking religious feature. That cause appears to be the strong religious sentiment, the firm faith that pervades the masses of Buddhists. The laity admire and venerate the religious, and voluntarily and cheerfully contribute to their maintenance and welfare. From its ranks the religious body is constantly recruited. There is scarcely a man that has not been a member of the fraternity for a certain period of time.

Surely such a general and continued impulse could not last long, unless it were maintained by a powerful religious conviction. The members of the order preserve, at least exteriorly, the decorum of their profession. The rules and regulations are tolerably well observed; the grades of hierarchy are maintained with a scrupulous exactitude. The life of the religious is one of restraint and perpetual control. He is denied all sorts of pleasures and diversions. How could such system of self-denial be ever maintained, were it not for the belief which the Rahans have in the merits that they amass, by following a course of life which, after all, is repugnant to nature? It cannot be denied that human motives often influence both the laity and the religious, but divested of faith and of the sentiments inspired by even a false belief, their action could not produce, in a lasting and persevering manner, the extraordinary and striking fact we witness in Buddhistic countries.

ARTICLE IV.

ORDINATION, OR CEREMONIES OBSERVED AT THE ADMISSION INTO THE SOCIETY.

We will now explain rather minutely, and describe as accurately as possible, the various ceremonies performed on the occasion of the promotion of a shyin to the rank of patzin, or professed member. It must be borne in mind that this ordeal through which he has to pass, or ordination, as we may aptly perhaps term it, which he has to receive, does not confer any peculiar character, or give any special spiritual power to the admitted candidate; but it merely initiates him to a more perfect course of life, and makes him the member of a society composed of men aiming at a higher degree of sanctity or perfection. The incumbent must be provided for the ceremony with a dress such as is used in the community; he must be found exempt from certain moral and physical defects that would render him unworthy of being admitted a member of the order; he must pledge himself to a rigorous observance of certain regulations which form the constitutions of the society.

The place where the ceremony is to be performed is a hall measuring at least twelve cubits in length, not including the space occupied by the Rahans whose presence is required on the occasion. The assembly of Phongyies, or Rahans, must include ten or twelve members at least if the ceremony be performed in towns, and four or six if it be in the country. He who presides over the ceremony is called Upitze, meaning master or guide; he has an assistant, named Cambawa Tsaia, whose office it is to read the sacred Cambawa, or book of ordination, to present the candidate to the Upitze and his assembled brethren, to put to him the requisite questions as prescribed by the ritual, and to give him instructions on certain points, the ignorance of which would prove highly prejudicial to and greatly offensive in a professed member of the order. All the regulations prescribed and the ceremonies observed on the occasion are contained in a book written in Pali, the sacred language. This book may be aptly termed the ritual of the Buddhists. It is held in great respect, and some copies written on sheets of ivory with gilt edges are truly beautiful, and bespeak the high value Buddhists set on the work. The copyists have retained the use of the old square Pali letters, instead of employing the circular Burmese characters. All the ordinances and prescriptions in this book are supposed to have been promulgated and sanctioned by no less an authority than Gaudama himself, the last Buddha and the acknowledged originator and founder of the Talapoinic order. Hence the high respect and profound veneration all Buddhists bear to its contents. The candidate, previously to the beginning of the ceremony, must be provided, as aforesaid, with his *patta*, or mendicant's pot, and a *tsiwaran*, the clerical dress or monkish habit. The *patta* is an open-mouthed pot of a truncated spheroidal form, wherein each member of the brotherhood must receive the alms which every morning he goes to collect in the streets.

The *tsiwaran* or yellow[3] garment, the only dress becoming a Rahan, is composed first of a piece of cloth bound to the loins with a leathern girdle, and falling down to the feet; second, of a cloak of a rectangular form, covering the shoulders and breast and reaching somewhat below the knee; and, third, of another piece of cloth of the same shape, which is folded many times and thrown over the left shoulder, the two ends hanging down before and behind. Another article always required for completing the full dress of the Rahan is the *awana*, a sort of fan made of palm leaves, set in light oval-shaped wooden frame, with a serpentine handle, somewhat resembling in appearance the letter S.

The Burmese translator of the Pali text has interpolated his work with many remarks tending to elucidate the text, and to show the various motives and reasons that have induced Gaudama to decree and publish as obligatory the regulations laid down in the sacred Cambawa. It must be borne in mind, too, that the omission of some essential parts of the ceremonies annuls *de facto* the ordination, whilst the non-compliance with others of minor importance, though not invalidating the act of admission into the sacred family, entails sin upon all members of the brotherhood assembled *ex officio* for the ceremony. The reader must be prepared to observe many points of close resemblance between the ceremonies observed at the reception of a monk, or the ordination of a priest, and those performed in these parts on the solemn occasion of admitting a candidate to the dignity of Patzin.

The preparations for the solemnity being completed, and the assembled fathers having occupied their respective

---

[3] Among southern Buddhists, preference is given to the yellow colour for the monk's habit. The juice extracted from the Jack-tree wood, by the process of boiling, supplies the necessary ingredient for dyeing.

seats under the presidence of the Upitze, the candidate is introduced into their presence attended by the assistant or reader of the Cambawa, and carrying his patta and yellow garments. He is enjoined to repeat distinctly thrice the following sentence to the Upitze, kneeling down, and his body bent forward, with his joined hands raised to the forehead: "Venerable President, I acknowledge you to be my Upitze." These words having been three times repeated, the assistant, addressing himself to the candidate, says: "Dost thou acknowledge this to be thy patta, and these thy sacred vestments?" To which he audibly answers, "Yes."

Upon this the translator remarks that, on a certain day, a Rahan that had been ordained without being supplied with either *patta* or *tsiwaran* went out quite naked, and received in the palms of his joined hands the food offered to him. So extraordinary, one would have said so unedifying, a proceeding having been mentioned to Gaudama, he ordered that henceforward no Rahan should ever be ordained unless he had been previously interrogated regarding the patta and the vestments. Any disobedience to this injunction would entail sin on the assembled fathers.

The assistant having desired the candidate to withdraw from the assembly to a distance of twelve cubits, and the latter having complied with his request, he turns towards the assembled fathers and addresses them as follows: "Venerable Upitze, and you brethren herein congregated, listen to my words. The candidate who now stands in a humble posture before you solicits from the Upitze the favour of being honoured with the dignity of patzin. If it appears to you that everything is properly arranged and disposed for this purpose, I will duly admonish him. O candidate, be attentive unto my words, and beware lest on this solemn occasion thou utterest an untruth or concealest aught from our knowledge. Learn that there are certain incapacities and defects which render a person unfit for admittance into our order. Moreover, when before this assembly thou shalt be interrogated respecting such defects, thou art to answer truly, and declare what incapacities thou mayest labour under. Now this is not the time to remain silent and decline thy head; every member of the assembly has a right to interrogate thee at his pleasure, and it is thy bounden duty to return an answer to all his interrogations."

"Candidate, art thou affected with any of the following complaints: the leprosy, or any such odious maladies? Hast thou the scrofula or other similar complaints? Dost thou suffer from asthma or coughs? Art thou afflicted with those complaints that arise from a corrupted blood? Art thou affected by madness or the other ills caused by giants, witches, or evil spirits of the forests and mountains?" To each separate interrogation he answers: "From such complaints and bodily disorders I am free." "Art thou a man?" "I am." "Art thou a true and legitimate son?" "I am." "Art thou involved in debts?" "I am not." "The bounden man and underling of some great man?" "No, I am not." "Have thy parents given consent to thy ordination?" "They have given it." "Hast thou reached the age of twenty years?" "I have attained it."[4] "Are thy vestments and sacred patta prepared?" "They are." "Candidate, what is thy name?" "My name is Wago," meaning, metaphorically, a vile and unworthy being. "What is the name of thy master?" "His name is Upitze."

---

[4] The writer does not think it worth repeating the reasons that induced Gaudama to lay down those several regulations. They owe their origin to the fact that some individuals contrived to be ordained though labouring under physical defects, and thereby became a sort of standing disgrace to the society. It was at the request of his father that Buddha forbade receiving to ordination sons who had not the consent of the parents, and fixed twenty years as the age requisite in him who would offer himself for the promotion to the order of Patzin. No slave, no debtor, could be ordained, because a man in such a condition does not belong to himself, and cannot dispose of his person, which to a certain extent is the property of his master and creditor.

The assistant, having finished the examination, turns his face towards the assembled fathers, and thus proceeds: "Venerable Upitze, and ye assembled brethren, be pleased to listen to my words. I have duly admonished this candidate, who seeks from you to be admitted into our order. Does the present moment appear to you a meet and proper time that he should come forward? If so, I shall order him to come nearer." Then turning to the candidate, he bids him come close to the assembly and ask their consent to his ordination. The order is instantly complied with by the candidate, who, having left behind him the distance of twelve cubits that separated him from the fathers, squats on his heels, the body bending forward and the hands raised to his forehead, and says: "I beg, O fathers of this assembly, to be admitted to the profession of Rahan. Have pity on me; take me from the state of layman, which is one of sin and imperfection, and advance me to that of Ṛahan, a state of virtue and perfection." These words must be repeated three times.

The assistant then resumes his discourse as follows: "O ye fathers here assembled, hear my words. This candidate, humbly prostrated before you, begs of the Upitze to be admitted into our holy profession; it seems that he is free from all defects, corporeal infirmities, as well as mental incapacities, that would otherwise debar him from entering our holy state; he is likewise provided with the patta and sacred vestments; moreover, he has asked, in the name of the Upitze, permission of the assembly to be admitted among the Rahans. Now let the assembly complete his ordination. To whomsoever this seems good, let him keep silence: whosoever thinks otherwise, let him declare that this candidate is unworthy of being admitted." And these words he repeats three times. Afterwards he proceeds: "Since, then, none of the fathers object, but all are silent, it is a sign that the assembly has consented; so, therefore, be it done. Let therefore this candidate pass out of the state of sin and imperfection into the perfect state of Rahan, and thus, by the consent of the Upitze and of all the fathers, let him be ordained."

And he further says: "The fathers must note down under what shade, on what day, at what hour, and in what season, the ordination has been performed."

This being done, the reader of the sacred Cambawa adds: "Let the candidate attend to the following duties, which it is incumbent on him to perform, and to the faults hereafter enumerated, which he must carefully avoid.

"1. It is the duty of each member of our brotherhood to beg for his food with labour, and with the exertion of the muscles of his feet; and through the whole course of his life he must gain his subsistence by the labour of his feet. He is allowed to make use of all the things that are offered to him in particular, or to the society in general, that are usually presented in banquets, that are sent by letter, and that are given at the new and full moon and on festivals. O candidate, all these things you may use for your food." To this he replies, "Sir, I understand what you tell me."

The assistant resumes his instructions: "2. It is a part of the duty of a member of our society to wear, through humility, yellow clothes, made of rags thrown about in the streets or among the tombs. If, however, by his talents and virtue one procures for himself many benefactors, he may receive from them for his habit the following articles, cotton and silk, or cloth of red[5] and yellow wool." The elect answers, "As I am instructed, so I will do."

The instructor goes on: "3. Every member of the society must dwell in houses built under the shade of lofty trees.[6] But if, owing to your proficiency and zeal in

---

[5] It is probable that the allusion to the red colour has a Thibetan origin. The Buddhist monks of that country have adopted the red for their dress, in preference to the yellow, which is the canonical colour of the habit of all the monks among the southern Buddhists.

[6] In this part of the regulations the elect is reminded of the primi-

the discharge of your duties, you secure to yourself powerful supporters who are willing to build for you a better habitation, you may dwell in it. The dwellings may be made of bamboo, wood, and bricks, with roofs adorned with turrets or spires of pyramidal or triangular form." The elect answers: "I will duly attend to these instructions."

After the usual answer, the instructor proceeds: "4. It is incumbent upon an elect to use, as medicine, the urine of the cow, whereon lime and the juices of lemon or other sour fruits have been poured. He may also avail himself, as medicines, of articles thrown out of bazaars and picked up in corners of streets. He may accept, for medicinal purposes, nutmegs and cloves. The following

---

tive condition of the members of the society. In imitation of their brethren of the Brahminical persuasion, and also for the purpose of living in seclusion, the Rahans, in the beginning, were satisfied with dwelling in huts raised at the foot of some tall tree. As soon, however, as Buddhism gained footing in various countries, we see that kings, nobles, and wealthy persons vied with each other in erecting splendid houses for the use of the monks. Gaudama himself was presented by King Pimpathara at Radzagio with the splendid Weloowon monastery. In Thawattie the rich man Anatapein offered him the famous Dzetawon monastery; and the rich lady Withaka of the same country gave him, as a gift, the no less splendid mansion named Pouppayon.

General A. Cunningham has discovered the ruins of Thawattie, fifty-eight miles north of Fyzabad, on the Rapti, in a place called Sahet Mahet, situated between Akaona and Bulrampur, five miles from the former and twelve from the latter. It was the capital of King Pathenadi, situated in north Kosala. In the Legend of Buddha we have seen how that monarch was dispossessed of his throne by one of his sons, and died while on his way to the capital of Adzatathat, his son-in-law. The ruins of the renowned Dzetawon monastery have been identified by means of the information supplied by the writings of the Chinese pilgrims we have often mentioned. The monastery was distant 1200 paces from the southern gate of the city. The scarcely less famous Pouppayon monastery was erected to the east of the Dzetawon. Mounds of ruins in that very same direction leave no doubt that in their bosom the last remains of that celebrated place are entombed. It is said that Gaudama, being fifty-five years old, began to reside permanently in monasteries built for him, and that he spent, out of the last twenty-five seasons, nineteen in the Dzetawon and six in the Pouppayon. According to Hwen Thsang, the place occupied by the Dzetawon monastery was a square, having 1000 cubits on each face or side. Besides the monastery, there were two temples and two tanks within the enclosure.

articles may also be used medicinally—butter, cream, and honey."

Now the assistant instructs the new religious on the four capital offences he must carefully avoid, under penalty of forfeiting the dignity he has just attained to, and solemnly warns him against committing one of them. Those sins are fornication, theft, murder, and spiritual pride. The committing of one of these sins by religious after their ordination, in the days of Gaudama, induced him to declare those excluded *de facto* from the society who had been guilty of such offences; and he enjoined that the assistant should immediately after the ceremony solemnly admonish the newly ordained Patzin carefully to shun such odious offences.

The assistant, without delay, proceeds as follows: "O elect, being now admitted into our society, it shall be no longer lawful for you to indulge in carnal pleasures, whether with yourself or animals. He who is guilty of such sin, can no longer be numbered among the perfect. Sooner shall the severed head be joined again to the neck, and life be restored to the breathless body, than a Patzin who has committed fornication recover his lost sanctity. Beware, therefore, lest you pollute yourself with such a crime.

"Again, it is unlawful and forbidden to an elect to take things that belong to another, or even to covet them, although their value should not exceed about six annas (one-fourth of a tical). Whoever sins even to that small amount is hereby deprived of his sacred character, and can no more be restored to his pristine state than the branch cut from the tree can retain its luxuriant foliage and shoot forth buds. Beware of theft during the whole of your mortal journey.

"Again, an elect can never knowingly deprive any living being of life, or wish the death of any one, how troublesome soever he may prove. Sooner shall the cleft rock re-unite so as to make a whole, than he who kills any being be readmitted into our society. Cautiously avoid so heinous a crime.

"Again, no member of our brotherhood can ever arrogate to himself extraordinary gifts or supernatural perfections, or, through vainglory, give himself out as a holy man; such, for instance, as to withdraw into solitary places, and, on pretence of enjoying ecstasies like the Ariahs, afterwards presume to teach others the way to uncommon spiritual attainments. Sooner may the lofty palm-tree that has been cut down become green again, than an elect guilty of such pride be restored to his holy station. Take care for yourself that you do not give way to such an excess." The elect replies as before: "As I am instructed, so I will perform." Here ends the ceremony. The elect joins the body of Rahans, and withdraws in their company to his own kiaong.

It has already been mentioned that this ceremony or ordination does not impart any spiritual character inherent in the person of the elect; but it is a mere formality he has to go through, to enter into the family of the perfect. The admitted member is not linked indissolubly to his new state; he is at liberty to leave it when it pleases him, and re-enter secular life. He may, moreover, if inclined, apply for re-admission into the order, but he must go through the same ceremonies that were observed on his first ordination. It is not very common to meet among the Burmese Rahans men who from their youth have persevered to an old age in their vocation. Those form the rare exceptions. They are very much respected, and held in high consideration during their lifetime, and the greatest honours are lavished upon their mortal remains after their demise. They are often designated by the honourable denomination of "pure from their infancy."

ARTICLE V.

RULES OF THE ORDER.

The obligations inherent in the dignity of Patzin, and the multifarious duties prescribed to the Buddhist monks, are contained in a book called Patimauk, which is, properly speaking, the manual of the order, and the *Vade Mecum* of every Talapoin, who is obliged to study it with great care and attention. It is even ordered that on festival days a certain number of recluses shall meet in a particular place called Thein, to listen to the reading of that book, or at least a part of it; that every brother should have always present to his mind the rules and regulations of his profession, and be prompted to a strict observance of all the points they enforce. This injunction is a very proper one, since it is a fact confirmed by the experience of ages that relaxation and dissipation find their way in all communities at the very moment the rules are partially lost sight of. So attentive to this duty are some Phongyies that they can repeat by heart all the contents of the Patimauk. We have read the book with a good deal of attention. Many wise and well-digested rules are to be met with here and there, but they are merged in a heap of minute, not to say ridiculous and childish, details, not worth repeating. In order, however, to give a correct and distinct outline of the mode of life, manners, habits, and occupations of the Talapoins, we will extract from it all that has appeared to be interesting and calculated to attain the above purpose, leaving aside the incongruous mass of useless rubbish.

Every member of the order, on his entering the profession, must renounce his own will and bend his neck under the yoke of the rule. So anxious indeed has been the framer of its statutes to leave no room or field open to the independent exertions of the mind, that every action of the day, the manner of performing it, the time it ought to last, the circumstances that must attend it, have all been minutely regulated. From the moment a Rahan rises in the morning to the moment he is to go to enjoy his natural rest in the evening, his only duty is to obey and follow the ever-subsisting will and commands of the founder of the society. He advances in perfection proportionately to his fervent compliance with the injunctions of, and to his conscientiously avoiding all that has been forbidden by, the sagacious legislator. The trespassing of one article of the rule constitutes a sin. The various sins a Rahan is liable to commit are comprised under seven principal heads. 1st, the Paradzekas; 2d, the Thinga-de-ceits; 3d, the Patzei; 4th, the Toolladzi; 5th, the Duka; 6th, the Dupaci; and 7th, the Pati-de-kani. These seven kinds of sins are subdivided and multiplied to the number of 227, which constitute the total amount of sins either of commission or omission that a Phongyie may commit during the time that he remains a member of the holy society. The Paradzikas are four in number: fornication, theft, killing, and vainglory in attributing to one's self high attainments in perfection. A recluse, on the day of his admission, is, as before related, warned never to commit these four sins, under the penalty of being excluded from the society. They are irremissible in their nature. The meaning of this is, He who has had the misfortune of yielding to temptation, and committing one of these four offences, is no longer to be considered as a member of the Thanga, or of the assembly of the perfect. He is *de facto* excluded from the society. He may exteriorly continue to be a member of the Thanga, but inwardly he really no longer belongs to it. All other offences are subjected to the law of confession, and can be expiated by virtue of the penances imposed upon the delinquent after he has made a public avowal of his sins.

The reader will no doubt be startled by the unexpected

information that the practice of confession has been established among the Talapoins, and is up to this day observed, though very imperfectly, by every fervent religious. Some zealous Patzins will resort to the practice once, and sometimes twice a day. Here is what is prescribed on this subject in the Wini, or book of scriptures, which contains all that relates to the Phongyies, the Patimauk being but a compendium of it: When a Rahan has been guilty of a violation of his rule, he ought immediately to go to his superior, and, kneeling before him, confess his sin to him. Sometimes he will do this in the Thein, the place where the brothers assemble occasionally to speak on religious subjects or listen to the reading of the Patimauk in the presence of the assembly. He must confess all his sins, such as they are, without attempting to conceal those of a more revolting nature, or lessening aggravating circumstances. A penance is then imposed, consisting of certain pious formulas to be repeated a certain number of times during the night. A promise must be made by the penitent to refrain in future from such trespasses. This extraordinary practice is observed now, one would say, *pro forma*. The penitent approaches his superior, kneels down before him, and having his hands raised to his forehead, says: "Venerable superior, I do confess here all the sins that I may be guilty of, and beg pardon for the same." He enters upon no detailed enumeration of his trespasses, nor does he specify anything respecting their nature and the circumstances attending them. The superior remains satisfied with telling him: "Well, take care lest you break the regulations of your profession; and henceforward endeavour to observe them with fidelity." He dismisses him without inflicting any penance on him. Thus an institution, so well calculated to put a restraint and a check upon human passions, so well fitted to prevent man from occasionally breaking commands given to him, or at least from slipping into the dangerous habit of doing it, is now, by the want of fervour and energy in the hands of that body, reduced to be no more than an useless and ridiculous ceremony, a mere shadow of what is actually prescribed by the Wini.

The punishments inflicted for the repeated transgressions of one or several points of the rule are, generally speaking, of a light nature, and seldom or never corporeal, as flagellations, &c. The superior sometimes orders a delinquent to walk through the courtyard during the heat of the day for a certain time, to carry to a distance a certain number of baskets-ful of sand, or a jug of water. Meekness, being a virtue most becoming a recluse, forbids the resort to penances of a more severe nature.

Humility, poverty, self-denial, and chastity are to him who has received the order of Patzin cardinal and most essential virtues, which he ought to practise on all occasions. He must, in all his exterior deportment, give unequivocal marks of his being always influenced by the spirit they inspire. The framer of the rules and regulations of the order seems to have had no other object in view than that of leading his brethren by various ways and means to the practice of these virtues, and inculcating on their minds the necessity of attending to the observances prescribed for this purpose. It is from this point we must view the statutes of the fraternity in order to understand them well and rightly, and appreciate them according to their worth and merit. We would indeed form a very erroneous opinion of institutions of past ages if we were to examine them, to praise or blame them, without a due regard being paid to the spirit that guided the legislator, and to the object he aimed at when he laid them down. Our own ideas, customs, manners, and education will often dispose us to disapprove at first of institutions made in former ages, amongst nations differing from us in all respects, under the pretext that they are not such as we would have them to be now, making unawares our own prejudices the standard whereby to measure the merit or demerit of all that has been established previously to our own times. The institutions of the middle ages, a celebrated modern historian has said, are intelligible to him that has entered into the spirit of those days, and who thinks, feels, and believes as did the people of those bygone centuries. This observation holds good to a certain extent, and, *mutatis mutandis*, in respect to Buddhistic institutions. The whole religious system must be understood, the object which the founder of the order had in view ought to be distinctly remarked and always borne in mind, ere we presume to pronounce upon the fitness or unfitness of the means he has employed for obtaining it.

For humility's sake every Talapoin is bound to shave every part of his body. In complying with this regulation he must consider that the hairs that are shaved off are useless things, serving merely for the purposes of vanity, and he ought to be as unconcerned about them as a great mountain which has been cleared of the trees on its summit. Influenced by the same spirit, the religious must always walk barefooted, except in case of his labouring under some infirmity, or for some other good reason; he is then allowed to use a certain kind of plain and unornamented slipper, the shape, colour, and dimensions of which are carefully prescribed by the rule. When the Rahans travel from one place to another, they are allowed to carry with them the broad fan, made of palm-leaves, and a common paper umbrella to protect their bare head from the inclemency of the weather, or screen it from the heat of the sun. Their dress, consisting, as above mentioned, of three parts, is as plain as possible. According to the Patimauk, each separate part must be made of rags picked up here and there, and sewed together by themselves. This regulation, though disregarded by many, is to a certain extent observed by the greater number, but in a manner rather contrary to the spirit, if not to the letter, of the rule. On their receiving from benefactors a piece of silk or cotton, they cut it into several small square parts, which they afterwards contrive to have stitched in the best way they can, so as to make their vestments according to the prescription of the statutes. The vestment ought to be of one colour, yellow in those countries in which Mahometanism does not prevail. The yellow colour is a mark of mourning, as the black is amongst most of the nations of Europe.

Seven articles are considered as essential to every member of the holy family, viz., the kowot, thin-bain, dugout (the three pieces constituting his vestment), a girdle, a patta, a small hatchet, a needle, and a small apparatus for straining the water he drinks. The entire number of articles he is permitted to use and possess amounts to sixty. They are all plain, common, almost valueless, offering no incentive to cupidity, and leaving him who is only possessed of them in the humble state of strict poverty.

The possession of temporal goods is strictly forbidden to the Rahans, as calculated to hinder them from meditating upon the law and attending to the various duties of the profession. Nothing indeed opposes a stronger barrier to the attainment of the perfect abnegation of self and a thorough contempt for material things, than the possession of worldly property. Hence a true Rahan has no object which he can, properly speaking, call his own. The kiaong wherein he lives has been built by benefactors, and is supplied by them with all that is necessary or useful to him. Food and raiment are procured for him, without his having to feel concerned about them. The pious liberality of his supporters assiduously provides for his wants. But it is expected that he shall never concern himself with worldly business or transactions, of whatever nature they may be. He can neither labour, plant, traffic, nor do anything with the intent of deriving profit therefrom. Agreeably to the maxim, "sufficient to the day is the evil thereof," the Rahan cannot make any stores for the time to come. He must trust in the never-failing generosity and ever-watchful attention of his supporters for his daily wants. Now, let it be said to the praise of the Buddhists, that he is seldom disappointed in the reliance he places on them.

That he may be more effectually debarred from a too easy and frequent use of the things of first necessity, a Talapoin is bound to go through a tedious ceremony, called Akat, or presentation, before he can lawfully touch anything. When he has occasion for food, drink, or anything else, he turns to his disciples and tells them to do what is lawful. Whereupon one of them, or several, as circumstances may require, rises from his place, and, taking the thing or things he wants with both hands, approaches him respectfully, and presents to him the articles, saying, This is lawful. Then the Rahan takes the things into his own hands, and uses them or lays them by, as may suit his convenience. When a thing is presented, the disciple must be at a distance of some cubits, otherwise the recluse is guilty of a sin; and if what he receives is food, he commits as many sins as he eats mouthfuls. Gold and silver being the two greatest feeders of covetousness, the rule forbids the Phongyies to touch them, and *a fortiori* to have them. But on this point, however, human covetousness has broken through the strong barriers the framer of the statutes has wisely devised for effectually protecting recluses from its dangerous allurement. Gold and silver are not indeed touched by the pious devotees, but the precious and dazzling metals are conventionally handed to the disciples, who put them into the box of the superior, who, whilst bowing obsequiously to the letter of the rule, disregards its spirit. Sometimes an innocent *ruse* is resorted to by a greedy religious for silencing the remorse of his conscience; he covers his hands with a handkerchief, and without scruple receives the sum that is offered to him. It would be unfair to pass a general and sweeping sentence of condemnation for covetousness upon all the members of the fraternity. There are some whose hands have not been polluted by the handling of money, and whose hearts have always been, we may say, strangers to the cravings of the *auri sacra fames;* but it cannot be denied that many among them are insatiable in their lust for riches, and not unfrequently ask for them.

No Rahan can ever ask for anything; he is allowed to receive what is spontaneously offered to him. In this point too the spirit of the rule is frequently done away with. The recluse will not ask an object he covets (I beg his pardon for making use of such a term) in direct words; but by some indirect means or circuitous ways he will give significantly to understand that the possession of such an object is much needed by him, and that the offering of it would be a source of great merits to the donor. In this manner he moves the heart of his visitor, and soon kindles in his breast a desire to present the thing, almost as eager as his own is to receive it.

Celibacy is strictly enjoined on every professed member of the society. On the day of his reception he is solemnly warned by the instructor never to do anything contrary to that most essential virtue. The founder of the order and the framer of its statutes has entered, on this subject, into the most minute details, and prescribed a multitude of regulations tending to fortify the Rahans in the accomplishment of the solemn vow they have made, and to remove from them all occasions of sin, even the most distant. We must give him credit for an uncommon acquaintance with the weakness of human nature, as well as with the violence of the fiercest passion of the heart, since he has laboured so much to strengthen and uphold the former, and bridle the latter by every means his anxious mind could devise. He was deeply read in the secrets of the human heart, and knew well that the surest tactics for carrying on successfully the warfare between the spirit and the flesh consist in rather avoiding carefully the encounter of the enemy, and skilfully manœuvring at a distance from him, than in boldly encountering him in the open field. Hence the repeated injunctions to shun all the occasions of sin.

The Phongyies are forbidden to stay under the same roof, or to travel in the same carriage and boat, with women; they cannot receive anything from their hands. To such a height are precautions carried that the religious are not permitted to touch the clothes of a woman, or caress a female child, however young, or even handle a female animal.[7]

When visited in their dwellings by women, who resort thither for the purpose of making offerings, or listening to the recital of a few passages of the sacred books, they must remain at a great distance from them, and be surrounded by some of their disciples. The Phongyies are to look upon the old ones as mothers and upon the young as sisters. The conversation must be as short as decency allows, and no useless or light expressions be ever uttered. On the festival days, when crowds of people, men and women, go to the kiaongs to hear the *tara*, or some parts of the law repeated, the Rahans, arrayed in front of the congregation, keep their fans before their faces all the while, lest their eyes should meet with dangerous and tempting objects. Much greater precautions are still required in their intercourse with the Rahanesses, a sort of female recluses, whose institute is greatly on its decline in almost all parts of Burmah. For better securing the observance of continence, a Phongyie never walks out of his monastery, or enters a private dwelling, without being attended by a few disciples. Popular opinion is inflexible and inexorable on the point of celibacy, which is considered essential to every one that has a pretension to be called a Rahan. The people can never be brought to look upon

---

[7] In treating of the precept of never touching women, it is added in the Wini that this prohibition extends to one's own mother; and even should it happen that she fall into a ditch, her son, if a Talapoin, must not pull her out. But in case no other aid is near at hand, he may offer her his habit, or a stick, to help her out; but at the same time he is to imagine that he is only pulling out a log of wood.

any person as a priest or minister of religion unless he live in that state. Any infringement of this most essential regulation on the part of a Rahan is visited with an immediate punishment. The people of the place assemble at the kiaong of the offender, sometimes driving him out with stones. He is stripped of his clothes; and often public punishment, even that of death, is inflicted upon him by order of government. The poor wretch is looked upon as an outcast, and the woman whom he has seduced shares in his shame, confusion, and disgrace. Such an extraordinary opinion, so deeply rooted in the mind of a people rather noted for the licentiousness of their manners, certainly deserves the attention of every diligent observer of human nature. Whence has originated among corrupted and half-civilised men such a high respect and profound esteem for so exalted a virtue? Why is its rigorous practice deemed essential to those who professedly tend to an uncommon degree of perfection? Owing partly to the weight of public opinion, and partly to some other reasons, the law of celibacy, externally at least, is observed with a great scrupulosity, and a breach of it is a rare occurrence. As the rule, in this respect, binds the Phongyie only as long as he remains in the profession, he who feels his moral strength unable to cope successfully with the sting of passion prefers leaving the fraternity and returning to a secular life, when he can safely put an end, by a lawful alliance, to the internal strife, rather than expose himself to a transgression which is to entail upon him consequences so disgraceful.

The sagacious legislator of the Buddhistic religious order, pre-occupied with the idea of elevating the spiritual principle above the material one, and securing to reason a thorough control over bodily appetites, has prescribed temperance as a fundamental virtue essential to every Rahan. In common with all their fellow-religionists, the Rahans are commanded to abstain from the use of spirituous liquors and of intoxicating substances. Such a prohibition is the wisest step that Gaudama could have adopted to preserve his followers from the shameful vice of drunkenness. All uncivilised people make use of spirits for the sole purpose of creating in them the effects of intoxication. Were it not for such an excellent regulation, the members of the Thanga would soon become, by their excesses, the laughing-stock of the laity. The time allotted for taking their meals extends from daybreak to the moment the sun has reached the middle of its course; but as soon as the luminous globe has passed the meridian, the use of food is strictly interdicted. A stomach, more or less loaded with nutritive substances taken in the evening, weighs down the body, enervates the energies of the soul, clouds the intellect, and renders a man rather unfit to devote himself to the high exercises of study, meditation, and contemplation, which ought to be the principal occupations of a fervent Rahan. He is allowed to make two meals in the forenoon, but it is expected that he will eat no more than is required to support nature. He must always take his meals in company with the members of his community. To stifle the craving of gluttony and eradicate immoderate desires, he ought to repeat frequently within himself the following sentence: "I eat this rice, not to please my appetite, but to satisfy the wants of nature;" just as he says when he puts on the habit, "I dress myself, not for the sake of vanity, but to cover my nakedness." Rice and vegetables are, according to the statutes, the staple food of the Phongyies; the use of fish and meat is tolerated, and now it has become a daily prevailing custom which has rendered the practice a lawful one. Strictly speaking, a Talapoin must remain satisfied with rice and various sorts of boiled vegetables which he has received in his patta during his morning perambulations through the streets of the place.

As it happened among the Romans that the law repressing convivial sumptuousness and luxury proved an ineffectual barrier against gluttony and other passions, so amidst the Rahans the strict regulations prescribing a poor and unsavoury diet have been obliged to yield before the tendencies to satisfy the ever-increasing demands of appetite. Most of the Phongyies give to dogs, or to the boys who live in the monastery, the vulgar food they have begged in the streets, and feed on aliments of better quality supplied to them regularly by some persons in easy circumstances, who call themselves supporters of the kiaong and of its inmates. The ordinary fare consists of rice and several small dishes for seasoning the rice, in which are some little pieces of flesh, dressed according to the culinary abilities of the cooks of the country, which are not certainly of the highest order. To this are added some of the fruits of the season, accompanied by sweetmeats, which female devotees are wont everywhere so carefully to prepare and so fondly to offer to those who are the objects of their pious admiration and respect. The aliments supplied to the humble recluses are of the best description for the country they live in. One would say that they live on the fat of the land. The most delicate rice and the finest fruits invariably find their way to the monasteries. But withal, the Phongyies are not to be charged with the sin of intemperance or gluttony.

The quantity of food they may take is also an object of regulation, as well as the very mode of taking, and even of swallowing it. Each mouthful must be of a moderate size; a second ought not to be carried to the mouth before the first has been completely disposed of by the masticatory process, and found its way down through the œsophagus. The contrary would be considered gluttony, and an evident sign that the eater has something else in view besides appeasing the mere wants of nature. It is rather an amusing sight to gaze at the solemn indifference of a Talapoin taking his meal. One would be tempted to believe that he is reluctantly submitting to the dire necessity of ministering to the wants of a nature too low and material. The rule forbids Talapoins to eat human flesh, or that of the monkey, snake, elephant, tiger, lion, and dog.[8] As a mitigation of the severity of the disciplinary regulation prohibiting the recluses from taking any food from twelve o'clock in the day until the next morning, the use of certain beverages is permitted during that time, such as cocoa-nut water, the juice of the sugar-cane, and other refreshing draughts.

The rule being silent regarding the consumption of the betel-leaf and other ingredients constituting the *delicious* mouthful for masticatory purposes, the Talapoins avail themselves largely of the liberty left to them on this subject. The quantity of betel and other accompanying substances which they consume is truly enormous. These articles hold a pre-eminent place amongst the objects that are presented to the inmates of monasteries. The dark-red substance adhering to the teeth and occasionally accumulating at the corners of the mouth, the incessant motion of the lower jaw, the stream of reddish spittle issuing frequently from the lips of the Talapoins, are unquestionable proofs of both their ardent fondness and copious consumption of that harmless narcotic. Except

---

[8] The Phongyies profess to have a tender compassion for the life of animals, and would not on any account allow themselves to be suspected of having contributed to the killing of an animal for the sake of feeding on his flesh. The writer has often taken a pleasure in taunting them on this account when he happened to see them eating pieces of boiled meat, by showing to them that their practice was little in accordance with their theory. They always answered that "they had not killed the animal, the flesh of which they were eating; but had merely received a piece of meat that had no life. As to the man who had deprived the animal of its life, he had certainly sinned, and would suffer for his misdeed. But that was an affair for which the perpetrator of the deed was alone answerable, and which concerned him alone." To this answer, of a rather elastic nature, the writer jocosely replied that "if there was no eater of meat there would be no killer of animals; and that, in his opinion, if sin there was, both had a share in it." Whereupon the yellow-dressed interlocutors invariably laughed, and feeling that they stood on insecure ground, adroitly changed the subject of conversation. There is no doubt that the Phongyies believe that it is sinful to kill animals, but at the same time they confess that it is difficult, nay, almost impossible, to live in this world without committing such a trespass.

during the short moments allotted for taking meals, a Rahan's mouth is always full of betel, and the masticating or chewing process is incessantly going on.

A great modesty must distinguish a member of the family of the perfect from a layman; that virtue must shine forth in his countenance, demeanour, gait, and conversation. Any sign on his face indicating the inward action of anger or any other passion is found unbecoming in a person whose composedness and serenity of soul ought never to be disturbed by any inordinate affection. He never speaks precipitately or loudly, lest it might be inferred that passion rather than reason influences him. Worldly or amusing topics of conversation are strictly interdicted, either with his brethren or laymen. The rule requires him to walk through the streets with affected simplicity, avoiding hurry as well as slowness, keeping his eye fixed on the ground in front, looking not further than ten or fifteen cubits.

Curiosity tends to expand the soul on surrounding objects; but a Rahan's principal aim being to attend diligently to himself, to prefer the care of self before all other cares, and to concern himself very little about all that takes place without, he assiduously labours to keep his soul free from vain inquiry, from eager desire of hearing news, and from an idle or unnecessary interference in things or matters strange to him. It seems that he has the wise saying always present to his mind, "Where art thou when thou art not present to thyself? And when thou hast run over all things, what profit will it be to thee if thou hast neglected thyself?" During his perambulations he never salutes or notices the persons he meets on his way; he is indifferent to the attentions and marks of the highest veneration paid to him by the people; he never returns thanks for offerings made to him, nor does he repay with a single regard the kindness proffered to him. Objects most calculated to awaken curiosity by their novelty and interest ought to find him cold, indifferent, and unconcerned. His self-collection accompanies him everywhere, and disposes his soul to an uninterrupted meditation on some points of the law. It is a counsel of the Wini to observe particularly the four cleannesses, viz., great modesty in the streets and public places, the confession of all failings, the avoiding of all occasions of sins, and the keeping oneself free from the seven kinds of sin. Such a wise injunction can only be attended to and observed by keeping a vigilant watch over the senses, which are the very gates leading into the sanctuary of the soul. We could enter into fuller and more particular details regarding the regulations of the Talapoinic order, but they would prove little interesting, and only corroborate what has been previously stated, that every action of a brother, even the most common, such as the manner of sitting, rising up, sleeping, eating, &c., has become the object of the legislative attention of the founder of the order. Nothing seems to have escaped his clear foresight, and he has admirably succeeded in leaving no room for the exercise of individual liberty. The rule is as a great moral being whose absolute commands must be always obeyed. Every individual is bound to lay aside his own self, and unconditionally follow the impulse of his guiding influence.

ARTICLE VI.

OCCUPATIONS OF THE BUDDHIST MONKS.

The whole life of a recluse being confined within a narrow compass, we will have very little to say regarding his daily occupations. As soon as a Talapoin has left at an early hour the sleeping horizontal position, he rinses his mouth, washes his face, and recites a few formulas of prayers, which he lengthens or shortens according to his devotion. He attires himself in his professional costume, gets hold of his mendicant's pot, and sallies forth, in company with some brethren or disciples, in quest of his food. He perambulates the streets in various directions, and, without any solicitation on his part, receives the rice, curry, vegetables, and fruits which pious donors have been preparing from two to three o'clock in the morning, watching at the door of their houses the arrival of the yellow-clad monks. Having received what is considered sufficient for the day, he returns to the monastery, and sets himself to eat either what he has brought, or something more delicate and better dressed which his supporter, if he has any, has sent to him.

On the principal festivals, or on extraordinary occurrences, abundant alms are brought to his domicile. Sometimes he is called by a pious donor to come and receive them in the pagodas, or in large temporary sheds erected for the purpose, reserved for the occasion. They consist chiefly of mattresses, pillows, betel-boxes, mats, tea-cups, and various articles he is allowed to make use of. On these occasions he repays his benefactors by repeating to them the five great precepts, and some of the principal tenets of the Buddhistic creed, and the chief points of the law. He enumerates at great length the numerous merits reserved to alms-givers. On this point it must be confessed that he is truly eloquent, and his language flowing and abundant: his expressions are ready at hand and most glowing, calculated to please the ears of his hearers and warm their souls to make fresh efforts in procuring him more copious alms. Occasionally he will recite long praises in honour of Gaudama, the last Buddha, for having during his previous existence practised eminent virtues, and thereby qualified himself for the high dignity of Phra. The sermon goes on sometimes in Pali or sacred language, which neither he nor his hearers can understand.

The Phongyies are sometimes requested to visit the sick, not so much for the purpose of ministering to the spiritual wants of the sufferer as for affording him some relief by his presence. It is believed that the appearance of a holy personage may have some effect in freeing the diseased from his distemper, and frightening the evil spirits that may be the mischievous agents in harming patients. The visitor repeats over them some points of the law that are intended to act as antidotes against the agency of the wicked one. Phongyies are very particular on the point of etiquette. When one of them has to enter into upper-storied houses, the yellow-habited religious, previous to his venturing into the lower story, will make it sure that there is no one, and particularly no woman, in the upper apartments, as it would be highly unbecoming that any man, and *a fortiori* a woman, should have their feet above his head. To avoid such an indecorous contingency, in case the sick person lies in a room upstairs, the Phongyie has recourse to an expedient few, I presume, would have thought of. By his direction a ladder is brought, the lower part of which rests on the street, and the upper leans on one of the upper windows; up goes the pious visitor, who by such a contrivance reconciles the observance of etiquette with the compliance to his duty. The writer confesses that he was much amused the first time that he witnessed such a feat performed at Penang by a Siamese Phongyie. The little crowd, attracted by this novelty, exhibited a curious mixture of feelings. Some laughed; many remained silent; but their deportment was evidently indicative of the respect and admiration that seemed to them to inspire the scrupulously-tender conscience of the religious.

We must allow that the Talapoins confer a truly invaluable benefit upon the people of these countries by keeping up schools, where the boys resort for the purpose of learning to read, write, and acquire the rudiments of arithmetic. In this respect they are eminently useful, and the institution, though to a certain extent burthensome to the people, in this respect deserves well of the country. The many abuses that at present attend it are almost fully atoned for by the great service its members gratuitously render to their countrymen. There are no other schools than those under their management. The tyrannical governments of Siam and Burmah do not take any steps to propagate instruction among their subjects, whom they look upon as slaves, fit only for bodily labour. The houses of Talapoins are so many little seats of elementary learning; and as they are very numerous throughout the country, every facility is afforded to male children to learn to read and write. The female children are excluded from partaking of this great boon by the strictness of the monastic regulations. It is a great misfortune, much to be lamented, as one-half of the population is thus doomed to live in perpetual ignorance. Owing to the gratuitous education given by the Buddhist monks, there are very few men throughout the breadth and length of Burmah who are not able to read and write. It is true that too often the knowledge thus acquired is very superficial and incomplete. But as regards the other half of the population, it may be stated that scarcely a woman among thousands can be found capable of spelling one word.

The Talapoins being much addicted to sloth and indolence, the schools are undoubtedly miserably managed. The boys are often left to themselves without regular control or discipline. When a boy enters the monastery as student, his teacher places into his hands a piece of blackened board, whereupon are written the first letters of the alphabet. The poor lad has to repeat over and over the name of the letters, crying aloud with all the powers of his lungs. He is left for several weeks at the same subject, until his instructor is satisfied that he knows his letters. In the next step the boy is directed to study the symbols of the vowels which are to be joined with consonants so as to form syllables and words. When this is done he is initiated into the art of uniting together and articulating properly the several consonants with the symbolic characters. He slowly shapes his course through the apparently much-complicated system of all the combinations of letters, so as to be able to spell correctly all the words of the language. Owing to the lack of order and method on the part of the teachers, boys spend a long time, sometimes one or two years, in mastering those difficulties, which, if properly explained, would much shorten the time usually devoted to such a study.

The Burmese alphabet, with the various combinations of letters and symbols for making words, is based on a most perfect and scientific methodical and simple process, borrowed from the Sanscrit. The method is plain and easy, as soon as it is understood. Any person that has received some education, and whose mind is somewhat developed, will be able, with the occasional assistance of an intelligent master, to go all over the various combinations in less than two months. The results derived from the method adopted by the Burmans are so great and complete that, after having gone over the general alphabet with attention, the beginner is able to read all the Burmese words he may meet with. We do not mean, of course, to say that he will be able to pronounce every word correctly. This is another thing altogether. But it is no less evident that the system used by Burmese in the combinations of letters leads to results infinitely more satisfactory than those obtained through the system of elementary reading and spelling used in Europe.

Unacquainted with the rules of grammar, the teachers are incapable of imparting any sound knowledge of the vernacular language to their numerous pupils. Hence writing, as far as orthography goes, is extremely imperfect; the spelling of words, having no fixed standard, varies to an indefinite extent. As soon as the scholars have mastered the difficulties of the long and complicated alphabet, some portions of the sacred writings are put into their hands for reading. The result is that the Burmese in general acquire some knowledge, more or less extensive, of their religious creed. Though none among them can be found who understands comprehensively the Buddhistic system, yet most of them are possessed of a certain amount of more or less limited information concerning Buddha and his law. In this respect they are perhaps ahead of many nominal Christians in several countries of Europe, who dwell in large manufacturing towns and remote country districts and belong to the lower classes, and who live without even a slight acquaintance with the essential tenets of the Christian creed.

In addition to the eminently useful task of teaching youth, the Buddhistic recluse devotes occasionally some portion of his time to the useful labour of copying manuscripts on palm-leaves, either for his personal use or to increase the small library of his monastery. The work is considered as a very excellent one, deserving of great merits, and much recommended by the rules of the society. It is a matter of regret that the native laziness of the Phongyies, as well as their total want of order in acquiring knowledge, thwart to a great extent the practical working of the wise provisions made by the framer of the rules. Were it not for such causes, copies of all the best and most interesting works on the religious system of Buddhism would be greatly multiplied, and could be easily procured; whilst now they are exceedingly scarce and hardly to be had at all. The few copies to be had with much difficulty are to be paid for very high. All the books are made of palm-leaves. The leaves are about twenty inches in length, and from three to four in breadth. On each face of the leaf from seven to nine or ten lines are written. A copyist uses a style of iron by way of pen. With the sharp point he scratches the epidermis of the leaf to form the letters. In order to render the letters perfectly visible, he rubs over the page just written with a piece of rag some petroleum, which, penetrating into the parts scratched by the style, causes the letters to become quite distinct and apparent.

The Talapoins spend the best part of the day sitting in a cross-legged position, chewing betel and conversing with the many idlers that are always to be found in great numbers about their dwellings. When tired of the vertical position, they adopt the horizontal one, reclining the head on pillows and gently submitting to the soporific influence of good Morpheus. They have always in their hands a string of beads, on which they are wont to repeat certain devotional formulas. The most common is the following, "Aneitsa, duka, anatta;" meaning that everything in this world is subjected to the law of change and mutability, to that of pain and suffering, and to that of entire and uninterrupted illusion. There is, indeed, an immense field opened to a reflecting mind by these three very significative expressions for carrying on serious and prolonged meditation; but none of the Talapoins, at least of those I have been acquainted with, are capable of understanding comprehensively their meaning. They often repeat the forty great subjects of meditation, and the rule enjoins them to be zealously addicted to contemplation, which is pronounced to be the chief exercise of a true follower of Buddha. But how can there ever be expected from weak and ignorant persons the habitual practice of so high an exercise, requiring an intellectual vigour of the very first order? They must repeat on their beads at least a hundred and twenty times a day the four following considerations on the four things more immediately necessary to men, food, raiment, habitation, and medicine: "I eat this rice, not to please my appetite, but to satisfy the wants of nature. I put on this habit, not for the sake of vanity, but to cover my nakedness. I live in this kiaong, not for vainglory, but to be protected from the inclemency of the weather. I drink this medicine merely to recover my health, that I may with greater diligence attend to the duties of my profession."

ARTICLE VII.

RELIGIOUS INFLUENCE OF THE PHONGYIES—RESPECT AND VENERATION PAID TO THEM BY THE LAITY.

When we speak of the great influence possessed by the religious order of Buddhist monks, we do not intend to speak of political influence. It does not appear that in Burmah they have ever aimed at any share in the management or direction of the affairs of the country. Since the accession of the house of Alomphra to the throne, that is to say, during a period of above a hundred years, the history of Burmah has been tolerably well known. We do not recollect having ever met with one instance when the Phongyies, as a body, have interfered in the affairs of the State. They also seem to remain indifferent to family or domestic affairs. The regulations they are subjected to, and the object which they have in view in entering the religious profession, debar them from concerning themselves in affairs that are foreign to their sacred calling. But in a religious point of view alone, their influence is a mighty one. Upon that very order hinges the whole fabric of Buddhism. From it, as from a source, flows the life that maintains and invigorates religious belief in the masses that profess that creed. We may view the members of the order as religious, and as instructors of the people at large, and principally of youth. In that double capacity they exercise a great control and retain a strong hold over the mind of the people.

There is in man a natural disposition and inclination to admire individuals who, actuated by religious feelings, are induced to leave the world and separate from society in order to devote themselves more freely to the practice of religious duties. The more society is corrupted, the more its members value those persons who have the moral courage to estrange themselves from the centre of vice, that they may preserve themselves from contamination. In fact, religious are esteemed in proportion to the extent of the contempt they have for this world. The Phongyies occupy precisely this position in the eyes of their co-religionists. Their order stands in bold relief over the society they belong to. Their dress, their mode of life, their voluntary denial of all gratification of sensual appetites, centre upon them the admiring eyes of all. They are looked upon as the imitators and followers of Buddha; they hold ostensibly before ordinary believers the pattern of that perfection they have been taught so fondly to revere. The Phongyies are as living mementoes, reminding the people of all that is most sacred and perfect in practical religion. No one will deny that the view of a body of religious existing in a community, keeping an intercourse with its members, must ever have a powerful tendency to foster religious feelings in the mind of a half-civilised people as the Burmese are. It is in this manner that the Phongyies command the respect and veneration of the people, and exercise a considerable amount of religious influence over the masses.

But in the capacity of instructors of the people, the members of the order act as yet more directly and actively upon the people. In Burmah there are no schools but those kept by the religious. The monasteries are as so many little seminaries where male children receive elementary instruction. The knowledge that is imparted to them by their masters is not secular, but purely religious. It is a point upon which the undivided attention of a keen observer must be centred in order to understand the full meaning of the following remarks. We do not mean to say that the instructor has always present to his mind, as a professor, the direct teaching of religious tenets; but the fact is that no information is conveyed to the pupils except that which comes from religious books. No other books are ever used in schools.

As soon as boys are able to read, religious books are put into their hands. During all the time they remain at school they go over books that have a direct reference to religion. Without even being aware of it, they imbibe religious notions, and become acquainted with some parts of the religious creed, particularly with what relates to Gaudama's preceding and last existence. When they grow up to manhood, if they happen to read, they have, as a general practice, no other books but such as have a reference to religion. When people assemble together, either in the dzeats on the occasion of festival days, or at home on other public occasions, particularly in the days following the death of some relatives, one or several elders read some passage of their scriptures, and thereby supply topics for conversation of a religious turn. This state of things originates almost entirely in the early education received in the monasteries at the hands of their masters, the Phongyies. It powerfully contributes to popularise and foster religious notions, whilst it indirectly heightens and brightens in the eyes of the people the position of the religious.

Moreover, the early intercourse between the youth and their masters tends to bring into closer contact and union both the religious and the laity. It draws nearer the ties that bind together these two fractions of the Buddhist society. The relation thus established between the teachers and the taught is further strengthened by the fact that the greatest number of the male portion of the community become affiliated, during a longer or shorter period, to the society, and subjected to its rules and regulations; they are cast in the mould of religious, and retain during the remainder of their life some of the features that have been at an early period stamped on their young minds. Their memory remains loaded with all that they learned by heart during the days they spent in the monasteries as students or members of the society.

Though the Phongyies or Talapoins are not remarkable

for their zeal in delivering instructions or sermons to the people, they discharge occasionally that duty on the eve of and during festival days, and on all occasions when considerable offerings are brought to them in their monasteries. Sometimes, too, they are requested to go to certain places prepared for that purpose, to deliver instructions and receive offerings tendered to them by some pious laymen. The preaching never consists in expounding the text of the religious books, and developing certain points of the law; it is a mere rehearsal and repetition of the precepts of the law or of regular formulas in praise of Gaudama, and an enumeration of the merits to be gained by those who bestow alms on them. These and similar circumstances much contribute to keep up the position of the religious, and aid them in retaining a powerful religious hold over their respective communities. We repeat it as our deliberate opinion, that upon the religious association under consideration principally rests, as on a strong basis, the great fabric of Buddhism. Were such an institution to give way and crumble to the dust, the vital energies of that false creed would soon be weakened and completely paralysed. Buddhism would yield before the first attack that would be skilfully and vigorously directed against it.

In Burmah the Phongyies are highly respected by every member of the community. When they appear in public, walking in the streets, they are the objects of the greatest attention. The people withdraw before them to leave a free passage. Women are seen squatting on both sides of the way, through respect for the venerated personages. When visited in their dwellings, even by persons of the highest rank, the etiquette is that every visitor should prostrate himself three times before the head of the monastery, uttering the following formula:—"To the end of obtaining the remission of all the faults I have committed through my senses, my speech, and my heart, I make a first, second, and third prostration in honour of the three precious things—Phra, his law, and the assembly of the perfect. Meanwhile, I earnestly wish to be preserved from the three calamities, the four states of punishment, and the five enemies." To which the recluse answers:—"For his merit and reward, may he who makes such prostrations be freed from the four states of punishment, the three calumities, the five sorts of enemies, and from all evil whatsoever. May he obtain the object of all his wishes, walk steadily in the path of perfection, enjoy the advantages resulting therefrom, and finally obtain the state of Neibban." On the visitor withdrawing from his presence, the three prostrations must be repeated; he then stands up, falls back to a distance of ten feet, as it would be highly unbecoming to turn the back suddenly on the holy man, wheels round on the right, and goes out. This usage is doubtless very ancient, and is at the same time looked upon as a very important one. In the Life of Gaudama we have seen it mentioned on all occasions when visitors went to pay their respects to him. Princes and nobles observed the ceremony with the utmost punctuality.

The best proof of the high veneration the people entertain for the Talapoins is the truly surprising liberality with which they gladly minister to all their wants. They impose upon themselves great sacrifices, incur enormous expenses, place themselves joyfully in narrow circumstances, that they might have the means to build monasteries with the best and most substantial materials, and adorn them with all the luxury the country can afford.[9]

---

[9] The writer, when he visited Bhamo two years ago, had the opportunity of witnessing a striking illustration of the above assertion. Living in a fine and substantial dzeat, in the vicinity of a large pagoda, he remarked an elderly Burmese woman coming every morning with some flowers, which she respectfully deposited in front of a niche tenanted by a huge marble idol. She was poorly dressed, but her mien and countenance indicated that she had seen better days. Entering into conversation with her, the writer learned from her that she was the widow of a wealthy man who had been the principal writer of the governor. Her husband had spent twelve thousand rupees in building the pagoda in front of us and the dzeat, and had just died when the work was completed,

Gold is often profusely used for gilding the posts, ceiling, and other parts of the interior, as well as several trunks or chests for storing up manuscripts. Two or three roofs superposed upon each other (a privilege exclusively reserved to royal palaces, pagodas, and kiaongs) indicate to the stranger that the building is a monastery. The recluse's house is well supplied with the various articles of furniture becoming the pious inmates. The individual who builds at his own expense such a house, assumes the much-envied title of *Kiaong-taga*, or supporter of a monastery. This title is for ever coupled with his name: it is used as a mark of respect by all persons conversing with him, and it appears in all papers or documents which he may have to sign. The best, finest, and most substantial articles, if allowed by the regulations as fit for the use of the Talapoins, are generously and abundantly afforded by benevolent persons. When the king is religiously inclined, the best and most costly presents he receives are deposited in the monasteries, to adorn the place or hall where the principal idol is.

Government does not interfere or give any assistance in building pagodas or kiaongs; nor does it provide for the support of the pious Rahans; but the liberality of the people amply suffices for all contingencies of the kind. When a man has made some profit by trading, or any other

---

leaving to her and her only daughter nothing but the house they now dwelt in. She was without any means of support. Having been asked whether she did not feel some regret that nothing had been left for her subsistence, and whether she did not think her husband would have behaved better in bestowing one-half of his money for religious purposes and keeping the other half for the maintenance of his family, the old lady gently smiled, and said, without hesitation or showing the least sign of repining, that her husband had acted very well and for the best; that she and her daughter, by their exertions, would always be able to support themselves in their humble and poor condition.

In many places the traveller's eyes are attracted by the site of a lofty and roomy kiaong, adorned with fine carvings. When he inquires about the individual whose pious liberality has erected that edifice, he is surprised and astonished to see him living in the poor and wretched house which is pointed out to him.

way, he will almost infallibly bestow the best portion of his lucre in building a kiaong, or feeding the inmates of a religious house for a few months, or in giving general alms to all the recluses of the town. Such liberality, which is by no means uncommon, has its root, we believe, in a strong religious sentiment, and also in the insecurity—nay, the danger—of holding property to a large amount.

When a Talapoin is addressed by a layman, the latter assumes the title of disciple; and the former calls him simply Taga, or supporter. The attitude of the layman in the presence of the Phongyie is indicative of the veneration he entertains towards his person. He squats down, and he never addresses the yellow-dressed individual without joining his hands in token of respect, and raising them up with a little motion indicative of intended prostration. As there is in Burmah a court language, so there is a language, or rather a certain number of expressions, reserved to designate things used by Talapoins, as well as most of the actions they perform in common with other men, such as eating, walking, sleeping, shaving, &c. The very turn of the commonest sentence is indicative of respect when speaking to a Rahan. He is called Phra, the most honourable term the language can afford. His person is sacred, and no one would dare to offer him the least insult or violence. The influence of the Talapoin upon the people is considerable, in proportion to the great respect borne to his sacred character. So extraordinary has it been on certain occasions, that Phongyies have been seen rescuing forcibly from the hands of the police culprits on their way to the place of execution. No resistance, then, could be made by the policemen without exposing themselves to the danger of committing a sacrilege, by lifting their hands against them when such an occurrence takes place. The liberated wretches are then forthwith led to the next monastery. Their heads having been shaved, they are attired in the yellow garb, and their persons become at once sacred and inviolable.

The veneration paid to Talapoins during their lifetime accompanies them after their death. Their state is considered as one of peculiar sanctity. It is supposed that their very bodies too partake of the holiness inherent in their sacred profession. Hence their mortal remains are honoured to an extent scarcely to be imagined. As soon as a distinguished member of the brotherhood has given up the ghost, his body is opened, the viscera extracted and buried in some decent place without any particular ceremony, and the corpse embalmed in a very simple manner by putting ashes, bran, and other desiccative substances into the abdominal cavity. It is then swathed with bands of linen, wrapped round it many times, and a thick coat of varnish laid upon the whole. On this fresh varnish gold leaves are sometimes placed, so that the whole body is gilded over from head to feet. When the people are poor and cannot afford to buy gold for the above purpose, a piece of yellow cloth is considered as the most suitable substitute. The body, thus attired, is laid in a very massive coffin, made, not with planks, but of a single piece of timber hollowed in the middle for receiving the earthly frame of the deceased. A splendid cenotaph, raised in the centre of a large building erected for the purpose, is prepared to support a large chest wherein the coffin is deposited. The chest is often gilt inside and out, and decorated with flowers made of different polished substances of various colours. Pictures, such as native artists contrive to make, are disposed round the cenotaph. They represent ordinarily religious subjects. In this stately situation the body remains exposed for several days, nay several months, until preparations are completed for the grand day of the obsequies. During that period festivals are often celebrated about it, bands of music play, and people resort in crowds to the spot for the purpose of making offerings to defray the expense to be incurred for the funeral ceremony. When the appointed day for burning the corpse at last arrives, the whole population of the town will be seen flocking in their finest dresses to witness the display of fireworks which takes place on the occasion of burning the corpse. A funeral pile of a square form is erected on the most elevated spot. Its height is about fifteen feet, and it ends with a small room made for receiving the coffin. The corpse having been hoisted up and laid in the place destined for its reception, fire is set to the pile in a rather uncommon way. An immense rocket, placed at a distance of about forty yards, is directed towards the pile by means of a fixed rope guiding it thereto. Sometimes the rocket is placed on a huge cart, and pushed in the direction of the pile. In its erratic and uncertain course it happens occasionally that it deviates from its course, and plunges into the ranks of the crowd, wounding and killing those it meets. As soon as it comes in contact with the pile, the latter immediately takes fire by means of combustibles heaped for that purpose, and the whole is soon consumed. The few remaining pieces of bones are religiously collected, and buried in the vicinity of some pagoda. Here ends the profound veneration, amounting almost to worship, which Buddhists pay to their recluses during their life and after their demise.

Two chief motives induce the sectaries of Buddha to be so liberal towards the Talapoins, and to pay them so high a respect; viz., the great merits and abundant rewards they expect to derive from the plentiful alms they bestow upon them, and the profound admiration they entertain for their sacred character, austere manners, and purely religious mode of life. The first motive originates from interested views; the second has its root in that regard men naturally have for persons who distinguish themselves from others by a more absolute self-denial, a greater restraint and control of their passions, a renouncement of permitted pleasures and sensual gratifications from religious motives. According to the fundamental dogma of Buddhism, any offering made to, or indeed any action done for the benefit of, a fellow-man is deserving of reward during future existences, such as digging a well, building a resting-place, a bridge, &c.; but far more abundant are the merits resulting from presenting a Talapoin with one or several articles necessary to his daily use, as they increase proportionately to the dignity of the person to whom the things are offered. We may judge from the following instance of the plentiful harvest of merits which a supporter of Phongyies is promised to reap hereafter: He who shall make an offering of a mendicant's pot or Thabeit shall receive as his reward cups and other utensils set with jewels; he shall be exempted from misfortunes and calamities, disquietude and trouble; he shall get without labour all that is necessary for his food, dress, and lodging; pleasure and happiness shall be his lot; his soul shall be in a state of steadiness and tranquillity, and his passion for the sex shall be considerably weakened. The offering of other objects secures to the donor wealth, dignity, high rank, pleasure, and an admittance into the fortunate countries or seats of the Nats, where all the things are to be met with and enjoyed that are calculated to confer on man the greatest sum of happiness. The people believe unhesitatingly all that is said to them in this respect, and they gladly strip themselves of many valuable things in order to obtain and enjoy, during coming existences, the riches and pleasures promised to them by their Rahans. The insecurity of property under tyrannical rulers may operate to a certain extent in determining people to part with their riches, and consecrate them to religious purposes, rather than see themselves violently deprived of them by the odious rapacity of the vile instruments of the avarice, tyranny, and cruelty of their heartless princes and governors.

It can scarcely be a matter of wonder that Buddhists so much honour and respect a Talapoin, when we consider that, in their opinion, he is a true follower of Buddha who strives to imitate his great prototype in the practice of the highest virtues, particularly in his incomparable mortification and self-denial, that he might secure the ascendancy of the spiritual principle over the material one, weaken passions which are the real causes of the disorder that reigns in our soul, and finally disengage her from their baneful influences, and from that of matter in general. He is exceedingly reserved and abstemious regarding food, the use of creatures, and the enjoyment of pleasures, in order to secure to reason the noblest faculty of an intelligent being, a perfect control over the senses. He is indeed in the right way leading to Neibban, the summit of perfection. In the opinion of a Buddhist, nobody can be compared to a true and fervent Rahan in sterling worth and merit. His moral dignity and elevation cast into the shade the dazzling splendour that surrounds loyalty. He is a pious recluse, a holy personage, a true member of the holy Thanga, and deserving, therefore, of the highest admiration and respect.

As a consequence of the profound veneration in which Talapoins are publicly held, they are exempted from contributing to public charges, tribute, *corvées*, and military service. It is an immense favour, particularly among the nations of eastern Asia, where the rulers look upon their subjects as mere slaves and tools under their command for executing the absolute orders of their capricious fancy. Under the present ruler of Burmah, the fathers and mothers of Phongyies are benefited by the fact of their sons being in a monastery. They are exempted from paying taxes, and are treated with some attention by the officials who wish to ingratiate themselves in the favour of his most Buddhist majesty. They have often the honorary affixes joined to their names.

In concluding this notice, we will briefly sketch the actual situation of the Talapoinic order in those parts where we have had the opportunity of observing it, and will allude to the causes that have operated in seducing it into vices, abuses, and imperfections which are lowering it greatly in the opinion of all foreigners and of a few well-informed natives.

The first and principal cause that has brought the Society into disrepute and opened the door to numberless abuses is the total absence of discernment in the selection of the individuals that seek for an admittance therein. Every applicant is indiscriminately received as a member of the brotherhood. No previous examination takes place for ascertaining the dispositions, capacity, and science of the postulant. No inquiry is ever made regarding the motives that may have induced him to forsake the world and take so important a step. His vocation is exposed to no trial. He has but to present himself and he is sure to be immediately received, provided he consent to conform exteriorly to the usual practices of his brethren. No account is taken of his former conduct. The very fact of his applying to be admitted into the society of the perfect atones amply for all past irregularities. The only respectability inherent in the modern Talapoins is that derived from the sacred yellow dress he wears. It may aptly be said of him that he is monk by the fact of his wearing the canonical dress. The houses of the order are, in many instances, filled with worthless individuals totally unfit for the profession, who have been induced by the basest motives to enter into them, chiefly by laziness, idleness, and the hope of spending quietly their time beyond the reach of want, and without being obliged to work for their livelihood. In confirmation of this, I will mention the following instance. During the second year of my stay in Burmah, I had with me, in the capacity of servant, an old stupid native. On a certain day he gravely told me that he intended to leave my service and become a Phongyie. I laughed at first at what I considered to be very presumptuous and impertinent language. The old man, however, kept his word. Having left my house a few days after our conversation on the subject of his new vocation, I heard no more of him till it happened a few months after that I met him in a monastery, attired in the full dress of a Phongyie, and so proud of his new position that he hardly condescended to put himself on a footing of equality with his former master.

Ignorance prevails to an extent scarcely to be imagined among the generality of the Phongyies. I have met with a great number of laymen who were incomparably better informed, and far superior in knowledge to them. Their mind is of the narrowest compass. Though bound by their profession to study with particular care the various tenets of their creed and all that relates to Buddhism, they are sadly deficient in this respect. They have no ardour for study. While they read some book, they do it without attention or effort to make themselves fully acquainted with the contents. There is no vigour in their intellect, no comprehensiveness in their mind, no order or connection in their ideas. Their reading is of a desultory nature, and the notions stored up in their memory are at once incoherent, imperfect, and too often very limited. They possess no general or correct views of Buddhism. I never met with one who could embrace the whole system in his mind and give a tolerably accurate account of it. The only faculty that they cultivate with great care is memory. It is surprising to hear them repeating by heart the contents of a book they have studied. As the number of books is very limited in countries where the art of printing has not been introduced, the pupils of the monasteries are compelled to commit to memory the greatest portion of the books they study. He who has lived in Burmah must have often heard, to his great surprise, laymen repeating, during sometimes a whole hour, formulas in Pali, or religious stories in Burmese, which they had learned in the school, or when they had put on the monkish habit.

Phongyies are fond of exhibiting their knowledge of the Pali language, by repeating from memory, and without stammering or stumbling, long formulas and sentences; but I have convinced myself that very few among them understood even imperfectly a small part of what they recited. Those who enjoy popularly a reputation for uncommon knowledge affect to speak very little, show a great reserve, despising as ignorant the person that approaches their abodes or holds conversation with them. But silence, which in a learned man is a sign of modesty, is too often with them a cloak to cover their ignorance, and a cunning device for disguising pride under the garb of humility. The latter virtue, though much recommended in the Wini, is not a favourite one with the Talapoins. It is indeed impossible that they could ever understand or practise it, since they are unacquainted with the two great ways that lead to it, viz., a profound knowledge of God and a thorough knowledge of self. Talapoins, who are distinguished among their brethren for their great austerity of manners and more perfect observance of their regulations, are the most unpleasing beings the writer has ever met with.

They are cold, reserved, speaking with affected conciseness: their language is sententious, seasoned with an uncommon dose of pretension. Sentences falling from their lips are half finished, and involved in a mysterious obscurity, calculated to fill with awe and admiration their numerous hearers; a certain haughtiness and contempt of others always shows itself through their affected simplicity and humble deportment. Vanity and selfishness, latent in their hearts, force themselves on the attention of an acute observer. In their manners they are occasionally so affected by a ridiculous reserve that one might be tempted to think that their brain is not quite sound. Talapoins, in general, entertain a very high idea of their own excellence; and the great respect paid to them by the people contributes not a little to foster it, and make them believe that nobody on earth can ever be compared to them. To such a height has their pride reached that they believe it would be derogatory to their dignity to return civility for civility, or thanks for the alms people bestow on them.

The most striking feature in the character of the Talapoins is their incomparable idleness. We may say that, in this respect, they resemble their countrymen, who are very prone to that vice. Two causes of a very different nature seem, in our opinion, to act together on the people of these countries to produce such a result. The first is a physical one; the heat of the climate, coupled with a perpetual uniformity in the temperature, producing a general relaxation in the whole system, which is never combated or counteracted by an opposite action or influence. The second cause is a moral one, the tyranny of the despotic governments ruling over the populations of Eastern Asia. Property is everywhere insecure. He who is suspected of being rich is exposed to numberless vexations on the part of the vile satellites of tyranny, who soon find out some apparent pretext for confiscating a part or the whole of his property, or depriving him of life, should he dare to offer resistance. In such a state of things every one is satisfied with the things of first necessity. Want forms the strongest tie that binds together individuals and races, and at the same time holds out the most powerful incentive to exertion. The people of these parts have but few wants, and therefore they lack inducement to labour for acquiring anything beyond what is strictly necessary. Emulation, ambition, the desire of growing rich, which are the main springs that move man to exertion, disappear and leave him in an abject and servile indolence, which soon becomes his habitual state, and the grave wherein is entombed all his moral energy.

Like their countrymen, Phongyies are exposed to the influence of the above causes, but their mode of life is a third additional reason why they are more indolent than others. They have not to trouble or exert themselves for the articles required for their subsistence and maintenance; these are abundantly supplied to them by their co-religionists. They are bound, it is true, to read, study, and meditate; but their ignorance and laziness incapacitate them for such intellectual exercises. They remain during the best part of the day sitting in a cross-legged position, or reclining, or sleeping, or at least attempting to do so. They occasionally resume the vertical position to get rid of *ennui*, one of their deadliest enemies, and by repeated stretchings of arms and legs, and successive yawnings, try to free themselves from that domestic foe. The teaching of their scholars occupies a few of them for a short time in the morning and in the evening. They are often relieved from their mortal *ennui* by visitors as idle as themselves, who resort to their dwellings to kill time in their company.

To keep up respectability before the public, the Rahans assume an air of dignity and reserve. They avoid all that could lead them into dissipation. Exterior continence is generally observed, and though there are occasional trespasses, it would be unfair to lay on them generally the charge of incontinence. Their life so far may be considered as exemplary. Though partly divested of that open-heartedness which is a peculiar characteristic of their countrymen, they are tolerably kind and affable with strangers. They, however, cannot relinquish in their conversation with them a certain air of superiority, inspired by the admiration of self and the high opinion they entertain of their exalted profession and sacred character. They are unwilling to see them sitting unceremoniously close to themselves; and when this cannot be avoided, they seek for an opportunity of removing to another place a little more elevated than that occupied by the visitor, as it would be highly unbecoming that laymen should ever presume to sit on a level with a recluse. Such a step would imply a sort of equality between them both, which is never to be dreamt of. Their smooth and quiet countenance, their meek deportment, are, as it were, slightly fretted with a certain roughness and rudeness peculiar to individuals leading a retired life, and estranging themselves, to a certain extent, from the place of society.

In the foregoing pages we have endeavoured to give a

faithful account of the great religious order existing in countries where genuine Buddhism is the prevailing creed. We have been obliged, for the sake of truth, to mention many abuses that have slowly crept into it; but we never entertained the slightest intention of casting a malignant contempt or a sneering ridicule upon its members. Most sincerely we pity those unfortunate victims of error and superstition who are wasting their time and energies in the fruitless pursuit of an imaginary felicity. No language can adequately express the ardour and intensity of our desires, sighs, and prayers to hasten the coming of the day when the thick mist and dark cloud that encompass their souls shall be dissipated, and the Sun of Righteousness shall shed into them his vivifying beams. However deplorable their intellectual blindness may be, we always felt that they have a right to be fairly and impartially dealt with. The religious order they belong to is, after all, the greatest in its extent and diffusion, the most extraordinary and perfect in its fabric and constituent parts, and the wisest in its rules and prescriptions, that has ever existed either in ancient or modern times without the pale of Christianity.

ADDENDA.

MANY persons have often put to the writer the following question:—Is it credible that the founder of Buddhism established from the beginning a body of religious, with so perfect an hierarchy and so complete an organisation as to elicit the wonder and astonishment of all those who contemplate it with a serious attention? No doubt, Buddhists attribute to Gaudama all the regulations contained in the Patimauk, or the book of the *enfranchisement;* they maintain that the contents of Cambawa, or book for the ordination of Patzins, have been arranged by the same hand. But the absurdity of such an assertion cannot fail to strike the eyes of even a superficial observer. These two books, with their elaborate divisions and subdivisions, must have been gradually prepared and arranged at an epoch when Buddhism had taken deep root and spread its branches far and wide, and had become the dominant religion in the countries where it is flourishing. To confer splendour on the admittance of individuals into the body of monks, the rules of the Cambawa were enacted. To render the life of religious an object of greater veneration in the eyes of the community, the regulations of the Patimauk were devised, and were very likely brought, by a slow process, to the state of completeness we see them at present.

Though Gaudama had nothing to do with the redaction of the books under examination, he is, nevertheless, the author of the principal and most important regulations.

It is in the Thoots or instructions he has delivered on different occasions that we must search for discovering the germ and origin of the principal points contained in the Patimauk and the Cambawa. At the conclusion of many of his instructions we find some hearers believing in him, and applying for admittance into the society of his disciples. When he approved of their dispositions, the applicants had but to renounce the ordinary pursuits of life, exchange their dress for the one regularly prescribed, and engage to live in a state of strict chastity: they then became at once members of the Thanga, without having to go through a prescribed ordeal. Faith in Buddha on the one hand, and on the other willingness to live in poverty and chastity, were the only requisites for obtaining admittance into the spiritual family of Buddha. The applicants were obliged to live in poverty, and depend for their food on the alms they could procure by begging. Hence they were called Bickus, or mendicants. They had to wear a dress made with rags picked up in cemeteries and stitched together. They placed themselves under the guidance of Gaudama, and denied to themselves all sensual gratifications. Such were the first and principal obligations imposed on the new converts who embraced a religious life. The Bickunies, or women who had embraced the holy profession, were gradually subjected to the same regulations. The minor details of the rule were introduced as consequences flowing from the general principles. This has been the work of time, and perhaps of one of the councils.

It does not appear from the instructions of Gaudama that the steps of the hierarchy were defined and fixed by him, as they have subsequently been. We remark in the assembly, the Bickus, or mendicants, constituting the great mass of the religious, then the *Thera*, or, as the Burmans write it, *Mathera*, the ancients, or members of the assembly distinguished by their age and proficiency in learning and virtue, and the Aryias, or those who had made the greatest progress in meditation and contemplation, and had entered into the current of perfection.

It has been asked also whether those who had reached one of the four Meggas—that is to say, who had become a Thautapan, a Sakadagam, &c.—were always members of the Thanga, and could not live in the world. From the tenor of certain passages in the life of Gaudama we see that many pious laymen became Thautapan, Sakadagam, and even Anagam; that is to say, followed the three first Meggas, though they continued to live in the world. The father of Buddha, King Thoodaudana, the father of Ratha and many others, reached one of the above-mentioned states, though they continued to follow the ordinary pursuits of life. This fact deserves attention, because it shows that the institutions of Gaudama rested on a broad basis, and that a life in the world was not an obstacle to following the ways of perfection.

ON THE WORD "NAT."

IN a note on the Nats, the writer, having expressed the opinion that the word "Nat," used by Burmans, was derived from the Sanscrit term Nath, which means lord, Major Phayre gave it as his decided opinion that the expression was a purely Burmese one, not at all derived from the Sanscrit. Leaving aside the etymological question, of which it may be said that *adhuc sub judice lis est*, we are happy to communicate to the reader the following reflections that have come from the pen of that distinguished scholar, who is so intimately acquainted with all that relates to Buddhism.

"The modern Burmans acknowledge the existence of certain beings which, for want of a better term, we will call 'almost spiritual beings.' They apply to them the name Nat. Now, according to Burmese notions, there are two distinct bodies or systems of these creatures. The one is a regularly-constituted company, if I may say so, of which Thagya Meng is the chief. Most undoubtedly that body of 'Nat' was unknown to the Burmans until they became Buddhists. Those are the real Dewah or Dewata.

"But the other set of Nats are the creatures of the indigenous system, existing among all the wild tribes bordering on Burmah. The acknowledgment of these beings constitutes *their only worship.* On these grounds I consider that the Burmese acknowledged and worshipped such beings before they were converted to Buddhism.

"Now, if they acknowledged such beings, they, no doubt, had a name for them, similar in general import to the 'fairy, elf,' and so on among the inhabitants of Britain for beings of a quasi-spiritual nature. I may observe there is a complete analogy in the state of Burmese belief in the existence of such beings and that which prevailed formerly in Europe, and some remnants of which may be found even now existing among the uneducated. I mean that before the Anglo-Saxon tribes were converted to Christianity the belief in fairies and elfs was universal. With Christianity came a belief in a different order of spiritual beings, and with that a new name derived from the Latin, angel. This is somewhat analogous to the state of things among the Burmese before and after their conversion to Buddhism.

"But to return to the Burmese. They, when they received Buddhism, appear to have generally retained their vernacular name for the beings called in Pali *Dewa.* Why this should be done is certainly not apparent. Why have the English and all Teutonic nations retained the ancient name *Evil*, and spirits, though they adopted with Christianity a new term for good spirits generally? I allude to the term *Devil*, which, there is no doubt, is philologically connected with that Pali word Dew-a or *Dev*-a.

"Regarding the meaning of the word *Nat* in Pali, I have no Pali dictionary, but I have the ordinary Oordoo Dictionary, which includes all ordinary Sanscrit words. I find there the Sanscrit word 'Nath,' and the meaning rendered 'master, husband, lord.' There is nothing to show that it refers to any supernatural being, but is only a term of respect. As such it might in Pali be made applicable to Nats. In Burmese, the people who *believe* in

Nats seldom use that word, but some honorific phrase. Some fishermen I knew quarrelled about their shares in a pool of water. In the case they constantly referred to the share of the 'Ashing-gyee,' who was no other than the presiding Nat of the said pool."

END OF VOL. II.